D0733791

# The Penguin Companion to Literature

## - 3 -

U.S.A.

*Edited by Eric Mottram and Malcolm Bradbury*

LATIN AMERICA

*Edited by Jean Franco*

PENGUIN BOOKS

Penguin Books Ltd, Harmondsworth, Middlesex, England
Penguin Books Inc., 7110 Ambassador Road, Baltimore, Maryland 21207, U.S.A.
Penguin Books Australia Ltd, Ringwood, Victoria, Australia

—

First published 1971
Copyright © Penguin Books Ltd, 1971

—

Made and printed in Great Britain
by Hazell Watson & Viney Ltd
Aylesbury, Bucks
Set in Monotype Times

# CONTENTS

*pp. 125, 187*

# CONTRIBUTORS

| | |
|---|---|
| AA | Arline Anglade |
| AG | Arnold Goldman, Lecturer in English and American Studies, University of Sussex |
| AH | Andrew Hook, Lecturer in American Literature, University of Edinburgh |
| BB | Brand Blanshard, Sterling Professor of Philosophy Emeritus, Yale University |
| BP | Barry Phillips, Assistant Professor of English, Wellesley College, Massachusetts |
| BS | Barry Spacks, Associate Professor in Humanities, Massachusetts Institute of Technology |
| BW | Brian Way, Lecturer in English, University College of Swansea |
| CA | Charles Angoff, Professor of English, Farleigh Dickinson University, New Jersey |
| DC | Dan Curley, Professor of English, University of Illinois |
| DG | Dorothy Goldman, Extra-mural Tutor, Universities of Sussex and Southhampton |
| DH | Mrs Deni Heyck |
| DKA | David K. Adams, Department of American Studies, University of Keele |
| EM | Eric Mottram, Lecturer in American Literature, King's College, University of London |
| GD | George Decker, Senior Lecturer in Literature, University of Essex |
| GW | Geoffrey Walton, Professor of English and Modern Languages, Ahmadu Bello University, Nigeria |
| HD | Howell Daniels, Secretary of the Institute of United States Studies, University of London |
| HB | Harold Beaver, Senior Lecturer, School of Literature, University of Warwick |
| JF | Jean Franco, Professor of Literature, University of Essex |
| JMC | J. M. Cohen |
| MA | Michael Allen, Lecturer in English Literature, University of Belfast |
| MB | Malcolm Bradbury, Professor of American Studies, University of East Anglia |
| MG | Michael Green, Lecturer in English Literature, University of Birmingham |
| RWB | R. W. Butterfield, Lecturer in Literature, University of Essex |

# PUBLISHER'S NOTE

*Bibliographies*

The bibliographies in small type which generally follow an entry are arranged as follows. The first paragraph lists editions of texts and translations of texts not already dealt with in the entry itself. The second paragraph lists critical works concerning the subject of the entry. In cases where only one paragraph occurs, it will be clear from the titles of the works listed whether they are texts or criticism.

The list of critical works is deliberately selective – further bibliographical information can usually be found in the listed works themselves.

The date of publication given is that of first publication. Thus in the U.S.A. section such dates are those of publication in the U.S.A. unless the work was first published elsewhere.

Abbreviated titles in the Latin American section are explained in the List of Abbreviations on pages 287–8.

Bibliographies have been compiled by the contributors of the relevant articles – their initials are placed before the bibliographies only for convenience.


*Cross-references*

Cross-references (◊ = see, ◊◊ = see also) from one article to another are made in the following cases: (a) when relevant information can be found in the articles cross-referred to; (b) when the writer cross-referred to is comparatively minor and the reader may wish to know who he is, even though he has not much relevance to the article in which cross-reference occurs. (A fruitless search is thus avoided – if a minor figure is not cross-referred to it can be assumed that there is no article under his name.)

# *U.S.A.*

# EDITORIAL FOREWORD

The editors have been allowed a full freedom in their selection of authors, and a word is needed about the principles of selection used and the emphasis of their interests. We have attempted to provide from our somewhat different cultural and critical standpoints, a broad coverage of the most important names in American writing from the early period of settlement through to the immediate present, including figures of historical as well as directly literary interest. We have, however, deliberately chosen to give particularly strong representation to twentieth-century writing. In this period American literature becomes markedly an international literature – and very much a *contemporary* international literature, influencing practice and attracting attention in many countries of the world. It is for this reason that we have laid special emphasis on including writers of the century and indeed of the immediate present who seem of interest, even though this has meant unequal coverage of minor figures – those of earlier periods are less fully represented (though we have attended throughout to minor figures who seem to us of cultural significance). The reader thumbing through the book may thus find in it many contemporary writers of whom he has probably not heard previously; indeed it could be read selectively through as a short guide to current developments and tendencies. Generally we have gone for liveliness rather than solemnity, and critical judgement rather than simple biographical record. So the reader might do well from time to time to check the author of an entry in the List of Contributors, since he has been encouraged to give a personal judgement.

In addition we have generally tried to suggest that American writing can be illuminated by seeing it in its cultural context. So influential American thinkers – Parrington and Veblen, William James and Marshall McLuhan, etc. – are included. So are figures of popular significance – McGuffey and Horatio Alger, Margaret Mitchell and James Whitcomb Riley, Zane Grey and Edgar Guest. There are also a small number of subject entries designed to suggest important features of American literary thought and experience – on the Connecticut Wits and the Transcendentalists, on Expatriates and the Lost Generation, on Realism, Naturalism and Veritism and on Little Magazines. Other non-author entries dealing with important publications – *The Bay Psalm Book*, *The Federalist*, etc. – are present.

We have normally followed the practice of dating works by their *first appearance*, whether in England or America. Many American works of the nineteenth century were first published in England to secure copyright advantages, just as certain colonial works appeared in London which still, despite the early appearance of American printing presses, remained as a central publishing capital. But, to avoid proliferating publishing details, we have thus diverged from the practice of the companion volumes in the series and have *not* given the place of a non-English publication *where it is American*.

The brief bibliography which concludes the section is intended to suggest where

13

the reader might discover a broad range of connections between the authors and topics of the Companion. Most of the works are well known and readable without sacrificing scholarship.

*King's College, London*                                        ERIC MOTTRAM
*University of East Anglia*                              MALCOLM BRADBURY

# A

**Adams, Brooks** (1848–1927). Historian, social commentator. Born in Quincy, Massachusetts, a younger brother of Henry ◊ Adams, of a distinguished family whose tradition he evoked in his preface to Henry's 'Letter to American Teachers of History' in *The Degradation of the Democratic Dogma* (1919); he was a profound influence on political and intellectual life during the progressive era. His first book, *The Emancipation of Massachusetts* (1887), argued that the early colonial ministry held the people imprisoned in a narrow, theocratic ideology; it attempted, thereby, to portray the moulding forces of a civilization. This led towards the large-scale, cyclical theory of history embodied in his greatest work, *The Law of Civilization and Decay* (1895; repr. 1955), which holds that the law of history is the law of centralization; but the centralized state contains the seeds of its own decay, since it invariably disintegrates under stress of economic competition. Not surprisingly, he set the virtues of the military over the commercial mind; he was a staunch nationalist, and an admirer of Theodore ◊ Roosevelt, over whom he had a significant influence. His intellectual influence is, like that of his more famous brother, in the promotion of a theoretical history accounting for progress through impersonal forces. But *The New Empire* (1902; repr. 1967) proposes a close integration of history and economics with geographical surroundings. [D K A/M B]

A. F. Beringause, *Brooks Adams: A Biography* (1955); Charles Olson, 'Brooks Adams' "The New Empire"', in *Human Universe* (1965); W. Berthoff, *The Ferment of Realism* (1965).

**Adams, Henry Brooks** (1838–1918). American historian. Born in Boston, Massachusetts. Of the fourth generation of distinguished statesmen (two of whom, John and John Quincy Adams, were Presidents of the United States), Henry, a man of thought and feeling rather than action, turned the family genius inwards to scholarship and writing. His formal education was at Harvard and in Germany. A secretary to his father, Charles Francis Adams, minister to England during the Civil War, he contributed to the newspapers on foreign and domestic affairs. From this it was an easy step to political journalism, history, fiction and, finally, the two master works, *Mont Saint-Michel and Chartres* (1913; private publ. 1904), a study of unity in the religion, art and architecture of the 12th century, and *The Education of Henry Adams* (1918; private publ. 1906), a study of multiplicity in the modern world of politics, science and technology, and an ironic analysis of the culture which formed him.

Adams taught history at Harvard, studied politics at first hand in Washington, and after the suicide of his wife in 1885 travelled to the East with his friend John La Farge and to the Sierras with the geologist Clarence King. His world travels are strongly reflected in the *Education* and in writings on Tahiti and Buddhism. For many years he was thought of only as a historian because of his thoughtful and discerning *History of the United States of America during the Administrations of Thomas Jefferson and James Madison* (9 vols., 1884–9, 1889–91), his *Historical Essays* (1891) and his biographies, *Albert Gallatin* (1879) and *John Randolph* (1882). But recently, with the republication of his political and social novels, *Democracy* (1880) and *Esther* (1884), and the appearance of his lively, voluminous letters, the imaginative power of these and of *Mont Saint-Michel and Chartres* and *The Education of Henry Adams* has been increasingly recognized. Adams's 'dynamic theory of history', expounded in the latter, is elaborated in *The Degradation of the Democratic Dogma* (1919, intr. Brooks Adams). Combining a layman's insights into both science and art with the perspective of the historian, Adams provided, in the symbols of the Virgin and the Dynamo, an interpretation of the intellectual and emotional foundations of subsequent American literature. He was one of the first to expound clearly the 20th-century need to ascertain ways of living with stability in what he called the 'multiverse'. [E M]

*Letters*, ed. W. C. Ford (2 vols., 1930, 1938);

*A Henry Adams Reader*, ed. E. Stevenson (1956). E. Samuels, *The Young Henry Adams* (1948), *Henry Adams: The Middle Years* (1958), *Henry Adams: The Major Phase* (1964); J. C. Levenson, *The Mind and Art of Henry Adams* (1957).

**Ade, George** (1866–1944). Humorist, playwright. Born in Indiana. *The Blond Girl Who Married a Butcher Shop Man* (1898) established the popular formula for this Chicago *Morning News* journalist: daily-life characters, colloquialism, erratic capitals. The one-per-week tales, written for 10 years, were collected in *Fables in Slang* (1900), *More Fables* (1900), *Forty Modern Fables* (1901), etc. His style consists not so much of slang as of Indiana Americanisms, his own racy manner and a cunning redemption of cliché by capital letters. F. D. Roosevelt used to educate his cabinet with Ade's *Fables*. His most famous plays are *The County Chairman* (1903) and *The College Widow* (1904), a hilarious and rather shrewd comedy of academics and athletes in mid-West college life, still regularly performed, and made into a musical, *Leave It to Jane*, by Jerome Kern. [EM]

Ed. Jean Shepherd, *The America of George Ade* (1962).

**Agassiz, Louis** (1807–73). Scientific writer. Born in Switzerland, he went to America in 1846, already famous for his work on glaciers and fish. At Harvard he made a reputation as lecturer, founded his Cambridge museum and the Wood's Hole Marine Biological Laboratory (1872), and compiled his chief work, *Contributions to the Natural History of the United States* (4 vols., 1857–63). His ice-age mania and anti-evolutionism did not prevent him from being a great naturalist and an inspiring and revolutionary teacher (William ◊ James and Sir Charles Lyell were his pupils); and probably he was a major influence on the naturalism of Emerson. Today his zoological studies are increasingly respected, and his example finds a place in Ezra Pound's pantheon. [EM]

Edward Lurie, *Louis Agassiz: A Life in Science* (1960); ed. E. C. Agassiz, *Louis Agassiz: His Life and Correspondence* (2 vols., 1885); Guy Davenport, *The Intelligence of Louis Agassiz: A Specimen Book of Scientific Writings* (1963).

**Agee, James** (1909–55). Poet, novelist, film critic. Born in Knoxville, Tennessee, he attended Harvard, published a collection of poems, *Permit Me Voyage* (1934), and worked for several magazines: *Fortune, Time* (1939–43), and the *Nation*, for which he reviewed films (1942–8). After 1948 his work was mainly for motion pictures. His brilliant film reviews and screenplays appeared in 2 volumes called *Agee on Film* (1958, 1960). A *Fortune* assignment of 1936 led to the eventual appearance in 1941 of *Let Us Now Praise Famous Men*, an account (with photographs by Walker Evans) of the social and economic conditions of poor-white sharecroppers in the South, re-creating the daily living of three representative tenant families. Agee's deep feeling for the land and its people emerges in a unique style of bitterness and passionate sympathy. Two novels followed, the second not quite finished when he died – *The Morning Watch* (1951), a short work about a day in the life of a 12-year-old boy in a Tennessee church school, and *A Death in the Family* (1957), which reports in meticulous detail a single episode in the life of a middle-class family in Nashville, Tennessee, in 1915. The novel presents straightforward people in an ordinary world, with great insight and compassion. Particularly successful is the handling of the children in the family, involved in troubles they only confusedly understand. [AH]

*Collected Poems*, ed. Robert Fitzgerald (1968); *Collected Short Prose*, ed. Robert Fitzgerald (1968); *Letters of James Agee to Father Flye* (1962).
Dwight MacDonald, *Against the American Grain* (1962); J. A. and H. Levitt, *A Way of Seeing* (1965); Peter H. Ohlin, *Agee* (1966).

**Aiken, Conrad** (1889–    ). Poet, novelist. Born in Savannah, Georgia. Early in his life, after his father killed his mother and committed suicide, he lived with relations in Massachusetts. At Harvard in 1911 he was in the famous class which included T. S. ◊ Eliot, Walter ◊ Lippmann, Robert ◊ Benchley and Van Wyck ◊ Brooks. His earliest influences as a philosophical poet and novelist were the French symbolists, the ◊ Imagists, Freud, William ◊ James and Havelock Ellis. But his great American antecedent is Poe, in both his insistence on the music of poetry and his psychological materials. In England, where he lived for a time from 1923, he was a friend of John Gould ◊ Fletcher and other younger poets. His first poems, *Earth Triumphant* (1914), and his criticism of contemporary poets,

*Scepticisms* (1919), aim for a concept of abstract aesthetic beauty which makes for Pateresque vagueness. From *The Jig of Forslin* (1916) onwards, Aiken's poetry shows the same mixture of psychological analysis and mellifluous sounds, without much development, through *Preludes for Memnon* (1931), *And in the Human Heart* (1940, a sonnet sequence) and *The Kid* (1947), a sequence of 9 poems on the curious legend of William Blackstone. *Three* (1968) is a short long poem celebrating everything and focused on the poet. Aiken's poetry is intermittently elusive and diffuse, brilliant in constructing atmosphere but weak in concentration. The musical ritualism of his poems tends towards hypnotic generalizations; but *Ushant* (1952) is a more clearly focused autobiographical prose work, and the criticism collected in *Reviewer's ABC* (1958) is completely lucid and useful. His stories tend to be illustrations of psychological ideas (from *Bring, Bring!*, 1925, to *Among the Lost People*, 1934). Of his 5 novels, *Blue Voyage* (1927) is a Joycean meditation of a playwright, *King Coffin* (1935) a meditation on a murder not committed, and *Great Circle* (1933) an analysis of the Oedipal breakdown of a marriage. Aiken's prose and poetry always have the integrity of his intense subjectivity; but also the narcissism. [EM]

*Selected Poems* (1961); *Collected Novels* (1964); *Collected Short Stories* (1960).
F. J. Hoffman, *Conrad Aiken* (1962); Jay Martin, *Conrad Aiken: A Life and His Art* (1962).

**Albee, Edward** (1928–    ). Playwright. Born Washington, D.C., and educated at Columbia University. His early one-act plays are brilliant absurdist analyses of contemporary social and psychological tensions: *The Zoo Story* (1958), *The Sandbox* (1959), *Fam and Yam* (1960) and the finest, *The Death of Bessie Smith* (1960), on the hysterical nature of Southern sexuality and politics. The dislocations and rituals of the theatre of the absurd are cunningly used in his first full-length play, *Who's Afraid of Virginia Woolf?* (1962), for the mutual destruction and reconciliation games of a history professor and his wife, and in *Tiny Alice* (1964), a psychological fantasy of sexual desire and manipulation in high camp manner. Albee has also adapted Carson ◊ McCullers's *The Ballad of the Sad Café* (1963) and James ◊ Purdy's *Malcolm* (1965) for the theatre, both studies

in adolescence and fantasy life. *A Delicate Balance* (1966) is in many ways the major synthesis of his dramatic talents for comic timing, masks and revels of relatively sinister threats to life, and the numbing agonies of the search for love within a family apparently bent on destruction. In 1968, Albee Americanized the British playwright Giles Cooper's *Everything in the Garden*, altering practically every word, turning a black comedy into his own form of tragicomedy. *Box-Mao-Box* (1968) is probably his most impressive work so far. It consists of 'Box', a monologue by an unseen speaker, with a menacing structure visible on stage, matching the criticism of contemporary American life, and 'Quotations from Chairman Mao Tse-Tung', a piece for four characters with differing points of view. Albee is one of the few American dramatists to have achieved a developing stature since the Second World War. [EM]

Christopher Bigsby, *Edward Albee* (1969); Richard E. Amacher, *Edward Albee* (1969).

**Alcott, Amos Bronson** (1799–1888). Philosopher, educator, poet. Brought up on a Connecticut farm, he had little schooling, worked in a clock factory, wanted to be a schoolmaster but in fact became a Yankee pedlar in Virginia and the Carolinas (1818–23). With the planters he found a range of books and manners unavailable in New England, and when he did become a teacher in Connecticut his methods – based on the 'self-realization' of the child by socratic dialogue, comfortable conditions, music and games – were radically opposed to Calvinist disciplines; but Boston allowed him to experiment. In 1830 he married (see the family of Louisa M. ◊ Alcott's *Little Women*) and in 1831 he was asked to found a school in Philadelphia, where he read Pestalozzi. He then began an infant school in Boston, the Temple School, where he put into practice the advanced but controversial theories outlined in *Record of a School, Exemplifying the General Principles of Spiritual Culture*, published in 1835 by his assistant Elizabeth Peabody, and in his *Conversations with Children on the Gospels* (2 vols., 1836–7). He refused to dismiss a Negro girl from the school and was then himself dismissed because of his abolitionist entanglements, his religious emphasis and his admission that he discussed human physiology with his pupils. By this time a leading ◊ Transcendentalist, an educational theorist admired by Emerson and W. E. ⋄ Channing (II), and a spiritual citizen of Concord, he moved in fact to the town and failed at farming. But his *Orphic Sayings* (1840, in the *Dial*; ed. William P. Randel, 1939) embodied his faith in innocence, intuition and the organic unity of all life 'agitated by the omnipresent soul', and were an important source of Transcendentalist ideas. In 1842 he visited England, and Carlyle, who found him 'a venerable Don Quixote . . . all bent on saving the world by a return to acorns', and returned to organize the 'Con-Sociate Family' community experiment at Fruitlands, near Harvard (his daughter Louisa M. Alcott's *Transcendental Wild Oats* is a fictional account), which failed after seven months. Thereafter he lived in Concord, neighbour to Emerson, Hawthorne, and Thoreau, supported by his wife and daughter Louisa, especially after the success of the latter's *Little Women*; until in 1859 he became Concord's Superintendent of Schools and 'travelling conversationalist'. From this work grew the Concord School of Philosophy (1879–88), run by a disciple, William T. Harris, and an important influence on American education. Most of Alcott's writing – poetry, reminiscences, sayings, a book on Emerson – belongs to the end of his life. He is no stylist or systematic thinker, and his real strength lay in endless learned conversations rooted in extreme neo-Platonism (Emerson said: 'As pure intellect, I have never seen his equal . . . the moral benefit of such a mind cannot be told'); but *Tablets* (1868) and *Table-Talk* (1877) reproduce something of his psychology of complexions and theory of relapsed creation. *Concord Days* (1872), based on his journals, and *New Connecticut, An Autobiographical Poem* (1887) have been reissued fairly recently. [MG]

*The Journals*, ed. O. Shepard (1938).
Ralph Waldo Emerson, 'Alcott', in *New American Cyclopaedia* (1858); O. Shepard, *Pedlar's Progress: The Life of Bronson Alcott* (1937); D. McCluskey, *Bronson Alcott, Teacher* (1940).

**Alcott, Louisa May** (1832–88). Novelist. In 1830 Bronson ⋄ Alcott married Abigail May; their daughters Elizabeth, Louisa, Anna and May were immortalized as Beth, Jo, Amy and Meg in Louisa's best-known work, the lastingly popular *Little Women*. Born in Pennsylvania while her father ran a school in Germanstown, educated at home

(though she also got some instruction from Thoreau, Emerson and Theodore Parker), forced to do menial work to support the household, she determined to write. *Flower Fables*, written when she was 16, appeared six years later (1855); considerable success came with *Hospital Sketches* (1863), about her experience as a Civil War nurse; her first novel, *Moods*, appeared in 1865; but fame arrived with *Little Women: Or Meg, Jo, Beth and Amy* (two parts, 1868, 1869). She followed this with *An Old-Fashioned Girl* (1870), *Little Men* (1871, about her nephews), *Aunt Jo's Scrap-Bag* (6 vols., 1872–82), *Eight Cousins* (1875), *Rose in Bloom* (1876), *Under the Lilacs* (1878), *Jo's Boys* (1886), etc., some of them for children, others showing her reform and suffrage interests. She visited Europe, edited a children's magazine, and died in Boston the day her father was buried. All her fiction is autobiographical, and most of her books are still in print in several languages. Her sentimental masterpiece not only provides several archetypal figures of American folklore but gives a lively rendering of mid-century Boston–Concord life. [MG]

*Louisa May Alcott: Her Life, Letters and Journals*, ed. E. D. Cheney (1889; repr. 1928).
Katharine Anthony, *Louisa May Alcott* (1938); Madeleine B. Sterne, *Louisa May Alcott* (1950).

**Aldrich, Thomas Bailey** (1836–1907). Novelist, poet. Born in New Hampshire. He became editor of the *Home Journal* at 20, and achieved national fame with his poem 'The Ballad of Babie Bell' (1855). His 'Marjorie Daw' was a famous short story of New York society (*Marjorie Daw and Other People*, 1873). Among his other works, *The Stillwater Tragedy* (1880), a detective story involved in anti-labour materials, and some of his academic lyrics, were most admired. He edited the *Atlantic Monthly* (1881–1900). But he is mainly remembered today for *The Story of a Bad Boy* (1870), a delightful autobiographical novel of his boyhood in Portsmouth (New Hampshire) and New Orleans. [EM]

Charles E. Samuels, *Thomas Bailey Aldrich* (1965).

**Alger, Horatio** (1834–99). Writer of children's books. Born in Revere, Massachusetts. After attending Harvard and going to Paris to lead a Bohemian life, he returned to become a Unitarian minister and then chaplain to the Newsboy's Lodging House in Manhattan. Here he wrote more than 100 tales of youthful self-improvement, generally about bootblacks and newsboys who made good through effort, resisting temptation and aiding elderly ladies. Subscribing to both the Victorian self-improvement myth and the American dream of success, they sold enormously well; over 20 million copies of each of the *Ragged Dick* series (1867 ff.), the *Luck and Pluck* series (1869 ff.) and the *Tattered Tom* series (1871 ff.) were published. He also wrote inspirational lives of Lincoln and Garfield. [MB]

Herbert B. Mayes, *Horatio Alger: A Biography without a Hero* (1928); J. Seelye, 'Who was Horatio? The Alger Myth and American Scholarship', *American Quarterly*, Winter, 1965; Kenneth S. Lynn, *The Dream of Success* (1955).

**Algren, Nelson** (1909– ). Novelist. Born in Detroit, he has lived mainly in or near Chicago, where much of his work is set. Graduating from the University of Illinois School of Journalism in 1931, at the bottom of the Depression, he wandered through the American South-west as a migratory worker, writing his first story from experiences as attendant at an unsuccessful, fraudulent Texas filling-station. He returned to Chicago, worked on a W.P.A. Writer's Project, and as venereal disease control worker for the Chicago Board of Health. He began systematically collecting material from the Polish neighbourhoods of the North-west Side, making friends with poverty-stricken workers and criminals, attending police line-ups for scraps of dialogue, reading local papers for stories. Out of this commitment emerge the novels *Somebody in Boots* (1935), *Never Come Morning* (1942) and *The Man with the Golden Arm* (1949); the short stories *The Neon Wilderness* (1947); and *Chicago: City on the Make* (1951), his impressions of the city. He gives a certain poetic intensity to the anonymous desolation of the American metropolis, especially in *Never Come Morning*; he also renders, with the nerve-racking force of the sophisticated thriller writer, a number of the violent situations fundamental to the American imagination – rapes, brutal police interrogations, stick-ups, street hoodlums, sport as aggression. All is suffused with a romantic nihilism suggested in Algren's admiration for Sartre and acknowledged debt to

Hemingway and Dostoyevsky. *The Man with the Golden Arm*, one of the first novels about drug addiction, brought him international fame.

This fiction all belongs to the pattern of tough Depression writing – the world of James T. ◊ Farrell – and it makes an occasional left-wing gesture (though nothing in it really suggests Algren's radical outspokenness as a citizen, as in his protest against the execution of the Rosenbergs). *A Walk on the Wild Side* (1956), which Algren himself calls a 'readers' book' rather than a book 'written for myself', is, however, a conscious and ill-judged attempt to write in a more up-to-date idiom and respond to the vogue of ◊ Beat Generation writers like Kerouac.

Algren writes best at moments and in episodes; his novels are structureless; his characters or situations rarely develop convincingly; the action moves in jerks from phase to phase. The style is uneven – sometimes genuinely poetic, or filled with the vitality of American speech, but often inflated with false romanticism. However, as a tough Chicago novelist he has a permanent though minor place in American literature. *Who Lost an American?* (1963) is a book of world travels, and *Notes from a Sea Diary* (1965) combines observations on Hemingway and his critics with anecdotes of a voyage to India and Hongkong. [BW]

*Nelson Algren's Own Book of Lonesome Monsters* (1963).

H. E. F. Donaghue, *Conversations with Nelson Algren* (1964); ed. Malcolm Cowley, *Writers at Work* (1958) (interviews with Alston Anderson and Terry Southern); Maxwell Geismar, *American Moderns* (1958).

**Allen, Hervey** (1889–1949). Novelist, poet, biographer. Born in Pittsburgh, educated at the U.S. Naval Academy and the University of Pittsburgh, he became a First Lieutenant of Infantry in the First World War, describing his experiences in an autobiographical novel, *Toward the Flame* (1926). He taught in high schools and at Vassar College. His novel *Anthony Adverse* (1933), a swashbuckling historical romance set in the Napoleonic era, enjoyed extraordinary success. It was followed by a Civil War novel, *Action at Aquila* (1938), and three novels about the New York state frontier collected together in *The City in the Dawn* (1950). Volumes of poetry included *Wampum and Old Gold* (1921), *Carolina Chansons* (1922) and *New Legends* (1929). But he will probably be best remembered for his excellent biography of Poe: *Israfel* (1926). [MG]

**Allston, Washington** (1779–1843). Painter, poet, novelist. Though best known as a painter of the romantic school, he produced work of great interest in verse, fiction and essays. He was born in South Carolina and graduated from Harvard, then studying painting in England and Rome. Two lengthy visits to England brought him close to the English romantics, including Wordsworth and Coleridge, who influenced his own romanticism in art and literature. His volume of poems *The Sylphs of the Seasons* appeared in London in 1813 and was republished in Boston; Coleridge praised it for its nature poetry. He wrote the first American novel set in Italy, *Monaldi* (completed 1822; published 1841); it is a Gothic revenge novel set among painters. Richard Henry ◊ Dana, Jr, a relative, edited the posthumous volume *Lectures on Art, and Poems* (1850), containing 4 theoretical essays, his poems, a story and some aphorisms. [MB]

Jared Flagg, *Life and Letters of Washington Allston* (1893); Edgar P. Richardson, *Washington Allston: A Study of the Romantic Artist in America* (1948); Nathalia Wright, *American Novelists in Italy: The Discoverers: Allston to James* (1965).

**Alsop, Richard.** ◊ Connecticut Wits.

**Anderson, Maxwell** (1888–1959). Playwright. The son of a Pennsylvanian Baptist minister, he graduated from the University of Dakota, and after teaching and journalism (from which he was sacked for his Christian pacifism) he went to New York in 1918 and began to write for the theatre. After his first play, *White Desert* (1923), he successfully collaborated with Laurence ◊ Stallings on *What Price Glory?* (1924), a disillusioned comment on the First World War whose fairly accurate language and decent debunking is spoiled by sentimentality. Neither of the following two collaborations was as successful as Anderson's own domestic comedy, *Saturday's Children* (1927), or his first blank-verse box-office seller, *Elizabeth the Queen* (1930). Subsequently hailed as America's leading dramatist, he joined the ◊ Playwrights

Company and won Pulitzer and Drama Critics' Prizes.

In *Elizabeth the Queen*, the interplay of Elizabeth and Essex is worked up to a certain richness by language intended to revive verse drama for modern audiences. The theme of conflict between public and private life appears in a contemporary Congress setting in *Both Your Houses* (1933), and in *Mary of Scotland* (1933) the nobility of the queen's faith is betrayed by the machinations of Elizabeth in a verse tragedy. The compromise idiom of ancient and modern is clever but unreal. *Winterset* (1935) is a second handling (*Gods of the Lightning*, 1928, came first) of the Sacco-Vanzetti materials, in which the son revenging his father's uncommitted crime is a Hamlet figure, averted from crime by love. After four lesser plays, *High Tor* (1936) again uses verse for a contemporary subject: allegory of American individualism in which the New York Dutch past competes with modern gangsters, and self-reliance is taken West by the defeated hero. In *Key Largo* (1939) a Spanish Civil War deserter sacrifices his life objectively, conforming to a theory expounded by Anderson in *The Essence of Tragedy* (1939), essays. Before his death he completed another nine plays, including a version of Alan Paton's *Cry, the Beloved Country* (1948), with music by Kurt Weill (with whom he wrote the musical *Knickerbocker Holiday*, 1938). Anderson's best plays have a seriousness of purpose and theme which raises them above the rut, but their very earnestness and self-conscious universalizing through verse is no more than service in an honourable cause. [EM]

*Eleven Verse Plays* (1940).
B. H. Clark, *Maxwell Anderson: The Man and His Plays* (1933); Mabel D. Bailey, *Maxwell Anderson: The Playwright as Prophet* (1957).

**Anderson, Robert** (1917–    ). Playwright. Born in New York City. He achieved fame with his first play, *Tea and Sympathy* (1953), on the problems of homosexuality and loneliness as they affect a New England schoolboy. Sex and sentiment also helped *All Summer Long* (1955) – the actual and symbolic flooding of a family in their riverside home – and *Silent Night, Lonely Night* (1959), in which husband and wife (not married to each other) find a Christmas Eve vigil strengthening. *You Know I Can't Hear You When the Water's Running* (1967) is four one-act plays with a sexual bias. [EM]

**Anderson, Sherwood** (1876–1941). Novelist, short-story writer. His fiction is auto-biographical, his autobiography – in *A Story-Teller's Story* (1924), etc. – no less fictional; and he saw both as expressing not only an individual truth but a national legend, a distinctively American experience. He was born into small-town life in an Ohio scarcely a generation from the first settling, when pioneer memories were strong; this world laid the foundations of a life-long suspicion of modern industrial society, and a respect for the imaginative individual craftsman. His own story was that of a Horatio ◊ Alger hero with a new ending. He found a talent for writing advertising copy, worked in a Chicago agency, then became manager of an Ohio paint factory. Meanwhile, growing dissatisfied with this life, he tried writing fiction; and, according to legend, he walked out of his factory and family and into his career as an artist. Whether this is true or not, he clearly felt it should be; and this is the one 'fact' universally known about him. He joined the active literary scene of Chicago; was briefly an expatriate in Paris, sitting at the feet of Gertrude Stein; then returned to New Orleans, where he encouraged Faulkner. He settled in Marion, Virginia, writing and editing newspapers.

His first novel was *Windy McPherson's Son* (1916), and thereafter in novel after novel the hero follows Anderson's steps from town to city, often to success greater than he ever achieved, then to disillusionment and rejection of the standard images of success, and finally to exploration of new ends and means. Often the discovery is of a kind of mindless communion with and acceptance by others. It is a semi-mystical vision, and at once the cause of his fictional successes and failures. Everything depends upon Anderson's finding an adequate place to stand to tell his story. Most of his novels fail through dead stretches of flat narrative summary and clogging patches of authorial comment. Only when he gets an adequate voice in the story – usually a first-person narrator – does he effectively express his insight, as in 'The Egg', 'Death in the Woods' and 'The Man Who Became a Woman', three stories involving an adult narrator looking back to the still-puzzling crucial events of his adolescence. *Poor White* (1920) is the best early novel; it exploits the personal legend but makes it into a broad and representative experience;

in later pages, however, the presentation of adult life and sexuality gives Anderson many problems he cannot quite solve. But best known is *Winesburg, Ohio* (1919), a series of interrelated tales of the thwarted lives of small-town people, men of one idea (he calls them 'grotesques') trapped in ignorance and intolerance, yet groping for life. In most of the tales appears the figure of George Willard, a young newspaper reporter, who finally rejects the town and sets out in search of the virtues he has seen dimly revealed . . . personal freedom, sexual vitality, lyric insight, blood brotherhood. At 51, Anderson returned to Winesburg – Virginia, not Ohio – having bought two country weeklies; between 1927 and 1931 he wrote personal essays in editorial form for them, character sketches and mood pieces edited by Ray Lewis White in *Return to Winesburg* (1967).

The *Portable Sherwood Anderson* (New York, 1949), with an introduction by Horace Gregory, contains most of Anderson's best (including *Poor White*) and enough of his worst to give a fair picture. Best individual volumes in addition to *Winesburg, Ohio* are *The Triumph of the Egg* (1921) and *Horses and Men* (1923), both collections of stories. [DC]

*Letters*, ed. H. M. Jones and W. B. Rideout (1953); *Memoirs* (1969); *Tar: A Midwest Childhood*, ed. R. L. White (1969).
Ed. R. L. White, *The Achievement of Sherwood Anderson* (1966); Irving Howe, *Sherwood Anderson* (1951).

**Antoninus, Brother** (William Everson) (1912– ). Poet. Born in California. During his term in a work camp for con-scientious objectors, he was a member of a group of writers whose Untide Press mimeo-graphed influential protest poetry in the Second World War. *The Residual Years: Poems 1934–1948* (1968) is a collection of poems which originally appeared in *These are the Ravens* (1935), *San Joaquin* (1939), *The Masculine Dead* (1942), *The Residual Years* (1944), *A Privacy of Speech* (1949), *In the Fictive Wish* (1967), *The Blowing of the Seed* (1966), *The Springing of the Blade* (1968) and *In the Year's Declension* (1961) (the first three of these appeared in *Single Source*, intr. Robert Duncan, 1966). These poems are an impressive achieve-ment of personal forms and rhythms intent on recording contact with landscape, experience of marriage, moral concern with Post-Depression America, and the years leading to a crisis of religious faith in 1949. The poet became a Catholic, was active in the Catholic Worker movement, and, in 1951, entered the Dominican Order as a lay brother. His monastic withdrawal ended in 1957 and he became a force in the San Francisco Renaissance of the 1950s (*Evergreen Review*, 2, 1957). *The Crooked Lines of God: Poems 1949–54* (1960) states directly the nature of his spiritual changes with exceptional honesty. *The Hazards of Holiness: Poems 1957–1960* (1962) delineate a dark night of the soul and recovery through prayer and renewed contact with that landscape of California as close to Antoninus as it was to Robinson Jeffers. The centre of *The Rose of Solitude* (1967) is his love for a young woman. *The City Does Not Die* (1969) is a poem commemorating the San Francisco earthquake. He left his order early in 1970. [EM]

David Kherdian, *Six San Francisco Poets* (1969).

**Arendt, Hannah** (1906–    ). The German-born scholar received her doctorate at Heidelberg, where she studied under Jaspers and Heidegger. She went to America in 1941, and has since taught at a number of universities and made a brilliant reputation with *The Origin of Totalitarianism* (1951, 1958; British title *The Burden of Our Time*), a superb account of imperialist and totalitarian systems, *The Human Condition* (1958), a vital revisionary rethinking of Marxism, *Between Past and Future* (1961), a collection of essays, *On Revolution* (1963), and the controversial *Eichmann in Jerusalem* (1963). *Men in Dark Times* (1969) contains essays on Rosa Luxemburg, Karl Jaspes, Walter Benjamin, Randall Jarrell, etc., and *On Violence* is a short book on power and rebellion. [EM]

**Arthur, Timothy Shay** (1809–85). Novelist. Born in Orange Co., N.Y., he wrote novels against gambling and drink and for the domestic virtues, but was not himself teetotal. One of his stories became a classic when it was made by William Pratt into a play, *Ten Nights in a Barroom and What I Saw There* (produced 1858). At one time even more in demand than *Uncle Tom's Cabin*, it contained the song of little Mary, 'Father, dear father, come home to me now', and is now produced regularly as burlesque. [EM]

**Asch, Shalom** (1880–1957). Novelist, playwright. One of the great figures of modern Yiddish literature. Though essentially cosmopolitan, and drawing on international subject matter, he has direct links with American life and letters as well as with a distinct racial culture. He was born in Poland and became resident in New York in 1910, writing for Yiddish newspapers and contributing to Yiddish-American literature. He has also lived elsewhere, in Berlin, Paris and London, and published his work in various countries. Most of his prolific writing was written in Yiddish or German, and much is still not translated into English; his works in Yiddish, collected in Warsaw in 1937, already ran to 28 volumes. His translated works include *Mottke, the Vagabond* (1917), retranslated by Edwin and Willa Muir as *Mottke, the Thief* (1935); *America* (1918); and *Kiddush Ha-Shem, An Epic of 1648* (1926), which has been regarded as a major contribution to modern Jewish literature. His *Three Cities: A Trilogy* (1933; again translated by the Muirs) deals with St Petersburg, Warsaw and Moscow in modern revolutionary periods, seen from a Jewish perspective. Another notable group of books were those that appeared in London in 1938 under the title of *Three Novels* – containing *Uncle Moses, Chaim Lederer's Return* and *Judge Not* . . . . A further major trilogy is the group which treats early Christianity in its Jewish context – *The Nazarene* (1939), *The Apostle* (1943) and *Mary* (1949). There are many other books to his name, but *East River* (1946), which deals with Jewish life in New York at the turn of the century, and explores the intermixture of American races, is an example of his use of American materials. He has also written numerous short stories, and the collection *From Many Countries* appeared in London in 1958. Native Jewish writing has played a large part in the growth of American literature, and also has found in American culture much of its modern material; Asch's work manifests both the contribution and the debt. Certainly his novels of Jewish life, both in the modern period and at the time of Jesus, etc., are classics of the Yiddish literature movement and have proved popular reading among much wider audiences. [MB]

**Ashbery, John** (1927–    ). Poet, playwright, art critic. Born in Rochester, N.Y., he studied at Harvard and Columbia, where he specialized in French literature, worked in publishing, and in 1955 he went to France, serving as art critic for the Paris *Herald Tribune* and writing on art for *Art News*, of which he later became an editor. He returned to New York in 1965. He was on the editorial panel for the 12 issues of *Art and Literature* (1964–7) and for the 5 issues of *Locus Solus* (1961–2), important magazines reflecting the work and interests of a group of mainly New York poets and artists which includes Kenneth ◊ Koch, Harry ◊ Mathews, James Schuyler and Frank ◊ O'Hara, and their younger friends and followers (including those associated with 'C' publications and the magazine *Mother*), including Ted ◊ Berrigan, John Perrault, Rod Padgett and Peter ◊ Schjeldahl. Ashbery's poems are highly original in their use of logical narrative, complex interlocking imagery and a sharp visual sense of landscape and town localities. His work has been one of the main channels for the employment of French surrealist poetry and prose in modern American poetry, although the compositional theories of Gertrude Stein are also involved. He has also written plays, including *The Compromise* (1955) and *The Heroes* (1950). His poems are in *Turandot and Other Poems* (1953), *Some Trees* (1956), *The Poems* (1960), *The Tennis Court Oath* (1962), *Rivers and Mountains* (1965) and *Double Dream of Spring* (1970). *Selected Poems* (1967) is a British edition of his work. *The Nest of Ninnies* (1969) is a shrewd, funny novel, written with James Schuyler. [EM]

Paul Carroll, *The Poem in Its Skin* (1968); Richard Howard, *Alone with America* (1969).

**Asimov, Isaac** (1920–    ). Science-fiction writer. Born in Russia, he received a Ph.D. from Columbia University. A professor of biochemistry, he has published many popular works, including the 2-volume *Intelligent Man's Guide to Science* (1960). Asimov's chief contribution to science fiction has been his use of robots, from the collection of stories *I, Robot* (1950) to *The Caves of Steel* (1954) and *The Naked Sun* (1957), both of which employ a robot detective, as does *Asimov's Mysteries* (1968), a collection which combines the science-fiction with the mystery story. His three laws of robotics, although crude, are now widely accepted by other writers in the genre. Under the pseudonym Paul

French he has also written for juveniles. Other works include *The Foundation Trilogy* (1963), a reprinting of three earlier novels, *Nine Tomorrows* (1959), a collection of tales, and *The Universe* (1967), a history of man's attitudes and discoveries within the cosmos from earliest times to the most recent. [HD]

**Atherton, Gertrude** (1857–1948). Novelist, biographer, historian. Born in San Francisco, she married a New Englander in 1876 and began her long, lively and very prolific career only in the late 1880s, after his death. Her extraordinarily diverse, patchy output includes a series of novels describing California from Spanish times to the present, the best known being *The Californians* (1898; rev. 1935) and *Before the Gringo Came* (1894; rev. 1902 as *The Splendid Idle Forties*); several society novels, typified by *Black Oxen* (1923), considered scandalous when it appeared; some international social fiction; and fictional, 'dramatized' biographies. That of Alexander Hamilton, *The Conqueror* (1902), was extremely successful, despite criticism that she had misrepresented the historical figures involved. An ardent feminist, she campaigned with verve in her novels against Puritanism, and was nominated a member of 'The Erotic School' (with Ellen Wheeler ◊ Wilcox) in a popular-newspaper phrase, *c.* 1868. In 1932 she produced a characteristically exuberant autobiography, *Adventures of a Novelist*. During the twenties she was reported in Europe as the most widely read contemporary American author. [MG]

**Auchincloss, Louis** (1917–    ). Novelist, short-story writer. Educated at Yale and the University of Virginia, in 1941 he became a lawyer in New York. His fiction displays his experience of law firms and the higher levels of New York society. Since *The Indifferent Children* (1947) he has been a prolific writer, publishing a novel or short-story collection almost annually, and the unfailing wit, elegance and subtlety of his work have often led reviewers to compare him with Edith Wharton, about whom he has written, and even Henry James. Among his novels, *Sybil* (1952) is notable for its powers of characterization, but perhaps his short stories contain his best work. Some of his collections, such as *The Romantic Egoists* (1954), have one unifying theme, and in others, such as *Powers* *of Attorney* (1963), the separate stories (here of a law firm) are so closely interrelated as almost to comprise a new form between short story and novel. [MG]

*The Injustice Collectors* (1951); *A Law for the Lion* (1953); *The Great World and Timothy Colt* (1956); *Venus in Sparta* (1958); *Pursuit of the Prodigal* (1959); *The House of Five Talents* (1960); *Edith Wharton* (1961) (criticism); *Reflections of a Jacobite* (1961) (criticism); *Portrait in Brownstone* (1962); *The Rector of Justin* (1964); *Pioneers and Caretakers* (1965) (criticism of 9 American woman novelists); *Tales of Manhattan* (1967); *A World of Profit* (1968).

**Audubon, John James** (1785–1851). Naturalist. Born in Santo Domingo, the son of a French navy captain, he spent his early life studying art in Louisiana, Pennsylvania and France; but when his father went bankrupt he opened a general store in Louisville, Kentucky, with a partner and a wife who let him travel in America on his real vocation, birds. His narratives and his paintings are equally fine: but he too went bankrupt, and was imprisoned at one time. *The Birds of North America* (1827–38) is a huge collection of plates whose text he published (with William MacGillivray) in 1831–9 as *Ornithological Biography*. The text for *The Viviparous Quadrupeds of North America* (1831–9) followed in 1846–54. His voluminous journals have been made into fascinating books, which include *Delineations of American Scenery and Character* (ed. F. H. Herrick, 1926) and *Journal of John James Audubon, Made during his Trip to New Orleans in 1820–21* (ed. H. Corning, 1929). Besides his beautiful bird drawings, he packed his journals with first-hand information about early American pioneers and the Indians. [EM]

*The Journals* (2 vols., 1960); *The Imperial Collection of Audubon Animals* (with J. Backman), ed. V. H. Cahalane (1968).

Alice Ford, *John James Audubon* (1965); Alexander B. Adams, *John James Audubon* (1966).

# B

**Babbitt, Irving** (1865–1933). Critic, teacher. Born in Ohio, he worked as a newspaper seller and cowboy before eventually graduating from Harvard (1889). After further study in Paris he taught in Montana, and became Professor of Romance Languages at Harvard in 1894. He was an outstanding scholar and teacher, and the most cogent and articulate member of the ◊ New Humanism movement. His lifelong advocacy of reason and his sustained and vehement opposition to romantic spontaneity had a lasting influence on the work of T. S. Eliot, and many others, including Yvor ◊ Winters.

All his favourite themes are present in the severe, elegant prose of *Literature and the American College: Essays in Defence of the Humanities* (1908). He recommends patience and discipline in literature as in life, attacking 'the moral impressionism' of modern society. 'The classical spirit, in its purest form, feels itself consecrated to the service of a high, impersonal reason. Hence its sentiment of restraint and discipline, its sense of proportion and pervading law.' In *The New Laokoön* (1910) he analyses 'the romantic confusion in the arts': 'Many of the greatest of our modern artists, Hugo, Wagner, Ibsen . . . have been eleuthéromaniacs. For over a century the world has been fed on a steady diet of revolt. Everybody is . . . taken up with his rights rather than with his duties. . . . We should have the courage to affirm . . . that a man may throw off the outer law only in the name of a higher law, and not in the name of universal sympathy.' In *Rousseau and Romanticism* (1919) he analyses with devastating force the characteristics of romantic literature, and despite much local unfairness the book remains a major study. Later came *Democracy and Leadership* (1924), his philosophy of modern civilization; *On Being Creative* (1932), contrasting classic imitation and romantic spontaneity; and a posthumous collection of essays, *Spanish Character* (1940, with a bibliography). Despite their rather wearisomely negative polemic, Babbitt's works are among the classics of modern criticism. [MG]

T. S. Eliot, 'The Humanism of Irving Babbitt' and 'Second Thoughts about Humanism', in *Selected Essays* (1932); R. P. Blackmur, *The Lion and the Honeycomb* (1955); Herbert Howarth, *Notes on Some Figures behind T. S. Eliot* (1965).

**Baker, Dorothy** (1907–68). Novelist. Born in Montana, she married the poet and teacher Howard ◊ Baker and lived in Paris, Cambridge, Massachusetts, and on her husband's orange farm in southern California. Her novels are clever and finished works, with an intensity of rendering and a concern with exactness of psychology that owe much to Hemingway but show the positive qualities of an individual style. Most of her books examine challenges to the aesthetic and emotional qualities of the young. *Young Man with a Horn* (1938), about a hero derived from Bix Biederbecke, deals intensively with the culture of the jazz world. *Trio* (1943), which has a university background, is a study of the influence of an authoritarian lesbian teacher on two young people, and *Our Gifted Son* (1948) concerns the problems of an artist of Mexican origin. *Cassandra at the Wedding* (1962), probably her best novel, reverts to exploring modern college and youth culture through a sensitive, strained heroine whose moral values are caught with superb precision. [MB]

**Baker, George Pierce** (1866–1935). Teacher, editor. Born in Providence, Rhode Island, he graduated from Harvard in 1887 and stayed on to become one of the most important teachers in America. In 1905 he opened his '47 Workshop' to teach young playwrights and allow them to see their works performed. The students eventually included ◊ O'Neill, ◊ Barry, ◊ Behrman, ◊ Howard, Robert Edmond Jones, ◊ Dos Passos, John Mason ◊ Brown, Rachel Field and Thomas ◊ Wolfe (who describes Baker, as Professor Hatcher, in *Of Time and the River*). But Harvard did not like him, and in 1925 Yale provided the facilities he needed to develop a graduate drama school. He edited *Plays of the 47 Workshop* (1918–25). [BM]

W. P. Kinne, *George Pierce Baker and the American Theatre* (1954).

**Baker, Howard** (1905–    ). Poet, novelist. He has lived much of his life in California, where he is now a fruit farmer, but has also lived in France and Greece, the locale of some of his verse. He has taught writing in universities, including Harvard and the University of California at Davis. His wife was the novelist Dorothy ◊ Baker. His *A Letter from the Country and Other Poems*, distinguished and finely finished poems, appeared in pamphlet form in 1941, and was recently reissued with some new verse as *Ode to the Sea and Other Poems* (1966). He is also author of a good novel, *Orange Valley* (1931), and a scholarly critical work, *Induction to Tragedy* (1939; repr. 1965). [M B]

**Baldwin, James** (1924–    ). Novelist, playwright, essayist. He was born in Harlem, New York City, and his earliest experiences of life and religion in the ghetto are memorably presented in his first novel, *Go Tell It On the Mountain* (1953), an important book in the renaissance of black American literature since the 1950s. Baldwin lived for a number of years in Paris, recovering from racialist America and discovering his Americanism. His second novel, *Giovanni's Room* (1956), partly and obliquely covers that ground, but it also reveals one of his constant themes, the redemptive features of sexual love. The destructive horror of racialism and the struggle for sexual stability are the interlocking themes of his third novel, *Another Country* (1961), which shows the penetration of the effect of the life and death of a jazz drummer on his New York friends, black and white alike. *Tell Me How Long the Train's Been Gone* (1968) marks a serious change in his methods: instead of poise and Jamesian continuities, his style is looser and discontinuous, to fit the themes of shocking sexual and intellectual waste: the centre is a Negro actor's self-establishment in the face of racialism in the theatre. Baldwin's great talent is more secure in his series of essays, analysing his own experience and every aspect of Negro life and literature with one of the finest prose styles of our time: *Notes of a Native Son* (1955), *Nobody Knows My Name* (1961) and *The Fire Next Time* (1963), one of the most powerful indictments of racial tyranny and

confusion ever written. *Going to Meet the Man* (1965) is a collection of stories on his characteristic themes, and his two plays are *Amen Corner* (1955) and *Blues for Mr Charlie* (1965). (◊ Negro Literature.) [E M]

Robert Bone, *The Negro Novel in America* (revised 1965); H. M. Harper Jr, *Desperate Faith* (1967); F. M. Eckman, *The Furious Passage of James Baldwin* (1968).

**Bancroft, George** (1800–91). Historian. Born Worcester, Massachusetts. Between 1810 and 1830 American scholarship developed a new professionalism, emphasizing the importance of original documentary sources. American historians went to German universities (especially Göttingen) for advanced study, returning usually to Harvard to apply German research methods. Bancroft went in 1818, returned to preach, teach and become a tutor at Harvard, to publish his *Poems* (1823), and also to write, largely on German subjects, for American reviews. His 10-volume *History of the United States from the Discovery of the American Continent* (1834–74; abridged and ed. R. B. Nye, 1967) was hailed as a classic on the appearance of the first volume. It still remains of interest, despite evident faults. Its highly rhetorical style was muted in the 6-volume edition of 1883–5, but other flaws remain. Certainly he remains a 'Father of American History', using philosophical concepts and original manuscript materials for his work; but cavalier use of quotations makes him unreliable, and his Jacksonian bias is strong. In fact, the work is best read as an expression of Jacksonian America: it sees the history of the colonies as an inevitable progression towards the establishment of separate national identity, is committed on the side of democracy and nationalism, and believes in the superior virtue of the American people. Significantly, Bancroft was involved in political and social reform movements before the Civil War, and was during periods as Secretary of the Navy and acting Secretary of War an open supporter of Manifest Destiny. He was minister to England (1846–9) and to Berlin (1867–74). [D K A/M B]

M. A. De Wolfe Howe, *The Life and Letters of George Bancroft* (2 vols., 1908); Russel B. Nye, *George Bancroft: Brahmin Rebel* (1944); Harvey Wish, *The American Historian* (1960).

**Barker, James Nelson** (1784–1858). Playwright. Born in Philadelphia, he became its mayor; later he worked in the Treasury Department. He wrote a number of plays, some of patriotic character, of which the best known are *Tears and Smiles* (1808), a comedy in which, in the manner of Royall ◊ Tyler, he draws the essential Yankee in his 'Nathan Yank'; *The Indian Princess, or La Belle Sauvage* (1808), on the story of John ◊ Smith and Pocahontas; a stage adaptation of Scott's *Marmion* (1816) and *Superstition, or The Fanatic Father* (1826), on the Salem Witch Trials. This last touches on the problem of mob-democracy and prefigures a number of treatments of this theme, in fiction by Hawthorne and others, in the theatre by Arthur Miller and others. [M B]

Paul M. Musser, *James Nelson Barker, 1784–1858* (1929).

**Barlow, Joel** (1754–1812). Poet. The son of a Reading, Connecticut, farmer, he was educated at Dartmouth College and Yale, where he associated with the ◊ Connecticut Wits but found himself less conservative. He became an army chaplain in 1780, probably as one way to keep writing poetry, but at the end of the revolutionary war he returned to law, edited the *American Mercury*, opened a bookshop in Hartford and collaborated with the Wits. He travelled to Europe as agent for an Ohio land deal and when it failed escaped to France, where he met the radical republicans Joseph Priestley, Horne Tooke, ◊ Paine, etc. and wrote the revolutionary tract *Advice to the Privileged Orders* (1792–3), and *The Hasty Pudding* (1796), three cantos on a Yankee dish, as an excuse for celebrating American agrarianism. In 1811 he negotiated a trade agreement with Napoleon, followed the Russian campaign, and then died of pneumonia during the retreat from Moscow. His fame rests on *The Columbiad* (1807), an expansion of his *Vision of Columbus* (1787), a turgid epic on 'the consequences of the discovery' of America whose 10 books absorb the founding of the colonies, colonial wars and the Yorktown surrender, as part of a divine plan. It was criticized in England for linguistic innovations like 'crass' and 'utilize'. [E M]

J. Woodress, *A Yankee's Odyssey: The Life of Joel Barlow* (1958); T. Grieder, 'Joel Barlow's "The Hasty Pudding": A Study in American Neo-Classicism', *BAAS Bulletin*, December 1965.

**Barnes, Djuna** (1892–    ). Novelist, playwright. Born in New York, she has spent many years in Europe. From the earliest work her essentially poetic and introspective imagination has created its own forms. *A Book of Repulsive Women* (1911; repr. 1948) combines poems and drawings. *A Book* (1923, reissued with three new stories as *A Night among the Horses*, 1929; British title *Spillway*) contained plays, stories, and poems analysing a variety of people temperamentally drawn more to animal than to human life. *Ryder* (1928) developed a monologue style with its close-patterned tracking of one man's relationship with mother, wife and mistress. The novel *Ladies' Almanack* appeared in 1928. With *Nightwood* (1936), praised by T. S. Eliot as 'so good a novel that only sensibilities trained on poetry can wholly appreciate it', she first won a public name; this story of five psychopathic characters, knotted together, moving irrevocably to their doom, has an inner claustrophobia which relates it to the suspense and horror of Jacobean tragedy. Her most recent publication, *The Antiphon* (1958), a poetic drama, seems to derive its stylized verse mannerism as much from the 17th century as the classics.

'In the acceptance of depravity,' the doctor in *Nightwood* remarks, 'the sense of the past is most fully captured. What is a ruin but Time easing itself of endurance? Corruption is the age of Time. . . . Crime itself is the door to an accumulation, a way to lay hands on the shudder of a past that is still vibrating.' While belonging to the experimental, expatriate twenties, Djuna Barnes's mood is closer to the *fin de siècle*. Her special contributions have been a fascination with lesbian relationships, a delight in baroque language to accompany the tortured drama of innocence and guilt, and a gust of macabre humour that sometimes recalls Webster's theatre. [H B]

U. Weisstein, 'Beast Doll and Woman: Djuna Barnes's Human Bestiary', in *Renaissance*, XV, i (Fall, 1962); A. Williamson, 'The Divided Image. The Quest for Identity in the Works of Djuna Barnes', in *Critique*, VII, i (Spring, 1944).

**Barry, Philip** (1896–1949). Playwright. Born in Rochester, N.Y. After a brief trial as a diplomat he attended George Pierce ◊ Baker's '47 Workshop' at Yale, where his work led to the prize-winning *You and I* (1922). He became one of America's most brilliant writers of light comedy about wealthy society: *White Wings* (1926), *Paris*

*Bound* (1927), *Holiday* (1929) and *Here Come the Clowns* (1938). *Hotel Universe* (1930) attempts the more solemn theme of a God–Freud figure handling a crowd of neurotics in the south of France villa. *The Animal Kingdom* (1932) returns to sophisticated comedy (mistress more of a wife than wife), and Barry's finest play, the perennially witty and critical *The Philadelphia Story* (1939), shows Tracy Lord throwing over the traces of upper-class traditions with a reporter on the eve of marriage number two, only to remarry husband number one, C. K. Dexter Haven. Barry's art here is a masterly replay of the eternal triangle, with social overtones which do not disturb any more than they penetrate below the glittering surface. [EM]

J. M. Brown, *Upstage* (1930); Gerald Hamm, *The Drama of Philip Barry* (1948).

**Barth, John** (1930–    ). Novelist. Born in Maryland, he was educated at Johns Hopkins University, and taught at Pennsylvania State University. He teaches now at the University of Buffalo. His short fiction has appeared in various journals including the *Kenyon Review* and *Esquire*. He has written four brilliant novels which have lately won him a high reputation among critics. *The Floating Opera* (1956) is a marvellously funny analysis of a nihilist who decides not to commit suicide; *The End of the Road* (1961) is an excellent Existential black comedy about a man who refuses definition and brings others to misfortune; and *The Sotweed Factor* (1960) builds a wild extravaganza, with, as usual, strong philosophical implications, around the supposed career of the real Ebenezer ◊ Cook, the Maryland Laureate, whose Marylandiad epic 'The Sot-Weed Factor' – i.e. the tobacco planter – provides part of the structure of this bulky, fanciful historical novel. *Giles Goat-Boy, or The Revised New Syllabus* (1966) is a brilliantly written, complex epic satire on the meanings of education, on the world as university and humanity as an infinitely malleable material. It includes a parody of Sophocles' *Oedipus the Tyrant*, elaborate Dantean allegories, and pagan and Christian myths about animals and gods. *Lost in the Funhouse* (1968) consists of stories and narratives set in the context of a brilliant fictive language game, with, though, a sometimes slightly ponderous working out. [MB]

Leslie Fiedler, in *On Contemporary Literature*, ed. R. Kostelanetz (1965); Robert Scholes, *The Fabulators* (1967).

**Barthelme, Donald** (1933–    ). Short-story writer. A Texan, he served in the army and now lives in New York. His *Come Back, Dr Caligari* (1964) is a collection of absurdist, surrealistic tales, with a satirical, black-humour approach. Most appeared originally in the *New Yorker*. Varied in quality, they are at best sharp and funny distillations of modern technological society. *Snow White* (1967) is a brilliant novel, with an elaborate satirical structure of deflated myths, dislocated contemporary ideologies and fads, and scepticism. These qualities are at their finest in *Unspeakable Practices, Unnatural Arts* (1968) and *City Life* (1970), important collections of stories in which surreal fragmentation and black humour are fully developed. [MB/EM]

**Bartram, William** (1739–1823). Botanist (like his father John). He was born in Philadelphia. A Quaker and an artist, he turned down ◊ Franklin's offer of a printing training, and, after a few years as a planter and merchant, accompanied his father on botanical expeditions (1773–7); it is his narrative of these journeys which constitutes his classic work of literary as well as scientific value, *Travels through North and South Carolina, Georgia, East and West Florida, the Cherokee Country, the Extensive Territories of the Muscogulges, or Creek Confederacy, and the Country of the Choctaws* (1791; repr. 1958). His scientific interests take shape within a love of American landscape and its life, and an elaborate prose Carlyle called 'a wondrous kind of floundering eloquence'. The *Travels* is in fact a work of primary romantic imagination. Chateaubriand read it, and there are traces in Wordsworth and Coleridge (see John L. Lowes, *The Road to Xanadu*, 1927). [EM]

*John and William Bartram's America: Selections from the Writings*, ed. H. G. Cruikshank (1957).

**Basso, Hamilton** (1904–    ). Novelist. Born in New Orleans, he began his writing career working there as a journalist, later joining the staff of the *New Yorker*. He has lived in South Carolina and also in Europe, and has drawn on both backgrounds for his fiction. Of his considerable number of novels, many have southern settings. They include *Courthouse Square* (1936), *Days be-*

*fore Lent* (1939), *The View from Pompey's Head* (1954), *The Light Infantry Ball* (1959) and *A Quota of Seaweed* (1960). These, particularly the more recent ones, have won him a considerable reputation in both England and America as a writer who explores interestingly and detachedly the social dimension and the character of community life. [MB]

**Baum, L(yman) Frank** (1856–1919). Novelist. Born in Chittenango, N.Y. His achievement is to have created the land of happiness and mystery called Oz and 14 best-selling books about it, from *The Wonderful Wizard of Oz* (1900) to *Glinda of Oz* (1920). Ostensibly for children, this impressive series is a serious and delightful American fairy tale, whose characters and adventures in Utopia dramatize, without terror, a dream rural America, and satirize chauvinism in this 'melting pot' of races. He wrote other children's books under various pseudonyms. [EM]

H. M. Littlefield, 'The Wizard of Oz: Parable on Populism', *American Quarterly*, Spring, 1964.

**'Bay Psalm Book'** (1640) (full title, *The Whole Booke of Psalmes Faithfully Translated into English Metre*). Undertaken in 1636, to ensure translations closer to the Hebrew, by 'thirty pious and learned ministers', and edited by Richard Mather, Thomas Welde and John Eliot, it is considered to be the first book printed in America (Cambridge, Mass.). The 1651 revised edition was used for over a century, in 27 editions, many of them in England and Scotland. It was the first American literature to be a success in the Old World. These metrical versions were to be sung to 'very neere fourty common tunes, as they are collected out of our chief musicians by Thos. Ravenscroft' – a basis of style in American music. [EM]

**Beach, Sylvia** (1887–1962). Bookseller, memoirist. Born in New Jersey, she kept a bookshop, Shakespeare and Co., at 12 rue de l'Odéon, in Paris, which became an important expatriate centre during the 1920s (◊ Lost Generation). It began in 1919 at a slightly different location, and at one point served as a publishing house, when no publisher could be found to print James Joyce's *Ulysses*. Her record of this period, *Shakespeare and Company* (1959), is a valuable document, and is usefully supp-

lemented by *Sylvia Beach: A Memorial Volume of Reminiscences* (1966) by 38 of her contemporaries. [MB]

**Beard, Charles Austin** (1874–1948). Political scientist, historian. Born in Indiana and a graduate of DePauw, he went to Oxford, where he helped to found Ruskin College. After teaching politics at Columbia University (1907–17), he resigned to write, his interests having shifted from European to American history. Though not accepting Frederick Jackson ◊ Turner's frontier thesis of American development, he admired and followed Turner's new emphasis on economic and social determinism. Beard was author or editor of over 50 books on history and government. The major theme of his *An Economic Interpretation of the Constitution of the United States* (1913) was that the Federalist sponsors of the new constitution of 1787 were the commercial, financial and manufacturing groups, and that there was a conflict of interest between these and the small farmers who constituted a majority of the population. *The Economic Origins of Jeffersonian Democracy* (1915) similarly analyses ◊ Jefferson's political support. His large-scale history of the U.S.A., written with his wife Mary Ritter Beard, began with *The Rise of American Civilization* (1927), and again stresses the importance throughout American history of the class of interest groups and – without denying the force of ideas or moral concepts the fundamental relationship of economics and politics. In *The Idea of National Interest* (1934) Beard applied his economic interpretation to recent American foreign policy; increasingly he urged that international economic interests were tending to involve America in world tensions and even war. In *America in Mid-Passage* (*The Rise of American Civilization*, iii; with Mary Beard, 1939), he vigorously advocated 'continentalism', a version of isolationism. In *American Foreign Policy in the Making: 1932–1940* (1946) and more strongly still in his last book, *President Roosevelt and the Coming of the War: 1941* (1948), he held that though Roosevelt's public statements stressed peace his foreign policy led the U.S.A. into war; this view became the basis of the 'revisionist' interpretation of American participation in the Second World War. Beard's interpretations (and his movement from progressivism to conservatism) have been attacked; but many of his bold generalizations remain to influence and challenge modern historians. [D K A/M B]

Bernard C. Borning, *The Political and Social Thought of Charles A. Beard* (1962).

**Beat Generation Writers.** A group of writers active in the 1950s, centred around William ◊ Burroughs, Allen ◊ Ginsberg, Jack ◊ Kerouac, and later Lawrence ◊ Ferlinghetti, Gregory ◊ Corso and Peter Orlovsky. The term 'beat' was first used in its new way by Kerouac and recorded in 1952 in an article by John Clellon ◊ Holmes in the *New York Times*. Roughly speaking, the Beats were a criticism of American complacency under the Ike–Nixon regime, an expression of new forms of prose and poetry and an exploration of consciousness, which joined the dissent of existing Bohemias in ◊ Greenwich Village (New York), North Beach (San Francisco) and Venice West (Los Angeles) to produce a distinctive style of literature and living, based on disaffiliation, poverty, anarchic individualism and communal living. A relaxation of 'square' (puritan, middle-class, respectable) attitudes towards sex, drugs, religion and art became the opposing uniformity of 'beat' (later fused into 'hip'). The word 'beat' has a range of meanings including depressed (to the point of wild escape from conventional living); exhausted; holy in poverty and beatific in joy and mystic illumination (with literary references back to Whitman, Blake and Rimbaud, and jazz associations with Lester Young and Charlie Parker), and to catching the note of spontaneous living (with references to Zen Buddhism, Indian peyote cults and visionary experience). In literature, the key works were Ginsberg's poem 'Howl' (1955), Kerouac's novel *On the Road* (1957), Gary ◊ Snyder's poems *Riprap* (1959), the early poems of ◊ Whalen and ◊ McClure, Ferlinghetti's *Pictures from the Gone World* (1955) (as well as the other work emanating from his City Lights bookshop in San Francisco), Corso's poems in *Gasoline* (1958), and Burroughs' *Junkie* (1953) and *The Naked Lunch* (1959). But there were a number of other significant figures, both in New York and in San Francisco, publishing in a number of beat magazines. Hangers-on developed into 'beatniks', a generally denigratory term, apparently coined by Herb Caen in the San Francisco *Chronicle*, for a form of living and writing partly created by

a frightened bourgeoisie and its sensation-seeking press. *The Beat* (ed. S. Krim, 1960) and *The New American Poetry* (ed. D. M. Allen, 1960) contained representative writings, and F. Rigney's *The Real Bohemia* (1961) attempted a sociological study of North Beach. [E M]

Lawrence Lipton, *The Holy Barbarians* (1959); ed. Thomas Parkinson, *A Casebook on the Beat* (1961); Ned Polsky, *Hustlers, Beats, and Others* (1967).

**Beecher, Henry Ward** (1813–87). Clergyman, editor, novelist, miscellaneous writer. Born in Litchfield, Connecticut. A graduate of Amherst College, he studied at a Cincinnati theological college of which his father, Lyman Beecher, a stern and rigorous Presbyterian, was president. Ordained in 1838, he became Congregational minister in Indianapolis (1839–47), then at Plymouth Church, Brooklyn. His success in New York as a vigorous preacher and as editor of the *Independent* (1861–4) and *The Christian Union* (1870–81) was later diminished by his involvement in a notorious adultery case (1874).

A strong anti-slavery spokesman, Beecher used extreme oratorical skill and a racy sense of humour in disseminating a mild, gentle and rather vague neo-Emersonian religion – he described God as 'one who loves a man in his sins for the sake of helping him out of them'. V. L. ◊ Parrington called him 'the high priest of emotional liberalism'; Thoreau, 'a magnificent pagan'. His aphoristic *Seven Lectures to Young Men* (1844) warned of temptations on the frontier; study of Darwin ensued in *Evolution and Religion* (1885). A novel *Norwood or Village Life in New England* (1867) contained pleasant descriptions of the New England landscape. He was a readable and intelligent essayist and also published lectures and sermons. He has no impartial biographer: Lyman Abbott published a laudatory *Henry Ward Beecher* (1903), and Paxton Hibben the hostile *Henry Ward Beecher: An American Portrait* (1927). [M G]

*Autobiographical Reminiscences*, ed. T. J. Ellinwood (1898).
Lionel G. Crocker, *Henry Ward Beecher's Art of Preaching* (1934); Robert Shapler, *Free Love and Heavenly Sinners* (1954).

**Behrman, S(amuel) N(athaniel)** (1893–     ). Playwright. Born in Worcester, Massachusetts. After working with George Pierce ◊ Baker's '47 Workshop' at Harvard (1916) his long theatre career began with the immediate success of *The Second Man* 1927), a comedy of two couple relationships, and he succeeded Philip ◊ Barry as the leading Broadway writer of high comedy in which wit and optimism overcome the corrupt pressures of the thirties. Of his huge output, the better pieces are *End of Summer* (1936) and *No Time for Comedy* (1939), which make laughter out of class shifts between 1900 and the Depression and the conflict of money and politics with creativity. He has also written *Duveen* (1952), a biography of the art dealer, and *Max* (1960), a study of Max Beerbohm, and worked on a number of famous Hollywood films, including Garbo's *Queen Christina* (1933). *The Worcester Account* (1954), stories, provides autobiography. *The Burning Glass* (1968), his first novel, is a social comedy of the thirties. [EM]

**Belitt, Ben** (1911– ). Poet. Born in New York City, he was educated at the University of Virginia, worked editorially for the *Nation*, and now teaches at Bennington College. His poetry, collected in *The Five-Fold Mesh* (1938), *Wilderness Stair* (1955) and *The Enemy Joy* (1964), is erudite, intellectually complex, emotionally intense and occasionally apocalyptic. He writes about nature, myth and poetry itself. He has also translated from Spanish, Mexican and South American verse. [BP]

**Bellamy, Edward** (1850–98). Novelist. He was born and lived most of his life in Massachusetts. Abandoning his profession of law – no lawyers are allowed in his ideal commonwealth – he became a journalist in 1871. His early novels possess no great originality; after *Six to One: A Nantucket Idyll* (1878), he published two romances which, as the titles indicate, owe something to Hawthorne: *Dr Heidenhoff's Process* (1880) and *Miss Ludington's Sister* (1884). *The Duke of Stockbridge*, a novel of Shay's rebellion, appeared serially in 1879 and in book form in 1900 (intr. J. Schiffman, 1962).

Despite Bellamy's growing interest in social reform there was nothing in these works to indicate that his next book would be the famous *Looking Backward: 2000–1887* (1888). Indeed, the work was originally intended to be a fantasy in the manner of his earlier productions. As he wrote, however, it became the 'vehicle of a definite scheme of industrial reorganization'. The new social and industrial order of the future is presented through the eyes of Julian West, a Bostonian who awakes 112 years after he has fallen into a mesmeric sleep in 1887. The action of the novel, strongly dependent on the vivid contrasting of past and future, has considerable dramatic tension; this, and the attractive imagery and style in which he advanced his theories, did much to ensure its phenomenal popularity and influence. A controlled yet savage attack on the existing social order, the book posited a unique American theory of state capitalism in a society from which economic individualism had been banished, with a consequent rise in the health and happiness of its members.

In order to disseminate Bellamy's views, over 150 'Nationalist' clubs were formed, and loosely linked to the Populist Party. Two journals, the *Nationalist* (1889–91) and Bellamy's own *New Nation* (1891–4), were additional organs of propaganda; but the movement was unable to exert any realistic political influence (*Talks on Nationalism*, 1938, reprints articles from the latter journal). Before his death Bellamy published a sequel to *Looking Backward*, *Equality* (1897), in which he vigorously attacked the profit motive; the book, however, lacked the verve of its predecessor and remained a rather dull economic tract. [HD]

*Edward Bellamy Speaks Again: Articles, Public Addresses, Letters*, intr. R. L. McBride (1937); *Edward Bellamy: Selected Writings on Religion and Society*, ed. J. Schiffman (1956).
Arthur E. Morgan, *Edward Bellamy* (1944); Sylvia E. Bowman, *The Year 2000* (1958); S. E. Bowman et al., *Edward Bellamy Abroad: An American Prophet's Influence* (1962).

**Bellow, Saul** (1915– ). Novelist. Born in Quebec, Canada, of immigrant Jewish background. His family moved to Chicago when he was 9, and he attended Chicago, Northwestern and Wisconsin Universities. Author of seven novels, as well as plays, short stories and essays, he is critically regarded as one of the best post-war American novelists. He has explored the situation of urban democratic man with intense sociological and psychological awareness, through a variety of fictional modes. His subject is the need to come to some adequate conception of selfhood in a world in which the romantic supports have been removed – a world crowded under the pressure of democratic numbers, hence encouraging deterministic philosophies which view man as the suffering victim of his environment. His heroes are concerned with man's desire to take on the duties of his humanity and understand the nature of responsibility for others. *Dangling Man* (1944), his first novel, showing obvious analogies with contemporary European Existential fiction, explores a man deprived of the capacity for effective choice by his city circumstances and by a draft notice which offers him the cancellation of freedom. *The Victim* (1947) deals with the difficulty of defining responsibility for others in a modern democratic city where the consequences of one's actions disappear into the crowd, no man has a defined place, and mechanical arrangements prevail. *The Adventures of Augie March* (1953) has a larger canvas, a more picaresque approach, and a joyous euphoria of tone and language as the hero is followed in a comic attempt to define the level of his humanity. *Seize the Day* (1956), a short, concentrated novel, meets the same question, concentrating on the challenge of human mortality. *Henderson the Rain King* (1959) has a broad comic scale and a large, extravagant hero who seeks the truth about the human scale in a semi-mythical African landscape, a landscape for adventures of the mind. On the same scale, *Herzog* (1964) restores the urban landscape. Its hero, a scholar and intellectual, confronts in a gladiatorial combat the question of his connexion with his society and the whole intellectual history of the West, exploring romantic optimism, deterministic pessimism, measuring the degree to which man must be seen as a suffering creature. Bellow exploits the double comedy involved; the world about his later heroes, depressing the nature of man, turns the quests of his heroes into intellectual farce; they are the Superman as clown. Though sometimes accused of unearned optimism, Bellow has a real capacity to render suffering and typify the conditions of modern life. Indebted to ◊ Dreiser and the Naturalists, he goes beyond them in intellectual and technical power, in his interpretation of society, and in his wry view of the new Superman. Among his contemporaries in the so-

called 'Jewish efflorescence' in post-war American fiction, he reveals an intellectual mastery and literary control that distinguish him clearly as a major writer. He has also written plays including *The Last Analysis* (1956) and *A Wen* (1965). His stories of the last 20 years are collected in *Mosby's Memoirs* (1969), in which a growing movement towards ironic reflection on man can be seen. *Mr Sammler's Planet* (1970) extends the ironic mode into a full-length novel. The book is centred around Mr Sammler, an ancient survivor of the pleasures (Bloomsbury) and the horrors (Auschwitz) of modern western civilization. He now lives out his last days amid the chaos and discordance of New York City in the moonshot age, with its cults of liberation and apocalypse, playing his one cold eye (the other was lost at Auschwitz) over modern vanities and reflecting whether man is in a state of self-destruction or moving toward a new state of being appropriate to its role in space: Sammler's wryness in this cool comedy of ideas is obviously Bellow's, too. [MB]

Tony Tanner, *Saul Bellow* (1965); K. M. Opdahl, *The Novels of Saul Bellow* (1968); Maxwell Geismar, *American Moderns* (1958); John J. Clayton, *Saul Bellow, In Defense of Man* (1968); Malcolm Bradbury, 'Saul Bellow and the Naturalist Tradition', *Review of English Literature*, October 1963.

**Bemelmans, Ludwig** (1898–1963). Novelist, essayist. He was the son of a Belgian painter and a Bavarian brewer's daughter. He is best known for his memoirs – humorous and elegantly caught observations on his Austrian youth, and his early days as a hotel waiter in the U.S.A. A writer for the *New Yorker* and other sophisticated journals, he specialized mainly in records of pre-war Europe and travel and gourmet pieces. Among his many books, *Life Class* (1938), *Hotel Splendide* (1941) and *The World of Bemelmans* (1955) best show his wit and charm, which also overflow into his fiction. Among his novels, *Dirty Eddie* (1947), a venture into the Hollywood novel, is a delightful spoof about a movie star pig; *Are You Hungry Are You Cold* (1960) tends to sentimentality. *On Board Noah's Ark* (1962) is a wry travelogue of the Mediterranean, and *The Street Where the Heart Lies* (1963) is an exotic tale of Americans in Paris. He has also written books for children. [MB]

**Benchley, Robert** (1889–1945). Humorist. Born in Massachusetts, educated at Harvard. He went into journalism, was managing editor of *Vanity Fair*, and then worked as drama critic for *Life* and the *New Yorker*. He is among the most hilarious and professional of modern American humorists; his main *forte* has been in the short essay, mostly written under the conditions of daily journalism. He commonly deals with ordinary situations, taking snippets of news or moral rules as a foil for his own incompetence and failures, or else his fantasies of power and prestige. One of his main comic techniques is the *non sequitur*, producing a nonsense method of writing evident in the titles of some of his books. He has published many collections of essays, including *Pluck and Luck* (1925), *20,000 Leagues under the Sea, or David Copperfield* (1928), *From Bed to Worse, or Comforting Thoughts about the Bison* (1934), *My Ten Years in a Quandary, and How They Grew* (1936), *Inside Benchley* (1942) and *Benchley Beside Himself* (1943). Various posthumous collections have been made, showing his continued popularity: *Chips off the Old Benchley* (1949) and *The Benchley Round-Up* (1954), etc. [M B]

Nathaniel Benchley, *Robert Benchley: A Biography* (1955).

**Benét, Stephen Vincent** (1898–1943). Poet, story writer, novelist. Born in Bethlehem, Pennsylvania. The son of an army officer, with whom he read history in widely scattered army quarters, he published his first book of poems before graduating from Yale (1919) and continued publishing successfully while a graduate student at Yale and the Sorbonne. Most of his major poetry and fiction was dedicated to exploring and understanding American national character, history and legend. Two long epic poems are among his best-known work – *John Brown's Body* (1928), exploring the Civil War, and *Western Star* (1943), unrevised at his death, dealing with American roots in the great 17th-century European migrations. Representative among his many short poems are 'The Hemp' (1918), a ballad depicting the destruction of a pirate at sea by an outraged Virginia planter; 'Ballad of William Sycamore' (1923), about a frontier character 'cradled on twigs of pine' at Plymouth; and the famous 'American Names' (1927), which compares European and American history by place-names (Salem, or Santa Cruz, or Sussex). He was a traditionalist in both his subjects and forms of expression (e.g. the ballad); but in these limits his craftsmanship was strikingly original. His fantasies and light verse are less impressive, though *King David* (1923) and numerous smaller poems reflect charming gifts of wit and satire.

Though his five novels are not particularly memorable, his short stories remain much admired, particularly those dealing with historical materials rather than contemporary life – 'Jacob and the Indians', a narrative tribute to the Jewish colonial-Americans,'The Devil and Daniel Webster', a comic folk-tale (made into an opera and a film) about the popular statesman who became legendary before his death, etc. In the depression and war years Benét became a literary defender of the democracies; and in speaking for his political and social liberalism over-exerted himself as lecturer and radio propagandist (see *We Stand United and Other Radio Scripts*, 1945). He wrote more and more on social themes – stories, articles and poems. *Burning City* (1936) interestingly represents the poetry of this phase. His writing continues to excite enthusiasm, though the only collection of his work is inadequate, and little of his criticism is reprinted. [R S]

*Selected Works* (2 vols., 1942); *Selected Letters*, ed. C. A. Fenton (1960).
Charles A. Fenton, *Stephen Vincent Benét: The Life and Times of an American Man of Letters* (1958).

**Benét, William Rose** (1886–1950). Poet, critic. Born in New York, elder brother of Stephen Vincent ◊ Benét, he married Elinor ◊ Wylie, whose poems he edited (1932). Active in magazine journalism, he helped found the *Saturday Review of Literature* in 1924; he also wrote for children. He was an exuberant and prolific poet; his volumes include *Merchants from Cathay* (1913), *The Falconer of God* (1914), *The Burglar of the Zodiac* (1918), *Moons of Grandeur* (1920), *Day of Deliverance* (1944) and *The Stairway of Surprise* (1947). The early work is high-spirited and romantic, whether the fantasy ranges to China or the prairies with cowboys and their ballads. Later he developed a free-verse medley of narrative, monologue, dialogue and lyric, seeking like his brother to catch semi-legendary meanings in daily experience. He also tried an experimental verse novel, *Rip*

*Tide* (1932), and a (Pulitzer Prize-winning) verse autobiography, *The Dust Which Is God* (1941). [HB]

**Berenson, Bernard** (1865–1959). Art critic, aesthetician. Born in Lithuania, he was brought to the United States as a boy and educated at Harvard. Sponsored by a group of Boston friends, he went to study in Europe and devote himself to connoisseurship. He spent most of his life near Florence, where his house I Tatti became an important artistic centre, not only for those interested in painting but also for writers. He was a dominant figure in shaping the modern attitude toward all the arts. An aesthetic philosopher, his notions of 'life enhancement' through art were widely influential and through books and conversations he established many themes in modern aesthetics. In addition to the famous volumes on Renaissance art – *Venetian Painters of the Renaissance* (1894), etc. – his books include *Aesthetics, Ethics and History* (1948), the autobiographical *Sketch for a Self-Portrait* (1949), the wartime diary *Rumor and Reflection* (1952), and *Sunset and Twilight: From the Diaries of 1947–1958* (1963). [MB]

*Selected Letters*, ed. A. K. McComb (1964); *The Bernard Berenson Treasury*, ed. Hannah Kiel (1962).
Sylvia Sprigge, *Berenson: A Biography* (1960).

**Bergé, Carol** (1928–    ). Poet. Born and educated in New York, she has worked in publishing and advertising, run a small art gallery (she is a painter herself), and co-founded Poetry Workshop in 1961. She appeared in *Four Young Lady Poets* (ed. LeRoi Jones, 1962) but her mature poems, finely made and deeply personal, appeared later in *Poems Made of Skin* (1968), *Circles, as in the Eye* (1969), *The Chambers* (1969), and, above all, in *An American Romance* (1969). *The Vancouver Report* (1965) is a useful account of a poetry conference involving some of the major contemporary American poets. [EM]

**Berger, Thomas** (1924–    ). Novelist. Born in Cincinnati, Ohio, he served in the Army in the Second World War, and has since lived in New York. His first novel, *Crazy in Berlin* (1958), established him as one of the most notable of contemporary ironists. Concerned with GIs in Germany,

its hero, Carlos Reinhart, reappeared in *Reinhart in Love* (1961), still moving through post-war western life as in a dream which is not his own. *Little Big Man* (1964) is a large-scale parody and serious appraisal of the Wild West and its myths and actuality. *Killing Time* (1967), his finest work to date, is a masterly dramatization of the confusions between law and criminality, normality and madness. In *Vital Parts* (1970) Reinhart encounters Bob Sweet, a shrewd caricature of the American as competitive individualist, a self-made monster who manipulates the younger generation with the skill of a sociologist and puts his main faith in cryonics, the science of freezing. Berger's dark humour and exceptional ability to create characters which represent the post-war scene are at the service of an ironical intelligence both debunking and alarmed. He is a major comic writer of the period. ([EM]

**Berrigan, Ted** (1934–    ). Poet. Born in Providence, Rhode Island, he joined the Army for three years in 1953, and then studied at the University of Tulsa, moving to New York in 1960. In 1963, he founded, with Lorenz Gude, *'C' Magazine*, whose 13 issues, along with the concurrent 'C' books, defined a new scene of poetry, centred on New York, and featuring such poets as Berrigan himself, Ron Padgett, Dick Gallup, Tom Veitch, Kenward Elmslie and Joe Ceravolo, and the artists Joe Brainard and George Schneeman. He has written for *Art News* and taught at the University of Iowa. *Sonnets* (1964) is a long and intricate set of interacting and permutated poems of considerable virtuosity; *Bean Spasms* (1967, with Ron Padgett) excellently represents the 'C' effect – parody, self-parody and an intense interest in procedure; *Many Happy Returns* (1968) collects his alternately introvertly wary and extrovertly exuberant recent poems. [EM]

**Berry, Wendell** (1934–    ). Poet, novelist. Born in Louisville, Kentucky. The south has been a basic part of the subject matter of his poetry and fiction. Graduated from the University of Kentucky, he taught at Stanford and New York University; now he teaches at the University of Kentucky, and farms. His precocious first novel, *Nathan Coulter* (1960), a study of a boy's coming-of-age in the tobacco-growing country, delicately evokes the way character develops from rural values and customs. In 1964 he published *November Twenty-Six, Nineteen Hundred Sixty-Three*, a long poem on the death of John F. Kennedy illustrated by Ben Shahn, and a first collection of verse, *The Broken Ground*. These poems, which show the same concern for land and roots in place and family as the novel, use a stark, imagistic approach to settings and subjects to catch carefully established subtleties of the spirit. His novel, *A Place on Earth* (1968), is a slow pastoral set in a sentimentalized Kentucky during the Second World War. In 1969 he published two books of poems, *Openings* and *Findings*, as well as a collection of social and political essays, *The Long-Legged House* [BS]

**Berryman, John** (1914– ). Poet. Born in Oklahoma, he graduated from Columbia and Cambridge, and has taught at Princeton, Washington and Cincinnati Universities, while his distinctive poetry appeared, since the thirties in little magazines and in 1940 in *Five American Poets*. After *Poems* (1942) and *The Dispossessed* (1948), *Homage to Mistress Bradstreet* (1956) presented Berryman's special abilities in a long and intricate work moving from Anne ◊ Bradstreet's life and spirit in 17th-century New England towards the present. *77 Dream Songs* (1964) is the first part of a projected series of complex, highly wrought dramatic commentaries on the poet and his times. The second sequence, *History, His Dream, His Rest* (1968), continues the forms, but draws in a wider range of American life. *Berryman's Sonnets* (1968) is a sequence of 115 love sonnets, written in the 1940s and reflecting the poetic fashions of the time (Empson, Donne, Hopkins). He has also written short stories and *Stephen Crane* (1950), the first major critical and biographical work on ◊ Crane. [EM]

**Beverley, Robert** (c.1673–1722). Historian. As a boy he was educated in England, returned to his parents in Virginia to manage the large plantation he inherited, and became Jamestown's representative in the House of Burgesses. His *The History and Present State of Virginia* (1705, 1722; ed. L. B. Wright, 1947) is a fascinating, brilliantly observed record, written in good plain 17th-century style – a history of the colony, drawing critically on John ◊ Smith;

a description of the country, including a first-hand report on the Indians; and an account of the government. His eye for nature is excellent, his account of the Indians respectfully recognizes their autonomous civilization, and his defence of the state is persuasive. But he cannot see that slavery besmirches his Virginian Eden. [EM]

**Bierce, Ambrose** (1842–1914?). Short-story writer, wit. Born in Ohio, he fought as a youth in the Civil War and went as a journalist to California. In London (1872–6) he published several books of sketches and epigrams and then returned to California, later to Washington; he finally disappeared into Mexico during a Civil War. An elegant and finished writer, his satirical objects and his California context never quite served him well enough. *The Devil's Dictionary* (1906; original title *The Cynic's Word Book*), a delightful compendium of misanthropic definitions – 'happiness' is the contemplation of the misery of another – shows that in concentration he was at his best. His concern with style is expressed in *Write It Right* (1909). The two best-known collections are *Tales of Soldiers and Civilians* (1891), in a later edition entitled *In the Midst of Life* (1892; revised 1898) and *Can Such Things Be?* (1893) – macabre tales, centred on death, given to fantasy, with a strong *fin de siècle* flavour. Bierce has been rather underestimated. A kind of Oscar Wilde, unsupported by his culture, his essentially Bohemian sensibility is at once sophisticated and in some sense derived – perhaps from European models (◊ Bohemianism). He has interested English readers for some time (though his London visit was not entirely successful), and A. J. A. Symons edited *Ten Tales* in 1925. [MB]

*Collected Works*, ed. Walter Neal (12 vols., 1909–12); *The Collected Writings*, selected Clifton Fadiman (1946); *The Enlarged Devil's Dictionary*, ed. E. J. Hopkins (1968).
Richard O'Connor, *Ambrose Bierce: A Biography* (1967); Paul Fatout, *Ambrose Bierce: The Devil's Lexicographer* (1951).

**Biggers, Earl Derr** (1884–1933). Playwright, novelist. Born in Ohio. He survives in his Hawaii Chinese detective, Charlie Chan, the plump philosophical American descendant of the oriental sage tradition of the West. He first appeared in *The House without a Key* (1925) and became an international hero through films in which he was portrayed by Warner Oland (see *The Chinese Parrot*, 1926, *The Black Camel*, 1929, *Keeper of the Keys*, 1932, etc.). [EM]

**Billings, Josh (Henry Wheeler Shaw)** (1818–85). Humorist. Born in Lanesboro, Massachusetts, he was one of the Civil War generation of vernacular comic commentators which took the age by storm, won Lincoln's admiration, and created the atmosphere in which a figure like 'Mark Twain' could become a significant writer. Most of this group – like 'Artemus ◊ Ward' and 'Petroleum V. ◊ Nasby' – used a single comic personality who lectured, wrote and commented on events in the voice of the illiterate crackerbarrel philosopher; 'Mark ◊ Twain' broke the pattern by making the pseudonym into the complex persona of a remarkable writer. The flowering of the group created a satirical era where agrarian folk-wisdom played against follies, government corruption and eastern pretensions for a popular audience.

Shaw, born in Massachusetts, was explorer in the West, farmer, steamboat captain, auctioneer and real-estate dealer until he turned to writing as 'Josh Billings', a Yankee countryman, comic essays based on his multifarious experiences, Artemus Ward, puns and bad spelling. He took on the part and lectured throughout the country. His fame was enormous and his output prolific, from *Josh Billings: His Sayings* (1865) through *Josh Billings on Ice* (1868) to *Josh Billings' Spice Box* (1881). Between 1869 and 1880 he produced the famous parody annual the *Farmer's All-minax*. [MB]

*The Complete Works of Josh Billings* (1919); *Uncle Sam's Uncle Josh*, ed. Donald Day (1953).
Cyril Clemens, *Josh Billings: Yankee Humorist* (1932).

**Bird, Robert Montgomery** (1806–54). Novelist, playwright. Born in Delaware, he became a doctor in Philadelphia, turned to drama and then to novels: *The Hawks of Hawk-Hollow* (1835), about a Tory family in the Revolution, and *Nick of the Woods* (1837), about post-Revolution struggles with the Indians, focused on a split-personality figure who is a Quaker and an Indian-killer, are the two best known. [MB]

**Bishop, Elizabeth** (1911– ). Poet. Born in New England, educated at Vassar,

she now lives in Brazil, the setting of some of her poems. She made her reputation with *North and South* (1946) and *Poems* (1955), a small body of striking and distinctive verse, more recently substantiated with *Questions of Travel* (1966), in which the indirectness and ironic understatement are even more prominent. Her work, often touched with fantasy, frequently suggests the mysterious operation of the universe and the terrifying face of its large cities ('Man-Moth', 'A Letter to N.Y.'). She sometimes celebrates nature, but can show its cruelty ('The Prodigal'); hence her verse has a pervasive sense of exile. Her poems are frequently long and carefully mannered, using elaborate rhyme or half-rhymes. An extraordinary meticulousness of craftsmanship marks all her work; exactitude of perception plays against inherently nostalgic or romantically tragic themes, to give great subtlety and toughness. [MB]

*Selected Poems* (1968): *Complete Poems* (1970).

**Bishop, John Peale** (1892–1944). Poet. Born in West Virginia, educated at Princeton, he settled on Cape Cod, where most of the poems collected in *Green Fruit* (1917), *Now With his Love* (1933) and *Minute Particulars* (1935) were written. At Princeton he first met Edmund ◊ Wilson, with whom he later collaborated on *The Undertaker's Garland* (1922). There are also stories, *Many Thousands Gone* (1931), and a novel, *Act of Darkness* (1935). He is said to be the prototype of Tom D'Invilliers, the radical young Princeton poet in his friend F. Scott Fitzgerald's first novel, *This Side of Paradise* (1920). He was very consciously the poet. With a controlled but gilded vocabulary he created neo-classic friezes – mothers by the seashore, a guilt-stricken Actaeon, a late Roman emperor retreating before Barbarians, a retiring senator, a sword dance, Hecuba in tears – as finely etched, but as evasive, as a Flaxman sculpture or a Robert Bridges lyric. His is a literature of literature, effectively muffling his own pulse. [HB]

*Collected Essays* (1948); *Collected Poems* (1948); *Selected Poems* (1960).
Ed. Allen Tate, *A Southern Vanguard*, The John Peale Bishop Memorial Volume (1947).

**Blackburn, Paul** (1926– ). Poet, translator. He was born in Vermont, spent his youth in New Hampshire, South Carolina and New York, served in the U.S. army, and studied at New York University, Wis-

consin and Toulouse, where he was a Fulbright teacher in 1955–6. During 1953–7 he
spent a good deal of time in Spain, and in
1962 was poetry editor of the *Nation*. He
has translated *El Cid Campeador* and his
fine Spanish translations appear in *Proensa*
(1953); he has recently completed an
anthology of Provençal poetry in translation. His earlier poetry is in *The Dissolving
Fabric* (1955), *Brooklyn–Manhattan Transit*
(1960) and *The Nets* (1961). His style here
is a personal version of the immediate
tradition of William Carlos ◊ Williams and
what is loosely called ◊ Black Mountain
poetry, meaning derivatives from 'projective
verse'. But *Sing-Song* (1966), *The Cities*
(1967) and *In. On. Or About the Premises*
(1968) show him to be a major original poet,
with a masterly rhythmic technique, a
humane but critical sense of humour, and
a feeling for urban living which is compassionate, satirical and wittily observant.
[EM]

**Black Mountain College.** Accompanied by a
handful of supporters, John Andrew Rice
left Rollins College, California – where his
attempts to found a liberal educational
centre in an illiberal town led to his dis-
missal – and in 1933 founded Black
Mountain, in the midst of the Depression,
and with little or no money, as a college
experiment in American community education. This centre, near Asheville, North
Carolina, became a focus for all those dissatisfied with academic methods and in need
of teaching and being taught creatively.
Among contributing teachers, students and
visitors were John ◊ Dewey, Josef Albers
(director in the 1940s), Charles ◊ Olson,
Louis Adamic, Eric Bentley and John ◊
Cage; among the painters and sculptors,
De Kooning, Kline, Stamos, Tworkov,
Vicente, Motherwell, Rauschenberg and
Guston; among writers Paul ◊ Goodman,
Robert ◊ Duncan, Robert ◊ Creeley,
Jonathan ◊ Williams, Fielding Dawson,
John ◊ Wieners, Joel ◊ Oppenheimer; and
among musicians and film-makers, Lou
Harrison, John Cage and Stanley Vander-
beek. Their work, and that of Paul ◊
Blackburn and Denise ◊ Levertov, was
published and considered in Cid Corman's
*Origin* (1951–6) and *Black Mountain Re-
view* (1954–7), edited by Creeley, with
contributing editors Allen ◊ Ginsberg,
Irving Layton, Olson, Jonathan Williams
and Robert Hellman. Among those

printed were also ◊ Zukofsky, Borges,
William Carlos ◊ Williams, Jack ◊
Kerouac, Philip ◊ Whalen, Ed ◊ Dorn,
Gary ◊ Snyder, Hubert ◊ Selby, Michael ◊
McClure and Michael ◊ Rumaker. These
writers have long since become a major
part of 20th-century American literature.
The college closed in 1956 but its work
fertilized art and literature to a degree rare
in the history of any culture. [EM]

**Blackmur, R(ichard) P(almer)** (1904–65).
Literary critic, poet. Born in Springfield,
Massachusetts. Partly self-educated, he
became Professor of English at Princeton.
Among the more important modern American speculative critics, he is generally associated with the tendency of the ◊ New
Criticism. The title of one of his critical
volumes – *Language as Gesture* (1952) –
suggests this kinship; he sought to identify
the character of literary language, and
develop a sophisticated analysis of it. But
he was also widely interested in the social
context of literature, writing on such topics
as literary expatriates and the development
of the modern literary intelligentsia. His
essay 'A Critic's Job of Work' – reprinted
in the useful paperback collection of his
writings, *Form and Value in Modern Poetry*
(1957) – presents criticism as 'the formal
discourse of an amateur', relevant in its
resistance to ulterior motive, dependent
finally on the critic's strength of mind.
Though particularly interested in modern
American poetry, Blackmur ranged widely
in his objects of study. He edited the Prefaces of Henry James – by whom his
criticism is influenced both in elegance and
in its weighty aesthetic emphasis – and
among his books are *The Double Agent:
Essays in Craft and Elucidation* (1935), *The
Lion and the Honeycomb: Essays in Solici-
tude and Critique* (1955) and *Eleven Essays
in the European Novel* (1964). His poems –
in various volumes, including *From Jordan's
Delight* (1937) – are dignified and speculative, moving between a classical rhetoric
and a lyricism drawn from song. [MB]

**Blechman, Burt** (1927–    ). Novelist. He
was born in New York, graduated at Vermont University, and studied at Columbia
and Chicago. He ran away from home to
join the merchant navy at 16 and then
supported himself with miscellaneous jobs.
He travels a good deal and was in Cuba
during the revolution. His fiction began with

one of the best satires on consumer society in the sixties, *How Much?* (1962), adapted as a play, *My Father, My Mother and Me*, by Lillian ♦ Hellman. His second novel, *The War of Camp Omongo* (1963), exposes the middle-class through its children at a holiday camp. *Stations* (1964) is as uncompromising in its style and form as his satire in the earlier work. The homosexual theme is presented surrealistically as the life of Everyman in a universe of pain (he is influenced by Céline and Genet). *The Octopus Papers* (1965) satirizes the American cultural establishment with an anger comparable to that of Nathanael ♦ West. *Maybe* (1967) is another black-humour novel concerning a widow squandering her husband's estate in an effort to counter the despair of her boring life. Blechman is rightly considered one of the best of contemporary American satirists. [EM]

**Bly, Robert** (1926– ). Poet, translator· Born in western Minnesota, he attended St Olaf's College and Harvard, went to Norway on a Fulbright award, and now lives on a farm in his native state. The poems in *Silence in a Snowy Field* (1962) are sparse, personal and observant, and repeatedly deal with the mysterious and affirming natural landscape of America, particularly of Minnesota, exploring silence, solitude and natural vigour in an immediate and modern idiom. In *The Light Around the Body* (1967) Bly responds in outrage to the warfare state, combining broad wit with a sense of the surreal hypocrisy of the Vietnam war. In an act of civil disobedience, he handed over the prize money from the National Book Award in 1968 to help young Americans 'defy the draft authorities'. As one of the founders and editors of the periodical magazine *The Fifties*, later called *The Sixties*, and of the Sixties Press, printing off-beat poetry and translations from little-known European and South American poets, Bly has been an important general influence in recent poetic movements. [BP/EM]

Richard Howard, *Alone with America* (1969).

**Bodenheim, Maxwell** (1893–1954). Poet, novelist, playwright. Born in Mississippi, he was associated with Chicago Bohemia until the 1920s, when he moved to New York and became an exotic if squalid figure in ♦ Greenwich Village circles. He published several volumes of poems, including *Minna*

*and Myself* (1918), *The Sardonic Arm* (1923), *Returning to Emotion* (1926), and *Selected Poems 1914–1944* (1946), sometimes anthologized but not easily available. His novels, cynical, 'shocking', often *romans à clef*, include *Crazy Man* (1924), *Replenishing Jessica* (1925) and *Naked on Roller Skates* (1931). He wrote plays with Ben ♦ Hecht. [MB]

**Bogan, Louise** (1897–1970). Poet. She belonged to what Yvor ♦ Winters has termed the 'reactionary generation', a group of brilliant minor poets who, though aware of the achievements of Pound, Eliot and Williams, chose traditional English forms and metres. Of this group, which included Winters himself, Allen ♦ Tate, and Hart ♦ Crane, she was probably the most accomplished metrist. Born and educated in New England (at Boston University), she moved to New York, where from 1931 she was the regular poetry reviewer for the *New Yorker*. Her first book of poems, *Body of This Death* (1923), sometimes reveals the influence of E. A. ♦ Robinson, a fellow New Englander transplanted to New York. Later poems show the too-obvious influence of Yeats. The catholic taste which made her a good reviewer, and her *Achievement in American Poetry 1900–1950* (1951), the best popular introduction to the subject, did some disservice to her poetry: there are too many tracks in the snow. Yet ten to twenty short lyrics in her *Collected Poems* (1954) are among the most perfect of their kind. Notable for their limpid diction, varied rhythms and dramatic structure, they are also important poems because of their intelligent preoccupation with such central human themes as sexual love and bodily decay. A fine technician, she quotes with approval Synge's dictum that 'the strong things of life are needed in poetry . . .'. *The Blue Estuaries, Poems 1923–1968* (1968) is her finest book. She won the Bollingen Prize in 1955. Her *Selected Criticisms* appeared in 1958. [GD]

Elder Olson, 'Louise Bogan and Leonie Adams', *Chicago Review*, VIII, 70–87 (Fall, 1954).

**Bohemianism.** Literary Bohemianism was already a well-established style in European literature before Murger's *Scènes de la vie de Bohême* (1851) popularized and ritualized its life of riotous poverty; and it has long attracted American writers. Much of the *avant garde* character of American (particularly modern) writing, and much of the movement of American writers to cities like Chicago, San Francisco and New York – and indeed to Europe (◊ Expatriates) – has been due to a strong neo-Bohemian pattern in American letters. Bohemianism may roughly be defined as characteristic of societies in which the absence of fixed social roles for the writer encourages him to devise a distinctive life-pattern of his own and gather into groups and communities of his peers; this in turn – because the standards are set by other writers and because technical discussion tends to ensue – encourages experimental and *avant garde* literature. Bohemianism – as Albert Parry in *Garrets and Pretenders: A History of Bohemianism in America* (1933; revised edn, 1960) has shown – has been a strong movement in the U.S.A. from ◊ Poe onward, developing through the Pfaff's Broadway beer-cellar group, including Whitman, in the 1850s, to a fashionable movement in the 1880s and thereafter. The aesthetic and dandyish style had many famous adherents – ◊ Huneker, ◊ Bierce, ◊ Hovey and so on to Pound. The expatriation and cosmopolitanism of the 1920s had much to do with the well-established Bohemian connexion with Paris; and the aesthetic, symbolist strain is strongly evident in American letters throughout this period – as in the early Faulkner, Wallace Stevens, and many others. Before 1920 the attractions of Bohemianism had created numerous expatriates – Lafcadio ◊ Hearn, Stephen ◊ Crane, Henry ◊ Harland – while Stuart ◊ Merrill and Francis Viélé-Griffin became fully fledged French symbolists, writing in French. The strong beatnik strain in current American writing is a later phase of the same movement, while the respectable Bohemian tone survives in the *New Yorker*, a derivative of a whole tradition of outrageous Bohemian literary journals. The distinct Bohemian habitats of the late 19th and early 20th centuries – ◊ Greenwich Village, Chicago, San Francisco, Carmel – survive in their roles. One might say that today Bohemianism has become a universal youth-style, with the modern university campus as one of the most familiar locales. [MB]

**Boker, George Henry** (1823–90). Poet, dramatist. Of wealthy Philadelphia background, he wrote many verse plays, the most celebrated being the tragedy *Francesca da Rimini* (1855), as well as sonnets on love and on public issues. He was a minister to Turkey and to Russia. [MB]

E. S. Bradley, *George Henry Boker: Poet and Patriot* (1927).

**Booth, Philip** (1925– ). Poet. Born in New Hampshire, educated at Dartmouth. He was an air force pilot in the Second World War, an experience that appears in his verse. Since then he has taught at various colleges, including Dartmouth and Wellesley, and produced a body of interesting personal poetry. *Letters from a Distant Island* (1957), *The Islanders* (1961) and *Weathers and Edges* (1967) have established him as a significant writer. [MB]

**Booth, Wayne** ◊ Chicago Aristotelians.

**Boucicault, Dion** (1820–90). Playwright. Born in Ireland, educated in England, he went to New York in 1853, already a famous actor-dramatist. He remained in the lead (with an occasional relapse) from 1853 to 1890. His most famous plays are *The Octoroon* (1859, on Mayne ◊ Reid's novel), *Rip Van Winkle* (1865, with Joseph Jefferson, on Irving's tale), and his Irish specialities – *The Colleen Bawn* (1860), with water spectacle, *Arrah-na-Pogue* (1864), in which 'The Wearing of the Green' was given new words and led to the shamrock business, and *The Shaughraun* (1874), all excellent melodramas. [EM]

**Bourjaily, Vance** (1922– ). Novelist. Born in Ohio. He founded and edited *Discovery* with John Aldridge (1952). His earlier novels, *The End of My Life* (1947) and *The House of Earth* (1955), have only some of the power of *The Violated* (1958), a huge but excellently organized novel of the forties generation, and *Confessions of a Spent Youth* (1960), a semi-autobiographical novel. *The Unnatural Enemy* (1963) is a brilliant history of American hunting and its complexes. In *The Man Who Knew Kennedy* (1967), Bourjaily attempts to probe the sickness around the President's assassination and the American glamour of successful men. [EM]

**Bourne, Randolph** (1886–1918). Social and literary critic. Born in Bloomfield, N.Y., he was crippled and disfigured by a childhood accident. He studied at Columbia and in Europe, and became an educationa and political radical, loathing war and American society so openly that his *New Republic* articles were suspended, in spite of their basically humanitarian protests for freedom. His major books are *Youth and Life* (1913), *The Gary Schools* (1916) and *Education and Living* (1917). Van Wyck ◊ Brooks posthumously edited *The History of a Literary Radical* (1920). Bourne's dissenting passion and clear prose, in the great tradition of ◊ Paine and ◊ Thoreau, is excellently represented in *War and the Intellectuals: Collected Essays 1915–1919* (ed. C. Resek, 1964). [EM]

Ed. L. Schlissel, *The World of Randolph Bourne* (1965); Sherman Paul, *Randolph Bourne* (U. of Minnesota Pamphlet, 1967).


**Bowers, Edgar** (1924–    ). Poet. Born in Georgia, he studied at the University of North Carolina and Stanford, and teaches at the University of California at Santa Barbara. His poetry is reflective but under an impressive control. He has published *The Form of Loss* (1956) and *The Astronomers* (1965), and has been represented in many anthologies, including *Five American Poets* (ed. Thom Gunn and Ted Hughes), published in England in 1963. [MB]

Richard Howard, *Alone with America* (1969).


**Bowles, Jane** (1918–    ). Novelist, short-story writer. She was born in New York City, married the novelist Paul ◊ Bowles in 1939, and wrote her first novel, *Two Serious Ladies* (1943), when she was 21. It describes the lives of two different women whose careers cross only twice, and is told in a prose style distinguished for its precision and poetry. Her play, *In the Summer House*, was produced in New York in 1953 and concerns an alcoholic woman maintaining her self-respect. All Jane Bowles's work shows 'the terrible strength of the weak' and their survival as failures. These works and 7 short stories make up *The Collected Works of Jane Bowles* (1967), which is introduced by Truman Capote. *Plain Pleasures* (1966) is the British title of her short stories. [EM]


**Bowles, Paul** (1910–    ). Novelist, short-story writer, translator, composer. He was born in New York, went to the University of Virginia because Poe had been there, and escaped from there to Paris, where his earliest poems had been published in *transi-*

*tion*. Returning to America, he took some lessons in musical composition from Aaron Copland, but soon returned to Europe. Gertrude Stein suggested Tangier to him in 1931, but he went to Africa permanently only after a spell as music critic for the *Herald Tribune* and writing theatre music (for two Tennessee Williams' plays, among others). In 1949 he went to Ceylon and now lives between there and Morocco. In 1941 he completed his opera *The Wind Remains* (libretto by García Lorca) in Mexico. He is married to the novelist Jane ◊ Bowles. Morocco is the locality for most of his fiction. *The Sheltering Sky* (1949) shows his remarkable feeling for the power of the African town and desert to generate existential fear and panic in characters exhausted and degenerated by western urban success and its values. He is a master of cruelty and isolation, and the ironies of the search for meaning in an inadequately understood environment. *Let It Come Down* (1952) again concerns the derangement of the senses of Europeans in an alien culture, moving towards an orgiastic climax: the hero is a young American committed to nothing but survival within corruption. Bowles's interests in the effects of kief and hashish are involved in the *dénouement*. *The Spider's House* (1955) again observes the effects of Africa on sophisticated westerners, but with more weight on the Moroccans themselves. This has been the direction of Bowles's career: the stories in *The Delicate Prey* (1950; British title *The Little Stone*) develop the theme of his novels, and contain some fine examples of controlled violence, like 'A Distant Episode', but in *A Life Full of Holes* (1964) he has tape-recorded and translated a story by an illiterate North African Moslem, Driss ben Hamed Charhadi, a moving life of stoic resignation to poverty. *Hundred Camels in the Courtyard* (1963), *Love with a Few Hairs* (1966), taped from Mohammed Mrabet, and *The Time of Friendship* (1967) all contain powerful insights into African sensibility and story-telling ability. *Up Above the World* (1967), a novel, is a black comedy exploiting his fascination with the darkness of sexual struggle, this time in Latin America, and the frontiers between reality and hallucination. In *Pages from Cold Point and Other Stories* (1968) the best stories are again located in North Africa, and *Their Heads are Green and Their Hands are Blue* (1963) is a collection of sharply observed travel notes.

*Scenes* (1968) is a small collection of poems from the 1940s. [EM]

C. E. Eisinger, *Fiction of the Forties* (1965).

**Boyd, James** (1888–1944). Novelist, poet. Energetic Philadelphian novelist of American history. His *Eighteen Poems* (1944) and *Old Pines and Other Stories* (1952) pale beside *Drums* (1925) – Johnny Fraser in the Revolutionary War – *Marching On* (1927) – a Civil War love story with descriptions of Antietam and Chancellorsville battles – and *Long Hunt* (1930), *Roll River* (1935) and *Bitter Creek* (1939). His historical localities are generally vivid and authentic. [EM]

**Boyle, Kay** (1903–    ). Novelist, short-story writer, poet. Born in Minnesota, her expatriate years in France before her return to the U.S.A. in 1941 provided her with much of the material for her fiction. Her interest in the international theme of Europe and America is matched, particularly in her early stories and novels, by an equally Jamesian interest in psychological character analysis. [A H]

Collections of stories: *Wedding Day* (1930); *First Lover* (1933); *The White Horses of Vienna* (1936); *The Crazy Hunter* (1940); *Thirty Stories* (1946); *The Smoking Mountain* (1951); *Nothing Breaks Except the Heart* (1966). Novels: *Plagued by the Nightingale* (1931); *Year before Last* (1932); *Gentlemen, I Address You Privately* (1933); *My Next Bride* (1934); *Death of a Man* (1936); *Monday Night* (1938); *The Youngest Camel* (1939); *Primer for Combat* (1942); *Avalanche* (1943); *A Frenchman Must Die* (1946); *His Human Majesty* (1949); *The Sea-gull on the Step* (1955); *Generation without Farewell* (1959). Poems: *A Glad Day* (1938); *American Citizen* (1944); *Collected Poems* (1962).
Richard C. Carpenter, 'Kay Boyle', *College English*, XV (November 1953); H. T. Moore, 'Kay Boyle's Fiction', *Kenyon Review*, Spring, 1960.

**Brackenridge, Hugh Henry** (1748–1816). Poet, novelist, political commentator. Born in Scotland, brought by Calvinist parents to Pennsylvania when he was 5, he was 15 when he began teaching in local schools. He attended Princeton with James Madison, and Philip ◊ Freneau, with whom he composed a satirical prose-tale, *Father Bombo's Pilgrimage to Mecca* (1770), and a famous Princeton commencement poem, *A Poem on the Rising Glory of America* (1772). Also with Freneau, he ran an academy in Maryland. He wrote two

patriotic dramas and served as chaplain in Washington's army. He then founded the short-lived *United States Magazine*, read law and practised in Philadelphia and Pittsburgh, and entered on a promising career in politics which collapsed with the decline of Federalism and because of the complexity of his own political position. For services to the Republican party he became justice to the Pennsylvania Supreme Court in 1799 and in late life revised Blackstone for American conditions.

He is best remembered for two things: the Princeton commencement poem and his massive documentary novel *Modern Chivalry*, published in instalments between 1792 and 1815 (ed. C. M. Newlin, 1937). Picaresque in structure, derived from English and European models, it has no concluded plot, being an episodic series designed as 'a mixture of images drawn from high and low life, with painting serious and ludicrous', formed into a loose satirical 'fable' of the adventures of Captain Farrago and Teague O'Regan. This classic Cervantean pair, the backwoods chevalier and the ignorant, conceited companion, travel through the corruptions of modern democracy. In Part One their travels expose local government and satirize ◊ Franklin's American Philosophical Society, the idiocy of Indian treaties, fashionable sexuality, duelling, the theatre and the tax system. Teague is successful in the French Revolution, and the captain returns home enlightened by his pragmatic truths. In Part Two, they found a new state on the frontier, and the book becomes a series of topical discussions on government and law. Brackenridge's description of American types has an edge, vigour and indigenous awareness not found again until Mark Twain; and his faith in democracy, finally, is complex enough to hold. *Modern Chivalry* is that rare thing, a neglected comic-satirical masterpiece, and a central achievement in 18th-century American fiction. [EM]

Claude M. Newlin, *The Life and Writings of Hugh Henry Brackenridge* (1932).

**Bradbury, Ray** (1920–    ). Science-fiction writer and novelist. Born in Illinois but has now lived for some years in California where he also writes for the screen (most notably the script for John Huston's *Moby Dick*). A prolific writer of short stories, he began his career with a collection of macabre fantasies entitled *Dark Carnival* (1947), some of which were reprinted in *The October Country* (1955). Thereafter followed other collections of stories and several novels.

There is some doubt whether Bradbury may be considered a science-fiction writer proper. Many of his tales are perhaps best described as essays in fantasy, excursions into a subjective world peopled by grotesques and inspired by recollections of childhood summers in the mid-West (the protagonists of *Dandelion Wine* and *Something Wicked* are both young boys in that region). His greatest asset is an imagination which allows him to indulge in a poetic rather than a scientific treatment of extra-terrestrial reality, a quality most in evidence in *The Silver Locusts*, a haunting account of Mars at the beginning of the 21st century. Though his work is not entirely devoid of the customary concerns of science fiction (*Fahrenheit 451* is a cautionary fable of a book-burning society of the future), his world is essentially private and poetic. His deceptively simple lyrical prose often reveals a subtle ear for the sound as well as the meaning of words; but sometimes his 'sensitivity' degenerates into whimsy and sentimentality. Whether we classify him as a writer of science fiction or of fantasies, here is a considerable talent which has done much to make respectable a new genre of fiction that goes beyond the confines of realism. [HD]

Stories: *The Martian Chronicles* (1950; English title *The Silver Locusts*), *The Illustrated Man* (1951), *The Golden Apples of the Sun* (1953), *The Day It Rained Forever* (1959), *The Machineries of Joy* (1964). Novels: *Fahrenheit 451* (1953), *Dandelion Wine* (1957), *Something Wicked This Way Comes* (1962), *I Sing the Body Electric!* (1969).

**Bradford, William** (1590–1657). Colonizer, historian. Bradford was a member of the dissenting congregation of Scrooby, Nottinghamshire, which fled to the Netherlands in 1609. Conditions there being harder and more uncertain than had been expected, a group from the Leyden congregation decided to emigrate to America. These famous Pilgrim Fathers who sailed from Plymouth on the *Mayflower* in September 1620 included William Bradford. Reaching the New World far to the north of their intended destination they established a colony in New England which they called Plymouth. On the death in 1621 of John Carver, their first governor, Bradford was elected his successor and held the office for 30 years. He began his history of the settlement in 1630 and probably finished it in 1650, but it remained unpublished until 1856. He tells the story of the exodus from Europe, the early years of hardship, and social and religious problems, and relations with the Indians as the history of a Chosen People. But the account, carefully checked, is accurate within its theological structure; hence it is a source for most later accounts of early settlement in New England, while its plain and eloquent prose makes it fine reading. [DKA/EM]

*Of Plymouth Plantation*, annotated S. E. Morison (1952).
Bradford Smith, *Bradford of Plymouth* (1951).

**Bradstreet, Anne** (1612?–1672). Poet. Born in England, she sailed in 1630 with her husband Simon and her father Thomas Dudley, former steward to the Earl of Lincoln. She settled in Ipswich and later North Andover, Massachusetts, her father and then her husband becoming Governors of the Massachusetts Bay Colony. She lived the life expressed in her poems – domestic, pious, alert to the quality of family life in a theocracy. Formally she hardly develops beyond her Elizabethan models, particularly Spenser and 'great Bartas', but her skill and feeling are her own. The first edition of her poems, *The Tenth Muse Lately Sprung Up in America* (1650), appeared in London without her supervision; the posthumous second edition, *Several Poems Compiled with a Great Variety of Wit and Learning* (1678), appeared in Boston, Massachusetts, with her corrections and a number of additions. The longer poems exploit her learning and include a dull versification of Ralegh's *History of the World*, a set of imitations of Du Bartas on the idea of fours (ages of man, seasons, etc.), and 'Contemplations', a typical long work in Spenserian stanzas on Spenserian themes (time, mutability, etc.). But there is an interesting domestic-provincial streak, which comes out finely in the shorter pieces – 'To My Dear and Loving Husband', 'Upon the Burning of Our House', etc. – which are significant contributions to metaphysical poetry. They are piously witty, informed by Puritanism, and reveal intense domestic emotions. Their merits still have fully to be recognized. Though her position as the first settler-writer of poetic imagination is secure, these introspective meditations on family life in a masculine, practical community need placing in an important 'domestic metaphysical' tradition in American letters. [MB]

Works, ed. J. Hensley (1967); Works, ed. J. H. Ellis (1867; reprinted 1962).
Helen S. Campbell, *Anne Bradstreet and Her Time* (1891); Josephine E. Piercy, *Anne Bradstreet* (1965).

**Brautigan, Richard** (1935–    ). Novelist, poet. He is above all a writer of the place in which he lives: the landscape and cities of the Pacific coast. His novels and stories are funny, quirkily original, and resist any categorization, just as his heroes are those whose freedom is anarchistic: *A Confederate General from Big Sur* (1964), *Trout Fishing in America* (1967), and *In Watermelon Sugar* (1968). His poems are collected in *The Pill versus the Springhill Mining Disaster* (1968). [EM]

**Brinnin, John Malcolm** (1916–    ). Poet, biographer, critic. He was born of American parents in Halifax, Nova Scotia, educated at the Universities of Michigan and Harvard, and has taught at various colleges, including Vassar and the University of California. His poetry is deft, often witty, with a wide range of voices from parody to philosophical meditation. Primarily a poet of occasions, he uses verse to comment upon prevailing issues and his own experience. His early volumes – *The Garden Is Political* (1942), *The Lincoln Lyrics* (1942), etc. – are chiefly political and show the influence of Auden. Later work, broader in theme and manner, is found in *The Sorrows of Cold Stone: Poems 1940–1950* (1951), while *Selected Poems* (1963) forms a useful introduction. He has been an important promoter of verse as Director of the Poetry Center of the New York Y.M.-Y.W.H.A., and as anthologist (e.g. the interesting *The Modern Poets: An American–British Anthology*, ed. with Bill Read, 1963). His memoir *Dylan Thomas in America* (1955) aroused controversy for its portrayal of Thomas's wildness; he also wrote a factually valuable biography of Gertrude Stein, *The Third Rose: Gertrude Stein and Her World* (1959), and a pamphlet on William Carlos Williams (1963). [MB]

'Phases of my Work', in *Contemporary American Poetry*, ed. H. Nemerov (1965).

**Bromfield, Louis** (1896–1956). Novelist, playwright, journalist. Born and raised on an Ohio farm, he went to Cornell and Columbia before service in the First World War interrupted his education; later he was a journalist and critic in New York, and a long-time expatriate in France. *Escape*, a highly praised tetralogy concerning men's efforts to free themselves from their background, began with *The Green Bay Tree* (1924), and continued with *Possession* (1925), *Early Autumn* (1926) and *A Good Woman* (1927). His work declined in quality with *The Strange Case of Miss Annie Spragg* (1928) and *Twenty-Four Hours* (1930), both studies of emotional stress, then fell off sharply in such novels as *Mrs Parkington* (1942). *Pleasant Valley* (1945) and *Out of the Earth* (1950) are excellent straight descriptions of life and work at Malabar, his highly advanced Ohio farm. In his later years, he became a well-known conservative spokesman. [MG]

Morrison Brown, *Louis Bromfield and His Books* (1956).

**Brooks, Cleanth** (1906–    ). Literary critic. A Southerner, born in Kentucky, educated at Vanderbilt and Tulane, then teacher of English at Louisiana State University (1932–47), he is now Professor of English at Yale (and was briefly cultural attaché at the American Embassy in London). During the 1930s (when with Robert Penn ◊ Warren he edited the *Southern Review*), he was closely associated with the movement of ◊ New Criticism, and the Southern literary revival. His many critical books and articles reveal a strongly 'structuralist' approach – an approach stressing the primacy of the text and the secondary nature of discussion of its origins or effects. *Modern Poetry and the Tradition* (1939) and *The Well-Wrought Urn: Studies in the Structure of Poetry* (1947) are documents of New Critical practice. The first, indebted to Eliot but possessing a strong practical criticism approach, distinguishes the characteristic poetic tradition as one of 'wit'; the second broadens the definition to consider the language of all poetry as that of paradox, and offers excellent close reading of a wide range of poems. But his criticism can have a strong social – almost a sociological – dimension, as more recently his *William Faulkner: The Yoknapatawpha County* (1963) has shown. His three text books *Understanding Poetry* (with Robert

Penn Warren, 1938), *Understanding Fiction* (with Warren, 1943), and *Understanding Drama* (with Robert Heilman, 1947), devoted to close reading, played a large part in introducing a critical approach into American teaching. His scholarly *Literary Criticism: A Short History* (1957), written with W. K. ◊ Wimsatt, with its exact analysis of critical concepts, is surely the best short general history available. [MB]

Stanley Edgar Hyman, *The Armed Vision: A Study in the Methods of Modern Literary Criticism* (1948).

**Brooks, Gwendolyn.** ◊ Negro Literature.

**Brooks, Van Wyck** (1886–1963). Literary historian, essayist. Born in Plainfield, New Jersey. He produced a monumental body of writing on American literary culture. In *America's Coming of Age* (1915), he outlined a concept of the autonomous nature of American literature and of the country's cultural reliance on its authors. Always biographical in nature, Brooks's work became increasingly popularized after the early thirties and increasingly conservative of a hypothetically pure American strain. Under the over-all title *Makers and Finders*, he produced a number of readable, if lightweight and unspecific, works, including *The Flowering of New England, 1815–1865* (1936), *New England: Indian Summer, 1865–1915* (1940) and *The Confident Years: 1885–1915* (1952). Brooks was not particularly hospitable to the work of immigrants later than the old Yankee stock. Earlier, he produced two influential studies, *The Ordeal of Mark Twain* (1920) and *The Pilgrimage of Henry James* (1925), which express his feeling for the harm done to these authors, by society and expatriation respectively. [AG]

Stanley Edgar Hyman, 'Van Wyck Brooks and Biographical Criticism', in *The Armed Vision* (1948); Gladys Brooks, *If Strangers Meet: A Memory* (1967); F. W. Dupee 'The Americanism of Van Wyck Brooks'; (*Partisan Review Reader*, 1946); W. Wasserstrom, *Van Wyck Brooks* (University of Minnesota Pamphlet, 1968).

**Brossard, Chandler** (1922–    ). Novelist. His first, under-estimated novel, *Who Walk in Darkness* (1952), explores, early, the sensibility of outsider withdrawal from American life, and is managed with great intelligence and fictional awareness. He

is also the author of two other novels, *The Bold Saboteurs* (1953) and *The Double View* (1960), and has edited a semi-sociological collection of essays about modern America. He has written a short book on Spain, *The Spanish Scene* (1968). He has worked as a journalist for *Look*, *Time* and the *American Mercury* and taught in various universities. [MB]

**Broughton, James** (1913–    ). Poet, film maker. Born in California. His finely formed and witty poems and films are part of the San Francisco Renaissance of the 1950s. His poems are in *The Playground* (1949), *Musical Chairs* (1950), *The Right Playmates* (1952), *An Almanac for Amorists* (1955) and *True and False Unicorn* (1957). His delightful films include *Mother's Day*, *Loony Tom*, *Adventures of Jimmy*, *Four in the Afternoon*, and *Pleasure Garden*. He has also written plays and revues. [EM]

**Brown, Charles Brockden** (1771–1810). Novelist. Born in a prosperous Philadelphia Quaker merchant family who fostered his early intellectuality while his health deteriorated. He came to loathe the law in which he was trained, as a mixture of 'endless tautologies' and 'lying assertions'. In the nationalism of his youth he contemplated the usual patriotic epics but found journalism more suitable, and his essays in the *Columbia Magazine* (1789) on the romantic solitary, the introspective 'rhapsodist' wandering in the American wilderness near his city, are a prelude to his later psychological fiction. In 1790 he met Elihu Smith, an extraverted medical student, who became his friend and with whose circle he founded the Society for the Attainment of Useful Knowledge. He visited Smith regularly in New York, to which he moved in 1796. He began to develop his fiction and that interest in psychosomatic phenomena which characterizes his work. In 1797, back in Philadelphia, he began the series of novels for which he should be famous, and, from 1799, his editing of the *Monthly Magazine and American Review*. His novels were decently received, but only his magazine work supported him. An importing business he was involved in failed in 1806 but a legacy kept him writing fiction, although it was now disappointingly conventional romances (*Clara Howard*, 1801, and *Jane Talbot*, 1801). Abandoning fiction, he edited a new magazine, and became increasingly depressed with the increase of his profits from Federalist journalism and the success of his *American Register* and his *Literary Magazine*. He married in 1804 and died six years later of 'pulmonary consumption'. *Wieland* (1798) is an important American transformation of the psychology of the European 'gothic' novel and concerns a German emigrant father, who explodes under some supposed divine judgement, and his son, who murders his family under the combined influences of religious mania and a ventriloquist under the power of a criminal philosophical aristocrat. *Ormond* (1799) is a variation on these themes, the central action being a campaign of seduction based on a philosophical system. Like the earlier novels, *Arthur Mervyn* (1799, 1800) has an astonishingly involved plot, this time the picaresque adventures of an American innocent in corrupt society. *Edgar Huntly* (1799), his finest work, uses American wilderness and Indian hostilities for a detection plot, with startling dream motivations and moral conclusions. Brown's novels are the first to use American landscape and natives, and his transformations of the 'gothic' began a long, important tradition in American fiction, from Poe and Hawthorne to Faulkner and Burroughs. [E M]

*The Novels* (1827, 7 vols; repr. 6 vols., 1887).
H. R. Warfel, *Charles Brockden Brown, American Gothic Novelist* (1949); D. L. Clark, *Charles Brockden Brown: Pioneer Voice of America* (1952).

**Brown, John Mason** (1900– ). War correspondent, essayist, drama critic. Born in Kentucky, he worked on the *Theatre Arts Monthly*, New York newspapers and the *Saturday Review*. His criticism, some of the most perceptive to have appeared in America, is collected in various volumes, including *The Modern Theatre in Revolt* (1929) and *As They Appear* (1952). [E M]

**Brown, Norman O.** (1913– ). Classical scholar, philosopher. Born in Mexico, educated at Oxford, Chicago and Wisconsin Universities, he has been professor of languages and classics in American universities and is now professor of humanities at the University of California, Santa Cruz. *Hermes the Thief* (1947) is an important study of the interrelation of Greek mythology and social

and economic history. In *Life against Death* (1959) he explores the radical revisions which should have followed Freud's model of human nature, especially in attitudes towards money, authority and sexuality. His analysis leads towards a revolutionary programme of 'polymorphous perversity' as a form of the resurrection of the body, and an end to the accumulation of wealth as a viable social aim. *Love's Body* (1968) is a superb collage of texts and opinions which clarify and extend the implications of *Life against Death*, towards a definition of freedom within what is known of human nature and the nature of the earth. These two works alone have made Brown a seminal figure of contemporary American thinking; he takes his place with John ◊ Cage, Buckminster ◊ Fuller, Marshall ◊ McLuhan and Noam ◊ Chomsky. His introduction to his translation of Hesiod's *Theogany* (1953) already provides precise mythical relevance for the study of such descriptive syntheses in our own time. [E M]

**Browne, Charles Farrar.** ◊ Ward, Artemus.

**Brownell, W(illiam) C(rary)** (1851–1928). Critic. Born in New York. Because of the moral and classical emphasis of his approach, he has been often associated with the ◊ New Humanism, though he precedes it and differs from it on many points. His critical volumes include *French Traits* (1889), *Victorian Prose Masters* (1901), *Criticism* (1914) and *Standards* (1917); the titles suggest his range and concern with principles. He stressed that criticism is an impersonal activity, concerned with the abstract forces behind concrete artistic expression; and that art is a rational activity to do with human enlightenment. Particularly important is his *American Prose Masters* (1909), recently reissued (1963) as a classic of criticism. Here his stress on the non-sensational, morally realistic quality of art prevents him from regarding highly the strong romance elements in American fiction, but he makes many usefully rigorous observations about Cooper, Hawthorne, Emerson, Poe, Henry James and others. [M B]

Morton Dawen Zabel, 'Introduction', *Literary Opinion in America* (3rd edn, 1962).

**Brownson, Orestes A(ugustus)** (1803–76). Journalist, novelist, writer on philosophy and theology. Born in Vermont, he passed through a series of religious denominations (Presbyterian, Universalist, Unitarian, etc.) and ended in 1844 as a Catholic convert, but was condemned for trying to found an individual 'American' Catholicism. His politics went through a similar series of individualisms in the grand New England manner; he was first a socialist, sending his son to Brook Farm (◊ Ripley) and joining up with Robert Owen, later a Democrat and later still a Republican. Despite these shifts his ideas were influential and in many ways representative; and both sides of his fascinating personality appeared in his *Boston Quarterly Review*, which he founded in 1838, and its successors, which attacked capitalism in tones like Marx's until he lost faith in the common people. (It was the first American journal popular in England.) He published many books on theological and general intellectual matters; *Charles Elwood, or The Infidel Converted* (1840) is a novel; and *The Convert, or Leaves from My Experience* (1857) describes his pragmatic changes of attitude. [MG]

*Works*, ed. H. F. Brownson (20 vols., 1882–1907); *The Brownson Reader*, ed. A. S. Ryan (1955).

H. F. Brownson, *Life* (3 vols., 1898–1900); Arthur M. Schlesinger, Jr, *Orestes A. Brownson: A Pilgrim's Progress* (1939); Theodore Maynard, *Orestes Brownson: Yankee, Radical Catholic* (1943); Americo D. Papati, *Orestes Brownson* (1965); C. Carroll Hillis, 'Brownson on Native New England', *New English Quarterly*, XL (1967).

**Bryant, William Cullen** (1794–1878). Poet, editor. His father was a country doctor in Massachusetts; he studied the classics and already imitated 18th-century poetic conventions at the age of 13, composing a satire against ◊ Jefferson; but the precocious Federalist and Calvinist later became a deistic democrat. He did not graduate but studied and practised law. At 16 he had produced one of his famous poems, 'Thanatopsis' (1817). In 1821 he married and delivered 'The Ages' as his Phi Beta Kappa poem at Harvard, and through his friendship with R. H. ◊ Dana, Sr, published his first *Poems* (1821). His literary reputation was high enough in 1825 for him to give up law and move to New York as an editor of the *New York Review*. From 1829 he edited the *Evening Post*, making it a redoubtable organ of liberalism. His poetic achievement was virtually complete by middle life with the 1832 collection of

*Poems*, though his later translations of Homer are of interest. 'Thanatopsis' characteristically contemplates the inevitability of death with that serenity which made Lowell refer to his 'supreme iceolation'. He believed poetry should provide 'direct lessons in wisdom' through 'truths which the mind instinctively acknowledges', and was strongly aware of the problem of literary relations with England; in his 1825 lectures he proclaimed 'all the materials for poetry exist in our own country, with all the ordinary encouragements and appointments for making use of them'. But his own poems are not especially American. His reading of Wordsworth is everywhere apparent. His poems on Indians, Africans, Greeks and 'William Tell' are typical of his humanitarian liberalism. His language is that of the transitional period between 18th-century diction and early-19th-century romanticism. His best poems philosophize about a carefully delineated natural object or scene – 'To a Waterfowl', 'The Snow Shower', 'The Song of the Sower' – and exemplify American literature's movement from New England puritanism to mild Republican, romantic transcendentalism. [EM]

*The Poetical Works*, ed. H. C. Sturges and R. M. Stoddard (1903); *William Cullen Bryant: Representative Selections*, ed. T. McDowell (1935).

H. H. Peckham, *Gotham Yankee: A Biography of William Cullen Bryant* (1950).

**Bryce, James** (1838–1922). Statesman' commentator on America. Born in Belfast' Ireland, the son of a Scottish schoolmaster; educated at Glasgow and Oxford Universities. His prize essay, *The Holy Roman Empire* (published in expanded form when he was 26), established him as a historian and scholar. From 1870 to 1893 he was professor of Civil Law at Oxford, and after being an M.P. for some years, he became Under-Secretary for Foreign Affairs in 1886 and, in 1905, Chief Secretary for Ireland. His interests in travel and politics combine in *Modern Democracies* (1921); his mountaineering ability was recognized by his presidency of the Alpine Club, his services to the state by a peerage, the presidency of the British Academy, and an O.M. in 1907. But it is as a student and interpreter – indeed as an admirer – of American life that Bryce is best remembered. He travelled extensively in America, and his insights were embodied in his classical book on American government, *The American Commonwealth* (1888), drawn largely from discussion with Americans and analysing political corruption, race prejudice and preoccupation with materialism as much as more positive qualities, summarized in his statement: 'America marks the highest level, not only of material well-being but of intelligence and happiness, which the race has yet attained'. He became a popular ambassador at Washington (1907–13). [BB]

H. A. L. Fisher, *James Bryce* (2 vols., 1927).

**Buchwald, Art** (1925– ). Humorous columnist. He left the University of Southern California without a degree to live in Paris and become a journalist. His column for the *New York Herald Tribune*'s Paris edition, a light-hearted commentary on social and political matters, was soon syndicated in American newspapers. In 1962 he moved to Washington, D.C., to apply his techniques of commentary to affairs in the nation's capital. His writing, though usually personal and whimsical, mixes high-spirited fantasy with political *savoir faire*. Collections include: *Art Buchwald's Paris* (1954), *A Gift from the Boys* (1958), *How Much Is That in Dollars?* (1961) and (on Washington) *I Chose Capitol Punishment* (1963). [MB]

**Buck, Pearl S(ydenstricker)** (1892– ). Novelist, story writer, biographer. Born in Hillsboro, Virginia. Her parents, Presbyterian missionaries to China, are portrayed in her fine biographies *Fighting Angel* (1936) and *The Exile* (1936), combined in 1937 as *The Spirit and the Flesh*. She grew up in China and returned for education at Randolph Macon College and Cornell University. After teaching psychology in Virginia, she returned to Nanking as an English teacher (1921–31). She has worked in a number of fields to encourage Chinese–American understanding. Her trilogy *The House of Earth* (1935), a saga of Chinese peasant life written in quasi-biblical prose, began with *The Good Earth* (1931, revised 1935; Pulitzer Prize, Howells Medal) and continued with *Sons* (1932) and *House Divided* (1935). In 1938 she became the first American woman to receive the Nobel Prize for Literature. Other novels include *East Wind – West Wind* (1930), *Dragon Seed* (1942), *Pavilion of Women* (1946) and *The Three Daughters of Madame Liang* (1969). She translated the Chinese classic

*Shui Hu Chuan* as *All Men are Brothers* (1933). [MG]

**Bukowski, Charles** (1920– ). Poet. Born in Germany, he was brought to America at the age of 2. He lives in Los Angeles. His prolific output began when he was 35, is anti-literary, strongly autobiographical and self-consciously the record of an outsider. His strength is an ability to record his vigorously alienated life in direct language, with neither self-pity nor the jargon of psychology and ideology. *Notes of a Dirty Old Man* (1969) is a prose record of his underground life (also in *Confessions of a Man Insane Enough to Live with Beasts*, 1965). His best poems are in *At Terror Street and Agony Way* (1968) and *The Days Run Away like Wild Horses over the Hills* (1969), which collects works from six earlier books. [EM]

*A Bukowski Sampler*, ed. Douglas Blazek (1969).
Ed. J. E. Webb, *The Outsider*, I, 3 (1963) (a Bukowski issue).

**Burke, Kenneth** (1897– ). Philosopher, literary critic, poet. Born in Pittsburg, associated with various expatriate magazines in the 1920s, later music critic for the *Dial* and the *Nation*, he is one of the freest-ranging and most exciting of modern American critics. His literary criticism, which despite certain analogies is radically at odds with the theory of the ◊ New Criticism, starts from essential social premises and moves out to an extended consideration of formal procedures. His three earliest books, *Counter-Statement* (1931, revised 1953), *Permanence and Change: Anatomy of Purpose* (1935; revised 1954) and *Attitudes toward History* (1937), while largely philosophical and ethical in emphasis, explore the social location of art and begin to ascertain its central character. In *The Philosophy of Literary Form: Studies in Symbolic Action* (1941), his most literary critical work, he considers that a work of literature involves the adoption of 'strategies' for encompassing 'situations', and these are 'the dancing of an attitude'. Critical and imaginative works are answers to questions posed by the situation in which they arose. Burke's approach, a genetic one, makes him treat writings as working objects, operating both for writer and reader in a social context. Later works – *A Grammar of Motives*

(1945), *A Rhetoric of Motives* (1950) and *A Rhetoric of Religion* (1961) – take the argument about the nature of art and language further into the realm of human relations. Attentive to the text and yet at a distance from it, Burke's highly sophisticated use of insights from sociology, psychology, philosophy and linguistics makes him sometimes abstruse and grandiose. His importance lies in his capacity to make associations between disparate disciplines and obtain a complex philosophy of form from them. He is essentially a literary theoretician of the works of man as 'the symbol-using animal'. The chapter 'The Philosophy of Literary Form', in the book of that title, is the most convenient introduction to his idea. *Language as Symbolic Form* (1966) is a brilliant collection of essays from the 1950s and 1960s. He is also a poet (*Books of Moments: Poems 1915–54*, 1955 and *Collected Poems: 1915–1967*, 1968) and a short-story writer (*The White Oxen and Other Stories*, 1924). *Toward a Better Life* (1932) is described by its subtitle: 'A Series of Declamations or Epistles'. In *Perspectives by Incongruity* (1964) and *Terms for Order* (1964), Stanley Edgar ◊ Hyman has edited selections which represent all Burke's resourceful writings. [MB/EM]

Stanley Edgar Hyman, 'Kenneth Burke and His Criticism of Symbolic Action', in *The Armed Vision* (1948); Denis Donaghue, 'Enigma Variations', *New York Review*, XI, 1 (1968).

**Burnett, Frances Eliza Hodgson** (1849–1924). Novelist, children's writer. An Englishwoman who settled in Knoxville, Tennessee, in 1865, she became a leading sentimental novelist with books like *Editha's Burglar* (1888), *The Secret Garden* (1911), a charming and nostalgic classic, and *The White People* (1917), about the supernatural. Her first novel, *That Lass o' Lowrie's* (1877), is set in Lancashire industry; but she is remembered best for *Little Lord Fauntleroy* (1886); a generation of boys in long curls and velvet and lace cursed her portrait of the little lord, the American-educated and precociously charitable heir to an English earldom. The original, her son Vivian, wrote a biography of his mother, *The Romantick Lady* (1927). Her autobiography is *The One I Knew Best of All* (1893). She established, through a lawsuit, the American author's control over his own work in England. [MG]

**Burnett, W(illiam) R(iley)** (1899–    ). Novelist. Born in Ohio, he made a fortune out of a series of filmed best-selling toughies, including *Little Caesar* (1929) and *The Asphalt Jungle* (1949), first-rate gangster novels. He is also the author of several historical novels; and screenplays. [EM]

**Burnham, James** (1905–    ). Social critic. This important figure in American social debate studied at Princeton and Balliol, founded the journal *Symposium* (1931–5) and was Professor of Philosophy at New York University 1932–54. He broke with Marxism in 1939, was one of the editors of the politico-literary *Partisan Review* in the 1940s, and became an editor of the conservative *National Review* in 1955. His most influential work is his analysis of modern bureaucracy, *The Managerial Revolution* (1941); and his books include *The Struggle for the World* (1947), *The Machiavellians* (1943), *Containment or Liberation* (1953) and *Congress and the American Tradition* (1959). His most recent work, *Suicide of the West* (1965), is a criticism of liberalism from Locke to Arthur Schlesinger, Jr. [EM]

**Burns, John Horne** (1916–53). Novelist. Born in Massachusetts, he studied at Harvard and served in Africa and Italy in the Second World War. He returned to the U.S.A. to write, but later settled in Italy. He died at 36, and his reputation has grown posthumously. *The Gallery* (1947) is a series of passionately written sketches about G.I.s in Naples and the corrupt idealism of democracy at war. *Lucifer with a Book* (1949) is a satirical novel exposing an American 'outward bound' type of private school, and *A Cry of Children* (1952) concerns complex love between two ex-Catholics. A further novel, *The Stranger's Guise*, was not published. [EM]

**Burroughs, Edgar Rice** (1875–1950). Popular novelist. Born in Chicago. With a career as soldier, policeman, Sears Roebuck manager, gold-miner, cowboy and storekeeper behind him, he became a best-selling novelist with science fiction and Tarzan stories – the first was *Tarzan of the Apes* (1914). He incorporated himself and had two towns named after him, but never visited either Mars or Africa. Tarzan lived on after his death in novels and films: he was the son of an English aristocrat, abandoned in Africa as a child and reared by apes into animal strengths and linguistics. He survived his adventures, married and eventually became a grandfather. By 1940, more than 25 million copies in 56 languages had been sold. The first film of a long series was *Tarzan of the Apes* in 1918 (remade with sound 1930). In 1929 Tarzan became a comic-strip hero, but he was already an international folk-hero. Burroughs wrote over 60 books, which made him rich; he once said: 'Most of the stories I wrote were the stories I told myself before I went to sleep.' The Martian and Pellucidar books are rapidly gaining some of the popularity of Tarzan, for example, *A Princess of Mars* (1917), *A Fighting Man of Mars* (1930–1), *Pellucidar* (1923) and *Tanar of Pellucidar* (1930). Venus is the subject of *The Pirates of Venus* (1934), *Lost on Venus* (1935), etc. [EM]

R. W. Fenton, *The Big Swingers* (1967).

**Burroughs, John** (1837–1921). Naturalist, essayist. Born in the Catskills section of New York State, he was deeply influenced by Emerson, became a friend of Whitman, and a leading figure in American natural history and a nature-dweller at Slabsides, a cabin on the Hudson River at Riverby, N.Y. His work mixes Transcendentalism and scientific exactness. His collections include *Wake-Robin* (1871), *Birds and Poets* (1877) and *Riverby* (1894). A poet himself, he wrote (with Whitman) *Notes on Walt Whitman as Poet and Person* (1867), the first study, later expanded as *Walt Whitman: A Study* (1896). Later work like *Accepting the Universe* (1920) presents his (very 19th-century) belief; *My Boyhood* (1922) is autobiography. The most convenient collection is *John Burroughs' America: Selections*, ed. F. A. Wiley (1951). [MB]

*Writings* (23 vols., 1904–22); *The Heart of Burroughs' Journals*, ed. C. Barrus (1928).
Dallas Lore Sharp, *The Seer of Slabsides* (1921).

**Burroughs, William** (1914– ). Novelist. Born in St Louis, he graduated from Harvard, worked through a number of jobs in Europe and America, and has since lived a semi-legendary life between Tangiers, London and Paris, creating a series of brilliant novels based on the international post-Second-World-War world of totalitarian Western states, their wars, homosexuality and addictions. In form and style his radical experiments extend certain methods of Joyce, Gertrude Stein and Dada into a new prose, which is the most influential among mid-century younger writers. *Junkie: Confessions of an Unredeemed Drug Addict* (1953, under the name 'William Lee') begins as a straightforward documentary of the underground life of the addict, but closes with materials on addiction, sex and the police which were to be permutated in his most important work to follow. *The Naked Lunch* (1959), *The Soft Machine* (1961, rewritten finally from two earlier versions 1968), *The Ticket That Exploded* (1962) and *Nova Express* (1964) is a brilliant tetralogy of novels whose importance is twofold: an extreme formal experimentation, using a range of techniques from conventional narrative to multispatial and temporal devices based on 'cut-up', 'fold-in', and permutational methods which extend 20th-century fictional innovations into a more thorough expressionist medium; and a radical and cosmically pessimistic analysis of his vision of the death of God and the universe given over to the licence of uncontrolled technological power groups. His presentation of parasitical sexuality, racialism, corporation capitalism, and medical and psychiatric tyranny is advanced in its satire and non-ideological scorn. His interest in the psychic action of drugs which extend consciousness informs *The Yage Letters* (1963, with Allen Ginsberg), letters written from South American travels in search of drugs. His literary and social revolutionary methods are demonstrated instructionally in *The Exterminator* (1960, with Brion Gysin) and *Minutes to Go* (1960, with Gysin, Gregory Corso and Sinclair Beiles). The rest of his voluminous work is scattered through innumerable *avant garde* magazines. *The Last Words of Dutch Schultz* (1970) is a film scenario on the gangster, and *The Job* (1970) is mainly an important interview on techniques. He is undoubtedly a major force in 20th-century literature. [EM]

'The Art of Fiction XXXVI: William Burroughs', *Paris Review* 35 (Fall, 1965); Ihab Hassan, 'The Subtracting Machine; The Work of William Burroughs', *Critique*, Spring, 1963; J. G. Ballard, 'Myth-Maker of the Twentieth Century', *New Worlds of Science Fiction*, May-June 1964; Mary McCarthy, 'Burroughs' Naked Lunch', *Encounter*, April 1963; Eric Mottram, *William Burroughs* (1970).

**Butler, Bill** (1934– ). Poet. Born in Washington, educated at Montana University, he has written most of his poetry while living and running a bookshop in England. It is highly wrought, complex in both rhythm and organization of materials, in the tradition of Hart Crane, with a technical accomplishment and range of vision unique in contemporary American poetry. His major work is: *Capricorn* (1963), *The Discovery of America* (1966), *A Long Slow Waltz* (1968) and *Byrne's Atlas* (1970). [EM]

**Byles, Mather** (1707–88). Poet and preacher. The nephew of Cotton ◊ Mather, he inherited his famous library but not his intellectual character. He was strongly British and was therefore dismissed from his Boston church in 1776. His poems are fearfully witty (he tried to emulate Augustan elegance, and actually corresponded with Pope), but they end in dullness. His preaching was, however, celebrated for its satire and word-play, rather unlike most Puritan sermons. [EM]

*Poems on Several Occasions* (1744); *Poems by Several Hands* (1775).

**Bynner, Witter** (1881–1968). Poet. He published his first volume of verse in 1907. After Harvard he travelled extensively, read widely, assimilating a variety of literary influences, and became active in the new movement of modern poetry in America (though he participated with Arthur Davidson Fricke in a famous hoax, their volume *Spectra*, 'by Emanuel Morgan and Anne Knish', which parodied ◊ Imagism and kindred poetic styles, in 1916). An important feature of his work is a strong oriental influence, and he travelled in the East studying and collecting Chinese literature, producing, with Dr Kian Kang-hu, *The Jade Mountain* (1929), a translation of Chinese poems from the Tang dynasty. Bynner's work showed the clarity and economy of the Chinese influence. Many of his early poems have clear lyrical echoes of the nineties; but, though a lyrical poet, the grandiloquence of some of his early influences gradually faded from his work. Bynner's other writing includes distinguished translations from several languages, verse-plays and *Journey with Genius* (1951), an account of his days with D. H. Lawrence in New Mexico, where he settled and where he sets many poems. He is a poet of real interest and considerable endurance, altering with half a century of poetic modes and fashions yet retaining a distinctive voice. *Selected Poems* (1936: revised edn, 1943, ed. Robert Hunt, intr. Paul Horgan) is a useful representative volume, while *New Poems* (1960) provides more recent work. [MB]

William Jay Smith, *The Spectra Hoax* (1961).

**Byrd II, William** (1674–1744). Planter. politician, writer. William Byrd of Westover, on the James River in Virginia, was in style a genuine aristocrat whose life helped to create the myth of a widespread Southern aristocracy. Virginia-born, English-educated (in the Middle Temple) he was elected to the Royal Society and to the House of Burgesses (at 18). As a businessman he was eminently successful, expanding his family estates from 26,000 to 180,000 acres. As a public servant he served for 37 years on Virginia's Royal Council. He was an amateur *littérateur* and scientist, and assembled a private library of over 4,000 volumes. For many years he kept a diary, written in an easy and attractive style, which is a valuable source for the social history of Virginia and for conditions in London where he spent many years. His *History of the Dividing Line betwixt Virginia and North Carolina: A Journey to the Land of Eden, A.D. 1733* (ed. W. K. Byrd, 1929) draws a sharp distinction between the two colonies, christening the undeveloped land to the south of his own province 'Lubberland'. Byrd was a secular-minded rationalist whose observations on the state of his times are of historical interest, but the *History* is also a witty, Smollettian book of anecdotes, aristocratic attitudes to the poor ('many of them seem to Grunt rather than Speak in ordinary conversation') and a surprising advocacy of English intermarriage with the Indians. [EM]

*The Prose Works*, ed. L. B. Wright (1966); *The Writings of 'Colonel William Byrd, of Westover in Virginia'*, ed. J. S. Bassett (1901); *A Great American Gentleman: William Byrd of Westover in Virginia, His Secret Diary for the Years 1709–1712*, ed. L. B. Wright and M. Trinling (1963).
Louis B. Wright, *The First Gentleman of Virginia* (1940); R. C. Beatty, *William Byrd of Westover* (1932).

# C

Cabell, James Branch (1879–1958). Novelist.
Born in Richmond, Virginia, a graduate of
William and Mary College, he always
stayed outside the mainstream of modern
American fiction, allowing his imagination
to flourish in idealistic romances. Most of
these, set in the medieval myth-country
of Poictesme, deal epically, in mannered
prose, with Dom Manuel, an adventurer
striving for ideals he pessimistically realizes
to be unattainable, with his descendants,
and with the legends that grow round him
after death. Two critical volumes (*Beyond
Life*, 1919, and *Straws and Prayer-Books*,
1924) are 'prologue' and 'epilogue' to his
Poictesme cycle, whose action, including
short stories and poems, is arranged in the
following genealogical sequence: *Figures
of Earth* (1921), *The Silver Stallion* (1926),
*Domnei* (1920; originally published as *The
Soul of Melicent*, 1913), *The Music from
behind the Moon* (1926), *Chivalry* (1909),
*Jurgen* (1919), *The Line of Love* (1905),
*The High Place* (1923), *Gallantry* (1907),
*Something about Eve* (1927), *The Certain
Hour* (1916), *The Cords of Vanity* (1909),
*From the Hidden Way* (1916), *The Jewel
Merchants* (1921), *The Rivet in Grand-
father's Neck* (1915), *The Eagle's Shadow*
(1904) and *The Cream of the Jest* (1917;
revised 1920).

*Jurgen* was the first book to win him a
wide reputation, partly because of a
charge of obscenity levelled against it. A
story of search and initiation, subtitled a
'comedy of justice', it concerns a middle-
aged pawnbroker who sets out to find his
wife, vanished under the influence of a useful devil. His wit and scepticism resist a
mythological world whose symbolic entities
include centaurs, Queen Helen, the land of
Cockaigne, Hell and God's throne. He
regains his wife and his prosaic life but the
novel is a criticism of conventional morality
and its tyrannies, hence the charges against
its eroticism. *The High Place* again opposes
dream and reality, placing comment on
America in a fictional medieval locality, but
*The Cream of the Jest* is more complex: a
Virginian writer enters the world of allegorical dreams of his own creation, more

exciting than his own life and the ageing
of his own body. But his dreams cannot be
sustained and he returns to his fate; and
again the hero's erotic dream of an 'ageless,
loveable and loving woman of whom all
poets had been granted fitful broken
glimpses' turns to chilly reality. The
deliberately archaic apparatus of image,
diction and symbol make the inner meanings
of Cabell's novels difficult to interpret with
security, and they have dated. But their
summaries do not do justice to their
search for ideal states, their charmingly
precise detail and their appeal to the
erotic dreamer in urban wastelands.
[HB/EM]

*Works* (18 vols., 1927–30); *Between Friends:
Letters of James Branch Cabell and Others*, ed.
P. Colum and M. F. Cabell (1932).
A. R. Wells, *Jesting Moses* (1963); Carl Van
Doren, *James Branch Cabell* (1932); Edmund
Wilson, 'The James Branch Cabell Case Re-
opened', *New Yorker*, 21 April 1955.

Cable, George Washington (1844–1925).
Story writer, novelist, historian. Born New
Orleans, the son of a Virginia slaveholder,
he served in the Confederate army from
1862, reporting the experience later in *The
Cavalier* (1901). After the war illness turned
him to writing; he produced a popular
humorous column under the pseudonym
'Drop Shot' for the New Orleans *Picayune*
and joined the paper as a reporter, leaving
when his Calvinism prevented him from
being theatre critic. He turned to account-
ancy and research into the history of New
Orleans, writing exact, careful local colour
stories collected as *Old Creole Days* (1879).
Their success encouraged *The Grandissimes*
(1880), a study of the Louisiana Creole
Negroes; *Madame Delphine* (1881), a
novelette about a quadroon woman's
anxiety to conceal her daughter's mixed
blood; *Dr Sevier* (1885); *Bonaventure*
(1888); and *Bylow Hill* (1902), which
narrates the unsuccessful marriage of a
Southern girl to a New England clergyman.

His history *The Creoles of Louisiana*
(1884) angered Creoles by its account of
their past; he has also been accused of mis-

representing them in fiction (typical objections are contained in Grace King's *Memories of a Southern Woman of Letters*, 1932). Always an enemy of slavery, he now became a determined reformer and further angered Southerners. *The Silent South* (1885) collects studies advocating the abolition of contract labour, better conditions for Negroes, and prison reform. Increasing opposition forced his move to Massachusetts, where he wrote *The Negro Question* (1888) and *The Southern Struggle for Pure Government* (1890).

Cable created a new province of American literature. He captured to the full picturesque scenes in the old French–Spanish city of New Orleans and the doomed plantations, especially in *The Grandissimes*, with its rich texture and atmosphere of mystery, yet quite avoided the excesses of later writers on this subject. His description of the French dialect of Creole Negroes was meticulously accurate; a keen dislike of caste and class oppression displays itself even in his early fiction; and an attractive sense of humour underlies his delicate and whimsical prose. [MG]

*The Negro Question, A Selection of Writings on Civil Rights in the South*, ed. Arlin Turner (1958).

Lucy L. C. Biklé, *George W. Cable: His Life and Letters* (1928); Arlin Turner, *George W. Cable, a Biography* (1956); Edmund Wilson, 'The Ordeal of George Washington Cable', *New Yorker*, XXXII (1957); P. Butcher, 'George Washington Cable', *American Literary Realism 1870–1910*, No. 1 (1967).

**Cage, John** (1912–    ). Composer, writer, mycologist. Born in Los Angeles, he studied music with Adolph Weiss, Arnold Schoenberg and others, adopted Zen Buddhism under the instruction of Daisetz Suzuki, worked with the dancer Merce Cunningham, the painter Robert Rauschenberg and the pianist David Tudor, and created the first 'happening' at Black Mountain College in 1952. He is internationally celebrated as one of the most important composers of this century; his compositional procedures involving chance, the *I Ching* and indeterminacy are central to modern art in general. His writings on music and the arts, in a style initially owing something to Gertrude Stein's terseness, are becoming as influential as his music (*Silence*, 1961, and *A Year from Monday*, 1967). He wrote the musical section of *Virgil Thomson* (1959, with Kathleen

Hoover) and in 1969 edited *Notations*, a large collection of instructions for the performance of music and other events. [EM]

Calvin Tomkins, *The Bride and the Bachelors* (1965); ed. Richard Kostelanetz, *The Theatre of Mixed Means* (1968), and *Master Minds* (1969).

**Cahan, Abraham** (1860–1951). Novelist, journalist. Born in Russia, he came to the United States in 1882 and took up journalism, finally becoming editor of the Socialist daily *Forward*. His first American novel was *Yekl: A Tale of the New York Ghetto* (1896), about the Americanization of a Jewish immigrant from Russia who adapts from being blacksmith to sewing-machine operator and changes wives in the process. But the classic treatment of the theme of Americanization occurs in his *The Rise of David Levinsky* (1917), an excellent, exemplary Jewish and immigrant novel, about a man who rises in the New World at considerable psychic and human loss. It is a prototype for many Jewish American novels since, and is his best-known book. [MB]

**Cain, James M(allahan)** (1892–    ). Novelist. Born in Annapolis, Maryland. His stories of violence and racketeering contributed to modern sensational realism and helped to produce a whole school of hard-boiled murder fiction. Born in Maryland, he was a newspaper reporter and screen-writer before producing his first, best-known and most influential novel, *The Postman Always Rings Twice* (1934), about a wife plotting with a hoodlum lover to murder her husband. His other novels likewise exploit the vividness and violence of life in a variety of settings; they include *Mildred Pierce* (1941); *Love's Lively Counterfeit* (1942), about racketeering in a mid-Western city; *Double Indemnity* (1943); *Past All Dishonor* (1946), a historical novel; *The Butterfly* (1947), about incest in Kentucky; and *The Magician's Wife* (1965). In prefaces to various books Cain has disclaimed the desire to be considered a 'tough' novelist, stressing rather his realism and the accuracy of his vernacular. [MB]

*Cain X3: Three Novels* (1969).

**Caldwell, Erskine** (1903–    ). Novelist. Born in Georgia, son of a Presbyterian home missionary, he came to early fame with vivid, humorous, strongly dramatized tales of Georgia share-croppers, tenant farmers and mill-hands, which seemed melodramatic to those sheltered from the violence of the South. The play of his novel *Tobacco Road* (1932) ran continuously on Broadway for over seven years: the economic poverty, social crudeness and degenerate sexuality are documented in such a way that the prurient could make the work, in either form, a success. The equally notorious novel *God's Little Acre* (1933) is again a powerful but entertaining indictment – there is this element of ambiguous intention in Caldwell's writing – of social conditions focused here on a cotton weavers' strike in Carolina. Both works brought censorship against Caldwell; the charges were dismissed, as they were against *Tragic Ground* (1944). Some of his best work is his earliest – the working-class novels *The Bastard* (1929) and *Poor Fool* (1930) – and here again, as in all his writing, the basis is first-hand experience. He has held a variety of jobs, including reporting, and the detail of his fiction is accurate. He is prolific: in 1949, for instance, it was estimated that 20 million copies of his books in all editions were in circulation. His novels about the South include *Journeyman* (1935), *Trouble in July* (1940), *This Very Earth* (1948), *A Place Called Estherville* (1949), *Episode in Palmetto* (1950) and *Close to Home* (1962), a brilliant study in relations between coloured women and white men. *Miss Mama Aimée* (1967) is a memorable collection of upper-class plantation grotesques. *The Weather Shelter* (1969) is a genre novel set in Tennessee. Among his novels set outside the South, *A Lamp for Nightfall* (1952) deals with Maine people and *All Night Long* (1942) with guerillas in Russia. Throughout his career he has written many short stories, most conveniently presented in *The Complete Short Stories of Erskine Caldwell* (1953); some of the best are in *Georgia Boy* (1943), *Certain Women* (1957) and *Men and Women* (1961). During his marriage with the photographer Margaret Bourke-White, they collaborated in a documentary book on Georgia share-croppers, *You Have Seen Their Faces* (1937). Further social criticism is contained in *Say! Is This the U.S.A.?* (1941) and *Around about America* (1964); *In Search of Bisco* (1965) is a humane and shrewd guide to Southern racialism, and *In the Shadow of the Steeple*

(1966) presents the Christian church in the South through the life of Caldwell's minister father. Caldwell's is a unique career combining social teaching (he lectured on Southern tenant farmers at the New School for Social Research – see his pamphlet *Tenant Farmer*, 1935), social documentary and fiction which ambivalently shocks with its picture of the ugliness and decay of American life. [HB/EM]

Calef, Robert (1648–1719). Polemicist. A cloth merchant who went to Boston in 1688, he attacked Cotton ◊ Mather's attitude towards witchcraft trials (*Wonders of the Invisible World*, 1693) in his *More Wonders of the Invisible World*. No Boston printer would handle it, so it appeared in London in 1700. Increase ◊ Mather had it burned in Harvard yard. [EM]

G. L. Burr, *Narratives of the Witchcraft Cases 1648–1706* (1914).

Calisher, Hortense (1911– ). Novelist. Born in New York. She is a major novelist of the intense movement of 'our common unusualness', presented in great detail and exactness. Her field is the American bourgeoisie, and her master is Henry James. *Absence of Angels* (1951), *Tales for a Mirror* (1962) and *Extreme Magic* (1964) are collections of short stories, and her novels are *False Entry* (1961), *Textures of Life* (1963), *Journal from Ellipsin* (1966), *The Railway Police* (1966), *The Last Trolley Ride* (1966) and *The New Yorkers* (1969). [EM]

Calverton, V(ictor) F(rancis) (pseud. of George Goetz) (1900–40). Critic. Born in Baltimore, Maryland. He is important both in the development of sociological literary criticism in America and in the campaign to assert that there was a distinctive tradition of American literature. Of Baltimore working background, and a Marxist, he published both polemical historical criticism and social commentary. His books include *The Newer Spirit: A Sociological Criticism of Literature* (1925), *The New Grounds of Criticism* (1930), *American Literature at the Crossroads* (1931) and *The Liberation of American Literature* (1932). Along with Van Wyck ◊ Brooks, Granville ◊ Hicks, Max ◊ Eastman and others, he did much to assert American literature's 'coming of age' and to establish its history.

He edited an *Anthology of American Negro Literature* (1929); founded a magazine, *The Modern Quarterly*; and wrote a novel, *The Man Inside* (1935). [MB]

Charles I. Glicksberg, 'V. F. Calverton: Marxism without Dogma', *Sewanee Review*, XLVI (1938).

**Capote, Truman** (1924–    ). Novelist, story writer, reporter. Born in New Orleans, where he lived until 1942. Since then has lived in New York City and travelled widely. His early work was associated with the development of post-war Southern gothic literature, but he has written in different modes and styles; and though some of his writing is disquietingly chic he has emerged as an enormously talented and successful literary professional. His first novel, *Other Voices, Other Rooms* (1948), hailed as the work of a youthful prodigy, takes its Southern hero into the hallucinatory and sinister world of the decadent and leaves him there. *The Grass Harp* (1951), a short novel, is a more benign exploration of the sinister and uncanny, with a stronger social theme. The surrealistic quality of this early writing comes out strongly in a collection of stories of this period, *A Tree of Night* (1949). They exploit sinister, monstrous and ghostly elements in exploring loneliness and lovelessness, and range from the tragic to the macabre comic. With *Breakfast at Tiffany's* (1958), made into a successful film, Capote shifts locale to New York and works much closer to the comedy of manners, exploiting more the stylish and quaint. But his work was turning more in the direction of reportage, much of it for the *New Yorker*. The collection *Local Color* (1950) brought together travel sketches and articles on famous people (particularly notable is a profile of Marlon Brando); *The Muses Are Heard* (1956) is a funny and well-observed study of a State Department-supported tour of Russia made by an American company playing *Porgy and Bess*; and the reportage manner reached its greatest success (both financially and in terms of its literary possibilities) in *In Cold Blood* (1966), a 'non-fiction novel' about the slaughter of a respectable Kansas farming family by two wandering psychopaths. The horrifying murder was intensively researched by Capote, who also came close to the murderers before their execution. Though over-promoted, the book is both powerfully terrifying and fascinating for its inside account of two distinct ele-

ments in the American national psyche, the orderly and the anarchic. [MB]

*Selected Writings* (1963).

Irving Malin, *New American Gothic* (1962); interview with Pati Hill, *Paris Review*, 16 (Spring-Summer, 1967); A. Kazin, *Contemporaries* (1962); Lee Baxandall, 'The New Capote and the Old Soviet Advice', *Studies on the Left*, VI, 2 (March-April 1966).

**Carman, (William) Bliss** (1861–1929). Poet. Canadian-born and Harvard-educated, he left business to become with Richard ◊ Hovey one of the Bohemian 'vagabond' school who stirred American verse at the end of the century (◊ Bohemianism). His first book was *Low Tide on Grand Pré* (1893), lyrics. With Hovey he wrote *Songs from Vagabondia* (1894), *More Songs from Vagabondia* (1896) and *Last Songs from Vagabondia* (1901). Between 1894 and 1898 he edited the early 'little' magazine the *Chap-Book* (◊ Little Magazines), worked for other papers, and, though an American resident, became Canadian poet laureate. His later work leaves the Bohemian image behind but stays strongly lyrical. He produced over 20 volumes, including *By the Aurelian Wall and Other Elegies* (1898), *Pipes of Pan* (5 vols., 1902–5), and *Ballads and Lyrics* (1923). He also wrote essays on art and nature. [MB]

*Poems* (1931).

Odell Shepard, *Bliss Carman* (1923).

**Carnegie, Andrew** (1835–1919). Industrialist, writer. This famous Scots-born industrialist worked his way up from work in a Pennsylvania cotton factory to domination of the steel industry; bought out by U.S. Steel in 1901 he turned to philanthropy and writing, contributing to letters not only the Carnegie Libraries but *Triumphant Democracy* (1886); *The Gospel of Wealth* (1889), about the stewardship obligations of the industrial oligarchs; an *Autobiography* (1920), etc. [MB]

Matthew Josephson, *The Robber Barons* (1934).

**Carnegie, Dale** (1888–1955). Popular educator. This famous lecturer and author of self-improvement manuals expressed a fundamental American remedial philosophy in best-sellers like *How to Win Friends and Influence People* (1936), which has had a world-wide sale of over 5 million; *How to Stop Worrying and Start Living* (1948); etc. [MB]

**Carter, Nick.** The hero of millions of readers may have been based on Allan Pinkerton (1819–84), who established the first United States detection agency in Chicago in 1850; but he was invented by John R. Coryell (1848–1924), whose mass of pop fiction appeared under a maze of pseudonyms and who worked in a writing team with T. C. Harbaugh and F. Van Rensselare Dey. Nick's first performance came in *The Old Detective's Pupil* (1886), and his character appeared also in stories by other writers, including George C. Jenks (1850–1929), who created another legendary hero, Diamond Dick (e.g. *Diamond Dick's Decoy Duck*, 1891). [EM]

**Cartwright, Peter** (1785–1872). Preacher, memoirist. A Virginia clergyman who spent his youth in the Kentucky region of Rogues Harbour, but became a Methodist itinerant preacher at 17 and was famous later on the frontier for his sermons and his courage. In 1842 he moved into Illinois and the Ohio valley, and opposed Lincoln as candidate for Congress. His *Autobiography of Peter Cartwright, the Backwoods Preacher* (1856) and *Fifty Years as a Presiding Elder* (1871) are essential readings on the frontier and revivalism. [EM]

**Caruthers, William Alexander** (1800–46). A Virginia-born physician, he is remembered for 3 novels: *The Kentuckian in New York, or The Adventures of Three Southerners* (1834); *The Cavaliers of Virginia* (1835), a romance about Bacon's Rebellion; and *The Knights of the Horseshoe, A Traditional Tale of the Cocked Hat Gentry in the Old Dominion* (1845). [MB]

C. C. Davis, *Chronicler of the Cavaliers: A Life of Dr W. A. Caruthers* (1953).

**Carver, Jonathan** (1710–80). Travel writer. Amid the controversies over his life and writings, it is clear that he was born in Weymouth, Massachusetts, grew up in Connecticut, served in the British army during the French and Indian wars, undertook an exploration of the western Great Lakes area in 1766–7, and at his death had a wife on both sides of the Atlantic. The preface to the third edition of his *Travels through the Interior of Parts of North America* (1778) fakes an aristocratic ancestry, and the text steals from other documents of the region, but the book carries an authentic grand vision of the American

West and some good accounts of the Plains Indians. It was admired and used by ◊ Bryant, Schiller, Chateaubriand, Wordsworth and Coleridge. [EM]

**Cary, Phoebe** (1824–71). Poet. She was born in Cincinnati and became, with her sister, a member of the New York circle of Horace Greeley and Rufus ◊ Griswold. Her poetry is thin, but her parodies are exceptionally good. [EM]

*Poems and Parodies* (1854).

**Cather, Willa** (1873–1947). Novelist, short-story writer, poet, journalist. Born in Virginia, she moved at 9 to Nebraska, still to some extent a pioneer community. Educated at the University of Nebraska, she became a teacher, later a journalist and finally a free-lance writer. Much of her best fiction is about immigrant and pioneer life in the agricultural West. But she is much more than simply a regional novelist; she is a complex and formal writer, who writes out of a deeply felt culture, and she must be regarded as among the important American writers of this century. Her collection of essays *Not under Forty* (1936) expresses her debt to a substantial tradition of fiction, particularly to Flaubert, Henry James, and Sarah Orne ◊ Jewett, whom she knew; and she exploits this tradition, the tradition of the socio-moral novel – and, in a sense, the European novel – in her fiction. Her pioneers are not primitives; nor are they devoid of traditional culture. She is often concerned with the threat to traditional – yet subtly presented – moral and spiritual standards that modern life has brought, and with the values of an old prairie aristocracy pursuing an idealistic and spiritual life in a materialist world. Her most admired heroes and heroines are deeply involved with life, and she conveys them to us with an intensity to the rendering of which her aesthetic was committed.

Willa Cather published a book of poems, *April Twilights*, in 1903 (revised 1933), a collection of stories, *The Troll Garden*, in 1905, and her first novel, *Alexander's Bridge*, in 1912. In 1912 she gave up regular journalism to write; and, advised by Sarah Orne Jewett to write from her knowledge of her own background, she went on to produce the pioneer and immigrant novels for which she is best known – *O Pioneers!* (1913), *The Song of the Lark* (1915), *My Ántonia* (1918) and *One of Ours* (1922;

Pulitzer Prize). All these books evoke, intensely, the life of men and women against the land and landscape of Nebraska, the mid-West and Colorado. In 1920 she collected some of her excellent short stories in *Youth and the Bright Medusa*. The next group of novels – *A Lost Lady* (1923), *The Professor's House* (1925) and *My Mortal Enemy* (1926) – is rather less well known, but these are in fact among her best work. In them, there is a change of manner, towards a growing delicacy of theme, a greater concern with the pressure of modern life upon traditional standards, and a developing symbolic mode of presentation. In her two next books, *Death Comes for the Archbishop* (1927) and *Shadows on the Rock* (1931), her Catholicism becomes more overt; both are historical chronicles of the early spiritual pioneering of the Catholic Church, in the first in New Mexico, in the second in Quebec. She is even here concerned with the notion of the good life, of Christianity as vitality. A further collection of stories, *Obscure Destinies*, containing some excellent work, appeared in 1932; and there are two later novels, *Lucy Gayheart* (1935) and *Sapphira and the Slave Girl* (1940). Her writings on literature are edited by B. Slote in *The Kingdom of Art: Willa Cather's First Principles and Critical Statements* (1967) [M B]

*The Novels and Stories* (1937-41); *Early Stories*, ed. Mildred R. Bennett (1957); *Collected Short Fiction* (1965).

E. K. Brown, *Willa Cather: A Critical Biography* (1953); ed. James Schroeter, *Willa Cather and Her Critics* (1967); J. H. Randall, *The Landscape and the Looking Glass* (1960); Mildred R. Bennett, *The World of Willa Cather* (1961).

**Catton, Bruce** (1899–   ). Journalist, historian. Born in Petoskey, Michigan. By training a newspaperman, he has lately emerged as a historian of particular gifts. His *Mr Lincoln's Army* (1951), *Glory Road: The Bloody Route from Fredericksburg to Gettysburg* (1952) and *A Stillness at Appomattox* (1953) together form a lavishly written and colourful 3-volume history of the army of the Potomac during the Civil War. More incisively written are *The Hallowed Ground* (1956), the story of the war from the viewpoint of the Northern armies, and *The Coming Fury* (1961), which was the first volume of *The Centennial History of the Civil War* (completed by *Terrible Swift Sword*, 1963, and *Never*

*Call Retreat*, 1965). Though his work has been criticized for its romanticism, its emphasis on personality, and its view of history as a crusade of ideals (rather than as a matter of economic factors and power conflicts) it represents popular history at a very high level of achievement. [D K A]

**Chandler, Raymond** (1888–1959). Mystery writer. Chicago-born, he went at 8 to England with his mother and was educated at Dulwich College. After a brief spell of journalism he left in 1912 for California, where after war-service he became a businessman associated with various oil companies. It was not until the Depression that he began, at 44, to write, publishing more than 20 stories between 1933 and 1939, most in *Black Mask*, then the leading vehicle for the hard-boiled school of detective fiction. Their success led him into the famous novels about racketeers, crooked cops and politicians. He lived in Southern California, the usual setting of his work, for most of his life, but was contemplating return to England when he died.

Chandler brought to the mystery novel the poetry of violence, a remarkable personal style, and an ability to develop character and situation dramatically. His essays in *The Simple Art of Murder* (1950) and the miscellany *Raymond Chandler Speaking* (1962) show his close concern for language and plot. The first novel, *The Big Sleep* (1939), was followed by *Farewell, My Lovely* (1940), *The High Window* (1942) and *The Lady in the Lake* (1943), these usually being considered his best works. The style of the later novels – *The Little Sister* (1949), *The Long Goodbye* (1954), *Playback* (1958) – becomes increasingly mannered, while his detective-hero Philip Marlowe is touched with sentimentality. This character, who first appears in *The Big Sleep*, owes something to the ruthless protagonists of other *Black Mask* writers, notably Dashiell ◊ Hammett; but he has a highly individual style and appeal. The Marlowe novels are extended morality plays, set in the finely depicted neon wilderness of Los Angeles, where the hero searches for a hidden truth without reference to either individual gain or abstract justice. The novels are collected in *The Raymond Chandler Omnibus* (1953) and *The Second Chandler Omnibus* (1962), the stories in *Killer in the Rain* (1964) and *The Smell of Fear* (1965). [H D]

Matthew J. Bruccoli, *Raymond Chandler: A*

*Checklist* (1968); Philip Durham, *Down These Mean Streets* (1963).

**Channing, Edward Tyrell** (1790–1856). Editor, lecturer. Born in Newport, Rhode Island, the younger brother of William Ellery ◊ Channing the Unitarian propagandist, he helped found and edit the *North American Review*, a major organ of Boston and America, the most important 19th-century American review. He is also important as a teacher, since as Boylston Professor of Rhetoric at Harvard he taught Emerson, Thoreau, Holmes, Lowell and R. H. ◊ Dana, Jr, who edited his *Lectures* (1856). [MB]

**Channing, William Ellery, (I)** (1780–1842). Clergyman, poet, essayist. Born in Newport, Rhode Island, he became tutor in a rich family in Virginia, where he read Rousseau, Wordsworth and Godwin – an introduction to European romanticism which modified his Christianity towards Transcendentalism (◊ Transcendentalists). A graduate of Harvard Divinity School, he was ordained a Congregational Minister in 1803. He visited Schiller, Goethe, Coleridge and Wordsworth and returned to his pulpit in Federal Street Church, Boston, as a man of 'no sectarian bonds', whose sermons brought together the Unitarian and Transcendental. His strong opposition to the Calvinist doctrine of human depravity came out in the ordination sermon for Jared Sparks and in two *Christian Examiner* articles in 1819, attacks which, added to previous work of Joseph Priestley and Henry Ware, encouraged the establishment of Unitarianism. He helped found and run *The Unitarian Church Register* (1821), founded the American Unitarian Association, and propagated a liberal religion which fed Transcendentalism and influenced Emerson, Longfellow, etc. He wrote four important works on slavery abolition between 1835 and 1842, and promoted the cause in the *Christian Examiner* and the *North American Review*. He told parishioners that 'justice is a greater good than property' but believed social advance could be furthered only through individual self-improvement, distrusting reform societies and arguing against the bureaucracy of charitable agencies.

Channing also won great reputation as a man of letters; he was one of the best-known literary figures of his day, famed particularly for his essays and reviews. His 'The Importance and Means of a National Literature' (1830) is the most cogent defence of cultural nationalism before Emerson's Phi Beta Kappa oration of 1837; it notes that while Americans protest against 'dependence on European manufacturers' they are content to import 'fabrics of the intellect'. But American faith in 'the essential quality of all human beings' favoured creative activity; hence the New World would beget 'great minds' and 'a nobler race of men'. [MG]

*Works* (6 vols., 1841–3; revised 1875; 1 vol. edn, 1886).
Arthur W. Brown, *Always Young for Liberty: A Biography of William Ellery Channing* (1956); David P. Edgell, *William Ellery Channing: An Intellectual Portrait* (1955); R. E. Spiller, 'A Case for W. E. Channing', *New England Quarterly*, III (1930).

**Channing, William Ellery, (II)** (1818–1901). Poet, biographer. Born in Boston. Nephew of the above, he left Harvard to go west and write poetry. He later moved to Concord to be near Emerson, who influenced him and also published him in the *Dial*; and became close to the members of that community, including Thoreau, of whom he wrote the first biography, *Thoreau, the Poet-Naturalist* (1873; revised 1902). A ◊ Transcendentalist, he published several volumes of verse, from *Poems* (1843) to *John Brown and the Heroes of Harper's Ferry* (1886). F. B. Sanbourn selected from his work in *Poems of Sixty-Five Years* (1902). [MB]

**Chapman, John Jay** (1862–1933). Critic, poet, playwright. New York born, he went to Harvard and became an adopted Bostonian, involving himself in the prevailing debates about literature, politics and religion. The influence of Emerson appears in *Emerson, and Other Essays* (1898). Other works include *Learning, and Other Essays* (1910), *Letters and Religion* (1924) and *New Horizons in American Life* (1932). One of his many plays was *The Treason and Death of Benedict Arnold* (1910); his poetry is in *Songs and Poems* (1919). For his involvement in Boston see his *Memories and Milestones* (1915) and his collected letters, a fascinating social document. [MB]

*Collected Works* (12 vols., 1970).
Mark A. De Wolfe Howe, *John Jay Chapman and His Letters* (1937); Richard B. Hovey, *John Jay Chapman: An American Mind* (1959).

**Chase, Mary Ellen** (1887– ). Novelist, essayist, scholar. Born and educated in Maine, she taught English at the University of Minnesota and Smith College. Her novels *Mary Peters* (1934) and *Silas Crockett* (1935), describing the past and present life of Maine seafarers, are impressive contributions to modern regional literature and have some excellent characterizations of women; later fiction includes *Dawn in Lyonesse* (1938), *The Edge of Darkness* (1957) and *Lonely Ambitions* (1960). She wrote humorous and descriptive essays about England (*This England*, 1936); two guides to the Bible, *The Bible and the Common Reader* (1944) and *Life and Language in the Old Testament* (1955); and *A Goodly Heritage* (1932) and *A Goodly Fellowship* (1939), interesting autobiographies about her teaching career. [MG]

Perry Westbrook, *Mary Ellen Chase* (1965).

**Chase, Richard** (1914–66). Literary critic, teacher. A Professor of English at Columbia, he was an important voice in the post-war critical movement that advanced beyond the ◊ New Criticism to myth and symbol studies and cultural analysis. His excellent *The American Novel and Its Tradition* (1957) stresses the 'romance' tradition of American fiction, and has advanced a general reappraisal of the distinctive symbolist and abstract quality of much American writing. *Quest for Myth* (1949) and the broader study of American culture *The Democratic Vista* (1959) are also important, as are various uncollected contributions to literary quarterlies. [MB]

*Herman Melville* (1949); *Emily Dickinson* (1951); *Walt Whitman Reconsidered* (1955).

**Chayefsky, Paddy** (1923– ). Playwright. A New Yorker, he began writing television plays about ordinary people's humdrum lives, the best of which is *Marty* (1953), the tale of a Bronx butcher's courtship of an old maid schoolteacher. His humorous, sympathetic realism continued in *The Bachelor Party* (1954) and *The Catered Affair* (1955). His first Broadway play was also originally a television script: *The Middle of the Night* (1956). His tape-recorder naturalism is modified towards stylization in *The Tenth Man* (1960), on the Jewish dybbuk theme, and *Gideon* (1961), in which a God-chosen man refuses even miracles as aids to belief. In *The Latent Homosexual* (1968) the poet hero, confronted by tax problems,

is manipulated back into circulation by a cunning lawyer. His *Television Plays* appeared in 1955. [EM]

**Cheever, John** (1912– ). Short-story writer, novelist. Born in Quincy, Massachusetts. The author of 5 collections of short stories and 3 novels, *The Wapshot Chronicle* (1957), *The Wapshot Scandal* (1964) and *Bullet Park* (1969), he is a prime exponent of the poignant, well-made story of the *New Yorker* school, in which magazine many of his stories have appeared. His novels have exposed his talents on a larger scale: there he has detailed a picture of the passing of rural America and its replacement by the new America of supermarket, superhighway and computer technology. His tone is of nostalgic regard for the old and satire for the new. Latterly, his writing has become increasingly satirical, its settings increasingly mechanized, and there are evident connexions with the work of William ◊ Burroughs and Terry ◊ Southern. His career shows that the contemporary trend to baroque satire and bizarre, black humour, especially in *Bullet Park* (1969), can be fed by a writer who has been working in his own personal strain for years and who has approached 'hard' satire only gradually. [AG]

Collections of stories: *The Way Some People Live* (1943); *The Enormous Radio* (1953); *The Housebreaker of Shady Hill* (1958); *The Brigadier and the Golf Widow* (1964).

**Chesnutt, C. W.** ◊ Negro Literature.

**Chicago Aristotelians.** A group of literary critics associated, from the 1940s on, with the University of Chicago and a major force in the development of modern American criticism. Their importance lies in their close philosophical analysis of criticism itself, and their challenges to the mechanical, over-simplified assumptions (about paradox, poetic language, symbols) of much modern critical writing. Their debt to Aristotle, a sophisticated one, derives from their approval of his pragmatic approach to the study of a text and his concern with poetics – with defining the structural parts of a work of art in terms of their relative importance. In particular, they are much concerned with defining 'plot' – the 'imitation of an action', and therefore that part of a work which subsumes all other parts of the imitation within itself.

The main statement of the group is to be found in *Critics and Criticism: Ancient and Modern* (1952; revised abridged paperback edn, 1957), edited by R. S. ◊ Crane, and containing essays by Crane, W. R. Keast, Richard McKeon, Norman Maclean, Elder Olson and Bernard Weinberg, all of whom base their critical approach – which, they insist, 'is one critical method among others' – on learned and wide-ranging scholarship and philosophical clarity. Weinberg, a Professor of Romance Languages and Literature, has produced an excellent *History of Literary Criticism in the Italian Renaissance* (1961); Elder Olson, *The Poetry of Dylan Thomas* (1954) and a general study, *Tragedy and the Theory of Drama* (1961); Crane an excellent theoretical study, *The Languages of Criticism and the Structure of Poetry* (1953). Deriving from the group is a most significant contribution to the study of fiction, Wayne Booth's *The Rhetoric of Fiction* (1961). [MB]

W. K. Wimsatt, *The Verbal Icon* (1954); René Wellek, *Concepts of Criticism* (1963); George Watson, *The Literary Critics* (1962).

**Chivers, Thomas Holley** (1809–58). Poet. Born in Georgia on a wealthy plantation. He trained as a physician but grew increasingly absorbed by any cult or sect he could join – Swedenborgian, ◊ Transcendentalist, Fourierist, Mesmerist, spiritualist, etc. His poems are unique; sometimes they have a curious free lyricism whose wild sounds and surreal juxtapositions have attracted poets ever since, however academics may scoff. His books, published at his own expense, include *The Lost Pleïad and Other Poems* (1845), *Memoralia, or Phials of Amber, Full of the Tears of Love* (1853), and *Virginalia, or Songs of My Summer Nights* (1853). Poe accused his *Eonchs of Ruby: A Gift of Love* (1851) of plagiarism, and the reverse was retorted. The correspondence of these mutual plagiarists is a fascinating study in shrewdness and misunderstanding. Chivers also wrote a theory of the unconscious, *Search after Truth, or a New Revelation of the Psycho-Physiological Nature of Man* (1848), and one of the earliest dramatizations of the Deirdre legend: *The Sons of Usna: Tragi-Apotheosis, in Five Acts* (1858). He is a poet of self-mesmerism, a linguistic swinger of great energy and perhaps mystic power. [EM]

S. Foster Damon, *Thomas Holley Chivers: Friend of Poe* (1930).

**Chomsky, Noam** (1928–    ). Linguist, political critic. Born and educated in Philadelphia, he studied at Harvard 1951–5, and since 1955 he has taught at the Massachusetts Institute of Technology, where he is professor of modern language and linguistics. His first reputation came in the field of linguistics, through both his lectures and his publications: *Syntactic Structures* (1957); *Current Issues in Linguistic Theory* (1964); *Aspects of the Theory of Syntax* (1965), an important work on transformational grammar; *Topics in the Theory of Generative Grammar* (1966); *Cartesian Linguistics* (1966); and *Language and Mind* (1968), a lucid statement of his philosophy of language. Chomsky's second reputation came through the effects of his radical Jewish background on his political opinions during the sixties. He is one of the American Establishment's most formidable critics. The political essays in his *American Power and the New Mandarins* (1969) includes 'The Responsibility of Intellectuals' and 'On Resistance', fine attacks on complacency and hidden power. Chomsky has transformed the status and relevance of theoretical linguistics in our time, and he goes on to make a remarkable connexion between the possibility of language as a biologically determined and transmitted structure, a criticism of extreme behaviourist psychology, and the responsibility of men of knowledge to challenge the authoritarian state in any of its agencies. [EM]

John Lyons, *Chomsky* (1970).

**Chopin, Kate** (1851–1904). Novelist, story writer. Born in St Louis, of part-French descent, she lived in New Orleans, then on a plantation, then again in St Louis after her husband's death. An admirer of Maupassant, she wrote stories, criticism and a play. Her stories are set largely among Creoles and Cajuns, and are to be found in *Bayou Folk* (1894) and *A Night in Acadie* (1897); they show great finesse and quality. Her novel *At Fault* (1890) is about the strain in sexual relations that occurs within the constraints of marriage – a theme vastly more successfully extended in her *The Awakening* (1899), a poised, textured book which Larzer Ziff has called 'a novel of the first rank'. It is about Edna Pontellier, a woman married with two children, well-to-do and intelligent, tempted into feeling, freedom and adultery. It was critically ill-received and she wrote little else. [MB]

Larzer Ziff, *The American 1890s* (1966).

**Churchill, Winston** (1871–1947). Novelist. Born in St Louis (no relation of the British statesman), he graduated from the Naval Academy at Annapolis in 1894 and immediately began to write successfully, spending most of his life in New Hampshire. *The Celebrity: An Episode* (1898), a satire on the flamboyant New York journalist Richard Harding Davis, was followed by his best-seller, *Richard Carvel* (1899), a romance set in the Revolutionary period. *The Crisis* (1901), concerned with St Louis at the time of the Civil War, enjoyed another huge success and typified the lengthy historical romances popular at the turn of the century. *The Crossing* (1904), a characteristically uneven work, described life on the frontier during the Revolution. Later came *Coniston* (1906), *Mr Crewe's Career* (1908), *A Far Country* (1915) and three novels about religion in modern society: *A Modern Chronicle* (1910), *The Inside of the Cup* (1913) and *The Dwelling-Place of Light* (1917). He described his religious convictions in *The Uncharted Way* (1940). [MG]

Charles C. Walcutt, *The Romantic Compromise in the Novels of Winston Churchill* (1951).

**Ciardi, John** (1916–    ). Poet. Born in Boston. He has taught at Kansas City University, Harvard, Rutgers and the Bread Loaf Writers Conference, and been poetry editor of the *Saturday Review*. His earliest collection is *Homeward to America* (1940), followed by eight further volumes of poems including *In Fact* (1963) and an excellent translation of Dante's *Divine Comedy* (1954, 1961). His poems are influenced by Eliot and Laforgue towards the humorous critical lyric. His latest book, *Person to Person* (1964), contains sharp images of contemporary America in rather literary poems. [EM]

Miller Williams, *The Achievement of John Ciardi* (1968).

**Clapp, Henry** (1814–75). Journalist, Bohemian. A leader of the group that gathered at Pfaff's beer-cellar on Broadway in the 1850s, known as 'King of Bohemia', he was born in Nantucket and promoted Whitman (another Pfaff Bohemian) and Fourier with equal energy. He founded the *Saturday Press*, where Whitman praised himself and where Twain and Billings appeared. He wrote *The Pioneer, or Leaves from an Editor's Portfolio* (1846). (◊ Bohemianism.) [MB]

**Clare, Ada** (pseud. of Jane McElheney) (1836–74). Novelist, poet, actress, Bohemian. She was 'Queen of Bohemia' to Henry ◊ Clapp's 'King', and was a leading figure in the Pfaff's beer-cellar group. Born in South Carolina, cousin of the poet Paul Hamilton ◊ Hayne, she made her own reputation as poetess and 'Love-Philosopher', producing an illegitimate child by pianist and composer Louis Gottschalk. A visit to bohemian circles in France encouraged her promotion of this advanced artistic life-style. Her writings themselves are relatively slender, but she published verse in Clapp's *Saturday Press* and on the west coast in the *Golden Era*, and distilled her affairs and her experience in a novel called *Only a Woman's Heart* (1866). (◊ Bohemianism.) [MB]

**Clark, Walter van Tilburg** (1909–    ). Novelist, poet, short-story writer. Born in Maine but brought up in Nevada, he has always identified his literary spirit with the West and explored frontier themes – those of man struggling for survival in the natural world, of justice and law confronted by forces of evil and anarchy, and of human action set against the motives for it. *The Ox-Bow Incident* (1940), set in the Nevada cattle country, is concerned with a posse's lynching of three men wrongly suspected of murder, and the forces and motives involved. *The City of Trembling Leaves* (1945), a less economically written book, describes the adolescence of a sensitive boy growing up in Reno. *The Track of the Cat* (1949) is a striking and exciting novel about the hunting of a panther, told with a density of symbolic meaning. *The Watchful Gods* (1950) is a collection of stories. Clark has also written poetry and taught creative writing. [AH]

Chester E. Eisinger, 'The Fiction of Walter van Tilburg Clark: Man and Nature in the West', *Southwest Review*, XLIV (Summer, 1959), and *Fiction of the Forties* (1965).

**Clark, William.** ◊ Lewis, Meriwether.

**Cleaver, Eldridge.** ◊ Negro Literature.

**Clemens, Samuel.** ◊ Twain, Mark.

**Clurman, Harold** (1901–    ). Stage director, critic. Born in New York City. In the 1920s, enthusiastic over the theory and practice of Copeau and Stanislavski, he joined with Lee Strasberg on his return from France, and together they founded the ◊ Group Theatre, a centre of creative hope in the Depression period. This experience is told in his excellent *The Fervent Years* (1945); and *Lies Like Truth* (1959) collects his first-rate theatre criticism. *The Naked Image* (1966) reports his theatre-going in America, Europe and Japan. He is drama critic of the *Nation*. [EM]

**Coates, Robert M.** (1897–    ). Novelist, short-story writer. Born in New Haven, Connecticut, he published his first novel, *The Eater of Darkness* (1929; revised edn reissued 1960), with Robert ◊ McAlmon's Contact Press while he was an expatriate in Paris; an experimental surrealist novel of considerable interest. His more recent novels are rather more conventional in character (*Yesterday's Burdens*, 1933; *Wisteria Cottage*, 1948, etc.). He is the author of some very good short stories, including *All the Year Round* (1943), *The View from Here* (1960) and *The Man Just Ahead of You* (1964), 13 *New Yorker* stories, his finest collection. He is art critic for the *New Yorker*. [MB]

**Coffin, Robert P(eter) Tristram** (1892–1955). Poet, novelist, biographer. A 'New Englander by birth, by bringing-up, by spirit' (but also educated at Princeton and Oxford), he devoted his life to the description and praise of his native State, Maine. A novel, *Lost Paradise* (1934), re-creates his boyhood life on a Maine salt-water farm; but he was primarily an energetic and prolific poet, among his best volumes being *Ballads of Square-Toed Americans* (1933), *Strange Holiness* (1935; Pulitzer Prize), *Maine Ballads* (1938) and *Poems for a Son with Wings* (1945). A preface to his *Collected Poems* (1939; expanded edition 1948) describes poetry as 'the art of making people feel well about life'. He also published biographies, including those of Laud (1930) and the Dukes of Buckingham (1931), and two critical works: *New Poetry of New England: Frost and Robinson* (1938) and *The Substance That Is Poetry* (1942). [MG]

**Collier, John** (1901–    ). Novelist, short-story writer. Born in England, a former poetry editor of *Time and Tide*, he moved to the U.S.A. in 1942 to live in Virginia and California. His inventive, surrealist vein, already established in novels like *His Monkey Wife* (1930) and *Defy the Foul Fiend* (1934) and volumes of stories like *Variations on a Theme* (1935), turned to American subjects, as in *Fancies and Goodnights* (1951), stories. [MB]

**Colman, Benjamin** (1673–1747). Minister, theologian, poet. Born in England, he was made pastor of Brattle Street Church, Boston, a liberal congregation. He published more than 90 books, mostly sermons – one is revealingly called *The Government and Improvement of Mirth* (1707) – but also poems. [MB]

**Combs, (Elisha) Tram(mell, Jr)** (1924–    ). Poet. He left Alabama to study physical sciences at five different Northern universities, then became an air-force meteorologist and oil-company chemist. In 1951 he migrated from science and the U.S.A. to St Thomas, Virgin Islands, where, using his talents as bibliophile, linguist, historian and poet, he ran a bookshop specializing in Spanish-American literature and history. His poetry, quietly intense, is collected in *Pilgrim's Terrace* (1957), *Ceremonies in Mind* (1959), *But Never Mind* (1961) and *Saint Thomas* (1965). Metrically and typographically experimental, he alternates between biting social reflection and sombre metaphysical meditation. [BP]

**Commager, Henry Steele** (1902–    ). Historian. Born in Pittsburgh. He has been professor of history and American studies at Amherst since 1956, and held the Pitt Professorship at Cambridge in 1947–8 and the Harmsworth Professorship at Oxford in 1952–3. His large output includes: editions of de Tocqueville's *Democracy in America* (1946) and *W. D. Howells* (1950, selected writings), *The American Mind* (1950, 'an interpretation of American thought and character since the 1880s'), *Theodore Parker* (1947), *The Growth of the American Republic* (2 vols., 4th edn 1950, with S. E. Morison), *Freedom and Order: A Commentary on the American Political Scene* (1966), *The Search for a Usable Past* (1967) and *The Commonwealth of Learning* (1968), an evaluation of American education. He is also the editor of *The Rise of the American Nation* (50 vols., in progress). [EM]

**Comstock, Anthony** (1844–1915). Censor. A Connecticut man, he founded and became life secretary of the Society for the Suppression of Vice. His merciless campaigns secured the 1873 Act excluding 'immoral' articles from the mails. His own moral nature seems not to have been outwardly corrupted by the mass of obscenity he read and saw. [EM]

H. Broun and M. Leech, *Anthony Comstock, Roundsman of the Lord* (1927).

**Condon, Richard** (1915–   ). Novelist. He specializes in the morality of crime and violence presented as comedy thrillers with a high degree of sophisticated invention. But the breaking of men, which occurs in so many of his fictions, is not frivolous. Within his humour lies a painful, almost despairing, sense of permanent human conflicts. His 'bad taste' is a weapon of analysis as well as a form of entertainment. [EM]

*The Oldest Confession* (1959); *The Manchurian Candidate* (1960); *A Talent for Loving* (1961); *Some Angry Angel* (1961); *Any God Will Do* (1966); *An Infinity of Mirrors* (1966); *The Ecstasy Business* (1967); *Mile High* (1969).

**Congdon, Kirby** (1924–   ). Poet. Born in Pennsylvania and brought up in New England, he has since lived mostly in New York and Florida. He edits *Magazine*, through which he has promoted what he has termed 'the mimeograph revolution', a rapid means of printing and circulating literary work without waiting for the cautious big publishing firms. His poetry takes the form of lyrics of the embattled self in a city context: *Iron Ark* (1962), *A Century of Progress* (1962), *Icarus* (1963), *Icarus in Aipotu* (1963) and *Juggernaut* (1965), a remarkable set of poems on the motor-cycle cult. He edited *Interim Books* with Jay Socin. [EM]

**Connecticut Wits.** Also known as the 'Hartford Wits'. The first American school of poets, flourishing in the 1780s and 1790s. They were all born in the 1750s, educated at Yale, amateurs, conservatives (i.e. Federalists), Calvinists and neo-classicists, with the possible exception of ◊ Barlow, and revolutionary satirists, modelled on Butler and

Churchill. They included ◊ Trumbull, Timothy ◊ Dwight and his brother Theodore, Lemuel Hopkins, David Humphreys, Richard Alsop and Elihu Hubbard Smith. Their group products include *The Anarchiad* (1786–7) and the verse satire in 20 instalments, *The Echo* (1791–1805). [EM]

Ed. V. L. Parrington, *The Connecticut Wits* (1926); L. Howard, *The Connecticut Wits* (1943).

**Connell, Evan S(helby), Jr** (1924–   ). Story writer, novelist. Born in Kansas City, Missouri, educated at Dartmouth, he has contributed finely written stories to many American magazines. Collections are *The Anatomy Lesson* (1957), *Mrs Bridge* (1958), a group of delightfully ironic sketches about a suburban matron, and *At the Crossroads* (1965). His novel *The Patriot* (1960) deals again ironically with an innocent hero in the air force during the Second World War. *Notes from a Bottle Found on the Beach at Carmel* (1963) is a long poem of 243 pages, dense with strange facts and lore. *The Diary of a Rapist* (1966) is a novelistic *tour de force* on the nature of sexual violence. To *Mrs Bridge* he has now added a companion, *Mr Bridge* (1969). [MB]

**Connelly, Marc** (1890–   ). Journalist, dramatist. From Philadelphia. His friendship with George S. ◊ Kaufman led to their successful collaborations in the theatre: *Dulcy* (1921) – in which a stupid woman ironically helps her husband's business career – *To the Ladies* (1922) – the same situation in verse – *Merton of the Movies* (1922) – a Hollywood satire – and *Beggar on Horseback* (1924) – a dream play against the industrialization of art. Connelly's own finest work is *The Green Pastures* (1930), based on Roark Bradford's *Ol' Man Adam an' His Chillun* (1928) – Old Testament myths enacted through the lives of Deep South Negroes treated with saccharine theatricality. His most recent books are *A Survivor from Qam* (1965), a novel, and *Voices Offstage: A Book of Memoirs* (1968). [EM]

**Conway, Moncure D(aniel)** (1832–1907). Biographer, novelist. Born in Virginia, he shifted to abolitionism and Unitarianism, was clergyman, editor and expatriate. He wrote biographies of Carlyle, Emerson, Hawthorne and Thomas Paine, whose writings he edited. His best-known novel is *Pine and Palm* (1887), about the Civil War, and his *Autobiography* (1904) records beliefs and personalities. [MB]

**Cook, Ebenezer** (*c.*1672–1732). Satiric poet. He was probably an English gentleman who went to buy tobacco in Maryland and returned to pour his disgust with greedy colonists into his hudibrastic satire 'The Sot-Weed Factor; or A Voyage to Maryland' (1708), a coarse, funny and probably realistic poem, which he may have followed up with *Sotweed Redivivus* (1730), a verse treatise on tobacco and its over-production. He may have written a comic poem on Nathaniel Bacon's 1676 revolution. He may have been an American and made 'laureate' by Lord Baltimore. He is certainly the hero of John ◊ Barth's *The Sotweed Factor* (1960). [EM]

**Cooke, John Esten** (1830–86). Novelist, biographer. This prolific Southern writer, best remembered for his ante-bellum romances, was born into a leading – and literary – Virginia family: his brother, Philip Pendleton Cooke, published a well-received volume of verse and his cousin was John Pendleton ◊ Kennedy. Amongst his novels, *Leather Stocking and Silk, or Hunter John Myers and His Times* (1854) is modelled on Cooper and deals with Virginia society; *The Virginia Comedians, or Old Days in the Old Dominion* (1854) and its sequel deals with pre-Independence actresses and aristocrats; *Surry of Eagle's Nest* (1866) fictionalizes the career of Stonewall Jackson; and *The Heir of Gaymount* (1870) deals with the Civil War, in which Cooke served on the Confederate side, and the need for agrarian reconstruction. He wrote biographies of Jefferson and Lee, and *Virginia: A History of the People* (1883). [MB]

**Cooper, James Fenimore** (1789–1851). Novelist. Born Burlington, New Jersey. The son of an enterprising and intelligent land speculator, Judge William Cooper, he spent most of his childhood in the frontier community of Cooperstown in upstate New York. This community later served as the model for 'Templeton' in *The Pioneers*, which was the first of his Leatherstocking tales. As the affluent Judge could afford to give his son a good education, he was sent to a school in Albany, where he received an excellent classical training and formed life-long friendships with the sons of the aristocratic Rensselaer and Jay families. After being expelled from Yale because of a prank, he went to sea as an ordinary merchant seaman, then as a midshipman in the U.S. Navy. His naval career, though successful, was brief: he gave up the sea in order to win the hand of Susan Delancy, whose distinguished ancestors had been governors of New York Colony. At 21 he prepared to settle down as a gentleman farmer, republican in his political principles but aristocratic in his sympathies. Apparently destined to a life of comfortable conservative mediocrity, he had in fact already absorbed the experience of ocean and wilderness which were to provide him with the raw materials for some 21 of his 34 novels.

His first novel, *Precaution* (1820), a clumsy imitation of Jane Austen, was written in 1819 on a dare, but with a secret hope that it might be successful enough to repair declining family fortunes; and during the remaining 32 years of his life he continued to write in order to maintain himself and his family at the social level to which they were accustomed. Yet in his second and third novels, *The Spy* (1821) and *The Pioneers* (1823), this American Gentleman created two outstanding democratic heroes – the patriotic pedlar Harvey Birch and the old hunter Natty Bumppo. In these, as in most of his later novels, the ostensible heroes and heroines are genteel characters whose actions, emotions and language are as stereotyped as possible: they provide the conventional 'love interest'; the lower-class characters come alive. Written in frank imitation of the early Waverley novels, *The Spy* and *The Pioneers* were so successful that Cooper, soon known as 'the American Scott', embarked seriously on a career of professional authorship. In 1822 he had moved to New York City. In his second and third works he had been the first writer to make successful novelistic use of authentic American scenes and manners; now in his fourth work, *The Pilot* (1823), he created the first novel in which strictly nautical action was of central importance. In this and subsequent sea romances, such as *The Red Rover* (1828), *The Water-Witch* (1830), *The Two Admirals* (1842), *Wing-and-Wing* (1843) and *The Sea Lions* (1849), he exhibited descriptive powers so remarkable that he became more famous as a sea novelist than as the creator of Leatherstocking. It was in this capacity that he was admired by Melville and Conrad. But he seems to have sensed quite early that in Leatherstocking he had created a mythical character who evoked the profoundest aspirations and regrets of expansive 19th-century white American civilization. In *The Last of the Mohicans* (1826) he wrote the first of four sequels to *The Pioneers*. This series of novels tells the life story of Natty Bumppo from the period of early manhood in *The Deerslayer* (1841), maturity in *The Last of the Mohicans*, unsuccessful courtship in *The Pathfinder* (1840), old age in *The Pioneers*, to extreme old age and death in *The Prairie* (1827). Read in this order, the series forms an artistically defective, yet intensely moving, epic of the Westward Movement. Not until *Moby Dick* did any other American write a work of comparable scope and power.

After the publication of *The Last of the Mohicans*, with its seemingly authentic portraits of American Indians, he found himself a world-famous author. Hoping to improve his health he took his family to Europe in 1826, where they were welcomed by many of the great literary and political figures of the age. He wished to manage publishing affairs in England, and have his children educated by peripatetic studies. He made friends with Scott, but his friendship with Lafayette was probably the decisive influence on his development during the seven years he spent in Europe. He incorporated Lafayette's tour of America into *Notions of America* (1828). He soon became an active supporter of democratic movements in England, France and Poland; he began to align himself with the Jefferson–Jackson faction in American politics. Though an uneasy democrat as soon as he returned to America, he was such an ardent supporter of European popular movements that *The Bravo* (1831), with its frankly proletarian ethos, greatly offended the Whig press in America, not to mention the Tory reviewers in Britain. During the 1830s, in fact, Cooper ceased to be a popular writer as he turned from tales of adventure to works of contemporary social satire like *Homeward Bound* and *Home as Found* (1838). Even before he returned to America in 1833, he was convinced that the republic had deteriorated during his absence into a mobocracy controlled by a licentious press, which was in turn controlled by commercial interests. He wished to retire from writing,

but he could not afford to; in any case, he had to strike back at his detractors. He struck back in print, and then, when he grew weary of being libelled, he personally conducted a series of libel suits which eventually silenced the Whig press.

The last decade of his life was an odd combination of great human sweetness in such works as *Satanstoe* (1845) and the double novel *Afloat and Ashore* (1844) and gloomy misanthropy in *Jack Tier* (1848), *The Crater* (1847) and *The Sea Lions* (1849). *Satanstoe* is the first of the Littlepage trilogy, which dramatizes the problems of land tenure in America, from the colonial period to the 1840s. *The Chainbearer* (1845) involves the Revolutionary war, and, in *The Redskins* (1846), Indians rescue the Littlepage family from exploiting agents and lawyers. Increasingly conservative in his social and religious views, he spent much of his energy supporting such bad causes as the American attack on Mexico and the Rensselaer family's attempt to force poor tenants to pay back rents. Though the latter was a bad cause, it incited him to write the Littlepage trilogy (1845–6), the first family chronicle novel in American literature.

Cooper was usually a slovenly writer; his plots were often loosely constructed, his action improbable and his genteel characters dull or insufferable or both. Yet at least a dozen of his novels have great imaginative vitality. His best novel, probably, is *Satanstoe*, though many critics prefer *The Pioneers*, *The Prairie* or *The Deerslayer*. Certainly the Leatherstocking tales, taken as a group, are his greatest work. But, as Robert Spiller has demonstrated, Cooper must not be judged only by his novels: he was probably the most acute social critic of his age, as he was also the most morally courageous writer America has ever produced. [G D]

*Letters and Journals*, ed. J. F. Beard (1960– ).
James Grossman, *James Fenimore Cooper* (1949); Yvor Winters, 'Fenimore Cooper and the Ruins of Time', in *In Defense of Reason* (1947); George Dekker, *James Fenimore Cooper the Novelist* (1967); Robert Spiller, *Fenimore Cooper, Critic of His Times* (1931); Kay S. House, *Cooper's Americans* (1965).

**Coover, Robert** (1932– ). Novelist. Born in Iowa, he studied at Indiana and Chicago Universities, served in the U.S. Navy 1953–7, has taught philosophy in universities and now lives in England. *The*

*Origin of the Brunists* (1965) is a first-rate first novel and concerns the founding of a mystical religion after a mining disaster. *The Universal Baseball Association, Inc., J. Henry Waugh, Prop.* (1968) is an allegorical novel using the American religious sport. *Pricksongs and Descants* (1969) contains his short fictions. [E M]

**Corso, Gregory** (1930–     ). Poet. Born in Greenwich Village, New York, he lived with foster parents, and spent his youth in poverty and violence until he met Allen ◊ Ginsberg and other ◊ Beat Generation writers who encouraged his gift for poetry. From *The Vestal Lady of Brattle* (1955) and *Gasoline* (1958), he developed the power of the longer poems in *The Happy Birthday of Death* (1960), some of the most personal and moving poetry since the Second World War, and the internationally located lyrics of *Long Live Man* (1962). *The Geometric Poem* (1966) is a long work in calligraphy on Egyptian materials. *American Express* (1961) is an amusing prose memoir. He contributed experimental work to *Minutes to Go* (1960) with William Burroughs and Brion Gysin, and to interviews (with Allen Ginsberg and William Burroughs) in *Journal for the Protection of All Beings* (1961). His plays include *In This Hurry-Up Age* (1962). [E M]

*Selected Poems* (1962).
John Fuller, 'The Poetry of Gregory Corso', *London Magazine*, April 1961.

**Cotton, John** (1584–1652). Theologian. Born in England, he was Dean of Emmanuel College, Cambridge, highly reputed as an Anglican theologian and orator. Drawn to Puritanism, he became rector of St Botolph's in Boston, Lincolnshire, but Archbishop Laud's enmity drove him to the Bay Colony in 1633. He arrived in Boston, Massachusetts, in part named in his honour, with a fellow graduate of Emmanuel, Thomas ◊ Hooker, and, with Hooker and Richard ◊ Mather, became one of the Colony's most important spiritual leaders. His grandson, Cotton ◊ Mather, called him 'indeed a most universal scholar, and a living system of the liberal arts, and a walking library'. His antinomian theory of grace direct from God inspired Anne Hutchinson, but he became more orthodox later, for example in *Bloudy Tenent Washed and Made White in the Bloude of the Lamb* (1647), a defence of theocracy against Roger ◊ Williams. Most of his works are theological argument with political implications, interpreting the function of the colony and the priesthood in it (he thought it should precede the magistracy). The titles of some of them suggest his interests: *An Abstract of the Lawes of New England* (1641), *The Covenant of God's Free Grace* (1645), *The Controversy Concerning Liberty of Conscience in Matters of Religion* (1646). *Milk for Babes, Drawn out of the Breasts of Both Testaments, Chiefly for the Spiritual Nourishment of Boston Babes in either England* (1646) is a stylish Puritan primer. His biography, John Norton's *Abel Being Dead Yet Speaketh* (1657), is the first American biography: this suggests his importance. [M B]

L. Ziff, *The Career of John Cotton: Puritanism and American Experience* (1963); Moses Coit Tyler, *A History of American Literature during the Colonial Period* (1949; repr. 1962).

**Cowley, Malcolm** (1898–     ). Critic, poet. Born near Balsano, Pennsylvania. Closely associated with the ◊ 'Lost Generation' of expatriates in Paris in the 1920s, where he was editorially involved with *Secession* and *Broom* (◊ Little Magazines), he has provided one of the most interesting objective records of this period in *Exile's Return* (1934; revised 1951). A general literary critic and a cultural historian, his *After the Genteel Tradition: American Writers since 1910* (1937; repr. 1959) is a useful broad study of American writing; and *The Literary Situation* (1954) has some fascinating cultural material on the conditions of American literary production. Volumes of poems: *Blue Juanita* (1929; reissued with additions, 1968) and *Dry Season* (1941). He has also edited several important volumes such as *The Portable Faulkner. The Faulkner–Cowley File: Letters and Memoirs, 1944-1962* (1967) is an important piece of literary history, and *Think Back on Us* (1967) is a collection of his writings from the 1930s arranged as a chronicle of the period by H. D. Piper. [M B]

**Cozzens, James Gould** (1903–     ). Novelist. Born in Chicago. After attending Harvard, he published in the 1920s four minor novels, which may be taken as apprentice fiction, before announcing in *The Last Adam* (1933; British title *A Cure of Flesh*) his characteristic subject: the subtle examination of moral predicaments and problems of conscience among the professional classes, whom he tends to regard as the guardians of a settled and traditional society. This theme, with variations, provides the material of *Men and Brethren* (1936), *The Just and the Unjust* (1942), *Guard of Honor* (1948) and *By Love Possessed* (1957).

The controversy aroused by the publication of the last succeeded in focusing attention upon Cozzens's achievement in earlier, strangely neglected novels – their central values and their formal adherence to the unities of time and place were apparently unfashionable virtues for their period. The protagonists are usually professional men – doctors, lawyers, clergymen – who are circumscribed by obligations and duties, limited in their actions by an awareness of responsibility to themselves and the society in which they live. Undoubtedly the best of these works is the long and complex *Guard of Honor*, one of the outstanding American novels to deal with the Second World War; here the civilian community is exchanged for a military air base in Florida, a setting which lets Cozzens analyse the dilemmas of leadership during three September days in 1943. All the novels are carefully constructed and accurately reflect their author's preoccupation with order, discipline, stability and hierarchy in social organizations. His early work includes two fine short novels: *S.S. San Pedro* (1931), a vivid tale of the sea, and *Castaway* (1934), a macabre fantasy of the isolation of modern man. *Ask Me Tomorrow* (1940), the story of a European education with autobiographical echoes, is among the least satisfying of the later works. *Children and Others* (1964) is a collection of short stories. His latest work is *Morning, Noon and Night* (1968). [H D]

Frederick Bracher, *The Novels of James Gould Cozzens* (1959); Dwight MacDonald, 'By Cozzens Possessed', in *Against the American Grain* (1962); D. E. S. Maxwell, *Cozzens* (1964); Granville Hicks, *James Gould Cozzens* (1968).

**Crane, Hart** (1899–1932). Poet. Born in Garretsville, Ohio. His parents separated while he was a child; as his mother was in need of sanatorium treatment, he lived with his grandparents. He began to write poetry at 13, and in 1916 went with his mother to his grandfather's fruit plantation on the Isle of Pines, south of Cuba, a crucial experience of exotic wild nature which supplied symbols for this poetry to place

with his childhood misery. He set himself against the Crane family's business life, and his alienation increased when his parents divorced. Leaving Cleveland for New York, already with a wide reading of poetry behind him, he worked briefly in his father's sweet business, as a munitions worker, labourer, advertising man, and even manager of a teashop, as his poems appeared in ♦ little magazines. Their broody Elizabethanisms and French symbolist images recorded his tensions and his homosexuality. His great efforts to shape his poetic skills while he was poor and exhausted increased his alcoholism. Living in Brooklyn in 1924 he began to think of his great poem 'The Bridge' (1930), but, sick and poor, restlessly moving between New York, the Isle of Pines and Europe, he found his creative periods difficult to maintain, in spite of financial help from the banker Otto Kahn. His first book of poems, *White Buildings*, appeared in 1926. After 1930, his unsettled life, the death of his father, and estrangement from his mother and many of his friends, he went to Mexico to write a poem on Montezuma. Returning from Vera Cruz, he leaped into the sea to drown.

'For the Marriage of Faustus and Helen' (1922–3), the long major poem in *White Buildings*, is a meditation in three sections on beauty, love and renaissance from death, 'an answer to the cultural pessimism' of T. S. Eliot which translates the two myths into contemporary symbols and localities in the vision of the poet, always the unifying agent present in Crane's poetry. 'Voyages' and 'At Melville's Tomb' show his persistent use of the sea as a complex Rimbaudian image throughout his career. In 'The Bridge', he again attempted a reply to *The Waste Land* by conceiving the span of Brooklyn Bridge as the symbolic creative curve of recurrent life which finally is to symbolize America as a new Utopia of the future. This masterpiece is a huge symphonic structure of movements which state major American myths: Pocahontas, Rip Van Winkle, Melville, Poe, Whitman, Columbus, the subway, Atlantis. The gist is relatively clear, but in detail the metaphors fuse myth, history, childhood memories and sensuous experience and need an exegesis of their brilliance.

Crane is one of America's finest poets. His visionary daring and seriousness of purpose have been a major influence on post-1946 poetry, especially through the West Indian poems, which were first brought together in the edition of *Collected Poems* (1933) edited by Waldo ◊ Frank. [EM]

*Complete Poems and Selected Letters and Prose,* ed. by Brom Weber (1966).
L. Dembo, *Hart Crane's Sanskrit Charge: A Study of the Bridge* (1961); R. W. B. Lewis, *The Poetry of Hart Crane* (1967); H. A. Leibowitz, *Hart Crane: An Introduction to the Poetry* (1968); R. W. Butterfield, *The Broken Arc: A Study of Hart Crane* (1969); J. Unterecker, *Voyages, A Life of Hart Crane* (1969).

**Crane, R(onald) S(almon)** (1886–1967). Critic, scholar. The best-known of the University of Chicago group of critics called the ◊ Chicago Aristotelians, Crane, a professor of English and an 18th-century scholar, made a signal statement of the need for criticism in literary studies in 'History versus Criticism in the University Study of Literature' (1935). But his view of criticism is that it is a mode of inquiry which always contains a covert aesthetic; hence the need is to expand the descriptive power of criticism, its 'poetics' element, so that it can account fully for the parts that make up the unity of a work. A classic example of his method is his famous essay 'The Concept of Plot and the Plot of *Tom Jones*', collected in *Critics and Criticism: Ancient and Modern* (1952; revised edn, 1957), a Chicago Aristotelian collection of essays which he edited. He is even more explicit in his Alexander Lectures at the University of Toronto, *The Languages of Criticism and the Structure of Poetry* (1953). For some subtle objections to his strong case, see W. K. ◊ Wimsatt, *The Verbal Icon* (1954). [MB]

**Crane, Stephen** (1871–1900). Novelist, short-story writer, poet. The youngest son of a Methodist minister in New Jersey. He studied at a military academy, Lafayette College and Syracuse University, and immediately set out on a career in New York journalism. The slum background of his first novel, *Maggie: A Girl of the Streets* (1893), was known at first hand: the book had to be published on borrowed money and under a pseudonym. *The Red Badge of Courage* (1895), which brought him success, was written partly out of war correspondent experience in Cuba and Greece, and partly from Civil War readings. It gained him the praise of Howells, Conrad, James, and H. G. Wells. A book of poetry and two further novels on contemporary American life followed in 1895–7, and his shipwreck in 1896 on the way to Cuba gave him the basis of his short story, 'The Open Boat' (1898). His marriage to a lady who had run a sporting house in Florida caused him to be ostracized, and his health was ruined by hardship and slum experience when he returned to England. Conrad looked after him, and Henry James visited the Cranes in their Surrey home. He died of tuberculosis in a Black Forest health centre. His work was given its present high critical evaluation only after the First World War, though it was deeply admired by many practising writers, including Conrad and Henry James.

*Maggie* is a terrifying and beautifully told story of poverty, seduction and suicide on the Bowery. *The Red Badge of Courage*, one of the greatest war novels, concerns the initiation of Henry Fleming into manhood and his violent conversion from chivalric heroics to a comprehension of battle and the relationships of men and nature, told in a prose which ranges from brilliant symbols to the most direct narrative of action. Jimmie Trescott, the hero of *Whilomville Stories* (1900), is one of the good bad boys of American fiction. *George's Mother* (1896) is a study of fear in the squalor of the Bowery. Among Crane's short stories the finest are 'The Bride Comes to Yellow Sky' and 'The Blue Hotel', masterpieces of slanted narrative whose influence on American fiction and films continues, and 'The Open Boat', a vivid description of the fear of death at sea, marred by confused determinism. *The Black Riders and Other Lines* (1895) and *War Is Kind* (1899) contain poems of originality, terse, inventive and strongly governed by symbols of ironic indifferent destiny. Less well known are his final works: *Active Service* (1899), on the Greco-Turkish war, *The Third Violet* (1897), in which a group of American matrons destroys the reputation of a painter who yields finally to a cigarette-smoking Bohemienne, and 'The Clan of No Name', a short story in which a young officer in the Spanish war places himself in a trap to test the law of fate. Little of this reaches the level of *The Red Badge*, but his whole career is a brilliant epitome of the early-19th-century writer grappling with urban corruption, war, and deterministic philosophies. [EM]

*Works*, ed. Wilson Follett (12 vols., 1925–6); *Stephen Crane: An Omnibus*, ed. R. W. Stallman (1952); *Letters*, ed. R. W. Stallman and Lillian Gilkes (1960); *The War Dispatches*, ed. R. W. Stallman and E. R. Hagemann (1964); *Uncollected Writings*, ed. O. W. Fryckstedt (1964); *Complete Short Stories and Sketches*, ed. T. A. Gullason (1963); *The New York City Sketches of Stephen Crane and Related Pieces*, ed. R. W. Stallman and E. R. Hagemann (1968). John Berryman, *Stephen Crane* (1950); Edwin H. Cady, *Stephen Crane* (1962); E. Solomon, *Stephen Crane: From Parody to Realism* (1966); R. W. Stallman, *Stephen Crane: A Biography* (1968).

**Crawford, F(rancis) Marion** (1854–1909). Novelist. Born in Italy, the son of the famous expatriate sculptor Thomas Crawford, he spent a considerable part of his life in that country, where much of his fiction is set; though extensive travels gave him world-wide locales for his more than 40 novels. *Mr Isaacs, A Tale of Modern India* (1882) established a popular following. His view of fiction as entertainment has diminished his reputation, but his narrative art and his powers of evocation of other lands and past history are considerable, and he was extremely successful. He dealt with romantic themes (as in *To Leeward*, 1884, *Pietro Ghisleri*, 1893, and *The White Sister*, 1909, all set in Italy); with political matters (as in *An American Politician*, 1884, set in the States in the Gilded Age); and with history (as in *Via Crucis*, 1899, about the Crusades). [M B]

Larzer Ziff, *The American 1890s* (1966).

**Creeley, Robert** (1926–      ). Poet, novelist, short-story writer. Born in Massachusetts, he studied at Harvard, ◊ Black Mountain College and New Mexico University. He has travelled widely in India, Burma, France and Spain, and lectured and read his poems all over America. His poetry first began to appear with *Le Fou* (1952), *The Immoral Proposition* (1953), *The Kind of Act of* (1953), *All That is Lovely in Men* (1955), *If You* (1956) and *The Whip* (1957). These issues mark the maturing of a terse, spare style of poem, inimitable and suited to his slow, deliberate explorations of the tensions of love and the struggle of men to ascertain what exactly they know. With *A Form of Women* (1959) and *For Love, Poems 1950–1960* (1962) this form seemed to be complete. In *Words* (1967) some of the poems are longer and more complex, but Creeley had hardly made any new depar-

tures. *Pieces* (1969), however, shows a new range of formal procedures shaped into a continuous work of considerable power. *The Charm* (1969) consists of early and uncollected poems. His short stories appeared in *The Gold Diggers* (1954, 1965), and they are like extended versions of his poetic themes, taking considerable risks in their tortuousness. His novel, *The Island* (1963), is a psychological study of married life in a prose which veers towards that of late Henry James. He co-edited *New American Story* with Donald Allen in 1965, introduced *The New Writing in the U.S.A.* (1967) and edited and introduced *Selected Writings of Charles Olson* (1966). [E M]

Ed. David Ossman, *The Sullen Art* (1963); Paul Carroll, *The Poem in Its Skin* (1968).

**Crèvecoeur, Hector St John de** (Michel Guillaume Jean de Crèvecoeur) (1735–1813). Travel writer and social historian. Born in Normandy, he received part of his education in Salisbury (England), and as a young man, while serving as lieutenant under Montcalm in Canada, took part in a map-making expedition to the Great Lakes; and after the fall of Quebec and Britain's annexation of Canada, he began to live in various parts of Pennsylvania and New York. In 1764 he became a citizen of New York, bought a farm in Orange County (1769) and married Mehetable Tippet of Yonkers. In a time of revolution, although he agreed with Franklin's independent artisan ideal, he retained an aristocratic attitude in some ways and was driven from his farm by 'patriots'. Leaving his wife and two children, he placed himself and his son under British protection, was promptly imprisoned, and on release returned to France, where his American experiences made him popular in society. He returned in 1783, but his wife had died and his children lived with a Boston merchant. He stayed as French consul in New York, New Jersey and Connecticut until 1790 and came to believe in the Revolution enough to devote himself to improving Franco–American understanding and American agriculture.

His reputation rests not with his large-scale *Voyage dans la haute Pennsylvanie et dans l'état de New York* (1801) but with *Letters from an American Farmer* (1782) and *Sketches of Eighteenth Century America* (1925). The *Letters* are an early and important answer to the question

'What is an American?' Crèvecoeur assumed that in an imperfect world the good society would weaken evil by having enough natural resources for subsidence, allowing men to work freely for self-interest and turn aggression into energetic productivity. America would fulfil this plan: men could be happy in this huge virgin territory where work had its immediate reward, where British government and Christian morality would be tempered to a liberal state, and restraint would prevent tyranny. He admired Quaker humanitarianism and the American farmer's independence, and loathed Virginian slavery. His ideal was the colonial freeholder whose environment bred a life without 'ancient prejudices and manners': 'here individuals of all nations are melted into a new race of men ... Americans are the western pilgrims, who are carrying along with them that great mass of arts, sciences, vigour, and industry which began long since in the east; they will finish the great circle'. Crèvecoeur's celebrated formulation of optimism is modified by warning against the lawless individualism of prosperity and he finally recommends the Indians as his model of peaceful community happiness, again with a warning against primitive regression. His images of agrarian freedom, self-reliance and the melting pot of nations have persisted into modern American thought. His understanding of the precise points at which law, community and freedom break down have a lasting relevance for America. [EM]

*Letters from an American Farmer* and *Sketches of Eighteenth Century America* (New American Library, 1963).
J. P. Mitchell, *St Jean de Crèvecoeur* (1916); M. Bewley, 'The Cage and the Prairie' in *The Hudson Review Anthology*, ed. F. Morgan (1961).

**Crockett, Davy** (1786–1836). Politician' story writer, legendary figure. This fabled comic hunter was actually born – in Tennessee. His rough childhood did include a little schooling, but his distinctions were dancing, singing and hunting bears. He won honour in the Creek War under General Jackson and turned politician, elected to the Tennessee legislature and then to Congress – 'the coonskin Congressman'. In 1829 he changed sides and became a Whig, and to right the confusion he wrote his *Narrative* (1834) and *An Account of*

*Col. Crockett's Tour to the North and Down East* (1835). He opposed Jackson on the national bank controversy and on the break with the Creek Indians. He died heroically fighting for Texas at the Alamo. His narrative is typical of his American frontier wit and boisterous yarning. In his own lifetime he was a legend, and the posthumous *Crockett Almanacs* (1835–56), ballads, J. K. ◊ Paulding's play *The Lion of the West* (1831), and many folk plays and books secured his myth down to the Davy Crockett song and the coonskin-cap fashion of the 1950s. [EM]

C. Rourke, *Davy Crockett* (1934).

**Cullen, Countee** (1903–46). Negro American poet. He was reared by foster parents in Harlem, N.Y., and graduated from New York University (1925), already a published poet before he took his graduate degree at Harvard. After his first book, *Colour* (1925), he produced *Copper Sun* (1927), *The Ballad of the Brown Girl* (1928), *The Black Christ* (1929, written in France on a Guggenheim scholarship), *The Medea and Some Poems* (1935) and the posthumous *On These I Stand* (1947). He edited the Negro magazine *Opportunity* and an anthology of Negro poets, *Caroling Dusk* (1927), and wrote one novel, *One Way to Heaven* (1931). He taught French in New York schools until his death, when he had become the living representative of the Negro poet struggling to write accurately about himself and his people without sentimentality, and yet to create poetry which was not only protest or description of a condition. His models were Keats and E. A. ◊ Robinson, but his themes were American, with poems like 'Heritage' showing his nostalgia for Africa. (◊ Negro Literature.) [EM]

**Cummings, E(dward) E(stlin)** (1894–1962). Poet, painter. His father was a teacher and a minister of the Old South Church in Boston, Massachusetts, and his boyhood was spent in the academic atmosphere and traditions of Cambridge and Harvard, where he received his B.A. in 1916 and against which he rebelled. In the First World War he served with the Norton Harjes Ambulance Service and through a grotesque bureaucratic error was imprisoned, for certain radical observations, in a French detention camp (*The Enormous Room*, 1922), where his sense of the individual against authority received its first practical reinforcement. After 1920, he painted and wrote poetry in Paris, and between 1923 and 1944 became a lively controversial poet with his 9 volumes (*Collected Poems*, 1938, and *Poems 1923–1954*, 1954). In 1925 he won the *Dial* award for distinguished services to literature and in 1952–3 gave the Charles Eliot Norton lectures at Harvard (*Six Non-Lectures*, 1953). He exhibited his paintings several times with the Society of Independent Artists in Paris, and in at least two shows in America (*CIOPW*, 1931, is a book of his drawings and paintings). His large output of poems over 40 years remained virtually unchanged in their themes, compressed language and syntax, and typographical layout. His song-like rhythms and lower-case and capitalized spatial patterns made his lyrics into reading-libretti in a modern baroque style which brought him a reputation for outrageous modernism. In fact his quirky individualism, his commonplace love themes, his satire against politicians, businessmen and salesmen, his sympathy with the underdog and his downright escapism were nothing if not reactionary, in a New England tradition stretching back to his real ancestor, Emerson.

Cummings is America's best popular poet, voicing self-reliant anarchism which is nearer Frost than Dada. *The Enormous Room* is a masterpiece of radical individualism and exuberant prose, and *EIMI* (1933) a first-rate critical book of travel in Russia. *Tom* (1935) is a satirical ballet burlesquing *Uncle Tom's Cabin*, and his plays, *Him* (1927) and *Santa Claus* (1946), mix fantasy, poetry and symbolism in a style which antedates Beckett and the absurdists. Read in bulk his poems tend to be a repetitious series on love, springtime, April and freedom, and hedonistic attacks on an amorphous 'Them'. Singly his works often have a lyrical tenderness and joy, or a scornful rejection of commercialism and humbug, which is altogether refreshing. [EM]

*Complete Poems* (2 vols., 1968); *Selected Letters*, ed. F. W. Dupee and G. Stade (1969); *A Miscellany Revised*, ed. and intr. G. J. Firmage (1965).

C. Norman, *The Magic-Maker: E. E. Cummings* (1958).

# D

**Dahlberg, Edward** (1890–    ). Novelist, essayist. His youth is described in a series of remarkable autobiographical books beginning with *Bottom Dogs* (intr. D. H. Lawrence, 1930): the Cleveland orphanage, his mother an itinerant lady barber, the life of Kansas City, his hobo boxcar existence until 1919, and his later meetings in New York with Alfred Stieglitz and his circle of artists and writers, including ◊ Garland, ◊ Dreiser and Randolph ◊ Bourne, whose opinions he appraises in *Alms for Oblivion* (1964), a collection of essays that ride his hobby horses in great style. His fictionalized life continued in *From Flushing to Calvary* (1932), *Those Who Perish* (1934), *Do These Bones Live* (1941), *The Flea of Sodom* (1950) and most recently *Because I Was Flesh* (1964), perhaps the definitive account of himself and his mother, told in a unique style as the life of Hagar and Ishmael in the American wilderness of cities. *The Sorrows of Priapus* (1957) is Dahlberg's didactic prophecy for the times, in his best aphoristic manner (see also *Reasons of the Heart*, 1965, a book of aphorisms). Further essays are collected in *The Leafless American* (1967); *Cipango's Hinder Door* (1966) is a volume of poems; and *Epitaphs for Our Times* (1967) is a collection of letters edited by Edwin Seaver. *The Carnal Myth* (1968) shows his collage methods at their most concentrated. He is a vehement agrarian, a fine chronicler, a stringent critic and an American stylist without imitators. [FM]

*The Edward Dahlberg Reader*, ed. P. Carroll (1967).

J. Williams, 'Edward Dahlberg's Book of Lazarus', *Texan Quarterly*, Summer, 1963; V. Lipton, 'The Sorrows and Joys of Edward Dahlberg', *Kenyon Review*, Autumn, 1958; H. Billings, *Edward Dahlberg: American Ishmael of Letters* (1968).

**Dana, Richard Henry, Jr** (1815–82). Writer, reformer, lawyer. Son of R. H. ◊ Dana, Sr, he was born in Cambridge, Massachusetts, and educated at Harvard. In 1834, at the end of his second year, he left the university because of eye trouble and shipped as a sailor round the Horn to California. After more than a year on the Pacific coast, gathering and curing hides, he returned to Boston to complete his studies at the Harvard Law School. In 1840, the year he was admitted to the Massachusetts bar, he anonymously published *Two Years before the Mast*, a narrative of 'the life of a common sailor at sea as it really is' based on a diary he had kept of the 150-day voyage on the brig *Pilgrim*, with all its minutiae of routine and off-duty hours and conversations, of the shore life in Santa Barbara, San Diego, Monterey and San Francisco, and of the stormy return trip on the ship *Alert*. Not only does it give an early important account of California; it also roused men's consciences – a central incident is the flogging of two shipmates and his vow 'to redress the grievances and sufferings of that class of beings with whom my lot has so long been cast'. Already earlier, in 1839, he had published an article in the *American Jurist*, 'Cruelty to Seamen', and in 1841 followed *The Seaman's Friend* (British title *The Seaman's Manual*), designed to show sailors their legal rights and duties; but the immediate popularity of *Two Years before the Mast* was due to its realism, its many portraits of officers and sailors, its detail. Dana became a founder of the Free-Soil Party; he was active before and during the Civil War in the slaves' cause; he became editor of a standard textbook on international law and author of *To Cuba and Back* (1859); nevertheless he felt, 30 years later, that his life had been an anti-climax, for 'my great success – my book – was a boy's work, done before I came to the Bar'. Hurt by failure, he withdrew to Rome in 1878 to continue his researches in international law; there he died. Posthumously collected were *Speeches in Stirring Times* (1910) and *An Autobiographical Sketch* (1953). [HB]

*Journal*, ed. R. F. Lucid (3 vols., 1968).

Charles Francis Adams, *Richard Henry Dana, a Biography* (1890); H. W. L. Dana, *The Dana Saga* (1941); James D. Hart, 'The Education of Richard Henry Dana, Jr', *New England Quarterly* IX, 1 (1936).

**Dana, Richard Henry, Sr** (1787–1879). Poet, journalist, editor. Born in Boston, he was one of the founders of the *North American Review*, the leading American 19th-century review; he wrote for many other journals and published *Poems* (1827). Much of his work was collected in *Poems and Prose Writings* (2 vols., 1833; enlarged 1850). [MB]

**Dannay, Frederic** ◊ Queen, Ellery.

**Davidson, Donald** (1893– ). Critic, poet. Born in Tennessee, a teacher at Vanderbilt University, he was a member of the ◊ Fugitive group there, one of the founders of the *Fugitive* magazine and later a contributor to the famous collection of southern agrarian essays *I'll Take My Stand* (1930). He has published four books of poetry – *An Outland Piper* (1924), *The Tall Men* (1927), *Lee in the Mountains and Other Poems, Including The Tall Men* (1938), and *The Long Street* (1961). *The Attack on Leviathan: Regionalism and Nationalism in the United States* (1938) is a vehement defence of the traditional Southern culture and economy, and a violent attack on the modern, capitalist state. *Still Rebels, Still Yankees* (1957) is a collection of essays; *The Spyglass* (1963) of views and reviews. *Southern Writers in the Modern World* appeared in 1958. Of the Fugitives, Davidson has become the most militant defender of every aspect of the *status quo* in the South. [AH]

**Davis, Richard Harding** (1864–1916). Journalist, novelist, playwright. Born in Philadelphia, the son of Rebecca Harding Davis, an early realist novelist, he became a famous journalist on the New York *Sun* and covered the Spanish–American war for the *Journal*, and thereafter became a leading and wide-travelled correspondent covering wars and making fact-finding tours. Collections of journalism include *Our English Cousins* (1894), *Cuba in War Time* (1897) and *With the Allies* (1914). His novels are sensational and sophisticated; they include *Soldiers of Fortune* (1897), *The King's Jackal* (1898) and *Vera the Medium* (1908). He also published many successful collections of stories, some of them providing the source of his more than 20 plays. [MB]

Larzer Ziff, *The American 1890s* (1967).

**Day, Clarence** (1874–1935). Essayist, artist. Born in New York City, the son of a Stock Exchange broker, he went to Yale, served in the navy during the Spanish–American war, ran a glove business in New York, and became a regular writer for the *New Yorker*. In four witty and unusual books Day immortalized his father as a typical representative of upper-class New York in the 19th century: they were *God and My Father* (1932), *Life with Father* (1935; successfully dramatized in 1939), *Life with Mother* (1937) and *Father and I* (1940). Other books include the delightful curiosity *This Simian World* (1920), a study of the ape-like nature of man with Day's own brilliant and fantastic illustrations, and *In the Green Mountain Country* (1934), an account of President Coolidge's funeral. [MG]

**De Forest, John W(illiam)** (1826–1906). Novelist, miscellaneous writer. Born in Connecticut, he returned from extensive foreign travel to serve three years as a Union Captain in the Civil War. His novel *Miss Ravenel's Conversion from Secession to Loyalty* (1867; intr. G. S. Haight, 1939) gave for the first time a harshly realistic treatment of the conflict and is also notable for its portrayal (without authorial retribution) of the spirited, independent and profligate Mrs Larue. Later work included *Kate Beaumont* (1872), about plantation society in Charleston and the 'poor whites' of South Carolina, and *Honest John Vane* (1875), a satire on political corruption. His war memoirs, *A Volunteer's Adventures*, appeared in 1946, and James H. Croushore and David Morris Potter edited *A Union Officer in the Reconstruction* (1948).

De Forest's complex novels, with their uncompromising though finally exhausting realism, never received sufficient attention in his lifetime, except from his constant admirer William Dean ◊ Howells, who commented that 'finer, and stronger workmen succeeded him, and a delicate realism, more responsive to the claims and appeals of the feminine oversoul, replaced his inexorable veracity'. [MG]

H. E. Starr, 'De Forest', *Dictionary of American Biography* (1930); W. D. Howells, *Atlantic Monthly*, XX (1867) and XXIX (1872) (reviews), and *Heroines of Fiction*, ii (1901); Edmund Wilson, *Patriotic Gore* (1962).

**Dell, Floyd** (1887– ). Novelist, playwright, editor. Born of a poor Illinois family, he worked as a factory hand, later became a journalist, first on a Davenport, Iowa, newspaper and then in Chicago, where he was associated with the mid-Western 'Chicago School' of writers, among them Carl ◊ Sandburg and Ben ◊ Hecht. He was a notable editor of the *Chicago Evening Post's Literary Review*. After 1914 he worked in New York, editing the socialist *Masses* (1914–17) and its successor *Liberation* (1918–24) (◊ Little Magazines). He received high praise for his first and best novel, *Moon-Calf* (1920), and its sequel, *The Briary-Bush* (1921). These were largely autobiographical studies of an idealistic youth who, frustrated by the atmosphere of a small Illinois town, seeks relief in Chicago, but returns to marry his first love after a hectic career in Chicago journalism. In *Janet March* (1923), *Runaway* (1925) and other novels he assumed his role of outspoken mouthpiece for Greenwich Village Bohemia and a confused twenties generation (◊ Bohemianism, Greenwich Village). He caused something of a sensation in 1930 with *Love in the Machine Age*, an account of his attitude towards sex. A humorous novel, *An Unmarried Father* (1927; dramatized 1928), gave a new phrase to the language; *Homecoming* (1933) was his autobiography. He and Paul Jordan Smith produced (1927) a fine text of Burton's *Anatomy of Melancholy*. [MG]

**Demby, William** (1922– ). Novelist. Born in Pittsburgh, he studied at West Virginia State College for Negroes and Fisk University, and has written a fine Existentialist novel, *Beetlecreek* (1950), set in West Virginia, an important contribution to novels of racial rejection in America. *Catacombs* (1965) is a novel set in Rome and employing considerable technical innovation. [EM]

R. Bone, 'William Denby's *Dance of Life*', *TriQuarterly*, 15 (1969).

**Dennie, Joseph** (1768–1812). Essayist, editor. Born in Boston, he went to Harvard, became a lawyer, and then one of the leading essayists of his age, writing pseudonymously and adapting the tradition of Addison and Steele. One of a group of Federalists of Anglophile sympathy, he edited in New Hampshire the *Farmer's Weekly Museum*. He later moved to Philadelphia and became central figure of an important literary circle, the Tuesday Club, and founder of one of the leading American literary weeklies, the *Port Folio*, in 1801. His pseudonyms were 'The Lay Preacher' and 'Oliver Oldschool, Esq.', and in the provincial atmosphere of American letters at this time he deeply influenced taste. His manner was imitated by Washington ◊ Irving, particularly for *The Sketch Book*. *The Lay Preacher* (1796, 1817; reprinted 1943) is collected essays. [MB]

Milton Ellis, *Joseph Dennie and His Circle: A Study of American Literature from 1792 to 1812* (1915).

**Deutsch, Babette** (1895– ). Poet, novelist, critic. Born in New York City, she began contributing to literary periodicals while studying at Barnard College. She was ◊ Veblen's secretary while he worked at the New School for Social Research, and active on the Committee for Cultural Freedom under John ◊ Dewey. She has taught in various New York colleges and translated Russian and German literature, particularly modern poetry and Yiddish writers, with her husband Avrahm Yarmolinsky, the Russianist. She is best known as a poet, her work being prolific, sophisticated and socially concerned (though not distinguished by a sensitive ear or memorable imagery), from the energies of *Banners* (1919), though the exhortation of *Epistle to Prometheus* (1931) to the lyrics of *Animal, Vegetable, Mineral* (1954), all included in *Collected Poems: 1919–1962* (1963). She has written 4 novels, including *In Such a Night* (1927), about Socrates, and *Rogue's Legacy* (1942), about François Villon; a book on Whitman (1941); a prose version of 15 Shakespeare plays; and some criticism. This includes *Poetry in Our Time* (1952), a good introductory study of modern poetry; and the very useful *Poetry Handbook: A Dictionary of Terms* (1957; revised 1961). [MB/EM]

*Collected Poems* (1969).

**De Voto, Bernard** (1897–1955). Editor, critical scholar. He edited the *Saturday Review of Literature* (1936–8) and worked on *Harper's Magazine* (1935–55). His finest work was for one writer: *Mark Twain's America* (1932, a famous reply to Van Wyck ◊ Brooks's *The Ordeal of Mark Twain*), *Mark Twain at Work* (1942) and *Mark Twain in Eruption* (1940), selections from Twain's autobiography. He left 5 books of essays, a number of historical works including *Across the Wide Missouri* (1947, about the 1830s exploration and destruction of the West), and novels and short stories. *The Hour* (1951) is a lyric fanfare for the martini and cocktail fad. [EM]

**De Vries, Peter** (1910– ). Novelist. Born in Chicago. Drawing his material almost exclusively from the successful, middle-class, East-coast America that has become the happy hunting-ground of organization men, status-seekers, and commuters in grey flannel suits, he has become the comic laureate of suburbia. Decency, Conn., is the setting for most of his novels, which delineate with zest and vitality the grotesqueries and idiosyncrasies of such a stable community. His characters are individuals trapped by patterns of behaviour often absurd in themselves. But De Vries, a talented comedian, a sharp social observer, is only in a limited sense a satirist; his work has no Swiftian intensity or disgust; he writes from inside an exurban world which amuses rather than offends him. At his best he writes a sophisticated, witty and entertaining novel of manners; but the energy and the punning verbal dexterity sometimes, not surprisingly, flag. Perhaps this is the reason why he has recently written a different kind of novel. In 1938 he became associate editor, and in 1942 co-editor of the magazine *Poetry*, and since 1944 he has been on the editorial staff of the *New Yorker*. His first book, *But Who Wakes the Bugler* (1940), was, appropriately, illustrated by the *New Yorker* cartoonist Charles Addams. Then followed *The Handsome Heart* (1943), *Angels Can't Do Better* (1944), *No, But I Saw the Movie* (1952), *Tunnel of Love* (1954), *Comfort Me with Apples* (1956), *The Mackerel Plaza* (1958), one of his best novels, and *The Tents of Wickedness* (1959), which incorporates some hilariously accurate literary parodies and burlesques. *Through Fields of Clover* (1961) concerns a gag-writer and his comedian. *The Blood of the Lamb* (1962) marks a change of manner; it is still funny and excellently written, but it changes tone to tragic seriousness. Through the characters' madness, suicide and tuberculosis, De Vries attempts a high level of sincere comment on religious faith. The result is disappointingly pseudo-profound, quite unlike the serious satire and dark underside of his usual comedy. *Reuben, Reuben* (1964) combines the quali-ties of both his manners – the comic exuberance and the critical – to present a Dylan Thomas sort of poet, or his myth. *Let Me Count the Ways* (1965) is a study in self-consciousness and its chaotic tendency to farce: again the tragi-comic manner shows De Vries's later form. *The Vale of Laughter* (1968) once again takes up his steady obsession with religion, with God's sport with man, with clowning as an expression of suffering. *The Cat's Pyjamas and Witch's Milk* (1968) are a pair of interrelated short novels. Throughout his career, he has developed a classic series of novels on the themes of religious comedy. [AH/EM]

**Dewey, John** (1859–1952). Philosopher Born in Burlington, Vermont, Dewey studied at the University of Vermont and the new graduate school of Johns Hopkins University. He taught at the University of Michigan, then at the University of Chicago, where he established a famous experimental school to try out his ideas on education. From 1905 till his retirement in 1929 he was a professor of philosophy at Columbia University.

An extremely prolific writer, he continued to pour out books and articles until his death at 93. His influence has been immense, partly because his pragmatic philosophy made a special appeal to the American mind, partly because he was the opposite of an ivory-tower philosopher: he had strong political interests – he was a liberal of 'socialist leanings – and was the leading educational reformer of his time. He gave the Gifford lectures (*The Quest for Certainty*) at Edinburgh in 1929; spent many months in Japan and China in 1918–20; and visited Turkey, Mexico and Russia, and in all these countries his educational influence was strong. In philosophy, he began as a Hegelian, but his studies of Darwin's biology led him to a new conception of the nature of thought, which he called 'instrumentalism'. Thinking, he said, is an activity of the organism, which, like swimming, walking and climbing, was generated as a means to adjustment and survival; it is an instrument brought into play when instinct and habit break down, in order to surmount obstacles in the way of behaviour. Hence its true test is practical – whether it succeeds in reaching the specific end for which it was adopted (*Studies in Logical Theory*, 1903). This insight required, he held, a reconstruction of philosophy. The speculative thought of the West since Plato had been dominated by a 'spectator view' of knowledge; the business of thought was to contemplate an eternal and changeless order. Repudiating this, Dewey substituted for contemplation 'creative intelligence', whose business was to transform the conditions of life so as to achieve the greatest practicable fulfilment for all. Since evolution implies continual change, our ideals themselves must be tentative; the ideal that is fixed and final tends to arrest advance (*Reconstruction in Philosophy*, 1920).

From his instrumentalism followed his views on education, politics and religion. If the right use of intelligence is no longer the pursuit of truth for its own sake, but rather as a preface to action, the old difference between cultural and vocational training is illusory. Throughout the United States progressive schools grew up in which children learned by doing – acquiring arithmetic by keeping store and studying literature by acting plays and stories. Dewey likewise held that only as citizens are encouraged to share the responsibilities of government will they become politically mature; hence his lifelong support of democracy (*Democracy and Education*, 1916). His philosophy demanded also reform in religion: for religion as the acceptance of creeds there should be substituted the religious attitude, conceived as dedication to the long-run good of mankind (*A Common Faith*, 1934). *Art as Experience* (1934) is an influential examination of formal structures and characteristic effects in all the arts. [BB]

S. Ratner, *Intelligence in the Modern World; John Dewey's Philosophy* (1939); ed. P. A. Schilpp, *The Philosophy of John Dewey* (1939); C. Wright Mills, *Sociology and Pragmatism* (1964).

**Dickens, Charles** (1812–70). English novelist. His famous tour of the United States (1842) produced later in the year *American Notes for General Circulation*, a series of descriptive sketches. He antagonized American readers by attacking slavery, certain penal systems and the absence of copyright protection. Later he rescued the failing *Life and Adventures of Martin Chuzzlewit* (1843–44) by dispatching his hero to the States, where Martin is ruthlessly cheated by the Eden Land Corporation (Cairo, Illinois). His swindlers delight in boasting of American success in 'the regeneration of man', and he hears several score people described

as 'one of the most remarkable men in this country'. Dickens returned for a reading tour (1867–8). [MG]

William Clyde Williams, *Charles Dickens in America* (1911); Philip Collins, *Dickens and Crime* (1962); 'Dickens in America', *The Times Literary Supplement*, 9 January 1943; Harry Stone, 'Dickens' Use of His American Experience in "Martin Chuzzlewit"', in *Publications of the Modern Language Association of America*, LXXII (1957).

**Dickey, James** (1923– ). Poet. Born in Atlanta, Georgia, he taught at Rice University and the University of Florida, and worked in advertising. He has published *Into the Stone and Other Poems* (1960), *Drowning with Others* (1962), *Helmets* (1964), *Two Poems of the Air* (1964), *Buckdancer's Choice* (1965) and *Babel to Byzantium* (1968). He is a lively critic and reviewer of poetry; a collection of essays, *The Suspect in Poetry*, appeared in 1964.

In verse he early found an individual voice, stylish yet deceptively conversational in tone. His poems frequently take natural settings as occasions for mystical contemplation. More recent verse reveals a stronger narrative element. He is a poet both of passion and of subtle insight, often understating what are really complex effects. *Poems 1957–1967* (1968) widens his subject matter, socially but not politically, notably in 'The Firebombing' and 'Slave Quarters'. *The Eye-beaters, Blood, Victory, Madness, Buckhead and Mercy* (1970) shows a considerable development in form and language. His novel, *Deliverance* (1970), about an allegorical canoe-trip in Georgia, has become a remarkable best-seller. [BS]

Laurence Lieberman, *The Achievement of James Dickey* (1968); Richard Howard, *Alone with America* (1969).

**Dickinson, Emily** (1830–86). Poet. Under a Calvinist father, dominatingly kind, she began an outwardly uneventful life at Amherst, Massachusetts. Apart from brief periods at Amherst Academy and Holyoke Female Seminary she ran the family home; she did not marry. She did send poems to a well-known literary man, Thomas Wentworth Higginson, but his criticism of their unorthodoxies in metre and style pushed her back into privacy. She hoarded her poems, among them love poems, apparently addressed to Benjamin Newton, a student in her father's office, with whom she corresponded until his death in 1853, and

Charles Wadsworth, a distinguished married clergyman who may have left America because of her. For the rest, and apart from a stay in Philadelphia, hers was a New England small-town puritan life in the atmosphere of the Civil War years. 'Pardon my sanity in a world insane', she wrote in a letter, a clue to her need to create a balanced life out of her passion and intellectual clarity.

In 1863 she probably wrote about 140 poems, and in 1864 nearly 200, the high point of her prolific output of about 1,775 poems, all written within the characteristic late-19th-century range of relationships between God, man and nature. Since she did not have the pressures of publication, her style is remarkably free, intense and idiosyncratic, the exact form of her complex personality. She may have dressed in white and enacted the role of subdued woman, but she concentrated on a 'lone orthography' which avoided genteel conventionality. Her weakness is a reliance on rhythmic cadences and metres from hymns and popular jingles. She was not a prosodic innovator, although her punctuation, derived from reading and pronunciation handbooks, looks odd, and her imagery continually startles with its freshness and penetration. Her modernity is her articulation of psychological experience and sceptical desire for faith.

Four years after her death her first volume was published, and augmented editions appeared in 1891 and 1896. A book of letters came out in 1894. But a true estimate of her genius began only after the First World War, and it was not until Thomas H. Johnson's magnificent editions of her poems and letters that a complete and accurate text was established. [EM]

*The Poems*, ed. T. H. Johnson (3 vols., 1958); *Letters*, ed. T. H. Johnson (3 vols., 1958).
G. F. Whicher. *This Was a Poet: A Critical Biography of Emily Dickinson* (1938); C. A. Anderson, *Emily Dickinson's Poetry: Stairway of Surprise* (1960); Richard Chase, *Emily Dickinson* (1951); T. H. Johnson, *Emily Dickinson: An Interpretative Biography* (1955); ed. C. R. Blake and C. F. Wells, *The Recognition of Emily Dickinson* (1964); R. B. Sewall, 'The Lyman Letters: New Light on Emily Dickinson and Her Family', *Massachusetts Review*, Autumn, 1965; R. W. Franklin, *The Editing of Emily Dickinson* (1968).

**Dickinson, John** (1732–1808). Born in Maryland, he studied law in London, and became a leader of the Revolutionary

whigs. Rich and conservative, he refused to sign the Declaration of Independence, since he hoped for conciliation. His writings had a major influence at a crucial time: they include, besides his famous 'Liberty Song' (1768), and two sets of *Letters of Fabius* (1788, 1797), the important *Letters from a Farmer in Pennsylvania* (1767–8), which had several American, French and English editions in 1768. The 12 letters hold that the Anglo-American controversy was legally wrong, that government should support property rights, and that legal petition and commercial tactics should precede possible resort to arms. Burke and Voltaire admired them (see R. T. H. Halsey's 1903 edition). [EM]

Charles J. Stillé, *The Life and Times of John Dickinson: 1732–1808* (1891).

**Dodson, Owen** (1914–    ). Poet, novelist. Born in Brooklyn, he studied at Bates College, Maine, and Yale School of Drama. He is head of the drama department at Howard University. Besides his volume of poems, *Powerful Long Ladder* (1946), and a number of unpublished but acted plays, he is best known for his novel, *Boy at the Window* (1951). [EM]

**Donleavy, J(ames) P(atrick)** (1926–    ). Novelist, playwright. Born in Brooklyn, but studied at Trinity College, Dublin, and in recent years has lived in Ireland and England. His first novel, *The Ginger Man* (1955) – originally published in Paris, now reissued in England and the U.S.A. – mixes English-style social observation with anarchic American humour. Its hero, Sebastian Dangerfield, is a well-elaborated American comic figure, an arrogant sensualist who romps through Dublin and London violating middle-class susceptibilities. Also dramatized as a play, the novel has strong elements of fantasy and violence as well as of very funny farce. This fantasy is further developed in his neo-surrealist play *Fairy Tales of New York* (1961) and in later fiction: *A Singular Man* (1963), a lively novel about a wealthy man with a complicated psyche and a persecution complex; *Meet My Maker, the Mad Molecule* (1964), short stories in similar vein; and *The Saddest Summer of Samuel S.* (1966), a novel about a sexual pilgrimage through Vienna. Donleavy's main gift is his ability to mix a comic inventiveness with an intense sense of personal loneliness. [MB]

**Donnelly, Ignatius** (1831–1901). Politician, historian, novelist. Born in Philadelphia, he became a lawyer and then moved west to found an ideal emigrant community in Minnesota. He became a Congressman and a leading figure in Populist protest, and in 1900 was the Vice-Presidential candidate of the party. He was a powerful orator and a devotee of many theories, including that of Delia Bacon that Sir Francis Bacon wrote Shakespeare's plays. His literary importance lies in his novel *Caesar's Column* (1891), a utopian – or rather anti-utopian – novel about a 20th-century world in which a capitalist aristocracy enslaves the working classes and is overcome by a revolution that itself degenerates into brutality, the story being seen from the standpoint of a moral agrarianism and, in addition, a melodramatic romanticism. [MB]

**Doolittle, Hilda (H. D.)** (1886–1961). Poet, novelist, translator. She was born in Pennsylvania and educated in Philadelphia. At Bryn Mawr she met Marianne Moore and – from Pennsylvania University – Pound and William Carlos Williams, all four poets representing the early stages of ◊ Imagism in America. H.D. appeared in Pound's *Des Imagistes* in 1914, as well as in the *Imagist Anthology* of 1930. In 1911 she left America, and in 1913 married Richard Aldington. She lived in England and in Switzerland. Her first volume, *Sea Garden* (1916), appeared in England, although some of the poems had already been published in Harriet ◊ Monroe's *Poetry*. *Hymen* (1921) is a masque with Greek figures, and her later poetry, in *Heliodora and Other Poems* (1924), *Red Roses for Bronze* (1929), and the *Collected Poems* of 1925 and 1940, maintained classical images and thought in a generally limpid and visual style. But her Greece was really a world of dream perfection whose modern symbolism rejected the complexity of the modern world between the wars – in spite of the intelligence of her prose love poem *Tribute to Freud* (1956). Her shorter poems are economical but not austere, their moments of arrested time and intense response to a revelatory landscape or object carefully composed, for all their apparent licence. Her search for moments of beauty and love are not as reactionary as is sometimes said. Later collections include *The Walls Do Not Fall* (1944), a response to

wartime London, *Tribute to Angels* (1945), devotional poems, and *Flowering of the Rod* (1946). *By Avon River* (1949) is a miscellany inspired by Shakespeare. She translated choruses from Euripides' *Iphigenia in Aulis*, *Hippolytus* and *Ion*, and *Hippolytus Temporizes* is a verse tragedy. Her novels include *Palimpsest* (1922), which is intent on cutting across boundaries of time and culture, *Hedylus* (1928) and *Bid Me To Live* (1960), ostensibly a First World War novel with leading literary figures, but better described by words which appear in it: 'Past the danger point, past the point of any logic and of any meaning, and everything has meaning. Start superimposing, you get odd composites, nation on nation.' One of her latest and finest works is *Helen in Egypt* (1961, posthumous), a 300-page lyrical poem. The usual estimation of H.D. as an Imagist in the minor key, with a restricted and rather precious beauty, is being radically changed by American poets who, in the 1960s, are reading her concentrated lyricism with renewed attention. The chief of these is Robert ◊ Duncan, whose articles in little magazines (*Coyote's Journal*, *TriQuarterly*, *Aion*, *origin* and *Caterpillar*) are parts of his forthcoming *H.D. Book*. [EM]

T. B. Swann, *The Classical World of H.D.* (1962); Glenn Hughes, *Imagism and Imagists* (1960); H. Gregory and M. Zaturenska, *A History of American Poetry 1900–1940* (1946).

**Dorn, Edward** (1929–   ). Poet. He was born in Illinois, studied at Illinois University and ◊ Black Mountain College, and has taught at Idaho State University and the University of Essex. He edited the magazine *Wild Dog* from Pocatello, Idaho. His poetry first appeared in substantial form in Donald Allen's anthology *The New American Poetry* (1960), and then in *The Newly Fallen* (1961) and *Hands Up!* (1964). They show an individual voice, uncertain in structure but able to convey attachments to the land and complex intellectual arguments with skill. *From Gloucester Out* (1964) was a turning point, a poem in which 'projective verse' methods were extended personally beyond the obvious reference to Charles ◊ Olson. This skill with long poems of varied materials and complex free form is clear, too, in *Geography* (1965) and *The North Atlantic Turbine* (1967), which contains mature work examining the nature of commitment to a particular locality and culture. *Gunslinger* (1968–9) is an extended poem of wit, verve and philosophical complexity. Of his prose, *What I See in the Maximus Poems* (1960) concerns Olson's poetry. *The Rite of Passage* (1965) is a first-rate novel of life on the land in the North-west of America, and *The Shoshoneans* (1966) a personal discovery of the plight of the Indians of the Basin-Plateau. [EM]

*Twenty-four Love Songs* (1969).
Ed. David Ossman, *The Sullen Art* (1963).

**Dos Passos, John** (1896–1970). Novelist, social historian. Born in Chicago, of Portuguese descent; educated at Choate School and Harvard, graduating in 1916. In Spain studying architecture when America entered the First World War, he joined the Ambulance Corps (as did Hemingway, E. E. Cummings and other idealistic young Americans). His disillusion with the experience of war and its social implication is given fictional form in *One Man's Initiation: 1917* (1920; reissued in unbowdlerized complete form, 1969) and *Three Soldiers* (1921). His next few years were spent as newspaper correspondent and journalist, and in 1922 he published a volume of poetry, *A Pushcart at the Curb*, and *Rosinante to the Road Again*, a collection of essays which explore the Iberian immigrant element in himself as well as aspects of Spanish culture. His next novel, *Streets of Night* (1923), begun while he was a student, begins to examine, however clumsily, the waste in urban American lives, the theme of so much of his mature writing, first exemplified in *Manhattan Transfer* (1925), which takes megalopolitan New York as its subject. This is his first attempt at composing a collective novel by means of a multiplicity of characters and scenes. The city itself seems to be of more oppressive importance than its citizens, and this determinist atmosphere makes the book a prelude to Dos Passos's central achievement, the trilogy *U.S.A.* (1937), a prose epic comprising *The Forty-Second Parallel* (1930), *1919* (1932) and *The Big Money* (1936). It traces, through interwoven biographies, the history of America from the early 20th century to the onset of the Depression in 1929. Gradually the numerous body of characters, fictional figures and real historical persons, forms a composite picture of society, expounding America's post-war aims and potentials, its whoring

after false materialistic gods, and its political and social injustices, with the execution of Sacco and Vanzetti (two anarchists accused of robbery and murder in Massachusetts in 1921) forming a focal disenchantment. The trilogy is an anti-epic in that it celebrates the *disestablishment* of an order, but as 'polyphonic' as the Renaissance epic in its complex structuring of fictional narrative, biographies of strategic socio-cultural figures like Edison, Ford, ◊ Veblen, Frank Lloyd Wright, Valentino and William Randolph Hearst, the prose-poetry of the impressionist 'Camera Eye' sections, and the newspaper montages of the 'Newsreel' sections.

Dos Passos's second trilogy, *District of Columbia* (1952), covers American social history and opinion in the thirties and forties: *The Adventures of a Young Man* (1939) concerns the disillusion of a young leftist in the Spanish Civil War, after bitter experiences among the workers of America; *Number One* (1943), based on the career of the southern politician, Huey Long, is a novel of political corruption; and *The Grand Design* (1949) is a criticism of the Roosevelt regime. Earlier experimental methods have been abandoned in this work, which is less brilliant as literature but still forceful as social analysis. *Mid-Century* (1961) returns to something of the structure of *U.S.A.* and has a broader scope, including a wider variety of public figures. But it is sentimentally patriotic, attacks the younger generations and the leaders of labour with considerable vehemence, and returns to the earlier attack on financiers. The main onslaught is against power men in any form; the defect is an abstract morality inside a deadened prose.

During the thirties Dos Passos progressively disengaged himself from the political left, ceasing to regard it as a solution to America's socio-economic problems. He espoused 'Jeffersonian' democratic conservativism (◊ Jefferson), expressed in *The Head and Heart of Thomas Jefferson* (1954), and a series of fictional and socio-historical works in which his wistfulness about the American past and his depression about the present grow side by side: *The Ground We Stand On* (1941), *The Prospect Before Us* (1950), *Chosen Country* (1951), *The Theme is Freedom* (1956), *The Men Who Made the Nation* (1957), *Prospects of a Golden Age* (1959); this is where the bulk of his work lay after *District of Columbia*. He also wrote two volumes of reportage, and several plays, which include *The Garbage Man* (1926), *Airways, Inc.* (1928) and *Fortune Heights* (1933). His later work includes *Mr Wilson's War* (1963), which uses his early dramatic and epic methods to document the First World War, *The Best Times* (1967), an account of a 1921 journey in the Near East and acquaintances in America (including Cummings, Hemingway and Hart Crane), *Brazil on the Move* (1963), a further examination of his ancestral preoccupations as well as a glance at modern South America, and *Occasions and Protests* (1965), a collection of essays with one redeeming piece, 'Satire as a Way of Seeing'. In *The Portugal Story* (1969) Dos Passos, the grandson of a Portuguese immigrant, describes three centuries of Portuguese history. In spite of this large output, it is *U.S.A.* that lasts as a major work of fiction, a great collective novel which gains in significance for its slow and painful abandonment of hopes, combined with modern technical scale and scope. [A G/E M]

J. H. Wrenn, *John Dos Passos* (1961); Maxwell Geismar, 'John Dos Passos: Conversion of a Hero', in *Writers in Crisis* (1942); Jean-Paul Sartre, 'John Dos Passos', in *Literary and Philosophical Essays* (1955); Robert Gorham Davis, *John Dos Passos* (University of Minnesota Pamphlet, 1962); John D. Brantley, *The Fiction of John Dos Passos* (1968).

**Douglas, Lloyd** (1877–1951). Novelist. Born in Indiana, he was a Lutheran and later a Congregational clergyman, mostly in university districts. He turned to fiction in his fifties, with *The Magnificent Obsession* (1929), about a Christian brain surgeon, and became an international best-selling writer. Other novels followed, usually dealing with success through piety. His formula of sex and religion, plus happy endings, plus a dash of spiritual fascism, reached case-history dimensions in *The Robe* (1942), the adventures of Jesus's last garment. *The Big Fisherman* (1948), the life of St Peter, had almost as incredible a global success. [E M]

**Drake, Joseph Rodman** (1795–1820). Poet, satirist. Born in New York. Only his 'Croaker Papers', satirical skits written with Fitz-Greene ◊ Halleck, were published during his short life, but *The Culprit Fay and Other Poems* appeared posthumously (1835), the title poem a striking work in the romantic mode about a fairy who loved a mortal, with a Hudson River setting. He was one of the important New York 'Knickerbocker' group, which included ◊ Irving, ◊ Bryant and ◊ Paulding. [M B]

Frank L. Pleadwell, *The Life and Works of Joseph Rodman Drake* (1935).

**Dreiser, Theodore** (1871–1945). Novelist. Born in Terre Haute, Indiana, the ninth child of German-speaking parents. Memories of his childhood, one of extreme poverty in which the family was dominated by the harsh and bigoted father, appear in his later fiction. After some months at Indiana University, Dreiser became a newspaperman on the Chicago *Globe* and worked in St Louis and Pittsburgh before arriving in New York in 1894. His first novel, *Sister Carrie* (1900), was rejected by Harper but enthusiastically received by Frank ◊ Norris, then working for Doubleday. But the publisher's wife apparently objected to the book's rawness, and while it was not exactly suppressed, a small, unpublicized edition ensured its commercial failure and another period of poverty for its author. Later, as editor for a firm which published magazines for a predominantly female readership, Dreiser achieved a considerable degree of financial independence. His second novel, *Jennie Gerhardt* (1911), was followed by two volumes of the 'Cowperwood' trilogy, partly based on the career of the Chicago traction magnate Charles T. Yerkes: *The Financier* (1912; revised edn, 1927) and *The Titan* (1914). (The third volume, *The Stoic*, appeared posthumously in 1947.) Dreiser's other novels are *The 'Genius'* (1915), an autobiographical and in some ways lamentable study of the artistic temperament; *An American Tragedy* (1925), a long and detailed novel based upon an actual murder case of 1906; and *The Bulwark* (1946).

In 1927 Dreiser visited Russia and expressed his new faith in *Dreiser Looks at Russia* (1928) and in *Tragic America* (1931). Thereafter he retained a strong sympathy for communism and shortly before his death joined the Communist Party.

Since the publication of his first novel Dreiser has remained a controversial figure. His prose has often been attacked for stylistic crudities; his novels tend to be loosely constructed; his opinions are often inconsistent and over-simple; his reduction of the complexities of human behaviour and motives to mechanistic 'chemisms' is obviously open to assault; his naturalistic universe often relies heavily upon the operations of chance. But he remains a writer of enormous power. In novel after novel he presents compulsive analyses of American life tragically illustrating the manner in which individual aspirations are thwarted or misdirected because of the perversion of American energies and ideals; his books are a bleak and ironical inversion of the Horatio ◊ Alger myth.

Profoundly influenced by his youthful reading of such authors as Hardy, T. H. Huxley and, in particular, Herbert Spencer, whose views left him 'intellectually in bits', Dreiser is usually included with those naturalist writers whose works express the principal tenets of Social Darwinism. Yet his novels reveal a redeeming sense of wonder and awe before the splendid if appalling mystery of life, while the quest of his characters for significance and self-fulfilment in the ordinary processes of living often invests them with dignity and pathos.

These qualities are well displayed by the heroine of *Sister Carrie*, about which Dreiser wrote: 'It is not intended as a piece of literary craftsmanship, but as a picture of conditions done as simply and effectively as the English language will permit.' It broke new ground in the subject matter of the American novel and in the objectivity with which the unconventional subject was treated. This and *An American Tragedy* probably constitute Dreiser's best work, and show his principal asset as a novelist: the relentless accumulation of detail to convey a vivid impression of reality. In its skilful use of the elementary symbolism afforded by houses, clothes and colours, *An American Tragedy* goes beyond the traditional confines of naturalistic writing; metaphor and symbol, as well as monumental descriptive narrative, indict the tawdry nature of the 20th-century American dream by illuminating the life and death of one lonely, but representative, individual. By contrast, in the Cowperwood trilogy Dreiser, for all his diligent research, sometimes failed to dramatize effectively the Nietzschean role he assigned to his prototypical financier; his real success comes in the presentation of Cowperwood's human relationships, not his business affairs.

Other works include *The Hand of the Potter* (1918), a full-length play which anticipates the theme of *An American Tragedy*;

*Twelve Men* (1919), which contains an affectionate portrait of his brother Paul Dresser, the songwriter; and a series of autobiographical volumes – *A Traveler at Forty* (1913), *A Hoosier Holiday* (1916), *A Book about Myself* (1922; reissued as *Newspaper Days*, 1931) and *Dawn* (1931). Dreiser also published *Hey Rub-a-Dub-Dub* (1920), a collection of essays which comes as near to expressing his philosophy as any single book by him, and 3 volumes of short stories: *Free* (1918), *Chains* (1927) and *A Gallery of Women* (1929). [H D]

*Letters*, ed. R. H. Elias (3 vols., 1959).
Helen Dreiser, *My Life with Dreiser* (1951); F. O. Matthiessen, *Theodore Dreiser* (1951); ed. Alfred Kazin and Charles Shapiro, *The Stature of Theodore Dreiser* (1955); Charles Shapiro, *Theodore Dreiser: Our Bitter Patriot* (1964); W. A. Swanberg, *Dreiser* (1965); Ellen Moers, *Two Dreisers* (1969).

**DuBois, William Edward Burghardt** (1868–1963). Negro sociologist, writer and propagandist. Born in Great Barrington, Massachusetts, he was educated at Fisk University and Harvard; his doctoral thesis there, on the suppression of the African slave trade with the U.S.A., was the first volume in the Harvard Historical Series. He went on to become prominent through his series of sociological studies of the status of the Negro in the U.S.A. Rejecting the views of the Negro leader Booker T. ◊ Washington, who believed in slow development through vocational training, he claimed more immediate equality and full citizenship for Negroes, and between 1903 and 1905 he emerged as leader of a militant radical, Negro wing. His writing is filled with passionate emotional concern for the fortunes of his race. Among his best early books is *Souls of Black Folk* (1903; repr. 1953), a series of sketches of Negro life. In 1909 he resigned from the faculty of Atlanta University to become a founder of the National Association for the Advancement of Coloured People, with whose moderate politics he later became disillusioned. In 1935 appeared his book *Black Reconstruction* (repr. 1955), in 1940 the autobiographical *Dusk at Dawn*. In 1949 he became director of the Peace Information Center in New York and was accused of communist sympathies. In 1961 he joined the Communist Party and, as director of the *Encyclopaedia Africana*, moved to Ghana, taking out citizenship in the year of his death. (◊ Negro Literature.) [D K A/M B]

An *ABC of Colour: Selections* (1963); *Autobiography* (1968).
F. L. Broderick, *W. E. B. DuBois: Negro Leader in a Time of Crisis* (1959).

**Dugan, Alan** (1923–    ). Poet. Born in New York City, he graduated from Mexico City College, returning to New York to work as model-maker for a medical supply house. He has published *Poems* (1961), which won the National Book Award and the Pulitzer Prize for Poetry, *Poems 2* (1963) and *Poems 3* (1967). His manner is brittle and determinedly anti-rhetorical, his subjects and style direct and plain. He writes at his best with a wit variously caustic, despairing and ferocious. [RP]

*Collected Poems* (1969).
Richard Howard, *Alone with America* (1969).

**Dunbar, Paul Laurence** (1872–1906). Poet. A leading poet of the 'Harlem Renaissance', he was the son of former slaves, born in Ohio and discovered working an elevator in Dayton in 1893, the year of his privately printed *Oak and Ivy*, which with *Majors and Minors* (1895) prepared for the book which brought him wider recognition, *Lyrics of a Lowly Life* (1896). Dunbar was the first Negro poet with a national reputation since Phyllis ◊ Wheatley, but (like her) he suffered from tuberculosis during his brief life. Written in tune with current regionalism, and with a good use of dialect (he admired Burns), his poems have strong rhythms and skilful folk quality, often humorous, though his attitudes seem conventionally pathetic and optimistic compared with later Negro protest poetry. He wrote leniently and sentimentally except in 'Ode to Ethiopia' and 'We Wear a Mask', which reveal the pain beneath the popular singer. (◊ Negro Literature.) [EM]

*The Complete Poems* (1940).
V. Cunningham, *Paul Laurence Dunbar and His Song* (1947).

**Duncan, Robert** (1919–    ). Poet. Born in Oakland, California, he has been a leading poet of the important San Francisco circle, which included Robin Blaser, Jack ◊ Spicer, Kenneth ◊ Rexroth and Helen Adam, active since the 1940s. At ◊ Black Mountain College he worked with Charles ◊ Olson, Robert ◊ Creeley and Denise ◊ Levertov (see his own biographical note in *The New American Poetry 1945–1960*, 1960), and is associated with the discontinuities and spatial improvisations of Californian painters of the mid-century. His career is marked by a dedication to the vocation of poet which is rare. The turning point in his earlier poetry, collected in *Heavenly City, Earthly City* (1947) and *Selected Poems (1942–1950)* (1959), is with 'The Venice Poem', in which he turned 'from the concept of a dramatic form to a concept of musical form in poetry'. His complex poetry explores the metaphysics of consciousness, the platonic relationship of man and nature, and what he calls 'the structure of rime'. His procedures and imagery are as erudite and wide-ranging as they are cunning and elusive. His books include *The Opening of the Field* (1959), *Roots and Branches* (1964) and *Bending of the Bow* (1968), which contains the first batch of 'Passages', the continuous open-ended series of poems in which his work is now contained. *Writing Writing* (1953) is a collection of pieces in the modes of Gertrude Stein. His prose includes *The Sweetness and Greatness of Dante's Divine Comedy* (1965), *As Testimony* (1965), a commentary on two poems, parts of a book on H.D. (Hilda ◊ Doolittle) which have appeared in *avant garde* magazines, and the introduction to a reissue of earlier work as *The Years as Catches: First Poems (1939–1946)* (1966). Other poetry has appeared as the pamphlet *Fragments of a Disordered Devotion* (1966) and *Of the War* (1966), which constitutes 'Passages 22–27', and in a special number of *Audit* magazine (IV, 3, 1967). Two of his plays are *Faust Foutu* (1960) and *Medea at Kolchis: The Maiden Head* (1965). *Letters* (1958) combines verse and prose, and is important for statements about his work, as is the essay 'Towards an Open Universe' (*Contemporary American Poetry*, ed. Howard Nemerov, no date). [EM]

*Selected Poems*, i, *The First Decade, 1940–1950*, ii, *Derivations, 1950–1956* (1969).

**Dunlap, William** (1766–1839). Playwright. Born at Perth Amboy, New Jersey, he was one of the first American professional writers, certainly the first professional playwright. First a portrait painter, he studied in London with Benjamin West, and grew involved with the theatre. Back in America, he became playwright, adapter of continental dramas, producer and manager. He wrote or adapted some 60 plays, in a vast variety of modes, and set in a variety of locales throughout the world. His *The*

*Father: or, American Shandyism* (1788) draws on Royall ◊ Tyler's *The Contrast. André* (1798; *American Plays*, ed. A. G. Halline, 1935) is a powerful drama about the British officer captured by the Americans during the War of Independence and hanged (it was later revised as a musical spectacle under the title *The Glory of Columbia Her Yeomanry!*). Others of his plays have the patriotic dimension familiar in the early American theatre. Dunlap also wrote many prose works, including *The Life of Charles Brockden Brown* (1815) and *A History of the American Theatre* (London, 1832). His translation of Kotzebue's play *The Stranger* (1798) was widely known. His work, now hard to obtain, was well known in England, as in the U.S.A., in the 19th century. [MB]

Van Wyck Brooks, *The World of Washington Irving* (1945); Oral S. Coad, *William Dunlap: A Study* (1917; 1962).

**Dunne, Finley Peter** (1867–1936). Journalist. Born in Chicago, where he became a reporter for the *Herald* (1884) and other papers. In 1896 he became editor of the *Evening Journal*, in 1900 of the New York *Morning Telegraph*, and later (1918–19) of *Collier's Weekly*. From 1903 he was famous as the creator of Mr Dooley, a witty and sceptical Chicago-Irish barman whose thoughts on events of the day appeared weekly in the press. Dooley's observations to his silent and gloomy comrade Malachi Hennessey were widely cherished, and often occasioned anxiety to politicians. They were collected in *Mr Dooley in Peace and in War* (1898), *Mr Dooley in the Hearts of His Countrymen* (1898), *What Mr Dooley Says* (1899) and so through to *Mr Dooley on Making a Will* (1919). Dooley thought only three books interesting – Shakespeare, the Bible and 'Mike Ahearn's history in Chicago' – but remarked 'What I like about Kipling is that his pomes are right off th' bat. ... No col' storage pothry f'r Kipling. All lays laid this mornin'.' [MG]

*Mr Dooley at His Best*, ed. Elmer Ellis (1938); *Mr Dooley on Ivrything and Ivrybody*, ed. Robert Hutchinson (1963).
Elmer Ellis, *Mr Dooley's America: A Life of Finley Peter Dunne* (1941).

**Duyckinck, Evert A.** (1816–78) and **George L.** (1823–63). Editors, literary critics and historians. Born in New York, these brothers were central figures in the post-

Knickerbocker, mid-19th-century New York literary scene, active with new writers and movements. Evert, a graduate of Columbia, originally hoped to become professor of literature there, studying in Europe for the purpose in 1838–9. When this did not come about, he became an active literary personality, a sponsor of ◊ Melville, friend of ◊ Hawthorne, ◊ Bryant, ◊ Irving, ◊ Lowell, ◊ Simms, etc., and a promoter of writers. He and Cornelius Mathews ran the critical magazine *Arcturus: A Journal of Books and Opinion* (1840–2). Then with his brother George and others he edited the even more brilliant *Literary World* (1847–53), a weekly journal of society, literature and art with remarkable contributors (Melville's 'Hawthorne and His Mosses' appeared there). The most significant venture of all was the two brothers' *Cyclopaedia of American Literature: Embracing Personal and Critical Notices of Authors, and Selections from Their Writings, from the Earliest Period to the Present Day* (1855; suppl. 1866, etc.), a 2-volume anthology and critical study which had major influence in establishing the significance and the study of American literature. [MB]

Perry Miller, *The Raven and the Whale* (1956).

**Dwight, Timothy** (1752–1817). Poet, miscellaneous writer. A precocious fellow-student of John ◊ Trumbull at Yale, he was born in Massachusetts, became tutor at Yale and, like his friend, collaborated on 'The Meddler' essays and in introducing more literature into the theology-bound curriculum, although he did become Professor of Theology as well as president of the college. He was an authoritative preacher (grandson of Jonathan ◊ Edwards) and administrator in many fields, but his fame rests on his work as a ◊ Connecticut Wit: *The Conquest of Canaan* (1785), which he claimed to be the first religious epic in America, is part of the large literature which celebrates America by biblical analogy, a deadening rehandling of the Book of Joshua in 10,000 lines of heroic couplets in 11 books; *The Triumph of Infidelity* (1788), in which Satan's historical perversions – paganism, Catholicism, Voltaire, Hume, etc. – are given a stolid run-through; and his better poem, *Greenfield Hill* (1794), a long praise of Connecticut agrarian life contrasted with European depravity, worse apparently than the massacre of the Pequod Indians in Part Four. He engaged little in the satirical activities of the Wits, but published Federalist political argument, many sermons, and a book of *Travels in New England and New York, 1769–1815* which contains valuable historical information. [MB/EM]

C. E. Cunningham, *Timothy Dwight, 1752–1817, A Biography* (1942); Leon Howard, *The Connecticut Wits* (1943).

# E

**Eastlake, William** (1917–  ). Novelist. Born in New York City, he was in the army and lives on a New Mexico ranch. His prose and fiction include *Go in Beauty* (1956), *The Bronc People* (1958), *Portrait of an Artist with Horses* (1963) and the outstanding *Castle Keep* (1965), a novel of an American garrison holding a 13th-century Ardennes castle. *The Bamboo Bed* (1969) is a satire based on his reports from the Vietnam war which appeared in the *Nation*. [EM]

**Eastman, Max** (1883–  ). Critic, poet. Born at Canandaigna, N.Y. One of the group of Marxist critics – others include V. F. ◊ Calverton, Waldo ◊ Frank and John ◊ Reed – who strongly influenced American criticism from the First World War onwards. He taught philosophy at Columbia before editing Marx, becoming editorially involved in two left-wing journals, the *Masses* (1911) and the *Liberator* (1917), and developing a deep interest in the social and scientific context of literature. His best-known books are *The Enjoyment of Poetry* (1913), *The Literary Mind: Its Place in an Age of Science* (1931), and then in 1934 two statements against totalitarian coercion of art: *Artists in Uniform: A Study of Literature and Bureaucratism* and *Art and the Life of Action*. He has produced some interesting works of memoirs (e.g. *Great Companions*, 1959), and his poetry is collected in *Poems of Five Decades* (1954). *Seven Kinds of Goodness* (1967) is a guide to Buddhism, Confucius, Socrates, Plato, Moses, Mohammed and Jesus. [MB]

Van Wyck Brooks, *Sketches in Criticism* (1932); Charles I. Glicksberg, 'Max Eastman: Literary Insurgent', *Sewanee Review*, XLIV (1936).

**Eberhart, Richard** (1904–  ). Poet, playwright. Born in Minnesota and educated at Dartmouth and Harvard, he tutored a Siamese prince, taught naval gunnery in the Second World War, worked with the Butcher Polish Company, served as poet-in-residence in universities, founded the Poet's Theatre, served the Library of Congress and National Culture Centre, and won the Bollingen Prize, with John Hall Wheelock,

in 1962. His first book of poems, *A Bravery of Earth* (1930), was followed by many others, including his *Selected Poems* (1951) and *Collected Poems* (1960). In his poems, the traditional religious moralist considers sin and war against a context of childhood wholeness and a mystical vision of Nature. A more direct and American speech emerged in *Burr Oaks* (1947) and reaches a high level of achievement in *Undercliff* (1953), his ninth book. His original explorations of baffling experience are as fine as ever in *Great Praises* (1957). His *Collected Verse Plays* (1962) tend to be undramatic discussions in a rather old-fashioned and extravagant idiom. *Thirty One Sonnets* (1967) was written 35 years earlier and put away, he says, 'as being too proud, too youthful, and too imitative'. His most recent work is *Shifts of Being* (1969). [EM]

Bernard F. Engel, *The Achievement of Richard Eberhart* (1968); Ralph J. Mills, *Richard Eberhart* (University of Minnesota Pamphlet, 1966).

**Edmonds, Walter D.** (1903–  ). Novelist. His native north-western New York State, with the Black River and the Erie Canal, is the stamping ground of an imagination which produced a series of energetic historical novels appearing since 1929, the most famous of which is *Drums along the Mohawk* (1936), a tale of Revolutionary rebels, British foes and Indian destruction, whose research he describes in *How You Begin a Novel* (1936). Other novels include *Rome Haul* (1929) and *Erie Water* (1933), about life on, and the building of, the Erie Canal; and *Young Ames* (1942), set in New York City in the 1830s. [EM]

**Edwards, Jonathan** (1703–58). Philosopher, scientist, theologian. Born in Connecticut, son and grandson of Puritan ministers. His boyhood sensitivity and precocity were curbed under a strict Calvinist education. The essays 'Of Insects' and 'Of the Rainbox', written at 11, already show his interest in natural science. At 13 he was studying at Yale, where he graduated at 16. His theological studies and experience of

Calvinist rigours were transformed into a sense of joy through mystical conversion and intellectually enriched through Locke's psychology and Newton's physics. The result was his firm belief in God's benevolence, expressed in two private works of self-examination and programmes for living, the 70 *Resolutions* and the *Personal Narrative*. He married Sarah Pierrepont in 1727, and in 1729 succeeded his grandfather in the ministry of Northampton, where the power of his sermons developed the religious revival known as the Great Awakening, which spread throughout New England in the 1730s and 1740s. Edwards' *Sinners in the Hands of an Angry God* (1741) is America's most celebrated sermon, insisting graphically on the realities of damnation and on the precariousness of life, which God holds like a spider 'or some loathsome insect over the fire'. His preaching terror and enthusiasm were opposed by religious rationalists, led by Charles Chauncey, minister in Boston, who stressed 'an enlightened Mind, and not raised Affections'. Edwards opposed the 'Half-Way Covenant' by which the Congregationalist bourgeoisie compromised between good living and the chance of damnation, and insisted that 'none ought to be admitted into the communion and privileges of members of the visible church of Christ in complete standing' unless they had experienced the 'sensible effect or sensation' of conversion or regeneration. On this issue he resigned and instead of forming a separatist movement moved to Stockbridge, Massachusetts, a frontier missionary church for the Mohawk and Housatonic Indians, where he expounded his organized philosophy in *Freedom of Will* (1754), *The Nature of True Virtue* (1765), *Concerning the End for which God Created the World* (1765) and *The Great Christian Doctrine of Original Sin Defended* (1758). Although his projected *History of the Work of Redemption* never materialized, his treatises gained him the presidency of the College of New Jersey (later Princeton University) in 1757; he died of smallpox inoculation after three months in office. *Freedom of Will* begins by opposing the idea of post-Adamite freedom to choose 'goodness' with the theory of God's choosing and rejecting whom he pleases. Edwards argues that will, like any effect, must have a cause and therefore cannot be 'free', since it is a consequence and therefore necessary. Will records only

choice made by a man's whole consciousness; a man has not freedom of will but of act; action not will must be morally judged, and man is morally responsible for his action. *Original Sin Defended* continues from these evasive but essential arguments on freedom, the great American cause, to announce man's two God-given principles, the one inferior – 'mere human nature' – and the other superior – 'spiritual, holy, man's divine nature'. But God is to be blamed for depriving man of the latter and he does inject his evolutionary creative urge or grace every now and then. It is at this point that Edwards' biology modified his theology. Adam, the American Adam, is the seed of the tree whose branches are later generations, and the finite universe can be resolved into sensations operating in the mind of both God and man. The types of the world are in moral correspondence with their anti-types in the spiritual world. It is the variations on freedom, determinism and the eternal Adam that make Edwards a significant American unifier of spirit and matter, of man's moral incapabilities with his scientific and literary endeavours. What Van Wyck ◊ Brooks termed his 'high-brow' legacy penetrated American thinking, the polar opposite of ◊ Franklin's self-reliant opportunism (see *America's Coming of Age* by Van Wyck Brooks). [EM]

*Representative Selections*, ed. C. H. Faust and T. H. Johnson (1935).

P. Miller, *Jonathan Edwards* (1949).

**Eggleston, Edward** (1837–1902). Novelist, historian, editor. He was educated in various Indiana country schools and brought up in the most rigid Methodism. At first a Methodist minister, he founded the creedless Church of Christian Endeavour in Brooklyn and became its minister (1874–9), also editing Sunday-school magazines. He campaigned enthusiastically for reform in many fields. He was responsive to the currents of literary realist and sociological thought of his time; and regional fiction makes an important advance in his varied, interesting novels, with their realistic descriptions of Indiana, the 'Hoosier State'. He seems to have written partly as a protest against the current literary obsession with New England, partly under the influence of Taine's remark in his *History of Art in the Netherlands* that 'the artist of originality will work courageously with the materials he finds in his own environment'. *The*

*Hoosier School-Master* (1871) describes adventures in a one-man village school, and reveals Eggleston's close study of Indiana dialect. *The End of the World* (1872) is an Indiana love story with a religious background; *The Circuit Rider* (1874), describing the confusion of a refined Methodist minister from the east when he meets religious ecstasies on the frontier, successfully captures the atmosphere of the frontier camps; and *Roxy* (1878) portrays a young woman against the setting of early-19th-century Indiana.

His two completed volumes of a projected *History of Life in the United States* (1896, 1900) are pioneering explorations of the country's social history; the second of these was reissued in 1933 as *The Transit of Civilization from England to America in the Seventeenth Century*, and has considerable analytical merits. [MG]

William Pierce Randel, *Edward Eggleston: Author of The Hoosier School-Master* (1946) and *Edward Eggleston* (1963).

**Eliot, John** (1604–90). Teacher and 'Apostle to the Indians'. Born in England, educated at Cambridge, he emigrated in 1631 and devoted himself to the conversion of the Massachusetts Indians. He established 'praying villages' and translated the Bible into the dialect of the Naticks, a branch of the Algonquins (1661, 1663). He wrote a variety of books about his mission and the Indians, some in their dialect; they include *The Glorious Progress of the Gospel among the Indians* (1649), *The Indian Primer* (1669) and *Up-Bookum Psalmes* (1663). Cotton ◊ Mather wrote his life (1691). [MB]

**Eliot, T(homas) S(tearns)** (1888–1965). Poet, critic, playwright. Though born and raised in St Louis, Missouri, he came from a Unitarian family whose roots were in New England: this twin heritage he was later to memorialize in 'The Day Salvages', the third section of his greatest poem, *Four Quartets* (1943). Harvard-educated, public-spirited and wealthy, the Eliot family made sure that he received an excellent classical training before he went up to Harvard in 1906. His mother, a gifted if very minor poetess, encouraged his early predilection for verse writing. Admirably prepared, he arrived at Harvard when it had much to offer: ◊ Santayana, Irving ◊ Babbitt and Barrett Wendell were among his teachers, and, as Herbert Howarth has shown in

*Notes on Some Figures behind T. S. Eliot* (1964), the influence of these men on the direction of Eliot's thought was decisive. From them, especially from Babbitt, he learned how the past could be used to measure, discipline and enrich the present. No less important during his Harvard days were his extracurricular studies: here he first read Dante, the poet whom he later considered the greatest permanent influence on his work. A more immediately utilizable discovery was Laforgue, whose wry ironic treatment of the modern urban landscape provided him with a voice which seemed and – in English – *was* strangely original and modern. His first attempts in verse have been published as *Poems Written in Early Youth* (1967; private edn, Stockholm, 1950). By 1911, at 23, he had completed 'The Love-Song of J. Alfred Prufrock', surely one of the most brilliantly precocious poems in the language. Already the master of the vivid sensuous imagery, the extraordinarily flexible tone, and the strongly expressive rhythms which were to be the chief characteristics of his mature poetry, he did not produce a comparable success again (though this is a disputable point) until 'Gerontion' (1920).

After obtaining his B.A. and M.A. degrees and embarking on doctoral study of the philosopher F. H. Bradley, and studying at Paris, Munich and Merton College, Oxford, he settled in London in 1915, where during the next few years he earned a precarious living by teaching, reviewing and working at Lloyds Bank. These were also the years when he wrote the remarkable satiric quatrain poems 'Whispers of Immortality' and 'Sweeney among the Nightingales', poems which, ostentatiously terse, grotesque and learned, had a programmatic significance for Eliot and his new mentor Pound, who wished to correct the delinquencies of the *vers libre* movement. *The Waste Land* (1922), written partly as a sequel to 'Gerontion', expressed what he took to be the spiritual and moral plight of post-war Europe. Abandoning (with Pound's help) the monologue form of 'Prufrock' and 'Gerontion', he created a poem in which an apparently random succession of images and points of view is presented, yet which is controlled (more or less) by a submerged symbolic narrative. The poem seemed to express the disillusionment of a generation, it was recognized by Pound and others as the chief masterpiece of the modern movement, and it established Eliot at once as the leading American poet of the day.

But it was as a critic that he first gained recognition among those in whose eyes poetic experimentation was suspect. Especially in his earlier criticism (*c.* 1917–25) he had an almost unprecedented gift for expressing with cogency and authoritative manner what others had often thought and said. Frequently muddled and contradictory as a theorist, and, compared with Johnson, Coleridge or Arnold, unoriginal and unadventurous as a practical critic, he has been perhaps the most successful dictator of literary taste in the history of English criticism. Thanks to his essays Milton and the romantics have been reexamined and revalued; the Metaphysical poets, the great Augustans, Dante and the French symbolists have gained a vastly larger and more appreciative audience. He did much, too, to encourage a popular awareness of the vitality of past literatures and the necessity to range outside English literature if one is to understand and evaluate it properly.

Eliot's interest in verse drama dated from the Harvard days, and the dramatic monologue, conceived partly as a development of the Jacobean soliloquy, was his favourite poetic form. This interest was extended during the early twenties by close study of the Senecan tradition, coupled with a perception that the Mass and the music hall might be exploited to help revive verse drama. The first result of this research was *Sweeney Agonistes* (1926–7), a brilliant fragment related in both tone and technique to the earlier quatrain poems. After 1927, when he was confirmed in the Church of England and shortly thereafter became a British citizen, he had powerful reasons to try to make contact with a larger community than his poetry could be expected to reach. True, two of his greatest poems, *Ash Wednesday* (1930) and *Four Quartets*, were yet to be written ; and they, no less than *The Waste Land*, could be called coterie poems. But after 1927, it can be inferred from his critical writings, he was aiming at a much larger, if still a minority, public. *Murder in the Cathedral* (1935) was his first artistically successful play ; to many critics it seems the only play he wrote (aside from *Sweeney*) in which Eliot the great poet is much in evidence. The later plays, however, show a more certain and

subtle command of dramatic technique; and they represent a serious attempt, as the two earlier plays do not, to deal with familiar contemporary society. Perhaps the best of these plays are *The Cocktail Party* (1950) and *The Confidential Clerk* (1954). He was awarded the Nobel Prize for Literature in 1948. [G D]

Donald Gallup, *T. S. Eliot; a Bibliography* (1953); Grover Smith, *T. S. Eliot's Poetry and Plays* (1956); ed. Hugh Kenner, *T. S. Eliot; a Collection of Critical Essays* (1962); Northrop Frye, *T. S. Eliot* (1963); ed. Allen Tate, *T. S. Eliot: The Man and His Work* (1966); George Williamson, *A Reader's Guide to T. S. Eliot* (1953); F. O. Matthiessen, *The Achievement of T. S. Eliot* (1935; 3rd edn 1958); Hugh Kenner, *The Invisible Poet* (1960).

**Elkin, Stanley** (1930–    ). Novelist. Born in St Louis. His first novel, *Boswell* (1964), is a black-humour tale of a teenager who becomes a wrestler and enters the top ranks of international society (including the Queen of England); it is a fine comedy of the pretensions of institutions and 'great names'. *Criers and Kibitzers, Kibitzers and Criers* (1966) is a collection of 9 stories with the same intelligence and imagination and similar themes of the destruction of illusions and the insanities of isolation. With *A Bad Man* (1967) Elkin penetrates into contemporary America through Leo Feldman, a man born with a homunculus inside him; he is the ultimate salesman who senses the madness of 'civilization' and operates his departmental store as a counterorganization. Elkin is one of the most important American novelists of the sixties. [D M]

**Ellison, Ralph** (1914–    ). Novelist. Born in Oklahoma. His *Invisible Man* (1952) is one of the most impressive post-war American novels. Its theme is that of much 20th-century literature: modern man's search for identity in an incomprehensible world. Its Negro hero emerges as an archetypal faceless underground man ; denied any basis for self-definition by his world, he remains invisible. His forays into society, in both North and South, result in violent rejection; and he ends a figure of total isolation, one who has chosen to live underground. This theme is articulated with an impressive richness of naturalistic detail; but what emerges from the density of minute particulars, often violent and terrifying, is a myth of man's search for meaning in chaotic experience. 'And Hickman Arrives' is a fragment from a second novel (*Noble Savage I*, 1960). *Shadow and Act* (1964) is a collection of essays, on a wide variety of aspects of the Negro and Negro culture in America. (◊ Negro Literature.) [AH]

Robert A. Bone, *The Negro Novel in America* (1958); Marcus Klein, *After Alienation* (1962); Ellin Horowitz, 'The Rebirth of the Artist', in *On Contemporary Literature*, ed. R. Kostelanetz (1965).

**Emerson, Ralph Waldo** (1803–82). Philosopher, poet. One of America's most important writers and a leading Transcendentalist, he was born in Boston, Massachusetts, descended from generations of New England ministers. When his father died, leaving the large family in poverty, the mother's self-reliance and endurance enabled four sons to be educated at Harvard. Emerson was no great scholar but read widely, already trusting his instincts – as his later philosophy would assert. He became Pastor of the Old Second Church of Boston; but, guided by W. E. ◊ Channing's reformed Unitarianism, his brother William's experience of Göttingen Bible criticism, and his own reading of Swedenborg and Coleridge, he came to decline the ministry traditional in his family. After the shock of his new wife's death in 1831, the mental derangement of his younger brother (1828) and his own psychosomatic symptoms when he preached, he doubted his vocation and in 1832 sailed for Malta, travelled through Italy and Switzerland, and reached Paris, where the Jardin des Plantes inspired him to almost mystical naturalism, the transcendental unity of men and nature. Disappointed with the ageing Coleridge and Wordsworth's conservativism, he obtained more nourishment from Carlyle, but returned to America to create 'pale face', as he called himself, into the great lecturer and writer he was ready to be. He remarried, settled in Concord, and crystallized his ideas in *Nature* (1836), combining the needed part of Puritan and Unitarian religion with 19th-century romantic ideology. *The American Scholar* (1837) calls for a national literature, and the 'Divinity School Address' (1838) rejects formal religion for intuitional experience of the World Soul. His sociability and lecturing reputation increased as he lectured as far west as the frontier and Mississippi valley.

For materials he drew on his journals, and the final form appeared as *Essays: First Series* (1841) and *Second Series* (1844). Although he met with the Transcendentalist Club and edited the *Dial*, he refused to join Brook Farm (◊ Ripley) in the name of individualism and doubt as to the artificiality of group experiment. He supported ◊ Thoreau's Walden Act and the Abolition cause in the 1850s. In 1847 he lectured successfully in London and Oxford, and met Arnold and Clough and renewed his friendship with Carlyle. Back in America he published *Representative Men* (1850) and *Conduct of Life* (1860) and gradually became an establishment figure himself. But his optimism grew bewildered and assertive as the Civil War drew nearer, and his voice after the war sounded forced. He was buried in Sleepy Hollow Cemetery, Concord, beside Thoreau and Hawthorne. His essays can be represented by 'Self-Reliance' ('society is everywhere in conspiracy against the manhood of every one of its members', therefore 'whosoever would be a man must be a non-conformist'), 'Spiritual Laws' ('there is a soul at the centre of nature, and over the will of man, so that none of us can wrong the universe'), 'Circles' (a man's own circle of thought should enclose earlier and contemporary circles), 'Art' (the artist 'employs the symbols in use in his day and nation, to convey his enlarged sense to his fellow men'), and 'The Poet' ('the complete man' using 'symbolic language'). The titular *Representative Men* are Plato, Swedenborg, Montaigne, Shakespeare, Napoleon and Goethe: the types of great men of 'a rich and related existence'. Of the relationship between his poetry and his essays he said, 'I can breathe at any time, but I can only whistle when the right pucker comes'. He championed Whitman in 1855 and his own poems often take free-verse organic forms to delineate his man-and-nature themes ('The Rhodora', 'Ode Inscribed to W. H. Channing', 'Brahma', 'Two Rivers'). His experiments with line and sound were of major use in developing American poetry. Although his thought and vocabulary have penetrated American culture, he was a great articulator of liberal ideas rather than a great artist. In his *Journals* the record of inner tension and joy is often finer than the published work of his lifetime. [EM]

*Complete Works*, ed. E. W. Emerson (12 vols., 1903–4); *The Journals*, ed. E. W. Emerson and W. E. Forbes (10 vols., 1909–14). Ralph L. Rusk, *The Life of Ralph Waldo Emerson* (1949); Sherman Paul, *Emerson's Angle of Vision: Man and Nature in American Experience* (1965); Stephen E. Whicher, *Freedom and Fate: An Inner Life of Ralph Waldo Emerson* (1953); Frederic I. Carpenter, *Emerson Handbook* (1953); W. M. Konvitz and S. Whicher, *Emerson: A Collection of Critical Essays* (1962).

**Enslin, Theodore** (1925–    ). Poet. Born and raised near Philadelphia, he has lived mostly on Cape Cod and in Maine. He studied music under Nadia Boulanger but gave it up for poetry. His considerable body of original work is published in *The Work Proposed* (1958), *The Place Where I am Standing* (1964), *New Sharon Prospect* (1966, which contains 'Pages from the Journals'), *This Do* (& *the Talent*) (1966), and *The Diabelli Variations* (1967). [EM]

**Eshleman, Clayton** (1935–    ). Poet. Born in Indianapolis, and educated at the local university, he lived often in Japan and South America, and now edits from New York *Caterpillar*, one of the most important little magazines of the sixties. In 1969 he published a major translation of the poetry of the Peruvian poet César Vallejo, *Poemas humanos/Human Poems*. His representative book of poems is *Indiana* (1969), which reads like the unhurried search of a man with more varied and complex experience than he can easily encompass. His projective verse forms are also worked out in *Walks* (1967), *Yellow River Record* (1969) and *The House of Ibuki* (1969). [EM]

**Everett, Alexander Hill** (1790–1847). Poet, essayist, editor. Born in Boston, Massachusetts, brother of E. ◊ Everett, he was a diplomat in Russia, Holland and Spain, where he assisted and befriended Washington ◊ Irving. Later he wrote the studies *Europe* (1822) and *America* (1827), and became a frequent contributor to, then editor of, the *North American Review* (1830–5), translating Goethe and encouraging attention to European romanticism. [MB]

*Essays, Critical and Miscellaneous* (1845–6).

**Everett, Edward** (1794–1865). Editor, essayist, orator, statesman. Brother of A. H. ◊ Everett, and like him an important figure in making American and Bostonian thought cosmopolitan. He was among the early group of Americans who studied at Göttingen and reformed and advanced American scholarship in theology, classics, history and European literature. First a Unitarian minister, then Professor of Greek at Harvard, he deeply influenced letters as editor of the important *North American Review* (1820–4) in one of its most cosmopolitan phases. He won great reputation as an orator, and his speeches, published as *Orations and Speeches on Various Occasions* (4 vols., 1853–68), had widespread popularity. Like his brother he turned to politics, and became in due course Minister to England and Secretary of State (1852–3). [MB]

**Expatriates.** The habit of literary expatriation, usually to Europe, is so well established in the history of American literature as to constitute a tradition. The circumstances of America's founding, as a colony intellectually dependent upon Europe, particularly on England, made this inevitable in the early days. Benjamin ◊ Franklin, who himself spent a large part of his life in England and France, observed that because Americans were not rich enough to encourage the fine arts 'our Geniuses all go to Europe'. During the 19th century many of the major writers – including Irving, Hawthorne, Cooper, James, Edith Wharton, Bret Harte and Stephen Crane – spent long periods in Europe. James became, at the end of his life, a British citizen. During this century the sentimental pilgrimage to what Hawthorne called 'our Old Home' developed; T. G. Appleton once spoke of the importance of Europe for the Yankee – 'it is the home of his protoplasm, of the long succession of forces which make him what he is.' In the early years of the present century, Ezra Pound and T. S. Eliot (who also became a British citizen) came to London to conduct their poetic revolution, and Gertrude Stein chose Paris as the city in which to seek 'glory'. Even after Van Wyck ◊ Brooks declared American literature officially of age, the pattern continued. A large part of the literary generation of the twenties, the so-called ◊ 'lost generation' – including Hemingway, Fitzgerald, Dos Passos, Katherine Anne ◊ Porter and Sylvia ◊ Beach – spent time in Paris, where a large American literary colony developed. A largish artistic colony still remains.

Expatriation became a conventional

mode of acquiring a literary apprenticeship, and later of expressing protest against
the provincialism or repression of American
life. At times – as with Theodore ◊ Roosevelt's complaints against 'hyphenated
Americans' – it came close to being a serious
political issue. There is a long debate about
it in American letters; it is much associated
with the literary dissatisfactions of American writers. At one time the essential opposition was between Europe's 'civilization'
and America's lack of it, but in the present
century the terms shift: it is Europe's
freedom, and the opportunities afforded
there for ◊ Bohemianism, that are contrasted with America's limitations. The
effect of such expatriation on American
letters is important; despite the repeatedly
expressed fears that this was leading to
intellectual servility and the Anglicization
or Europeanization of American writing,
its effect has been to make American letters
remarkably cosmopolitan and international, and the cosmopolitan ideal was
repeatedly expressed by expatriates like
James and Pound. Recently there have
been signs that the tide is flowing the other
way; from ◊ Nabokov, Auden, Isherwood
and the German refugees from Hitler onward, the expatriate from Europe has
played an important part in American
letters. [MB]

R. P. Blackmur, 'The American Literary Ex-
patriate' in *Foreign Influences in American Life:
Essays and Critical Bibliographies*, ed. D. F.
Bowers (1944); Malcolm Cowley, *Exile's Re-
turn* (1934); ed. Philip Rahv, *Discovery of
Europe: The Story of American Experience in
the Old World* (1947); Ernest Hemingway, *A
Moveable Feast* (1964).

# F

**Fair, A. A.** ◊ Gardner, Erle Stanley.

**Falkner, William C.** (1825–79). Novelist. Now best known as the great-grandfather of William ◊ Faulkner (who changed the spelling of the family name), this Mississippi railroad builder, lawyer and soldier was once esteemed as the author of *The White Rose of Memphis* (1880), an exotic Southern romance. He also wrote, in reply to *Uncle Tom's Cabin*, *The Little Brick Church* (1882) and a travel book, *Rapid Ramblings in Europe* (1884). [M B]

**Farrell, James (Thomas)** (1904–  ). Novelist, short-story writer. Born on Chicago's South Side, he lived in that city until 1931. He attended classes at the University of Chicago (where he wrote the sketch that would eventually grow into his best-known work, the Studs Lonigan trilogy) and worked in various jobs, including advertising and undertaking. Since the early 1920s he has lived more or less continuously in New York City, writing and lecturing extensively. *It Has Come to Pass* (1958) records his visit to Israel in 1956.

Farrell's reputation rests upon three distinct yet related cycles of fiction: the Studs Lonigan trilogy, the Danny O'Neill pentalogy and the Bernard Carr trilogy. The first, comprising *Young Lonigan* (1932), *The Young Manhood of Studs Lonigan* (1934) and *Judgment Day* (1935), dispassionately records the brutalized Chicago life and pathetic death at 29 of Farrell's inarticulate hero. Danny O'Neill, who appears in *A World I Never Made* (1936), *No Star Is Lost* (1938), *Father and Son* (1940), *My Days of Anger* (1943) and *The Face of Time* (1953), succeeds in escaping the destructive forces of the family and the larger environment of Chicago. His literary aspirations are indirectly fulfilled in the Bernard Carr trilogy: *Bernard Clare* (1946), *The Road Between* (1949) and *Yet Other Waters* (1952). Among Farrell's other novels are *Gas-House McGinty* (1933) and *This Man and This Woman* (1951). *New Year's Eve 1929* (1968) is a short allegory of a woman's life and *Lonely for the Future*

(1966), a story of 1927 Chicago's clubs. *The Silence of History* (1963) inaugurates a new series based on another young man from Chicago; the second volume is *What Time Collects* (1964). *A Brand New Life* (1968) makes a return to his earlier vigour. A prolific writer of short stories, he has now published over 200, many of which were brought together in *The Short Stories of James T. Farrell* (1937) and *An Omnibus* (1956). His literary criticism and occasional essays are collected in *A Note on Literary Criticism* (1936), *The League of Frightened Philistines* (1945), *Literature and Morality* (1947), all exploring his proletarian-naturalist aesthetics, and *Reflections at Fifty* (1954). Luna Wolf has edited *Selected Essays* (1964).

Farrell's work has been unfashionable in literary circles, and critics tend to view his novels with an air of patronage. Since the early 1930s he has remained in his fiction very much an unreconstructed naturalist (though he professes allegiance to Sherwood ◊ Anderson rather than to ◊ Dreiser), exploiting the monotony, boredom, cruelty and violence of modern urban life, concentrating upon the relationship of the individual to the family unit and to the larger, frequently hostile environment in which the family finds itself. Certainly, Farrell's work tends to lack variety; so does his prose style, despite the stylistic experimentation of *Gas-House McGinty*. But if his achievement is limited, it still represents a positive, substantial contribution to modern American literature. The Bernard Carr trilogy (the name was changed after a libel suit) is less interesting and convincing than the earlier sequences; but it too forms part of Farrell's avowed overall intention to create 'as complete a story of America as I knew it, of the hopes, the shames, the aspirations'. In this sense much of his work is an immense *roman fleuve* which offers an effective, at times moving and indignant, history of 20th-century America. [H D]

Edgar M. Branch, *A Bibliography of James T. Farrell's Writings, 1921–1957* (1959); Edgar M. Branch, *James T. Farrell* (University of Minnesota Pamphlet, 1963); C. C. Walcutt, *American Naturalism: A Divided Stream* (1956); B. H. Gelfant, *The American City Novel* (1954); W. M. Frohock, *The Novel of Violence in America* (2nd edn, 1957); ed. S. J. Krause, *Essays on Determinism in American Literature* (1964).

**Fast, Howard** (1914–    ). Novelist. Born in New York City, he travelled through the States during the Depression, taking a variety of jobs, and became a leading American left-winger; his *The Naked God* (1957) is a famous document of disenchantment with the Communist Party, though not with the left. His writing, mostly historical, tends to deal with revolutionary situations, often touched with 'propaganda' emphasis. One group of his novels is concerned with the American Revolutionary war (*Two Valleys*, 1933, *The Unvanquished*, 1942, *The Proud and the Free*, 1950, etc.), while *Citizen Tom Paine* (1943) is a persuasive study of ◊ Paine as European-American revolutionary. He has also set novels in the Reconstruction period, in more contemporary American settings – *Clarkton* (1947), for instance, deals with a strike in a Massachusetts mill town – and in the biblical and Roman past. His romantic historical epics, some of them filmed, include *My Glorious Brothers* (1948), set in pre-Christian Israel; *Spartacus* (1952), set in Rome; *Moses, Prince of Egypt* (1958); and *Agrippa's Daughter* (1965). *Power* (1963) is a portrait of a labour leader, which includes an account of the origins of the coal miners' union, in the 1920s or 1930s. Fast can write sentimentally and splashily; but a sophistication not only political but historical invigorates his work. [M B]

S. Meistler, 'The Lost Drums of Howard Fast', in *A View of the Nations*, ed. H. M. Christian (1960).

**Faulkner, William** (1897–1962). Novelist, short-story writer, poet. Born in New Albany, Mississippi, and brought up in Oxford, seat of the University of Mississippi, he left school early, joined the Royal Flying Corps in Canada in the First World War (which ended before he had completed training), and studied briefly at the University in Oxford. Supporting himself with odd jobs, he began to write (writing was in the family and the fame of his great-grandson has renewed the reputation of William C. ◊ Falkner, the model for Faulkner's Colonel Sartoris). Faulkner's first book,

*The Marble Faun* (1924), is a collection of derivative (Keatsian, Georgian) pastoral verses of little distinction. (A second volume of poetry, *A Green Bough*, appeared in 1933.) The following year he was helped by Sherwood ◊ Anderson in New Orleans, wrote journalism, and began work on his first novel, *Soldiers' Pay* (1926), in which a wounded First World War soldier returns to the South. He returned from travel in Europe that year and thereafter spent most of his life in Oxford. *Mosquitoes* (1927), a mildly satirical novel of New Orleans literary Bohemia, was followed, on Sherwood ◊ Anderson's advice, by fiction about his home area, and *Sartoris* (1929) begins the series of novels and stories about life in north Mississippi, re-created as Yoknapatawpha County, in which his full creative powers were to develop. A world-weary, lost generation approach still impregnates *Sartoris*, but parts of it rise to that level of emotional and historical realism which the Yoknapatawpha work attains: *The Sound and the Fury* (1929), *As I Lay Dying* (1930), *Sanctuary* (1931), *Light in August* (1932), *Absalom, Absalom!* (1936), *Go Down, Moses* (1942), *Intruder in the Dust* (1948), the trilogy of *The Hamlet* (1940), *The Town* (1957) and *The Mansion* (1959), and *The Reivers* (1962), his last novel.

Although Faulkner renders the physical reality of Yoknapatawpha's inhabitants, soil, river, sand and brush country, Negro cabins, small farms, decaying mansions, small towns with their court-house, jail, stores, square and statue to the Confederate dead, he is not limited by this particularity of time, place and history: he is not simply a regional novelist. His fiction moves continually towards the condition of myth through which he is able to express and define an imaginative vision of human existence.

Faulkner's world, though often regarded as a compound of Jacobean horror and a naturalistic emphasis on the brutal and violent in human nature, does affirm the human values he spoke of in accepting the Nobel Prize (1950) – 'courage and honor and hope and pride and compassion and pity and sacrifice'. He reveals a tragic sense of man's failure to sustain these ideals, seen specifically in the failure of the South, buttressed by flawed notions of religion, to recognize the humanity of the Negro, and in his outrage at the existence of men, in both North and South, obsessed by the desire for self-aggrandizement, who fail even to know such ideals exist. Faulkner's key merits are regional, and idealistic, though formally his novels reveal a readiness for modernist experiment. He frequently employs such devices as Joycean stream of consciousness, scrambled chronology, mythic and biblical parallelism, and the manipulation within a single novel of apparently disparate narrative lines: *The Wild Palms* (1939), which consists of two wholly distinct stories printed in alternating chapters, provides the extreme example of this last technique. The style can be equally complex; though sometimes undisciplined and rhetorically extravagant, its page-long sentences, involuted and parenthetical, can often create a richly significant verbal texture. Structural and stylistic devices, however, are usually related to major thematic preoccupations: for example, Faulkner's frequent departures from standard narrative chronology have much to do with his idea of time, his sense that past events continue into the present.

*The Sound and the Fury* (1929) employs most of the devices mentioned to tell the history of the decline of the Compson family in Jefferson, Mississippi, due to its failure to love. The novel's four sections rehearse the story from the differing points of view of four characters, the first being a brilliant *tour de force* told by an idiot, Benjy. *As I Lay Dying* (1930), also technically complex, is the story of the poor-white Bundren family's journey to bury Addie Bundren in Jefferson – on a naturalistic level, grotesquely humorous, but ritualistic and symbolic in its elaborate telling. *Light in August* (1932), Faulkner's most penetrating and dramatic analysis of contemporary Southern society, tells the two stories of Joe Christmas, victim of the South's racial prejudice, and Lena Grove searching for the father of her unborn child; both come together to define the strength and weaknesses of the South's way of life, the clash between white and black finally seen in terms more universal than those of Southern racial conflict. *Absalom, Absalom!* (1936), also often of extraordinary rhetorical and structural complexity, is about Thomas Sutpen's doomed attempt to build up a plantation and found a family; his design founders on Southern racial prejudice and the inability to love; his fate becomes an emblem for the whole

South. In *Go Down, Moses* (1942), which includes the superb story 'The Bear', Faulkner brilliantly unites the idea of a promised land cursed by slavery and the destruction of America's pastoral wilderness – a recurring symbol in his work for man's urge to exploit and violate. In contrast, *The Unvanquished* (1938) relates his Southern preoccupations in a more conventional prose form. *Intruder in the Dust* is a good example of Faulkner's attempt to come to terms with his inheritance of Negro and white relations, and the short story 'Red Leaves' shows something of his interest in native American Indians and their declining culture. The *Hamlet–Town–Mansion* trilogy concerns the growth to power of the Snopes clan, Faulkner's image, at once realistic and grotesque, of greed and licence inherent in the development of the South. *Requiem for a Nun* (1951) develops material in *Sanctuary* concerning the nature of moral law, and includes some definitive statements about the history of Yoknapatawpha, complex prose passages placed between the dramatized main narrative. Of the novels not directly concerned with Yoknapatawpha, *Pylon* (1935) concerns the courage of aviators during a New Orleans Mardi Gras, and *A Fable* (1954) is a grandiose, verbose allegory of power based on mutinies on the Western front in the First World War.

Faulkner's many first-rate short stories appeared in *These Thirteen* (1931), *Doctor Martino and Other Stories* (1934), *Knight's Gambit* (1949), *Collected Stories* (1950) and *Faulkner's County* (1955; includes the Nobel address, *As I Lay Dying*, and extracts from the Yoknapatawpha novels). *The Portable Faulkner* (1946, ed. Malcolm Cowley) arranges selections of Yoknapatawpha fiction materials to form a chronological 'saga', for which Faulkner provided a map and a history of the Compson family. The generation of this important work is given in *The Faulkner–Cowley File* (1967). *New Orleans Sketches by William Faulkner* (1955) is a collection of his contributions to the *Times-Picayune* in 1925. His direct expressions of opinion are contained in *Essays, Speeches and Public Letters* (ed. J. B. Meriwether, 1967), *Faulkner at Nagano* (1956; included in *Lion in the Garden: Interviews with William Faulkner, 1926–1962*, ed. J. B. Meriwether and M. Millgate, 1968), *William Faulkner in the University* (1959) and *Faulkner at West Point* (1964). [AH/EM]

Michael Millgate, *The Achievement of William Faulkner* (1967); Cleanth Brooks, *William Faulkner: The Yoknapatawpha Country* (1963); Edmond L. Volpe, *A Reader's Guide to William Faulkner* (1964); C. H. Nilon, *Faulkner and the Negro* (1965); Dorothy Tuck, *A Handbook of Faulkner* (1965).

**Fearing, Kenneth** (1902–61). Poet, novelist. Born in Oak Park, Illinois. After the University of Wisconsin he worked at various jobs until he became a freelance writer in New York. His commercial work appeared under several pseudonyms while he wrote poetry for little magazines, collected in his first volume, *Angel Arms* (1929). His first novel was *The Hospital* (1939) and the best known is *The Big Clock* (1946). Fearing's poetry definitively concerns urban, mechanized society, in which faith and love are thinned away. His typical poem uses newspaper and police-report styles to document satirically some disgrace of bourgeois neglect and greed, or some city criminality. His use of city slang is as masterly as his handling of the accumulative line. [EM]

*New and Selected Poems* (1956).

**'Federalist, The'** (written by Alexander Hamilton, 1755–1804, John Jay, 1745–1829, and James Madison, 1751–1836). The constitution of 1781 under which the 13 newly emancipated colonies were held together in a loose union of States provided for a national congress to which the States delegated certain defined powers. Gradually the desire to establish a more effective and efficient national government grew, and in 1787 a convention was appointed in Philadelphia to propose such revision. As the debates progressed it became clear that what was emerging was not an amended constitution but an entirely new one setting up a tripartite national government with much more positive powers. The question of whether or not the new constitution would be ratified by the States dominated politics in 1787 and 1788. It was particularly controversial in New York State, where the governor, George Clinton, opposed ratification. After letters advocating non-ratification appeared in the New York press, an opposition series supporting the constitution appeared between 27 October 1787 and 4 April 1788 over the

pen name 'Publius'. Some of these letters were published in book form on 22 March 1788; a complete collection appeared on 28 May 1788. The volume was called *The Federalist*, a name which had been assumed by the proponents of a new constitution. In 1792 it was revealed that 'Publius' was the collective pseudonym of Alexander Hamilton, John Jay and James Madison. Madison, a delegate to the Philadelphia convention, had probably contributed more to the drafting of the constitution than any other of the Founding Fathers. Hamilton, although a delegate, had missed many of the meetings, but he and Jay (who had not been at Philadelphia) were keenly interested in both ratification and the local political battles within New York State.

Of the 85 letters which make up *The Federalist*, Hamilton is credited with the authorship of 51, Madison with 27, and Jay with 5. Numbers 62 and 63 are disputed, but Professor B. F. Wright has recently attributed them to Madison. *The Federalist* is less a comprehensive work of political philosophy than a series of observations aimed at winning voter support by urging that the objects of government, which are assumed rather than analysed, can best be attained through stronger central government, and that the type of federalism advocated cannot, because of the system of checks and balances and separation of powers, become despotic. But inherent in the letters is a concept of property right and individual liberty. Society is believed to be composed of a collection of interest groups, and the main function of government is seen to be arbitration between these, since, man being essentially selfish, he must be persuaded that unrestricted pursuit of self-interest cannot but be prejudicial to society as a whole and thus eventually to himself. It is debatable whether *The Federalist* letters had much effect in winning support for the constitution of 1787, but since that time they have been acclaimed as a cogently argued and practical defence of the federal form of government. [DKA]

*The Federalist*, ed. B. J. Wright (1961).

**Federal Theatre.** The only American theatre nationally sponsored, as the Works Progress Administration, a project to rescue unemployed theatre artists and staff during the Depression and to bring their work to an American audience which had hardly experienced theatre at all. It was begun (1935) and directed by Hallie Flanagan, a pupil of George P. ◊ Baker, and a woman of outstanding knowledge of the theatre. She organized five regional theatres to provide work, a stage as an incentive to dramatists and technicians alike, and to encourage experiment in form and production, through such projects as a children's theatre, a Negro theatre, a marionette theatre, a topical 'Living Newspaper', a popular-price theatre for new authors, an experimental theatre and a try-out theatre. Hallie Flanagan understood that the Federal Theatre could continue its social purpose and survive only by becoming a national theatre. In four years, thousands of productions were created throughout the country in 31 States. By 1937 alone it had played to approximately 16 million people, at an average audience price of 30 cents. Productions included an all-Negro *Macbeth* and T. S. Eliot's *Murder in the Cathedral*, both of which were major successes; Labiche's *The Italian Straw Hat* (*Horse Eats Hat*, in America), directed by the then unknown Orson Welles, with music by Virgil Thomson; Blitzstein's important political musical *The Cradle Will Rock*; and on 27 October 1936, 21 simultaneous productions of Sinclair ◊ Lewis's and John C. Moffit's *It Can't Happen Here*, which concerned the establishment of a Fascist dictatorship in America. Accused of communism, this superb achievement was assassinated by Congress in 1939 in a disgraceful 'trial' without adequate evidence. [EM]

Hallie Flanagan, *Arena: The Story of the Federal Theatre* (1940); Jane De Hart Matthews, *The Federal Theatre, 1935–1939* (1968).

**Feldman, Irving** (1928– ). Poet. Born and educated in New York City, he travelled and taught abroad and at Kenyon College and the State University of New York at Buffalo. His two books of poems, *Works and Days* (1961) and *The Pripet Marshes* (1965), employ Yiddish inflections, usually in short, quick run-on lines, to explore Old Testament themes as they are translated and transformed by the fate of Jewish civilization in the 20th century. [BP]

**Ferber, Edna** (1887–1968). Short-story writer, novelist, playwright. Born in Michigan, she was a reporter for newspapers in Wisconsin, Milwaukee and Chicago, and later a war correspondent, before becoming a full-time writer. *Dawn O'Hara*, her first novel, concerns a newspaper woman in Milwaukee. Her early stories described with great success a new American type, the woman in business; they were collected in *Roast Beef, Medium* (1913), *Personality Plus* (1914) and *Emma McChesney and Co.* (1915). Women were also the protagonists in her early novels, *Fanny Herself* (1917); *The Girls* (1921), about three generations of a family; and *So Big* (1924; Pulitzer Prize), a study of a widowed school-mistress and mother in a rough rural community. Two big popular novels, *Show Boat* (1926), about a Mississippi river family, and *Cimarron* (1930), which concerned the Oklahoma land rush of 1889, were filmed. Later novels, though less successful, have tackled with relish an extraordinary variety of subjects; they include *American Beauty* (1931), *Come and Get It* (1935), *Saratoga Trunk* (1941), *Great Son* (1945) and *Ice Palace* (1958). Texans were enraged by the unflattering *Giant* (1952), and Edna Ferber comments on the book's reception and the making of a film version in the second of two lively autobiographies, *A Peculiar Treasure* (1939) and *A Kind of Magic* (1963). With George S. ◊ Kaufman she wrote a series of plays, among them *The Royal Family* (1927), a satire on the Barrymores; *Stage Door* (1936); and the famous *Dinner at Eight* (1932). [MG]

**Ferlinghetti, Lawrence** (1919– ). Poet. Born in New York, he studied at Columbia and the Sorbonne, and with his poetry and his publishing centre the City Lights Bookshop helped to make San Francisco a by-word as a city of new literature during the 'San Francisco Renaissance' and the ◊ Beat Generation period of the fifties. His poems in *Pictures from The Gone World* (1955), *A Coney Island of the Mind* (1958) and *Starting from San Francisco* (1961) are partly finely made personal lyrics and partly long public poems – frequently written for declamation, with and without jazz. His public readings in the 1950s were part of the rejuvenation of spoken poetry on the West Coast. He has perfected a kind of public poem made up of topical and critical references, light-toned but serious satire, and literary references which is extremely effective in performance. He published some of his poems as broadsides, to facilitate their display and general availability:

these are included in *Starting from San Francisco* and continue in, for example, 'Berlin' (1961), 'Where is Vietnam' (1965) and 'Moscow in the Wilderness, Segovia in the Snow' (1967). Ferlinghetti has always been conscious of the need for direct statement and clear responsibility in poetry. *Unfair Arguments with Existence* (1962) is a collection of experimental plays, and *Routines* (1963) are scenarios for happenings. *Her* (1960) is a novel in the form of an interior and surreal monologue. *After the Cries of the Birds* (1967) is a poem with an essay on its genesis. *The Secret Meaning of Things* (1969) contains six long poems, and *Tyrannus Nix?* (1969) is the latest of his 'political-satirical tirades'; the target is President Nixon. [E M]

**Fiedler, Leslie** (1917– ). Literary and social critic, novelist, storywriter. Born in Newark, New Jersey, he was head of the English Department at Montana State University until moving recently to the University of Buffalo. Most influential as a critic, he has combined sociological interests with concern with psychology and myth to produce eccentric but stimulating critical studies, mostly of American literature. He came to prominence with long essays on the Alger Hiss and the Rosenberg espionage cases and a piece on *Huckleberry Finn* attributing repressed homosexual emotion to Huck and Jim; these are collected in *An End to Innocence: Essays on Culture and Politics* (1955). This notion is expanded into a general theory of white American psychological inability to face up to 'coloured' races in its midst; of American literature and culture as a series of accommodations and rejections of 'love' for men of other races; of the cultural dominance of the white American female and the male attempt to escape it. *Love and Death in the American Novel* (1960), Fiedler's most connected work, is a bulky study of American literature seen in this light, concentrating on the Sentimental (love) and Gothic (death) traditions in the novel. A monograph, *The Jew in the American Novel* (1950), assimilates the Jew into his notion that 'outsider' groups like Indians and Negroes are akin to the major American writers who at their best produced works severely critical of American life – as argued in *No! in Thunder: Essays in Myth and Literature* (1960). *Waiting for the End* (1964) looks at modern American writing

in the light of cultural shifts from expatriate through Jewish to Negro mentality, and is depressed and apocalyptic. *The Return of the Vanishing American* (1968) develops the thesis that the Indians carry the sacred energies of America. His complex and elaborately constructed novels include *The Second Stone* (1963) and *Back to China* (1965); *Pull Down Vanity* (1962) and *The Last Jew in America* (1967) are collections of very lively stories. *Being Busted* (1970) concerns the implications of his being tried on narcotic charges in Buffalo. [A G]

**Field, Eugene** (1850–95). Poet, newspaperman, prankster. Born in St Louis, Missouri, he seems to have been expelled from three colleges for practical jokes. Working on papers in St Louis, Kansas City and Denver, he found his vocation in Chicago on the *Daily News*. His column made fun of current idiocies; his poetry churned out sentimentalities by the foot. His parodic *Tribune Primer* (1881) advised children to mutilate flies, eat lye, beat the baby, etc., but his normal target was Chicago philistinism. His range runs from Western ballads and hymns to corny children's verse. Most of it is awful. His fame may well rest with 'Wynken, Blynken and Nod' and 'Little Boy Blue'. [E M]

**Fisher, Vardis** (1895– ). Novelist, poet. He was born in a Mormon family in Idaho and has taught English at Utah and New York Universities. During the Works Progress Administration years he directed the Federal Project for the *Idaho State Guide* (1937). As a novelist, his reputation began with a tetralogy about Vridar Hunter – *In Tragic Life* (1932), *Passions Spin the Plot* (1934), *We Are Betrayed* (1935) and *No Villain Need Be* (1936). *Children of God* (1939) is a historical novel about the early Mormons, and *Darkness and the Deep* (1943) begins his series of novels on the development of primitive man, continued in *Peace like a River* (1958), *My Holy Satan* (1959) and *Orphans in Gethsemane* (1960). His recent works include *Suicide or Murder: The Strange Death of Meriwether Lewis* (1962) and the novel *Mountain Man* (1965). His poems are found in *Sonnets to an Imaginary Madonna* (1927). [E M]

**Fiske, John** (1842–1901). Philosopher, historian. Born in Hartford, Connecticut. One of the leading intellectual figures of his day, he was a Christian evolutionist who promoted the views of Comte, Herbert Spencer and other neo-Darwinians in such books as the influential *Outlines of Cosmic Philosophy* (1875) and *Darwinism and Other Essays* (1879). He taught philosophy at Harvard and later history at Washington University, St Louis. He wrote numerous historical works, mostly dealing with the U.S.A., and including *The Beginnings of New England* (1889), *The American Revolution* (1891) and *How the United States Became a Nation* (1904). Both as evolutionary positivist and historian he was an eloquent popularizer rather than an originator; his skill in presentation, both as lecturer and writer, and his tendency to reconcile evolution with Christian providence – both seemed to work in favour of the U.S.A. – won him great general prestige. [M B]

*Writings* (24 vols., 1902).

J. S. Clark, *The Life and Letters of John Fiske* (2 vols., 1917); Thomas S. Perry, *John Fiske* (1906).

**Fitch, Clyde** (1865–1909). Dramatist. Born in Elmira, N.Y. His series of successes began with *Beau Brummel* (1890). His professionalism produced a large number of realistic social plays of topicality and caricatural detail, including *Barbara Frietchie* (1899), using Whittier's Civil War poem (and the basis of Romberg's musical *My Maryland*), *Captain Jinks of the Horse Marines* (1901) and *The Girl with Green Eyes* (1902), a melodrama of neurotic jealousy and some satire of New York society. [E M]

**Fitts, Dudley** (1903–     ). Poet, translator. Born in Boston, he was educated at Harvard and teaches at Philips Academy, Andover. *Poems: 1929–1936* (1937) collects some of his verse. Amongst his chief work have been his vigorous translations from the Greek – notably of Aristophanes (*Lysistrata*, 1954, *The Frogs*, 1955, etc.) and of Sophocles, whose *Oedipus* he translated with Robert Fitzgerald. [M B]

**Fitzgerald, F. Scott** (1896–1940). Novelist. Born in St Paul, Minnesota, with an ancestry from poor Irish and old Maryland. His family had become prosperous, and had included the author of 'The Star-Spangled Banner'. At Newman School, New Jersey, his tentative and aborted grooming as America's great Catholic writer began in the

hands of Father Fay. At Princeton he wrote for the Triangle Club, but literary success did not compensate for not being rich or an athletic hero. Nor did the army send him abroad in 1917, although he found time to write in camp *The Romantic Egoist*, rewritten as his first published novel, *This Side of Paradise* (1920), an autobiographical work using extracts from letters, episodes from his relations with Fr Fay, and his failed Princeton dreams. But his personal disillusion, his sense of youthful fling being all a man had, and his moral message of waste and the need for responsibility suited post-war urban America; the book became a best-seller and made him rich. He had described 'a generation grown up to find all Gods dead, all wars fought, all faiths in man shaken'; he defined the Jazz Age, the boom reaction to the First World War, and bitterly knew it was mistaken and doomed. He now lived like a hotel playboy, and *Flappers and Philosophy* (1920, stories) confirmed the image he and his wife Zelda projected, the decayed underside of which he described in *The Beautiful and the Damned* (1922), with its world of parties, petting, aesthetics and anxiety over money. But this novel's satirical gloom and noisy barrenness did not suit Fitzgerald's public. He and his wife now paraded through American and European hotel society on the cash he could make only through writing fiction as entertainment. The need for wealth is projected in 'The Diamond as Big as the Ritz' in *Tales of the Jazz Age* (1922). But during his wrangling life with Zelda he managed to write his masterpiece, *The Great Gatsby* (1925), and *All the Sad Young Men* (1926). In spite of praise from T. S. Eliot and Edmund Wilson, *Gatsby* had little success. Back in America Fitzgerald tried to write a Hollywood comedy, and lived in Delaware, but he returned to Europe in 1928. Zelda spent an increasing amount of time in asylums, for which he felt guilty, and he dramatized some of their experience in *Tender is the Night* (1934), a disordered novel written desperately after a long period of sterility and hackwork, and *Taps at Reveille* (1935), a last collection of stories. The breakdown he suffered in America he brilliantly recorded in three essays in *Esquire* in 1936 (see *The Crack-Up*, ed. Edmund Wilson, 1945). He died exhausted from Hollywood hackwork and a ruined constitution. But he had managed, during this final period, to write 17 fine tales (*The Pat Hobby Stories*, 1962).

It is clear from his letters to his daughter that his understanding of capitalist society intensified as he read Marx: his sense of Western decay gives a dimension of the epic to his last and unfinished novel, *The Last Tycoon* (1941). His work as a whole is a serious analysis of the need for 'responsibility' of action between the wars and dramatizes how potential leaders fail from under-nourishment as they search for alternatives to capitalism, Catholicism and communism. The 'ability to function' is betrayed by materialism and ignorance. The hero of *The Great Gatsby* is a *nouveau riche* whose Prohibition loot corrupts an idealism based on American myths of self-reliance and endless opportunity. In spite of its structural flaws, the meticulous style and insights into the American class system make this one of the most gifted novels of the century. *Tender is the Night* is in some ways a profounder study of the talented man exhausted before maturity by the society which needs him. *The Last Tycoon* is a brilliant account of the misgivings of the last Hollywood producer with faith in the moral and social necessity of films. Fitzgerald, more than any other American novelist, presents understandingly the interior exhaustion and the decline of leadership in America during the inter-war years. His melancholy is the sadness of the breakdown of the American dream itself. [EM]

Letters, ed. Andrew Turnbull (1963); *The Apprentice Fiction*, ed. J. Kuehl (1969).

A. Mizener, *The Far Side of Paradise: A Biography of F. Scott Fitzgerald* (1951); Andrew Turnbull, *Scott Fitzgerald* (1962); *F. Scott Fitzgerald, The Man and His Work*, ed. Alfred Kazin (1951); H. D. Piper, *F. Scott Fitzgerald: A Critical Portrait* (1967).

**Fitzgerald, Robert S.** (1910– ). Born in Geneva, N.Y., he studied at Trinity College, Cambridge, and Harvard, worked on the New York *Herald Tribune* and *Time*, and in 1946 began his distinguished university teaching career. Apart from his own work in *A Wreath for the Sea* (1943) and *In the Rose of Time* (1956), he has collaborated with Dudley ◊ Fitts on a magnificent translation of Sophocles' Oedipus plays (1939) and made a brilliant version of the *Odyssey* (1961). [EM]

**Fletcher, John Gould** (1886–1950). Poet. Born in Arkansas, of 'Mugwump' or

intellectual-populist background, he studied at Harvard during the lively period when the French symbolists and Chinese verse were being discussed. The receipt of an inheritance decided him to throw up his studies, pursue his aesthetic interests in these fields, and become a poet. In 1909 he settled in London, 'an interloper on the charmed circle of London literary life' – as he said in his interesting autobiography *Life Is My Song* (1937) – and produced a considerable quantity of poems, publishing five volumes at his own expense. He came under the influence of Pound and ◊ Imagism, but, disquieted by some of the more radical implications of the movement, linked himself with Amy ◊ Lowell's breakaway wing, with its more exotic and highly coloured poetry. In 1932, after long vacillation between Europe and America, he chose the U.S.A. and associated with the ◊ Fugitives, contributing to the Southern agrarian anthology *I'll Take My Stand*. Asserting more strongly his Southern heritage, Fletcher's later poetry – *The Epic of Arkansas* (1936), *The Burning Mountain* (1946), *Arkansas* (1947) – draws on national and regional themes.

As a poet, Fletcher participated in several modern movements, but he is primarily an impressionist. He was fascinated by the analogy between poetry and other arts, particularly painting; and his aesthetic speculations have real substance to them. With Amy Lowell he worked on 'polyphonic prose' and 'colour symphonies'. He was devoted to elaborate visual and rhythmic effects; the title of his best-known volume, *Irradiations: Sand and Spray* (London, 1915), suggests the kind of aesthetic texture he sought. There is a strong *chinoiserie* element in his verse, and if in the long run it seems touched with dilettantism it is never without real interest. He undoubtedly contributed to the development of Southern poetry, and his *Selected Poems* (1938) won him belatedly considerable admiration. [M B]

Amy Lowell, *Tendencies in Modern American Poetry* (1917); Glenn Hughes, *Imagism and the Imagists* (1931).

**Foerster, Norman** (1887– ). Critic, editor, teacher. Born in Pittsburg, Pennsylvania, he has been Professor of English at the University of North Carolina (1914–30) and at the University of Iowa (1930–44) (where as Director of the School of Letters he recognized novels, poems and plays as work towards a Ph.D.). A leader of the ◊ New Humanist movement, he edited its manifesto, *Toward Standards* (1930). His own most important book is *Nature in American Literature* (1923), which explores the development of the 'naturalistic movement in American literature from Bryant to Whitman and the typical essayists of the present century ... at the same time, by studying the movement in relation to the Classical and Christian tradition which it has more and more supplanted, we may determine in some measure how far it has enriched man's life and how far it has tended to imperil his self-knowledge.' The characteristic values and concerns expressed here are also found in his other books: *American Criticism: A Study in Literary Theory from Poe to the Present* (1928); *The American Scholar* (1929); *The Humanities after the War* (1944) and *The Humanities and the Common Man* (1946). He has edited many anthologies. [MG]

**Ford, J. H.** ◊ Negro Literature.

**Frank, Waldo** (1889–    ). Novelist, social commentator. Born in Long Branch, New Jersey, he co-founded and edited the magazine *Seven Arts* (1916–17), which sought a literary regeneration; and was active in *avant garde* and social reformist circles, gradually moving to Marxism. His revolutionary position and interest in sociology and economics are reflected in some of his many novels – *City Block* (1922), *Holiday* (1923), *The Bridegroom Cometh* (1938) etc. – though others have a more mystical or more poetic aspect. As a social commentator he wrote on Latin America (where he has a high reputation), Spain and Russia, as well as criticizing American life from a semi-Marxist position. His *Our America* (1919; British title *The New America*, 1922) was an influential item in the protest against American stuffiness and contempt for the arts that lay behind the expatriate movement of the twenties; it is one of many non-fiction books. He was Hart Crane's first editor. [MB]

Gorham B. Munson, *Waldo Frank: A Study* (1923); W. R. Bittner, *The Novels of Waldo Frank* (1958); R. L. Perry, *The Shared Vision of Waldo Frank and Hart Crane* (1963).

**Franklin, Benjamin** (1706–90). Printer, statesman, natural philosopher and miscell-

aneous writer. Born in Boston, he was the first fully self-made Man of the Enlightenment, American style. The son of a candlemaker, he went to Philadelphia at 17 and by the range and vigour of his activities helped to make that city the cosmopolitan capital of the infant republic that it later became. His *Do-good Papers* (1722) – essays modelled on the *Spectator* and Defoe, which praised the artisan class for their self-taught middle way of industriousness – appeared while he was a printer. Under the patronage of the governor of Pennsylvania he travelled to London (1724–6) and there formed his rational life plan based self-consciously on his balance of character, and wrote *A Dissertation on Liberty and Necessity, Pleasure and Pain* (1725), a conventional 18th-century tract. He returned to Philadelphia, married, opened his own shop in 1728, and by 1748 was rich and celebrated, living a career based on thirteen points conducive to prosperity, social comfort and the minimum disturbance to self-esteem. Through the annual 10,000 copies of *Poor Richard's Almanack* (1732–58), aphoristic prefaces and notes (including the last preface 'The Way to Wealth'), his ideas penetrated the populace via his mouthpiece, 'Poor Richard' Saunders, and his sayings or 'gleanings' were largely rephrased folk-sayings made from 'the sense of all Ages and Nations' (e.g. 'Love your neighbour; yet don't pull down your hedge', 'If you would be loved, love and be loveable', and 'A plowman on his legs is higher than a gentleman on his knees'). He founded and supported the Junta' (1727) for the self-improvement of artisans and tradesmen, the Library Company (1731), the American Philosophical Society (1744) and the Academy of Philadelphia (1749; later the University of Pennsylvania). One of his main publications was his *Pennsylvania Gazette*, which became the *Saturday Evening Post*. From local government posts he rose to be the State delegate to the Albany Convention, the first colonial move towards confederation, and in 1757 the Pennsylvania Assembly sent him to London to appeal through Parliament concerning the proprietorship of their territory. He returned to America in 1762, but was sent to England, returning only in 1775. His huge journalistic output records his interests in science and invention; his tall stories, whimsical *Bagatelles*, satires,

'Remarks Concerning the Savages of North America' (1784), his electrical experiments, his practical development of bifocal spectacles, a smokeless street-lamp globe, a stove, etc., all testify to his endless pragmatic curiosity and utilitarian habits. His scientific papers and international correspondence contain important contributions to knowledge and terminology (he seems to have pioneered 'armature', 'battery', 'conductor', 'electrician', 'charge' and 'discharge', and 'positive' and 'negative' for the language of electricity). From 1776 to 1784 he lived in France as colonial negotiator and ambassador, the living embodiment of America to the Europeans, a role he played with entertaining skill. But he died in Philadelphia; his tomb inscription reads: 'Benjamin Franklin, Printer'. He is best known in literature for his *Autobiography*, covering the years 1731–59, which was not fully published until 1868. His claim to literary distinction rests more on the style than on the usually utilitarian subjects of his essays; for his writing followed his interests, from men and manners through politics, education, religion, cultural institutions, science, military and maritime policies, spelling, swimming, and back to the more trivial amenities in old age. Combining wit and morality, ingenuity and clarity, force and fancy, the best of his essays are models of literary expression. A gift of mild irony lightens the heaviest subjects and gives weight to the lightest. As a political satirist, particularly during the period of debate with England on the rights of the colonies, he rivalled Swift and Voltaire and the best of his contemporaries, and his *Autobiography* deserves the reputation it has achieved for candour and insight; the record of a man's life, it is also a major document for the birth of the American republic. [E M]

*Writings*, ed. A. H. Smyth (10 vols., 1905–7); *Papers*, ed. L. W. Larabee, etc. (12 vols., 1960–    ); *Representative Selection*, ed. C. E. Jorgensen and F. L. Mott (revised edn 1962). Carl Van Doren, *Benjamin Franklin* (1938); I. Bernard Cohen, *Benjamin Franklin: His Contribution to the American Tradition* (1953); A. O. Aldridge, *Benjamin Franklin: Philosopher and Man* (1965); P. W. Connor, *Poor Richard's Politicks* (1965).

**Frederic, Harold** (1856–98). Newspaperman, novelist. Born in New York State, he became permanent London correspondent of the *New York Times* in 1884. He wrote nine novels, some of them historical, most dealing with New York State, mixing naturalism and romanticism. They include *Seth's Brother's Wife* (1887), a dramatic tale set in upper New York State; *The Lawton Girl* (1890); and *The Return of the O'Mahony* (1892). The work for which he is remembered is *The Damnation of Theron Ware* (1896; ed. Everett Carter, 1960; British title, *Illumination*). A friend and admirer of W. D. ◊ Howells, Frederic went well beyond Howells's limited realism in this frank account of a Methodist minister losing his faith. [H D]

*Harold Frederic's Stories of New York State*, ed. T. F. O'Donnell (1966). T. F. O'Donnell and H. C. Franchere, *Harold Frederic* (1961).

**Freeman, Mary E(leanor) Wilkins** (1852–1930). Novelist, story writer. Born in Randolph, Massachusetts. Her subject-matter was New England rural life, which she caught with a local-colourist's exactness and an objectivity that makes her comparable with Sarah Orne ◊ Jewett. Two collections of stories, *A Humble Romance and Other Stories* (1887) and *A New England Nun and Other Stories* (1891), with their ironies and their grim spinsters, are usually thought her best work. Among her novels, *The Portion of Labor* (1901), with its social analysis of a New England mill, is the most highly regarded. [M B]

Edward Foster, *Mary E. Wilkins Freeman* (1956).

**Freneau, Philip** (1752–1832). Poet. Born in New York City, he grew up in the New Jersey house he lived in for the rest of his life. As a Princeton student, he associated with such youthful revolutionary patriots as James Madison, H. H. ◊ Brackenridge and Aaron Burr, and his political nationalism began to form, although his earlier poems imitate 18th-century English pastoral and 'graveyard' verse, and Goldsmith. He and Brackenridge wrote a class poem for commencement called 'The Rising Glory of America' (1772) – as part of the British Empire, however, and he had to revise it later to suit his Americanism. After graduation in 1771, and a period of teaching and pamphleteering, in 1776 he became secretary to a West Indian planter for two years and wrote his early militant poems far from the bloodshed, together with exotic landscape and mutability poems, and the long 'gothic' 'The House of Night'. On his way home a British privateer captured and released him; he enlisted in the militia, served on American privateers, published patriotic verses, and was again captured by the British in 1780, an experience he described in 'The British Prison Ship' (1781). In the same year he pugnaciously edited the *Freeman's Journal* and wrote satires and eulogies for the republican cause ('Columbia shall never be ruled by an isle'), the most readable of which are 'The Political Balance' and 'To the Memory of the Brave American'. For health and fortune he became a sea captain; his poetic reputation increased and he now wrote against American money-grubbing, the neglect of poetry, and uncertain justice in the new democracy ('On the Emigration to America and Peopling of the Western Country'). He married, and from 1789 onwards edited ◊ Jefferson's *National Gazette*. His poems celebrated now the ideals of ◊ Paine's *Rights of Man*. Later he turned to nature poetry. Some of his most famous works of distinctly American quality are: 'The Wild Honey Suckle', 'The Indian Burying Ground' and 'The Dying Indian: Tomo Chequi'. The hero of the latter became his mouthpiece of noble savagery in *The Jersey Chronicle* (1795), a prose soliloquy of romantic primitivism and deism. Poverty sent him back to sea in 1803, but he continued his philosophical nature poems ('On the Religion of Nature', 'On a Honey Bee'). In 1809 he gave up the sea, published the third edition of his *Poems Written and Published during the American Revolutionary War*, and settled on the remains of his estate. The 1812 war roused him to poems like 'The Volunteer's March', but in 1815 his house was burned down; he began to drink ; he was found dying of exposure after a December snowstorm. Most of his poetry has lost its special appeal with the passing of the political occasion, but his work is the first body of professional journalism and poetry in American literature. His talents were turned towards polemics for a nation struggling for independence. He had little time to develop his art while fighting poverty, federalism and the British. [EM]

*Poems*, ed. Fred L. Pattee (3 vols., 1902–7; repr. 1963); *Poems*, ed. H. H. Clark (1929; repr. 1960) (selection).
Lewis Leary, *That Rascal Freneau: A Study in Literary Failure* (1941); Philip M. Marsh, *The Works of Philip Freneau: A Critical Study* (1968).

**Friedman, Bruce Jay** (1930–    ). Novelist. He was born in New York City, studied at the University of Missouri, and served in the air force. He has emerged as a leading figure in the satirical-fantasy genre and black-humour movement of the sixties, about which he has written. His novels are *Stern* (1962), about a melancholy urban Jew undergoing fantasies of comic paranoia and undermining persecution mania, and *A Mother's Kisses* (1964), which concerns a Jewish adolescent's struggles with college, mother and American mores. His short stories are collected in *Far from the City of Class* (1963), which includes '23 Pat O'Brien Movies' from which a play was made in 1966, and *Black Angels* (1966). *Scuba Duba* (1967) is a play farcically sending up the current fads of skin-diving, psychiatry and so on. He has also edited an anthology, with an important introduction, *Black Humor* (1965). [EM/MB]

**Fromm, Erich** (1900–    ). Psychoanalyst and philosopher. Born in Germany, he studied at Heidelberg, Munich and Berlin. From Frankfurt psycho-analytic and social research institutes he went to the International Institute of Social Research in New York in 1934. He has taught in many universities and written important books, mainly on his major theme: the correction of puritanism and authoritarianism. The most celebrated are *Escape from Freedom* (1941; British title *The Fear of Freedom*), a study of the meaning of freedom and authority, and *Man for Himself: Inquiry into the Psychology of Ethics* (1947). His later books include *The Forgotten Language* (1951, dreams, fairy tales, myths), *The Sane Society* (1955), *The Art of Loving* (1956), *Zen Buddhism and Psychoanalysis* (1960), *The Dogma of Christ* (1966) and *You Shall Be as Gods* (1966), a non-theistic interpretation of Jewish scriptures. [EM]

**Frost, Robert** (1874–1963). Poet. Born in San Francisco, he was brought to New England when he was 10, at his father's death. He went to Dartmouth College, married, studied at Harvard, and between 1900 and 1905 farmed in New Hampshire and worked in mills in Lowell, Massachusetts, and as editor and teacher. But although his first published poem appeared when he was 19 ('My Butterfly'), only 14 poems were printed before 1918, and *A Boy's Will*, his first book, published in England when he was 39. He had sold his farm, gone to London and cultivated the friendship of Edward Thomas. After three years and *North of Boston* (1914), he returned to America well known and settled in New Hampshire again. *New Hampshire* (1923) shows one of his few developments – towards politics and satire. *A Further Range* (1936) is more philosophically theoretical than earlier work, while the two *Masques* (1945, 1947) mark a third stage – concern with man's relations with God and ultimate metaphysical conditions. Frost by now had a wide public and numerous prizes and university posts and degrees, and was on the way to becoming America's unofficial laureate, tacitly acknowledged by his trips to Russia and Israel, and the invitation to read 'The Gift Outright' (1942) at President Kennedy's inauguration.

From first to last (*In the Clearing*, 1962) Frost did not experiment much with line and rhythm; *A Boy's Will* already includes 'Mowing' and 'The Pasture', which fix a part of his poetic character, unaltered in 'Mending Wall', 'The Death of the Hired Man' and 'After Apple Picking' (1914), 'The Witch of Coos', 'The Star-Splitter', and 'Stopping by Woods on a Snowy Evening' (1923), 'Design' (1936) and 'Directive' (1947). These poems take the even, Georgian movement and tune of Frost's English friends, such as Lascelles Abercrombie and Edward Thomas, and combine it with Emersonian and New England poetic and speech styles to project his characteristic assertive sentence of the Yankee farmer, sometimes wise, sometimes the anti-political village wiseacre, sometimes the broadly sceptical determinist. His finest lyrics and narrative poems create a non-urban relationship between man, landscape and sky, which is romantic and frequently uneasy inside the assured tone. The 'design of darkness' and the uncertainty of meaning and action which recur in his work and life were made bearable by the creative act and the stance of public poet. As recent volumes of his letters show (*Selected Letters of Robert Frost*, ed. L. Thompson, 1964, and *Letters of Robert Frost to Louis Untermeyer*, 1963), his 44 honorary degrees and national respect came at the end of a life of stoic loneliness, family misfortunes, fear of

mental unbalance, and profound distrust of the 'deep shadow' of melancholy. As he once said, 'irony is simply a kind of guardedness' and 'humour is the most engaging cowardice'. Poetry was his 'momentary stay' against disaster, and he had made his readers feel his own need for 'a word of assurance'. [EM]

*The Complete Poems* (1951); *Selected Prose*, ed. H. Cox and E. C. Latham (1966).
Sidney Cox, *A Swing of Birches: A Portrait of Robert Frost* (1957); ed. J. M. Cox, *Robert Frost: A Collection of Critical Essays* (1963); Daniel Smythe, *Robert Frost Speaks* (1965); Reuben A. Brewer, *The Poetry of Robert Frost* (1963); Lawrance Thompson, *Robert Frost: The Early Years* (1966); ed. E. C. Latham, *Interviews with Robert Frost* (1966).

**Frye, Northrop** (1912–    ). Literary critic. Though Canadian-born and now principal of Victoria College in Toronto, Frye has taken a central place in the development of modern American criticism and is one of the most influential of post-war theoretical critics. His general position is stated in *Anatomy of Criticism* (1957): criticism is a species of humane studies, a form of organized knowledge that can work by general principles deriving from the theoretical classification of various fundamental elements. These elements are a mixture of traditional generic classifications and mythological universals – which can, nonetheless, be seen as related to the changing cultural context of literature. [MB]

*Fables of Identity: Studies in Poetic Mythology* (1963); *The Well-Tempered Critic* (1963); *Fearful Symmetry : A Study of William Blake* (1947); *T. S. Eliot* (1963); *A Natural Perspective: The Development of Shakespearean Comedy and Romance* (1965); *The Return of Eden: Five Essays on Milton's Epics* (1965); *Fools of Time: Studies in Shakespearean Tragedy* (1967); *The Modern Century* (1967).
Ed. M. Krieger, *Northrop Frye in Modern Criticism* (1966).

**Fuchs, Daniel** (1909–    ). Novelist. Born in New York City. In 1961 his early novels – *Summer in Williamsburg* (1934), *Homage to Blenholt* (1936) and *Low Company* (1937) – were republished as *Three Novels* and re-established his reputation as a realist of Jewish slum life in Brooklyn, a closed world seen with humour and without political comment. He has lived and worked in Hollywood since the thirties and received the 1955 Academy Award for his scenario of *Love Me or Leave Me*. [EM]

**Fugitives, The.** A group of Southern poets, contributors to the *Fugitive*, a poetry magazine, 19 numbers of which were published in Nashville, Tennessee, from April 1922 to December 1925. The group comprised Donald ◊ Davidson, James Marshall Frank, Sidney Mttron Hirsch, Stanley Johnson, John Crowe ◊ Ransom, Alec B. Stevenson, Allen ◊ Tate, Walter Clyde Curry, Merrill ◊ Moore, William Yandell Elliott, William Frierson, Jesse Wills, Ridley Wills, Robert Penn ◊ Warren, Laura ◊ Riding (Gottschalk) and Alfred Starr. Andrew ◊ Lytle and Cleanth ◊ Brooks became closely associated with the group at the time of the magazine's demise. With the exceptions of Hirsch, a playwright, Frank and Stevenson, Nashville businessmen, and Laura Riding, wife of a faculty member of the University of Louisville, Kentucky, all the contributors were associated with Nashville's Vanderbilt University, as either students or teachers.

The Fugitives represent the most talented, cohesive group of creative writers America produced since the ◊ Transcendentalists. After 1925, Ransom, Tate and Warren all went on to make major contributions to American poetry; a psychiatrist in Boston, Merrill Moore continued to produce his 'American sonnets' with fantastic facility; Tate and Warren also became important novelists, and with Brooks and Ransom became the founders of the so-called ◊ 'New Criticism', which transformed the formal teaching and study of literature in America and elsewhere. Curry and Frierson produced works of literary scholarship, Elliott of political science ; Stanley Johnson published a novel, *The Professor* (1925), and Ridley Wills two novels: *Hoax* (1922) and *Harvey Landrum* (1924). Davidson remained most strongly pro-Southern, and has published poems and essays; Lytle has published four fine novels.

Despite its responsibility for the emergence of the New Criticism, the Fugitive movement, as its social and economic thinking most clearly reveals, was essentially a conservative one. Founded at a time when a rapid expansion of industrialism was widely seen as the answer to most of the South's problems, the group remained firmly committed to a traditional, regionalist, agrarian, Southern ideal. Ransom, Tate, Davidson, Warren and Lytle were among the 'Twelve Southerners' who defended an agrarian South in *I'll Take My Stand: The South and the Agrarian Tradition* (1930). The same group was joined by Brooks in the publication of a second agrarian volume, *Who Owns America? A Declaration of Independence* (1936). The Fugitive vision of a rural, non-industrial South reflected a wider philosophical conservatism. The Fugitive movement focused a rather Eliot-like reaction against many social, political and philosophical aspects of the modern world: progressive liberal optimism, Marxism, capitalism, philosophical relativism and rationalism. The campaign to preserve the agrarian tradition produced little effect; but by the end of the 1930s the movement's conservative ideology, touched with modernist overtones, had penetrated deeply into literary and intellectual circles in America.

The dominant tone of the poetry of the *Fugitive* was set by John Crowe Ransom. Ransom on the whole turned away from such contemporary doctrines as ◊ Imagism and free verse. His poems are classical in their attention to matters of formal discipline, metaphysical in their mannered verbal complexity and ironic wit. What they express with an elegance and sophistication of tone is a rather bleak view of the imperfect nature of the human condition. Fugitive criticism largely mirrors this kind of poetry, though it has dealt well and ably with modern literature and is influenced by some of its aesthetics. It finally arrives at a position of aesthetic formalism in which the work of literature is seen as autonomous – a complex verbal structure largely independent of any social, historical or philosophical background. The critic's work is the analysis of that independent verbal structure.

The Fugitive movement ended the idea that the South represented a cultural backwater; indeed its major figures launched that literary renaissance in the South which remains one of the most striking features of 20th-century American literature. [AH]

*Fugitives, An Anthology of Verse* (1928).
John M. Bradbury, *The Fugitives, A Critical Account* (1958); ed. R. R. Purdy, *Fugitives' Reunion: Conversations at Vanderbilt* (1959); Louise Conran, *The Fugitive Group: A Literary History* (1959); John L. Stewart, *The Burden of Time: The Fugitives and Agrarians* (1969).

**Fuller, Henry Blake** (1857–1929). Novelist. Born in Chicago. He wrote in a cosmopolitan vein that drew on numerous short visits to Europe and contributed important pieces of international fiction to American letters; but he is now best remembered, perhaps a little unfairly, as a 'realist'. Like several contemporaries he seesawed between realism and romance. His first two novels, *The Chevalier of Pensieri-Vani* (1890; written under the pseudonym 'Stanton Page') and *The Châtelaine of La Trinité* (1892), are historical romances set in Europe. His next two, *The Cliff-Dwellers* (1893), his best-known work, about workers in a skyscraper, and the excellent *With the Procession* (1895), were realist, with Chicago settings. Then followed other books of various kinds – *From the Other Side: Stories of Transatlantic Travel* (1898), which united his realistic American and his European materials; *The Last Refuge: A Sicilian Romance* (1900); *Under the Skylights* (1901), with a Chicago setting; *Waldo Trench and Others: Stories of Americans in Italy* (1908); *On the Stairs* (1918), which reverts to Chicago materials; *Not on the Screen* (1930), etc. A novelist of manners and a pioneer of the American city-novel, Fuller also wrote for Chicago newspapers and was closely involved with the Chicago magazine *Poetry* (◊ Little Magazines). [MB]

**Fuller, Margaret** (1810–50). Critic, Transcendentalist. She was educated by her father in her birthplace, Cambridgeport, Massachusetts, to a point where his will and possessiveness wrecked her childhood. She grew up a disturbed prodigy, with – as she said – 'a man's ambition with a woman's heart'. Emerson remarked that her friendships were 'chemical' in their demands. After her father's death she became a leading ◊ Transcendentalist, a friend of Emerson, Alcott's assistant, head teacher of a Providence school, and famous for her 'Conversations' and femininism. For two years she edited the *Dial*, an important collection of poetry, criticism, philosophy and translations of eastern literature. Her part in Brook Farm (◊ Ripley) is fictionalized in Hawthorne's *The Blithedale Romance*. *Summer on the Lakes* (1844) is a fascinating account of this gifted New England intellectual's confrontation with the frontier, the Indians in Oregon, and the immigrants in Milwau-

kee. *Woman in the Nineteenth Century* (1845) idealizes America as the redemptive centre of the world in which women would overcome man's tyranny and harmony would ensue. After her last job, writing first-rate criticism of American literature for Horace Greeley's New York *Tribune*, she sailed in 1846 for Europe, visited Wordsworth, Carlyle, Mazzini, George Sand, Chopin and, in Rome, the Marquis Ossoli, with whom she fell in love. The ship they and their son returned to America on was wrecked off Fire Island, and they were drowned. [EM]

*Writings*, ed. Mason Wade (1941).
Mason Wade, *Margaret Fuller: Whetstone of Genius* (1940); Madeleine B. Stern, *The Life of Margaret Fuller* (1942); ed. Perry Miller, *Margaret Fuller American Romantic* (1963).

**Fuller, R. Buckminster** (1895–    ). Engineer, poet, philosopher. Born in Milton, Massachusetts, he was educated at the U.S. Naval Academy and at Harvard, but received no academic degrees. His inventions are part of his life programme of intention to benefit mankind as directly as possible, and are too numerous to list completely; they include houses, an electric car, a world map, and geodesic and tensegrity structures. His first book, *Nine Chains to the Moon* (1938), contains most of his basic ideas for 'comprehensive anticipatory design science', the recycling of resources in order 'to do more with less', the rationalization of the Earth on a 'One Town World Plan', and the elimination of scarcity as the basis of both wretched human conditions and the philosophical basis of their perpetuation. His major works include: *Education Automation* (1962), *Untitled Epic Poem on the History of Industrialization* (1962), *No More Second Hand God* (1963), *Ideas and Integrities* (1963) and *Operating Manual for Spaceship Earth* (1969). *What I am Trying to Do* (1968) is a set of drawings with an introduction. Fuller's international influence has reached the prophetic stage. [EM]

Robert W. Marks, *The Dymaxion World of Buckminster Fuller* (1960); John McHale, *R. Buckminster Fuller* (1962); ed. James Meller, *The Buckminster Fuller Reader* (1970).

# G

**Gaddis, William** (1922– ). Novelist. His single major work is *The Recognitions* (1955), a large experimental, and elaborately organized novel on ruse and forgery rather in the manner of *Tristram Shandy*; it is based on the palindrome 'trade ye no mere moneyed art'. [DM]

**Gale, Zona** (1874–1938). Novelist, story writer, poetess, dramatist. Born in Portage, Wisconsin, she began a career in journalism which took her to New York. Her early stories reverted to mid-Western materials, treating them sentimentally in the local colourist manner, as titles like *Friendship Village* (1908) and *Heart's Kindred* (1915) suggest. But when she returned home with unpopular progressive and pacifist views she began to develop a more detached attitude to the region, and works like *Birth* (1918) and *Miss Lulu Bett* (1920), which she dramatized, reveal the repressiveness and middle-class conventionality of the mid-West and link her work with that of Sinclair ◊ Lewis. *When I Was a Little Girl* (1913) and *Portage, Wisconsin* (1928) are autobiography. Her later work, which includes the novel *Faint Perfume* (1923) and *Yellow Gentians and Blue* (1927), short stories, had great success. [MB]

August Derleth, *Still Small Voice: The Biography of Zona Gale* (1940).

**Gardner, Erle Stanley** (1889–1970). Detective-story writer. Born in Malden, Massachusetts. One of the literary phenomena of our time, he was for many years a prolific author of stylistically undistinguished but phenomenally successful novels which for the most part feature either the lawyer Perry Mason (*The Case of . . .*) or the District Attorney Douglas Selby (*The D.A. . . .*). Publishing also under the pseudonyms A. A. Fair and Charles J. Kenny, among others, Gardner, a lawyer, produced over 100 books since he first began writing in the early 1920s. Among his non-fictional works are several books about Baja California and *The Court of Last Resort* (1952), an account of his attempts to help men unjustly convicted of murder. [HD]

Alva Johnston, *The Case of Erle Stanley Gardner* (1947).

**Garland, Hamlin** (1860–1940). Novelist, story writer, memoirist. Born in West Salem, Wisconsin. An important voice in the mid-Western literary upsurge, and a significant spokesman for new realist techniques in writing, he grew up amid the hard realities of life in Iowa and South Dakota. He went to Boston, still a major literary centre, in 1884 to study, write and lecture, and here was influenced by the aesthetic theories of the realist William Dean ◊ Howells and the economic ideas of the reformer Henry ◊ George. He read in science, economics and social matters, as well as in American writing. The poverty and monotony of frontier life deeply affected him and, adopting a form of realism he called 'veritism', he wrote the tales in his first book, *Main-Travelled Roads: Six Mississippi Valley Stories* (1891), drawing on boyhood experience to explore the rural poor of the prairies and the social and economic forces behind agrarian hardship. Others in the same mood were collected in *Prairie Folks* (1893) and *Wayside Courtships* (1897) – later combined as *Other Main-Travelled Roads* (1910). In the 1890s active in the reform movement, he wrote several novels illustrating Populist principles. *Jason Edwards: An Average Man* (1892) dramatizes George's single-tax theory; but the most sustained is *Rose of Dutcher's Coolly* (1895), a realistic narrative of a Wisconsin girl's attempt to escape the brutalizing drudgery of farm life. All these exemplified 'veritism', a theory made explicit in the essay-collection *Crumbling Idols* (1894; repr. 1960), a statement of his literary radicalism (◊ Realism).

In 1893 he moved back to the mid-West and associated with a Chicago group of writers, which included Henry Blake ◊ Fuller, interested in regional realism. He now began to travel widely through the West, writing articles, joining a gold rush; and in 1899 made his first trip to England (where he came to know Shaw and Zangwill) and France. Over this period he published – in addition to *Her Mountain Lover* (1901), caricaturing English society – many works of fiction, most of them popular, sentimental romances of the Far West. Late in life he published eight volumes of rambling reminiscences, marked by a fascinating neo-scientific approach to experience – four deal with his family background, the others with his literary acquaintances. The first, *A Son of the Middle Border* (1917), has claims to be considered with *Main-Travelled Roads* as his best work. *A Daughter of the Middle Border* (1921; Pulitzer Prize) deals with the early years of his marriage; *Trail-Makers of the Middle Border* (1926) with his father's migration from Maine to Wisconsin; *Back-Trailers from the Middle Border* (1928) with his literary career. *Roadside Meetings* (1930) and *Companions on the Trail: A Literary Chronicle* (1931) are the more interesting of the accounts of literary contemporaries.

Though the literary revolution he in part pioneered was taken further by others, he remains interesting for his literary mode and his strong regional flavour. The long-established view that he was a victim of the genteel tradition (symbolized by his transfer from the radical journal *The Arena* to the more conventional *Century*) is now being modified. ◊ Fuller's portrait of him as Abner Joyce in *Under the Skylights* (1901) offers too simple an explanation of his defection from early literary ideals. His reputation, however, still rests on the stories of frontier life and the re-creation of the background to them in the autobiography. Although the theories of *Crumbling Idols* – an ultimately disappointing book – were never fully incorporated into the fiction, the accuracy with which he presented little-publicized aspects of American life marks an important development in the history of American literary realism and naturalism, while the memoirs do constitute a valuable and still interesting record of a vanished era. [HD]

*Diaries*, ed. D. Pizer (1968).
Donald Pizer, *Hamlin Garland's Early Work and Career* (1960); Jean Holloway, *Hamlin Garland: A Biography* (1960); ed. L. A. Arvidson, *Centennial Tributes* (1962).

**Garrigue, Jean** (1914– ). Poet. Born in Indiana, educated at the University of Chicago, she has taught at several colleges, including the University of Iowa and Bard, and travelled in Europe, where a number of

106

her poems are set. Though her range is not wide, and she deals usually with natural objects interfused with states of emotion, she is an able, convincing poet who works her material intensively, at length and with great vigour. Her best poems are probably those in which the background detail gives way to her argument, which is frequently in favour of hope or permanence found through love or poetry itself. Her volumes are *The Ego and the Centaur* (1947), *The Monument Rose* (1953), *A Water Walk by Villa d'Este* (1959), *Country without Maps* (1964), which contains some of her best poems to date, and *The Animal Hotel* (1966), a novel. [MB]

**Gass, William** (1924– ). Novelist. Born in North Dakota, he teaches philosophy at Purdue University. Gass has emerged as a major fiction writer of the 1960s, with an exciting insight into provincial life and a prose style of considerable power: *Omensetter's Luck* (1966), *In the Heart of the Heart of the Country* (1968 – a set of excellent stories – and *Willie Master's Lonesome Wife* (1968) – a hilarious fiction in the manner of Sterne and Blast. [EM]

**Gelber, Jack** (1932– ). Playwright. Born in Chicago. His reputation was made through the Living Theatre's New York production of *The Connection* (1959) by Julian Beck and Judith Malina, in which heroin addiction is the metaphor for other forms of social addiction and alienation. The jazz of Freddie Redd and Jackie McLean considerably helped the action. *The Apple* (1961), as the title implies, concerns temptation in New York, employing a variety of Brechtian and Absurd effects. *The Cuban Thing* (1968) uses the Castro revolution. *On Ice* (1964), his first novel, forsakes the inflexions of Pirandello and Charlie Parker for conventional picaresque meandering in New York. [EM]

**George, Henry** (1839–97). Political economist, editor. He was born in Philadelphia, left school at 14, and after various jobs became a compositor and editor in California. After years of near-poverty he became a journalist and essayist, a self-taught man making use of his experience to understand economic and social problems. What he termed his 'ecstatic vision' (in 1869), that land value is related to the growth of the community around it more than man's labour on it, inspired his *Our Land and Land Policy* (1871), a pamphlet attacking land grants for railway companies. His work as editor of the Oakland *Transcript*, experience of land speculation in California, and first-hand knowledge of economic inequalities led to his best-selling *Progress and Poverty* (1879), which gained him an international reputation. Its basis is the 'single-tax' argument that a tax on unearned increment from land would prevent the absorption of surplus wealth through land rents and enable the community to reap the land's value according to their creation of its value. His now largely discounted ideas were helped into circulation by his vivid jargon-free prose. Clubs were established in support of his doctines, which influenced many reformist figures, including William Dean ◊ Howells, Hamlin ◊ Garland, Tolstoy and Bernard Shaw. [DKA/HD]

*The Complete Works* (10 vols., 1906–11).
George R. Geiger, *The Philosophy of Henry George* (1933); Charles A. Barker, *Henry George* (1955).

**Gibson, William** (1914–   ). Playwright. Born in New York. His *Two for the Seesaw* (1959) is a neat dialogue between a Bronx girl with ulcers and a mid-Western lawyer. *Dinny and the Witches* (1959), a fantasy, appeared off Broadway, and *The Miracle-Worker* (1960), the story of Helen Keller's early training, became an international success. *A Cry of Players*, originally written and produced in 1947, was revived in 1968. *A Mass for the Dead* (1968) is a prose autobiographical work. [EM]

**Gilbert, Jack** (1925–   ). Poet. He has spent most of his literary life on the West Coast and been involved in the recent movements in poetry there. He taught creative writing at the University of California and San Francisco State College. His one volume, *Views of Jeopardy* (1962), translates classical myth into a vision of the modern Orpheus singing obsessively to the unattentive hell of New York or San Francisco. [BP]

Ed. Howard Nemesov, *Poets on Poetry* (1967); *Genesis West*, I, 1 (1962).

**Gilder, Richard Watson** (1844–1909). Newspaperman, poet. He was born in New Jersey and went into newspapers there,

later becoming an influential figure as editor of *Scribner's Monthly* and *The Century Magazine*. He had great contemporary fame as a poet for volumes such as *Five Books of Songs* (1900). [MB]

**Gill, Brendan** (1914–   ). Novelist, story writer. He was born in Hartford, Connecticut, and after graduating from Yale joined the editorial staff of the *New Yorker*, in which many of his stories have appeared. He is an elegant and amusing writer of social observation. His first novel, *The Trouble of One House* (1950), takes as its subject a dying woman, and *The Day the Money Stopped* (1957) is a delightful character comedy with a social point. [MB]

**Ginsberg, Allen** (1926–   ). Poet. Born in New Jersey, the son of the poet and teacher Louis Ginsberg; his mother was a Russian emigrant, active on the left, whom he laments in one of his finest poems, 'Kaddish', in which he emotionally bridges the political gaps between the crucial American generations of the thirties and fifties. After school in Paterson and study at Columbia University, he worked at various jobs – café dish-washer, seaman, welder, night porter and book reviewer for *Newsweek*. Meanwhile he studied and absorbed the particular inspirations of his poetry, Blake and Whitman, and experimented with states of consciousness with drugs. He exploded into the literary scene with *Howl and Other Poems* (1956) as a major poet, and, with Kerouac and Burroughs, as the centre of the ◊ Beat Generation group. He consolidated his poetic art in *Kaddish and Other Poems* (1960), *Reality Sandwiches* (1963) and *Planet News* (1969). *Empty Mirror* (1960) is a collection of poems which are mostly preparations for his central achievement, and *The Change* (1963) is two poems written in India and Japan in 1963. 'Howl' is a lament for the sickness of urban America and for poets, artists and intellectuals in the Ike–Nixon era, written in long-breathed lines and highly wrought language developed from Blake, Whitman, Melville, William Carlos Williams and Hart Crane. Ginsberg's characteristic poems at this stage were either short, intensely personal lyrics or long rhapsodic celebrations of ecstasy, the search for the godhead, and the expansion of consciousness. His visionary ability to invite the reader to an open exchange of honesty and tenderness is valuable and extraordinary, both in his poetry and in his life generally. His more recent work develops a long, discursive and socially conscious and critical poem, partly based on transcriptions of verbal recording into a tape-recorder of ideas, images and responses while travelling. A good example is 'Wichita Vortex Sutra' (1966, in *Planet News*), and *TV Baby Poems* (1967) contains two such poems. The method is developed in *Ankor Wat* (1968) and *Airplane Dreams* (1968). From being a Beat Generation poet Ginsberg has responded to the America of his time to become an intensely political poet, a man active throughout the world in promoting the free life, and attacking authoritarianism in Czechoslovakia, Russia and America alike. [EM]

*A Casebook on the Beat*, ed. T. Parkinson (1961); *The Beats*, ed. S. Krim (1960).
E. Lucie-Smith, *Mystery in the Universe: Notes on an Interview with Allen Ginsberg* (1965); J. Clellon Holmes, *Nothing More to Declare* (1967); Lawrence Lipton, *The Holy Barbarians* (1959); *Paris Review* 37 (Spring, 1966) (interview with Thomas Clark); Jane Kramer, *Allen Ginsberg in America* (1969).

**Glasgow, Ellen** (1874–1945). Novelist, poet. Born in Richmond, Virginia, the Old Dominion to which she limited her fiction and which in her time was part of the post-Reconstruction South. As a child her health prevented her from attending school and her education came from her father's library and her later reading of the great European novelists and the British evolutionists. She did not marry. After destroying an adolescent novel, she published *The Descendant* (1897), a novel concerning a New York Bohemia she hardly knew. Although she often travelled, and did live in New York for a short time, Richmond was her home. She published a volume of poems, *The Freeman*, in 1902. *Virginia* (1913) brought her popular acclaim, and *Barren Ground* (1925) established her critical success. *In This Our Life* (1941) gained a Pulitzer Prize (1947). Besides her 19 novels she wrote short stories, essays, and an autobiography, *The Woman Within* (1954). Her fiction is an acute account of the old agrarian South invaded by industrialization, of a society dying under out-moded manners, opinions and methods, and of a woman's place in these changes. In *A Certain Measure* (1943) a collection of criticism, her 19th-century philosophy of

nature against human nature insists on the courage of an inner integrity to carry a person through bad times. *The Voice of the People* (1900), *The Battle-Ground* (1902) and *The Deliverance* (1904) are social historical novels with this interior action. *Barren Ground* and *Vein of Iron* (1935), her finest novels, both present the survival of girls, from declining Southern families, by their stoicism of work and gritty selfhood. Ellen Glasgow's realism rejects both the despair and the arrogance of the South, and although approaching sexual relations rather drily, her delineation of family life is keen. [EM]

*Collected Stories*, ed. R. K. Meeker (1963); *Letters*, ed. B. Rouse (1958).
F. P. W. McDowell, *Ellen Glasgow and the Ironic Art of Fiction* (1960); Louis Auchincloss, *Ellen Glasgow* (University of Minnesota Pamphlet, 1964); M. Geismar, *Rebels and Ancestors: The American Novel 1890–1915* (1953).

**Godfrey, Thomas** (1736–63). Playwright, poet. Born in Philadelphia, he was the author of the first play by a native American to be acted professionally on the American stage. *The Prince of Parthia: A Tragedy*, written before 1763, published in 1765 and acted in Philadelphia in 1767, draws on Elizabethan and Jacobean dramatic conventions and language, and deals with passion and violence in oriental Parthia. Godfrey also published *The Court of Fancy: A Poem* (1762) and *Juvenile Poems on Various Subjects*, printed with *The Prince of Parthia* in 1765. [MB]

**Goetz, George.** ♢ Calverton, Victor Francis.

**Goggan, John Patrick** ♢ Patrick, John.

**Gold, Herbert** (1924–    ). Novelist. He was born in Ohio, studied in Paris and at Columbia, and lives in San Francisco, after finding New York 'too nervous' for a writer. He has taught in universities, received prizes, but remains a highly independent writer and critic. With his first five novels – *Birth of a Hero* (1951), *The Prospect before Us* (1954), *The Man Who Was Not with It* (1956), *The Optimist* (1959) and *Therefore Be Bold* (1960) – he established himself as a professional novelist of the anxieties and tensions of the fifties. His collected stories, written in the same racy, topical style, appear in *Love and Like* (1960).

His best novel to date is *Salt* (1963), a hectic account of New York middle-class degeneracy. *The Age of Happy Problems* (1962) is 18 sharp essays on American society. Gold's taut, highly metaphored style is the exact vehicle for that contemporary vision he shares with the writers in his shrewdly introduced collection, *Fiction of the Fifties* (1959). *Fathers* (1967) takes the form of a memoir novel about first- and second-generation Americans in this century. *The Great American Jackpot* (1970) adopts a sour attitude towards San Francisco in the 1960s. [E M]

*Genesis West*, II, 2 and 3 (1964) (interview).

**Gold, Michael** (pseud. of Irving Granich) (1894–      ). Novelist, playwright. Born on New York's Lower East Side, he was, under his pen-name, an important contributor to American 'proletarian realist' letters. One of the group of political radicals with literary interests that included Max ◊ Eastman and Floyd ◊ Dell, and gathered around the magazines the *Masses*, the *Liberator* and the *New Masses*, he edited the last in a particularly revolutionary phase (◊ Little Magazines). He was also associated with the ◊ Provincetown Players, along with John ◊ Reed, Dell and of course Eugene O'Neill, and wrote several plays. With the upsurge of literary-social criticism in the 1920s, he became, through his *New Masses* mouthpiece, an influential voice advancing virtually a Stalinist line, promoting socialist–communist theories of literature, attacking 'genteel' writing (Thornton Wilder was a famous victim). Plays include *Fiesta* (1925), set in Mexico, and *Battle Hymn* (1936; with Michael Blankfort), about John Brown. *120 Million* (1929) and *Change the World!* (1937) are articles. But his best-known work is a novel, *Jews without Money* (1935), drawing on the world of his childhood. [M B]

*The Mike Gold Reader*, ed. S. Sillen (1954); *Proletarian Literature in the United States*, ed. Granville Hicks (1935).
Daniel Aaron, *Writers on the Left* (1961).

**Golden, Harry** (1902–      ). Essayist, humorist. Of New York Jewish background, he moved to Charlotte, North Carolina, and started the *Carolina Israelite*, a monthly 'personal journal' written by himself and with a national circulation which unfortunately ceased publication in 1968. Four selections of his notes and essays from it

have appeared – *Only in America* (1958), *For 2c Plain* (1959), *Enjoy! Enjoy!* (1960) and *The Harry Golden Omnibus* (1962). Golden is the Jew as cracker-barrel philosopher, and exploits the irony of the mixture; his pieces are mainly nostalgic reminiscence or shrewd comic social commentary, but he excoriates segregation and supports the Negro struggle. He has also published a biography of Carl ◊ Sandburg. [M B]

*The Right Time* (1969) (autobiography).

**Goldman, William** (1931–      ). Novelist. *The Temple of Gold* (1957), an immensely popular novel on Fitzgerald themes transferred to the sixties, sympathetically explores adolescence and 'delinquency'. There followed *Your Turn to Curtsey, My Turn to Bow* (1958), *Soldier in the Rain* (1960) and *Boys and Girls Together* (1964), a highly successful novel on his familiar youth themes. But *No Way to Treat a Lady* (1964) treats themes of sexual violence and murder within a blandly innocent prose, very much part of the black humour of the sixties. *The Season* (1969) is a critical attack on Broadway and theatre critics. *Butch Cassidy and the Sundance Kid* (1969) is the screenplay of George Roy Hill's film. [E M]

**Goodman, Paul** (1911–      ). Novelist, poet, playwright, psychologist, philosopher. He was born in New York and studied at the City College and Chicago University. The range and quality of his work and his ability to speak directly without the obscuring jargon of his special fields has made him a figure of major importance in the revolutionary American situation of the fifties and sixties. Since his first work in *New Directions* in the forties his reputation as a comprehensive critic and creative writer has grown. *Drawing the Line*, which brings together his *May Pamphlet* and additional materials written in 1962, is the clearest statement of his anarchist principles and his attack on political and psychological ideologies and 'sociolatry', the fetishism of over-organized society and its theory. *Communitas* (1947, with his brother Percival Goodman) is a comprehensive study of comparative city planning, with concrete recommendations. *Gestalt Therapy* (1951, with F. S. Perls and Ralph Hefferline) is a textbook of psychology and analysis, influenced by the psychologist Wilhelm ◊ Reich. The highly influential *Growing Up Absurd* (1960) is a study of youth and delinquency, using materials from literature, psychology and political theory. *Utopian Essays and Proposals* (1962) is a collection of articles on subjects ranging from Reich to American *avant garde* writing. *The Community of Scholars* (1963) and *Compulsory Mis-Education* (1964) criticize, respectively, the idea and practice of the university in America, and the notion and effects of 'formal schooling' within a structure of compulsory education. The nonconformism, constructiveness and practicability of these materials is the basis of *People or Personnel* (1965), and the same radicalism, pacifism and clarity penetrates his plays: *The Cave of Machpelah* (1959), and those in *The Facts of Life* (1965) – *Faustina* (1949), *The Young Disciple* (1955) and *Jonah* (1965). His short stories are collected in *The Break-Up of Our Camp* (1949) and *Our Visit to Niagara* (1960). His very individual and rather didactic poems are in *The Lordly Hudson* (1962), *Hawkweed* (1967) and *North Percy* (1968). His criticism appears in *Art and Social Nature* (1946), *Kafka's Prayer* (1947) and *The Structure of Literature* (1954), a really useful study of plot structures. *The Empire City* (1959) is a large complex novel of New York from the thirties to the fifties, and comprises *The Grand Piano* (1942), *The State of Nature* (1964), *The Dead Spring of* (1950) and *The Holy Terror* (1959). *Making Do* (1963) is a novel about a group of unconventional young men and women whose behaviour challenges middle-class standards. *Five Years: Thoughts during a Useless Time* (1967) is a frank autobiographical study, and *Like a Conquered Province* (1967) a study of 'the moral ambiguity of America' through examinations of education, planning, ecology, decentralization and the media. Goodman is a prime example of fertile discontent and original thinking in America, part of a great tradition which includes Thoreau and other anarchists and rebels. His influence on contemporary dissent and reconstruction is inestimable. [EM]

*Adam and His Works: Collected Stories* (1968).

**Gordon, Caroline** (1895–    ). Novelist, short-story writer, critic. Born in Todd Co., Kentucky. Married Allen ◊ Tate in 1924. A sense of failure and disintegration, both personal and social, and a consequent

search for salvation, characterize her fiction; hence the history of the South provides her with a powerful image for her vision of the human predicament. Her first four novels are set in the region around Clarksville, Tennessee, including part of Kentucky, where she grew up. *Penhally* (1931) relates the history of four generations of a Kentucky plantation family as an index of the disruption of a culture. *Aleck Maury, Sportsman* (1934) shows an individual's search to resolve this same disintegration of social values. *The Garden of Adonis* (1937), which confronts the social and economic conflicts of the changing South more directly, also shows another form of personal salvation, agrarian retreat, as inadequate. *None Shall Look Back* (1937) returns to the Penhally family and shows how the Civil War is largely responsible for the destruction of the social basis of its way of life. With *Green Centuries* (1941), she moves back to frontier North Carolina and Tennessee in the 18th century, bringing together European and Indian cultures to illuminate Western man's ultimately self-destructive drives. *The Woman on the Porch* (1944) once again employs a passionate, sensitive woman as the principal victim of life's failures. *The Forest of the South* (1946) and *Old Red and Other Stories* (1963) are fine collections of stories.

Her most recent novels, *The Strange Children* (1951) and *The Malefactors* (1956), show Miss Gordon's controlled, almost clinical, vision of individual disintegration leading her towards a religious definition of the meaning of salvation. *How to Read a Novel* (1957) is a valuable contribution to criticism of fiction; and with Allen Tate she edited *The House of Fiction; An Anthology of the Short Story* (1950). [AH]

Andrew Lytle, 'Caroline Gordon and the Historic Image', *Sewanee Review*, LVII (Autumn, 1949); Vivienne Koch, 'The Conservatism of Caroline Gordon', in *Southern Renascence*, ed. L. D. Rubin, Jr, and R. D. Jacobs (1953); F. P. W. McDowell, *Caroline Gordon* (U. of Minnesota Pamphlet, 1966).

**Gover, Robert** (1929–    ). Novelist. His first novel, *One Hundred Dollar Misunderstanding* (1962), won considerable attention for its relationship between Kitten, a 14-year-old Negro prostitute, and a college sophomore ; his third novel, *Here Goes Kitten* (1964), returns to the same two characters with the same white liberal fun.

Between these two came *The Maniac Responsible* (1963), a highly wrought and rhetorical study of a murderer, and after them, *Poorboy at the Party* (1966). *J. C. Saves* (1968) is the third instalment of Kitten's adventure. Gover is skilful, amusing and culturally observant, but also sentimental. [M B]

**Goyen, William** (1915– ). Novelist. Born in Texas, he went into the navy and later taught at the University of Houston, Texas, and the New School for Social Research, New York. His first novel, *The House of Breath* (1950), already showed his characteristically virtuoso poetic and mythic style in which the plot and characters are embedded. In his short stories *Ghost and Flesh* (1952) it is again the charged style which impresses; *The Faces of Blood Kindred* (1960) contains highly atmospheric stories of chance revelations of family connexions. His second novel, *In a Farther Country* (1955), is a series of stories centred on a Spanish-American woman and again written in a richly wrought manner, which recognizes the fact that the normal is frequently uncanny. *The Fair Sister* (1963), a novel expanded from an earlier story called 'Savata, My Fair Sister', shows Goyen firmly established in the body of Southern writers of the fantastically normal – Eudora ◊ Welty, Carson ◊ McCullers, Flannery ◊ O'Connor – with his poetic versions of local idiom and relish for warped intensities of life. But through the wrought-up prose the comic satire on the popular religion of camp meetings and preachers is clear. So is his old-fashioned condescension towards Negroes. [EM]

**Granich, Irving.** ◊ Gold, Michael.

**Grau, Shirley Ann** (1929– ). Novelist, short-story writer. Born in New Orleans. Her early fiction is concerned with the primitive inhabitants of the coastal islands and bayous west of the mouth of the Mississippi River; these people, mixed French and Spanish in origin, isolated by geography, poverty and race, are well documented in *The Black Prince and Other Stories* (1955) and *The Hard Blue Sky* (1958), an episodic novel. Action and event are more prominent than psychological complexity, but characters and setting are observed with clarity. *The Hard Blue Sky* is particularly impressive for its sense of the subordination of human action to the power of the natural world. In *The House on Coliseum Street* (1961), a more introspective, psychological novel, the enervating heat and humidity of the New Orleans summer match the passivity and pointlessness of the life of the protagonist. *The Keepers of the House* (1964) is wider in scope than any of her earlier novels – the story of a Southern family destroyed by divisions within itself, but fighting back against a corrupt community. But here as previously a strain of over-simplifying primitive romanticism prevents her from the fullest exploration of the issues her novel raises. [A II]

Louise Y. Gossett, 'Primitives and Violence: Shirley Ann Grau', in *Violence in Recent Southern Fiction* (1965).

**Green, Paul Eliot** (1894– ). Dramatist. From North Carolina, he has written conventional plays about his home State, including *Abraham's Bosom* (1926), a courageous work about race conflict in the South, *The House of Connelly* (1931), landowners and tenant farmers in conflict, and *Native Son* (1941; with Richard Wright). But his reputation rests with his open-air productions derived from legend, folklore and history, a native American theatre whose plays he calls 'symphonic drama'. His achievement, independent of Broadway, is a combination of ambitious experiment, poetic language and a real feeling for America's past. *The Lost Colony* (1937) uses music, dance, pageant and dialogue to present the origins of Roanoke Island, where it was played. *The Highland Call* (1939) does the same for the Scots North Carolina settlement of Cape Fear River Valley, and *The Common Glory* (1947) uses the history of Jefferson and Virginia, 1775–82. *The Founders* (1957) dramatizes the Jamestown colony. *Texas* (1966) is one of his most recent outdoor dramas. He also wrote the libretto for Kurt Weill's musical, *Johnny Johnson* (1936). [EM]

*Five Plays of the South* (1963).
Ed. R. Walser, *Paul Green of Chapel Hill* (1951).

**Greenberg, Samuel** (1843–1917). Poet. He was born in Austria and reached the U.S.A. when he was 7. He survived lower East Side New York squalor and, while suffering from tuberculosis in hospital, read poetry for the first time and began to write poems. Nothing was published in his lifetime, but the manuscripts reached Hart ♢ Crane, who was impressed enough with his sensuously powerful metaphors to use them and their method in his own work. [EM]

*Poems: A Selection from the Manuscripts*, intr. Allen Tate (1947).

**Greenwich Village.** A section of New York City in Lower Manhattan which has had long literary associations – with ♢ Paine, ♢ Poe, ♢ James, ♢ Whitman, ♢ Twain and others. From about 1910 onward it became a distinct artistic and literary community, because of its low rents, European flavour and literary associations; its cold-water flats and studios and its general freedom made it a centre of American ♢ Bohemianism. During the 1920s it became a stepping stone for expatriation (♢ Expatriates) and Paris, a movement encouraged by rising rents. Caroline Ware, in *Greenwich Village, 1920–1930: A Comment on American Civilization in the Post-War Years* (1935), gives an interesting sociological analysis of this phase. Again after the Second World War it became a thriving Bohemian centre, spreading outward from the now fashionable and expensive core, and its proliferation of coffee houses, jazz centres and off-Broadway playhouses gives it a distinctive pattern of life. Throughout this century it has abounded in ♢ little magazines and movements. The magazines include the *Little Review*, the *Masses*, the *Seven Arts* and the *Quill*; it also now produces an interesting paper, *Village Voice*. Those associated with it include Floyd ♢ Dell, Maxwell ♢ Bodenheim, Eugene ♢ O'Neill, Edna St Vincent ♢ Millay, E. E. ♢ Cummings, John ♢ Reed, Willa ♢ Cather and Max ♢ Eastman, and more recently many 'hip' and 'beat' writers including Norman ♢ Mailer, who has contributed important pieces to the *Village Voice*. Among its many theatre groups special mention should be made of the Greenwich Village Players, an outgrowth of the ♢ Provincetown Players. Reminiscences appear in Alfred Kreymbourg, *Troubador* (1925), Max Eastman, *Enjoyment of Living* (1948), Alyse Gregory, *The Day is Gone* (1948) and Henry W. Lanier, *Greenwich Village Today and Yesterday* (1949). The active and exciting post-Second-World-War phase is best reported in Albert Parry, *Garrets and Pretenders* (1960), and in two articles in the special New York number of *Dissent*, VIII (Summer, 1961). [MB]

**Gregory, Horace** (1898– ). Poet, translator, critic. He was born in Milwaukee, Wisconsin, and after attending the university there became a writer in New York, publishing his first volume of poems, *Chelsea Rooming House*, in 1930 (it appeared in England as *Rooming House*, 1932). He then taught classics and modern poetry at Sarah Lawrence College, and has published many further volumes of poems, translations from the classics, literary criticism and essays on art. As a poet he is conveniently represented in *Poems 1930–1940* (1941), *Selected Poems* (1951) and *Collected Poems* (1964), which won the Bollingen Prize. Gregory's poetry has strongly marked social concerns and a strong vernacular element; at the same time there is a clarity and distillation drawn from his devotion to the classics. His excellent idiomatic translation of the *Odes of Catullus* (1931) shows the force of this influence. (He has also translated Ovid's *Metamorphoses*, 1958.) His literary criticism includes a sympathetic early book on D. H. Lawrence, *Pilgrim of the Apocalypse* (1933), a volume of essays on American poetry, *The Shield of Achilles* (1944), and *The Dying Gladiator* (1961). *The World of James McNeill Whistler* (1961) is the best biography of this painter. With his wife, Marya ♢ Zaturenska, he wrote the very useful *A History of American Poetry: 1900–1940* (1946). [MB]

**Grey, Zane** (1875–1939). Best-selling Western novelist. Born in Zanesville, Ohio. In the development of the Western into a convention with enormous popular appeal and distinct codes of chivalry and toughness, the novels of Zane Grey – originally an Ohio dentist – have played a great part. He produced over 60 books, selling over 15 million copies. His characters, heroes and villains, are usually cowboys. *The Last of the Plainsmen* (1908), an early book, is said by *aficionados* to be one of the best; but it was *Riders of the Purple Sage* (1912) that won him his first popular success, and thereafter came a wealth of others, many published posthumously. [MB]

Jean Kerr, *Zane Grey: Man of the West* (1950).

**Griffin, John Howard** (1902– ). He was born in Texas, served in the Pacific in the Second World War, travelled in Europe, and has been a professional lecturer in music, aesthetics and history. He was blinded in the war and recovered his eyesight recently. His novel *The Devil Rides Outside* (1952) is outstanding, and he has since written *Nuni* (1956); but he is famous for his experiences, disguised as a Negro, through the South, which appeared in *Sepia* magazine and subsequently as *Black Like Me* (1961). [EM]

*The John Howard Griffin Reader* (1968).

**Griswold, Rufus W(ilmot)** (1815–57). Editor, anthologist. Born in Benson, Vermont. He replaced Edgar Allan ◊ Poe as editor of the famous and well-paying *Graham's Magazine* in Philadelphia, and through that, his editorship of the *International Literary Monthly*, and his famous anthologies – *The Poets and Poetry of America* (1842), *Prose Writers of America* (1847) and *Female Poets of America* (1848) – exercised great influence over mid-century taste. He promoted Poe but, as his literary executor and 'friend', presented him in a biography and a memoir to his edition of Poe's works (1850) as 'satanic' and corrupt. This and factual dishonesties in biography and editing have not endeared him to subsequent scholars and Poe-defenders. [MB]

**Grossman, Alfred** (1927–    ). Novelist. Grossman writes with confidence and panache of the milieu of New York City office-and-apartment life, though his well-shod heroes drop from time to time into the seedier world of delinquency and dereliction. His usual pattern, followed in each of his three novels – *Acrobat Admits* (1959), *Many Slippery Errors* (1963) and *Marie Beginning* (1964) – is to take a hero who feels constricted by the niceties and exigencies of his buttoned-down life and plunge him for a while into a more-or-less self-willed topseyturveydom. From his contact with the 'forbidden' and *outré*, the hero returns to the upper world more integrated. Recently, as his fiction has begun to approximate the 'black humour' of Terry ◊ Southern and Thomas ◊ Pynchon, he has shifted his focus on to the female guide-figures to his underworlds. [AG]

**Group Theatre.** An important association of actors, dramatists and producers, some from the ◊ Theatre Guild, who under Harold ◊ Clurman, Cheryl Crawford and Lee Strasberg formed their own organization for plays of 'social significance' in 1931. Their first success on Broadway was Paul ◊ Green's *The House of Connelly* (1931), and subsequently they offered 23 productions, including work by ◊ Anderson, ◊ Lawson, ◊ Kingsley, Irwin ◊ Shaw, ◊ Saroyan and ◊Odets. The Group was united in radical politics and Stanislavskian acting and production methods. After its dissolution in 1941, its method principles at least were continued into Strasberg's Actor's Studio. [EM]

H. Clurman, *The Fervent Years* (1945).

**Guest, Edgar A(lbert)** (1881–1959). Journalist, famous bad poet. Born in England, he came to the U.S.A. at 10. He wrote a daily poem for the Detroit *Free Press*, full of folksy morality. Among the many collections are *A Heap o' Livin'* (1916) ('It takes a heap o' livin' in a house t' make it home') and *Just Folks* (1917). *Collected Verse* appeared in 1934, though Guest had many, many more poems to come. [MB]

**Gunther, John** (1901–70). Journalist. Born in Chicago, he became a reporter on the Chicago *Daily News* in 1922 and gained a reputation particularly for his reports from Germany in the thirties. In 1936 he produced the first of his famous books, *Inside Europe*, which set the pattern of the series which followed: *Inside Asia* (1939), *Inside Latin America* (1941), *Inside USA*, (1947), *Inside Africa* (1955), *Inside Russia Today* (1958), *Inside Europe Today* (1961). These are digests of facts, entertainingly put together with a minimum of commitment. He also wrote *The High Cost of Hitler* (1940), *Roosevelt in Retrospect* (1950), *General Douglas McArthur* (1951), *President Eisenhower* (1952), *Death, Be Not Proud* (1949, on the brain cancer of his young son), and *A Fragment of Autobiography* (1962). [EM]

# H

**Hadas, Moses** (1900–66). Scholar. Born in Georgia and educated at Emory University, the Jewish Theological Seminary and Columbia University, where he was Professor of Greek from 1953. His eminence as a Hellenist was famous through *Hellenistic Culture: Fusion and Diffusion* (1959), *Humanism* (1960) and many other volumes. He was also a scholar of Old Testament period culture and introduced and translated the delightful *Three Greek Romances* (1954). [EM]

**Hale, Edward Everett** (1822–1909). Popular author, clergyman, scholar. A Boston Unitarian clergyman, at one time chaplain to the United States Senate, he published widely in a variety of fields. Stories were collected in *If, Yes, and Perhaps* (1868), containing his famous tale 'The Man without a Country', about a naval officer who suffers from a wish never to see the States again. He wrote various kinds of social, historical, satirical and supernatural fiction; utopian and philanthropic promotion; and two excellent volumes of memoirs, *A New England Boyhood* (1893) and *Memories of a Hundred Years* (2 vols., 1902). [MB]

Edward Everett Hale, Jr, *The Life and Letters of Edward Everett Hale* (2 vols., 1917).

**Hall, Donald** (1928–    ). Poet. He was born in Connecticut, educated at Harvard and Oxford, where his poem 'Exile' won the Newdigate Prize and was published by the Fantasy Press. He has published several volumes – *To the Loud Wind and Other Poems* (1955), *Exiles and Marriages* (1955), *The Dark Houses* (1958) and *A Roof of Tiger Lilies* (1964). Like several young American poets he has united the ironical formalism of much post-war English poetry and the more speculative, subjective manner of much recent American verse. Some of Hall's poems reach out towards social themes, and towards overt discovery ('Man learns by love, and not by metaphor'); others are concerned with rendering the vigour of a thing, a relationship, a cultural heritage. He has also edited an encyclo-

pedia of modern poetry and several anthologies, including the Penguin *Contemporary American Verse* (1962). *String Too Short to Be Saved* (1962) is a series of reminiscences of boyhood holidays in New Hampshire. [MB]

**Hall, James** (1793–1868). Journalist, editor. The Philadelphian banker and lawyer was one of the first Americans to record frontier legends. His books include *Letters from the West* (1828), *Tales of the Border* (1835) and *Sketches of History, Life and Manners in the West* (2 vols., 1834–5). He founded and edited the *Illinois Monthly Magazine* (1830–2), the first Western literary journal, and the *Western Monthly Magazine* (1832–6). [EM]

J. T. Flanagan, *James Hall: Literary Pioneer of the Ohio Valley* (1950).

**Hall, James N.** ◊ Nordhoff, Charles.

**Halleck, Fitz-Greene** (1790–1867). Poet. Born in Guilford, Connecticut, he became an important figure in the lively literary scene of early-19th-century New York, in its 'Knickerbocker' period. A friend of Washington Irving and James Fenimore Cooper, he was first a clerk in a banking house, then personal secretary to John Jacob Astor, the merchant and a patron of literary men. In 1819 Halleck and Joseph Rodman ◊ Drake produced the famous 'Croaker' poems, a series of humorous and satirical odes printed anonymously in the New York *Evening Post*; in 1860 they appeared in book form as *The Croakers*. Halleck's other famous satire was *Fanny* (1821), which mocked contemporary *nouveaux riches*. A tour to Europe in 1822 produced two of his best poems, 'Alnwick Castle' and 'Burns', collected in *Alnwick Castle, with Other Poems* (1827). Campbell, Byron and Scott particularly influenced him, and he was an editor of Byron and of *Selections from the British Poets* (1840). His work shows ways in which English romanticism, both as a sensibility and as a literary technique, could be adapted by American writers to American materials –

as in 'Red Jacket' (1828), about an Indian chief, 'The Field of Grounded Arms' (1831), about the Battle of Saratoga, 'Young America' (1865), and the unfinished 'Connecticut'. A minor poet, highly regarded in his day, he undoubtedly helped to form a whole phase of American literary sensibility. *The Poetical Works* first appeared in 1847 and went through three revised editions in the poet's lifetime. [MB]

*The Poetical Writings*, ed. J. G. Wilson (1869).
James G. Wilson, *The Life and Letters of Fitz-Greene Halleck* (1869); Nelson F. Adkins, *Fitz-Greene Halleck: An Early Knickerbocker Wit and Poet* (1930).

**Hammett, Dashiell** (1894–1961). Detective-story writer. He served in the army in the First World War, and subsequently worked as a private detective for a Pinkerton Agency, in San Francisco, before he began to write his famous tough detective novels. He re-enlisted for the Second World War, and served in the Aleutians. His heroes, Sam Spade and the Thin Man, are universally known, and his reputation has been strong in intellectual as well as popular quarters (he was admired by Sinclair Lewis, Robert Graves, André Gide, etc.) because of his economical style and capacity to catch the tone of a cool American toughness. He helped to sketch a new American folk-hero, akin to the Hemingway hero, whose apotheosis came in film (for which Hammett wrote). His novels are *Red Harvest* (1929), now often considered the best, with its anonymous Continental Operative hero; *The Dain Curse* (1929); *The Maltese Falcon* (1930), which introduces Sam Spade and which had most influence on subsequent detective writers like Raymond ◊ Chandler; *The Glass Key* (1931); and *The Thin Man* (1932). Five of these were reissued by his friend Lillian ◊ Hellman in *The Novels of Dashiell Hammett* (1966). Hammett's detectives (particularly the Continental Operative), though tough, also use intelligence and observation to meet crime. Many of his stories and novels first appeared in the popular detective magazine *Black Mask*. Some of the stories appeared in *The Adventures of Sam Spade* (1944) and *The Creeping Siamese and Other Stories* (1950), and a selection with a biographical introduction by Lillian Hellman, *The Big Knockover* (1966), includes *Tulip*, an unfinished autobiographical novel. [MB]

**Hansberry, H.** ◊ Negro Literature.

**Harland, Henry** (1861–1905). Novelist, story writer, editor. Best remembered as an important figure in the Aesthetic movement in England, where he edited the *Yellow Book* (1894–7), his earlier career is fascinating and his biography confusing (most sources give it incorrectly). He claimed to have been born in St Petersburg, and later announced English aristocratic parentage; in fact he was born in New York of parents from Connecticut. He went to Paris and then briefly to the Harvard Divinity School, and in New York began writing under the pen-name 'Sidney Luska' realistic novels of New York Jewish life. This early work includes *As It Was Written: A Jewish Musician's Story* (1885), *Mrs Peixada* (1886), *My Uncle Florimund* (1888) and *A Latin Quarter Courtship and Other Stories* (1889). Several of these novels are touched with sensationalism and cosmopolitan matter, but it was not until he advocated intermarriage with Gentiles in *The Yoke of the Thorah* (1887) that his pretence of being Jewish was unmasked. Harland then moved to Paris and in 1889 to London with an introduction from his godfather, Edmund Clarence Stedman, to Henry James. He now became an aesthete and a Jamesian stylist, tempted by Paris Bohemia, and was converted to Catholicism. Thereafter came historical novels and Left-Bank romances – *Mademoiselle Miss and Other Stories* (1893), *Grey Roses* (1895), *Comedies and Errors* (1898) and two books which caught the full tide of historical fiction and have survived well, *The Cardinal's Snuff Box* (1900), his most successful novel, a romance about an Italian duchess, and *My Friend Prospero* (1904). James said of the fiction of his expatriate aesthete period that it was lost in a whimsical picturesque vision of palace secrets, rulers and pretenders, of the heavy air of Rome 'where Cardinals are part of the furniture'. [MB]

Henry James, 'The Story-Teller at Large: Mr Henry Harland', in *American Essays*, ed. Leon Edel (1956).

**Harrington, Alan** (1919– ). Novelist. He was born in Massachusetts and graduated from Harvard in 1939; he has worked in public relations and advertising. *The Revelations of Doctor Modesto* (1955) is a highly entertaining novel satirizing philosophical universal panaceas. *Life in the Crystal Palace* (1959) takes on organization men in an American corporation, and *The Secret Swinger* (1966) tells of the disastrous adventures of a middle-aged man attempting to rejuvenate himself in young 'beat' circles and free himself from family and marriage with hip permissiveness. *The Immortalist* (1969) is a non-fiction account of salvation through medical engineering. [EM]

**Harris, George W(ashington)** (1814–69). Southern humorist. He was born in Pennsylvania, apprenticed to a jeweller, captained a Tennessee river-boat and wrote technological articles. Then he turned to sketches in the South-western tall-tale tradition and produced *Sut Lovingood: Yarns Spun by a 'Nat'ral Born Durn'd Fool'* (1867), frontier-dialect writing founded in Sut's practical joking and rough-neck humour. This kind of early pop-writing drew heavily on folklore. Mark Twain knew this work and was undoubtedly influenced. [MB]

Milton Rickels, *George Washington Harris* (1965)

**Harris, Joel Chandler** (1848–1908). Novelist, short-story writer. He was born in Georgia and as a boy began work in a printing shop. Work on a plantation gave him a contact with Negro folklore. He put this to profit in comic sketches for the *Atlanta Constitution*, which he joined in 1876 and where, in 1879, the first Uncle Remus story appeared: 'Negro Folklore. The Story of Mr Rabbit and Mr Fox, as Told by Uncle Remus' (the 1880 introductory story for *Uncle Remus, His Songs and His Sayings*). *Nights with Uncle Remus* (1883) maintained the popularity of the tales and introduced Daddy Jack, whose Gullah dialect of the Sea Islands made the stories less accessible. Where the earlier stories were post-Civil War, these concerned a generally affectionate master–slave relationship, although Uncle Remus is permitted shrewd individuality. After *Uncle Remus and His Friends* (1892) and *Mr Rabbit at Home* (1895), further volumes (1905 and 1910, posthumous) were backed with 5 children's books (1894–9) and many stories and novels not in the Uncle Remus series. *Mingo and Other Sketches in Black and White* (1884) concerns a faithful black Georgia servant and white class contrasts; *Sister Jane* (1896) deals with ante-bellum Georgia, *Free Joe, and Other Georgian Sketches* (1887), whose main story concerns the problems of an ex-slave, and *Gabriel*

*Tolliver* (1902) with the Reconstruction. *On the Plantation* (1892) is an autobiographical fiction of his early years.

The Uncle Remus tales preserve dialect, lore and attitudes of Southern 19th-century Negroes as seen by a white Southerner fascinated by the animal mythology through which they came to terms with their condition. Harris newly presented this material to Americans without black-faced minstrel crudeness. In his later stories he was more conscious of the international beast–folklore tradition of which the Afro-American oral tradition was part, but the Remus pattern stayed: the philosophical old Negro reciting to the 7-year-old son of 'Marse' John and 'Miss' Sally, or his descendant. Today the characters are part of American folklore, and Brer Rabbit is a major American, the cunning trickster who survives oppression by a craft which challenges physical domination. The European Reynard the Fox has become the Afro-American rabbit, accompanied by Brer Tarrypin, the hero of the cautious, who may often master the strong and crafty, Brer Fox, the predator who himself is preyed upon, and many more. Although Harris believed he was a transcriber, his tales are finished literary works, drawn, however, from plantation tradition. [EM]

*Joel Chandler Harris: Miscellaneous Writings*, ed. J. C. Harris (1931); *The Favorite Uncle Remus*, ed. G. Van Santvoord and A. C. Coolidge (1948).
Julia C. Harris, *The Life and Letters of Joel Chandler Harris* (1918); Alvin F. Harlow, *Joel Chandler Harris* (*Uncle Remus*): *Plantation Storyteller* (1941); Francis P. Gaines, *The Southern Plantation: A Study in the Development and the Accuracy of a Tradition* (1924); P. M. Cousins, *Joel Chandler Harris: A Biography* (1968).

**Hart, Moss** (1904–61). Playwright, librettist. He began his career in 1925, his first success being *Once in a Lifetime* (1930), written with George S. ◊ Kaufman, his collaborator in many future works. It is a typical comedy-farce, composed, like all his best work, with wit, speed and broad humanity. With Kaufman he also wrote *Merrily We Roll Along* (1934) and, one of their best, *You Can't Take It with You* (1936). There followed *I'd Rather Be Right* (1937) and *The American Way* (1939). *George Washington Slept Here* (1940), *Winged Victory* (1943), *Light Up the Sky* (1948) and *The Climate of Eden* (1952) are his own plays.

Best of all the collaborations with Kaufman is *The Man Who Came to Dinner* (1939), a caricature of Alexander ◊ Woolcott's career, superficial and funny. He wrote the librettos for Irving Berlin's *Face the Music* (1933) and Kurt Weill's *Lady in the Dark* (1941). His work with Kaufman epitomizes Broadway show business of the thirties at its finest. [EM]

**Harte, Bret** (1836–1902). Short-story writer. Born in Albany, New York, he went as a youth to California (1854) where he worked as an itinerant gold-miner, schoolmaster, Wells Fargo expressman, journalist and printer, gaining prominence through the prose sketches and verses he contributed to the *Golden Era* and the *Californian* (for which later, as editor, he engaged Mark Twain to write weekly articles). In 1863 he was appointed secretary of the U.S. branch mint in San Francisco. In 1867 appeared *The Lost Galleon*, a collection of his poems, and *Condensed Novels and Other Papers* (1867), clever satirical parodies of Dickens, Cooper, Victor Hugo and others, whose aptness suggests Harte's real qualities as a critic (he was an effective, sharp reviewer). A year later he helped to establish the famous *Overland Monthly*, a centre for western writing (including the work of Mark Twain). Harte edited the paper for two years, until 1870, and in it appeared some of his most famous work, stories of western life like 'The Luck of Roaring Camp', 'The Outcasts of Poker Flat', 'Tennessee's Partner', 'Brown of Calaveras', and the humorous ballad 'Plain Language from Truthful James', better remembered as 'The Heathen Chinee'.

Their collection in *The Luck of Roaring Camp and Other Sketches* (1870) had a triumphant reception, which he promptly followed up by resigning a professorship at the newly founded University of California and returning East to write for the *Atlantic Monthly*. He sought desperately to maintain his talents, collaborated with Twain, etc. But his life thereafter was to be a decline, though he made frequent contributions of stories to magazines and collected them in book form: *Mrs Skaggs's Husbands* (1873), *Tales of the Argonauts* (1875), *An Heiress of Red Dog* (1879), *A Sappho of Green Springs* (1891), *Colonel Starbottle's Client* (1892), as well as writing novels and plays. From 1878 to 1885 he was U.S. consul in Germany and Scotland,

spending the last years of his life in London. He never returned to the U.S.A.

A deceased prostitute's child who softens the hardened hearts of the miners so that, when the river rises, one of them drowns with the child in his arms; a gambler, two prostitutes and a thief snow-bound with an eloping couple whose true love thaws their hearts until all starve, die or shoot themselves in an effort to save the innocents; a faithful friend willing to give his entire mining stake in return for the life of a partner, captured as a highwayman, who had once eloped with his wife: out of such rhetorical contrasts of moral black and white Bret Harte captured the imagination of his Victorian reading audience. The formula is still effective. This brawling world of miners, prospectors, gamblers, robbers and prostitutes is perhaps even more attractive, a century after, to a generation brought up on Hollywood and the Wild West: while something of a young man's sharp ear and eye, stirred heart and mind, lives for ever in the bravado of these tales which an older Harte could never recapture. [HB]

*Letters*, ed. G. B. Harte (1926); *Representative Selections*, ed. G. B. Harrison (1941).
R. O'Connor, *Bret Harte: A Biography* (1966).

**Hartford Wits.** ◊ Connecticut Wits.

**Hawkes, John** (1925– ). Novelist, dramatist. Born in Connecticut, he studied at Harvard and teaches creative writing at Brown University, Rhode Island. One of the few post-war American writers convincingly exploiting the experimental tradition of modern fiction, he has had a considerable cult reputation that has lately widened to broader acclaim. His surrealistic fiction is founded on a sense that nightmare consciousness reveals a fundamental mythology; and he is extraordinarily inventive in his creation of symbolic moments and nightmare landscapes. His novels, set in post-war Germany, in wartime England, in deserts, on islands, explore the elemental, grotesque experience of the psyche. The blurred settings, fantastic landscape, and use of powerful horror devices make for an extremely intense fiction. At times, however, the effect seems overworked and literary; in *The Lime Twig* (1960) he clearly derives his landscape and world, that of wartime England (a country he had not visited), from Graham Greene and others. His other books include *The Cannibal* (1949), *Charivari* (a novella, 1949), *The Beetle Leg* (1951), two short novels called *The Owl* and *The Goose on the Grave* (1953), and *Second Skin* (1964), which seems to mark a development in his work in that the hero finds a pattern of escape and rediscovery. *The Innocent Party* (1967) contains four of his plays. *Lunar Landscape* (1969) collects shorter fiction from the 1940s onwards. [M B]

S. K. Oberbeck, 'John Hawkes: The Smile Slashed by a Razor', in *Contemporary American Novelists*, ed. Harry T. Moore (1964); I. Malin, *New American Gothic* (1962); R. Scholes, *The Fabulators* (1967).

**Hawthorne, Nathaniel** (1804–64). Novelist, short-story writer. The Hawthornes of Salem, Massachusetts, declined from colonial prominence (one was a witch-trial judge) to Nathaniel's sea-captain father, who died on a voyage when his son was 4. While recovering from a leg injury, the boy took to reading and solitude in the remote Maine village to which his mother had removed when he was 12. When he returned to Salem from Bowdoin College (Longfellow was a classmate), he began to write professionally in a seclusion reflected in the hero of his 'gothic' first novel, *Fanshawe* (1828), unsold copies of which he burned; he wrote no more novels for 21 years. Nor did his tales, also anonymous, bring him reputation until the *Twice-Told Tales* of 1837. He worked in the Boston Custom House (1839–41) as salt and coal measurer, and when this political appointment ended bought a share in Brook Farm (◊ Ripley), later withdrawing from its impracticable utopian ends, disillusioned with agrarian ideology and liberal evasions about the nature of leadership and community – major materials of all his work. In 1842 he married and lived in the Old Manse, Concord, where Emerson had written *Nature*. He did know the ◊ Transcendentalist circle but did not share their optimism and reforming faith. *Mosses from an Old Manse* (1846) appeared the year he left for his Salem custom surveyorship, from which political change again removed him in 1848. In his freedom he wrote his 'hell-fired' masterpiece *The Scarlet Letter* (1850), on which his reputation grew. Living at Lenox, in the Berkshires, he was contacted by Melville, and brought out *The House of the Seven Gables* (1851), *A Wonder Book for Boys and Girls* (1851) and

*The Snow Image and Other Thrice-Told Tales* (1851). At West Newton he wrote *The Blithedale Romance* in 1852, the year he returned to Concord and published a campaign biography for his college friend Franklin Pierce, the Democratic presidential nominee. After election Pierce gave him the consulship at Liverpool (1853), where he served for four years before going to Italy in 1857, where he began *The Marble Faun* (1860). He returned to Concord in 1860, and after writing *Our Old Home* (1863) his creativity relaxed. Family ill health and the Civil War depressed him. The Abolitionist movement conflicted with his scepticism about reform. He died leaving three unfinished novels.

His masterworks are 'romances', by which he meant an imaginative fictional projection of moral life rather than detailed naturalism. One major group of his works translates 17th-century American life into 19th-century moral and political concerns. *The Scarlet Letter* takes the ancestral New England confrontation of witch and judge and delineates it as a 19th-century conflict of ideas and ways of living which include female emancipation, the nature of sexuality in marriage and adultery, the personal character of religious or philosophical vocation, and the ontology of psychological independence. The greatness of this novel is supported by a group of important short stories on related themes of guilt, intellectual pride, suppressed sensuousness and the heroism of speculative and emotional living. These dramatic moral fables include 'The Maypole of Merrymount' (the effects of the implantation of traditional paganism into the puritan New World), 'The Gray Champion' (the beginnings of independence in the colonies), 'The Minister's Black Veil' (the refusal of love and sympathy), 'Young Goodman Brown' (witchcraft as necessary parallel to puritanism), and 'My Kinsman Major Molineux' (a boy becoming a man at the time colonial America begins to throw off England). Another group of stories concerns intellectual power in the scientist and artist, the head's conflict with the heart, and Faustian hubris of challenge to established ideas and ways of living. 'Ethan Brand' deals with the 'unpardonable sin' of using another human being instrumentally, 'Rappacini's Daughter' and 'The Birthmark' with the scientific alteration of nature and human nature, and 'The Artist of the Beautiful' with the ways in which art and science cut a man off from the chain of common humanity. These are constant themes in Hawthorne's work as a whole and are deeply embedded in the nature of American literature and culture in the 19th century. In his other novels he begins with the conflict between social inheritance and the needs of the present. In *The House of the Seven Gables* two young people seek to be released from an archaic New England family whose tradition of public probity has become warped into criminal fraud and enfeebled amoral delicacy. Opposed to the ancient house and its ghosts are the technology of the railway and the daguerreotype, as well as the freedom symbolized by nature. *The Blithedale Romance* is a critique of the Brook Farm experiment and a superb analysis of the urge to Utopia, the corrupting effects of unexamined desires for leadership, and the undetermined and tragic effects of feminist emancipations. For his last completed novel, *The Marble Faun* (1860), Hawthorne places his action in Italy: the Italian count Donatello, the mysteriously European Miriam, and an American couple form a triangulation of his familiar themes. Apart from long passages of not unpleasant travelogue, it is a romance of crime and punishment, a myth of the fortunate and necessary fall from innocence to maturity, and the relative purity of New World youth in wicked old Europe. The stylization and dogma are far more schematic than in *The Scarlet Letter*, and earlier uncertainties of tone and address in his prose have a field day, but it is an important extension of his fundamental issues. Besides these major works various fragments were published after his death, including *Septimius Felton: or, The Elixir of Life* (1872), *The Dolliver Romance and Other Pieces* (1876) and *Doctor Grimshawe's Secret* (1883; ed. from manuscript 1954). Passages from his American, English, and French and Italian notebooks have been edited by Randall Stewart (1932 and 1941) and Sophia Hawthorne (1872) respectively. His letters have not yet been published in a reliable edition, but a collection of love letters appeared in 1907, and some letters to Ticknor, the publisher, in 1910. But the collected letters is being prepared, and an annotated Centenary Edition of all his works has been initiated by Ohio State University with *The House of the Seven Gables*,

*The Blithedale Romance* and *Fanshawe* (1966). This attention is justified for a great fiction writer whose career is at the centre of the American tradition of apprehension concerning the nature of permanent evil in a society dedicated to and capable of infinite progress. His influence extends powerfully through Henry James, especially in his treatment of the 'international theme' of the American in Europe, to William Faulkner and mid-20th-century 'gothic' novelists of the American power structure. [EM]

*The Portable Hawthorne*, ed. Malcolm Cowley (1948).

H. H. Waggoner, *Hawthorne: A Critical Study* (1955); Randall Stewart, *Nathaniel Hawthorne* (1948); E. Wagenknecht, *Nathaniel Hawthorne: Man and Writer* (1961); R. R. Male, *Hawthorne's Tragic Vision* (1957); ed. J. D. Crowley, *Hawthorne: The Critical Heritage* (1970).

**Hay, John** (1838–1905). Diplomat, historian, poet, novelist. Born Salem, Indiana, he grew up in the Illinois region of Pike County, setting of his famous ballads. After attending Brown University, he began to study law in an office next door to Abraham ◊ Lincoln's in Springfield, Illinois. On Lincoln's election to the Presidency, Hay went with him to Washington as an assistant private secretary. A posting to the American legation in Paris deflected him towards the arts. In 1870 he returned to America and to journalism. He published many poems and ballads, collecting them in *Pike County Ballads and Other Pieces* (1871). In 1878 he went to Washington as an assistant secretary of state and was the neighbour and friend of Henry ◊ Adams. He appears recurrently in Adams' *Education of Henry Adams*. Like Adams, Hay published a novel anonymously: *The Bread-Winners: A Social Study* (1884), which defended capitalism against labour and is notable for its expression of the post-Civil-War discontent of the 'dispossessed' upper class in the mercenary Gilded Age. In 1890 he published (with John Nicolay) the 10-volume *Abraham Lincoln: A History*. In the same year *Poems*, his collected verses, appeared. Afterwards American ambassador to England and, briefly, Secretary of State, he worked for peace on many fronts in his remaining years. But his literary fame rests firmly on his dialect poems of Pike County, such as 'Little Breeches' and 'Jim Bludso of the Prairie Bell'. [A G]

*The Complete Poetical Works* (1916).

William Roscoe Thayer, *The Life and Letters of John Hay* (2 vols., 1915); W. D. Howells, 'John Hay in Literature', *North American Review*, September 1905; T. Dennett, *John Hay: From Poetry to Politics* (1933).

**Hayne, Paul Hamilton** (1830–86). Poet. Born in Charleston, South Carolina, he was one of the important group of pre-Civil-War Southern writers who gathered in that city, others being William Gilmore ◊ Simms and Henry ◊ Timrod, whose works he edited. His elegant and reflective nature poetry appeared in the *Southern Literary Messenger*, and with Timrod he founded *Russell's Magazine*. *Poems* (1855) and *Sonnets and Other Poems* (1857) appeared before the Civil War, during the course of which he wrote patriotic Confederate verse. After the war, in difficult circumstances, he vowed to live by writing, and produced *Legends and Lyrics* (1872) and other poetry and biography. [MB]

*Collected Poems* (1882).
Kate H. Becker, *Paul Hamilton Hayne: His Life and Letters* (1951).

**H. D.** ◊ Doolittle, Hilda.

**Hearn, Lafcadio** (1850–1904). Novelist, travel-writer, translator. Though usually regarded as an American writer because he exerted most influence in the U.S.A., Hearn spent only a part of his life there. Born on the Ionian island of Santa Maria, son of a surgeon-major in the English army and a Greek mother, he was reared in Dublin by an aunt who sent him to Catholic schools and finally to America in 1869. He settled in Cincinnati and became a journalist. In 1877 he went on an assignment to New Orleans, where he studied Creole literature with George Washington ◊ Cable. He began translation from Gautier, Flaubert and Anatole France; his first book, *One of Cleopatra's Nights* (1882), translates six Gautier tales. A professed romantic, impressionist and hunter of the exotic, he began exploring through a variety of literatures, and *Stray Leaves from Strange Literature* (1884) consists of articles founded on literary exotica. He published two novels, *Chita* (1889), on the destruction of an island off Louisiana by a tidal wave, and *Youma* (1890), about slave rebellion in Martinique (see also *Two Years in the French West Indies*, 1890). Already interested in the orient – *Some Chinese Ghosts* (1887) is a collection of oriental legends – he went in 1890 to Japan on a commission from *Harper's*. He married a Japanese woman and settled there, becoming a citizen and a Buddhist, working as a teacher – for a time at Tokyo University – and an interpreter of Japanese life to the west.

Japan realized for Hearn his impressionism, mysticism and taste for the exotic, and it was in these lights that he interpreted it to American and English readers. Most of his later books are studies of the richer aspects of Japanese life – *Glimpses of Unfamiliar Japan* (2 vols., 1893), *Gleanings in Buddha Fields* (1897), *In Ghostly Japan* (1899), *Shadowings* (1900), *Japan: An Attempt at Interpretation* (1904), etc. – or else collections of stories and legends. His journalism and his lectures on literature, English, American, European and oriental, have been collected only since his death: *Occidental Gleanings* (2 vols., 1925), *Appreciations of Poetry* (1916), and *Life and Literature* (1922). The important *Leaves from the Diary of an Impressionist: Early Writings*, which states his aesthetic, was collected in 1911 by Ferris Greenslet. His Japanese wife, Setsuko Koizumi, wrote a memoir, *Reminiscences of Lafcadio Hearn* (1918); so did his son, Kazuo Koizumi, in *Father and I: Memories of Lafcadio Hearn* (1935). Yone Noguchi's *Lafcadio Hearn in Japan* (1910) contains a useful Japanese appreciation of the man.

Hearn's reputation is somewhat uncertain, not least because of the complications of his citizenship and his publishing history. His importance in international literature is that he made accessible the long-closed world of Japan and *japonisme* to the modern arts, he also led the way into much of the 20th-century interest in imagism and impressionism. His Bohemian sensibility (◊ Bohemianism), his taste for the exotic, his fascination with symbolism, make his aesthetic development important. His mind is highly sophisticated and critically interesting; and its cosmopolitanism (as Earl Miner shows in *The Japanese Tradition in British and American Literature*, 1958) gave many new hints to the poets of England and America from about 1910 onwards. His *Letters from the Raven* (1907) are an important source for his autobiography. [MB]

*Writings* (16 vols., 1922); *The Selected Writings*, ed. H. Goodman, intr. Malcolm Cowley (1949). Vera McWilliams, *Lafcadio Hearn* (1946); Elizabeth Stevenson, *Lafcadio Hearn* (1961);

Albert Parry, *Garrets and Pretenders* (1960); Elizabeth Bisland, *The Life and Letters of Lafcadio Hearn* (2 vols., 1906).

**Hecht, Anthony** (1923– ). Poet. A former student of John Crowe ◊ Ransom at Kenyon College and now a teacher, he won considerable poetic reputation both in the U.S.A. and England with *A Summoning of Stones* (1954), a collection of excellent verse. The book takes its title from Santayana's phrase suggesting that poetry's aim is to 'call the stones themselves to their ideal places, and enchant the very substance and skeleton of the world'. Hecht's verse is both witty and moralizing, and it ranges between poems of occasions and philosophical quandaries deriving from painfully felt experience. *The Hard Hours* (1967) confirms his talent and elegance, includes a nice parody 'The Dover Bitch' and extends the autobiographical tendency of the earlier book (some of whose poems are reprinted here). [MB]

**Hecht, Ben** (1893–1964). Novelist, dramatist journalist. Born in New York, he made his career in Chicago, beginning in the 'literary renaissance' there in the thirties. His first novel, *Erik Dorn* (1921), uses his reporter experience in Berlin (1918–19) as well as his admiration for Huysmans. From 1922, he wrote novels and stories, edited his *Literary Times*, and worked on plays and films: *The Front Page* (1920, with Charles MacArthur), *Wuthering Heights*, *Nothing Sacred*, *Scarface*, *Notorious* (1946), etc.; his plays include *The Scoundrel* (with Noël Coward). In the 1940s he advocated extreme forms of Zionism, and all his life remained a mid-Western radical journalist using all literary forms, including autobiography, with *A Child of the Century* (1954). [EM]

**Heggen, Thomas** (1919–49). Novelist dramatist. Born in Iowa. He left the *Reader's Digest* to serve in the navy in the Pacific during the Second World War and put that experience to work in *Mister Roberts* (1946), a money-making novel, film and play, which is an uninhibited satire on the service, a study in boredom and revolt. He died of talented inertia in what Budd ◊ Schulberg called 'that gold-plated bear trap' of early success ('Taps at Reveille', in *Esquire*, November 1960). [EM]

**Heinlein, Robert A(nson)** (1907– ). Science-fiction writer. Born at Butler, Missouri. A trained physicist, he began writing in 1939 and has since published many influential and widely translated novels and stories for juvenile as well as adult audiences. Several of his works are now accepted as classics of the genre; they include *Orphans of the Sky* (1951; originally published as a 2-part serial in 1941) and *Methuselah's Children* (1958; serial version, 1941), both of which form part of his 5-volume *History of the Future*. Others in the series are *The Man Who Sold the Moon* (1950) and *The Green Hills of Earth* (1951). His many works include *The Puppet Masters* (1951), *The Star Beast* (1954), *The Door into Summer* (1957), *Stranger in a Strange Land* (1961), *Glory Road* (1963) and *The Moon is a Harsh Mistress* (1966). [HD]

**Heliczer, Piero** (1937– ). Poet. Born in Rome, he went to America at 10, studied at Harvard, was an expatriate in Paris, and has made films and written poems, both extremely individual in their imagery and form, in England and New York. His films include *Autumn Feast*, made in Brighton, Sussex, and the unfinished *Dirt*. His poems are included in *You Could Hear the Snow Melting and Dripping from the Deer's Mouth* (1958), *I Dreamt I Shot Arrows in my Amazon Bra* (1960) and *Second Battle of the Marne* (1961). *The Soap Opera* (1967) is his most mature work to date, and is illustrated by artists which include Andy Warhol and Jack Smith. Heliczer combines surrealist imagery, direct expressions of love and clear lyricism with a complexity of form partly derived from his training in music. [EM]

**Heller, Joseph** (1923– ). Novelist. Born in Brooklyn, he studied literature at New York University, Columbia and Oxford. He has taught writing at Pennsylvania State College but spent more time in advertising, now heading the promotion department of *McCall's* magazine. In the Second World War a bombardier in the air force, he flew 60 combat missions from Corsica over Italy and France – an experience that lies behind his one novel, *Catch–22* (1961). Among the best novels to appear since the war, it is funny, compassionate, technically original and morally concerned, using the methods of black humour and the theatre of the absurd to satirize the army, the capitalist state and the host of doctors and psychiatrists modern living demands. His air force is less

121

a fighting unit than a bureaucracy perpetuating itself through flagrant but persuasive use of authoritarian logic – Catch–22 – which constantly thwarts the hero Yossarian, a kind of *homme moyen sensuel*, in his attempts to enjoy life and survive. His play *We Bombed in New Haven* (1968) shows war as a game of role-playing and spectatorism. [B W]

Brian Way, 'Formal Experiment and Social Discontent: Joseph Heller's *Catch-22*', *Journal of American Studies* (October 1968).

**Hellman, Lillian** (1905–   ). Playwright. Born in New Orleans, she has lived mainly in New York. Her first important play with a Broadway run was *The Children's Hour* (1934). She visited Russia in 1936 and 1945, was active on several leftish organizations, and was therefore called before the House Un-American Activities Committee in 1952, but refused to testify against friends and colleagues. *The Children's Hour* concerns sexual scandal in a girl's boarding school and analyses abnormal psychology. In *The Little Foxes* (1939) she presents an Alabama aristocratic family in decline through a new rapacious social class, *The Watch on the Rhine* (1941) exposes pre-war complacency about Nazism, and *The Searching Wind* (1944) delineates the appeasement of fascism in the thirties. *Another Part of the Forest* (1946; the earlier chronicles of the *Little Foxes* family) and *Toys in the Attic* (1960) again concern the South in decline and neurosis. Her most recent work is a version of Burt ◊ Blechman's satirical novel *How Much?* called *My Mother, My Father and Me* (1963). All her plays are notable for their psychological intensity, strongly motivated violence and liberal critical attitudes. She also adapted Voltaire's *Candide* for Leonard Bernstein's musical, which had lyrics by Richard Wilbur, Dorothy Parker and John La Touche. *An Unfinished Woman* (1969) is autobiography oddly omitting her life in the theatre. [E M]

**Hemingway, Ernest** (1898–1961). Novelist. Born in Oak Park, Illinois. In boyhood he developed that passion for active outdoor pursuits which so deeply marked his life and fiction. He hunted and fished in the forests of the Great Lakes region, which still kept some of their frontier characteristics. His independence, and his compulsion to bury himself in the American wilderness, indeed to identify with the primitive everywhere,

can be traced to this time and place, and to his experiences with his father, who was a doctor, and with the Indians. After a stylistically formative spell as a journalist, he joined a volunteer ambulance unit (before America entered the war). Severely wounded near the Austrian frontier in 1918, he was awarded the Croce di Guerra. The wound altered his consciousness profoundly, bringing him face to face with death and terror of annihilation; he said that he 'ceased to be hard-boiled' and, discovering his own vulnerability (a feeling intensified by his father's suicide), he set out to exorcise his fears by confronting death or observing others confront it as often as he could. Hence his obsession with violence – bullfighting, boxing, safari, big-game hunting and war – and the skills of games and writing. At his most confident – as in the superb story 'The Undefeated' – he holds off terror with the virtues of the born fighter, courage and nobility in the face of death, a stoical resistance to pain, a perfect sympathy with one's physical environment. The hero is a Spanish bullfighter; his virtues are those of the idealized American redskin.

Sent after the war to Paris as correspondent for Hearst newspapers, he began to write under instruction from Gertrude ◊ Stein and Ezra ◊ Pound and emerged with Scott ◊ Fitzgerald as the most gifted of the ◊ 'Lost Generation' writers. Influenced by *Huckleberry Finn* and the discipline of journalism, he developed a distinctive fictional manner, vernacular, terse, unabstract, concerned with 'the real thing, the sequence of emotion and fact which make the emotion'. Apart from some privately printed ventures, his first book was *In Our Time* (1925), short stories using the expatriate perspective to define his sense of America, the central figure in the finest ones being Nick Adams, a young man shaped by the mid-West and the war. *The Torrents of Spring* (1926), a comic masterpiece, begins as a burlesque of Sherwood ◊ Anderson's *Dark Laughter*, and becomes a successful enterprise in self-mockery, a satire on the cult of American maleness. His more popular success came with *The Sun Also Rises* (1926; British title *Fiesta*), usually considered his best novel. Jake Barnes, an American, and Brett, an Englishwoman, cannot consummate their love because Jake is impotent, 'wounded in the war'. In the religion, bull-fighting and drinking of the fiesta at Pamplona they are forced to confront the emptiness of their lives, from which the pleasures of the expatriate round in Paris had protected them; they are sustained, if at all, only by that stoical fortitude in the face of the intolerable which is the last resort of the Hemingway hero. The novel conveys with equal brilliance the ritual or turbulence of the fiesta, the pleasures of fishing and drinking, and, through its dialogue, the flat surface of Paris lost-generation life. *Men without Women* (1927), his finest collection of stories, shows many such confrontations with death and emptiness; its heroes are soldiers, bull-fighters, boxers, gangsters; it evokes the feel of violent action with unequalled economy and force. *A Farewell to Arms* (1929) deals with a love-affair conducted against the background of the war in Italy. Its excellence lies in the delicacy with which it conveys a sense of the impermanence of the best human feelings; the unobtrusive force of its symbolism of mountain and plain; above all the vast scope of its vision of war – the retreat from Caporetto is one of the great war-sequences of literature.

After 1930, with the exception of a few stories and episodes, Hemingway reworks less and less successfully the situations of the earlier books. *Death in the Afternoon* (1932) and *Green Hills of Africa* (1935), about bull-fighting and safari, already contain much of the attitudinizing and simple-pretentious writing that mar later novels. *Winner Take Nothing* (1933) has one excellent story, 'A Clean Well-Lighted Place'. *To Have and Have Not* (1937), a short novel about a Caribbean smuggler, is marred by an inept attempt at fashionable social criticism; but *The Fifth Column and The First Forty-Nine Stories* (1938) contains, along with a play and the stories from the earlier collections, some fine new stories using recent African and Spanish experiences – the best work of the later years. His next novel, *For Whom the Bell Tolls* (1940), set in the Spanish Civil War, is impressive, his most ambitious book; but its moulded attitude to politics confuses its direction and its dialogue, attempting epic simplicity, is often portentously absurd.

Hemingway by now was living in Cuba; during the Second World War he took active part as correspondent and irregular soldier in France, experiences reflected in *Across the River and into the Trees* (1950), an unconscious parody of his earlier work

and his worst novel. *The Old Man and the Sea* (1952), a fable about a Cuban fisherman's struggle with a great marlin, though dignified and often beautiful, does not entirely succeed, though it won him the Nobel Prize. Work he left after his death is now appearing posthumously. As he aged, Hemingway found it growingly difficult to keep up the active life he loved and, after treatment for mental disturbance, he shot himself at Ketchum, Idaho, in 1961, just as his father had done many years before. *Islands in the Stream* (1970), though never properly revised, possesses some of the intensity of his best work, and the lonely, almost broken hero, Thomas Hudson, has the tragic qualities of the later Hemingway himself.

He is one of the great American writers, not only because he superbly evokes action and the surface of things, but even more because of the uncanny force with which his work asks ultimate questions about life and death. A nihilist for whom the emptiness of modern life was perhaps most adequately symbolized by modern war, a nightmare of darkness, blood, confusion and treachery, he still held an ideal of the decent life. A man may sustain himself with the ephemeral pleasures of physical sensation, such as sex, alcohol and sport; he may acquire skills that make him precise and controlled, may possess a stoical resistance to his fate, may take sustenance from organized religion. But when these fail, he may prefer the nothingness of death to the nothingness of life. No writer has so effectively expressed this tension between the extreme pleasures and extreme terrors of being alive. [B W]

Stewart Sanderson, *Hemingway* (1961); Philip Young, *Ernest Hemingway* (1952; revised edn, 1959); Carlos Baker, *Hemingway: The Writer as Artist* (1956: revised edn, 1963); Edmund Wilson, 'Hemingway: Gauge of Morale', in *The Wound and the Bow* (revised edn, 1952); W. William White, *By-Line: Ernest Hemingway* (1967); Carlos Baker, *Ernest Hemingway* (1969); ed. Carlos Baker, *Hemingway and His Critics* (1961).

**Henry, O(liver)** (pseud. of William Sidney Porter) (1862–1910). Short-story writer, humorist, journalist. One of the most prolific writers ever, he was born in North Carolina and, without much schooling and virtually orphaned, worked in his uncle's drugstore, gradually retreating into a shy, poverty-stricken world of fantasy escape. After two years on a Texas ranch, he ran through a series of unskilled jobs, developing talents for cartooning and singing. In 1894 he founded *The Rolling Stone*, a comic magazine which soon failed, and two years later he was charged with embezzlement of funds from an Austin, Texas, bank and fled to New Orleans and Honduras. He returned when his wife was dying and served a long sentence in the Federal Penitentiary, Colombus, Ohio. Here he began to write and publish as 'O. Henry', from 1899 onwards, his first story, 'Whistling Dick's Christmas Stocking', already concluding with the twist for which he became famous. On release, he worked in New York, gathering material from a detailed contact with every aspect of the city's life. Overwhelming success brought him a salaried contract with the *World* for a story a week. He became a central figure in this peak period of the American magazine short story. The fatalism of his stories penetrated his life as well, and he died in drunkenness.

*Cabbages and Kings* (1904), his first collection, is a linked series of South American yarns. The New York tales of *The Four Million* (1906) include some of his perfect stereotypes, in works such as 'The Skylight Room' and 'The Furnished Room'. *Heart of the West* (1907) is a Western collection, and the hero of *The Gentle Grafter* (1908) is Jeff Peters, a confidence man in a main American tradition. *Roads of Destiny* (1909) embodies strongly his crude notion of fate, the basis of his twist. His style is almost anonymous, his use of dialect completely authentic, and his range of locality wide and vivid. But to entertain he resorted to cheap suspense and caricature. His strength is the startling surfaces of paradox and the grotesque, combined with commendable skill at plotting irony. [EM]

*The Collected Works*, intr. H. Harrison (2 vols., 1953); *Best Short Stories of O. Henry*, ed. B. Cerf and Van H. Cartmell (1945).

G. Langford, *Alias O. Henry: A Biography of William Sidney Porter* (1957); E. H. Long, *O. Henry: The Man and His Work* (1949).

**Hergesheimer, Joseph** (1880–1954). Novelist. He studied art in his home town, Philadelphia, and in Italy, before returning first to Virginia, then Pennsylvania, to write. Like James Branch ⟡ Cabell, whom he knew and who wrote a short book about him, he admired aristocracy and idealism, and his early novels like *Mountain Blood*

(1915), set in Virginia, *The Three Black Pennys* (1917), about several generations of a Pennsylvania ironmaster family, *Java Head* (1919), about Salem in its great days of the China trade, *Linda Condon* (1919), and *Balisand* (1924), about post-Revolution Virginia, are classics of twenties exoticism, based both on devotion to 'beauty' and on an evocative power derived from research or feeling for regional history. But it is usually agreed that the later romances – like *Tampico* (1926) and *The Limestone Tree* (1931) – lack the earlier finesse and convincing exoticism. He also produced accounts of travel and two interesting autobiographical volumes, *A Presbyterian Child* (1923) and *From an Old House* (1925). [MB]

R. E. Martin, *The Fiction of Joseph Hergesheimer* (1966).

**Herrick, Robert** (1868–1938). Teacher and novelist. Born in Cambridge, Massachusetts, he joined the English Department at the nascent University of Chicago in 1893 and taught there for 30 years. He thought highly of his self-styled 'idealistic' novels, which include *The Real World* (1901), *A Life for a Life* (1910), *The Healer* (1911) and *Clark's Field* (1914), but his best work is to be found in a series of realistic novels which examined the materialism and corruption of contemporary Chicago: *The Gospel of Freedom* (1898); *The Web of Life* (1900); *The Common Lot* (1904); and *The Memoirs of an American Citizen* (1905; reissued, intr. Daniel Aaron, 1963). [HD]

Blake Nevius, *Robert Herrick: The Development of a Novelist* (1962).

**Hersey, John** (1914– ). Novelist, reporter. Born in China, once secretary to Sinclair Lewis, during the Second World War a correspondent with a literary flair, he made his reputation as a war novelist with *A Bell for Adano* (1944), dealing with peasant life in American-occupied Sicily. Then came a remarkable piece of reportage about the first atomic bomb explosion, *Hiroshima*, which occupied an entire issue of the *New Yorker* (31 August 1946) – for which Hersey had been a writer – before achieving vast circulation as a book. His later novels have a journalist's sense of relevance and efficiency of manner, and have sometimes moved towards a broadly allegorical purpose; they are *The Wall* (1950), *The Marmot Drive* (1953), *A Single Pebble* (1956), *The War Lover* (1959), *The*

*Child Buyer* (1960), and *Under the Eye of the Storm* (1967). *Too Far to Walk* (1966), a Faustian novel about university students, is his best yet. *The Algiers Motel Incident* (1969) documents police and National Guard killings in the black ghetto of Detroit in 1967. [MB]

**Heyward, DuBose** (1885–1940). Novelist, poet, playwright. His best-known work is his novel *Porgy* (1925), about Negro life in Catfish Row in old Charleston, South Carolina, his home town. He and his wife Dorothy Heyward, herself a well-known playwright and novelist, adapted it into a successful play (1927), which George Gershwin then adapted into the famous opera *Porgy and Bess* (1935). Heyward was at his best as a local-colour writer, exploiting his deep knowledge of regional conditions, local vernacular, humour and folk-philosophy. Earlier he had produced a romantic collection of poems with Hervey ◊ Allen, *Carolina Chansons* (1922), and he continued to publish verse. Other fiction includes *Mamba's Daughters* (1929), also about Charleston Negro life, and *Peter Ashley* (1932), about Charleston during the Civil War. [MB]

Frank Durham, *DuBose Heyward: The Man Who Wrote 'Porgy'* (1954).

**Hicks, Granville** (1901– ). Literary critic. Until his famous resignation from the Communist Party in 1939, one of the group of literary radicals who interpreted American literature from a Marxist point of view – see, for instance, his *The Great Tradition: An Interpretation of American Literature since the Civil War* (1933, revised 1935) and also his *Figures of Transition* (1939) on late-19th-century English literature. He was the literary editor and staff critic of *New Masses*, edited the collection *Proletarian Literature in the United States* (1935), and wrote a study of John ◊ Reed. More recently he has written fiction and edited a good collection of criticism of fiction, *The Living Novel* (1957). *Part of the Truth* (1965) is a modest but essential account of his career, which now seems part of American intellectual history. [MB]

**Hillyer, Robert** (1895–1961). Poet, novelist, translator, critic. Born in East Orange, New Jersey, he graduated from Harvard and served in the ambulance corps and in the army during the First World War. He

taught at various American universities, including Harvard and Kenyon College. His poetry, with its links with the Georgians and an acknowledged debt to Robert Bridges, tends toward the romantic-pastoral: *Sonnets and Other Lyrics* (1917); *In Time of Mistrust* (1939); *Collected Verse* (1933); *Collected Poems* (1961). He also wrote novels and three useful volumes of criticism – *Some Roots of English Poetry* (1933), *First Principles of Verse* (1938) and *In Pursuit of Poetry* (1960). [MB]

**Himes, Chester** (1909– ). Novelist. He was born in Missouri, studied at Ohio State University and worked on the Cleveland *Daily News*. He is one of the leading Negro novelists in America, in direct descent from Richard ◊ Wright. *If He Hollers Let Him Go* (1945) violently delineates the conflict of black and white in a wartime shipyard in California, with a hero whose neurotic race-consciousness is a stage beyond Wright's Bigger Thomas. *Lonely Crusade* (1947) concerns race discriminations in the labour unions and the betrayal of a black American by the Communists. *Cast the First Stone* (1952) is about prison life, with largely white characters. *The Third Generation* (1954) is a penetrating study of middle-class Negro experience and the Negro college. *The Primitive* (1955) concerns inter-racial sexuality, treated with tragic passion. *Pinktoes* (1965) is a funny and highly topical satire on the sexual levelling between black and white, and *Cotton Comes to Harlem* (1965) is again a serious treatment of his familiar themes in a comic form. *The Heat's On* (1966) is a Harlem detective novel and *Blind Man with a Pistol* (1969) combines all his effects into a high point of his career. (◊ Negro Literature.) [EM]

**Hoffman, Charles Fenno** (1806–84). Novelist, poet, travel-writer. Born in New York, editor of several journals including the *Knickerbocker Magazine*, and one of the Knickerbocker group that included ◊ Irving, he wrote two famous accounts of prairie travels, *A Winter in the West* (1835) and *Wild Scenes in the Forest and Prairie* (1839), and three volumes of poems, many with Hudson River settings, brought together in *The Poems of Charles Fenno Hoffman* (1873). Best known is his novel *Greyslaer: A Romance of the Mohawk* (1840), dealing with the struggles of Whigs and Tories during the Revolution. [MB]

**Hofstadter, Richard** (1916–70). Historian. Born in Buffalo, N.Y., he taught in New York City universities. One of the leading historians of American political, social and cultural thought, his *Social Darwinism in American Thought* (1944, 1960), *The American Political Tradition* (1948) and *The Age of Reform: From Bryan to F.D.R.* (1955) are definitive, excellently written works. *Anti-Intellectualism in American Life* (1963) is an important and pioneer book whose effect ought to be salutary. *The Paranoid Style in American Politics* (1965) is a collection of essays and *The Progressive Historians* (1968) concerns F. J. Turner, C. Beard and V. L. Parrington. [EM]

**Hollander, John** (1929– ). Poet, critic. Born in New York, he teaches at Yale and is poetry editor of *Partisan Review*. His volumes of verse are *A Crackling of Thorns* (1958), *Movie-Going and Other Poems* (1962) and *Visions from the Ramble* (1965). His critical work, besides numerous articles, includes *The Untuning of the Sky: Ideas of Music in English Poetry, 1500–1700* (1961). His verse is usually reflective and philosophical, the steady rigorous analysis of a given situation, moving towards an abstract insight. [MB]

**Holmes, John Clellon** (1926– ). Novelist. Born in Massachusetts. His novel *Go* (1952) described the ◊ Beat Generation at first hand before it became a popular subject. 'The Philosophy of the Beat Generation' is an important essay reprinted on the same matter, *The Horn* (1958) an interesting jazz novel, and *Get Home Free* (1964) a sophisticated bleak story of New York and Louisiana. He has also published poems, and *Nothing More to Declare* (1968), a personal account of writing in the last two decades, with portraits of Allan ◊ Ginsberg, Jack ◊ Kerouac, Gershon Legman, etc.: an essential document for understanding the Beat Generation. [EM]

*The Beats*, ed. S. Krim (1960) (anthology).

**Holmes, Oliver Wendell** (1809–94). Essayist, poet, humorist, scientist, teacher. A descendent of Anne ◊ Bradstreet, he was born in Cambridge, Massachusetts, and brought up among the upper-class Boston 'Brahmins' he described as 'the harmless, inoffensive, untitled aristocracy'. During his time at Harvard (graduated in 1829, celebrating his class in a long series of reunion poems), a group of Calvinists

ousted his father Abiel from his Cambridge parish; Holmes was to attack Calvinism throughout his life, especially in his poem 'The Deacon's Masterpiece' (1858), in which he satirizes Calvinist reliance on logic and compares their theology to a 'one-hoss shay' which suddenly collapsed. Abandoning law for medicine, he received his Harvard M.D. in 1836, and was Professor of Anatomy at Dartmouth (1838–40), then at Harvard (1847–82), publishing between appointments his important *Homeopathy and Its Kindred Delusions* (1842) and *The Contagiousness of Puerperal Fever* (1843). His aesthetic delight in physiognomy was shown in such poetry as the excellent *The Stethoscope Song* (1849), *The Living Temple* (1858) and *La Griesette* (1863). His pioneering *The Physiology of Versification* (1883) tried to find a common law governing metre and the pulse rate. Three 'medicated novels' were revealed as early studies in psychiatry by Clarence P. Obendorf in his abridgement *The Psychiatric Novels of Oliver Wendell Holmes* (1944; revised 1946). The best, *Elsie Venner* (1861), is a penetrating study of a schizophrenic girl, and also a thrust at Calvinism; Holmes said he tried in it to 'test the doctrine of "original sin" and human responsibility'. *The Guardian Angel* (1867) analyses multiple personality and the possibility of conflict between heredity and environment; *A Mortal Antipathy* (1885) examines a severe phobia. Both are inferior as novels.

Meanwhile Holmes had become famous as a witty and stimulating lecturer, clubman and conversationalist. From two early papers he developed his mastery of anecdotes, stories and epigrams ('Do not put your trust in money, put your money in trust'; 'Man has his will, woman her way') into *The Autocrat of the Breakfast Table* (1858), a series of brilliant and wide-ranging conversations, and its successors *The Professor at the Breakfast Table* (1860), *The Poet at the Breakfast Table* (1872) and *Over the Teacups* (1891). Other essays, written for *Atlantic Monthly*, became *Soundings from the Atlantic* (1864) and *Pages from an Old Volume of Life* (1883).

His biographies of Motley (1879) and of Emerson (1885) were disappointing except, significantly, for a chapter on Emerson's verse; Holmes himself hoped to be remembered primarily as a poet. From the appearance of 'Old Ironsides' (1830), a widely reprinted poem opposing the destruction of the frigate *Constitution*, he was a prolific writer of occasional verse. His work is always skilful, but only a few of his poems are much read, among them 'The Ballad of the Oysterman' (1830), a parody on the romantic ballad; 'The Lost Leaf' (1831), a half-sentimental, half-satirical character study; and his own favourite, the mystical 'The Chambered Nautilus' (1858). [MG]

*Complete Poetical Works*, ed. H. E. Scudder (1895); *Works* (13 vols., 1892); *Oliver Wendell Holmes: Representative Selections*, ed. S. I. Hayakawa and H. M. Jones (1939).
John T. Morse, *The Life and Letters of Oliver Wendell Holmes* (1896); William L. Schroeder, *Oliver Wendell Holmes: An Appreciation* (1909); Mark A. de Wolfe Howe, *Holmes of the Breakfast Table* (1939); Miriam R. Small, *Oliver Wendell Holmes* (1962).

**Hooker, Thomas** (1586–1647). Theologian. An Emmanuel College, Cambridge, Congregational divine, he went to New England in 1633 and three years later removed his congregation from Massachusetts to Connecticut, founding the town of Hartford in moderate opposition to rigid Calvinism. *Survey of the Sum of Church Discipline* (1648; with John Cotton) summarizes his tolerant reconciliatory role in the discussion of theocracy. Most of his other works survive in shorthand versions by admirers. An important early American democrat, he believed in the abolition of property and religious tests for the franchise, and that 'the foundation of authority is laid in the free consent of the people'. [EM]

G. L. Walker, *Thomas Hooker, Preacher, Founder, Democrat* (1891).

**Hooper, Johnson Jones** (1815–62). Southern humorist. He was born in North Carolina, edited the Montgomery, Alabama, *Mail* until 1861, and made a name as a humorist chiefly with *Some Adventures of Captain Suggs, Late of the Tallapoosa Volunteers* (1846) about an early dialect picaro whose principle is that 'it is good to be shifty in a new country'. Hooper became secretary of the Provisional Congress of the Southern States in 1861. [EM]

**Hopkins, Lemuel** ◊ Connecticut Wits.

**Hopkinson, Francis** (1737–91). Poet, satirical novelist. Born in Philadelphia, where he became a lawyer and Federal judge. He was the first student at the Academy of Philadelphia (University of Pennsylvania) and

claimed to have been the first American-born composer (in 1781 he wrote the 'dramatic allegorical cantata' *The Temple of Minerva*). He also signed the Declaration of Independence as New Jersey's delegate and wrote for the Revolutionary cause. *Battle of the Kegs* (1778), his best-known work, is a satirical poem (to be sung to *Yankee Doodle*) based on the incident of the mechanical gunpowder kegs sent down the Delaware to blow up the British fleet (the British burned his home town in revenge), and *A Pretty Story* (1774) is a satirical allegory of revolutionary politics. Hopkinson designed New Jersey's State seal and helped to design the American flag. John Adams unfairly described him as 'one of your pretty, little, curious, ingenious men'. [EM]

**Hovey, Richard** (1864–1900). Poet. Born in Normal, Illinois, he graduated from Dartmouth College, where he wrote early verse, and studied art before finally committing himself, stylishly, to poetry. He was one of the underestimated group of American *fin de siècle* poets who prepared for the transition to 'modern' verse. Perhaps more significant than for the kind of sensibility he expressed than for the quality of his writing, he was devoutly 'Bohemian', celebrating in life and verse the vagabond existence (◊ Bohemianism). In 1891–2 he visited Europe and came under strong influence from the French symbolists, then strongly affecting writing in English; he translated Mallarmé and eight plays of Maeterlinck, who stirred his dramatic ambitions.

Hovey's wandering-poet ideal is best revealed in the three series of *Songs from Vagabondia* (1894, 1896, 1901), written with the Canadian Bohemian poet Bliss ◊ Carman. He early planned a cycle of poetic dramas on the Arthurian legends which he did not live to complete, though several parts of the work appeared between 1891 and 1907 (the posthumous *Holy Grail*). Other work includes *Seaward* (1893), an elegy on a friend's death, and the collections *Along the Trail* (1898) and *To the End of the Trail* (1908). [MB]

Bruce Weirick, *From Whitman to Sandburg in American Poetry* (1924); A. H. Macdonald, *Richard Hovey: Man and Craftsman* (1957).

**Howard, Sidney Coe** (1891–1939). Playwright. Born in Oakland, California. He studied at the University of California and in George Pierce ◊ Baker's 47 Workshop at Harvard. After war service he produced his first play, a Renaissance melodrama, *Swords* (1921). He died at the height of his career through a tractor accident in Massachusetts. His first prize-winner was *They Knew What They Wanted* (1924; musical version, *The Most Happy Fella*, 1957), a sensational but tender and truthful social drama of an ageing Italian vine-grower in the Napa Valley, California, who marries a mail-order wife. *The Silver Cord* (1926) exposes neurotic mother-love in New England; *The Late Christopher Bean* (1932) satirizes the art-dealing world; and *Alien Corn* (1933) opposes the Babbitt personality with an émigré musician from Vienna. Howard's competent abilities and realistic dialogue correspond to the social observation fiction of ◊ Marquand. [EM]

**Howe, Julia Ward** (1819–1910). Biographer, poetess. A New Yorker by birth, she was a famous female suffrage leader, promoter of prison reform and international peace, biographer of Margaret ◊ Fuller, and composer of 'The Battle Hymn of the Republic' (1862) and a mass oᵣ ᵤther poems. [EM]

**Howells, William Dean** (1837–1920). Novelist, critic, playwright. Born in Ohio, entirely self-educated, he began work at 9 in the printing office of his father and by 15 was contributing essays and poems to Ohio newspapers. Two autobiographical volumes, *A Boy's Town* (1890) and *Years of My Youth* (1916), re-create these years, while *My Literary Passions* (1895) shows the phenomenal reading he undertook to become a writer (it equipped him later to become Professor of Modern Languages at Harvard). In 1860 he published *Poems of Two Friends* (with John J. Piatt) and a campaign biography of Lincoln, and visited Boston to meet Lowell, Fields, Emerson and Hawthorne, while Holmes prophetically spoke of 'the apostolic succession'. The Lincoln biography won him the Consulate at Venice (1861–5), where he spent a happy and fruitful period recorded in the engaging sketches of *Venetian Life* (1866), *Italian Journeys* (1867) and the more scholarly *Modern Italian Poets* (1887). He returned to work on the *Nation* and attained the eminence of editing the *Atlantic Monthly*. His move from Boston to New York in 1888 signalled a change in the relative

cultural power of the two centres and also in Howells's thought, bringing a Tolstoyan social concern into his later novels. A prolific writer of highly esteemed, successful and influential books, he was the close friend of many major writers, including Stephen Crane, Frank Norris and Henry James, finely discussed in *Literary Friends and Acquaintance* (1900). He became first president of the American Academy of Arts and Letters (1908); celebrations marked his seventy-fifth birthday; he achieved the rarely filled role of 'Dean of American letters', though a new generation of writers was often disrespectful – Mencken called him 'an Agnes Repplier in pantaloons'.

Howells deserved much better; he is an important novelist in a distinctive mode, a central figure in American social fiction, as well as a superb memoirist and a significant cultural figure. His first novel, *Their Wedding Journey* (1872), is pleasant but slight; ᵤₑₐᵣ *Chance Acquaintance* (1873), *A Foregone Conclusion* (1875), *The Lady of the Aroostook* (1879), *The Undiscovered Country* (1880), *A Fearful Responsibility* (1881) and *Dr Breen's Practice* (1881) strike a distinctive note in the history of American fiction. Howells used his European experiences to develop the new species of the international novel; he also began to create, with subtle psychological realism, a novel of manners entirely American in inspiration and setting. His work reaches great distinction with his two most successful novels, *A Modern Instance* (1881) and *The Rise of Silas Lapham* (1885), the latter a fascinating, deep-rooted analysis of the social and moral predicaments of a newly rich New England family.

With *Indian Summer* (1886) Howells became the acknowledged leader of the American 'realist' school. In later novels his irony shifts further away from love-relationships into crucial social issues. *Annie Kilburn* (1888) indicts labouring conditions and false philanthropy; *A Hazard of New Fortunes* (1890) shows the clash of labour and capital in a strike; *An Imperative Duty* (1892) introduces a heroine of Negro blood; and *A Traveler from Altruria* (1894), with its sequel *Through the Eye of a Needle* (1907), contrasts American society with a well-ordered Utopia. Of his last novels, some revert to earlier themes or to scenes of youth and childhood. The best are *The Landlord at Lion's Head* (1897) and *The Kentons* (1902), while *The Vacation of the Kelwyns* (1920), is a delightful idyll set in the Centennial summer of 1876. Most of Howells's works are now being reprinted in a series of authoritative texts.

Howells wrote plays, four volumes of indifferent poetry, and numerous works of criticism, travel and autobiography. For many years the leading exponent of realism in the U.S.A., his insistence on the 'smiling aspects' of American life and the weight of his statements in *Criticism and Fiction* (1891) separated him from younger writers. This was not timidity. He believed the commonplace and average were typical of America, and made for genuine democratic art. Unobtrusively his often underrated novels assert that 'fidelity to experience and probability of motive' which he thought the essential condition of imaginative literature, and his great sense of community makes him that rare thing, an American *social* novelist. [HD]

*Complete Plays*, ed. W. J. Meserve (1960); *William Dean Howells*, ed. Clara and Rudolph Kirk (1950) (selections); *Selected Writings*, ed. H. S. Commager (1950).

Edwin H. Cady, *The Road to Realism: The Early Years, 1837–1885, of William Dean Howells* (1956) and *The Realist at War: The Mature Years, 1885–1920, of William Dean Howells* 1958); Everett Carter, *Howells and the Age of Realism* (1954); G. N. Bennett, *William Dean Howells: The Development of a Novelist* (1959); ed. K. E. Eble, *Howells: A Century of Criticism* (1962); C. Marburg Kirk, *William Dean Howells and Art in His Time* (1965).

**Howes, Barbara** (1914–     ). Poet. Born in Boston, Massachusetts, she edited in New York the magazine *Chimera* and, after marrying the poet William Jay ◊ Smith, spent considerable time in Italy and France. Her poetry in *In the Cold Country* (1954) and *Light and Dark* (1959) is written in a cultivated tradition, developing occasions drawn from domestic settings, life in foreign lands, and paintings and works of art into a kind of mythological intensity. Concerned primarily with delicate shades and the intricate pathways of human love, she has been praised by Louise ◊ Bogan, who has influenced her. Her latest volume is *Looking Up at Leaves* (1967). [MB]

**Hughes, Langston** (1902–67). Poet, novelist satirist, playwright. Born in Joplin, Missouri. His boyhood was spent in midWestern towns, and as a young man he taught in Mexico, worked his father's ranch

there, became a Staten Island farmer, a seaman, a Montmartre night-club cook and a bus-boy in a Washington hotel – where he got Vachel ◊ Lindsay to read his poems at a recital (see his autobiography in *The Big Sea*, 1940, and *I Wonder as I Wander*, 1956). His first book of poetry, *The Weary Blues* (1926), began a long and admirable career as one of America's leading men of letters and Negro poets. His blues, ballads and lyrics have appeared in at least 7 volumes. His plays include *Mulatto* (1936) and *The Prodigal Son* (1964), and he has written opera libretti, lyrics for musicals, and the cantata *The Ballad of the Brown King. Not without Laughter* (1936) is a novel, and *The Ways of White Folks* (1934) short stories. Hughes' satirical sketches, written originally for a Negro paper, have been collected in *Simple Speaks His Mind* (1950), *The Best of Simple* (1961) and *Simple's Uncle Sam* (1965), the wry, witty adventures of one of American literature's most endearing characters, Jesse B. Simple of Harlem, U.S.A. Throughout his career Hughes has created a body of Negro American writing in which he uses the tradition of Whitman, ◊ Lindsay, ◊ Sandburg and ◊ Dunbar for his own genial irony and caustic humours. The recording of his *Weary Blues* is one of the few jazz-and-poetry performances of any quality. (◊ Negro Literature.) [EM]

*Selected Poems* (1959); *The Panther and the Lash* (1969).

**Humphrey, William** (1924–     ). Novelist. Born in Clarksville, Texas, he has made the South-west the chief subject matter of his fiction. But though writing in the Southern tradition of novels concerned with communities and families responding to forces of change, he has a psychological and sociological awareness that makes him much more than a regionalist. His two novels, *Home from the Hill* (1958) and *The Ordways* (1965), set in contrast legends from the past and present-day Texas, the latter concerning the Southern diaspora following the Civil War and the changes in Texan life. Though sometimes sentimental, his accuracy of rendering and his scope make him a figure of considerable interest in the recent fictional scene. [MB]

**Humphreys, David.** ◊ Connecticut Wits.

**Huneker, James Gibbons** (1860–1921). Critic, novelist. Born in Philadelphia, he studied music in Paris and was music critic on Philadelphia and New York newspapers; in this role he became the leading spokesman of Impressionism and did much to promote European *avant garde* tendencies in the U.S.A. He was a glutton of the arts, was closely associated with the cosmopolitan-Bohemian phase of the late-19th-century American arts (◊ Bohemianism), and hence not only advanced American modernism but promoted a style of aestheticism that was to come through to the *Smart Set* and the *New Yorker*. ◊ Mencken, a later version of the same kind of sensibility, admired him as 'the chief man of the movement of the nineties on this side of the ocean'. His early books are chiefly on music. Then came *Iconoclasts: A Book of Dramatists* (1905) and *Egoists: A Book of Supermen* (1909) on the little-known modernists of the European theatre, etc. *Promenades of an Impressionist* (1910) conveys his aesthetics and his highly Parisian sensibility. He is a sharp and colourful critic, if in what is now a faded manner. Among other works are two volumes of stories, *Melomaniacs* (1902) and *Visionaries* (1905), and *Painted Veils* (1920), a highly elaborated, fanciful, 'daring' novel about the New York art world. *Steeplejack* (2 vols., 1920), his autobiography, asserts his commitment to all the arts. [M B]

*Letters*, ed. J. Huneker (1922); *Intimate Letters* ed. J. Huneker (1924).
Arnold T. Schwab, *James Gibbons Huneker, Critic of the Seven Arts* (1963); Benjamin de Casseres, *James Gibbons Huneker* (1925); Alfred Kazin, *On Native Grounds* (1942); Albert Parry, *Garrets and Pretenders* (1960).

**Hunter, Evan** (1926–    ). Novelist. Born in New York, he has published several novels under his own name – including *The Blackboard Jungle* (1954), *Buddwing* (1964) and *Last Summer* (1968) – and consider-ably more under the pseudonym Ed McBain. For the most part these are realistic and well-constructed accounts of crime and detection in the 87th Precinct of a large American city. Hunter has often been praised for the way in which his detailed knowledge of police procedure communicates a sense of reality. [H D]

*Cop Hunter* (1956); *Lady Killer* (1958); *King's Ransom* (1959); *Give the Boys a Great Big Hand* (1960); *The 87th Squad* (1960); *See Them Die* (1961); *The Empty Hours* (1962); *Axe* (1964); *Fuzz* (1968); *Shotgun* (1968); *Sons* (1969).

**Hutchinson, Thomas** (1711–80). He was born in Boston, went to Harvard at 12, and by the age of 21, having made money, entered public life. His Toryism helped George III appoint him a chief justice and, later, governor of Massachusetts. It was he who provoked James Otis to remark 'Taxation without representation is tyranny'. In 1774 martial law was proclaimed and he had to account for his failures in England: he never went back. His chief work was *A Collection of Original Papers Relative to the History of the Colony of Massachusetts* (1764, 1767, 1818), the best account of his times. [E M]

**Hyman, Stanley Edgar** (1919–70). Critic. He was born in New York City, graduated at Syracuse University and taught at Bennington. His original and wide-ranging criticism includes *The Armed Vision* (1948), an important analysis of modern critics (some of the basic texts he edited in *The Critical Performance*, 1956), *Poetry and Criticism* (1961), concerning literary taste, *Nathanael West* (1962), *The Tangled Bank: Darwin, Marx, Frazer and Freud as Imaginative Writers* (1962) and *The Promised End* (1963), collected essays and reviews, also assembled in *Standards: A Chronicle of Books of Our Times* (1966). [M B]

**Ignatow, David** (1914–    ). Poet. Author of *Poems* (1948), *Gentle Weight Lifter* (1955), *Say Pardon* (1961), *Figures of the Human* (1964) and *Rescue the Dead* (1968), he left college during the Depression and, until he turned to full-time teaching in 1965, worked as a businessman in his native New York City, lecturer at the New School for Social Research, editor of the *Beloit Poetry Journal* (1949–59) and poetry editor of the *Nation* (1962–3). His flat, colloquial style re-creates Brooklyn speech rhythms in the telling of concentrated episodes which suggest an ironic mythic vision of modern city life. *Poems 1934–1969* (1970) contains previously uncollected and unpublished poetry. [B P]

**Imagism.** A poetic movement flourishing in England and the United States between 1912 and 1917, and originating in the theories, expounded in London from 1908 onwards, of the anti-romantic aesthetician T. E. Hulme and the polyglot poetry reviewer F. S. Flint. Ezra ◊ Pound's *Ripostes* (1912) included five miniature poems by Hulme, his 'Complete Poetical Works', and during this year Pound coined the term 'Les Imagistes'. A platform for Imagism was found in Harriet ◊ Monroe's *Poetry* (Chicago), where in March 1913 Flint and Pound published a few definitions and principles (◊ Little Magazines). *Des Imagistes: An Anthology* (1914) included poems by Flint, Pound, Richard Aldington, H.D. (Hilda ◊ Doolittle), Ford Madox Ford, William Carlos ◊ Williams, and Amy ◊ Lowell, thus associating English and American poets. By then Pound's interest in the movement was waning, and after a row with Amy Lowell over the distribution of her financial resources, he dissociated himself from the group. *Some Imagist Poets* (1915) contained a new statement of Imagist doctrine by Aldington and Amy Lowell, and poems by Aldington, Lowell, Flint, H.D., John Gould ◊ Fletcher and D.H. Lawrence. These six poets were represented in similarly entitled anthologies issued in 1916 and 1917, after which by general consent no further collections appeared.

The brief history of Imagism is one of irascibility and recrimination, with Pound as the chief source of disturbance. However, the foremost Imagist theoreticians, Hulme, Flint, Pound and Aldington, were largely in agreement on the following principles: that Japanese *haiku* and *tanka*, certain lesser-known Greek and Latin writers, 19th-century French poetry and theory, and a few neglected English figures had more to teach the contemporary poet than most of the conventionally accepted 'great English poets'; that Victorian verbosity, heavy-handed didacticism, platitudinous ornamentation and fondness for ethereal abstractions were crimes against art; that the poetic virtues include precision, concentration, firmness of outline, freshness and clarity of vision, and the use of striking, arresting analogies; and that each emotion has its distinctive rhythm and need not pay heed to obsolete metrical rules, i.e. free verse, Flint's 'unrhymed cadence', is to be preferred.

To these purificatory rather than revolutionary postulates the ten poets most closely associated with Imagism remained for a very few years more or less loyal. Of these poets, Fletcher, Ford and Amy Lowell were always more impressionistic than Imagistic; Lawrence and Williams were affected by the movement rather than dedicated to it; Flint and Hulme were more influential as theorists than as practitioners; and Aldington and Pound were either too adventurous or too versatile to be long fulfilled within the self-imposed limitations of Imagism. The purest, finest and most consistent application of Imagist principles is to be found in the poetry of H.D.

Imagism, as a self-proclaiming movement, died in 1917. Almost by definition it was a movement destined to produce minor poetry, and apart from H.D. all the chief Imagists soon went in search of broader horizons. But its influence upon subsequent poetry has nonetheless been considerable and for the most part salutary. Imagism was the first organized attack in this century upon sloppy approximation in description, rhythmic monotony, staleness of perception and cultural parochialism. Further, one of its most striking features was that it was Anglo-American in character, and for a time closely linked two poetic traditions. [R W B]

Glenn Hughes, *Imagism and the Imagists* (1960); Stanley K. Coffman, Jr, *Imagism* (1951).

**Imlay, Gilbert** (1754?–1828?). Novelist, propagandist. He was born in New Jersey, fought in the Revolution, and in 1783 involved himself in shady land sales in Kentucky. He fled the lawsuits and turned up in the 1790s in London and Paris radical circles with Joel ◊ Barlow and Tom ◊ Paine. In 1793 he was in the Girondist plot to seize Louisiana from Spain, and he fathered a boy on Mary Wollstonecraft. The next known fact is his burial on the island of Jersey. *A Topographical Description of the Western Territory of North America* (1792) takes the form of 11 enthusiastic letters to an English friend. *The Emigrants* (1793) is the first novel of the area between Pittsburg and the Mississippi, and an early version of the 'American innocence versus wicked Old Europe' myth, with its basis in 'natural rights', including the rights of women and divorce. America sustains men's natural goodness and is free from 'the commercial spirit', the class system and 'the tyranny of custom'. Imlay's epistolary novel is readable, psychologically fairly full in the Richardson manner, and designed to tempt Englishmen to America. [E M]

**Inge, William** (1913–    ). Playwright. He was born in Kansas, taught in Missouri and was general arts critic on the St Louis *Times* (1943). He produced his first play, *Farther Off from Heaven*, in 1947, inspired by Tennessee Williams' *The Glass Menagerie*. His very successful plays are psychodramas involving the solution of personal and social problems by introspection and togetherness among average mid-Westerners: *Come Back Little Sheba* (1950), *Picnic* (1953), *Bus Stop* (1955) and *The Dark at the Top of the Stairs* (1957). *A Loss of Roses* (1960), *Natural Affection* (1963) and *Where's Daddy?* (1966) show a distinct easing towards melodrama and routine. [E M]

R. Baird Shuman, *William Inge* (1965).

**Irving, Washington** (1783–1859). Short-story writer, historian. Born in New York City. His father was an ex-petty officer, a hardware dealer and a Calvinist deacon. Irving was very different and needed the less strict encouragement of his mother for the development of his sensibility, which preferred dreamy out-of-doors wandering to school. While he trained as a lawyer, his bookishness turned towards literature. His first and anonymous work was *The Letters of Jonathan Oldstyle, Gent* (1802–3) in the *Morning Chronicle*, followed by the *Salmagundi Papers* (1807–8), again a series of sketches and essays. In 1809 appeared his *History of New York*, called the 'Knickerbocker History' after its supposed author; it begins as a comic parody of historical scholarship and ends as a straight account of Dutch colonization. Financial and critical success decided him on a literary career, slightly interrupted by war service in 1812. In 1815 he travelled to Europe and stayed 17 years; when he needed money he wrote *The Sketch Book of Geoffrey Crayon, Gent* (1819–20), published in instalments in New York and as a book in London (with the help of Scott). Irving's reputation as a gentleman of letters was established. *Bracebridge Hall* (1822), a dullish celebration of the English squire, and *Tales of a Traveller* (1824), a hack assemblage of stories, were blasted by critics, and he left for Spain and wrote a life of Columbus (1828), which swelled his patriotism, his reputation and his pocket. *The Conquest of Granada* (1829) is a wretched historical romance of the Moors in Spain but it gained him Spanish honours and a room in a palace where he wrote a better book, *The Alhambra* (1832). He reluctantly left Spain to become American Legation secretary in London, resigning in 1832 to return to America and be shocked by its 'all pervading commonplace'. But his extensive journeys made *Tours on the Prairies* (1835), and the Astors commissioned a fur-trade epic based on the family manuscripts: *Astoria* (1836, 1849) – after which he bought a Hudson valley cottage and decorated it with ivy from Scott's own house. He returned to Spain as ambassador in 1842 and back in New York wrote lives of Goldsmith, Washington and Astor before he died. The 32 pieces of his *Sketch Book* contain his best work. Embedded in whimsy and bland Anglicized stylishness in imitation of English essayists, and in sentimental landscape descriptions, are two famous tales, 'Rip Van Winkle', with a hero whose easy-going Dutch ancestors retain him in the Kaatskill mountains where he misses

20 years of American progress, and 'The Legend of Sleepy Hollow', in which a Yankee schoolmaster, Ichabod Crane, finds his belief in old New England witchcraft disables him before the supposed ghost of a headless Hessian left-over from the Revolutionary War, and loses him the hand of an heiress. Irving transformed the German originals of these tales into American myths. He encouraged American cultural life by his professional example. [EM]

*Works* (40 vols., 1910).

Pierre M. Irving, *The Life and Letters of Washington Irving* (4 vols., 1862–4); Stanley T. Williams, *The Life of Washington Irving* (2 vols., 1935); W. L. Hedges, *Washington Irving* (1965).

# J

**Jackson, Shirley** (1919–65). Novelist. She was born in San Francisco, and after her marriage to Stanley Edgar ◊ Hyman settled in Vermont to a middle-class intellectual life she described in *Life among the Savages* (1953) and *Raising Demons* (1957). The dark obverse side to these humorous chronicles is her novels of mental morbidity and the supernatural in ordinary localities – *The Road through the Wall* (1948), *Hangsaman* (1951) and *The Bird's Nest* (1954). The personal nightmare penetrates the weird allegory of *The Lottery* (1949), *The Sundial* (1958), *The Haunting of Hill House* (1959) and *We Have Always Lived in the Castle* (1962). *The Witchcraft of Salem Village* (1956) is a children's account of the 1690 trials. *Come Along with Me* (1968) includes posthumous work and is edited by her husband. [EM]

The Magic of Shirley Jackson, ed. Stanley E. Hyman (1966).

**James, Henry, Sr** (1811–82). Philosopher. Of wealthy Albany, New York, background, he withdrew from Princeton Theological Seminary in revolt against Calvinism and in due course became a Swedenborgian with ◊ Transcendentalist overtones. A friend of many major European and American thinkers, including Emerson and Carlyle, he travelled in Europe and lectured widely in the States, while his own family became a remarkable community in itself (Henry ◊ James, William ◊ James). He was a complex social thinker and reformer, as books like his *Christianity the Logic of Creation* (1857), *Substance and Shadow* (1863) and *Society the Redeemed Form of Man* (1879) show. His influence on both his sons, the philosopher and the novelist, has come more and more to light. [MB]

F. O. Matthiessen, *The James Family* (1947); Austin Warren, *The Elder Henry James* (1934); Frederick H. Young, *The Philosophy of Henry James, Sr* (1951).

**James, Henry** (1843–1916). Novelist, short-story writer, playwright, critic, essayist. He was born in New York City, the second of the five children of Henry ◊ James, Sr, the Swedenborgian philosopher, who later took his family to Europe in order that the children might receive a better 'sensuous education'. Henry was educated intermittently at schools in Geneva, Paris, Boulogne and Bonn; during 1862–3 he attended Harvard Law School. In 1869 he made his first extended adult trip to Europe, and the record of these months and the later period 1872–4, also spent abroad, is to be found in his first published books: *A Passionate Pilgrim and Other Tales* (1875) and *Transatlantic Sketches* (1875), travel essays which complement and interact with the fiction to present a young American's highly enthusiastic European impressions. For a year James lived in Paris, but in 1877 he decided to settle in London, where he remained, with the exception of frequent excursions to the continent and fewer to his native land, until 1896. During his last years he lived and wrote in Lamb House, Rye; from this period the famous 'legend of the master' takes its origin. Returning to London in 1912, he felt the advent of the First World War keenly, and in protest against what he considered to be American tardiness assumed British nationality in 1915. Next year he suffered a stroke ('So here it is at last, the distinguished thing', he is reported as saying), and on his death-bed received the Order of Merit.

It is customary and convenient to divide James's career into three periods. In the first he made his reputation as the originator of the international novel and story. His first published novel, *Roderick Hudson*, about the moral and artistic disintegration of an American in Rome, appeared in 1876; it was followed by *The American* (1877), the first self-conscious and consistently serious attempt to dramatize in fiction the social relationships between the Old World and the New; *The Europeans* (1878), a subtle examination of the impact of two slightly raffish Europeans upon their cousins in the rural Boston of the 1830s; *Washington Square* (1881); and such charming productions as 'Daisy Miller' (1879), probably James's most popular single work in his lifetime, and the witty tale 'An International

Episode' (1879). This period culminated in the undisputed masterpiece *The Portrait of a Lady* (1881), where the accepted contrasts of the international theme are subordinated to the psychological realization of the heroine's character in a way which foreshadows his later subject matter and experiments in technique; the central focus shifts to the single observing consciousness and to the growth of that moral consciousness as a result of the incompatibility of the demands of the individual and those of society. The novels and tales of these six years present James's fullest and most complex use of the international subject for primary rather than secondary effects. During this period he created the twin figures of the American girl and the American businessman in Europe, and also discovered, most notably in *The Portrait of a Lady*, the artistic possibilities offered by the Europeanized American. Manipulating his favourite theme for a variety of purposes and with differing emphasis, James eschews any easy preference for one civilization over another, allowing a hypothetical ideal combination of moral values to emerge from the interplay of two societies and the concomitant mixture of manners.

The themes of the second period, from the mid-1880s to 1897, are more specifically English, though earlier contrasts appear in such tales as 'Lady Barberina' (1884) and *The Reverberator* (1888). Major works of this decade are *The Bostonians* (1886) and *The Princess Casamassima* (1886), the one a satiric account of female emancipation in Boston, the other a richly observed novel of anarchists and aristocrats in London, which together effectively refute the charge that James was neither interested in nor capable of rendering immediate social concerns and actualities. During 1890–5 an intense preoccupation with the possibilities of the stage, which first emerges in *The Tragic Muse* (1890) and which lasted until the disastrous first night of *Guy Domville* in 1895, did not prevent him from writing an impressive group of stories centring on the nature and predicament of the creative artist. His unsuccessful experiments in dramatic technique nevertheless profoundly influenced the structure of his later novels.

The third period of James's literary career opens with *The Spoils of Poynton* (1897) and *What Maisie Knew* (1897), and includes such works as *The Turn of the Screw* (1898), *The Awkward Age* (1899) and *The Sacred Fount* (1901). If criticism is still undecided as to the merits of some of these last works, an even sharper division of opinion is observable in the case of the three novels *The Wings of the Dove* (1902), *The Ambassadors* (1903) and *The Golden Bowl* (1904), in which, it is sometimes claimed, an over-elaboration of motive is accompanied by an over-refinement in style. In them James develops most fully his commitment to the single point of view and his theories on 'scenic' progression in a subtle and intricate prose which is capable of reproducing every nuance of the fine moral intelligence with which he endows his characters. These novels have been praised and denigrated in a wide variety of interpretations, which ranges from their acceptance as moral fables of a high order to a consideration of them as James's reworkings of his father's Swedenborgian theology and ethics.

In 1904 James visited the United States for the first time since 1883. The result was *The American Scene* (1907), at once a fine travel book and James's farewell to a country he could not live in. On his return he began the prodigious task of revising his novels and tales for the selective 'New York' edition of his works (24 vols., 1907–9). Two posthumously published novels, *The Ivory Tower* (1917) and *The Sense of the Past* (1917), were later added.

James was also a remarkable critic who ranged widely in European and American literature. Throughout his career he was preoccupied with questions of form, from his early plea in the often reprinted essay 'The Art of Fiction' (included in *Partial Portraits*, 1888) to his final assessments in *Notes on Novelists* (1914). His prefaces to the volumes in the 'New York' edition, conveniently collected by R. P. Blackmur as *The Art of the Novel* (1934), established categories and principles which have deeply affected – and not always for the best – later developments in criticism. Among his many other works one may mention the biographies *Hawthorne* (1879) and *William Wetmore Story* (1903); his engaging travel essays, the best of which were issued as *The Art of Travel* (ed. M. D. Zabel, 1958); and the unfinished autobiography: *A Small Boy and Others* (1913), *Notes of a Son and Brother* (1914) and *The Middle Years* (1917), together edited by F. W. Dupee as *Henry James: Autobiography* (1956).

The 'New York' edition has been recently reprinted (1961–6), a text followed in *The Novels and Stories of Henry James* (35 vols., 1921–3) which includes all the fiction published in James's lifetime. Leon Edel has edited the *Complete Tales*, which reprints the 112 short stories (12 vols., 1962–7) and the *Complete Plays* (1949). Robert E. Spiller's excellent survey of James criticism up to 1954 appears in *Eight American Authors* (ed. Floyd Stovall, 1956); the revised edition of 1963 contains a check list covering 1955 to 1962. See also 'Criticism of Henry James: A Selected Checklist', *Modern Fiction Studies*, III (1957) and *Modern Fiction Studies*, XII (1966). [HD]

*Letters*, ed. Percy Lubbock (1920); *Selected Letters*, ed. L. Edel (1956); *The Notebooks*, ed. F. O. Matthiessen and K. Murdock (1947).

Leon Edel, *Henry James: The Untried Years, 1843–1870* (1953), *Henry James: The Conquest of London, 1870–1883* (1962), *Henry James: The Middle Years, 1884–1895* (1963), *Henry James: The Treacherous Years, 1895–1901* (1969); F. O. Matthiessen *Henry James: The Major Phase* (1946); ed. F. W. Dupee, *The Question of Henry James* (1945); Richard Poirier, *The Comic Sense of Henry James* (1960); Oscar Cargill, *The Novels of Henry James* (1961); Dorothea Krook, *The Ordeal of Consciousness in Henry James* (1962); Maxwell Geismar, *Henry James and His Cult* (1964); Douglas Jefferson, *Henry James and the Modern Reader* (1964); L. B. Holland, *The Expense of Vision* (1964); S. Gorley Putt, *A Reader's Guide to Henry James*; ed. Tony Tanner, *Henry James: Modern Judgements* (1968); ed. R. Gard, *Henry James: The Critical Heritage* (1968).

**James, William** (1842–1910). Philosopher, psychologist. James was born in New York City of a father, Henry ◊ James, Sr, himself a considerable philosopher, and rich enough to send his sons abroad for much of their education. In Paris, the young James conceived the ambition of being a painter; at Harvard, which he entered at 19, his interests shifted to biology, and in 1865 he went with ◊ Agassiz on a scientific expedition to Brazil, returning to Harvard to enter the Medical School, and taking his M.D. in 1870. In 1872 he began his teaching career of 35 years at Harvard as an instructor in physiology, but his interest gradually shifted again, first to psychology and finally to philosophy. In 1860 he published his *Principles of Psychology*, which is a classic in its field. In 1901–2, he gave the Gifford lectures in Edinburgh on *The Varieties of Religious Experience*. The development of his pragmatic philosophy came late in his life; *Pragmatism* was published in the year of his retirement from Harvard in 1907, and *A Pluralistic Universe* in 1909. He died at his summer home in Chocorua, New Hampshire, on 26 August 1910. He was the elder brother of the novelist, Henry James.

Regarding James's achievements as a philosopher opinions vary, but there is no doubt that his thought was influential on writers as various as his brother Henry and Gertrude Stein and that he was a remarkable writer with a unique personality. He had an 'artistic temperament' whose ups and downs were accentuated by a life-long frailty of health. He was impatient of pedantry, of the formal side of teaching, and even of philosophy as a purely intellectual pursuit; he was impulsive, imaginative, deeply affectionate, unconventional in his tastes, sympathetic with spiritualism and mysticism, and broadly democratic in his feelings – 'a sort of Irishman among the Brahmins', as Santayana put it. These traits appear in his writing, and give it colour and vitality. *The Varieties of Religious Experience*, especially, is remarkable for its balance of rationality and sympathy for extreme religious experiences.

The leading idea running through James's thought is that of the will as the dominant factor in experience. His studies as a biologist suggested to him that man is an organism made for action. Even the emergence in our experience of distinct things and concepts is due to the attempt to satisfy practical needs. Life begins for the infant as 'a blooming, buzzing confusion', in which balls and bottles are slowly singled out because they satisfy some interest. When concepts are formed, they are usually fashioned in terms of utility; spoons are things to eat with and knives to cut with; 'the meaning of essence is teleological,' said James in the *Psychology*. His dynamic way of conceiving the mind appears again in the James-Lange theory of emotion: 'we feel sorry because we cry, angry because we strike, afraid because we tremble.' Some object sets up a reaction in us, and the emotion *is* our feeling of this reaction. The secret of emotional control is therefore the control of the bodily responses.

The most famous expression of James's view of primacy of the will is found, however, in his pragmatism. He did not believe that wholly disinterested thought was possible; a philosophy is accepted as much because it satisfies the heart's desire or is congenial to one's temperament as because it convinces the intellect. But James did not adopt his pragmatism all at once. *The Will to Believe* (1897) was a half-way house to the later doctrine. In that much-discussed essay, he held that, if probabilities were balanced and the doctors disagreed, we were justified in accepting the belief which worked best, in the sense of leading to the most satisfying results in practice. But he came to see that he could not stop there; if the practical consequences of a belief were really relevant to its truth in such a case, they must be so generally.

Pragmatism was essentially a doctrine of truth. Whereas philosophers of the past had held that the truth of a belief lay in its correspondence with fact or its coherence with experience as a whole, James held that 'the true . . . is only the expedient in our way of thinking'. If the belief in God or in immortality leads to lives of more courage, peace and happiness, it is, so far, true. This teaching was heard gladly by many persons concerned to hold their religious beliefs, but it has not worn well. It is in trouble, for example, when it comes to beliefs about the past or to those scientific beliefs which are without practical effects.

James was not afraid of the unconventional. He was an eager investigator of spiritualistic mediums. In religion he was inclined to the view of a finite and struggling Deity, warring like ourselves against evil; and in the *Varieties* he regards certain mystical experiences as probable revelations of a superhuman consciousness. In later life he developed an ingenious theory of the relation of the mental and physical realms. There existed only one neutral stuff, which became mental or physical according to context; tables and chairs when taken in the context of our thoughts and feelings were mental; taken merely in their relations of space and causality, they were physical. This theory of 'neutral monism' found an advocate for a time in Bertrand Russell.

Though not a rigorous thinker, James's insight into human nature, his power of describing it, and his capacity for friendship were extraordinary. Fortunately he has been made the subject of one of the best biographies of the century (see Perry, below). [BB]

*Letters*, ed. Henry James (2 vols., 1920); *The Writings*, ed. John McDermott (1968).

R. B. Perry, *The Thought and Character of William James* (2 vols., 1935); F. O. Matthiessen, *The James Family* (1947); G. W. Allen, *William James: A Biography* (1967).

**Jarrell, Randall** (1914–65). Poet, critic, novelist. He was born in Nashville, Tennessee, served in the air force in the Second World War, taught at a number of universities, was consultant in poetry at the Library of Congress 1956–8, and worked on the *Nation*. His distinguished poetry began with *Blood for a Stranger* (1942) and subsequently appeared in *Little Friend, Little Friend* (1945), *Losses* (1948), *The Seven-League Crutches* (1951), *Selected Poems* (1955), *The Woman at the Washington Zoo* (1960) and *The Lost World* (1965). His characteristic subjects were the victims of war and historical crisis as examples of the ineradicable human condition, only briefly and uncertainly ameliorated in childhood. Although his poems have the tight elliptical quality of much ◊ New Criticism verse, there is an unmistakable anguish and compassion entirely personal to him, as if the ills of the unstable and violent forties had penetrated into his own sensibility and had to be exorcized. Poems in the last two books have the additional poignancy of the self-irony of the poet whose own condition hardly seems to him to warrant his analysis and evaluation of his fellow men. The added intensity raised his freer forms to a fresh quality. Of his criticism, *Poetry and the Age* (1953) is incisive and generous, and is especially valuable for its estimations by careful quotation, and *A Sad Heart at the Supermarket* (1962) includes good studies of Kipling and Malraux and a classic essay in wry disillusionment with western chances of literacy. His novel of academic life, *Pictures from an Institution* (1954), is both hilariously funny and a comment on the hopeless condition of certain liberal arts colleges. Jarrell stood for a level of critical integrity and independent poetry which is rare in a culture which tended towards inimical groups. [EM]

*The Complete Poems* (1969); *The Third Book of Criticism* (1969).

Ed. Robert Lowell, Peter Taylor and Robert Penn Warren, *Randall Jarrell 1914–1965* (1967); S. Stepanchev, *American Poetry since 1945* (1965); M. L. Rosenthal, *The Modern Poets* (1960).

**Jeffers, Robinson** (1887–1962). Poet. He was born in Pittsburg, and as a boy, tutored by his father, a theologian and classical scholar, his education continued lengthily in Switzerland, Germany and America. When he was 16 the family settled in California; he graduated from Occidental College, California, in 1905. His studies in medicine, forestry and literature in various colleges resulted in that broad scholarly and geographical interest which penetrates his poetry. But he could not give his complete time to poetry until he received an inheritance and married a woman whose secure vitality warmed his own austerity. He settled in Carmel, on the Monterey coast of California, whose mountains over the Pacific and timeless, barbaric natural life are so active in his work – 'people living – amid magnificent unspoiled scenery – essentially as they did in the Idylls or the Sagas, or in Homer's Ithaca. Here life was purged of its ephemeral accretions.' At Point Sur he built a granite house and worked out his solitude in its tower.

His first two volumes of poetry, *Flagons and Apples* (1912) and *Californians* (1916), are most conventional, but *Tamar and Other Poems* (1924) marks the beginning of his impressively unique career. 'Tamar', based on Samuel 11:13 and Shelley's *The Cenci*, is his first long narrative poem, transposing the Old Testament story of cursed heredity, incest and revenge to California: it is representative of Jeffers's vision of mankind doomed with introspection and lust. 'The Tower beyond Tragedy' is a brilliant drama based on the *Oresteia*, and the title poem of *Roan Stallion* (1925) concerns a man killed by his horse, identified with a woman as a primitive god. His following volumes include *The Women at Point Sur* (1927), *Cawdor* (1928), *Dear Judas* (1929), *Descent to the Dead* (1931), *Thurso's Landing* (1932), *Give Your Heart to the Hawks* (1933), *Solstice* (1935), *Such Counsels You Gave Me* (1937), *Selected Poetry* (1938), *Be Angry at the Sun* (1941), *Medea* (1946), *The Double Axe* (1948), *Hungerfield* (1954) and a version of Euripides' *Hippolytus*.

Of the poems and plays in these, 'Cawdor' is an American Hippolytus myth, 'Thurso's Landing' a powerful poem of lust, impotence and insanity in Monterey, and 'Give Your Heart to the Hawks' the embodiment of his philosophy that humanity must develop the peace and endurance of rocks, the solitude of hawks, and respect for a God who is 'hardly a friend of humanity'. *Medea* (staged in New York in

1947 and 1965) is his greatest play. His shorter poems are elegies and conversations on similar themes: the steady background of nature, the pessimistic human foreground of men, a dark vision influenced by Nietzsche and Freud. His sensibility seems to look longingly away from human life towards the cold mysteries of nature, viewed from the heights of his own Sierras. He returned repeatedly to the theme of incest to embody his visionary drama of sterile life and inturned passion cut off from nature and inviting disaster. Merely to reject Christianity for a faith based on lust and energy, like the ranting of Dr Barclay in *The Women at Point Sur*, is to invite bloodshed and waste. Not anarchy of impulse, but 'to uncentre the human mind from itself' is what man needs. Jeffers's aim was 'to awake dangerous images and call the hawks'. His language and line reject modern symbolism and rhetoric, and speak directly and passionately in classical clarity. His brutality can be monotonous, but where his characters grow archetypal against monumental nature, his poems have a unique grandeur. [HB/EM]

*The Selected Poetry* (1959); *Selected Poems* (1965). L. C. Powell, *Robinson Jeffers: The Man and His Work* (revised edn, 1940); R. Squires, *The Loyalties of Robinson Jeffers* (1956).

**Jefferson, Thomas** (1743–1826). Reformer, third President of the United States. He was born in Virginia, graduated from William and Mary College in 1762, became a lawyer and was elected to the Virginia House of Burgesses in 1769. His paper *A Summary View of the Rights of British Americans*, sent to the Virginia convention in 1774, claimed 'natural rights' for emigrant settlement, the end of British taxation, and the need for a trade agreement with Britain. Its sane, clear, flexible prose illuminates the *Declaration of Independence* in 1776, drafted by Jefferson, with changes by John Adams and ◊ Franklin; it was partly indebted for ideas to John Locke's *Two Treatises of Civil Government* (1690) and *Letters Concerning Toleration* (1689, 1690, 1692), and influenced by George Mason's *Virginia Declaration of Rights* (1776). Jefferson was a member of the Virginia House of Delegates (1776–9) and governor of Virginia (1779–81), his main legislature concerning laws of inheritance and religious freedom. He tried to establish free education and the gradual abolition of slavery. In retirement at his magnificently designed Monticello he worked on his great *Notes on the State of Virginia* (1784–5). Where the *Declaration* set out a general philosophy of the Revolution and the reasons for colonial resistance, *Notes* places the idea of freedom in a wider context. After 7 chapters on the geography and resources of Virginia, 16 chapters delineate its social and political history, and through this scheme Jefferson set out to show that nature and man were not inferior in the New World, that America had already produced men of genius, and that the Indians themselves were 'formed in mind as well as in body on the same module' as Europeans. But he believed Negroes were inferior, although entitled to freedom and opportunity. The master–slave relationship was degrading; a Negro insurrection was to be feared; freedom was more expedient (Jefferson owned over 100 slaves). He also believed country workers were God's chosen people; towns bred vice as well as bad health. The independent farmer is the ideal: law and order are based on his property-owning self-reliance. Jefferson modified this view later ('our people have a decided taste for navigation and commerce'), but it is his agrarian opinions that have had a lasting effect on American belief.

Jefferson was elected to Congress in 1783 and in 1784 was appointed Franklin's assistant on the trade treaties with France. He observed the early French Revolution and deplored its later violence and imperialism. In Europe, he studied the classical architecture which became the basis of his plans for Virginia's state capitol and the subsequent national architectural style. After his appointment as first American secretary of state in 1790, he became the Republican leader in opposition to the Federalists under Alexander Hamilton, whom he suspected of monarchism, aristocracy and commercial industrialism. He was Vice-President under John Adams (one result was his *Manual of Parliamentary Practice*, 1801) and President in 1800, his main achievements being the Louisiana Purchase of 1803 and the subduing of pirates who had menaced shipping for some years past. The last years of his life he spent at Monticello, experimenting with agricultural methods, inventing and studying. He sold his large library to Congress in 1814 (the basis of the Library of Congress), to replace what the British had burned. Between 1811 and 1814 he carried on an important correspondence with John Adams.

The University of Virginia, founded on his plans and curriculum, opened in 1825. Jefferson's knowledge was extensive and utilitarian: he was an architect, a gardener and farmer, a mathematician and scientist, a lawyer, an inventor and a musician. As a deist, like Franklin and Paine, he believed in tolerance and the separation of church and state. As a founder of the Democratic Party, he advocated the abolition of slavery, freedom of the Press, States rights and isolationism. Apart from *Notes on Virginia*, his writings are mainly political pamphlets and papers, letters, and an *Autobiography* (1820; mostly on public life). All his writing is practical, since, as he said, 'literature is not yet a distinct profession with us . . . the first object of young societies is bread and covering'. The standard edition of *The Papers of Thomas Jefferson* (Princeton, various editors) runs to nearly 20 volumes. [F M]

*Life and Selected Writings*, ed. A. Koch and W. Peden (Modern Library, 1944); *The Basic Writings*, ed. P. S. Foner (1944).

Claude G. Bowers, *The Young Jefferson* (1945), *Jefferson and Hamilton* (1925), *Jefferson in Power* (1936); Leonard W. Levy, *Jefferson and Civil Liberties: The Darker Side* (1963); Albert J. Nock, *Jefferson* (1961); Dumas Malone, *Jefferson and His Times* (3 vols., 1962).

**Jewett, Sarah Orne** (1849–1909). Novelist, story writer. Though she went to Berwick Academy, she seems to have derived her main education accompanying her doctor father on calls to farms and fishing villages around South Berwick, Maine, where she was born and about which she wrote. Early stimulated by Harriet Beecher Stowe's novels of New England life to describe the declining harbours and deserted farms of the Maine Coast, she published her first sketch at 19 in the *Atlantic Monthly*; it was republished in a series assembled as *Deephaven* (1877). Then followed *A Country Doctor* (1884), *A Marsh Island* (1885) and *A White Heron* (1886), tales of a New England girl declining marriage for a medical career, a planter's love for a farmer's daughter, and a girl's heart torn between a white heron and a predatory ornithologist. But her best book is *The Country of the Pointed Firs* (1896), a series of sketches written in a compact evocative style, modelled in part on Flaubert's, to catch (as in *Deephaven*) the spirit of the isolated Maine seaport of Dunnet ('more like one of the lazy English seaside towns . . . not in the least American') as seen by a summer visitor. She hears landlady's gossip, meets the local characters (the Queen's twin, born in the same hour as Victoria; shy William Blackett, courting for 40 years a girl who lives with an invalid mother; poor fisherfolk, retired sea-captains old gentlefolk) and draws together the cross-threads of reminiscence till a delicately humorous fabric is woven of a people, a place and its past – making this her most successful attempt at conveying the atmosphere of loss, decay and regret haunting a coast once bustling with West Indian trade. Other books and stories include: *The King of Folly Island* (1888), *A Native of Winby* (1893), *The Life of Nancy* (1895), the historical romance *The Tory Lover* (1901) and the posthumously collected *Verses* (1916). Her life-long friend Annie Fields edited her *Letters* (1911); Willa ⟡ Cather, who deeply admired and was much influenced by her work, edited her stories. [H B]

The Best Stories, ed. Willa Cather (2 vols., 1925; reissued as *The Country of the Pointed Firs and Other Stories*, 1 vol., 1955).
F. O. Matthiessen, *Sarah Orne Jewett* (1929); Richard Cary, 'Sarah Orne Jewett', *American Literary Realism 1870–1910*, No. 1 (1967).

**Johnson, Edward** (1598–1672). Historian. A Canterbury joiner, he went to Boston, Massachusetts, in 1630 with Winthrop and became distinguished in the colonial militia and government. In 1650 he began his history of the colony, *The Wonder-Working Providence of Sion's Saviour in New England* (published anonymously in 1654; ed. W. F. Poole, 1867), in which the structure of historical Providence takes the form of a military revolution of release from bondage organized by the forces of Christ. Its style is grandiose and bathetic, and includes doggerel praises of the Puritan leaders. But Johnson is good on daily life and on the Indians. [E M]

**Johnson, James Weldon** (1871–1938). Poet. Born in Jacksonville, Florida, he became one of the first Negroes admitted to the Florida bar since Reconstruction. As his fascinating autobiography, *Along This Way* (1933), records, he was a New York song-writer, a consul in Venezuela and Nicaragua, executive secretary of the NAACP, and professor of creative literature at Fisk University. The best of his poetry is in *God's Trombones* (1927), an important collection of folk

sermons. He also edited an anthology of Negro poetry and two books of spirituals. (⟡ Negro Literature.) [E M]
*Selected Poems* (1935).

**Jones, James** (1921– ). Novelist, short-story writer. He was born in Illinois, joined the regular army, and in 1945 submitted the manuscript of a novel to the editor Maxwell Perkins, who, although returning the book, backed his talent as he had backed Thomas Wolfe, Jones's own inspiration, years earlier. His first novel, *From Here to Eternity* (1951), was a best-seller, which, in spite of some weak love scenes, is a remarkably fine account of frustrated and fulfilled creativity, of authority in conflict with independence, within the heavily detailed army setting. Private Robert E. Lee Prewitt is outstanding amongst the fictional heroes of the fifties and sixties who fight the system. *Some Came Running* (1957) is another large novel which repeats some of the earlier materials, in a different form, before moving on to a study of Illinois small-town society. The naturalism tends to be obsessed with detail, but the characterization is excellent. *The Pistol* (1950) is a powerful short novel whose material – the consuming desire of a soldier to own his own pistol as a means to manhood – begins *The Thin Red Line* (1962), a large-scale novel about the war in the Pacific islands. Jones handles clearly and vividly a wide range of characters and a complex campaign, and has the courage and knowledge to describe with almost unique accuracy the nature of killing, fear and leadership. In *Go to the Widow-Maker* (1967) he returns once again to his themes of masculinity attained through war and war-substitutes, but this time the sexual scenes have some vigour, even if they are protracted and repetitious. Jones's handling of the excitement and neuroses of skin-diving and the exhaustion of urban literary life is first-rate. He is one of the few intelligent writers in his field. *The Ice-Cream Headache* (1968) is a collection of his short stories within a running commentary on his methods. [E M]

**Jones, LeRoi** (1934– ). Playwright, novelist, editor. Born in New Jersey. His long education included scholarships to schools, studies at Rutgers, Howard and Columbia, air-force service as a gunner, and being a leading Negro thinker, speaker and writer during the revolution of the 1950s and 1960s. His plays – *Dutchman, The Slave* and *The Toilet* (1964) – and his poetry – *Preface to a Twenty Volume Suicide Note* (1961), *The Dead Lecturer* (1964) and *Black Art* (1966) – articulate the anger and anguish of an intelligent man faced with the violence of a segregated society. *Blues People: Negro Music in White America* (1963) is an insider's book on jazz as the social response of Negro America, and *The System of Dante's Hell* (1965) is both a passionate autobiographical novel and an exploration of post-Joyce, post-Kerouac prose styles. His *Yugen* magazine (1957) and Totem Press have encouraged a large number of contemporary poets. While he was director of the Black Arts repertory theatre in Harlem, financed by the HARYOU Act (a government anti-poverty programme), he produced a number of plays articulating 1965 definitions of Black Power: his own play *Slave Ship* (undated, duplicated typescript) is typical in its scorn for Uncle Toms and their white masters. *Home: Social Essays* (1966) collects his articles into the chronicle of his experience between visiting Cuba in 1960 and the death of Malcolm X in 1965. *Tales* (1967) is a collection of his short stories, and *Black Music* (1968) of articles on contemporary jazz. LeRoi Jones is an important writer: as a black American writer his significance is even greater. (✧ Negro Literature.) [E M]

**Josephson, Matthew** (1899–    ). Literary, social critic. Born in Brooklyn, N.Y., he was one of the ✧ 'Lost Generation' expatriates in Paris in the 1920s, where he was editorially involved with *Secession, Broom,* and *transition* (✧ Little Magazines); he was later assistant editor of the *New Republic*. Strongly influenced by surrealism in the twenties, he made, like other writers, a transition to social interests in the thirties. His *Portrait of the Artist as American* (1930), an interesting piece of socio-literary criticism, gives a historical analysis of the American writer's instinct towards exile. Other books include *Zola and His Time* (1928), *Jean-Jacques Rousseau* (1931), a notable biography, and *Life among the Surrealists* (1962). His strongly social emphasis is best indicated by his lively left-wing analysis of the great Gilded Age American capitalists, *The Robber Barons* (1934). *Infidel in the Temple* (1967) is a lively account of personal and journalistic experience in the 1930s, vital for any estimate of this period. *Al Smith: Hero of Cities* (1970, with Hannah Josephson) is a study of the presidential candidate of 1928. There is an interesting portrait of Josephson in Malcolm Cowley's *Exile's Return* (1934; 1962). [M B]

**Josselyn, John** (fl.1638–75). Naturalist. An Englishman who spent 10 years in New England, mostly in Maine with his brother; they were shareholders in Sir Fernando Gorges' company, whose disputes with the Puritans caused some of the rancour in Josselyn's *An Account of Two Voyages to New England* (1674). His important work is *New England's Rarities Discovered in Birds, Fishes, Serpents and Plants of That Country* (1672), the earliest naturalist account of the area with any pretensions to science amid the fantasy. [E M]

**Justice, Donald** (1925–    ). Poet. Born in Florida, he has taught at the State University of Iowa. *The Summer Anniversaries* (1960), and *A Local Storm* (1963), show him to be a formalist, in the manner of Richard ✧ Wilbur or John Crowe ✧ Ransom. He has experimented with verse modes and shows a delicate feeling for language and a powerful musicality. His latest volume is *Night Light* (1967). [B S]

Richard Howard, *Alone with America* (1969).

# K

**Kanin, Garson** (1912–    ). Actor, director, playwright. He was born in Rochester, N.Y., and has been active in Hollywood and on Broadway most of his adult life, and acted in a number of stage successes. In 1937 he joined Samuel Goldwyn's organization, and in 1947 he and the English film director Carol Reed made *The True Glory*, a documentary war film. His best-known play is *Born Yesterday* (1946), an archetypal drama of the not-so-dumb-blonde-and-her-gangster-friend sort of star vehicle. Among his other works are *A Double Life* (1948), with his wife, Ruth Gordon), his direction of the film *The Diary of Anne Frank* (1955), and a novel, *Blow Up a Storm* (1959). [EM]

**Kantor, MacKinlay** (1904–    ). Novelist. Born in Webster City, Iowa, a prolific writer of highly competent fiction, he is probably best known for his historical novels, particularly the group dealing with the American Civil War. His first novel, *Diversey* (1928), is set among Chicago gangsters, an early example of literary exploitation of the theme. The first Civil War novel was *The Jaybird* (1932), but great success came with *Long Remember* (1934), a detailed fictional treatment of the Battle of Gettysburg. *Arouse and Beware* (1936) and more recently *Andersonville* (1955) return to the same area of interest. Other books include *Gentle Annie* (1942), set in the Oklahoma of 1901; *Happy Land* (1943), touching on the Second World War; *Signal 32* (1950), about life in a New York police precinct; and *Spirit Lake* (1961). All are carefully researched, the wide range of subjects suggesting his professionalism. He has written for Hollywood, and published books for children and a childhood autobiography, *But Look, the Morn* (1947). [MB]

**Kauffmann, Stanley** (1916–    ). Novelist, playwright, critic. Born in New York, he was already writing for the theatre as a student at New York University. After working with the Washington Square Players and in publishing, he became a leading critic of film and theatre in such journals as *New Republic* and *Commentary* and is now the influential drama critic of the *New York Times*. His work, critical, theatrical, fictional, mixes professionalism with intelligence. His novels, which commonly deal with the world of writers, artists and musicians, and their moral and emotional problems, include *The King of Proxy Street* (1941), *This Time Forever* (1945), *The Hidden Hero* (1949), *A Change of Climate* (1954), *The Philanderer* (1954) – the subject of a famous obscenity case in the English courts – and *Man of the World* (1956). [MB]

**Kaufman, Bob** (?    –    ). Satirist, poet. He was born on the West Coast and, after spending 20 years in the merchant navy, was working in the Los Angeles Hilton when ◊ Kerouac and ◊ Ginsberg found him and he became part of the 'San Francisco Renaissance' of the 1950s. ◊ Ferlinghetti published his satires in *Abomunist Manifesto* (1959) and the prose poems *Second April* (1960) as City Lights broadsides. They are collected with interesting shorter pieces in *Solitudes Crowded with Loneliness* (1965). *Golden Sardine* (1967) contains poems and montage sequences which have some of the sardonic social criticism and lonely passion of Bob Dylan's lyrics. [EM]

**Kaufman, George S(imon)** (1889–1961). Playwright, columnist. Born in Pittsburg, he had a long list of popular plays to his name, mostly Broadway hits, mostly in collaboration with Moss ◊ Hart and Marc ◊ Connelly (including *Dulcy*, 1961), and *Merton of the Movies* (1922). Apart from his columns in the Washington *Mail* and the New York *World*, *Tribune* and *Times*, he collaborated on *The Royal Family* (1927), *Dinner at Eight* (1932) and *Stage Door* (1936) with Edna ◊ Ferber; *Of Thee I Sing* (1932) with Morris Ryskind and George Gershwin; *June Moon* (1929) with Ring ◊ Lardner; *The Solid Gold Cadillac* (1952) with Howard Teichmann. His film scripts include the Marx Brothers' *Animal Crackers* and *Coconuts*, and he collaborated with J. P. ◊ Marquand [on the film script for this novelist's *The Late George Apley* (1946). [EM]

**Kazin, Alfred** (1915–    ). Autobiographer, critic. He writes excellently about his Brooklyn childhood in *A Walker in the City* (1951) and of his later literary life in *Starting Out in the Thirties* (1965). *On Native Grounds* (1942) is a standard critical discussion of American literature since 1900, and three further critical volumes maintain his usefulness: *The Inmost Leaf* (1955) and *Contemporaries* (1962), two collections of essays, and *F. Scott Fitzgerald* (1951). [EM]

**Keast, W. R.** ⟡ Chicago Aristotelians.

**Kees, Weldon** (1914–55). Poet. Born in Nebraska, he worked on the Federal Works Project, became director of the Bibliographical Centre for the Rocky Mountain Region, wrote for *Time* in New York, made documentary films, and exhibited paintings in shows with De Kooning, Hofmann and the abstract expressionists. In 1951 he went to San Francisco, began to compose music, made more films and collaborated with Dr Jurgen Ruesch on *Non-Verbal Communication*, also contributing the magnificent photographs. His car was found abandoned on the approach to the Golden Gate Bridge on 18 July 1955, and he has not been seen since. The bitter, distinctively dislocating poems of this brilliant man appeared in *The Last Man* (1943), *The Fall of the Magicians* (1947), and *Poems 1947–1954* and have been republished as part of *Collected Poems*, edited by Donald Justice (1960). [EM]

**Kelley, W. M.** ⟡ Negro Literature.

**Kelly, Robert** (1935–    ). Poet. Born in Brooklyn, he studied at the City College of New York and at Columbia, and launched the *Chelsea Review* and, with George Economou, *Trobar*, an important magazine of new verse (1960). He has taught at various colleges. With other poets he has been associated with *The Sixties* magazine, and with the subjective surrealism of 'deep image' poetry ('Notes on the Poetry of the Deep Image', *Trobar* 2, 1961). With seven other poets, he formed The Blue Yak, a poets' cooperative in New York in 1961. His earlier poems in *Armed Descent* (1961) and *Her Body against Time* (1963) are mainly short lyrical pieces, placing personal experience in intellectual and religious contexts. *Lunes* (1965) shows a masterly

handling of the extremely brief form. But it is with *Finding the Measure* (1968) that this poetry achieves its unique combination of experimental form, wide-ranging intellectual knowledge and a personal voice. He has since then published prolifically; *Sonnets* (1968), *Songs I–XXX* (1968), *The Common Shore, Books I–V* (1969), *A California Journal* (1969), and *Kali Yuga* (1970). His most carefully worded poetry is still *Axon Dendron Tree* (1967). [EM]

**Kennedy, John Pendleton** (1795–1870). Novelist, satirist, memoirist. He was born in Baltimore, practised law, served in Congress and was Speaker to the House and secretary of the navy (he organized the Perry expedition to Japan and Kane's second expedition to the Arctic). He sponsored Poe, was a friend of Irving and Holmes, and supplied Thackeray with material for *The Virginians*. Of his Southern romances the most important is *Swallow Barn* (1832), which eulogizes the Virginian planter in a tale of boundary disputes and love affairs between two families. *Horseshoe Robinson* (1835) concerns a backwoodsman in the Revolution, and *Rob of the Bowl* (1838) is a satire of Jacksonian democracy. [EM]

C. H. Bohner, *John Pendleton Kennedy: Gentleman from Baltimore* (1961).

**Kennedy, X. J.** (1929–    ). Poet. He was born in New Jersey, studied at Columbia and the Sorbonne, and has taught at several universities. His poems in *Nude Descending a Staircase* (1961) move easily between a world of bawdry, irreverent high spirits and apt contemporary reference, and one of traditional poetic elegance. He is a serious wit and a good poetic craftsman. A second collection of poems, *Growing into Love*, appeared in 1969. [BS]

**Kerouac, Jack** (1922–69). Novelist. He was born in Lowell, Massachusetts, studied in local Catholic schools and at Columbia University (1941), and began to write and live in the image of his early reading: Jack London, Hemingway, Saroyan, Wolfe and Joyce, and the free style of prose and living of his friend Neal Cassady, the Dean Moriarty of *On the Road*. With William ⟡ Burroughs and ⟡ Ginsberg in New York and San Francisco in the late 1940s and early 1950s, he practised the ⟡ Beat Generation life, after a period in the merchant navy and bumming around America. After his first published novel, *The Town and the City* (1950), an excellent work in Wolfeian autobiographic style, *On the Road* (1957) soon came to represent his generation throughout the world: its record of a new Bohemian style of living, the 'spontaneous bop prosody' of its rapid physical movement, urgent absorption of experience and jazz sense, all contributed to a heady fiction which is still influencing young writers. Drink, sex, drugs and jazz again form the San Francisco life of *The Subterraneans* (1958); but *The Dharma Bums* (1958) includes more oriental philosophical practices and a direct contact with nature in the North-west mountains (see also *The Scripture of Golden Eternity*, 1960, an American *sutra*).

*Doctor Sax* (1959) is a *tour de force* of Kerouac's style, evoking boyhood experiences with unique exhilaration, and *Maggie Cassidy* (1959) and *Visions of Gerard* (1963) are simpler written memories of boyhood. *Tristessa* (1960) concerns Mexican experience, *Big Sur* (1962) returns to the earlier complex style to describe breakdowns of the self on the Californian coast, *Satori in Paris* (1966) is about the search for ancestral identity in Brittany, and *Desolation Angels* (1965) is a fine re-working of Beat Generation experiences in an apparently definitive if mournful and nostalgic tone. All these books constitute parts of the continuous *Duluoz Legend* series, whose most recent addition is *Vanity of Duluoz: An Adventurous Education, 1935–46* (1968), a disappointingly sentimental re-animation of the past: middle-age did not suit Kerouac, and he grew garrulous. As in Wolfe's case, his autobiographical passion makes for looseness of form and a prose of rhapsodic repetition; but his vision of the post-war world of youth is an authentic and tragically exuberant response in an original prose style. *Lonesome Traveller* (1960) is a collection of travel sketches, and *Book of Dreams* (1961) a book of his sources. *Mexico City Blues* (1959) is an influential volume of poetry experimenting with jazz forms, *Rimbaud* (1960), a broad-sheet poem, and *Pull My Daisy* (1961), the printed form of an ad-libbed commentary to film incorporating an unproduced play, and starring Allen Ginsberg, Gregory Corso, Peter Orlovsky and the painter Larry Rivers. [EM]

Ann Charters, *A Bibliography of the Works of*

*Jack Kerouac* (1967); ed. Thomas Parkinson, *A Casebook on the Beat* (1961); John Clellon Holmes, *Nothing More to Declare* (1968); *Paris Review* 43 (Summer, 1968) (interview with Ted Berigan).

**Kesey, Ken** (1935–     ). Novelist. He grew up in the timber country of Oregon, studied at the University of Oregon, where he was a champion wrestler, and came south to Stanford University to attend creative writing classes held by Wallace ♢ Stegner and Malcolm ♢ Cowley. He worked in a mental hospital for a time, and later became the centre of a new-style ♢ Bohemianism in the Bay Area of San Francisco, before being arrested, hunted from the country and re-arrested, and imprisoned, in 1966. His first novel, *One Flew over the Cuckoo's Nest* (1962), draws on his mental hospital experience for a brilliant, funny and mordant satire on the dehumanization of western society, one of the most important novels of the post-war years. His second, *Sometimes a Great Notion* (1964), concerns the conflicts and solidarities in a logging family in the North-west – a large, ambitious novel with the pretentions and scale of Thomas ♢ Wolfe. His messianic LSD scene is the subject of *The Electric Kool-Aid Acid Test* (1968) by Tom ♢ Wolfe. [EM]

**Keyes, Frances Parkinson** (1885–1970). Novelist, biographer. Born in Virginia, daughter of a Professor of Greek, Mrs Keyes was educated in Boston and Switzerland. A journalist, she was associate editor of *Good Housekeeping* (1923–35), editor of the *National Historical Magazine* (1937–9). Mrs Keyes won enormous success with a long series of novels, usually set in the South or New England. Among them are *The Ambassadress* (1938), *Queen Anne's Lace* (1930), *All That Glitters* (1941), *Dinner at Antoine's* (1948) and *Steamboat Gothic* (1952). She wrote two biographies: *Written in Heaven* (1937; rev. as *St Teresa of Lisieux,* 1950), and *The Sublime Shepherdess*, concerning Bernadette of Lourdes (1940; enlarged 1953). [MG]

**Killens, J. O.** ♢ Negro Literature.

**Kingsley, Sidney** (1906–     ). Actor, playwright. Born in New York, he gained his first prize on Broadway with *Men in White* (1933), probably the archetype of hospital soap-opera, with accurate details. But *Dead*

*End* (1935) is a good social drama (and an even better film, 1937) about the struggles of children in an East River slum, overshadowed by the rich and the gangster Baby Face Martin. Social purpose impregnated Kingsley's plays for all their sensationalism. His 'dead end kids' went into American mythology. His later career is best represented by *Ten Million Ghosts* (1936), a protest play against munitions profiteering and war; *Detective Story* (1949); and an adaptation of Koestler's *Darkness at Noon* (1951). *Night Life* (1962) is a Manhattan night-club melodrama in which the meek are supposed to inherit the earth, and die doing so. [EM]

**Kinnell, Galway** (1927–     ). Poet. Born in Rhode Island, educated at Princeton and the University of Rochester, he has taught in universities in the U.S.A. and abroad, and been a freelance writer. Lucid and at best finely detailed, his verse has tended toward the experimental, particularly in recent work. It is often concerned with semi-religious matter, as in the fascinating long poem 'The Avenue Bearing the Initial of Christ into the New World', in his first collection, *What a Kingdom It Was* (1960). He has since published *Flower Herding on Mount Monadnock* (1964), *Poems of the Night* (1968) and *Body Rags* (1969), and translated *The Poetry of François Villon* (1964). *Black Light* (1966) is a novel set in Persia. [MB]

**Kizer, Carolyn** (1925     ). Poet. Born in Spokane, Washington, she has been associated with a group of poets residing in and around Seattle and publishing in *Poetry North-West*. Besides writing her own personal but tough-minded poetry, collected in *The Ungrateful Garden* (1961) and *Knock upon Silence* (1965), she has done a number of translations from the Chinese, particularly from the great 8th-century poet Tu Fu. The formal verse and violent imagery of her earlier poems have recently given way, perhaps via an influence from Chinese, to poems of quiet situation in which free verse and plain speech dominate. [BP]

**Knight, Sarah Kemble** (1666–1727). Travel writer. A merchant's daughter and sea-captain's widow who travelled from Boston, where she was born, to New York and back in 1704–5 and described her difficult and dangerous experiences on horseback in the *Journal* (ed. and pub. Theodore Dwight, 1825), a vivid, humorous and authoritative impression of the times and an image of early American self-reliance. [EM]

**Koch, Kenneth** (1925–     ). Poet, playwright, novelist. Born in Cincinnati, served in the army in the Pacific, studied at Harvard and Columbia. With John ◊ Ashbery and Frank ◊ O'Hara, with whom he was linked in the Poet's Theatre, he represents the American extension of modern French poetic methods, a group who with Edward Field, Barbara Guest, James Schuyler and Harry ◊ Mathews were associated with the Artist's Theatre, *Locus Solus* magazine, and New York abstract expressionist painters of the 1950s. His is a poetry and drama of witty juxtapositions, cubist and dadaist dislocations, and anti-symbolism, in direct line from Raymond Roussel and Gertrude Stein and influenced by Pierre Reverdy and Max Jacob. Koch's main work is in *Poems* (1953); *Ko, or A Season on Earth* (1959), an exhilarating multi-plotted novel in verse; *Thank You and Other Poems* (1962); the long and dazzling 'When the Sun Tries to Go on' (*The Hasty Papers* 1960; reissued with illustrations by Larry Rivers, 1969); *Poems from 1952 and 1953* (1968) and *The Pleasures of Peace* (1969). *Bertha and Other Plays* (1966) is a collection of 17 plays in 130 pages. [EM]

F. W. Dupee, 'Kenneth Koch's Poetry', *The King of the Cats* (1965); Richard Howard, *Alone with America* (1969).

**Kopit, Arthur L.** (1937–     ). Playwright *Oh Dad, Poor Dad, Mamma's Hung You in the Closet and I'm Feelin' So Sad* (1960) is a hilarious take-off of 'absurd' drama ending with the nice line 'What is the meaning of this?' Kopit has also published *The Day the Whores Came Out to Play Tennis* (1965), a collection of 6 expert plays, one of which, 'The Hero', has no dialogue, and *Indians* (1968), a satirical drama on the myths of the 'West'. [EM]

**Krutch, Joseph Wood** (1893–     ). Teacher, critic. Born in Knoxville, Tennessee. His main fields are represented by *The American Drama since 1918* (1938, 1957), *Edgar Allan Poe* (1926), an early psychological literary study, *The Modern Temper* (1929), an important analysis of 'meaninglessness' during the twenties, and *The Desert Year* (1952), reflections on man and nature. *More Lives Than One* (1962) is his entertaining autobiography. [EM]

The Best Nature Writings of Joseph Wood Krutch (1970).

**Kunitz, Stanley** (1905–    ). Poet. Born in Worcester, Massachusetts, he was educated at Harvard, served in the Second World War, and has taught in several universities. Though a volume, *Intellectual Things*, appeared in 1930 it is not until lately that he has received considerable notice. *Pass-port to the War* appeared in 1944. With *Selected Poems 1928–1958* (1958) he made a powerful impact on critics, other poets and a wider reading public (he won the Pulitzer Prize), perhaps because now a poetry made out of intense personal experience, and concerned with the intricacies and tensions of a man's relations with the world, was found more important. His poems have a strong metaphysical speculativeness coupled with great intellectual and rhythmic resource. Kunitz is a joyous, celebratory poet of great craft and real substance, capable of wisdom, wit and balance. [MB]

# L

**La Farge, Oliver** (1901– ). Novelist. The greatest American expert on the Indians. Born in New York City. At Harvard he specialized in anthropology and archaeology, and made expeditions to Arizona, Mexico and Guatemala for his universities. His understanding of Indian culture is complete, and he writes about it in a first-rate style in the form of novels and stories: *Laughing Boy* (1929), *Sparks Fly Upward* (1931), *The Year-Bearer's People* (1931), *Long Pennant* (1933) and *The Enemy Gods* (1937). *Behind the Mountains* (1956) concerns a New Mexico village, and *Raw Material* (1945) is an autobiography. [E M]

Ed. Winfield Townley Scott, *Oliver La Farge: The Man with the Calabash Pipe* (1966).

**Lamantia, Philip** (1927– ). Poet. He was born in San Francisco and is one of the foremost contemporary poets of drug experience and the surreal image. His visionary poems appear mostly in ◊ little magazines, but his books include *Erotic Poems* (1946), *Narcotica* (1959), *Ekstasis* (1959), *Destroyed Works* (1962), *Touch of the Marvelous* (1966), a collection of early poems, and *Selected Poems 1943–1966* (1967), which includes new work. He was published at the age of 15 by *View* magazine and praised by André Breton. His poems have retained the essential surrealist quality of revealing inner life through explosive images and ecstatic vision. [E M]

**Langer, Susanne K.** (1895– ). Philosopher. Born in New York City, she studied at Radcliffe and has taught in American universities. *The Practice of Philosophy* (1930) and *An Introduction to Symbolic Logic* (1937) preceded her more influential syntheses of aesthetics and symbolism in *Philosophy in a New Key* (1942) and *Feeling and Form* (1953), extensions of Emile Cassirer's and other modern theories of significant form, which she usefully supports with *Problems of Art* (1955) and *Reflections on Art* (1958), an extremely useful source book of writings by artists and critics. *Philosophical Sketches*

appeared in 1962, and *Mind: An Essay on Human Feeling* (1967) inaugurates a new 3-volume project. [E M]

**Langland, Joseph T.** (1917– ). Poet. He was born in Spring Grove, Minnesota, and educated at the State University of Iowa; before turning to college teaching in 1941, he was a farmer and rural schoolteacher. *The Green Town* (1956) and *The Wheel of Summer* (1963) contain his poems; he has edited anthologies and been poetry editor of the *Massachusetts Review*. Much of his work is searching and ponderous, employing a great deal of verbal density; more recent poems have tended to be wryly observant and more relaxed. [B P]

**Lanier, Sidney** (1842–81). Poet, novelist, critic. Born in Georgia, he was the first significant poet of Southern experience. His family were not planter 'aristocrats' but urban middle class. In his lawyer father's library he found Scott, Froissart, Bulwer-Lytton and *Gil Blas* – the staple of 19th-century chivalric nostalgia in the South. Although he was an excellent musician he felt that God had made music 'so small a business in comparison with other things' that he refused his natural vocation. During the Civil War he fought for a romantic-medieval South he saw later as 'the conceit of a whole people'. Captured by the Union army, he spent 1864–5 in prison, where he resisted ill health enough to translate Heine and Herder. Finding a living in the ravaged post-war South was difficult for a sick poet and musician. He taught, served in his father's law office, and wrote a novel, *Tiger-Lilies* (1867), a farrago of romantic themes and war which at least enabled him to realize the inferior provincialism of the South; his best poems in the *Round Table*, in the late 1860s, present a broken society through his own uncertainty and instability. In 1873 he played in the Peabody Orchestra of Baltimore, a good career interrupted by sickness. 'Corn', published in *Lippincott's Magazine*, began his late reputation as a poet. He lectured at Johns Hopkins and at the end of his life wrote *The Science of English Verse* (1880), on the theory that poetry was basically music, and *The English Novel and the Principle of its Development* (1883), slightly wild but interesting works.

Whitman's physicality and directness, which he admired, might have corrected Lanier's extravagantly Keatsian imagery and musicality, but his achievement was skilful and perhaps heroic, considering his life and times. Poems like 'Tyranny' and 'Laughter in the Senate' criticize the Reconstruction, and 'Nirvana' is a lament for the war obstructions to his development. 'Corn' dramatizes the case for replacing cotton with corn to revive Southern economy: the imagery and rhythm are surprisingly effective and seem to have influenced the ◊ Fugitive poets of the 1930s. In 'The Symphony' (1875) textures and metaphors imitate musical instruments in a discussion of social themes and reconciliation through love, an ambitious affair. His lyrics are better, and his best poem is 'The Marches of Glyn' (1878), a Transcendentalist transformation of nature in Georgian swamps and live-oaks. Lanier's effort to write genuinely contemporary poetry during Civil War and Reconstruction is one of the most interesting causes in American literatur . [EM]

*Collected Works: Centennial Edition*, ed. C. R. Anderson, etc. (10 vols., 1945).

A. H. Starke, *Sidney Lanier: A Biographical and Critical Study* (1933).

**Lardner, Ring** (1885–1933). Journalist, short-story writer. Born in Michigan, he was a reporter in South Bend, Indiana, and Chicago, before editing (1910–11) a St Louis baseball weekly. He covered sport for various newspapers and became a syndicated columnist, after which he lived in New York. He made his name as a satirist through publishing, in the Chicago *Tribune*, *You Know Me, Al: A Busher's Letters* (1916; revised edn, 1925), a series of letters by 'Jack Keefe', an imaginary newcomer to a professional baseball team, which revealed Lardner's keen sense of humour, unsparing accuracy of observation, and gift for rendering American vernacular speech which earned him the admiration and gratitude of H. L. ◊ Mencken. A collection of verse, *Bib Ballads* (1915), though not well received, again shows the satirist's delight in the comic

flaws of the average American which was to be developed in *Gullible's Travels* (1917; revised edn, 1925) and in several collections of short stories, the best of which are *How to Write Short Stories* (*with Samples*) (1924), and *The Love Nest and Other Stories* (1926), whose title story is perhaps his best single piece. In these and later volumes the stupidity and dullness of his protagonists – typists, barbers, sportsmen – are analysed with sardonic wit and a growing pessimism. Unlike Hemingway, he did not suffer from hero-worship: as a news-reporter he simply exposed ignorance and ineptitude without enjoying it. He won a large popular audience long before the critics discovered him.

Lardner's autobiography, *The Story of a Wonder Man* (1927), is characteristically ironic and entertaining. There is a full and accurate biography in Donald Elder's *Ring Lardner* (1956). [MG]

*The Collected Short Stories* (1941); *The Portable Ring Lardner*, ed. G. Seldes (1946).

John Berryman, 'The Case of Ring Lardner', *Commentary*, XXII (1956); W. Goldhurst, *F. Scott Fitzgerald and His Contemporaries* (1963).

**Larner, Jeremy** (1937– ). Novelist. Born in Indianapolis, he studied at Brandeis and Berkeley. His novel *Drive, He Said* (1964), an excellent example of satirical humour and social criticism of the sixties, is the story of a college sportsman spoiled by grafting intellectual and business society. His second novel, *The Answer* (1968), deals with psychedelic trippers and their disillusion. *The Addict in the Street* (1964, with Ralph Tefferteller) is a documentary commenting on the statements of drug addicts; it is one of the best works of its kind. He has recently edited with Irving Howe a collection of essays, *Poverty: Views from the Left* (1968). *Nobody Knows* (1970) is a study of the 1968 Eugene McCarthy campaign. [EM]

**Laurents, Arthur** (1918– ). Dramatist. Born in Brooklyn, N.Y. He first achieved recognition with *Home of the Brave* (1946), a penetrating war play. His work generally shows concern for the individual in oppressive environment and for experiments in dramatic form. *The Bird Cage* (1950) presents tyranny in the relations between a chorus girl and a night-club owner, both *The Time of the Cuckoo* (1953) and *A Clearing in the Woods* (1957) concern a woman's self-discovery, and *Invitation to a March* (1960) is a comic fantasy based on the Sleeping Beauty. Laurents is respected also for his film scripts, *Rope*, *Anastasia* and *The Snake Pit*, and his stories for musicals, including *West Side Story* (1957) and *Gypsy* (1959). [E M]

**Lawson, John Howard** (1895–    ). Playwright. He was born in New York City, served in the American ambulance service in the First World War, marched for Sacco and Vanzetti and became a communist as well as one of America's leading radical dramatists (at least since his early Freudian Expressionist play, *Roger Bloomer*, 1923). *Processional* (1925), a 'jazz symphony of American life', in which Dynamite Jim, the proletarian hero, is attacked by anti-Marxist forces in West Virginia during a coal strike, is his earliest typical work: the twenties bitterness is brilliantly alleviated by the sharp humour of racial and social types. Then came *Loud Speaker* (1927), again dealing with worker persecution and injustice, and *The International* (1928), in which love provides a surprisingly bourgeois solution to the class war. *Success Story* (1932) is more concerned with the individual than the communist class pattern, and after *Gentlewoman* (1934) Lawson revaluated his orthodoxy, organized his *Theory and Techniques of Playwriting and Screen writing* (1936), and in 1937 wrote *Marching Song*, as a model revolutionary play whose collective hero is the Auto Workers Union. Then he went to Hollywood and wrote good film scripts (see *Film in the Battle of Ideas*, 1953). He was one of the Hollywood artists imprisoned by the House Un-American Activities Committee during its witch-hunting 1950s. Lawson's work is a lively dramatization of social power in America, even if some of his stereotypes age badly. His most recent work is *Film: The Creative Process* (1965). A neglected and most interesting work is *The Hidden Heritage* (1950), a radical appreciation of social and political ideas prior to the founding of America in the 17th century. [E M]

M. Y. Himelstein, *Drama Was a Weapon: The Left-Wing Theatre in New York 1929–1941* (1963); G. Rabkin, *Drama and Commitment: Politics in the American Theatre of the Thirties* (1964).

**Leary, Timothy** (1920–    ). Psychologist. Born in Springfield, Massachusetts, he studied classical psychology at Berkeley and was dismissed from the Harvard University Centre for Research in Personality in 1963, when the faculty discovered that he, his associates and volunteers had taken part in controlled experiments with psilocybin, the chemical derivative of a certain sacred mushroom. In 1960, Leary had been given the mushroom in Cuernavaca by a scientist from the University of Mexico. The illumination he experienced radically changed his attitude towards consciousness and the nature of traditional religious mysticisms. His teachings on expanded consciousness, the use of L S D and other drugs, and the transformation of Western society have a strongly religious bias. He has a large following both in America and beyond, through his lectures and his writings in *The Psychedelic Reader* (1965, with G. M. Weil and R. Metzner: articles from *The Psychedelic Review*), *The Psychedelic Experience* (1964, with R. Metzner and R. Alpert) and *The Politics of Ecstasy* (1969). *High Priest* (1969) is autobiographical, and *Psychedelic Prayers* (1966) draws on the Tao Te Ching to form a manual of preparation for psychedelic experience. [E M]

**Lee, Manfred B.** ◊ Dannay, Frederic.

**Legman, Gershon** (1919–    ). The most erudite scholar of erotic folklore alive, his career is marked by unique courage and persistence. *The Horn Book* (1964), a large-scale account of erotica and bawdy, is a standard work. *Love and Death* (1949) is a short, definitive study of censorship, and his other works include *Oragenitalism* (1940), *The Guilt of the Templars* (1964), *The Fake Revolt* (1967 – a severe criticism of the so-called sexual revolution) and *Rationale of the Dirty Joke* (1968, first series), a superb analysis of sexual humour using over 2,000 examples. He also edited *Neurotica*, an important journal which appeared between 1948 and 1951, and Robert Burns's *Merry Muses of Caledonia* (1965). An account of his life in New York is lovingly given in John Clellon ◊ Holmes's *Nothing More to Declare* (1968). [E M]

**Leland, Charles Godfrey** (1824–1903). Humorist. Born in Philadelphia; educated in New Jersey and Germany. He became an important figure in journalism, and a man of many learned interests; but he is best remembered for his Pennsylvania German dialect-humour, particularly for the Hans Breitmann ballads. His first work in this vein was *Meister Karl's Sketch-Book* (1855); then came *Hans Breitmann's Barty and Other Ballads* (1868). Leland continued to produce more of these comic mock-German poems, and they were collected in *Hans Breitmann's Ballads* (1914). [MB]

**Lerner, Max** (1902–    ). Critic, social commentator. Born in Russia, he belongs to the tradition of critical social analysis so active in America in the 1930s, a tradition less concerned for literature as such than for its expressive function in revealing the culture. His numerous books and articles include *It Is Later Than You Think* (1938) and the monumental, useful study *America as a Civilization: Life and Thought in the United States Today* (1957), which clearly shows his social-historical approach. Lerner has taught at Sarah Lawrence, Harvard and Brandeis Universities; recently he has become widely known as a newspaper columnist commenting on social and literary matters. [MB]

**Levertov, Denise** (1923–    ). Poet. She grew up in Ilford, Essex, but after marrying the American writer Mitchell Goodman moved to the U.S.A. in 1948. Though an early volume, *The Double Image*, appeared in London in 1946, it is in America that she has really formed her poetic manner. She employs that kind of concentrated pictorial approach bequeathed by the ◊ Imagists to both English and American poetry, but taken further in the U.S.A. Her incantatory quality and her visionary ecstatic dimension separate her from the British tradition and link her closely with the ◊ Beat Generation and ◊ Black Mountain poets. Like them, she has been influenced by William Carlos ◊ Williams in her concern with celebrating the life residing in particular things and responding innocently to 'authentic' experience. Her volumes include *Here and Now* (1957), *Overland to the Islands* (1958), *Jacob's Ladder* (1961), which contains some interesting pieces on the Eichmann trial and reprints poems from the 1958 volume, *O Taste and See* (1964), which includes her first published story, and *The Sorrow Dance* (1967). She translated *In Praise of Krishna: Songs from the Bengali* (1968) with E. C. Dimock. [MB]

**Levin, Harry** (1912–    ). Critic. He has been teaching at Harvard since 1934; his erudition and range are exceptional in a critical scholar. He has edited Jonson, Rochester and Flaubert, and the novelist himself praised his *James Joyce* (1941). His major works are *The Broken Column: A Study in Romantic Hellenism* (1931), *Toward Stendhal* (1945), *The Overreacher* (1952; on Marlowe), *The Power of Blackness: Hawthorne, Poe, Melville* (1958) and the essays in *Contexts of Criticism* (1957). *The Gates of Horn* (1963) is an important study of French fiction. His advocacy of comparative literature is a major contribution to a possible Atlantic culture. [EM]

**Levin, Meyer** (1905–    ). Novelist. A Chicago-born journalist, in his first novel, *Reporter* (1929), he dealt with newspaper life. He lived for a while in Europe, including Palestine; his novel *Yehuda* (1931) is about a Zionist community there, while *Golden Mountain* (1932) retells traditional Jewish folk-tales. His other novels, most of them realistic and reportorial in character, usually treat Jewish themes; they include *The Old Bunch* (1937), about Chicago immigrant children; *Citizens* (1940), about a strike; *Compulsion* (1956), based on the Leopold-Loeb case; and *The Fanatic* (1964), where he treats of such serious matters as Jewish experience under Hitler and anti-semitism in America, with characteristically false portentousness. *In Search* (1950) is autobiography. [MB]

**Lewis, (Harry) Sinclair** (1885–1951). Novelist. Born at Sauk Center, Minnesota. He attended Yale and held various jobs – he joined briefly in Upton ◊ Sinclair's Helicon Hall venture, and later sold plots to Jack ◊ London – before devoting his full time to writing from 1915. His first novel, *Our Mr Wrenn* (1914), was followed by *The Trail of the Hawk* (1915), *The Job* (1917) and *Free Air* (1919). With *Main Street* (1920) and *Babbitt* (1922) he rapidly established an international reputation, officially sealed by the award of the Nobel Prize in 1930, the first time it had gone to an American author. This marked the apogee of Lewis's literary career. In the melancholy period from *Ann Vickers* (1933) to the posthumously published *World So Wide* (1951) Lewis produced 10 novels that testified to the progressive decline in his creative powers. During his last years he wandered extensively in Europe, and after his death in Rome his ashes were appropriately returned to his birthplace.

A journalist rather than an artist, Lewis wrote too much too quickly, and his later work is mostly negligible. Yet, as his biographer has stated in a definitive survey, although Lewis was one of the worst important writers in modern American literature 'without his writing one cannot imagine modern American literature'. The authentic voice of the mid-West, he liberated new areas of experience for the American novelist. Again, rather in the manner of Cooper a century earlier, he gave to Europeans an image of the United States which they recognized and which, to a certain extent, they wanted. His novels are often confused in style and sprawling in structure, and he tended to indulge in caricature and not character. The strengths and weaknesses of his books derive ultimately from those in the man. Although he became known primarily as a satirist of the American scene, Lewis's own reaction to the vulgar materialism and cultural impoverishment of his time was ambivalent. The Gopher Prairie of *Main Street* may exhibit a provincial complacency, but the values which the culture-bearing Carol Kennicott attempts to impose upon the town are so jejune as to render her a fool as well as a prig. Similarly, in *Babbitt*, which with *Arrowsmith* (1925) is probably his best work, the satiric force of Lewis's portrait of Zenith tends to be dissipated by his recognition of the rebelliousness, albeit stifled, in George F. Babbitt himself. The victory for another businessman in *Dodsworth* (1929) is less equivocal; in a leisurely reworking of one of James's major themes and with a backward glance to his own first novel, Lewis presents the liberating effect of Europe upon Sam Dodsworth. These novels and *Elmer Gantry* (1927), a broad and vigorous satire on the excesses of American religion, constitute the most permanent of his sociological fictions. In them he offered, especially in his dialogue, a sharp and easily assimilated image of the American middle class; and, as a result of his concentration upon a single representative individual, who often stood in the same ambiguous relation to his society as he did himself, Lewis was able to define dramatically the best and the worst in that culture. Characteristically, in his novel *It Can't Happen Here* (1935), he examined the

triumph of an American dictator without examining the nature of political power or the impotence of liberalism. [H D]

Mark Schorer, *Sinclair Lewis: An American Life* (1961); ed. Mark Schorer, *Sinclair Lewis: A Collection of Critical Essays* (1962); D. J. Dooley, *The Art of Sinclair Lewis* (1967).

**Lewis, Meriwether** (1774–1809). Soldier, explorer. Born in Albemarle, Virginia. In 1802 Thomas Jefferson sponsored an expedition to explore the headwaters of the Mississippi and to discover a water route to the Pacific. It would have to pass through French territory at a time when the Louisiana Purchase was being negotiated and the boundaries disputed with Britain. Command was given to Lewis, a Virginian who had served in the state militia during the Whiskey rebellion, in the regular army and as one of President ◊ Jefferson's private secretaries. He chose as his associate commander William Clark (1770–1838), an old Virginian friend who had resigned from the army in ill health in 1796. The expedition set out in 1804 and in 1805 reached the three forks of the Missouri, ascended the Jefferson to its source, and crossed to the Columbia river. They returned in 1806, and Lewis was rewarded with the governorship of Missouri territory, but he died, possibly by his own, and, possibly murdered, in 1809 (see Robert Penn ◊ Warren's *Brother to Dragons*). Clark was governor of Louisiana and the Missouri territories, and later superintendent of Indian affairs in St Louis from 1822 to his death. Both men kept extensive journals of their exploration but publication was delayed by their later duties and the death of Lewis. In 1810 Clark secured Nicholas Biddle to prepare an edition, and this too was delayed until 1814. The *Journals* stimulated interest in the West and encouraged the idea of a trans-continental trade route to the Pacific. [D K A/E M]

*The Journals of Lewis and Clark*, abridged and ed. Bernard De Voto (1953).

Ed. Elliott Cowes, *History of the Expedition under the Command of Lewis and Clark* (3 vols., 1965); Richard Dillon, *Meriwether Lewis: A Biography* (1965).

**Lewisohn, Ludwig** (1882–1955). Novelist, literary and social critic. Born of Jewish background in Berlin and brought to the U.S.A. as a child, he grew up in Charleston, South Carolina. After graduate work at

Columbia he taught European literature in various universities, including Wisconsin and Brandeis. He was a participant in American social debate and was for a time associate editor of the liberal periodical the *Nation*. At first a liberal idealist urging the America of the 1920s out of its Puritan phase – many of his novels and articles turn on emancipated human and social relationships – he later became a devout Zionist. Two volumes of autobiography, intense, strongly voiced documents, expose his background and position – *Up Stream* (1922) and *Mid-Channel: An American Chronicle* (1929). Both reveal his sense of being persecuted in the States for his German-Jewish background, particularly during the war, and a feeling that American culture is narrow and repressive. Among his numerous novels, some of them concerned with marital problems, are *The Broken Snare* (1908); *The Case of Mr Crump* (1926), first published in Paris and praised by European critics, only lately available in the U.S.A.; *The Island Within* (1928); *Steʰen Escott* (1930); *An Altar in the Fields* (1934), about a couple sent by a psychiatrist to solve their marital problems in the African desert; and *Trumpet of Jubilee* (1937), touching on the experience of Jews under Hitler.

As a literary critic Lewisohn comments valuably and from an enlightened viewpoint on European literature in studies like *The Modern Drama* (1915), *The Spirit of Modern German Literature* (1916), *The Poets of Modern France* (1918), *The Creative Life* (1924) and on American literature in two highly useful studies, *Expression in America* (1932) and *The Story of American Literature* (1937). His concern with the Jewish problem appears in several books, including *Israel* (1925) and *The American Jew* (1950). [MB]

**Liebling, A(bbott) J(oseph)** (1904–63). Journalist, social commentator. Born in New York City. His early career was with various semi-popular newspapers whose shortcomings he later analysed in cultural critiques of the press in the *New Yorker*, to which journal he became a leading contributor. A stylist, humorist and writer of strong cultural opinions, he has documented not only the press (*The Wayward Pressman*, 1947, *The Press*, 1961), but also the war in Europe (*The Road Back to Paris*, 1944), boxing (*The Sweet Science*, 1956),

and Southern politics (*The Earl of Louisiana*, 1961). [MB]

**Lincoln, Abraham** (1809–65). The sixteenth President of the United States. He was born in Kentucky, grew up on the frontier in Illinois, where he learned Western storytelling and humorous rhetoric, and worked variously as storekeeper, surveyor, postmaster and army captain in the Black Hawk War (1832) before being elected in 1834 to four terms in the State legislature. After being called to the bar, he moved to Springfield in 1837 and married, following a problematic courtship. His lawyer reputation helped him to be elected in 1846 to Congress, where he voted against both Abolition and the Mexican War. He did not run for re-election. The Dred Scott case (1857) increased his feeling for the anti-slavery cause, and after his 1858 acceptance of Republican nomination for the Senate he engaged Stephen Douglas in a series of debates which made him nationally famous. It is in these and in the *Cooper Union Address* (1860) that Lincoln's mastery of persuasive language is first clear. When he was nominated for the presidency, his virtual silence during the campaign did not prevent his overwhelming victory. Then, in 1861, his *Farewell Address* at Springfield (perhaps revised later) again shows his rhetorical individuality – that combination of alliteration, rhythm, cadence and timing of clauses which has long since degenerated in the mouths of presidential imitators and others. In the *First Inaugural Address* (1861) Lincoln increased his power by making his chief concern the preservation of the Union, even at the expense of Abolition, although when the War of Secession came he refrained from employing a dictatorial manner even in the face of generals he could not approve of, a free press which abused him and a cabinet largely unsympathetic. His *Emancipation Proclamation* (1862), originally a war measure, became a foundation of the Reconstruction, and his *Gettysburg Address* (1863) is the standard Lincoln speech. Phrases from its 260 words are part of American folk-speech. The magic lies in the King James Bible rhythms and common American diction employed to carry unoriginal ideas with tremendous articulation of common feeling. The *Second Inaugural Address* (1865), delivered six weeks before his assassination, again includes no new ideas but is powerful in its directive of feeling based on 17th-century cadence and references to God and America in united action. The other side of the great man was the melancholy faced joker who admired Artemus ◊ Ward (see Lloyd Dunning's *Lincoln's Funnybone*, 1942), and inherited the tradition of Western humour (see Constance Rourke's *American Humour*, 1931). Among the hundreds of books on Lincoln and collections of his writings, a beginning may be made with Philip Van Doren's *Life and Writings of Abraham Lincoln* (1940), a comprehensive selection with notes, and R. P. Basler's *Abraham Lincoln: His Speeches and Writings* (1946), a large number of authentic texts with a useful analysis of his progress as a writer. [EM]

James G. Randall, *Lincoln the President* (4 vols., 1945–55); Allan Nevins, *The Emergence of Lincoln* (1950).

**Lindsay, (Nicholas) Vachel** (1879–1931). Poet. Among the earliest writers of the modern American 'renaissance' of literature. He was born in Springfield, Illinois, and family associations made him early acquainted with the rural life of the mid-West, where devotion to Lincoln as Emancipator and Andrew Jackson as 'friend of the common man' merged with the moral earnestness of evangelical fundamentalism, its social philosopher William Jennings Bryan. Lindsay embraced the prevailing millennialism, but not his parents' ambition for him to enter the ministry. He left his college programme unfinished in 1900, and earned his way for several years while studying in art school in Chicago and New York. He taught social settlement and YMCA programmes, and while developing theories of community art prepared to become the prophet of those visionary Utopias which were to be expressed in later prose writings (for instance, *The Golden Book of Springfield*, 1920). At 30, still a poet without a subject, he began walking tours in which he played the mendicant minstrel, trading 'rhymes for bread', in poetry recitations through the eastern highlands and the South. Here indigenous myths and ballads gave him his effective inspirations, as did his search for an 'American' rhythm – which he related to the sounds of galloping herds and shrieking motors, Negro dancing and revival singing, and what he called 'vaudevilles' and 'circuses'.

With *General William Booth Enters into Heaven, and Other Poems* (1913) and *The Congo, and Other Poems* (1914) he won astonished attention for poetry. The two title poems established his mastery of a new – though not untraditional – ballad. With *The Chinese Nightingale and Other Poems* (1917), we find in the title poem an excellent example of his characteristic fantasy of contemporary common life – while such poems as 'The Ghost of the Buffaloes' and 'In Praise of Johnny Appleseed' continue his gift of transmitting living regional American folklore, as had the earlier Lincoln poems and 'The Santa-Fé Trail'. Famous first volumes by ◊ Masters and ◊ Sandburg were simultaneously advancing the growth of a new mid-West literature, celebrated and concentrated in the Chicago review *Poetry* (◊ Little Magazines). But beyond the accomplishment of these st three volumes, his *Collected Poems* (1923) added little – though some of h later poems about childhood and his poem-games retain a wistful charm. In the four negligible volumes of the later period sentimentality predominates. He supported himself by recitals of his own verse until the novelty of his spectacular dramatization wore thin; then as audiences and readers dwindled he suffered poverty and an emotional depression, which resulted in his suicide in 1931. [RS]

*Selected Poems*, ed. Mark Harris (1964).
Edgar Lee Masters, *Vachel Lindsay: A Poet in America* (1935); Eleanor Ruggles, *The West-Going Heart* (1959).

**Lippmann, Walter** (1889–    ). Columnist, social analyst. Born in New York. For a long time an influential, civilized voice in the American scene, Lippmann taught at Harvard, served in government under Woodrow Wilson and then, after writing for the *New Republic*, became the powerfully influential political columnist of the New York *Herald Tribune*. Lippmann remarkably mixes the insider's knowledge of government with the outsider's detachment and idealism. A radical moderate with a commonsense mind, he has the rare power to provide his readers with both inside analysis of contemporary issues and an ideal of a humane society (one of his books is called *The Good Society*, 1937). Among numerous other books and lectures are *A Preface to Morals* (1929), *Interpretations, 1933–1935* (1936), *The Cold War* (1947), the reflective *The Public Philosophy* (1955) and *The Communist World and Ours* (1959). [MB]

*The Essential Lippmann*, ed. Clinton Rossiter and James Lare (1963).

**Literary Reviews.** ◊ Little Magazines.

**Little Magazines.** In this century little magazines and small-circulation journals have played an important part in establishing the modern movement in literature and the consolidating movement in literary criticism which followed it. In *The Little Magazine: A History and a Bibliography* (1946) F. J. Hoffman, Charles Allen and Carolyn Ulrich argue that they 'have stood, since 1912 to the present, defiantly in the front ranks of the battle for a mature literature', and have done this by first publishing 'about 80 per cent of our most important post-1912 critics, novelists, poets, and story-tellers'. The growth of these magazines is in fact a fairly direct indication of the growth of a specialist or *avant garde* attitude towards literature, which has been very evident in this century, particularly in the U.S.A.; and during this century they have existed in very large numbers, deriving from Bohemian groups, expatriate groups, regional movements and even individuals (◊ Bohemianism, Expatriates, Lost Generation). The modern movement in literature, the experimental revival from about 1910 onwards, cosmopolitan, complex, often allusive and private, has depended on strong aesthetic motivations and the tendency of writers to form into movements and groups; this has been a feature of the American literary scene. Little magazines, flourishing in all parts of the U.S.A., and the expatriate centres of Europe (London, Paris, Rome, etc.), have presented these movements and *avant garde* tendencies. And more sober critical journals, often though not always centred on universities, also in terms of circulation and specialized interest 'little', have elaborated a new criticism as well as promoting many original poets and story writers – many of them also major critics (e.g. Allen ◊ Tate, John Crowe ◊ Ransom, Robert Penn ◊ Warren).

The early little magazines arose directly out of an atmosphere of experiment, renaissance, rebellion, often out of centres with active Bohemian movements. Early

models of the type are the *Chap-Book* (1894–8), from Chicago, printing Stephen ◊ Crane, Hamlin ◊ Garland, Henry James, William Vaughn ◊ Moody and others; *M'lle New York* (1895–9), involving James Gibbons ◊ Huneker and European experimental writers; and the *Lark* (1895–7), from San Francisco. But it was not until a strong vein of experimentalism established itself in American letters that the great journals began. In 1912 in Chicago Harriet ◊ Monroe began *Poetry: A Magazine of Verse*, which played a large part in establishing the new experimenters of the 1910s and 1920s, including Eliot, Vachel ◊ Lindsay, Amy ◊ Lowell, Edgar Lee ◊ Masters and Carl ◊ Sandburg, and is still alive. *The Masses* (1911–17) gradually began to turn into a ◊ Greenwich Village Bohemian journal, linking its founding socialist and pacificist attitudes with a strong interest in the arts. The Greenwich Village spirit promoted Alfred Kreymbourg's the *Globe* (1913–14), which printed the first *Des Imagistes* anthology from Ezra Pound and others (1915–19); while the lively literary movement in Chicago, linked with the London expatriates through Pound, was the source of a second review, Margaret Anderson's *Little Review* (1914–29), printing Hart ◊ Crane, Pound, Eliot, Sherwood Anderson, Hemingway, and some of Joyce's *Ulysses*; it ended its days with Dada in Paris.

In such magazines many distinguished writers, young and experimental, began to gain attention – William Carlos ◊ Williams, Marianne ◊ Moore, Wallace ◊ Stevens, E. E. ◊ Cummings and Robert ◊ Frost should be added to the names already mentioned. At the same time Pound in London was tirelessly promoting their work among the little magazines there and providing them with international reputations, as well as acting as agent for English experimentalists with the American reviews. In America the number of reviews was growing, including *Bruno's Weekly*, *Contemporary Verse*, and the *Liberator*. From New York came the monthly *Seven Arts* (1916–17), edited by James Oppenheim, which spoke of a renaissance in American letters and printed much remarkable criticism supporting the view from Waldo ◊ Frank, Randolph ◊ Bourne, Van Wyck ◊ Brooks and others; Sherwood Anderson and Eugene O'Neill were among those who contributed fiction; Robert Frost, Carl

Sandburg and Amy Lowell were among the poets. It was later absorbed by the *Dial*, the famous review for which ◊ Emerson and Margaret ◊ Fuller had written; in 1916 it was taken over by new editors, including Randolph Bourne and Van Wyck Brooks; and from 1920, under Scofield Thayer, the *Dial* printed many new writers of importance, ranging from T. S. Eliot to Thomas Mann; later Marianne Moore became its editor.

In 1920, at the beginning of an even more exciting period, William Carlos Williams and Robert ◊ McAlmon produced *Contact* (1920–32), printing most of the writers already mentioned and Kenneth ◊ Burke, Yvor ◊ Winters and others. From New Orleans came the lively *Double-Dealer* (1921–6), which published important Southern writers like Tate, Ransom and Faulkner – as well as Hemingway, Anderson, Thornton Wilder and others – and so helped to promote the Southern renaissance. In 1922 appeared the *Fugitive* (◊ Fugitives). Other little magazines over this period were *Laughing Horse, S4N* and *Bozart*. But in the twenties, Paris became the new European centre, and many young writers went there (◊ Lost Generation), taking along or founding their reviews. Alfred Kreymbourg and Harold Loeb went to Italy, where costs were low, to produce *Broom*, which printed American and European experimentalists side by side (1921–4). Arthur Moss brought out *Gargoyle* (1921–2) in Paris, with surveys of Cubist art. Gorham B. ◊ Munson started *Secession* (1922–4), which printed Stevens, Marianne Moore, Matthew ◊ Josephson and Malcolm ◊ Cowley and pursued an expatriate flirtation with Surrealism and Dada. Ford Madox Ford had Hemingway as his assistant editor and a strong American contribution for his *transatlantic review* (1924–5), where Gertrude Stein, the experimentalists' folk-heroine, appeared with part of her *The Making of Americans*, along with Joyce, Ford himself, various young American writers and some English ones. Ernest Walsh's *This Quarter* (1925–32) brought out three issues containing Pound, Hemingway, Joyce, Yvor Winters, and others; then after the death of its editor it passed to Ernest Titus, who recast it and printed Williams, Cummings, Hemingway, Anderson, James T. ◊ Farrell and others.

In New York, H. L. ◊ Mencken and George Jean ◊ Nathan began the provocative, anti-expatriate, anti-aesthetic *American Mercury* (1924–33); it circulated fairly widely and had a popular-satirical tone which was very much Mencken's own, and it spoke for a new urban sophistication, attacking the 'booboisie' and other middle-class or provincial targets; Sinclair ◊ Lewis and Ernest Boyd were among the contributors. Also in New York, the *Masses* tradition was revived with *New Masses* (1926 on; various editors), preparing the way for the political interests of the 1930s. The vein of social criticism was strong in journals of this type (which include the *Freeman*, 1920–4, the *Nation*, the *New Republic* and V. F. ◊ Calverton's *Modern Quarterly*, 1923–40), but close connexions with literature were preserved; and *New Masses* in its early years printed some remarkable work by Robinson ◊ Jeffers, Sherwood Anderson, Floyd ◊ Dell, Carl Sandburg, Witter ◊ Bynner and others. The following year saw the *Hound and Horn* (1927–34) from Harvard, one of the earliest of the critical little magazines, printing Eliot, Kenneth ◊ Burke, R. P. ◊ Blackmur and Allen Tate as critics; fiction by Katherine Anne ◊ Porter, John ◊ Dos Passos, etc.; and verse by many important poets and now well established in the smaller journals. The number of regional reviews, many of them with a literary-critical flavour, was now growing; from Lincoln, Nebraska, for instance, came the *Prairie Schooner* (1927 onwards), university-centred but with a regional emphasis. The development of such journals became important in the thirties as the critical movement grew in force, as academic study of literature expanded, and as literary debate widened.

During the late twenties, another group of expatriate magazines developed in Paris and elsewhere; there was Pound's *Exile* (1927–8), printing Hemingway, McAlmon, Louis ◊ Zukofsky, etc., and some remarkable items by Pound himself; there was Eugene Jolas's remarkable *transition* (1927–38), printing Joyce's *Work in Progress*, Gertrude Stein, Hart Crane, Allen Tate, Kay ◊ Boyle, Harry Crosby, Horace ◊ Gregory, Archibald ◊ MacLeish and many other distinguished writers, and promoting the famous 'Revolution of the Word'; there was the *Tambour* (1928–30), and the *New Review* (1931–2), which printed Henry ◊ Miller. But by the 1930s the expatriate

155

movement was fading, the experimental-aesthetic impetus diminishing, and the new reviews tended either towards overtly political or literary critical perspectives. Some, in particular *Partisan Review* (1934 onwards), were both; beginning as a publication of the John Reed Club of New York, *Partisan Review* grew increasingly emancipated from the party line and published remarkably good criticism, usually with a sociological emphasis, from Lionel ◊ Trilling, Philip ◊ Rahv, Edmund ◊ Wilson, and Blackmur, as well as the poetry of Stevens, Tate, ◊ Jarrell, Karl ◊ Shapiro, etc., and the fiction of Delmore ◊ Schwartz, Saul ◊ Bellow, Katherine Anne Porter, etc. The experimental tradition found a new centre in James Laughlin's *New Directions in Prose and Poetry* (1936 onwards), printing most of the major moderns. From the South came Cleanth ◊ Brooks' and Robert Penn Warren's *Southern Review* (1935–42); in 1938 came John Crowe Ransom's excellent *Kenyon Review*, printing most of the major new critics and poetry by many important poets of both the experimental and a new semi-academic generation, as well as similar fiction; and from New Haven, Connecticut, came *Furioso* (1939 onwards), linking poetry with analytical criticism of it (poets printed include Marianne Moore, Stevens, Cummings, Horace Gregory, John Peale ◊ Bishop, Richard ◊ Eberhart). These critical reviews had from the 1930s on a powerful influence on American writing, rationalizing the position of the literary intellectual, now more likely to be on the university campus than in Bohemia.

By the 1940s and 1950s, the Bohemian-experimental and the critical phase tended to merge as the university became more Bohemian, the Bohemian centres more academic; and though the two groups have often battled they were closely linked. A typical situation was that of the *Chicago Review*, which from 1946 was produced from the University of Chicago, printing many new writers like J. F. ◊ Powers along with older ones like Kenneth ◊ Patchen and James T. Farrell; it gradually grew associated with the Beat Generation (at the same time holding a lively sociological interest) and fell out with the university appearing independently as *Big Table*. *Western Review*, *Folio*, the *Antioch Review*, the *Hudson Review*, as well as the old *Sewanee Review* (founded 1892) and the

*Yale Review* (1892), took on new importance in this phase; all came out of academic contexts and ranged from a strongly critical to an experimental emphasis. They virtually dominated the creative scene in the late 1940s and 1950s and are still important.

But in the 1950s there developed an increasing number of challengers. For example there was competition from the many magazines produced by the ◊ Beat Generation and the growing number of Bohemian and hippie literary enclaves, as well as from various experimental, free expression and liberation movements. *Evergreen Review* since its foundation in 1957 has been a major centre of new experimental writing, European as well as American, printing a lot of the best (as well as some spuriously sensational) work of the Beat writers, and has featured William ◊ Burroughs, Jack ◊ Kerouac, Gregory ◊ Corso, John ◊ Rechy and many others, though its quality has now declined severely. A strong competitor was the *Noble Savage* (1960 onwards; Saul Bellow was an editor), which published many important new writers. Both of these came from paperback publishers, and, seeing the small magazine as a good promotional device, other such publishers have produced *New World Writing* (1947 onwards), *Discovery*, and the *Anchor Review*, ranging in character from the experimental and academic to the slightly glossy. The important inheritor in this line is the *New American Review*. But the Beat Generation and other new forces produced in addition numerous smaller publications, such as those deriving from Jonathan ◊ Williams or from Lawrence ◊ Ferlinghetti's City Lights Bookshop. Some of these had a strong anarchist emphasis, like the *Journal for the Protection of All Beings*. More important were ventures like the *Black Mountain Review*, which was a centre of new experimental poetry by Robert ◊ Creeley, Charles ◊ Olson, etc.; Robert ◊ Bly's *The Sixties* (formerly *The Fifties*); and LeRoi ◊ Jones's *Yugen*. The tradition of dissent periodicals (*Dissent, Commentary*) was reinforced by a variety of ventures like Paul Krassner's *Realist*, printing writers like Terry Southern and Joseph Heller, and *Ramparts*. The expatriate tradition in the magazine continued too, most solidly with George Plimpton's *Paris Review* and J. F. McCrindle's *Transatlantic Review*; while with the coming into existence of a new reviewing newspaper with radical bias, the *New York Review of Books*, the entire balance of the media in relation to the literary scene was transformed.

In fact this phase saw a media explosion which has continued into the late sixties and played a large part in the expansive, radical cultural climate of this period. Through the 1960s the numbers of magazines went on increasing, but the forms of publication were changing significantly. What the poet-editor Kirby Congdon has called the 'mimeograph revolution' (indeed the general availability of cheap means of typographical reproduction) enabled poets and movements to issue their own magazines; publication has become far less a special achievement, and has lost the scarcity structure of editorial costs and selection; the capitalist market of narrowed enterprise has been relaxed as large numbers of magazines, printed regularly and circulated by a handful of booksellers but mainly by post, produced an expansive, creative climate. Then there is an underground newspaper press drawing in materials previously found in small journals; publications like *East Village Other*, *Los Angeles Free Press*, and *Rolling Stone* (there are scores more) provide a context for exploration of political protest, rock music, esoteric religion and relaxed sexuality, in the main line of American anarchism. Of more literary publications, with the demise of Lita Hornick's *Kulture* and *Art and Literature* (John ◊ Ashbery and others), two brilliant magazines, the best general magazines now are perhaps Charles Newman's *TriQuarterly* and Clayton Eshleman's *Caterpillar*. After the cessation of *C Magazine* (Ted ◊ Berrigan) and *Mother* (Peter ◊ Schjeldahl and Lewis Mac-Adams), the New York poetry scene is best seen in *Angel Hair* (Ann Waldman and Lewis Warsh) and *Adventures in Poetry* (Larry Fagin). For the more general scene: *Works* (John Hopper and Robert Brotherson), *Sumac* (Dan Gerber and Jim Harrison), *Some Thing* (Jerome ◊ Rothenberg and David Antin), *Floating Bear* (Diane di Prima), *The San Francisco Earthquake* (Jacob Herman and Claude Pelieu), etc. The best of the black literary magazines is David Henderson's *Umbra*. But selection is invidious in the extreme; the sheer vitality of the little magazine scene in 1970 is impossible to cover briefly. Today experimentalism is no longer an oddity, nor the

little magazine the place that harbours the writer too daring to sell. The climate of experimentalism has a general dominance in the literary and in the social scene; the clear categorization of the market which was once possible is no longer viable; the counter-culture so extensive and vigorous that the entire previous structure of the cultural scene is under challenge. [MB/EM]

Reed Whittemore, *Little Magazines* (U. of Minnesota Pamphlet, 1963); 'The Little Magazines', *Times Literary Supplement*, 25 April 1968; 'The Small Presses',*Works*, 11, i (1969); *Directory of Little Magazines*, ed. Leonard V. Fulton and Kavan McCarthy); James Gilbert, *Writers and Partisans* (1968).

**Living Theatre, The.** Founded in 1947 by Judith Malina and Julian Beck it has remained, with a few brief breaks, a centre of new theatre, first in America and later in Europe. In its initial New York centre, it put on experimental plays by Gertrude ◊ Stein, Paul ◊ Goodman, Kenneth ◊ Rexroth, T. S. ◊ Eliot, John ◊ Ashbery and William Carlos ◊ Williams, and Yeats, Brecht, Lorca, Strindberg, Jarry and Cocteau, thus injecting a variety of life into American theatre. The last productions before it left for Europe in 1963 included *The Connection* by Jack Gelber, Pound's version of Sophocles' *Women of Trachis*, and Kenneth Brown's *The Brig*, all strong works directly connected with the social and political protests against victimization which were to absorb the company in the sixties. Even when the acting and production standards may have been relaxed, the company generated a sense of commitment to the social function of theatre. In 1963 the Living Theatre was seized by the Internal Revenue Service for non-payment of taxes. The government showed no lenience and this seemed to fulfil the message gathering in the company's plays. The Becks, with 26 of their group, moved to Europe, where they developed the idea of a theatre company as creative political critics and emotional gurus. They became part of the radicalism of the late 1960s. Their major productions were Jean Genet's *The Maids*, the Sophocles Brecht *Antigone*, and three works which were created by the company as a group – *Frankenstein* (1965, partly based on Mary Shelley's character), *Mysteries and Smaller Pieces* (1966) and *Paradise Now* (1968). In 1964 and 1969 they performed in England,

and in 1968, as almost legendary heroes, returned triumphantly to America, and became part of both the new radicalism in politics and the developments in audience-participation and actor-activism in drama. The Becks' early work was aesthetic and poetic; their later theatre of revolution owes ideas to Antonin Artaud's 'theatre of cruelty', the pacifism and anarchism of Paul Goodman, Reich's psychology of sexual liberation, the epic theatre of Erwin Piscator, with whom Judith Malina studied in the late 1940s, and Hassidic Judaism, both the service and the mysticism. [E M]

'The Return of the Living Theatre', *Tulane Drama Review*, XIII, 3 (1969).

**Lloyd, Henry Demarest** (1847–1903). Journalist, reformer. Born in New York. After qualifying as a lawyer in 1869 he joined a New York group trying to reform Tammany Hall, the Democratic Party organization in the city. He then moved to Chicago and in the Chicago *Tribune*, part-owned by his father-in-law, pointed out the dangers of unrestrained big business and monopoly, and the unsavoury political practices of many large corporations. He investigated conditions among the miners in the Spring Valley, Illinois, coal strike, championed the demonstrators convicted after the Haymarket Riots of 1886, and in the early 1890s worked for the Populist party, becoming disillusioned later and turning to the Socialist-Labor party. In later life he held that socialism was the only sound alternative to the established American parties, though he believed firmly in a pragmatic, not a doctrinaire, approach to contemporary problems. His positive aims are expressed in *A Strike of Millionaires against Miners* (1890), an attempt to formulate the rights of labour, and in his most famous book, *Wealth against Commonwealth* (1894; ed. T. G. Cochran, 1963), he sought to produce a valid alternative to the prevailing concept of Social Darwinism. [D K A]

Daniel Aaron, *Men of Good Hope* (1951).

**Locke, David Ross.** ◊ Nasby, Petroleum Vesuvius.

**Lockridge, Ross** (1914–48). Novelist. Born in Indiana, he was educated at the Sorbonne and Harvard, and taught at Indiana University and Simmons College. By his early death he had completed one novel, the ambitious and extended *Raintree County* (1948), which takes in some of the great

political and social occasions of an imaginary Indiana county through the 19th century. Its scope and rhetoric link it with the work of Thomas ◊ Wolfe, whom the author admired. [M B]

**Logan, John** (1923–      ). Poet. Born in Iowa, educated at Coe College and the University of Iowa, he became editorial director of the Poetry Seminar in Chicago and a teacher at Notre Dame University. His volumes, which include *A Cycle for Mother Cabrini* (1955), *Ghosts of the Heart* (1960) and *Spring of the Thief* (1963), are marked by an extremely personal, vivid and erudite Catholicism. The earlier poetry is violent in imagery, coarse in diction; the latest volume shifts to a quieter, more assured and more directly personal kind of confessional poetry. [B P]

Paul Carroll, *The Poem in Its Skin* (1968).

**London, Jack (John Griffith London)** (1876–1916). Novelist. His father was an astrologer, his mother came from a comfortable Ohio fam²ly. In San Francisco he spent his boyhoc ᵢ on the waterfront and from the age of ' ⁄ worked in a cannery and became a fight' ₁g, drinking outlaw, and a voracious reaᵤer, beginning with Irving's *Alhambra* and working his way through the Oakland library with travel adventures, Smollett, Wilkie Collins, Kipling, Ouida, etc. He switched allegiance and became a government hero – see the stories in *Tales of the Fish Patrol* (1905) – and went to the Arctic in a sealing ship (material for *The Sea Wolf*, 1904). He returned in the 1893 depression, sank to the bottom of the labour scale, and joined Coxey's Army's march on Washington in 1894, just after winning first prize in a newspaper story competition. The four crucial elements of his youth were complete: heroic sea adventure, fiction of romance and exploration, the taste of success with his first story, and an understanding of the conditions of labour in America. Now he discovered the *Communist Manifesto*, enrolled at the University of California (he was 20) and became an active socialist. At Berkeley he read the 19th-century social evolutionists, and, in 1897, took off for the Klondike gold rush carrying Darwin, Haeckel and *Paradise Lost* in his bag.

His education in natural law, determinism and authority continued. His life was legendary. He now read Frazer, the 19th-century economists and Nietzsche, and was drawn to Shaw's philosopher-athlete in *Man and Superman*. In 1903 he wrote *The People of the Abyss*, an account of poverty in London's East End, and *The Call of the Wild*, an all-time best-seller. *The Sea Wolf* had an advance sale in America of 40,000. From 1900 to 1916, 50 books earned him over a million dollars, which he spent fast. *The War of the Classes* (1905) and *The Human Drift* (1917) work out his economic determinism and reformism, and *Martin Eden* (1909) dramatizes his own rise into the moneyed class as a betrayal of idealism, while *John Barleycorn* (1913) concerns his alcoholism. His travels ended on his ranch, Wolf House, in California: he died a public figure, exhausted and in despair.

In *The Call of the Wild* the transformation of a pet dog into leader of a Yukon wolf pack is the example of Darwinian survival, written in a swiftly moving style; *White Fang* (1906) is nearly as brilliant, telling the reverse story. *The Sea Wolf* concerns the career of Captain Wolf Larsen as he puts Spencer and Nietzsche into superman practice, defeated by symbolic blindness and the skill of an ex-dilettante pressed into his service. *The Iron Heel* (1907) is an early 20th-century nightmare Utopia, a warning against fascist dictatorship in Chicago. *The Assassination Bureau*, left unfinished, has recently been rescued and completed by R. L. Fish (1963); the plot concerns a millionaire socialist's scheme to kill the head of a bureau dedicated to eliminate enemies of society. In many ways London is the archetypal popular 20th-century novelist: his conflicts are still central. [EM]

*Letters from Jack London*, ed. K. Hendricks and I. Shepard (1965).

Ed. P. S. Foner, *Jack London: American Rebel* (1947); R. O. Connor, *Jack London: A Biography* (1965); Joan London, *Jack London and His Times* (1939; reissued with new introduction, 1968).

**Longfellow, Henry Wadsworth** (1807–82). Poet. One of the most popular poets who ever lived, he was born in the seaport and forest frontier of Portland, Maine, and educated with Hawthorne and the future president Pierce at Bowdoin. He modelled his early literary ambition on ♢ Irving, who received him in Spain during his 1826–9 study journey. His linguistic abilities gained him a professorship at Bowdoin and, in 1834, at Harvard, after a second European trip to encounter Scandinavian and German romantic poetry, and Carlyle. The early death of his wife and child are reflected in the mild stoicism of his ensuing poetry and philosophy. He remarried in 1843 and lived in enough wealth to resign from Harvard in 1854, but in 1861 his wife died from burns: this ended a period of happiness during which most of his famous poems were written. His popularity in his own lifetime was great, unbroken by the Civil War, honoured by Oxford and Queen Victoria, and finally by Westminster Abbey. But 'A Psalm of Life' (1838) is typical, a work of melancholic cliché on mutability. *Ballads and Other Poems* (1842) includes 'The Wreck of the Hesperus', 'The Village Blacksmith', 'Excelsior' and 'The Rainy Day' – sentimental classics of bathetic rhetoric and self-pity raised by their readers to levels of myth, as was 'Evangeline' (1847), whose theme was intended to be and is American – the plight of the Acadian exile from Nova Scotia to Louisiana in slow, crude hexameters. *The Song of Hiawatha* (1855) versifies historical sources in hypnotic trochaic tetrameters, said to derive from the Finnish *Kalevala*. After his 'Indian Edda' appeared *The Courtship of Miles Standish* (1858), the last of his three 'epics', a New England courtship interrupted by Indian wars. *Tales of a Wayside Inn* (1863) includes 'Paul Revere's Ride', and his final poems included a poor translation of Dante (1865–7). The art of Longfellow is an outstanding example of popular taste. Recent efforts to raise him to the level of mythopoeic poetry have not been convincing, although his narrative poems are good fun. His synthetic folk-poems are internationally known but have little depth or linguistic talent. [EM]

*Letters*, ed. A. Hilen (2 vols., 1967); *Representative Selections*, ed. O. Shepard (1934).

Newton Arvin, *Longfellow: His Life and Work* (1933); E. Wagenknecht, *Longfellow: A Full-Length Portrait* (1955).

**Longstreet, Augustus Baldwin** (1790–1870). Born in Georgia, educated at Yale, he became a judge, a clergyman, a professional college president and a newspaper editor. But he is remembered for his comic tales and sketches in *Georgia Scenes* (1835), an entertaining collection of Georgia wit and folktales he apparently felt ashamed of later and tried to suppress. [EM]

J. D. Wade, *Augustus Baldwin Longstreet* (1924).

**Loos, Anita** (1893–    ). Novelist, playwright, film-script writer. Born in California, she was writing scenarios for D. W. Griffith at 15. Besides her screenplays of many well-known films, she has won fame and best-sellerdom for two celebrations of the female gold-digger in *Gentlemen Prefer Blondes* (1925), the witty, self-exposing narrative of Lorelei Lee, 'a Professional Lady', and its sequel *But Gentlemen Marry Brunettes* (1928). Both books are marked by an eye for the age, an ear for its speech and a sense of its values. More recently Miss Loos satirized Hollywood in *No Mother to Guide Her* (1961). Her plays include *Happy Birthday* (1947), *A Mouse Is Born* (1951) and the stage version of Colette's *Gigi*; her autobiographies are entitled *This Brunette Prefers Work* (1956) and *A Girl Like I* (1966), in which she describes her experiences in Hollywood and New York ('I reported Gertrude Stein as the most manly of the lot', is the level). [MB]

**Lost Generation.** 'You are all a lost generation': Gertrude Stein is credited with the remark in one of the epigraphs to Ernest Hemingway's *The Sun Also Rises* (1926). Though Hemingway subsequently regretted the phrase, and Gertrude Stein denied using it, it stuck as the description of the literary generation of the 1920s, particularly that part of it which expatriated to Paris (◇ Expatriates) and led a wild Bohemian-literary life. The phrase suggests the sense of alienation and philosophical uncertainty which has often been felt to be the defining characteristic of much American writing of the twenties; it also suggests the awareness of being a generation which existed among many of the writers of the period, and their sense that in a period of rapid change and uncertainty they had lost touch with the attitudes and norms of their parents. The generation was alienated, separated, lost (though all one needed do to find them was to go to Paris). There have been many chronicles of this 'mass-alienation', but few real explanations. The two best are by R. P. ◇ Blackmur in his essay 'The American Literary Expatriate' (in *Foreign Influences in American Life: Essays and Critical Bibliographies*, ed. David F. Bowers, 1944) and Malcolm ◇ Cowley in *Exile's Return* (1934; revised edn, 1951). Blackmur's semi-sociological argument is that this was the first time a country had attempted to detach its cultural capital from its political and economic capital, and that it was bound to lead to tension and failure. Cowley sees a pattern of development from the socially hostile art of the twenties to the socially committed art of the thirties; he regards the 'lost generation' as being detached both from previous generations and from the aims of their society, and sees them as involved in a rebellion whose character was not political but artistic. Their background was largely middle-class, and they regarded art as a traditional mode of escape from this class, because it was associated with Bohemianism, liberalism and radicalism. Lacking a strong social interest, having the middle-class sense of estrangement from power and its distrust of political action, they found France an appropriate centre for their creed, which was literary formalism. However, they found 'a crazy Europe in which the intellectuals of their own middle class were more defeated and demoralized than those at home', and this gradually turned them either towards political action or to extreme tension leading in a number of cases to suicide.

This was, nonetheless, a highly productive period for American letters, and this should not be forgotten in any account of it. Samuel Putnam, in *Paris Was Our Mistress: Memoirs of a Lost and Found Generation* (1947), stresses the disreputable quality of much of the activity, and also the remarkable size of the group present. But this included Hemingway, Fitzgerald, Ezra Pound, John Dos Passos and many others of importance; Hemingway distinguished between those who came to be Bohemians, and those who actually wrote. The strongly experimental atmosphere threw up numerous salons, magazines and small presses printing in English. Connexions were made with surrealism and Dada. A remarkable amount of important writing did emerge; this is the essential literary importance of the phase.

But it has another kind of significance in that it represents a phase in which the writer's life became – because of increased education and of the convenient economic arrangements which made Parisian Bohemian life extremely cheap for Americans – within the reach of a much larger group than previously; therefore the role of the writer changed. One aspect of the phenomenon was that a vastly enlarged generation of intellectuals found an attractive *modus vivendi* which however encouraged insecurity and tension. The result was that a very large group of writers and aspirants formed a kind of peer-group stimulating to technical advance and elaboration. The climate of the period is best evoked in Hemingway's *The Sun Also Rises* and Fitzgerald's *Tender Is the Night* (1934). Robert ♢ McAlmon's *Being Geniuses Together: An Autobiography* (1938) and Ernest Hemingway's *A Moveable Feast* (1964) give convenient pictures of lost-generation life, showing the personalities and famous occasions involved. [MB]

**Lovingood, Sut** ♢ Harris, George W.

**Lowell, Amy Lawrence** (1874–1925). Poet. Born in Brookline, Massachusetts, she was educated privately, and in her youth travelled much abroad. *A Dome of Many-Colored Glass* (1912) consists of poems conventional in form and sentimental in attitude, but after meeting Pound in London in 1913 she became an enthusiastic convert to ♢ Imagism, in whose anthologies she was liberally represented. Pound, having broken with the Imagist group, petulantly renamed the movement 'Amygism'. She died of a stroke after years of excessive literary industry and a series of operations.

Her collections of poetry include *Sword Blades and Poppy Seed* (1914), *Men, Women, and Ghosts* (1916), *Pictures of the Floating World* (1919) and *What's O'Clock?* (1925). Versatile rather than original, scintillating rather than substantial, her poetry lacks the firmness and concision advocated by Imagist theoreticians, and is in fact less Imagistic than impressionistic. Self-consciously exotic and extravagant, it is ablaze with flowers and rich fabrics. Although a devoted New Englander, she would often wander nostalgically to pre-Revolutionary France or to an oriental never-never land. She possessed an amazing facility for rhyming, but her characteristic form is an unrhymed free verse. She also experimented with polyphonic prose, an intermittently rhymed prose-poetry.

Her study of contemporary poetry, *Tendencies in Modern American Poetry* (1917), is less witty and succinct than *A Critical Fable* (1922), a similar survey in verse, modelled on *A Fable for Critics* by her relative James Russell ♢ Lowell. Just before her death she completed a massive, exuberant, but disorganized biography, *John Keats* (1925). Her *Complete Poetical Works* appeared in 1955. Richard Alding-

ton's estimate seems fair: 'In Amy there was something of an artist and a real aesthetic appreciation.' [RWB]

Stanley K. Coffman, Jr, *Imagism* (1951); S. Foster Damon, *Amy Lowell* (1935); Horace Gregory, *Amy Lowell* (1958).

**Lowell, James Russell** (1819–91). Poet, essayist, editor, diplomat. Born into a distinguished New England family, educated at Harvard, he came rapidly to prominence as a poet. His first book, *A Year's Life and Other Poems*, came out in 1841, and *Poems* in 1844, the year he married Martha White, who appears to have encouraged his interest in the Abolitionist cause and other liberal movements (he wrote many political essays and addresses). His liberal opinions had in them a distinct conservative strain, in that he was concerned with the survival of an 'exemplary' aristocracy. In 1848 his reputation as a poet increased with the publication *Poems: Second Series. A Fable for Critics*, a long satirical poem on his contemporaries, published anonymously (the title page describes it as 'By A Wonderful Quiz, who accompanies himself with a rub-a-dub-dub, full of spirit and grace, on the top of the tub'); *The Vision of Sir Launfal*, a Grail story in verse; and the first series of his famous *Biglow Papers*, Yankee dialect poems on contemporary issues, satirically treated, and attacking particularly American policy in the Mexican war. In 1855, two years after the death of his wife, he became Professor of Belles Lettres at Harvard; in 1857 he became editor of the *Atlantic Monthly*; and in 1867 he published the second series of *Biglow Papers*, which the Civil War stirred him to write. In the years after the war he continued to publish poetry, but grew increasingly well known as an essayist and literary critic. In two series of essays called *Among My Books* (1870, 1876), and elsewhere, he published studies of Chaucer, Dante, Spenser, Shakespeare, Keats, etc., which are still highly regarded. His *The English Poets: Lessing: Rousseau* (1888) circulated widely in England. By this time he had become American minister to the Court of Spain (1877–80); and then from 1880 to 1885 American minister in Britain (where he delivered his famous address 'Democracy'). To England he became closely attached, and he reveals in his later life a kind of fondness for the English social pattern which became a popular American nostalgia during these Gilded Age years.

The striking feature of his work is its range of manners and styles, a range so great that he later became convinced that he dissipated his gifts. Later criticism has tended to agree with his judgement. He has a variety of tones of voice, a variety of themes, the themes and voices of the wide-ranging Victorian intellectual. His interest in provincial vernacular, his exuberance, and his literary nationalism co-exist with a much more cosmopolitan vein, particularly evident in his substantial literary criticism. In his poetry, perhaps his most characteristic technique is descriptive or reflective, but he will move suddenly to exhortation, assailing poverty, tyranny and religious doubt. His satirical vein is important, but it often lacks direction and falls back on exuberance. A major figure, he is too varied to have produced any definitely major works. Probably his odes and longer poems – 'Commemoration Ode' (1865), 'The Cathedral' (1870) and 'Agassiz' (1874) – are among his best. [MB]

*The Complete Writings*, ed. Charles Eliot Norton (16 vols., 1904).
H. E. Scudder, *James Russell Lowell: A Biography* (2 vols., 1901); Leon Howard, *Victorian Knight-Errant: A Study of the Early Literary Career of James Russell Lowell* (1952); Martin Duberman, *James Russell Lowell* (1967).

**Lowell, Robert** (1917–    ). Poet. He was born in Boston, Massachusetts, and inherits New England introspection, dissent and spiritual exploration. After Harvard, he studied with John Crowe ◊ Ransom at Kenyon College, and with Robert Penn ◊ Warren and Cleanth ◊ Brooks at Louisiana State University. He became a Roman Catholic, and in 1943 was gaoled for conscientious objection to allied bombing of civilians. His training in the classics and with the ◊ New Criticism poets shows in his first two volumes of poetry, *Land of Unlikeness* (1944) and *Lord Weary's Castle* (1946). His international reputation began with *Poems 1938–1949* (1950). The title poem of *The Mills of the Kavanaughs* (1951) is a 20-page psychological novelette, and *Life Studies* (1959) consists of lengthy poems and a prose section concerned with his immediate family and his own experience of hospital, prison and married life in the 1940s and 1950s. *For the Union Dead* (1964) develops the forms of his later poetry

and shows an increased scope of social criticism. His free translations – *Phaedra* (1960) and *Imitations* (1962) – are among his finest work, and his three plays, based on stories by Hawthorne and Melville, *The Old Glory* (1965), have transformed the possibilities of verse drama. What Alfred Kazin called 'the elegantly turned tumult of style and evocation of Catholic glory and order' of his earlier poems is modified into the freer tradition of William Carlos ◊ Williams in the *Life Studies* poems of direct, non-exegetical confession, self-exposure and spoken-voice rhythms. Lowell's career, itself a remarkable achievement in poetic discipline, also reflects a crucial change in American poetry from academic verse to the renewal of the line from Whitman. But his nervous, slightly timid approach to contemporary affairs enervates the poems in *Now the Ocean* (1967), while his verse play treatment of the Aeschylean theme in *Prometheus Bound* (1967, with pictures by Sidney Nolan) is too oblique to be as politically effective as its intention seems to be. (Nolan also illustrates *The Voyage*, the Baudelaire poems from *Imitations*.) *Notebook 1967–8* (1969) is a remarkable poetic witness to the conflicts of the sixties. Lowell now reflects the American liberal intellectual's struggle to save what he can from increasing chaos. [EM]

H. B. Staples, *Robert Lowell: The First Twenty Years* (1962); Jerome Mazzaro, *The Poetic Themes of Robert Lowell* (1966).

**Lowenfels, Walter** (1897–    ). Poet. He was associated with many of the great American ◊ expatriate writers who lived in Paris after the First World War, publishing some half-dozen small volumes of poetry there. In 1934 he gave up Europe and poetry, returning to the States to be a journalist; in 1955, after his arrest during the McCarthyite purges, he returned to poetry, publishing recently *American Voices* (1959), *Song of Peace* (1959), *Some Deaths: Selected Poems, 1929–1962* (1964) and *Land of Roseberries* (1965). His important efforts to keep the spoken word alive on the page and the sometimes witty, sometimes poignant compassion he expresses for the victims of this world have won him the admiration of two different generations of the *avant garde*. In 1961 he edited the valuable *Walt Whitman's Civil War*, in 1964 *Poets of Today*, and in 1967 *Where is Vietnam? American Poets Respond. Thou Shalt not Kill* (1968) contains his peace poems. *We Are All Poets Really* (ed. Allen de Loach, 1967) and *The Portable Walter* (ed. Robert Gover, 1968) are collections of his work. *To an Imaginary Daughter* (1964) is a prose record of relationships between generations. [B P]

A. Guttman, 'Poetic Poetics', *Massachusetts Review*, Autumn, 1965.

**Lowry, Robert** (1919– ). Novelist, story-writer. He is one of the group of vigorous realists produced by the experiences of the Second World War. He served in the army in Africa and Italy and drew on this for several novels – including *Casualty* (1946) and *Find Me in Fire* (1948) – and the Italian-set stories in *The Wolf That Fed Us* (1949). He is a vigorous and often a funny writer concerned with the horrors of war and the threat of modern experience to individual decency. [M B]

**Luhan, Mabel Dodge** (1879–1962). Patroness of the arts, memoirist. Born in Buffalo, N.Y. Her salons in different parts of the world linked her in many of the modern movements in American and European letters. In 1902, married to the architect Edward Dodge, she went to live in Florence, Italy; in 1913 she returned to New York and set up her salon on Fifth Avenue near Greenwich Village; in 1918 she settled in Taos, New Mexico, in an adobe house and married Antonio Luhan, a Pueblo Indian. Her various houses were literary centres, drawing important writers of each period; and she really participated in three distinct movements, one expatriate, the second New York revolutionary, the third Western. Gertrude Stein wrote a famous 'portrait' of her, 'Portrait of Mabel Dodge at the Villa Curonia', and she has been found to be the model for other characters in literature, in the work of writers as different as Carl ◊ Van Vechten and D. H. Lawrence. Others associated with her include Bernard ◊ Berenson, John ◊ Reed, Max ◊ Eastman, Walter ◊ Lippmann, and E. A. ◊ Robinson. Her life is crucial for any understanding of intellectualism or feminism in the first half of this century.

*Lorenzo in Taos* (1932) is her record of her connexion in New Mexico with Lawrence, and gives insight into Indian culture

and its artistic attraction. Her major work is *Intimate Memories*, four volumes of literary reminiscence which give important records of the whole period between about 1900 and 1935; the volumes are *Intimate Memories: Background* (1933), *European Experiences* (1935), *Movers and Shakers* (1936) and *Edge of the Taos Desert: An Escape to Reality* (1937). [M B]

Christopher Lasch, *The New Radicalism in America, 1889–1963* (1965).

**Lynd, Robert S(taughton)** (1892–1949) and **Helen M(errell)** (1896– ). Teachers, sociologists. Born in Indiana and Illinois respectively. Their reputation was established with the classic studies of an American small town, *Middletown* (1929) and *Middletown Revisited* (1937). Robert Lynd became Professor of Sociology at Columbia in 1931, and his wife is Professor of Social Philosophy at Sarah Lawrence College. Her two major works are *England in the 1880s: Toward a Social Basis for Freedom* (1945) and the brilliant *On Shame and the Search for Identity* (1958). [E M]

**Lytle, Andrew** (1902– ). Novelist, story-writer. Born in Tennessee, he graduated from Vanderbilt and associated there with the ◊ Fugitive group. He has taught at the University of Florida and the University of the South at Sewanee, Tennessee, where he now edits the *Sewanee Review* (◊ Little Magazines). He began, following the example of fellow-Fugitives ◊ Tate and ◊ Warren, by writing a biography with a Civil War setting, *Bedford Forrest and His Critter Company* (1931). Four novels followed – *The Long Night* (1936), a historical romance of the Civil War; *At the Moon's Inn* (1941), a more serious historical fiction dealing with DeSoto and the Spanish conquest of the Florida Indians; *A Name for Evil* (1947; reprinted in *A Novel, A Novella and Four Stories*, 1958), a fable of the clash between modern and traditional values; and his best work to date, *The Velvet Horn* (1957), superbly rendering a boy's initiation to manhood in the Civil War and after. All are in the Southern tradition, and the best resemble Faulkner in their concern with exploring a culture and creating a regional mythology. [A H]

# M

**McAlmon, Robert** (1895–1956). Editor, publisher, novelist, poet, story writer. Born at Clifton, Kansas. An important figure among the ◊ Lost Generation in Paris in the 1920s, he left one of the best records of the period in his autobiography, *Being Geniuses Together* (1938). From Kansas, McAlmon went to New York and became co-editor with William Carlos ◊ Williams of the magazine *Contact* (◊ Little Magazines). Marriage to the English writer 'Bryher' brought him first to London and then to Paris, where he became deeply involved in expatriate life, helping James Joyce, editing magazines, and founding, in 1922 with William Bird, two small presses – Contact Editions and the Three Mountains Press – which became important centres of expatriate publishing (Hemingway, Williams, Pound, Stein and H.D. were among their authors). Several of McAlmon's own books appeared from these presses – the story-collections *A Hasty Bunch* (1922) and *A Companion Volume* (1923) and the novel *Post-Adolescence* (1923), etc. McAlmon's fiction, intensely realized, poetic, modern, has both the cosmopolitan and regional interests typical of expatriate writing – he writes, for instance, about Paris and the Riviera, and Kansas and childhood. For the latter, see particularly *Village: As It Happened Through a Fifteen-Year Period* (1924). His poetry, loosely ◊ Imagistic, appeared in several volumes, the most complete being *Not Alone Lost* (1937). [MB]

**McBain, Ed.** ◊ Hunter, Evan.

**McCarthy, Mary** (1912–    ). Novelist, critic, travel writer. She was born in Seattle, orphaned at the age of 6 and raised by relations of Catholic, Protestant and Jewish backgrounds. Her childhood complexities are carefully described in one of her best books, *Memories of a Catholic Girlhood* (1957). She graduated from Vassar in 1933 (see her novel *The Group*, 1963) and began her career as critic and reviewer on progressive magazines including the *Nation*, the *New Republic* and *Partisan Review*. She has taught at Bard and Sarah Lawrence (which

provided material for *The Groves of Academe*, 1952), and has since lived in Paris. She has always been at the centre of sophisticated opinion in New York intellectual life, from her participation in the American left of the thirties, and her admiration for Trotsky, to her visit to Vietnam in the war of the 1960s. She began her literary career with *The Company She Keeps* (1942), which includes the well-known 'The Man in the Brooks Brothers Suit', the story of an intellectual woman's seduction by a businessman (Robert Penn ◊ Warren published her first story in the *Southern Review*). *The Oasis* (1949) is a satire on liberal utopians and *The Groves of Academe* (1952) shrewdly analyses a leftist academic's urge to martyrdom. *A Charmed Life* (1955) and her short stories collected in *Cast a Cold Eye* (1952) are sharply observant studies of contemporary manners, especially malicious towards intellectuals. *The Group* follows the lives of a set of young women who had known each other at college as they choose between emancipation, careers and family traditionalism. It is a smartly written novel, whose social and sexual analysis is not as superficial as the smooth style might suggest. *Venice Observed* (1956) and *The Stones of Florence* (1959) are highly personal travel books, containing critical information on the condition of Italy. *Sights and Spectacles* (1956) is a collection of surgical theatre reviews, and *On the Contrary: Articles of Belief 1946–1961* (1962) is a set of unevenly critical essays, travel pieces and estimations of classical authors. *The Writing on the Wall* (1970) is a collection of her literary criticism. *Vietnam* (1967) and *Hanoi* (1968) are critical reviews of America's war and its implications. She brings an independent eye and a sharp pen to everything she tackles, but her fiction does not have the qualities she admires in her criticism. [EM]

Doris Grumbach, *The Company She Kept* (1967); Irvin Stock, *Mary McCarthy* (U. of Minnesota Pamphlet, 1968).

**McClure, Michael** (1932–    ). Poet. He was born in Kansas but has lived most of his life in San Francisco. He is one of the most original and vital poets in America, developing some extreme personal forms of typographical, spatial and ejaculatory effects which combine ideas from both Antonin Artaud and Charles ⋄ Olson (his and Robert ⋄ Creeley's 'projective verse') and form a profoundly intimate poetry of love and transcendental experience. His extensive poetry in book form includes: *Passage* (1956), *For Artaud* (1959), *Hymns to St Geryon* (1959), *Dark Brown* (1961), which contains some uniquely open love poems, and *A New Book / A Book of Torture* (1961). *Ghost Tantras* (1964) combine words and phonetic phrases and are intended to be read and growled aloud. *Thirteen Mad Sonnets* (1964) is a printed version of handwritten poems, and ● (1966) is a set of poems completed by designs of the artist and filmmaker Bruce Connor. *Meat Science Essays* (1963) presents the philosophy of McClure's emergence from his 'dark night' into possession of his flesh and spirit, and *Love Lion Book* (1966, issued as *Writing II*) is a rather more overtly philosophical version of earlier poetic ideas, while *Poisoned Wheat* (1965) is a poetic blast against the warfare state. Among his plays the best known are *The Blossom, or Billy the Kid* (1967) and *The Beard* (1967), an extended erotic scene between Jean Harlow and Billy the Kid. *Freewheelin Frank, Secretary of the Angels* (1967), 'as told to Michael McClure by Frank Reynolds', concerns the Hell's Angels motorcycle gang of San Francisco. His recent works include *Hail Thee Who Play* (1968), *The Sermons of Jean Harlow and the Curses of Billy Kid* (1968) and *Little Odes and the Raptors* (1969). [E M]

Marshall Clements, *A Catalogue of the Works of Michael McClure* (1965).

**McCullers, Carson** (1917–67). Novelist, short-story writer, playwright. The world of her fiction is filled with violence, perversion and injustice, and deformed by conflict, frustration, pain and grief. She was born in a small town in Georgia, and such a town provides the unromantic setting for most of her work: long summers of glaring heat, drab houses, cafés and small factories, the smells of poverty and decay, an overpowering impression of bleak ugliness. Most of the inhabitants live locked in physical or spiritual isolation, suffering grotesque physical or psychological disfigurement as freaks, oddities, the dispossessed and out-cast. Yet Carson McCullers does not create such a world to gain cheap, sensational effects; her central theme is love, its thwarting and failure, occasionally its grace. Without love, the human community disintegrates before the pressures of hatred and fear, social, racial and economic injustice, sexual violence and perversion.

*The Heart is a Lonely Hunter* (1940) explores the problems of isolation and communication as reflected in the central character, John Singer, a deaf-mute, whose loneliness focuses that of the four other main characters, who try to achieve some kind of communion with him. *Reflections in a Golden Eye* (1941) is more extravagantly scored by violence and perversion in a variety of forms within an army camp in the South, and its handling of characters owes too much to the psychologist's case-book. *Member of the Wedding* (1946) finely portrays the emotional anxieties and conflicts endured by an imaginative adolescent as she tries to come to terms with her maturing self. *The Ballad of the Sad Café* (1951) is a collection of stories which provides an excellent introduction to Carson McCullers' fictional world. *Clock without Hands* (1961), a novel more subdued in tone than most of her previous work, deals largely with the racial problems of Southern society, and states rather than dramatizes its solutions. Carson McCullers successfully dramatized *Member of the Wedding* in 1950; *The Square Root of Wonderful* (1958) is another play. [A H]

Ihab H. Hassan, 'Carson McCullers: The Alchemy of Love and Aesthetics of Pain', *Modern Fiction Studies*, v (Winter, 1959–60); Louise Y. Gossett, 'Dispossessed Love: Carson McCullers', in *Violence in Recent Southern Fiction* (1965); Oliver Evans, *Carson McCullers: Her Life and Work* (1965).

**Macdonald, Dwight** (1906–   ). Political writer. After graduating from Yale, he worked editorially on *Fortune* and *Partisan Review* (1944–9) and founded *Politics* (1944), an important journal of philosophical anarchism and pacifism, some of whose essays are contained with other political writings in *Memoirs of a Revolutionist* (1957). He has also written *Henry Wallace* (1948), *The Ford Foundation* (1956), *Against the American Grain* (1962), a collection of his essays including those on Mass Cult and Mid-Cult, Cozzens and Twain, and *The Ghost Conspiracy* (1965), a critique of the

Warren Commission report on the assassination of President Kennedy. He is one of the very few political and social thinkers since 1940 to have maintained independence of mind and a style uncorrupted by the editorial policies of the journals he has contributed to. [EM]

Hannah Arendt, 'He's All Dwight', *New York Review*, XI, 2 (1968).

**McGinley, Phyllis** (1905– ). Poet. Oregon-born, she lives in New York. One of a school of sophisticated light-verse commentators more common in the U.S.A. than elsewhere, she is, along with Ogden ◊ Nash, among the most successful and satisfying. Her witty, satirical and urbane poems comment on the American scene with a variety of tones and subjects, contrasting urban and country life, observing commuters, patterns of taxation, fashions and foibles. Her work, published in the *New Yorker*, the *Saturday Review*, etc., has been collected in numerous volumes, including *A Pocketful of Wry* (1940), *Husbands Are Difficult* (1941) and the delightful and successful *Love Letters of Phyllis McGinley* (1954). *Times Three: Selected Verse from Three Decades* (1960) is a collection which shows the range of her work. She has also written books for children and a book on saints, *Saint-Watching* (1969). [MB]

**McGrath, Thomas** (1918– ). Poet. Born in Dakota, he studied at three universities, served in the army in the Aleutians, and then worked and taught in a number of colleges. His power is revealed in long autobiographical poems such as *Letter from an Imaginary Friend* (1962), which evokes Dakota farm life of the twenties, the character of the I.W.W., and his youthful struggles during the Depression. He tends to be garrulous but it is out of exuberance and lack of interest in academic forms. His shorter poems, appearing since 1940, are represented in *New and Selected Poems* (1964). [EM]

**McGuffey, William Holmes** (1800–73). Teacher. Born in the Ohio wilderness, he graduated at Washington College with honours. His great linguistic gifts he used teaching at a number of universities; he became famous through his textbooks, which taught Americans how to read, a series opening in 1836 with his *First* and *Second Eclectic Readers* and continued in 1837, 1841 and 1857. These works, often written in collaboration with his brother, sold over 120 million copies, the most recent edition being in 1920. (One Wisconsin school board used the 1879 edition as late as 1961.) Harvey C. Minnick's *William Holmes McGuffey* (1936) shows how the *Readers* helped to release children from Calvinist Christian gloom and terror by creating a child's work of familiar toys, animals and friends. Richard V. D. Mosier's *Making the American Mind: Social and Moral Ideas in the McGuffey Readers* (1947) shows their moral and political purposes, strongly conservative within the Jefferson–Hamilton argument. [EM]

**McKeon, Richard.** ◊ Chicago Aristotelians.

**Maclean, Norman.** ◊ Chicago Aristotelians.

**MacLeish, Archibald** (1892– ). Poet, playwright. Born at Glencoe, Illinois. His long public career began after he had graduated from Yale, returned from the First World War, and received his degree from Harvard, where he later taught law. *Tower of Ivory* (1917) was the first of many books of poems, collated in *Collected Poems 1917–1952* which gained three national awards. In 1923 he was an expatriate among the Paris ◊ Lost Generation; later he was an editor of *Fortune*, Librarian of Congress (1939–44), and in the United States government from 1941 to 1945 (finally becoming assistant secretary of state); he represented America in the organization of UNESCO. Naturally, his poetry concerns the interrelation of social and political action and the poet's responsibility. In his essay 'The Irresponsibles' (1940) he attacked his American contemporaries for their disillusioned disengagement from large American interests. He has served the state himself, and so his *Poetry and Experience* (1961) describes his theory that poetry must serve and be involved in society as a form of knowledge the state needs. In 1949 he became Boylston Professor at Harvard, and his poetry has always had about it a certain academic topicality. His early work is dominated by symbolism, Pound and Eliot (e.g. 'The Hamlet of A. MacLeish', 1928), and his professional skill did not conceal a certain superficiality. His best poems were meditative lyrics like 'You, Andrew Marvell'. *Conquistador* (1932), the result of a desire to use an American subject, concerns Cortez's conquests in New Spain. MacLeish pioneered the verse radio play with a message in *The Fall of the City* (1937) and *Air Raid* (1938), and *The Trojan Horse* (1952) is an interesting if ambiguous comment on the Red scare. His most successful verse play is *J.B.* (1958), in which Job, God and Satan enact conflict under the Big Top, while *Herakles* (1967) dramatizes the conflict between reason, work and science, and love of human life, the non-political, and the eternal feminine. All his work is eclectic, immediate and apprehensive; he has consistently worked out his idea of a public poetry. But his articulation of liberal uneasiness and the need for clear action suffers from the absence of risk in both form and content. *A Continuing Journey* (1968) is a collection of his essays and addresses on the American scene since the Second World War, poetry and art, libraries and teaching, and those men he has elegiacally memorialized. His latest poems are in *The Wild Old Wicked Man* (1968). [EM]

H. H. Waggoner, *The Heel of Elohim: Science and Values in Modern American Poetry* (1950); Signi Falk, *Archibald MacLeish* (1965).

**McLuhan, Herbert Marshall** (1911–    ). Critic. Born in Alberta, Canada, he studied at Manitoba University, and gained his Ph.D. at Cambridge University with a thesis on Thomas Nashe. He has taught at various American and Canadian universities, and returned to his Centre for Culture and Technology, University of Toronto, in 1969. He became a Catholic in 1937 and has taught only at Catholic institutions. His excellent literary criticism is collected in *The Literary Criticism of Marshall McLuhan, 1943–1962* (ed. E. McNamara, 1969), and with Richard J. Schoeck he has edited *Voices of Literature* (1964), a high school anthology. His popular reputation lies with a series of books (which overlap repetitiously, in spite of their concern with experimental format) concerning the media of communication. *The Mechanical Bride* (1951) is a warning analysis of advertising. *The Gutenberg Galaxy* (1962) is a brilliant study of the cultural effects due to the changes from script to print and to electronic circuitry. *Understanding Media* (1964), which first gained him an international fame, covers a wide range of communication and environmental matters, and is influential particularly for a controversial analysis

of the written and printed word in a society dominated by film and television. McLuhan uses a wide range of information from experts in various fields in order to state, aphoristically and trenchantly, a stream of ideas about technology and communications media, irrespective of overt content. His influence on business procedure and environmental studies is reflected in his *Dew-Line Newsletter*, designed largely for capitalist organizations. His work continues that of his predecessor, H. A. Innis, whose *The Bias of Communication* (1951) he introduced in an edition of 1964. In 1953, he founded, with Edmund S. Carpenter, the anthropologist, *Explorations*; some of the journal's essays, by various contributors, appear in *Explorations in Communication* (1960), and number 8 is reissued as *Verbi-Voco-Visual Explorations* (1967) – the title is from Joyce's *Finnegans Wake*, a major source for McLuhan. *The Medium is the Massage* (1967, with Quentin Fiore) is a collage of visual and typographical materials on environmental themes. *War and Peace in the Global Village* (1968, with Quentin Fiore) backs a programme for the elimination of current social and political disasters with apposite quotations from *Finnegans Wake*. *Through the Vanishing Point* (1968, with Harley Parker), one of his best works, is an analysis of space in poetry and painting. *Counter Blast* (1969, with Harley Parker), whose title acknowledges a typographical forerunner in Wyndham Lewis's *Blast* (1914), is another restatement of familiar materials. [EM]

Eric Mottram, etc., 'The World and Marshall McLuhan', *The Journal of Canadian Studies*, vol. 1, No. 2 (1966); ed. Gerald E. Stearn, *McLuhan Hot and Cool: A Critical Symposium* (1967); Sidney Finkelstein, *Sense and Nonsense of McLuhan* (1968); Richard Kostelanetz, *Master Minds* (1969).

**Mailer, Norman** (1923–    ). Novelist, short-story writer, poet, essayist, playwright. He was born in New Jersey, grew up in Brooklyn, graduated from Harvard in 1943, and served with the 112th Cavalry (San Antonio, Texas) in the Pacific campaign of the Second World War, as clerk and rifleman. The recurring image in his writings is a man on patrol against an enemy, moving warily and with as much intelligent appreciation of the terrain, whether jungle or city, as he can muster. His war experience went primarily into his first novel, *The Naked and the Dead* (1948), a best-seller which also launched his critical reputation. Within the basic scheme of an operation on a Pacific island, Mailer provides a critical analysis of American society, through inset biographical sketches of main characters, in the manner of ◊ Dos Passos's *U.S.A.*, and an examination of authoritarian character and its place in recent Western history, through the character of General Cummings. The literary and social fame generated by this book rather dogged Mailer in the years that followed. His next two novels were radically misread and mistreated by the public and the critics, who wanted a repetition of his war novel and not risky explorations of a cancerous and plague-ridden society. Also his kind of public confessional openness and his sense of needing to be 'the champ' of his profession has not endeared him.

His first story appeared in 1941, and he wrote an early unpublished novel, *A Transit to Narcissus*, while awaiting draft into the army. His early work is contained in *Advertisements for Myself* (1959), in which short stories, essays and parts of novels are linked with an autobiographical commentary, designed as a therapeutical self-estimate and in fact a brilliant study of a talented writer growing up in the post-war scene. It includes 'The Man Who Studied Yoga', one of his finest stories, 'The Time of Her Time', an important section of what was then 'a novel in progress', and a key essay, 'The White Negro', a study of the hipster-outsider figure who represents significant aspects of the fifties and sixties and who is the heroic centre of Mailer's fiction and philosophy: the man who acts existentially, manufacturing his values in a world whose standards he largely rejects. *Barbary Shore* (1951), his second novel, is a Kafkaesque political allegory, elaborately written as a rehearsal of the struggle between socialism and the agents of capitalism. It is also a preparation for *The Deer Park* (1955), which dramatizes some of his existential ideas through the story of a film director in the thirties under pressure from the House Un-American Activities Committee, an air-force veteran trying to achieve some kind of life in post-war America, and Marion Faye, Mailer's most important single character, a philosophical pimp with Faustian ambitions. The scene is Hollywood and the Californian desert, whose failure of nourishment reflects a national sickness. *An Ameri-*

*can Dream* (1965) presents the diseased society in an advanced state in the form of a continuing battle between evil, both the supernatural and the Mafia, and those who at least partly understand the nature of spiritual and social decadence. *Why Are We in Vietnam?* (1967) takes the supernatural, Reichian psychological and existential themes a stage further: a hallucinated Texas disc-jockey pours out a complex story of a bear-hunt in Alaska, on which he accompanies his father and his friend. The nature of hunting, killing, exposure to the nature of the earth, and his future embarkation for Vietnam service are projected through a dazzling pyrotechnic prose. Parallel with these two novels, Mailer has written two volumes of essays, *The Presidential Papers* (1963), which includes a vision of President Kennedy as existential president-hero of America and a famous account of the Democratic Convention of 1960, 'Superman Comes to the Supermarket', and *Cannibals and Christians* (1966), which includes with political and literary essays his short science fiction, 'The Last Night'. *The Idol and the Octopus* (1968) collects his writings on the Kennedy and Johnson administrations. *The Deer Park* was successful as a play in New York in 1967, and his poems appear in *Deaths for the Ladies and Other Disasters* (1962). He has always been a politically committed writer and it is this moral energy that makes *The Armies of the Night* (1968) one of his finest books, an account of the march on Pentagon by various protest groups in which he took part with Robert ◊ Lowell, Dwight ◊ Macdonald and others in 1967. But *Miami and the Siege of Chicago* (1968) is often a strained piece of reporting, only intermittently penetrating. He has recently made his first films, *Wild 90* (1968) and *Beyond the Law* (1968). His work is as unevenly brilliant as one might expect from a writer who explores the possibilities of prose and form and is committed to an honesty made difficult by his knowledge of psychology and theology, politics and the history of the novel. His intelligence is intensely individual in its seriousness and completely characteristic of mid-century America. [EM]

*The Short Fiction* (1969).

Richard Foster, *Norman Mailer* (U. of Minnesota Pamphlet, 1968); D. L. Kaufman, *Norman Mailer: The Countdown* (1969); B. H. Leeds, *The Unstructured Vision of Norman Mailer* (1969).

**Malamud, Bernard** (1914–    ). Novelist, short-story writer. Born in Brooklyn; educated at City College, New York, and Columbia. He has been teaching in universities since 1939.

*The Natural* (1952), a remarkable first novel, tells of the brief glory and final ruin of Roy Hobbs, a baseball hero, through a mocking yet sympathetic exploration of the myth of American baseball and the legend of the Grail. In his novel *The Assistant* (1957), Malamud takes up the specifically Jewish themes with which he is most closely associated. Morris Bober, a 'good Jew', a man incapable of dishonesty or malice but imprisoned in a desperately poor grocery store, takes on Frank Alpine, turned from hold-up man to remorseful assistant. When Morris dies, Frank succeeds him and becomes a Jew, accepting the exacting Jewish heritage of imprisonment and righteousness. Malamud's theme is redemption in a squalid world illuminated by extraordinary bursts of love. *A New Life* (1961) is a novel about a New Yorker who goes to teach at a land-grant college in the Pacific North-west looking for self-renewal. Malamud fails to avoid the two main clichés of the American academic novel: the lone liberal faculty crusader against a reactionary administration; and sexual adventures with students and faculty wives. *The Fixer* (1966), a novel, takes the theme of Jewish suffering back to the Tsarist Russia of pre-1914. It presents the ordeal of Yakov Bok, a poor Jewish handyman, falsely accused of the ritual murder of a Christian child. In spite of some moving passages, Malamud's handling of the material shows a certain woodenness and lack of warmth.

In the two short-story collections, *The Magic Barrel* (1958) and *Idiots First* (1963), the finest stories belong to the world of *The Assistant* or take the form of brilliant Jewish parables like 'The Magic Barrel' and 'The Jewbird'. The poorer ones are tales of academic life or Americans in Italy. *The Fixer* (1966) fictionalizes the notorious case of Mendel Beiliss, a Jewish Russian worker in Kiev, accused in an anti-semitic murder case in 1911. Malamud's theme here is the tribal solidarity of Jews and the individual Jew's solitariness. 'My short stories,' Malamud has said, 'acknowledge indebtedness specifically to Chekhov, James Joyce, Hemingway, Sherwood Anderson, and a touch perhaps of Sholem Aleichem and the films of Charlie Chaplin.' *Pictures of Fidelman* (1969), short stories, continues the theme of the American–Jewish artist in Italy.

Malamud's range is wide, his moral sensibility extraordinarily fine, and his humour complex and subtle. Although he can evoke actual places and atmospheres with unequalled force, his special talent is for the fable and the symbolic tale. With Saul ◊ Bellow, he is the most impressive figure among American urban Jewish writers. [B W]

*A Malamud Reader*, intr. Philip Rahv (1967).
Jonathan Baumbach, 'The Economy of Love: the Novels of Bernard Malamud', *Kenyon Review*, Summer, 1963; Leslie Fiedler, 'Malamud: The Commonplace as Absurd', in *No! in Thunder* (1960); Marcus Klein, *After Alienation: American Novels in Mid-Century* (1962).

**Maltz, Albert** (1908–    ). Dramatist, fiction writer. Born in Brooklyn, N.Y. He was a member of George Pierce ◊ Baker's Yale workshop and wrote, with his fellow student George Sklar, *Merry-Go-Round* (1932), a celebrated play of New York City corruption, and the pacifist *Peace on Earth* (1933). His most powerful work is *Black Pit* (1935), a Marxist tragedy in which a miner, forced to spy and betray, is ostracized by his fellow workers. In *Private Hicks* (1936), the National Guard hero refuses to act as strike-breaker. Maltz's stories and novels have similar attitudes. Although two of his scripts became official Marine Corps and Navy films, he was thrown out of work by the Hollywood anti-Left bullying in the 1950s. [E M]

**Marcuse, Herbert** (1898–    ). Philosopher. Born in Berlin, he studied under Heidegger at Freiburg and wrote a doctoral thesis on Hegel. With the Nazis dominating Germany, in 1933 he left to teach in Geneva. From 1933 to 1934 he worked with the Institute of Social Research, which had emigrated from Frankfurt University to Columbia University, New York (its founders were T. W. Adorno and Max Horkheimer). Its journal, *Zeitschrift für Sozialforschung*, printed Marcuse's papers on Marx and Hegel. *Reason and Revolution: Hegel and the Rise of Social Theory* (1941; 2nd edn, with additional material 1954) concerns the bases of social freedom; Marcuse tries to exonerate Hegel from intellectual involvement in the pre-history of Nazism. In 1950, after a period with the government's Office of Intelligence Research, he returned to Columbia. The result of Russian studies both there and at Harvard became *Soviet Marxism* (1958). Marcuse has since taught at Brandeis and California universities and increasingly become a focus for the New Left in both America and Europe. *Eros and Civilization* (1955) attempts to make Freud usable for socialist sociology. *One Dimensional Man* (1964) concerns the dehumanizing effects of capitalist technology, and the essay entitled 'Repressive Tolerance', in *A Critique of Pure Tolerance* (1967, with R. P. Wolff and Barrington Moore), proposes 'the withdrawal of toleration in speech and assembly from groups and movements which promote aggressive policies, armament, chauvinism, racial and religious discrimination, or which oppose the extension of public services'. *Negations* (1968), which reprints essays from the thirties, shows the unresolved conflicts between philosophical universals and historical particulars in Marcuse's programme from the beginning. *An Essay on Liberation* (1969) tones down his radical despair with optimism based on the necessary operation of dialectical theory in the shape of the 'diffused rebellion among the youth and the intelligentsia'. Marcuse places his faith in a 'union of liberating art and liberating technology' but he is caught in a 19th-century web of Marxist and Freudian dogma and a 20th-century mystique of Youth and the New. [EM]

**Marquand, J(ohn) P(hillips)** (1893–1960). Novelist. Though born in Wilmington, Delaware, he spent his boyhood in Newburyport, Massachusetts, and after graduating from Harvard in 1915 served on the staff of the *Boston Transcript*. There he began writing popular romances – *The Unspeakable Gentleman* (1922), *The Black Cargo* (1925), *Warning Hill* (1930), *Ming Yellow* (1934) – and first won prominence with Mr Moto, the Japanese detective, in the *Saturday Evening Post*. It was not until 1937, with the publication of *The Late George Apley*, which won him the Pulitzer Prize, that his serious reputation was established for ironic comedies of New England and New York upper-class manners, There followed *Wickford Point* (1939), *H. M. Pulham Esq.* (1941), *So Little Time* (1943), *B.F.'s Daughter* (1946), *Point of No Return* (1949), *Melville Goodwin, U.S.A.* (1951), *Sincerely Willis Wayde* (1955), *Stopover:*

*Tokyo* (1957), *Life at Happy Knoll* (1957), and *Women and Thomas Harrow* (1958). *Lord Timothy Dexter* (1925) is the life of an 18th-century New England eccentric. *Thirty Years* (1954) contains his collected stories and articles.

Marquand's world, set among Boston Brahmins, New Englanders and the white-collar New York suburbanites, is similar to that of Galsworthy's *Forsyte Saga*; but whereas Galsworthy's Forsytes still lived with an effortless, unquestioning confidence in their inherited values, the inner drive of Marquand's heroes, recorded by him with wry realism, is at constant odds with the outer conformity and inherited manners of their caste. He ranged increasingly among the professional classes with stories of a failed doctor, a domineering industrialist's daughter, a middle-aged banker, an army officer, a businessman: all are frustrated; all are failures, at least to themselves; for the impulse of their private lives and of their careers separated long ago, leaving them shipwrecked in middle age, divided against themselves. Out of these conflicts of the inner man withdrawn from the outer code of his career, his class or his society, Marquand has created the satirical comedy of his best novels. [HB]

Philip Hamburger, *J. P. Marquand*, *Esquire* (1952); John J. Gross, *John P. Marquand* (1963); C. Hugh Holman, *John P. Marquand* (University of Minnesota Pamphlet, 1965).

**Marquis, Don** (1878–1937). Humorist, novelist, playwright. Born at Walnut, Illinois. As a columnist on various newspapers, particularly on the New York *Sun* and the New York *Tribune*, he produced vast amounts of short humorous commentary, much of it ephemeral; but several of the comic characters he invented are still remembered and still relevant. He satirized the pretensions of ◊ Greenwich Village 'advanced thought' through a little group of would-be advanced gossips, collected as *Hermione and Her Little Group of Serious Thinkers* (1916). His 'Old Soak', an inebriated social commentator and a one-man challenge to Prohibition, was commemorated in several books and a successful play, *The Old Soak* (1922). He wrote several novels, comic and serious, including *The Cruise of the Jasper B* (1916) and the semi-autobiographical *Sons of the Puritans* (1939). His plays include a serious drama on the life of Christ, *The Dark Hours* (1924).

But his best-known work is the whole sequence of books beginning with *archy and mehitabel* (1927), and consisting of the comic verse and prose of a cockroach, archy, who had a former existence as a *vers libre* bard. archy types with his head, to produce typographical oddities. The whole series has a virtuosity of style and a comic vigour that gives it a special value in his work. 'i see things from the under side now,' says archy, commenting on various social matters and on his relations with mehitabel, the alley cat, a reincarnation of Cleopatra ('toujours gai is ever her word'). Marquis interestingly demonstrates the way in which the newspaper columnist made a valuable contribution to the American comic and vernacular tradition. [MB]

Edward Anthony, *O Rare Don Marquis: A Biography* (1962).

**Masters, Edgar Lee** (1868–1950). Poet. Raised in rural Illinois, Masters practised as a Chicago lawyer before retiring to New York. From 1898 onwards he published over 50 volumes of poetry, fiction and biography. However, he found no individual voice until *Spoon River Anthology* (1915), a collection of casual free-verse epitaphs, spoken by the dead from their cemetery in a mid-Western town. Their stories interact to form a fragmentary history of a decaying community, which has forsaken the ideals of its founders and fallen prey to acquisitiveness and hypocrisy. In Spoon River, men of integrity are derided or persecuted by the complacent and the corrupt, thwarted lovers driven to drink or suicide, and the decent and industrious rewarded only with poverty or misfortune. The few tales of fulfilment are significantly less memorable than those of defeat and oppression. Conspicuous above all is man's egocentricity, the cause of life-long tragic misunderstandings. The virtues of the anthology rest in its concentration upon essentials and in the ironic humour that variegates this flat record of human failure.

Masters never repeated this success. His later verbose works include *The Domesday Book* (1920), *The New Spoon River* (1924), a Jeremiad against urbanization, and *The New World* (1937), a populist agrarian's outline for an epic of America. Among the several biographies he wrote is the hostile *Lincoln, the Man* (1931). Masters' poetic achievement is slight, but he is important because in *Spoon River Anthology* he dealt a death-blow to the more obtuse forms of sentimental regionalism and clarified some of the reasons for the disintegration of small communities and the collapse of traditional American values. *Spoon River Anthology* was made into a theatre entertainment in 1963. [RWB]

Bernard Duffey, *The Chicago Renaissance in American Letters* (1954); M. Yatron, *America's Literary Revolt* (1959).

**Mather, Cotton** (1663–1728). Minister, historian, scholar. He was born into the New England ministry, his father Increase ◊ Mather and his grandfathers Richard Mather and John ◊ Cotton being clergymen and central figures in New England affairs. He entered Harvard at 12, and at 22 became assistant to his father at the North Church in Boston, where he served until his death. His interests were multifarious; he was a man of monumental learning on a vast range of subjects, possessing a personal library that rivalled that of William ◊ Byrd of Westover for size. Though somewhat conservative in his religion at a time when an increasingly liberal tone was creeping into Puritan theology, and a believer in witchcraft at a time of scientific progress (his *The Wonders of the Invisible World*, 1693, analyses – yet with scientific detachment – the work of devils among the Salem witches), he was on some issues, such as his advocacy of inoculation for smallpox, well in advance of his age. Indeed his conservatism has been much exaggerated at the expense of his scientific curiosity. He was elected to the Royal Society in 1713, and was in close communication with men of learning throughout Europe.

He was a prolific writer; and though no collected edition of his work has been assembled some 450 items are traced to him. They include sermons, verse, history, comments on economic, educational and political matters, scientific commentary, folklore, etc. He often forsook Puritan 'plain style' for elegant writing, influenced – as in his *Political Fables* – by Jacobean elaboration and Restoration elegance. His most famous work, the *Magnalia Christi Americana* (1702), a learned and vastly documented history of New England, showed how God was at work in the new land. Mather considered it important enough to send it to London for publication, and its elegance and fineness make it clear it was to speak for New England to the world. The body and range of his work are a remarkable testament to New England learning and energy as well as to piety. [MB]

*Selections*, ed. Kenneth B. Murdock (1926; 1960); *On Witchcraft* (1956).

Perry Miller, *The New England Mind: From Colony to Province* (1953); Barrett Wendell, *Cotton Mather: The Puritan Priest* (1891; 1926); R. P. and L. Boas, *Cotton Mather* (1928).

**Mather, Increase** (1639–1723). Writer on theology, history and politics. He was the youngest son of Richard Mather (1596–1669), the first generation New England minister and one of the authors of the ◊ *Bay Psalm Book*. His son, continuing this important dynasty, was Cotton ◊ Mather, a powerfully influential figure of the next generation of Puritan divines. Increase was educated at Harvard, of which he later became president, and Trinity College Dublin, and later married John ◊ Cotton's daughter in Massachusetts. He became minister at North Church, Boston, the most influential centre of Puritan theocracy of which he was a leading theorist and preacher. In 1692, he gained the new charter for Massachusetts from England, an act which ironically weakened theocratic power by basing suffrage on property-ownership. During the witchcraft fears of the 1690s in Salem and elsewhere he warned the early Americans that the Devil was taking over New England, but he did not fully support the trials and some secularization seems to have alleviated his mind before his death. His large output (at least 102 works is known to be by him) includes *The Life and Death of . . . Richard Mather* (1670), *An Arrow against Profane and Promiscuous Dancing* (1684), histories of New England, *Cases of Conscience Concerning Evil Spirits Personating Men* (1693) and *An Essay for the Recording of Illustrious Providences* (1684), a strange amalgam of superstitious natural history and supernatural special pleading, but a valuable record of the 17th-century state of mind. [EM]

Kenneth B. Murdock, *Increase Mather: The Foremost American Puritan* (1925).

**Mathew, Harry** (1930–    ). Novelist, poet. He was born in New York and lives in Paris. He edited *Locus Solus* magazine with ◊ Ashbery, ◊ Koch and ◊ Schuyler, his poems appear in *avant garde* journals, and he has written two brilliant imaginative novels: *The Conversions* (1962), a highly

complex quest in the form of answers to a game, satires on contemporary opinions, and invented cults; and *Tlooth* (1966), again modelled somewhat on the puzzle structures of Raymond Roussel's fiction, but less surrealist, more consciously directed, and certainly as startling and gripping as any bizarre detective story ever written. [EM]

**Matthews, Brander** (1852–1929). Literary historian, critic. Born in New Orleans. He is significant here for his early contribution – along with the work of E. P. ◊ Whipple, Moses Coit ◊ Tyler, W. C. ◊ Brownell, etc. – to the study of American literature. His *An Introduction to the Study of American Literature* (1896), though brief, opens up the 19th century as a subject for study. Professor of Literature and Dramatic Literature at Columbia between 1892 and 1924, he also wrote several important books on drama, with a practical and theatrical emphasis – they include *The Development of the Drama* (1903), *Molière* (1910), *Shakespeare as a Playwright* (1913) and *The Principles of Playmaking* (1919). He also wrote three plays in collaboration, and some fiction – the novel *A Confident Tomorrow* (1899), etc. [MB]

**Matthiessen, F(rancis) O(tto)** (1902–50). Critic, scholar. Born in California, educated at Yale and Harvard, he taught at Yale for two years and at Harvard for most of his life, becoming famous for his tutorial work in literature. In 1947 he taught at the Salzburg Seminar and Charles University, Prague, an experience recorded impressively in *From the Heart of Europe* (1948). In 1949–50 he worked on his *Oxford Book of American Verse* (1950) and on *Theodore Dreiser* (1951), left unrevised at his death. He committed suicide, 'terribly oppressed by the present times', a profound and symbolic shock to his friends and colleagues. His life's work was 'to search for a usable tradition in American literature' (Malcolm Cowley), and his teaching always emphasized the social context of literature. His major work is *American Renaissance* (1941), subtitled 'Art and Expression in the Age of Emerson and Whitman' and consisting of a detailed examination of those two authors, together with Thoreau, Hawthorne and Melville, in relationship to the 17th-century English and American cultural inheritance, in order to establish the nature of the first great blossoming of a distinctively American literature. Matthiessen shows how the reformist spirit of the 1840s precedes and informs the masterpieces of the 1850s, and his basis is Pound's statement that 'the history of an art is the history of masterwork, not of failures or mediocrity'. *Sarah Orne Jewett* (1929) is a biographical and sociological study of the American writer, and after *Translation: An Elizabethan Art* (1931), he wrote *The Achievement of T. S. Eliot* (1935, revised 1947), a relatively aesthetic literary study placing the poet in the American tradition of Puritanism and Dante studies at Harvard, as well as the European line; *Henry James: The Major Phase* (1944), one of whose important and pioneering sources was James's then unpublished notebooks; and a fascinating study, *The James Family* (1947), based on the lives and works of Henry James, his father, and his brother William, the philosopher. *F. O. Matthiessen, 1902–1950: A Collective Portrait* (ed. P. M. Sweezy and L. Huberman, 1950) reprints the special edition of the *Monthly Review* (October 1950) devoted to recollections of his friends and colleagues. It is said that May ◊ Sarton's novel, *Faithful Are the Wounds* (1955), is partly a version of his last years. [EM]

Stanley Edgar Hyman, *The Armed Vision: A Study in the Methods of Modern Literary Criticism* (1948).

**Mead, Margaret** (1901–   ). Psychologist, anthropologist. Born in Philadelphia, she was a pupil of Franz Boas in 1923, and in 1925 studied adolescent girls in Samoa, before taking her Columbia doctorate. *Coming of Age in Samoa* (1928) was both good anthropology and a best-seller, beginning the pattern of her later books, *Growing Up in New Guinea* (1930), *Sex and Temperament in Three Primitive Societies* (1935) and books on Polynesian and Indian societies. Her most popular success was *Male and Female* (1949), an application of anthropological discoveries to the contemporary urban West. All her work has ultimately been devoted to developing 'a war-less world' through re-education for racial understanding, whether through her *Redbook* column or *New Lives for Old* (1956). [EM]

**Meltzer, David** (1937–   ). Poet. He was born in New York but left for Los Angeles at 14 and has since been associated with poetry in the 'San Francisco renaissance' of the fifties. He took part in the efforts to read poetry to jazz, and was represented in Donald Allen's *The New American Poetry* (1960). His poems appeared in *Ragas* (1959), which uses oriental instances and references and is largely unified by intensely personal moods, *The Process* (1965), *We All Have Something to Say to Each Other: Being an Essay Entitled Patchen and Four Poems* (1962), which includes one of the very few good accounts of Kenneth ◊ Patchen's poetry, and *The Dark Continent* (1967), a less overtly experimental collection but substantial in its extension of subjects. *Yesod* (1969) and *Round the Poem Box* (1969) are his recent poetry. *Journal of a Birth* (1967) is a prose work which originally appeared in 1961. His novels include a trilogy of sexual madness and erotic organizations, *The Agency, The Agent,* and *How Many Blocks in the Pile?* (1968), the four books of *Brain-Plant* (1969), which concerns totalitarian eroticism, and two single novels, *Orb* and *The Martyrs* (1969). [EM]

David Kherdian, *David Meltzer: A Sketch and a Checklist* (1965), and *Six Poets of the San Francisco Renaissance* (1967).

**Melville, Herman** (1819–91). Novelist, poet, short-story writer. One of America's greatest writers, complex, original and profound. He was born in New York City, of Boston Calvinist and New York Dutch ancestry, into an atmosphere of security and comfort, well educated and socially happy. In 1830 his father went bankrupt and became the poor failure the American success ethic insists on for the financially fallen. He died insane from overwork and worn-out nerves. Melville worked as bank clerk, salesman, farm-hand and schoolteacher in New York and Massachusetts, tried an engineering and surveying course, began writing, but in 1839 signed on as cabin boy, a deeply shocking experience of menial squalor and crude vice, both at sea and in Liverpool, which he used in *Redburn* (1849). On his return he taught, travelled to Illinois and the Great Lakes and down the Mississippi to Cairo, and in 1841 sailed as seaman on the whaler *Acushnet* into the Pacific. After eighteen months he deserted in the Marquesas Islands and escaped from there in an Australian whaler whose crew mutinied: he was imprisoned in Tahiti for his share. From there he sailed for Hawaii, where he worked in a pin-bowling alley and in a store, and returned to Boston in 1844. Backed by extensive reading and research, these events were the shaping experience of his life and served as bases for the series of books beginning with *Typee* in 1846. In 1850 he lived with his wife in Pittsfield, Massachusetts, near Hawthorne. Deeply disturbed by the stupid reception of his complex political and religious allegory *Mardi* (1849), he turned to the sea stories with which he could attract the reading public (*White Jacket*, 1850, and *Redburn*), but *Moby-Dick* (1851) combines sea story and allegory into the central masterpiece of American literature, written partly under the inspiration of the parallel achievement by Hawthorne, whom he met in 1850 and on whom he wrote an important essay, 'Hawthorne and His Mosses' (1850).

But *Moby-Dick* was 'broiled in hell fire' and too difficult for critics and public in a sentimental time, nor could they read *Pierre* (1852), rebarbative in its psychological complexity and elaborate prose. Melville, dubbed mad and obscene, was not supported by his family and friends, and his sense of vocation cut him off from the readership he needed. In 1853–4 he wrote magazine stories. *Israel Potter* (1855) is an amusing historical and satirical burlesque, and *Piazza Tales* (1856) and *The Confidence Man* (1857) are superb works of his maturity. He failed to gain a possible consulship, and his family had increased, but in 1856 his father-in-law paid for a tour for his health in Europe and the Near East (*Clarel*, 1876, and *Journal of a Visit to Europe and the Levant, October 11, 1856 – May 6, 1857*). The poetry he wrote in his later New York years is collected in *Battle Pieces* (1866), *John Marr and Other Sailors* (1888) and *Timoleon* (1891), the last book published in his lifetime. In 1866 he was appointed deputy customs inspector in New York, a job that left him little time for writing until in the 1870s he worked on *Clarel*. He resigned in 1885, his literary reputation nearly vanished, his writing restricted to poems; he left *Billy Budd, Sailor: An Inside Story* in manuscript at his death.

Apparently diverse, Melville's career has a splendid singleness of complex design. *Typee* tells of entry into and escape from a Pacific island community whose customs deeply disturb the American bourgeois hero. *Omoo* (1847) is a sequel less interesting but containing important material on the Pacific islands. The next four novels constitute a huge exploration of the historical and

psychological origins and development of self, society and the desire to create and destroy gods and heroes. *Mardi* is a detailed allegory of religion, government and philosophic principles. In *Moby-Dick* the religion and commercial acumen of the New England whaling industry and its captains is a metaphor of the hunt for absolute truth, heroic leadership and Faustian self-discovery. Ahab and Ishmael, captain and seaman, represent the opposites of doomed hubris and pacific survival on the *Pequod*, itself the symbol of American, and therefore universal, society. *Pierre* explores Oedipal relationships, the isolation of a man seeking integrity, and the American country–city hostility, and *The Confidence Man, His Masquerade* is a brilliant narrative of passengers on a Mississippi river-boat as the image of the inherent moral destructiveness of the Protestant ethic, demonstrated with complete scepticism. *Redburn, White Jacket* and *Billy Budd* (1924; ed. H. Hayford and M. M. Sealts, 1962) show the world of the ship as the power structure into which a young man is initiated for survival against social and sexual oppression; Billy Budd transcends the enacted ideas of both Paine and Burke to become a man-made god. The finest of Melville's short stories explore his themes of the isolated self, the failure of conventional worldly knowledge and the 'power of blackness' penetrating love ('Bartleby', 'Benito Cereno', 'The Paradise of Bachelors and the Tartarus of Maids', and 'The Encantadas'). In the 18,000 lines of octosyllabic couplets of *Clarel*, an American theological student explores Palestine in hopes of finding secure faith, and makes a final ambivalent plunge away from theology and introspection and towards the common people.

Melville's great career is capped by his highly original poems, small-scale forms for his large themes. He died virtually unnoticed. His genius, recognized and evaluated only since the 1930s, is part of the first great period of American literature, the flowering which includes Poe, Emerson, Hawthorne, Whitman and Thoreau. [EM]

*The Complete Works* (Hendricks House edition, in progress); *Writings* (Northwestern Newbery edition, 1967 ff.) (*Typee, Omoo* published).
Merlin Bowen, *The Long Encounter: Self and Experience in the Writings of Herman Melville* (1960); Leon Howard, *Herman Melville: A Biography* (1951); Howard P. Vincent, *The Trying-Out of Moby-Dick* (1949); W. Berthoff, *The Example of Melville* (1962); H. Bruce Franklin, *The Wake of the Gods* (1963).

**Mencken, H(enry) L(ouis)** (1880–1956). Editor, journalist, literary critic. Born in Baltimore, his home all his life, Mencken had little more than a high-school formal education, and while still in his late teens he plunged into newspaper work. He was reporter, editorial writer, columnist and editor for the Baltimore *Sunpapers* from 1906 till his death. He became literary editor of the *Smart Set* in 1908 and six years later co-editor with George Jean ◊ Nathan. In 1924 he and Nathan founded the *American Mercury*. Nathan left the following year, and thereafter Mencken edited the magazine till the end of 1933. Meanwhile he had been collecting his essays into volumes, chiefly into a series of six *Prejudices* (1919, 1920, 1922, 1924, 1926, 1927). In 1919 he published the *American Language*, a brisk journalistic survey of the differences between English English and American English, and also an attempt to present the richness of American English. The book went into three editions and was expanded into two *Supplements* (1945, 1948). The general reading public was overwhelmed by its scholarship, though professional linguists saw in it little more than a lively rewriting of their researches. Mencken's *Book of Prefaces* (1917), a selection of critical essays, was far more impressive.

As an editor Mencken was enormously industrious and daring, and he had a good eye for writers with original ideas, especially in the realms of sociology, history and biography, though for a while he also was hospitable to novelists and short-story writers beginning their careers. He did a great deal to wake America up to the values in the novels of Theodore Dreiser, Sinclair Lewis and Sherwood Anderson. He was surprisingly blind to the works of Ernest Hemingway, Thomas Wolfe and William Faulkner. As a critic of poetry he was almost totally ignorant and inept.

The depression of 1929 robbed him of his vast audience among college students and their younger professors, and he went into a decline. For a long time, while the breadlines were multiplying, he denied the reality of the Depression, calling it 'newspaper talk'. His books on politics (*Notes on Democracy*, 1926), religion (*A Treatise on the Gods*, 1930) and morals (*A Treatise on Right and Wrong*, 1934) are of little value. They reveal Mencken as more a night-school scandalizer than a genuine and original scholar. He gradually returned to public attention with the publi-

cation of his 3 volumes of a ⬦ *Happy Days* (1940), *Newspaper* and *Heathen Days* (1943). The make pleasant reading, but since t. many 'stretchers' in them they ca. be taken too seriously as autobiography or history. Mencken also wrote much on music in the *American Mercury* and the *Baltimore Sun*, but he was never more than an amateur musicologist.

Above all else, he was a superb editor. His editing of the *American Mercury* during its first five years, 1924–8, was historic in its influence. The other quality periodicals were never the same afterwards. He was also a superb newspaper man. His sheer good reporting, yet to be properly sifted and collected, was of a high order. Thus his influence as a journalist was great, and this influence will probably keep his memory alive longer than his more ambitious writings. Perhaps the best all-round selective anthology of his writings was made by himself in *A Mencken Crestomathy* (1949). [CA]

Charles Angoff, *H. L. Mencken: A Portrait from Memory* (1956); Ernest Boyd, *H. L. Mencken* (1925); Edgar Kemler, *The Irreverent Mr Mencken* (1950); ed. M. Moos, *A Carnival of Buncombe* (1957); Carl Bode, *Mencken* (1969).

**Meredith, William** (1919– ). Poet. Born in New York City, he was educated at Princeton and has taught at various American universities. His books, which have won various literary awards, include *Love Letter from an Impossible Land* (1944), *Ships and Other Figures* (1948), *The Open Sea* (1958), *The Wreck of the Thresher* (1964) and translations from Apollinaire (1964). His naval experience in the Second World War and the Korean war provides an important theme – 'the sea schools us with terrible water'. But his most typical poems celebrate nature and domestic life, about which he writes with decorum, directness and wit. [BP]

**Merrill, James** (1926– ). Poet, novelist, playwright. Born in New York, he studied at Amherst College, has travelled widely, particularly in Greece and Italy, and taught in American universities. Several volumes of his poems – including *The Black Swan and Other Poems* (1946), *The Country of a Thousand Years of Peace and Other Poems* (1958), *Water Street* (1962) and *Nights and Days* (1966) – have appeared; *Selected Poems* came out in 1961. Merrill has pubushed a novel, *The Seraglio* (1957), and written a play, *The Immortal Husband* (1955). He is an elegant, intellectual and sometimes very elliptical writer, drawing on classical knowledge and cultural contrasts between other civilizations and his own. He can be witty and elegant and also excitably and exactingly involved in his matter; he has a considerable range of voice and artistic resource, not confined to poetry. [MB]

Richard Howard, *Alone with America* (1969).

**Merrill, Stuart** (1863–1915). Poet. Born in Hempstead, New York, and educated in France, his father being an American lawyer there. In this way he became a long-term expatriate, and is perhaps most properly located as one of the French symbolist movement. Nearly all his writing was produced in French and came out of the Parisian Bohemian literary context (◊ Bohemianism). He published two collections of good symbolist verse, *Les gammes* (1887) and *Les fastes* (1891), and a socialist poem about the oppressed, *Une voix dans la foule* (1909). His one work in English is a collection of translations from the prose-poems of French symbolists (Huysmans, Baudelaire, Mallarmé, etc.) called *Pastels in Prose* (1890), which appeared with an introduction by W. D. ◊ Howells. [MB]

Edmund Wilson, *Axel's Castle* (1931).

**Merton, Thomas** (1915–69). Poet, religious writer. Born in France of an English father and an American mother, his advanced education was at Cambridge University and Columbia, where he did graduate work. He became a Catholic, and in 1941 a Trappist monk, entering the Abbey of Gethsemane at Trappist, Kentucky. His writings, all subsequent to his religious experience, explore it in various forms of contemplation, spiritual autobiography, and study of theological and moral problems. An interesting figure of modern devotion, he was influenced by Blake as well as St Augustine. He published first as a poet: *Thirty Poems* (1944), *Man in the Divided Sea* (1946), *Figures for an Apocalypse* (1947), *Emblems of a Season of Fury* (1963), *Cables to the Ace* (1968) and *The Geography of Lograine* (1969). In 1948 his spiritual autobiography, *The Seven Storey Mountain*, became an American best-seller. He later published many volumes of meditation, often touching on current problems of philosophy

or conduct: *Seeds of Contemplation* (1949), *No Man Is an Island* (1955), *The Silent Life* (1956), *Secular Journals* (1959) and *Life and Holiness* (1963), etc. Merton's monastic experience did not close him to contemporary events and processes; and his studied, religious approach to such matters made him a valuable commentator – exemplified by his introduction to and essay in *Breakthrough to Peace* (1964), and his essays and fables in *Raids on the Unspeakable* (1964). *Zen and the Birds of Appetite* (1968) and *Mystics and Zen Masters* (1969) show the congruencies of Christian mysticism and Buddhism. His last work was *Contemplative Prayer* (1970), composed for the community. [R W B]

**Merwin, W(illiam) S(tanley)** (1927– ). Poet, translator. After study at Princeton, he went to France and Spain and finally to England, where he first established a reputation as a poet. He has published several volumes of verse, including *A Mask for Janus* (1952), *The Dancing Bears* (1954), *Green with Beasts* (1956), *The Drunk in the Furnace* (1960), *Moving Target* (1963) and *Lice* (1967) and some important translations – notably of *The Cid* (1959) – many collected in *Selected Translations, 1964–1968* (1969). He now lives in the U.S.A. and France. His earlier poems resembled those of the English 'Movement', though he is more philosophical and enigmatic. He has a fondness for the curious and metaphysical turn of thought and image. His attitude to modern civilization is often satiric or despairing, yet always vigorous and passionate. His nature poems, particularly, show an exciting baroque energy – especially the ones about the great beasts of the animal world. He has had considerable influence on contemporaries, showing the possibilities of a dignified, elaborated poetry as a relevant means of dealing with modern subjects. [BS]

**Mezey, Robert** (1935– ). Poet. He was born in Philadelphia and, in a classic pattern for many mid-century American poets, went to Kenyon College and the State University of Iowa, thereafter teaching in various American universities. *The Lovemaker* (1961) shows an assured manipulation of traditional verse forms that reflects the tutelage of John Crowe ◊ Ransom and Paul Engle; but at its best his verse displays very personal and unacademic concerns. [BP]

**Michener, James A(lbert) (1907– ).** Novelist, short-story writer. He was born in New York and travelled widely in early life; during the Second World War he served in the South Pacific. Out of these experiences he wrote his widely known fiction. *Tales of the South Pacific* (1947), a collection of stories told by a naval officer about American servicemen and the inhabitants of the South Pacific islands, was made into a romping musical. Essentially the novelist as story-teller, Michener exploits colourful settings and the charm of places; other novels and stories, such as *Sayonara* (1954) and *Hawaii* (1959), deal colourfully with the South Pacific and Japan, though he also writes of home ground – *The Fires of Spring* (1949) is set in Pennsylvania. *Caravans* (1963) is a conventional search for a lost girl set in a detailed Afghanistan background. *Iberia* (1968) is a further instalment of the American intellectual flirtation with Spain. [MB]

A. Grove Day, *James A. Michener* (1964).

**Miles, Josephine (1911– ).** Poet, literary scholar. She teaches English at the University of California at Berkeley. Her poetry is extremely intellectual, abstruse and witty, in a manner particularly associated with the 1930s, though it has been adapted in more recent work. Books of verse include *Lines at Intersection* (1939) and *Prefabrications* (1955), the most convenient representation being in *Poems 1930–1960* (1960), which selects from earlier volumes. *Kinds of Affection* (1968) has a less strenuous style, more direct and less filtered. Her literary studies have largely been devoted to the analysis of poetic vocabulary; these analyses, using word counts and statistical comparisons, have been of radical importance in systematic discussion of literary language. The several books devoted in different ways to this large-scale task include *The Vocabulary of Poetry* (1946), *The Continuity of Poetic Language* (1951) and *Eras and Modes in English Poetry* (1957). Also important is her study of the changing relationship between object and emotion in literature, *Pathetic Fallacy in the Nineteenth Century* (1942). [MB]

**Millay, Edna St Vincent (1892–1950).** Poet. Born in Rockland, Maine. She presented in her early volumes – of which the witty and rebellious collection *A Few Figs from Thistles* (1920) is a striking example – a woman writer's position in the twenties' revolt against conventionality. This Greenwich Village Bohemianism she soon outgrew. In 1923 *The Harp-Weaver and Other Poems* revealed the mature poet and recalled her first success in 1912, 'Renascence', a reflective poem still admired for its depth and lyric felicity. Its proponents provoked a controversy when it lost an award in competition with an established poet; but it gained her a sponsor who helped her to complete her college years at Vassar (1917). Her girlhood at Camden on the coast of Maine gave her intimate knowledge of the frugal living and intellectual energy then characteristic of that region, and enriched her natural imagery and shrewd knowledge of character.

Her writing increasingly reflected the sophistication of her literary environment and her married life. From the Elizabethan and Cavalier poets of England she discovered the roots of her own sensibility and won her freedom. Her style was independent and flexible, witty and brilliant if seldom profound, and nearly as precise as that of ◊ MacLeish, who surpassed her in imagination and depth. Like him and S. V. ◊ Benét, she participated prominently in the democratic literary propaganda of the war, of which her poem *The Murder of Lidice* (1942) was a noteworthy example. Following *The Harp-Weaver*, her best-accomplished work is found in *The Buck in the Snow and Other Poems* (1928) and *Fatal Interview* (1931), inspired by a love affair, but remarkable for its objective psychological interest. It is also uniquely a successful modern sonnet sequence, in the Elizabethan tradition. Her mastery of the sonnet was manifest from the beginnings, in form impeccable, but adapted to many moods, and to subjects as diverse as the logical paradigm, 'Euclid Alone . . .' and the passionate Endymion poem. With comparable success she maintained independent control of her swift-moving ballads without disguising their Pre-Raphaelite affinity. Her poetic dramas are remarkable for their survival in the little theatres, and one, *The King's Henchman* (1927), with a score by Deems Taylor, was performed by the Metropolitan Opera. After three volumes of declining appeal (1939–40) she virtually ceased publication during her last decade and she died in 1950. [RWB]

*Collected Poems* (1956) (comprises the bulk of *Collected Sonnets*, 1941, and *Collected Lyrics*,

1943); *Letters,* ed. A. R. MacDougall (1952). Elizabeth Atkins, *Edna St Vincent Millay and Her Times* (1936); Vincent Sheean, *The Indigo Bunting: A Memoir of Edna St Vincent Millay* (1951).

**Miller, Arthur** (1915–    ). Playwright. The most distinguished of contemporary liberal dramatists in America, he was born and educated in New York City. After his father's business failed in the Depression (he was a Jewish manufacturer and shop-owner), he worked at a number of prole-tarian jobs, studied journalism at Michigan University in 1934, and began to write plays and radio scripts which gained him prizes and a living. He worked briefly with the ◊ Federal Theatre project and during the war worked as a fitter in the Brooklyn navy yard and on an army training film (*Situation Normal,* 1944). In 1945 he published *Focus,* a novel on anti-semitism in American cities. His first performed play was *The Man Who Had All the Luck* (1944); it was not a success but here already were some of his major themes of the insecure relationships between a man's honour, his work and his family, and the nature of business ethics and personal ethics under capitalism. His life has always been public and committed. In 1960–1 John Huston filmed his script of *The Misfits,* a brilliant work concerning the end of cowboy masculinity and the Western pastoral myth. Miller's wife, Marilyn Monroe, played a leading role. In 1956 he refused to betray left-wing associates to the House Un-American Activities Com-mittee; in 1965 he was elected the first American international president of P.E.N. All these elements of his career appear in one form or another in his plays and stories. In 1968 he appeared in Paris as the leader of an American pacifist group with a plan for peace in Vietnam.

His plays all concern the nature of a man who, under pressure from his society's stated and assumed laws, is driven to actual or virtual suicide, whether in America or in Europe, today or in the 17th century. In *The Man Who Had All the Luck* the mechanism of determinism and luck is too obvious and philosophically confused. Business success or failure is again central in *All My Sons* (1947), with moral equivocations surround-ing betrayals of faith in public and family situations during the Second World War. Miller allows his businessman hero suicide after his cry 'a man can't be Jesus in this world!', but he has no idea how to change

'this world'. In *Death of a Salesman* (1947) the stocking salesman Willy Loman goes to his death bewildered by his failures and his sons' loss of respect for him, but the only positive is his wife's cry that 'attention must finally be paid to such a person'. Both plays were successful in the New York theatre. The basis of *The Crucible* (1953) is the 1690 witchcraft hunt and trial series in Salem, Massachusetts, related to the contemporary McCarthy hysteria. Again the hero, John Proctor, is confronted with a conflict be-tween laws of self-judgement and judgement by society, with the relationship between the man and his wife and family stretched to breaking point under social pressure. What survives is a man's integrity and the love of his wife. But the end is death. The stylization of language begun in *Death of a Salesman* is developed here, but Miller has returned to earlier naturalist settings; his characteristic combination of expressionis t decor, semi-stylized language and thorough-ly naturalistic characterization is at its best in *A View from the Bridge* (1955; *A Memory of Two Mondays* was produced the same year but it is hardly a major part of Miller's career). Here the clash is between Sicilian law embodied in Eddie Carbone and his dockland slum community, and the law of the wider society of America. Eddie's 'good name' is lost in the confusion of values, and his death is part of the logic of ancient law. In *After the Fall* (1964) the centre of lost values and lost integrity is a liberal-leftist lawyer; the expressionist action takes place inside his head as an act of recovering his past. In *Incident at Vichy* (1964) a group of Frenchmen and an Austrian aristocrat are under interrogation as Jews in 1942; the arguments for self-sacrifice put forward are cynical and the writing is even looser than in the previous play. *The Price* (1968) still concerns guilt, responsibility and the con-flict between self and society, this time be-tween two brothers, a policeman and a surgeon, as they define their relationship with their dead father, their own innocence and their own moral superiority. Miller is a serious dramatist of the American liberal middle class, his post-ideological plays exactly representing the irresolution and worry of the post-war years. His many theoretical essays reinforce the delineation of family, personal honour and sexual in-security in his plays, themes and their method of exposition which he partly in-herits from Ibsen, a version of whose *An*

*Enemy of the People* he has made (1951), and O'Neill. His short stories are in *I Don't Need You Any More* (1968). *Collected Plays* (1957) contains five plays and an important introduction. *In Russia* (1969) combines his prose with Inge Morath's photographs. [EM]

Dennis Welland, *Arthur Miller* (1961); Robert Hogan, *Arthur Miller* (1964); S. Haftel, *Arthur Miller: The Burning Glass* (1965); J. Goode, *The Story of the Misfits* (1963); Edward Murray, *Arthur Miller: Dramatist* (1967).

**Miller, Henry** (1891–    ). Novelist. He was born in New York City of German ancestry, and brought up in Brooklyn. After attending the City College of New York for two months, he worked at various odd jobs before becoming employment manager of the messenger department of the Western Union Telegraph Company of New York. In 1924 he gave this up to write, and settled in Paris in 1930. Here he wrote *Tropic of Cancer* (1934), an American classic. Usually classed as a novel, it is, like many other books of Miller's, an intermediate form, fictional autobiography. The first-person narrator is clearly Miller, but the material is shaped into novelistic episodes, not left in the accidental order imposed by the actual chronology of events. *Cancer* records Miller's life in Paris as poverty-stricken artist, amorist, good companion and receptive soul. It is sharply anecdotal, with enormous comic verve, bringing together the traditions of European bawdry and of American humour. Its use of obscene words was revolutionary, reflecting with a new realism the ordinary callousness of male talk and the destructive potential of such words. When the sexual act is performed without love, Miller feels, it becomes an index of all human futility, and only obscene words can render its emptiness. *Black Spring* (1936) is a Parisian companion-piece to *Cancer* with important developments in prose style, and *Tropic of Capricorn* (1939) its American counterpart, with classic opening scenes in a telegraph company.

In 1939, Miller left Paris and visited Greece, publishing *The Colossus of Maroussi* (1941) in which he describes his transformation under the effects of ancient and modern forces. He returned to America in 1940, toured the country in 1941–2, and produced *The Air-Conditioned Nightmare*, recording his repudiation of modern American life and his championing of individual American artists and eccentrics. In 1944, he settled at Big Sur on the Californian coast, where he has lived ever since. His main literary enterprise there has been the trilogy *The Rosy Crucifixion*, his most ambitious exercise in fictional autobiography, consisting of *Sexus* (1945), *Plexus* (1949) and *Nexus* (1960). But the sharp sense of life and the delightful humour of the Parisian books have given way to a philosophical examination of sexual experience, which tends to repetition and loose style. Besides the stories in *Nights of Love and Laughter* (1955), the rest of his large output consists of collections of essays and personal reminiscences: *Max and the White Phagocytes* (1938), *The Cosmological Eye* (1939), *The World of Sex* (1940), *The Wisdom of the Heart* (1941), *Sunday after the War* (1944), *Remember to Remember* (1947), *The Smile at the Foot of the Ladder* (1948), *Books in My Life* (1952), *Rimbaud* (1952), which became *Time of the Assassins* (1956), *Big Sur and the Oranges of Hieronymus Bosch* (1957) and *Stand Still Like the Hummingbird* (1962), which contains an important essay on Thoreau, who, with Lawrence, stands at the head of the major influences of Miller's explorations of sex and anarchistic liberty. *Just Wild about Harry* (1963) is a play, *The Michael Fraenkel–Henry Miller Correspondence Called Hamlet* (1939; repr. 1952), a fascinating clash of intelligences and styles of literary consideration. *The Red Notebook* (no date) is a reproduction of a notebook which he began while touring America prior to *The Air-Conditioned Nightmare* and which he finished in 1944 before going to live at Big Sur. *To Paint is to Love Again* (1960) is illustrated by his own paintings (he has had a number of exhibitions over the years). *Maurizius Forever* (1959) is analysis of crime, and he contributed an essay to the volume on tribute to *Joseph Delteil* (1962). *Order and Chaos Chez Hans Reichel* (1966), a memoir of friends, is a magnificently produced book from the Loujon Press, Tucson, Arizona, one of the great little presses of the world. Of Miller's huge correspondence 3 volumes have appeared: *Art and Outrage* (1959, with the major contributions by Alfred Perlès and Lawrence Durrell), *Lawrence Durrell and Henry Miller: A Private Correspondence* (1963) and *Letters to Anaïs Nin* (ed. Gunther Stuhlmann, 1965). Miller is the major 20th-century participant in the increasingly important American line of dissent and pacifist anarchism. His writing is mainly autobiographical, and this is both an advantage in its direct personal commitment and its tendency to garrulousness. His sexual frankness has been of positive value for readers, internationally, and his dedication to literature as an instrument of self-development has created for him a large following, especially among the dissenting generations of the fifties and sixties. [B W/E M]

*The Henry Miller Reader*, ed. Lawrence Durrell (1960).

Alfred Perlès, *My Friend, Henry Miller* (1955); William A. Gordon, *The Mind and Art of Henry Miller* (1967); Kingsley Widmer, *Henry Miller* (1967); George Orwell, 'Inside the Whale', in *England, Your England, and Other Essays* (1954).

**Miller, Joaquin** (Cincinnatus Hiner Miller) (1841–1913). Poet and dramatist. Born in Indiana, he was, like Bret Harte and to some extent Mark Twain, one of the literary figures who represented the pioneer West to the literary East. As a child he travelled the Oregon trail with his family, later became a cook in the California mines, and later still lived with the Digger Indians. He acquired some education and in 1860 was admitted to the bar, but after various other ventures he went to San Francisco with literary ambitions. But his success came when he went to London. He printed *Pacific Poems* (1871) at his own expense and won acclaim in many quarters, particularly among the Pre-Raphaelites, as 'the Byron of Oregon'. Rossetti helped him to revise his work to produce *Songs of the Sierras* (1871), and he acquired international reputation. His verse dramas and histories of his own past and of various parts of the country were only a part of his considerable later publication. Their documentary interest is damaged by literariness and exaggeration, but he draws on an evidently fascinating culture. Some of his poems, and his *Life among the Modocs* (1873), about living among Indians, have survival value. [M B]

**Miller, Perry** (1905–63). Scholar and critic. Born in Chicago, he left college in 1923 for three years of adventure as bum and seaman, discovered his vocation in the Congo, and began his teaching career at Harvard in 1931. His life-work was the study of the American puritans and their tradition in a series of important works beginning with *Orthodoxy in Massachusetts* (1933) and continuing with *The New England Mind: The Seventeenth Century*

(1939) and *From Colony to Province* (1953). His authoritative biographical study *Jonathan Edwards* (1949) was backed by an edition of *Images or Shadows of Divine Things* in 1948. *The Raven and the Whale* (1956) studies the backgrounds of Poe and Melville, and *Errand into the Wilderness* (1956) collects his best essays. He is one of America's greatest intellectual historians, and his final, unfinished work, *The Life of the Mind in America* (1965), is as masterly as ever. [E M]

**Miller, Warren** (1921–66). Novelist. Born in Pennsylvania, he studied at the University of Iowa, served in the U.S. Army in Europe in the Second World War, and lived his literary life in New York. Some of his books appeared under the pseudonym of Amanda Veil, and he also wrote children's books with Edward Sorel. But he is best known for novels under his own name: *The Cool World* (1959), a remarkable account of teenage Harlem gang activity; *Looking for the General* (1964), a satire; and *The Siege of Harlem* (1965), concerning the founding of Harlem as a separate state. [E M]

**Mills, C(harles) Wright** (1916–62). Sociologist. Born in Texas, he was professor at Columbia from 1945, writing some of the most influential political commentaries of the century in America. He was a polemicist for social change rather than an academic 'pure' sociologist. His earliest work (with H. H. Gerth) was *From Max Weber: Essays in Sociology* (1946), followed by a study of labour leaders, *The New Men of Power* (1948) and (with Clarence Senior and Rose Goldstein) *The Puerto Rican Journey* (1950). His wider public came with *White Collar* (1951), a brilliant and relentless penetrating analysis of American middle-class society, and *The Power Elite* (1956), which poses the three controlling power-groups in America: corporation capitalists, militarists and politicians. These were extended and followed up with *The Causes of World War Three* (1958), an acutely persuasive description of war momentum, and *Listen, Yankee* (1960), an outspoken commentary on the Cuban revolution. *The Marxists* (1962) is 'a primer on marxisms', written to educate Americans away from mere hearsay on some fundamental modern ideas. Mills' broader sociological works began with his dissertation *Sociology and*

*Pragmatism* (published in 1964), and included *Character and Social Structure* (1953, with H. H. Gerth), one of the best introductions to modern sociology, *The Sociological Imagination* (1959), a criticism of the methods and assumptions of modern sociologists, and *Power, Politics and People* (collected essays, ed. I. L. Horowitz, 1963). Mills' work has considerable influence with the New Left, both in America and Britain, and among the student revolutionaries in Europe in the 1960s. [EM]

**Mitchell, Margaret** (1900–49). Novelist. Born in Georgia, she became a journalist, and later world-famous as the author of *Gone with the Wind* (1936), the classic best-seller of the century. The novel is a variant on the tradition of Southern romance fiction, and is set in Georgia during the Civil War and Reconstruction. A historical romance with exciting characters and epic dimensions, more than 8 million copies were sold in 40 countries. Its action turns on the attempts of the exotic and mercenary heroine, Scarlett O'Hara, to restore Tara, the family plantation, and on her love-relationships: its ably presented sentimentality and its mixture of daring and morals made it an incredible success of great cultural significance. [MB]

Finis Farr, *Margaret Mitchell of Atlanta: The Author of Gone with the Wind* (1966); Frank Luther Mott, *Golden Multitudes: The Story of the Best-Seller in the United States* (1947).

**Monroe, Harriet** (1860–1936). Editor, poet, autobiographer. Born in Chicago. She is best known for founding and editing *Poetry; A Magazine of Verse*, which first appeared in Chicago in October 1912 and was thereafter one of the leading journals of the new movement in American poetry, printing most of the distinguished names of the poetic revolution – Pound, Eliot, H.D., Sandburg, Masters and Hart Crane, among others (◊ Little Magazines). Her selection was helped radically by Pound, the London editor, whose *Letters* (ed. D. D. Paige, 1950) show much about the review's development. Her own verse – collected in *Valeria and Other Poems* (1892), *You and I* (1914) and *Chosen Poems* (1935) – is not particularly distinguished; but her autobiography, *A Poet's Life: Seventy Years in a Changing World* (1937), is a fascinating document of the literary revolution of the early years of the century, also revealing much about the Chicago revival of which she was part. [MB]

**Moody, William Vaughn** (1869–1910). Playwright, poet. A brilliant teacher at Harvard, and other colleges. His early poems were Elizabethan and Miltonic. But *Gloucester Moors* (1901) is an individual work of some originality on the theme of oppressive power, and *An Ode in Time of Hesitation* (1900) and *On a Soldier Fallen in the Philippines* (1900) are bitter attacks on American imperialism. His largest work is the verse trilogy *The Masque of Judgement* (1900), a play about American sin obsession written in high Miltonic language, *The Fire-Bringer* (1904), a promethean work with a celebrated lyric section, 'The Song of Pandora', and *The Death of Eve*, planned to complete the dramatic sequence by making woman the mediator between man and God, but never completed. His positivist romantic inheritance also comes out in his prose plays, *The Faith Healer* (1909), concerning mysticism, and *The Great Divide* (1909), which ran for a thousand performances in New York, contrasting Puritan New England with the Arizona West and featuring the ways to end guilty sexual repression. [MB/EM]

*The Poems and Plays*, ed. J. M. Manley (2 vols., 1912); *The Selected Poems*, ed. B. M. Lovett (1931).
David D. Henry, *William Vaughn Moody: A Study* (1934).

**Moore, Julia A.** (1847–1920). Poet. The 'Sweet Singer of Michigan' was a notoriously bad poetess whose *The Sweet Singer of Michigan Salutes the Public* (1876) – later called *The Sentimental Song Book* – had wide circulation and eventually became the subject of wide humorous commentary; Ogden Nash says he learned the possibilities of bad versifying from her work. It stands in American literary history as a cultural document – widely remembered, almost totally unread. [MB]

**Moore, Marianne** (1887– ). Poet. Born in St Louis, she graduated from Bryn Mawr in 1909. After teaching stenography for five years, she began contributing poems to the English magazine of the ◊ Imagists, the *Egoist*. Her first volume of *Poems* (1921) was chosen from that magazine by friends without her knowledge. In the same year she became an assistant in the New York Public

Library. The second volume, *Observations* (1924), she prepared herself. From 1925 until its demise in 1929 she edited the *Dial*, the fortnightly literary review which had moved in 1918 from Chicago to New York, attracting such writers and associates as Conrad ◊ Aiken, Van Wyck ◊ Brooks, John ◊ Dewey, Thomas Mann and T. S. Eliot (◊ Little Magazines). Her *Selected Poems* (1935), introduced by T. S. Eliot, was followed by *The Pangolin, and Other Verse* (1936), *What Are Years?* (1941), *Nevertheless* (1944), and *Collected Poems*, which won the Pulitzer Prize in 1951. *Predilections* (1955) contains essays on her favourite writers. Her most recent publications are *The Fables of La Fontaine* (1954), a verse translation, *Like a Bulwark* (1956), *O To Be a Dragon* (1959), *The Arctic Fox* (1964) and *Tell Me, Tell Me* (1966).

'I tend to write', she has said, 'in a patterned arrangement, with rhymes . . . to secure an effect of flowing continuity.' Her line is long, gathering in its wake a host of observed detail and sharply drawn images, which she leaves to stir their own unaided ripples in the reader's imagination. Her mood is at once elegant and ironical, conversational yet restrained, the starting point of her meditations often being rare or fabulous animals – hippopotamus, wild ostrich, basilisk, pelican, buffalo, monkey, mongoose, octopus, unicorn or peacock. 'There is a great amount of poetry in unconscious/fastidiousness. Certain Ming/products', she writes, ' . . . are well enough in their way . . . ', but passes on to a puppy eating off a plate, a swan under the willows in Oxford, ants scurrying round an ant-heap. 'What is/there in being able/to say that one has dominated the stream in an attitude/of self-defence,' she ends, 'in proving that one has had the experience/of carrying a stick?' 'Self-reliant like the cat,' her father used to say, 'that takes its prey to privacy . . . the deepest feeling always shows itself in silence; not in silence, but restraint.' As much can be said of her poems. [HB]

*The Complete Poems* (1968).
Eugene P. Sheehy and Kenneth A. Lohf, *The Achievement of Marianne Moore: A Biography 1907–57* (1958).

**Moore, Merrill** (1903–57). Poet. Born in Tennessee, he was educated at Vanderbilt and associated there with the ◊ Fugitive Group. By profession a doctor and psychiatrist, he later taught at Harvard. Throughout his life he wrote sonnets on a playfully prolific scale, even dictating them to a tape-recorder in his car. Over 100,000 are said to exist, only a small proportion in print – in volumes like *The Noise That Time Makes* (1929), *Six Sides to a Man* (1935), *M: One Thousand Autobiographical Sonnets* (1938), and *Case Record from a Sonnetarium* (1951). The high rate of production does not detract from their elegance and formal control; the Fugitive voice is there in the stylish accuracy of diction. The subjects, though usually simple, are carefully analysed with strong psychological awareness. [MB]

Henry W. Wells, *Poet and Psychiatrist: Merrill Moore, M.D.* (1955).

**More, Paul Elmer** (1864–1937). Critic, philosopher. He was born in St Louis, Missouri, and had a Calvinist upbringing. After graduating from Washington University in 1887 he taught for five years, then went to study at Harvard, where he met Irving ◊ Babbitt. He now abandoned his planned doctorate and conceived his task as 'the formulation of conscious and deliberate standards'; he thus became a leader in the ◊ New Humanism. A journalist and critic for many years, he edited the *Nation* (1909–14) before returning to lecture at Princeton in semi-retirement.

His chief work was the long series of *Shelburne Essays* (11 vols., 1904–21) and the later *New Shelburne Essays* (3 vols., 1928–36), from which selections were published in 1935. Most of these essays concern English and American literature, but he also wrote on other subjects and became virtually an equivalent of Matthew Arnold. He was a life-long student of the Upanishads, and a distinctive, curious blend of Platonism and mysticism runs through the series. His main concern is to show the qualities of classical writing and to scourge the modern value of romanticism, 'the infinitely craving personality'. This he did time and again, from *The Drift of Romanticism* (1913) to 1928, when his outburst against ◊ Dos Passos's *Manhattan Transfer* (which he described as 'an explosion in a cesspool' in his *Demon of the Absolute*, 1928) provoked serious attacks on New Humanism in general, and on More from an old foe, H. L. ◊ Mencken. [MG]

*The Religion of Plato* (1921); *The Christ of the New Testament* (1924); *Pages from an Oxford Diary* (1937); *The Greek Tradition* (5 vols., 1921–31).

Robert Shafer, *Paul Elmer More and American Criticism* (1935); Arthur H. Dakin, *Paul Elmer More* (1960); Francis X. Duggan, *Paul Elmer More* (1966).

**Morison, Samuel Eliot** (1887–    ). Historian. Born in Boston. His major work derives from his passionate interests in early New England and the history and practice of seafaring, happily combined in *The Maritime History of Massachusetts* (1921), *Builders of the Bay Colony* (1930) and the brilliant *Admiral of the Ocean Sea* (2 vols., 1942), a full-scale study of Columbus's voyages. His most recent works have been a 15-volume *History of United States Naval Operations during World War II* (1947–62), *Freedom in Contemporary Society* (1956) and *The Oxford History of the American People* (1965). He has also notably contributed to literary history with his studies of the pattern of colonial New England intelligentsia, especially in *The Intellectual life of Colonial New England* (1956). [DKA/EM]

**Morley, Christopher** (1890–1957). Novelist, poet, essayist. Born in Pennsylvania, he was educated at Haverford College and, as a Rhodes Scholar, at Oxford, where he published a rare first volume of poems (*The Eighth Sin*, 1912). Oxford is the scene of his novel *Kathleen* (1920). He went on to become active in New York publishing and literary journalism. An intelligent and prolific writer, he was an influential columnist for various papers (notably the *Saturday Review of Literature*) and produced more than 50 books, many of them novels, all marked by charm, erudition and elegance. His witty, informal essays are brought together in *Shandygaff*...(1918), *Mince Pie* (1919), *Forty-Four Essays* (1925), etc.; *Essays* (1928) is a selection from earlier volumes. Among the novels are *Where the Blue Begins* (1922), and *Kitty Foyle* (1939); *Poems* (1929) is a collection of verse. [MB]

G. R. Lyle and H. T. Brown, Jr, *A Bibliography of Christopher Morley* (1952).

**Morris, Wright** (1910–    ). Novelist. The emptinesses of the great plains of Nebraska, where he was born, have had much to do with the qualities of his fiction; where objects are few those present gain a peculiar richness of meaning. His early novels reveal a tremendous sense that things, looked at closely, may show what life really is for those who made and used them. Hence *The In-habitants* (1946) and *The Home Place* (1948), the story of a man who brings his family back to a Nebraska farm, combine text with photographs. Morris made his home more recently in Tamalpais Valley, California.

The later novels, in the main about personal and family relationships and cleavages in the mid-West, are equally concerned with revelation and reality. 'Objects' are replaced by characters and situations, actions and events, more publicly available. But the underlying preoccupation remains – the search for a genuine reality usually arrived at by an imaginative transformation momentarily produced by heroes or an act of heroism, or by the power of love, or by the creative consciousness itself. In *The World in the Attic* (1949) the imaginative attic world is more real than mundane reality outside; *Man and Boy* (1951) is about the struggle towards imaginative transformation of an empty, dry life; *The Works of Love* (1952) describes the quest for love and communion with others; *The Huge Season* (1954) concerns escape from limitation via an imaginative understanding of the meaning of the past – in this case the glamorous, heroic twenties. In *The Field of Vision* (1956) a bizarre group of American tourists in Mexico seek some kind of vision that will lead them out of the unreality of their lives. Other novels are *My Uncle Dudley* (1942), *The Man Who Was There* (1945), *The Deep Sleep* (1953), *Love among the Cannibals* (1957) and *Ceremony in Lone Tree* (1960). *What a Way to Go* (1962) makes a break with his earlier novels in that it deals, comically and sharply, with American and European tourists in Europe, and a middle-aged professor's encounter with the eternal feminine. *Cause for Wonder* (1963) isolates the awareness of his American characters once again in Europe, and *One Day* (1965), like its predecessor, concerns an individual's experience in time, but the plot deals with a small community near San Francisco. *In Orbit* (1967) shows Morris, with his next novel, still terse, oblique and deeply serious: it concerns the impact of a school drop-out on a university town of the South-west. Morris's novels are written in complex stream-of-consciousness structures but do not lose touch with human realities. With humour, wit and technical accomplishment, they evoke sensitively and poignantly the recent American past and present in the mid-West and South-west. His distinguished intelligence is acutely at work also in *The*

Territory Ahead (1958), critical essays on 19th- and 20th-century American writers. But *A Bill of Rites, A Bill of Wrongs, A Bill of Goods* (1968) is an angry and too sweepingly scornful indictment of American culture in the 1960s: the sense of doom has no sense of satirical direction. *God's Country and My People* (1968) links 85 photographs into an autobiographical statement. [AH/ EM]

*Wright Morris: A Reader* (1970).
David Madden, *Wright Morris* (1965); Wayne C. Booth, 'The Two Worlds in the Fiction of Wright Morris', *Sewanee Review*, LXV (Summer, 1957); Leon Howard, *Wright Morris* (U. of Minnesota Pamphlet, 1968).

**Morton, Thomas** (1575?–1647?). A wild London lawyer who arrived in New England as shareholder in Mount Wollaston, a Puritan settlement (later renamed Merrymount) which he managed to divert to atheism, maypole-dancing and licentious living, according to the Puritans, who also claimed he sold arms to the Indians and consorted with their women. Returning from banishment in 1643 he was imprisoned in Boston, and after release died a few years later in York, Maine. His Anglican settlement and commercial aplomb, in what is now Quincy, Massachusetts, are celebrated, and his enemies are satirized in *New English Canaan* (Amsterdam, 1637; ed. C. F. Adams, 1883). William Bradford's *History of Plymouth Plantation* is critical of Morton. Morton's experience is the basis of Hawthorne's 'The Maypole of Merrymount' (1836) and an opera by Howard Hanson and Richard Stokes (1934). Robert ◊ Lowell's play *Endecott and the Red Cross* (1965) treats him fairly. [EM]

**Moss, Howard** (1922–     ). Poet, critic. He was born in New York, taught at Vassar, and is now poetry editor of the *New Yorker*. He has published several volumes of verse – including *The Wound and the Weather* (1946), *A Swimmer in the Air* (1957), *A Winter Come, A Summer Gone: Poems 1946–1960* (1960), *Finding Them Lost* (1965) and *Poems* (1968) – as well as a critical work, *The Magic Lantern of Marcel Proust* (1962). His poems possess the power of making something close to light verse both dignified and revealing through skilful use of varied verse forms and elaborately detailed urban observation. [MB]

**Motley, John Lothrop** (1814–77). Historian, diplomat. Born at Dorchester, Massachusetts, the son of a prosperous New England family, he spent several years studying in Europe after graduating from Harvard in 1831. He published two fictional works, *Morton's Hope: or, The Memoirs of a Young Provincial* (1839), which was based on his experiences in Germany as a student at Göttingen, and *Merry-Mount: A Romance of the Massachusetts Colony* (1849). Later he was secretary of legation in St Petersburg, Minister to Austria, and Minister to Great Britain. His historical interests became focused on the Netherlands, and he published his best-known and most successful work, *The Rise of the Dutch Republic* (3 vols.), in 1856, following it with *The History of the United Netherlands* (1860–67) and *The Life and Death of John of Barneveld* (1874). His approach as a historian was chiefly political and religious; like his contemporary Prescott, he saw history as a branch of literature. But despite skilfully drawn portraits and a strong sympathy for his subject-matter his work is ponderously laden with reference and quotation, though his place in the history of American history is unquestioned. [DKA]

**Motley, Willard** (1912–65). Novelist. Born in Chicago, as a young man he worked his way across America as emigrant labourer, waiter, cook, ranch-hand, etc. His reputation began with his novel *Knock on Any Door* (1947), the story of a Chicago slum boy growing into a criminal in the corrupt pre-war city environment. In the forties, Motley had joined the Chicago writers of the thirties, and other city writers of America in condemning the urban environment which so much excited them. After this success, his big house on Wells Street became a Bohemian centre. He followed up with *We Fished All Night* (1951) and *Let No Man Write My Epitaph* (1958), which substantially and effectively covered the same ground, the chosen fields of ◊ Dreiser and ◊ Farrell before him. But the repetitions began to lack vitality. His experience as an American Negro living in Mexico, where he had been for 12 years before his death, went into *Let Noon Be Fair* (1966), which records the corruption of a fishing village by bored Americans and their money. It is a not successful study of triviality and hedonistic degradation. As Nelson ◊ Algren wrote: 'He was a Negro and a writer but he was not a Negro writer. His scene was always White Bohemia.' [EM]

**Mumford, Lewis** (1895–    ). Teacher, literary critic, writer on architecture, town planning and philosophy. Born in New York, he was educated at City College, Columbia and the New York School of Social Research, where he heard Thorstein ◊ Veblen. He helped to found the Regional Planning Association of America (1924), and taught at numerous universities. He is now best known for his lucid and stimulating essays on architecture and town planning, such as those collected in *From the Ground Up* (1956) and *The Highway and the City* (1963); but these are only a small part of his lifetime's work on the relations between man and his environment, a study greatly influenced by his early reading of Patrick Geddes, the Scottish biologist and city planner. A great American polymath, his early publications were *The Story of Utopias* (1922); *Sticks and Stones* (1924), a history of American civilization seen through its architecture; *Herman Melville* (1929), a critical biography with a strong psychological emphasis; and two valuable studies in 'American experience and culture' with special reference to literature, *The Golden Day* (1926), examining New England from 1830 to 1860, and *Brown Decades* (1931), surveying the arts between the Civil War and 1895. But his major work is a tetralogy, *Renewal of Life*, which presents his philosophy of modern civilization and is based on a study of Western cities from the 10th century; it consists of *Technics and Civilization* (1934), *The Culture of Cities* (1938), *The Condition of Man* (1944) and *The Conduct of Life* (1951), in which he stresses his plea that men should be sceptical of all 'systems'. His passionate concern with problems of metropolitan development has also produced *City Development: Studies in Disintegration and Renewal* (1945) and his most important single work, the classic *The City in History* (1961). His other works include *Green Memories* (1947), a biography of his son, *Art and Technics* (1954), *In the Name of Sanity* (1954), and *The Transformations of Man* (1956). *The Urban Prospect* (1968) is a collection of recent articles.

He has said: 'As time has gone on I have become more, rather than less, radical. Though brought up as an Episcopalian, my religion is that of the traditional American humanist, like Emerson or Whitman.' And: 'The issues that I raised have proved discussable; and the rigid methods and regimented goals that once seemed as inevitable as they were ominous, since they were based on the latest findings of science and technology, have begun to collapse like pricked balloons under rational examination.' These views receive their latest discussion in *The Myth of the Machine* (1967). [MG]

*The Human Prospect*, ed. Harry T. Moore and Karl W. Deutsch (1955) (selections).

**Munson, Gorham B(ert)** (1896–    ). Critic and editor. Born in Amityville, N.Y., he was, as an expatriate in the 1920s, editor of *Secession* (◊ Little Magazines, Lost Generation). Among his numerous books of criticism and economic commentary are *Waldo Frank* (1923); *Robert Frost: A Study in Sensibility and Good Sense* (1927), an early appreciation; *Destinations: A Canvas of American Literature since 1900* (1928), a useful survey; and some books on the teaching of creative writing, including *The Writer's Workshop Companion* (1951). [MB]

# N

**Nabokov, Vladimir** (1899– ). Novelist. One of the finest of present-day novelists, and now American by adoption, Nabokov was born in St Petersburg to an eminent Russian family whose fortunes collapsed in the Revolution: they went into exile in 1919. After finishing his education at Trinity College, Cambridge, he lived in England, Germany and France, writing in Russian and making his reputation in Russian émigré circles (about whom he has written considerably). During 20 years of this life he worked at a series of Russian novels, only later translated into English. In 1940 he went to America, began writing in English, became a citizen in 1945, taught at various colleges, used a research fellowship at Harvard in lepidoptera (his other main field), and spent an 11-year period as Professor of Russian at Cornell. He is now a full-time writer and lives in Switzerland.

The main springs of his fiction lie in the Russian and European literary tradition. In addition to an obvious debt to Gogol, on whom he wrote a curious study (1944), his style and sensibility are European, his aesthetic experiments emerging from those of the early 20th-century masters. His fiction is highly stylized, oblique in techniques, self-conscious in language, and playing elaborate jokes to present his materials with maximum indirection and to invent the maximum changes in form. Sartre said he has the exile's desire to knock down the material he has constructed. His work conveys a deep sense of loss and disintegration, exploiting the tension between his great capacity to re-create places, sensations and values, and his bold authorial detachment. Essentially a comic novelist, indulging in infallible wit and whimsy, he writes from penetrating political and cultural awareness. In 1923 he published two books of poetry and in 1926 his first novel, *Mashenka*; there followed *King, Queen, Knave* (1928; in English, 1968), a traditional romance parodied; *The Luzhin Defense* (1929; in English as *The Defense*, 1964), a chess novel; *The Eye* (1930; in English 1965), a nostalgic story of a Russian émigré in Berlin; *The*

*Return of Chorb* (1930), a collection of stories and poems; *The Exploit* (1931); *Camera Obscura* (1932; in English 1938); *Despair* (1934; in English 1966), a *doppelgänger* crime novel; and *Invitation to a Beheading* (1935; in English 1959).

Two plays, *The Event* and *The Waltz Invention*, appeared in 1938, and *The Gift* (1937; in English 1963), his last novel in Russian, shows his ability at its height in the story of another émigré in Berlin, this time a writer like Nabokov. In 1941 he published *The Real Life of Sebastian Knight* (written in English while he was still in Paris). Then came *Speak Memory: An Autobiography Revisited* (1967), originally pieces in the *New Yorker, Atlantic Monthly, Partisan Review* and *Harper's Magazine*, and appearing in earlier form as *Inconclusive Evidence* (1951). His second English novel was *Bend Sinister* (1948) and then followed his two 'American' novels: *Pnin* (1957), a superb comic novel about a teacher of Russian in an American college, and the novel that first established his reputation with a large audience, *Lolita* (1955 in Paris, 1958 in America), a *tour de force* of comic satire on sex and the American ways of life focused on the love of a middle-aged European for an American 'nymphet'. *Pale Fire* (1962) is a supreme example of Nabokov's formal games: a novel hidden in a poem and its commentary. *Ada or Ardor: A Family Chronicle* (1969) summarizes his life-long fascination with puzzles and games, and his obsession with family sexuality. *Nabokov's Dozen* (1958) is a collection of thirteen stories and *Nabokov's Quartet* (1967) collects four stories from between 1930 and 1959. *Nabokov's Congeries* (1968) is Page Stegner's selection from all his work. In 1964 appeared a translation (and commentary) of *Eugene Onegin* by Pushkin: of the 4 volumes' 2,000 odd pages, 228 are devoted to the translation. His work cannot be quickly summarized. He once urged that it is hard to judge work written in 'my untrammelled, rich, and infinitely docile Russian tongue' against the work written in a 'second-rate brand of English'. But his English writings show him to be an excellent and unique stylist. He is a major 20th-century novelist. [MB/EM]

Andrew Field, *Nabokov: His Life in Art* (1967); Page Stegner, *Escape into Aesthetics: The Art of Vladimir Nabokov* (1967); ed. L. S. Dembo, *Nabokov: The Man and His Work* (1968); Robert Scholes, *The Fabulators* (1967).

**Nasby, Petroleum Vesuvius** (pseud. of David Ross Locke) (1833–88). Humorist. Born in New York State, Locke was an itinerant printer and then a journalist in Ohio. It was in the Finlay, Ohio, *Jeffersonian* that 'Nasby' made his appearance as bigoted and illiterate Copperhead – a pro-Southern Northerner – during the Civil War years. In 1865 Locke went to the Toledo *Blade*, which he was to own, and produced more Nasby letters for the paper. Nasby is in the convention of 'Artemus ◊ Ward' and 'Josh ◊ Billings' and is presented with the usual grammatical illiteracies and vernacular spirit of this movement in humour. But Locke used Nasby ironically, to represent Southern white-supremacy views which he opposed, and he is, like other humorist-figures of the period, a congenital defector and rogue. *The Nasby Papers* (1864) first collected these newspaper pieces; other volumes followed including *Swingin' Round the Cirkle* (1867), *The Diary of an Office Seeker* (1881) and *Nasby in Exile: Or, Six Months of Travel* (1882), which, again typically, takes the character abroad. *The Nasby Letters* appeared posthumously in 1893. Locke also wrote novels – *A Paper City* (1879) satirizes land speculation, and *The Demagogues* (1881) political life. [MB]

Cyril Clemens, *Petroleum V. Nasby* (1936); James C. Austin, *Petroleum V. Nasby* (1965).

**Nash, Ogden** (1902–    ). Humorous poet. His verse, widely and internationally known, has been collected in numerous volumes, from the 1930s onwards, and includes *Versus* (1949), *Family Reunion* (1950), *Everyone But Thee and Me* (1962), and *Marriage Lines* (1964). Nash has confessed a debt to American 'bad' poetry, such as Julia A. ◊ Moore's; its clumsy prosody is at the heart of his method. But he is periodically very inventive and exploits many of the devices of modern poetry; his superbly ostentatious bad rhymes and his use of the long line have a 20th-century spirit, so much so that a number of serious poets confess to having learned from him. Nash's main themes are those of witty social commentary and the charming cele-bration of domestic life and d[...] disaster. A poet to please children, h[...] Belloc or Lear – which comic tradit[...] he continues – more than a children's poet. Too genial and elegant to deserve the title of satirist, his books do often comment sharply on society; but his main persona in his poems is as husband and father or else as aphorist, questioning the world's platitudes, pieties and even grammar. Much of his work has appeared in the *New Yorker*, on which he has served editorially. [MB]

*Collected Verse from 1929 On* (1961).

**Nathan, George Jean** (1882–1958). Dramatic critic. A native of Indiana and a graduate of Cornell University, Nathan 'did time' on New York newspapers and popular magazines as a reporter and feature writer, but by the age of 30 he found himself and devoted the remainder of his life to dramatic criticism. He wrote for a variety of periodicals, but his name is chiefly associated with *Arts and Decoration*, *Vanity Fair*, the *Smart Set* and the *American Mercury*. His style was inclined to be slapstick, which prevented many people from noting the vast knowledge and extraordinary perception in his critical essays. He was probably the most learned, the most acute and the most influential dramatic critic the United States has yet produced. In the twenties and much of the thirties he could, pretty much, make or break a play or a playwright. He, more than any other individual critic, helped to educate the American public to look down upon the theatrical merchandise of the Belascos and to appreciate the full stature of Eugene O'Neill. He also laboured heroically to bring the works of Sean O'Casey, Molnar, Wedekind and Hauptmann to the attention of Broadway. Most of his two dozen books are collections of his critical reviews. He also wrote on morals, history, marriage, religion and politics, but what he had to say on these subjects is considerably inferior to his discussion of the theatre. His most representative and best books are *Mr George Jean Nathan Presents* (1917), *The Autobiography of an Attitude* (1925) and *The Theatre in the Fifties* (1953). [CA]

*The World of George Jean Nathan*, ed. C. Angoff (1952); *The Magic Mirror*, ed. T. Q. Curtiss (1960).
Charles Angoff, 'George Jean Nathan: A Candid Portrait', *Atlantic Monthly*, December 1962; Isaac Goldberg, *The Theatre of George Jean Nathan* (1926).

**Neal, John** (1793–1876). Novelist, essayist. A Maine Quaker. He wrote, quickly, a number of fairly melodramatic novels, including *Keep Cool* (1817) and *Randolph* (1823), and between 1824 and 1827 lived in London, where he contributed to *Blackwood's* a series of essays on American writers which did much to make American writing known in England. He asserted the need for a vernacular American literature and, in his later novels particularly, endeavoured to use native speech, themes and styles. His *Brother Jonathan* (1825), *Rachel Dyer* (1828) and other books drew on strongly Yankee materials. He settled again in Portland, Maine; founded *The Yankee*, a literary journal; and presented a record of his attitudes and experiences in his autobiography, *Wandering Recollections of a Somewhat Busy Life* (1869). [MB]

**Negro Literature.** 'Negro', like 'Indian', is a term invented by colonizing white Europeans to designate certain imported, or indigenous, human beings whom they intended to retain in subservient control. 'Negro' labelled a required stereotype, and most Negroes accepted this typification, under whatever duress, until nearly 350 years after the first importation of slaves into the New World in the 1620s (John Hope Franklin, *From Slavery to Freedom*, revised edn 1956). 'Negro' meant, and still does mean for many whites, a person who may be used as part of a cheap labour force because he can be considered as part of the myth of the Christianizing West that some men are nearer to beasts, can be called 'black' to associate them with darkness, the Devil and Hell, and may be lumped with that eternal underground force of the sexually potent and naturally wicked. The 'Negro' of mythical stereotype must therefore be kept down. But in the 1950s and 1960s black Americans, along with black people throughout the world, began to designate themselves 'black' without the malign connotations of the term. The movement of literature follows therefore the development from slavery to post-Civil War partial liberation, from incipient protest to full protest, and finally to the revolutionary 'black power' movement of the 1960s. The increase in information about black Americans grew considerably over this last period. The nature of slavery is documented in: Stanley Elkins, *Slavery, A*

*Problem in American Institutional and Intellectual Life* (1959); D. P. Mannix and Malcolm Cowley, *Black Cargoes: A History of the Atlantic Slave Trade* (1962); and David Brion Davis, *The Problem of Slavery in Western Culture* (1966). In 1944 appeared Gunnar Myrdal's pioneering study, *An American Dilemma* (a useful condensed edition prepared by Arnold M. Rose, *The Negro in America*, 1948). The inadequate treatment of Negroes in books on history, economics, politics and sociology, and in school texts, is being slowly challenged by studies arguing the hypocrisies of democracy, including: Herbert Aptheker's pioneering *Documentary History of the Negro People in the United States*, 1951); Howard Brotz, ed., *Negro Social and Political Thought, 1850–1920* (1966); and Leslie Fishel and Benjamin Quarles, *The Negro American: A Documentary History* (1967). Of the many works delineating the movement towards a less oppressed life, some of the more significant are: Booker T. ◊ Washington, *Up from Slavery* (1901); William E. B. ◊ DuBois, *Souls of Black Folk* (1903); *George Washington Carver: An American Biography* (1942); *Narrative of the Life of Frederick Douglass, An American Slave* (1845); Virginia Cunningham, *Paul Laurence Dunbar* (1947 – a life of the poet); James Weldon ◊ Johnson, *The Autobiography of an Ex-Coloured Man* (1912); Edwin P. Hoyt, *Paul Robeson* (1958); Constance Webb, *Richard Wright* (1968); R. G. B. Reisner, *The Legend of Charlie Parker* (1962); and Dick Gregory, *Nigger* (1964). The more general challenge to the Negro condition is documented in: M. Ahmann, ed., *The New Negro* (1961); Harold Isaacs, *The New World of Negro Americans* (1963); and Kenneth B. Clarke, *Dark Ghetto* (1965). Naturally, few Negroes have ever been able to achieve status as writers, rather than entertainers in the fields of sport, music and the stage. Only the freak sustained or transcended the compulsory physical labour, the enclosure in rural or city ghetto, the absence of education for self-realization and freedom and the deliberate condition for subordination from childhood onwards. Even black music, which until the 1960s always had a quality superior to black writing, was largely suppressed as racial expression throughout the 200 years before the Civil War, and in the years following either patronized as entertainment or used as a basis for sociology. The gap between rural and city folk music and blues, and compositions by artists such as Duke Ellington, Charles Parker, Ornette Coleman and Cecil Taylor, is exactly the gap between the permitted semi-anonymous artistry of the 'invisible' Negro and the public manifestations of important, sophisticated, minority art. The watershed between the two in literature occurs between the 1920s and 1960s, between the so-called Harlem Renaissance and the literature of Black Power, between literature which largely attempts to compete with and imitate general American forms and literature which focuses protest and revolt without necessarily being bound to those forms. This development has been hamstrung by the means of communication and production being in the hands of white publishing houses, theatres, television and radio networks. But since 1960, books on or about Negroes have become good business, and the amount of material published itself constitutes something of a revolution. As the novelist John A. Williams observes: 'the presence of black editors in large numbers would do as much for black writing as Jewish or Anglo-Saxon editors did for Jewish and Anglo-Saxon literature'. Black Americans are a minority and if their literature is to be differentiated from general American works, the problem of definition can only be made as part of the historical process of change in the Negro condition. This development is given in: August Meier, *Negro Thought in America 1880–1915* (1963), Leonard Broom and Norval Glenn, *Transformation of the Negro American* (1965) and the documentary and autobiographical writings of Negroes including Langston ♦ Hughes, James ♦ Baldwin, Ralph ♦ Ellison, LeRoi ♦ Jones and Martin Luther King Jr (*Stride Toward Freedom*, 1958, and *Why We Can't Wait*, 1964). The Black Muslim movement, so strong in the early 1960s, became considerably less powerful after the assassination of Malcolm X (E. Essien-Udom, *Black Nationalism*, 1962; Louis Lomas, *When the Word is Given*, 1963). The growth of the secular civil rights movement, both before and after Mrs Rosa Parks' refusal to step to the back of an Alabama bus in 1954 and the sit-ins of 1960, is documented in: John P. Roche, *The Quest for the Dream* (1963); Arthur I. Waskow, *From Race-Riot to Sit-In, 1919 to the 1960s* (1966); Ronald

Segal, *The Race War* (1966); and Louis E. Lomax, *The Negro Revolt* (1962). Detailed accounts of Negro culture in the crucial period of the 1960s are given in: Charles Silberman, *Crisis in Black and White* (1964); Harold Cruse, *The Crisis of the Negro Intellectual* (1967); and *In Black America* (ed. Pat Romero), a large volume of information and articles by leading black writers (1969). The development of the Black Power movement is given in: Joanne Grant, ed., *Black Protest: History, Documents and Analyses 1619 to the Present* (1968); Stokeley Carmichael and Charles V. Hamilton, *Black Power* (1967); and Floyd B. Barbour, ed., *The Black Power Revolt* (1968). The importance of the major black leader of the post Second World War period is given in his own excellent *Autobiography of Malcolm X* (1965) and George Breitman, *The Last Year of Malcolm X* (1967); *Malcolm X Speaks: Selected Speeches and Statements* (1965); A. Epps, ed., *The Speeches of Malcolm X at Harvard* (1969); and John Henrik Clarke, ed., *Malcolm X, The Man and His Times* (1969). The experience of the only man to inherit so far any of Malcolm's charisma is contained in Eldridge Cleaver's *Soul on Ice* (1968) and *Eldridge Cleaver: Post-Prison Writings and Speeches* (1969) – to which must be added a major influence on Negroes in America today, Frantz Fanon's *The Wretched of the Earth* (1963; tr 1965).

Negro slaves and their descendants had no choice but to live out their roles as stereotypes of Western imagination, 'an oversimplified clown, a beast or an angel', in Ralph Ellison's words, but always placed outside the 'democratic plan'. The plea of the black writer has always been, in the cry of J. Saunders Redding, 'I am tired of giving up my creative initiative to these demands' – of being a victim, a Negro, a type. LeRoi Jones speaks for the 1960s condition: 'The Negro writer can only survive by refusing to become a white man.' But M. B. ♦ Tolson speaks for those who wish to reach further: 'I, as a black poet, have absorbed the Great Ideas of the Great White World, and interpreted them in the melting-pot idiom of my people. My roots are in Africa, Europe and America.' Jupiter Hammon (1720–1800) was a slave poet praised for his verses by white critics; his 'Address' (1787) pleads for patience in the slave state. Phyllis ♦ Wheatley wrote in a similarly enchained condition. In 1789 appeared 'Negro Slavery by Othello, a Free Negro', a first protest against slavery. But the verbal creativity of Negroes was all the time going into the anonymous or semi-anonymous work-songs, ballads, blues and spirituals which did not need white praise (Newman I. White. *American Negro Folk-Songs*, 1928; Samuel Charters *The Poetry of the Blues*, 1963). The folk literature also included those stories handed on now through anthropological collections and the work of white men like Joel Chandler ◊ Harris. The most sophisticated Negro poets of the later nineteenth and early twenthieth centuries – ◊ Dunbar, Johnson, Jean Toomer, Langston Hughes, Arna Bontemps, Gwendolyn Brooks, and many more – are good but not major poets. The main movement within Negro poetry lies between Johnson's preface to his *Book of American Negro Poetry* (1922) – the need to find 'a form that will express the racial spirit' – and ◊ Cullen's *Caroling Dusk: An Anthology of Verse by Negro Poets* (1927) – the need for universal rather than black poetry, 'the individual diversifying ego transcends the synthesizing hue'. This is the growing division in fiction and theatre as well. The first Negro novels are *Clotel, or The President's Daughter* (1853) by William Wells Brown and *Blake, or The Huts of America* (1859) by Martin Delany. After 1890 the numbers increased but were no better than the mass of American sentimental and naturalistic fiction. The fact of their being written by Negroes is their importance; the most representative include: Dunbar's *The Uncalled* (1898); Charles W. Chesnutt's *The Colonel's Dream* (1905); Claude McKay's *Home to Harlem* (1928); and Arna Bontemps' *Black Thunder* (1936). Jean Toomer's *Cane* (1923) is a rare affirmation of blackness written both passionately and complexly. From the 1930s onwards Negro fiction begins to take its place in the pattern of American writing, with outstanding work from Richard ◊ Wright, Chester ◊ Himes, Ralph Ellison and James Baldwin. (See also R. Boné, *The Negro Novel in America*, 1958; Margaret J. Butcher, *The Negro in American Culture*, 1956; J. Saunders Redding, *To Make a Poet Black*, 1939; ed. Seymour L. Gross and John E. Hardy, *Images of the Negro in American Literature*, 1966; ed. Herbert Hill, *Soon, One Morning*, 1963, and *Anger and Beyond* (1968).) The development of a Negro theatre is far

slower. At first it was restricted to Negroes playing their stereotypical roles in racial plays (and films later). Henry James remembered seeing the stage version of *Uncle Tom's Cabin* as a child, and Mrs Stowe dramatized her novel *Dred* in 1856, such entertainments were popular, and were, for white audiences, largely voyeuristic pleasures – for example, Dion Boucicault's *The Octoroon* (1959) and, as late as 1920, O'Neill's *The Emperor Jones,* and, more harmfully, the stage version of Thomas Dixon's *The Clansman* (1905). In the 1930s a handful of stage works presaged the changes in attitude to come: DuBose and Dorothy ◊ Heyward's novel *Porgy* (1927) made into a first-rate opera, *Porgy and Bess* (1935) by George Gershwin, and Marc Connelly's *The Green Pastures* (1930). The Federal Theatre encouraged Negro playwrights. But in 1958, Lorraine Hansberry's sentimental Negro family drama, *Raisin in the Sun,* was an exception on the New York stage, even if its characters were acceptable stereotypes. The crucial movement in Negro literature in the 1960s is from protest to revolution in its aims. James Baldwin's play *Blues for Mr Charlie* (1964) is a protest play for white audiences. LeRoi Jones's later plays are for black audiences and preach revolt, and therefore sharply differ from the general work of the Negro Ensemble Company of New York, whose style and programme is largely for bi-racial audiences. The New York Shakespeare Festival's Hamlet when asked what he is reading replies '*Ebony,* baby'; black actors have their television soap-opera series; and one of the 'hits' of Broadway in the 1960s was Howard Sackler's *The Great White Hope* (1968), largely based on the life of the boxer Jack Johnson. But the new black theatre is remote from any such games of entertainment. It uses modern theatre techniques to fire a black audience to action against white supremacy (Ed Bullins, *Five Plays,* 1969; Ed Bullins, *New Plays for the Black Theatre,* 1969; ed. William Couch, Jr, *New Black Playwrights,* 1969). The beginning was the Black Arts Repertory Theatre School (1964) and the Black Arts Alliance (1967) and what is termed 'guerrilla theatre', designed to awaken black audiences (*Tulane Drama Review,* Vol. 12, No. 4, 1968; *Black Theatre;* Loften Mitchell, *Black Drama: The Story of the American Negro in the Theatre,* 1969; Doris E. Abramson, *Negro*

*Playwrights in the American Theatre 1925–1959*, 1969). The tone is given in explicit statements by major black writers. John Oliver Killens: 'Everywhere Western man went on the earth, "Christianizing" and "civilizing", he made men into the "niggers", the better to conquer and exploit. And made men believe they were niggers. To deniggerize the earth is the black writer's challenge' ('The Black Writer and Revolution', *Tulane Drama Review*, op. cit.); LeRoi Jones: 'The Black Artist's role in America is to aid in the destruction of America as he knows it' (*Home*, 1968). As Calvin C. Hernton wrote in the 1966 edition of his polemical *Sex and Racism in America*: 'when racism disappears, the nature of the American political-economic system . . . will have changed'. The changes in poetry are registered in: LeRoi Jones and Larry Neal, ed., *Black Fire: An Anthology of Afro-American Writing*, 1968; Clarence Major, ed., *The New Black Poetry* (1969); and to some extent in Langston Hughes, ed., *New Negro Poets: USA* (1964). The African affinities, frequently stated in this period, can be found in Mercer Cook and Stephen E. Henderson, *The Militant Black Writer in Africa and the United States* (1969) and checked in Melville J. Herskovits, *The Myth of the Negro Past* (1941). A summary of the variety of opinions on Negro literature today may be read in Edward Margolies, *Native Sons* (1969), which examines a wide range of writers, from DuBois to LeRoi Jones, and Addison Gayle Jr, ed., *Black Expression: Essays by and about Black Americans in the Creative Arts* (1969). The new Negro fiction develops in: Paule Marshall's *Brown Girl Brownstones* (1959); William Melvin Kelley's *A Different Drummer* (1962), *A Drop of Patience* (1966) and *Dem* (1967); Earle Conrad's *The Premier* (1963); John Oliver Killens' *And Then We Heard the Thunder* (1963); Jesse Hill Ford's *The Liberation of Lord Byron Jones* (1965) and *The Feast of Saint Barnabas* (1969); Ishmael Reed's *The Freelance Pallbearers* (1967); and especially in the development of John A. Williams through *Night Song* (1961), *Sissie* (1963), *The Man who Cried I Am* (1967) and *Sons of Darkness, Sons of Light* (1969). Shorter fiction is collected usefully in: *American Negro Short Stories* (1967, ed. John Henrick Clarke) and *The Best Short Stories by Negro Writers* (1967, ed. Langston Hughes). Reference may be made to: *Negro American Literature Forum* (Indiana State University: quarterly) and *The Guide to African–American Books* (Negro Book Club). [EM]

**Nemerov, Howard** (1920–    ). Poet, novelist, critic. Born in New York and educated at Harvard. He edited the little magazine *Furioso*, and has taught at Hamilton College and Bennington. His poems in *The Image and the Law* (1947), *Guide to the Ruins* (1950), *The Salt Garden* (1955) and the useful collection *New and Selected Poems* (1960) have a considerable range of tone and manner, from an Eliot-like philosophical manner to something nearer light verse, where he responds more directly to immediate occasions or domestic experience. The intellectual moralist in Nemerov appears in his fiction. Besides his lively short stories in *A Commodity of Dreams and Other Stories* (1959), he has written novels dealing with the moral dilemmas of the intellectual in advertising and the academic among his students (*The Homecoming Game*, 1957). They include *The Melodramatist* (1949) and *Federigo, or the Power of Love* (1954). His criticism has appeared widely and is partly collected in *Poetry and Fiction: Essays* (1963). An impressive and interesting writer, with deep moral scruples, he can be ponderous and slight. *The Next Room of the Dream* (1963, poems and two plays) and *The Blue Swallows* (1968) contain too many conventional and dull 'serious' poems among the lighter ironical political pieces. *Journal of the Fictive Life* (1965) is a mixed bag of diary, sketches for novels, some uninteresting dreams and a few poems. [MB]

Peter Meinke, *Howard Nemerov* (U. of Minnesota Pamphlet, 1968).

**Nevins, Allan** (1890–    ). Historian. Born at Camp Point, Illinois. He rose to the highest ranks of the historical profession without having acquired the benediction of the doctorate; his first historical works were written while a practising journalist in New York City. Not until 1931, when he became Professor of American History at Columbia University, did he devote himself fully to teaching and research. His major work falls into two fields: biography, and a narrative history of the United States from 1847. All his work reflects an awareness of social and economic trends, and he is generally sympathetic to the rise of big business. His conservatism and pre-occupation with character can be seen in his biographies *Grover Cleveland* (1932), subtitled 'A Study in Courage', and *Hamilton Fish* (1936). He rejects the muckraking interpretation of the rise of the corporation, stressing the qualities of leadership behind the huge personal fortunes of the late 19th and early 20th centuries. Particular application of his admiration for leadership in the economic sphere came with his 2-volume life *John D. Rockefeller: The Heroic Age of American Enterprise* (1940), revised and reissued as *Study in Power: John D. Rockefeller, Industrialist and Philanthropist* (1953) – in which emphasis was placed on the constructive aspects of economic consolidation. *Ford* (with F. E. Hill, 2 vols., 1954, 1957) also celebrates the heroic age of American business activity, showing Ford as an enlightened leader, though the authors criticize his increasingly autocratic ways during the inter-war years.

Nevins's history of the United States since 1847 began with *The Ordeal of the Union* (2 vols., 1947) and continued in *The Emergence of Lincoln* (2 vols., 1950) and *The War for the Union* (2 vols., 1959). This excellent, well-written narrative illustrates his belief that history should be seen whole, with the complete culture of the age displayed before the reader, and that only by an acknowledgement of the complexity of society can the historian hope to detach a satisfactory interpretation of climactic events. Nevins suggests that behind the slavery issue lay a race question; the crucial fact was not that the Negro was a slave, but that the slave was a Negro. However, he does not seem to accept the irrepressible conflict theory, feeling that had there been a series of strong instead of weak presidents during the 1850s some compromise solution might have been worked out to keep the union intact. [D K A]

**New Criticism, The.** A movement in American academic criticism starting in the 1920s, dominating most subsequent critical and educational approaches, and still influential. 'New Criticism' can be broadly characterized by its emphasis on the *autonomy* of a given literary work; it has made its purpose the 'close reading' of a single text, regarding biographical material, information about the writer's ideas, the work's reception, etc., as secondary. A work

of art is a concrete whole, a complete experience in itself, an unparaphrasable entity. It is also a *verbal* experience, a pattern of language working – unlike, say, science or discursive prose – by concentration, irony and ambiguity. The distinctiveness of literature lies in its capacity to be simultaneously particular and universal; hence it has a clear function (virtually an anti-scientific one) and great educational value in training responsiveness.

The movement's assumptions (and its philosophical emphasis) derive fairly directly from the criticism of Eliot and Pound and, through them, of Hulme and Bergson; particularly in its stress on the discreteness of literature. Hence it is closely linked with the modern movement in literature itself, and has certainly influenced much literary practice. Out of it has come some of the best of modern criticism, particularly of poetry – its emphasis on possessing a work as a sustained, complete experience, as an 'image', has made it rather less effective with fiction and drama. But the names associated with it – John Crowe ◊ Ransom, Allen ◊ Tate, Robert Penn ◊ Warren, Cleanth ◊ Brooks, R. P. ◊ Blackmur, Yvor ◊ Winters – are among the most important in modern criticism (some are also leading creative writers). Not all were totally united, and among the names mentioned there are clear differences of perspective (Blackmur and Winters particularly show clear temperamental and theoretical differences). But, like the *Scrutiny* group in England, the tendency profoundly influenced all critical practice; books like Brooks' and Warren's *Understanding Poetry* (1938) spread its influence widely, and its theories had great educational importance, replacing the prevailingly scholarly emphasis of literary study. Like Leavis, these critics had considerable concern with culture and tradition (many of them belonged to the ◊ Fugitives group and were Southerners), and also tended to prefer poetry created in metaphysical or 'concrete' traditions, hence distrusting romanticism.

The term 'the New Criticism' was used as the title for a book by Ransom (1941), one of the most explicit statements. The movement's general premises have been usefully questioned by W. K. ◊ Wimsatt and R. S. ◊ Crane, who represent dissenting but not entirely dissociated tendencies in modern American criticism. Its importance generally lies in its sophistication of practice and of theory; its remarkable critical integrity and insight, a condition of the very high quality of its exponents; and its general cultural influence – on writers, on the condition of letters, on education. Indeed it is because the movement existed that we can regard the 20th century as a great age of criticism.

For discussion of the movement and examples of its work, see *Critiques and Essays in Modern Criticism* (1949), ed. R. W. Stallman; *The Critic's Notebook* (1950), ed. R. W. Stallman; and *Essays in Modern Literary Criticism* (1952), ed. Ray B. West. [MB]

René Wellek, *Concepts of Criticism* (1963); S. E. Hyman, *The Armed Vision* (1948); George Watson, *The Literary Critics* (1962); ed. John Crowe Ransom, *The Kenyon Critics* (1967).

**New Humanism, The.** The name given to the literary and philosophical writings of a group of conservative critics, notably Irving ♦ Babbitt, Norman ♦ Foerster, Paul Elmer ♦ More and Stuart Sherman, who drew together to defend and clarify their literary and moral principles when under attack in the late 1920s. Such common beliefs as the group possessed derived partly from their shared admiration for W. C. ♦ Brownell (1851–1928), who in such works as *Victorian Prose Masters* (1901) advised writers to pay closer attention to the traditions of their culture, and emphasized the central importance of 'discipline' – both ideas central to the Humanist movement.

Probably the most significant common factor in Humanist writing is its stress on the distinctions between God, man and nature, and on man's unique possession of moral and ethical ideas. These interests underline More's long and widely read series, *Shelburne Essays* (1904–21), to which Foerster paid tribute in attempting his own definition: 'humanism should be confined to a working philosophy seeking to make a resolute distinction between man and nature and man and the divine'. The common Humanist attitudes consequent upon this 'philosophy' may be briefly stated. First, they believe man's true nature is that of a controlled and rational being, so that the individual's proper business is the discriminating cultivation of all his faculties. 'The humanist, then as opposed to the humanitarian, is interested in the perfecting of the individual rather than in schemes for the elevation of mankind as a whole, and although he allows largely for sympathy, he

insists that it be disciplined and tempered by judgement' (Babbitt). Second, they wish to encourage and inhabit a society based on reason and control. Babbit attacked contemporary society for its worship of 'the quantitative life' adulterated with 'moral impressionism', claiming that the word *humanitas* 'implies doctrine and discipline, and is applicable not to men in general but only to a select few – it is, in short, aristocratic and not democratic in its implication'. But few of this group would have supported More's notorious claim (in *Aristocracy and Justice*, 1915) that property rights were more important than the human right to life. Third, they believe that a literature which truly reflects and explores man's nature will be primarily ethical and concern itself with moral values, and not with the ideal of self-expression introduced by romanticism. More chronicled *The Drift of Romanticism* (1913), and in 1919 came Babbitt's polemical and scathing *Rousseau and Romanticism*. New Humanist critics unite in praising the restraint of classical writing and in lamenting nearly all modern literature. Fourth, they reassert the supreme value of literature and the study of moral experience in education, and oppose the fashionable rise of the natural sciences. 'The humanities need to be defended today against the encroachments of physical science, as they once needed to be against the encroachments of theology' (Babbitt). (Accounts of the particular qualities of More, Babbitt and Foerster will be found under their separate entries. The early works of Stuart Sherman (1881–1926) – *Matthew Arnold: How to Know Him* (1917) and *On Contemporary Literature* (1917), attaching 'the chaos of naturalism' – are in the Humanist mainstream. Later he took up different and more moderate standards.)

The central document of the movement is *Humanism and America: Essays on the Outlook of Modern Civilization*, edited by Norman Foerster in 1930, to which T. S. Eliot was a contributor. It immediately provoked vigorous and hostile replies in the same year from, among others, Kenneth ♦ Burke, Malcolm ♦ Cowley, Lewis ♦ Mumford, Allen ♦ Tate, Edmund ♦ Wilson and Yvor ♦ Winters in *The Critique of Humanism: A Symposium*, edited by C. Hartley Grattan. The intellectual force of these objections and the marked trend in the thirties towards criticism with a sociological or Marxist bias severely weakened

New Humanist influence; but a deeper reason may have been an ultimate contradiction behind their work. A statement such as this, by Babbitt, appeared to represent the misapplication of a religious ideal: 'The individual who is practising humanistic control is really subordinating to the part of himself which he possesses in common with other men that part of himself which is driving him apart from them.' In 1927 Eliot asked prophetically: 'Is it, in the end, a view of life that will work by itself, or is it a derivative of religion which will work only for a short time in history, and only for a few highly cultivated persons like Mr Babbitt – whose ancestral traditions, furthermore, are Christian, and who is, like many people, at the distance of a generation or so from definite Christian belief? Is it, in other words, durable beyond one or two generations?' [MG]

N. Foerster, *Towards Standards: A Study of the Present Critical Movement in American Letters* (1930); Louis J. A. Mercier, *The Challenge of Humanism* (1933) and *American Humanism and the New Age* (1948).

**Nin, Anais** (1914–    ). Novelist. Born in Paris, of French, Spanish, Danish and Cuban descent, she went to America at 11, and there began the journals – an experiment with language and a life-long confession, as well as the source of her fiction. Volumes 1, 2 (1967) and 3 (1970) are already recognized as masterpieces of self-absorption and analysis. Encouraged by the *avant garde* in Paris in the twenties and thirties (which included Henry ◊ Miller and Antonin Artaud) she began her unique series of novels with *Winter of Artifice* (1939). After a period in her other two professions, dancing and psychology, she returned to America in 1940 and continued to write books which, because publishers turned them down, she printed herself, until Dutton brought out *Ladders to Fire* (1946), a chronicle of erotic attachments among four women written in the form of a lyric series of streams of consciousness. *A Spy in the House of Love* (1954) has been filmed and *The House of Incest* (1949) set to music by Varese. Her other fiction includes *Under a Glass Bell and Other Stories* (1944), *This Hunger* (1945), *Children of the Albatross* (1947), *The Four-Chambered Heart* (1950), *Seduction of the Minotaur* (1961) and most recently *Collages* (1964), a series of portraits of actual people fused into the life of a central fictional character, a young woman painter living in Los Angeles. *Cities of the Interior* (1959) is a collection of five of her fictions (including *Solar Barque*). She has also written *D. H. Lawrence: An Unprofessional Study* (1932) and *The Novel of the Future* (1969), on the theory and technique of fiction. Anais Nin is a master of the *roman fleuve*, whose central theme, she has said, is 'the quest of the self through the intricate maze of modern confusion'. She employs the methods of symbolism, surrealism, psychoanalysis and various kinds of painting, together with technical influences from Lawrence, Henry Miller and Djuna ◊ Barnes. [EM]

Oliver Evans, *Anais Nin* (1968).

**Nordhoff, Charles** (1887–1947). Novelist. Born in England of American parents. After studies at Stanford and Harvard, and ambulance and Lafayette Flying Corps service in France in the First World War, he and James N. Hall went in 1920 to live in Tahiti. Their most famous collaboration was the trilogy *Mutiny on the Bounty* (1932), *Men against the Sea* (1934) and *Pitcairn's Island* (1934). [EM]

**Norris, Frank** (1870–1902). Novelist. He was born in Chicago and lived there until 1884, when his family moved to San Francisco. He then studied art briefly in Paris, where the principal influence upon him was not Zola but Froissart: *Yvernelle*, a juvenile poem which reflects his interest at this time in the Middle Ages, was privately published in 1892. In 1890 he entered the University of California at Berkeley and began to contribute to periodicals and magazines; during a year spent at Harvard (1894–5) he began to write novels. As a war correspondent, he travelled to South Africa and Cuba, then became publisher's reader for Doubleday, where he strongly recommended ◊ Dreiser's *Sister Carrie*. His first published novel, *Moran of the Lady Letty* (1898), was followed by *McTeague* (1899), *Blix* (1899) and *A Man's Woman* (1900). At the time of his death from peritonitis he was engaged on a trilogy on the production, distribution and consumption of wheat; *The Octopus* appeared in 1901, *The Pit* posthumously in 1903, and the third volume was never written. Other posthumously published works were *The Responsibilities of the Novelist* (1903); two collections of tales, *A Deal in Wheat* (1903) and *The Third Circle* (1909); and *Vandover and the Brute* (1914), the manuscript of which was lost for several years. Oscar Lewis edited *Frank Norris of 'The Wave'* (1931), a collection of occasional contributions, and Donald Pizer collected *The Literary Criticism of Frank Norris* (1964).

Norris's first attempt at fiction have little to offer the reader today. *Moran of the Lady Letty* is a short and vigorous sea-story with an improbable heroine engaged in improbable adventures, *Blix* a slight autobiographical tale. Of the two naturalist novels which Norris began at Harvard under Professor Lewis E. Gates, *McTeague* is superior to *Vandover and the Brute*. The latter, set in San Francisco, charts the social descent and final degradation of a lycanthropic artist-hero. It is a youthful and immature work. The downfall of McTeague, an enormous and slow-witted dentist, produces, despite its romantic elements, its melodrama and its overt symbolism, an interesting novel which comes close to being a textbook for naturalistic fiction (◊ Realism). McTeague himself is a living illustration of the naturalist thesis: a man of prodigious strength and low intelligence, he rapidly reverts to a primitive state when his carefully assembled world collapses about him, even developing a sixth sense which warns him of approaching danger.

Norris's most satisfying novel is *The Octopus*, a long and complex book based upon an actual clash in 1880 between farmers in the San Joaquin valley and the Southern Pacific Railroad, the octopus of the title. The vitality and sweep of the writing enable the characters to be more effectively realized than in the earlier works; they are no longer stiff embodiments of a typically naturalistic preoccupation with the forces of heredity, environment and economic determinism. Norris himself would seem to agree with the shadowy Shelgrim, the head of the railroad, who denies the significance of human effort in the inexorable struggle between the major forces of the Wheat and the Railroad. Though the vagueness of these affirmations may be related to Vanamee's mystical vision of the wheat as a dynamic and irresistible natural force, its equation with the man-made iniquities of monopoly produces an evasive rather than a persuasive conclusion. *The Pit* concentrates upon the distribution of the wheat, with the attempt of Curtis Jadwin to corner the market in Chicago.

Though Norris was influenced by Zola, his debt is technical rather than philosophical; there is a great deal in his work that belongs to the older American tradition of romantic protest. He was a consistent thinker, and his novels are often confused and contradictory, sometimes excessively reliant upon traditional devices such as coincidence or upon perversions of naturalist theories of behaviour. Although his criticism shares with his fiction enthusiasm and sincerity, the essays collected in *The Responsibilities of the Novelist* (1903) are finally disappointing. Despite the guarded treatment of sexual relationships and the modish elevation of the Anglo-Saxon in his work, despite the crudities of half-assimilated naturalist doctrines and rather naïve philosophizings, his writing is important in that it represents a sharp break with the genteel tradition in American literature and looks forward to the work of Theodore Dreiser and John Steinbeck. [HD]

*Letters*, ed. F. Walker.
Ed. K. Lohf and E. P. Sheehy, *Frank Norris: A Bibliography* (1959); Franklin Walker, *Frank Norris: A Biography* (1932); Ernest Marchand, *Frank Norris: A Study* (1942); Warren French, *Frank Norris* (1962); Donald Pizer, *The Novels of Frank Norris* (1966).

**Norton, Charles Eliot** (1827–1908). Editor, critic, translator. Son of the American biblical scholar Andrews Norton, he was an active figure in Cambridge, Massachusetts, during the period 1850–1900 when Boston/Cambridge was an important intellectual centre. Professor of Fine Art at Harvard, co-editor of the *North American Review*, critic of literature and art, translator of Dante, editor of Donne's poems, Carlyle's letters and many other volumes, he had close connexions with writers, intellectuals and scholars in the U.S.A., and throughout Europe, which he visited often (see, for instance, his *Notes of Travel and Study in Italy*, 1860). His *Letters* (2 vols., 1913), in addition to revealing his critical viewpoint on the arts, are a cultural record of the Cambridge intellectual aristocracy in its cosmopolitan phase (or, as its critics would say, at the height of the genteel tradition) and a valuable document. [MB]

Edward W. Emerson, *Charles Eliot Norton* (1912).

# O

**O'Brien, Fitz-james** (c. 1828–62). Poet, fiction writer. He was born in Ireland and went to New York in 1852 to enter its Bohemian life and continue his prolific output of poems, stories and plays. He died in the Civil War at the battle of Bloomery Gap. His science fiction is imaginative and well written; three of the best tales are *The Diamond Lens*, *What Was It?* and *The Wondersmith.* [EM]

*Poems and Stories*, ed. W. Winter (1881).
Sam Moskowitz, *Explorers of the Infinite* (1963).

**O'Connor, Edwin** (1918–68). Novelist. Born in Providence, Rhode Island. A former radio announcer, O'Connor developed this experience into a sharp satirical novel about a broadcaster who moves toward demagoguery in *The Oracle* (1951). Another form of demagoguery provides the subject of his second novel, *The Last Hurrah* (1956), which treats Boston political life and the history of an Irish-American party-machine politician. Fascination with Irish-American locations is taken further in *The Edge of Sadness* (1961), a study of a Catholic priest in a decaying city parish. *I Was Dancing* (1964) is about a superannuated vaudeville performer resisting old age. *All in the Family* (1966) concerns the further life of Jack Kinsella, the secretary of the hero of *The Last Hurrah*, Frank Skeffington. [MB]

**O'Connor, Flannery** (1925–64). Novelist and short-story writer. She was born and died in Georgia, and studied in Writer's Workshop at the University of Iowa. She is usually said to be a Southern Gothic and/or Catholic writer. Both are probably true, subject to severe qualification. Her typical characters are indeed God-ridden but not in a way that appears to be uniquely Catholic. Rather they seem the essence of Protestantism, seeking an individual and immediate relationship with God. They stalk him, defy him, try to trick him into some sign by doing the things 'that people have quit doing – like boiling in oil or being a saint or walling up cats'. Even the psychopathic murderer of 'A Good Man Is Hard

to Find' (*The Artificial Nigger*, 1957) commits his murders in an attempt to force God to reveal himself. But grace can be attained only through the kind of self-knowledge arrived at in *The Violent Bear It Away* (1960) by Rayber, who has his eyes burned clean and is able at last to look into his own heart and recognize his real place in the world. Love, however, is not the clue to a saving communion with the world as it is in so many writers. The clue is suffering, and Hazel Motes (*Wise Blood*, 1952) burns out his eyes with quicklime so that he can see better. It is only in the last story she wrote, 'Parker's Back' (*Everything That Rises Must Converge*, 1965), that the vision of harmony underlying all the grotesqueness and agony becomes visible and the wild humour achieves its tragic focus. O. E. Parker is unable to achieve in his own flesh the vision of beauty he once saw in a tattooed man in a circus. Each new tattoo only adds to the mess he is making of himself. Then he has a stern Byzantine Christ tattooed on his back, not for his own eyes this time, and suddenly his very soul becomes an arabesque. He can now confess his secret name, Obadiah, worshipper of God. Clearly Flannery O'Connor is religious if not clearly Catholic, and clearly she is Gothic, although the horror and outrage are subordinated to the God passion and are not ends in themselves. [DC]

S. E. Hyman, *Flannery O'Connor* (University of Minnesota Pamphlet, 1966); ed. M. J. Friedman and L. A. Lawson, *The Added Dimension: The Art and Mind of Flannery O'Connor* (1966); Robert Drake, *Flannery O'Connor* (1966).

**Odets, Clifford** (1906–63). Playwright. He was born in Philadelphia, grew up in New York City, and after high school and work in radio, as an actor, and with Theatre Guild, joined the ◊ Group Theatre in 1930. His early work is the epitome of the socially conscious drama of the thirties and the Stanislavski realism of the Group which he organized with Harold ◊ Clurman and Herbert Biberman. He joined the Communist Party in 1934 and left in 1935, the year of his establishment as a leading dramatist. He left for Hollywood in 1936, an act which shocked the committed theatre of the time. In 1952 he testified before the House Un-American Activities Committee that he resigned from the C.P. when asked to write propaganda.

In 1935 he had four plays on Broadway: *Waiting for Lefty*, a brilliant short play on the New York taximen's strike, with a celebrated agitprop ending and an influential use of European expressionist methods; *Till the Day I Die*, about a communist agent in Nazi Germany; *Paradise Lost*, in which the middle-class Gordon family is pushed by Depression degradation into social rebellion; and *Awake and Sing!*, his finest work, in which a poverty-ridden Jewish family are raised to the level of universal drama; the awakening of Ralph Berger develops through his family: the atheist Marxist grandfather, the mother obsessed by money and acquiescence in the present, Moe's bourgeois dream of paradise, and so on. The Bronx speech and Odets's sentimental progressive optimism are still capable of moving. In *Golden Boy* (1937), the money-success theme is sentimentally embodied in the story of a young boxer-violinist corrupted by the fight world. After these excellent plays appeared the less impressive *I Can't Sleep* (1936), *Night Music* (1940) and *Clash by Night* (1941). But *The Big Knife* (1948) is a first-rate play on success and failure in Hollywood. The loneliness of *Rocket to the Moon* (1938) and so many of his plays is again the centre of *The Country Girl* (1950). *The Flowering Peach* (1954) re-creates the Noah story. Odets's best work concerns the loneliness enforced by people's efforts to succeed in the city. His plays act better than they read and have an authentic life which is unique in the social theatre of the thirties. [EM]

*Golden Boy and Other Plays* (Penguin Plays, 1963); *Six Plays* (Modern Library, 1939).
J. W. Krutch, *The American Drama since 1918* (1939).

**O'Hara, Frank** (1926–66). Poet. He was born in Baltimore, served in the navy 1944–6, studied at Harvard and Michigan, and lived and worked in New York most of his highly productive life. He joined the Museum of Modern Art in 1951, resigned to give more time to his writing, and rejoined it in 1955. As assistant curator he was responsible for the organization of major exhibitions of work by David Smith, Robert Motherwell, Reuben Nakian and Jackson Pollock; among his books on painting are *Jackson Pollock* (1959) and *Robert Motherwell* (1965). A number of his poems were published in collaboration with artists, for example *Odes* (1960), with serigraphs by Michael Goldberg. In 1956 he worked as playwright in residence at the Poet's Theatre, Cambridge, Massachusetts: his plays include *Love's Labour*, *Awake in Spain!*, *What Century?*, *Try! Try!* (in *Artist's Theatre*, ed. H. Machiz, 1960), and *The General Returns from One Place to Another* (in *Eight Plays from Off-Off Broadway*, ed. N. Orzel and M. Smith, 1966). His plays were produced in many *avant garde* theatres: his verse play *The Houses at Fallen Hanging* was played by the Living Theatre in 1956. His poetry is associated with that of Kenneth ◊ Koch and John ◊ Ashbery in Donald Allen's *The New American Poetry* (1960), as part of the 'New York Poets', but his poems have a decided originality of their own: *A City Winter and Other Poems* (1952), *Oranges* (1953), *Meditations in an Emergency* (1957), *Second Avenue* (a long poem issued as a pamphlet, 1960), *Odes* (1960), *Lunch Poems* (1964), and *Love Poems* (*Tentative Title*) (1965). His poems have a visual detail and accuracy which is the location of their exuberance and joy; but they contain a certain melancholy confronted with cruelty and callousness. His musical references are witty and surprising; his love poems are tender and inventive. His sense of New York is unique. His forms are elegant without being fussy, poised and sophisticated without being exhibitionist. His tragic death in an accident was a major loss to American poetry and painting. [EM]

Ed. M. Anania and C. Doria, *Audit-Poetry*, IV, 1 (1964).
Richard Howard, *Alone with America* (1969).

**O'Hara, John** (1905–70). Novelist. Born in Pittsburg, Philadelphia. He began as a journalist ('I have done everything . . . on the editorial side, from covering girls' field hockey to a Congressional investigation') and in 1964 his byline was still to be read in the weekend edition of the Long Island *Newsday*. His literary credo appears clearly in the preface to *Sermons and Soda Water* (1960), three novellas which are among his best work: 'I want to get it all down on paper while I can. . . . I want to record the way people talked and thought and felt, and to do it with complete honesty and variety.' His first short stories concerned the life of country clubs, bars and the theatre, and throughout his career he has turned out a huge number of stories, works where is best located what Lionel ◊ Trilling calls his 'exacerbated social awareness'. The volumes include *The Doctor's Son* (1935), *Files on Parade* (1939), *Pipe Night* (1945), *Hellbox* (1947), *Assembly* (1961), *The Cape Cod Lighter* (1962), *The Horse Knows the Way* (1964) and *Waiting for Winter* (1967). The last two volumes are notable for their refusal to glamorize the bleak lives they record and their understated style, tense with underground alienated life, either evaded or panicky. *Waiting for Winter* is an extraordinary series of studies in slow ageing and seedy frustration. *And Other Stories* (1968) is a cycle of 12 deftly told stories of wealthy misery.

O'Hara's novels include *Appointment in Samarra* (1934), *BUtterfield 8* (1935), of which the historian Allan Nevins has said no one could understand 1930s America without reading it, *Hope of Heaven* (1938), *A Rage to Live* (1949), *The Farmer's Hotel* (1951) and *Ten North Frederick* (1955). *From the Terrace* (1959) is an over-large novel with most of O'Hara's vices: heaped-up detail, soupy nostalgia and boring sexuality. *Elizabeth Appleton* (1963) is another college novel, redeemed by its nailing down of campus life, suburban sex and wretched small-town power drives. *The Big Laugh* (1962) is a good novel of Hollywood in its 1930s heyday, and *The Lockwood Concern* (1965) is O'Hara's best since 1934 – a large novel of four generations of business family in Pennsylvania, a plot typically packed with suicide, murder, big deals and romantic social and sexual power ploys. None of these novels moves technically into the 20th-century area of experimental forms: the nearest would be *Ourselves to Know* (1960), which builds the story of a respectable Pennsylvanian who shoots his girl wife from the narrator's interpretation of documents, letters and manuscripts. *Lovely Childs* (1969) is a late study of wild oats sown and happy marriage reaped. *Pal Joey* (1940), a series of letters from a night-club singer, dramatized by O'Hara with others, became a most successful musical comedy, one of the finest scripts of its kind. *Five Plays* appeared in 1961 and

*Sweet and Sour* (1954) is a collection of some of his literary journalism.

O'Hara's fiction is preoccupied with social distinctions, the social and sexual codes of the wealthy and not so wealthy, located in Gibbsville, and other fictional forms of the native Pennsylvania, which is his Yoknapatawpha. But he also mastered the environments of New York and Hollywood for characters which appear much the same in all his work. His tone is jaunty and ironic, the equivalent of his refusal to reach introspectively too far into the life which obsesses him. His theme is the ironic gap between social and private selves. His strength lies in excellent dialogue which embodies social differences and a shrewd knowledge of a class stratum shunned by most intellectuals and their novelists as untouchable. But his later novels cannot resist a sheer accumulation of details about the external lives of his privileged Americans and their squandered affluence. If America has reared the Trollope it deserves, O'Hara is just that. [HB/EM]

Edward R. Carson, *The Fiction of John O'Hara* (1961).

**Olson, Charles** (1910–      ). Poet, critic. He was born in Worcester, Massachusetts, and formally educated at the Universities of Yale, Harvard and Wesleyan. He taught at Clark, Harvard and at ◊ Black Mountain College (instructor and rector 1951–6), where he began his continuing influence on American poetry, both in his theories of form and content, and in his own extensive practice. His first publication was an essay, 'Lear and Moby Dick' (1938, in *Twice-a-Year*). In 1952 he studied Mayan hieroglyphics in Yucatan. Until recently he was a governing force in the Department of Further Studies at New York State University, Buffalo. Of his prose, *Call Me Ishmael* (1947) is a searching essay on the meaning of Melville's *Moby Dick*; *Mayan Letters* (1953), letters to Robert ◊ Creeley on Mayan remains, is also an initiatory part of his personal rhetoric and his creative anthropology, the bases of his poetic vocation as well; and *Human Universe and Other Essays* (1965) is a massive collection of important essays, issued since 1950. They include the highly influential article 'Projective Verse' (1950), a discussion of 'composition by field', form as extension of content, and the line as a structure of syllable and 'breath'. Some of Olson's ideas extend principles in Pound and E. F. Fenollosa, the oriental art critic, but also derive from the work done at Black Mountain College with other poets. In *Letters for Origin 1950–1956* (1969) Olson discusses his philosophy of form and the idea of a literary journal (*Origin* being the important magazine founded by the poet Cid Corman). His poetry is some of the finest written this century, and is included in *In Cold Hell, in Thicket* (1953) and *The Distances* (1961), poems which make precise statements of personal experience given meaning in a discriminated historical and geographical context, strongly critical of urban democratic capitalism and its depredations of basically agrarian life. This work receives its most complete form to date in *The Maximus Poems* (1–10, 1953; 11–22, 1956; combined in 1960; and *Maximus IV, V, VI*, 1968), a remarkable series of lyrical, sociological and formal experimental poems, which together with Pound's *Cantos* and William Carlos ◊ Williams's poetry makes up the basic poetics of a great deal of American poetry since the 1950s. *O'Ryan* (1965) is 10 witty poetic examinations of the myth punned in the title. *A Bibliography on America for Ed Dorn* (1964) extends Pound's methods out of Frobenius and Williams's *In the American Grain* to form a plan of the process of the formation of America – in 16 pages. *Proprioception* (1965) is another bibliographic reading plan, in Olson's characteristic rhetoric of prose and verse together. *West* (1966) does this for the Red Indian and the land, and *Stocking Cap* (1966) is a reprint of a short story of 1951. *Charles Olson Reading at Berkeley* (1966) is a rough transcription of a reading at the Poetry Conference of 1965, available on tape. In *Causal Mythology* (1969) he states the basis of his use of myth. [EM]

Selected Writings, ed. Robert Creeley (1966).
G. F. Butterwick and A. Glover, *A Bibliography of Works by Charles Olson* (1967); Ann Charters, *Olson/Melville: A Study in Affinity* (1968).

**Olson, Elder.** ◊ Chicago Aristotelians.

**O'Neill, Eugene** (1888–1953). Playwright. Born in New York City, America's greatest playwright was the son of actors James O'Neill and Ellen Quinlan. After Catholic and private schools, he took a year at Princeton in 1906, married in 1909, divorced in 1912, and after a period of unsatisfying jobs became a seaman, a career which furnished him with subjects and characters for the rest of his life. A spell of acting and reporting ended when he entered a sanatorium after a breakdown; recovering there from tuberculosis, he read the great dramatists of the world, looked back into his sea life and his family's unstable complexities, and wrote his first play, *The Web* (1913–14). In 1914 he joined George Pierce ◊ Baker's 47 Workshop at Harvard. The Provincetown Players produced his first performed play, *Bound East for Cardiff*, in 1916, the date of the beginning of serious American theatre. They put on three more of his sea plays and produced ten of his works when the company moved to New York (1917–20). Between 1918 and 1929 he won the Pulitzer Prize for *Beyond the Horizon* (1920) and *Anna Christie* (1921), married again, divorced, and married Carlotta Monterey, who survived him. The great cycles of plays he worked at in the later thirties and forties were frustrated by Parkinson's disease and repeated suffering from alcoholism and family neuroses. For 12 years after *Days without End* (1934) he had no play on Broadway, although he won the Nobel Prize in 1936. The last and finest stage of his career began with *The Iceman Cometh* (1946).

O'Neill had no serious theatre tradition to work on: he created his own out of his reading and first-hand practice. He is part of the generation of Joyce and Eliot, deeply concerned with European expressionism (Strindberg in particular) and with modern psychology as an instrument to analyse the classical and biblical myths. Nietzschean philosophy reinforced his American need to explore the nature of self-reliance and heroic individualism. His experimental forms were the expression of this complexity. *The Emperor Jones* (1920) is the monologue of the Negro dictator of a West Indian state, declining Darwinianly to the accompaniment of accelerating drums and stage sets which symbolize his fears. In *The Hairy Ape* (1922), the stoker Yank, dislocated from nature and society, is crushed by a gorilla at the conclusion of a symbolic search for himself. This is the theme and manner of *Desire under the Elms* (1924), with its opened-house set, *All God's Chillun Got Wings* (1924), a high stylization of miscegenation problems, and *The Great God Brown* (1926), an extraordinary conflict of private and external selves displayed through masks and Greek and Nietzschean references. In *Marco Millions* (1928) O'Neill transposes satire on American commercialism to the Venice of Marco Polo. The search for self, already treated through the Ponce de Leon story in *The Fountain* (1925), is best handled at this period in *Strange Interlude* (1928), a long psychological study of a woman, using a modern version of soliloquy to express inner life. The symbolism of *Dynamo* (1929) is too crude, the dynamo being 'science', which fills the gap left by 'religion'. *Lazarus Laughed* (1926), which O'Neill mistakenly believed was his best play, is a choral drama of huge forces and ecstatic affirmative laughter.

The masterpiece of his middle career is *Mourning Becomes Electra* (1931), a trilogy transposing the House of Atreus into the New England Mannon family during the Civil War, with Aeschylean fate reinterpreted through modern psychological destiny. *Ah, Wilderness!* (1933) and *Days without End* (1934) are family plays of less importance. Between 1934 and 1943 O'Neill planned and began to execute a cycle of one-act plays, *By Way of Orbit* (of which *Hughie*, 1942, is a small masterpiece), and a cycle of full-length plays, *A Tale of Possessors Dispossessed*, the dramatic developments of interrelated families. In what O'Neill managed to write, Sarah Harford appears as a girl in *A Touch of the Poet* (1958) and as a married woman in *More Stately Mansions* (1965); and the superb *Long Day's Journey into Night* (1956) and *A Moon for the Misbegotten* (1957) present members of the Tyrone family. To these magnificent achievements can be added *The Iceman Cometh* (1946), which deals simply and grandly with the illusions and disillusions of a group of men in an archetypal bar – the measure of the final climax of a long strenuous career.

O'Neill's best work has an intensity of passion and a sense of theatre action which his faults of rhetoric and symbolism can withstand. His courage and endless experiment created an American theatre out of nothing, a series of plays which represent American culture between the wars and which can be compared only with the finest poetry and novels. [EM]

A. and B. Gelb, *O'Neill* (1962); ed. O. Cargill, etc., *O'Neill and His Plays* (1962); Edwin A. Engel, *The Haunted Heroes of Eugene O'Neill*

(1953); B. H. Clark, *Eugene O'Neill: The Man and His Plays* (1947); L. Sheaffer, *O'Neill, Son and Playwright* (1968).

**Oppen, George** (1908– ). Poet. He was born in New Rochelle, N.Y., and lives in Brooklyn. His first book of poems, *Discrete Series* (1934, repr. 1966), was prefaced by Ezra Pound, who wrote: 'I salute a serious craftsman.' It is the terse, concentrated quality of these short poems that impresses; they are an epitome of the Objectivist movement with which he was associated with Louis ◊ Zukofsky, Charles ◊ Reznikoff and others. His poems appeared in the *Objectivists Anthology*, *Active Anthology* (ed. Pound), *Poetry, Hound and Horn* and a number of little magazines of the thirties, and were part of the extension of ◊ Imagist and Objectivist precision of language and form which came to be of major importance in Pound, Williams and Zukofsky. In the forties his work appeared in the little magazines and finally in two important volumes, *The Materials* (1962) and *This Is Which* (1965), poetry whose craft and inquiring intelligence are a significant influence on contemporary American poetry. His finest book is his most recent: *Of Being Numerous* (1968). [EM]

**Oppenheimer, Joel** (1930– ). Poet, playwright. He was born and educated in New York, studied at Cornell and Chicago Universities and went to ◊ Black Mountain College. He worked as a printer-typographer until recently, when he became programme director of a Federal arts project centred on St Mark's-in-the-Bowerie, New York. His first two books of poetry were published by Jonathan Williams's Jargon Press: *The Dancer* (1952) and *The Dutiful Son* (1956), personal lyrics deeply in the tradition of lyrical poetry of private life since the Provençal poets, and with the same wary respect for and challenge to women. This style is excellently developed in *The Love Bit* (1962). *A Treatise* (1966) is a long poem of social criticism. *The Great American Desert* (1966) is a collection of plays, the title drama being a brilliant short epitome of the Western myth. *Bad Times in Bummersville* was produced in 1968. Oppenheimer's strength lies in durably honest and drily passionate poems of love and friendship, and a witty critical eye for the urban-pastoral relationship. [EM]

# P

**Pack, Robert** (1929–    ). Poet. Born in New York City and educated at Dartmouth College and Columbia University, he taught for a number of years at Barnard College. Besides four volumes of poetry – *The Irony of Joy* (1955), *A Stranger's Privilege* (1959), *Guarded by Women* (1963) and *Home from the Cemetery* (1970) – he has written a book on Wallace ◊ Stevens, translated Mozart's librettos, composed children's books and helped to edit the influential series *New Poets of England and America*. The metaphysical speculations of his own poetry depend largely on concentrated verbal effects. [BP]

**Page, Thomas Nelson** (1853–1922). Novelist. Born in Hanover, Virginia, he was a lawyer many of whose romantic works were devoted to a sentimental reconstruction and justification of the old South. From 1913 to 1919 he was ambassador to Italy. *Marse Chan*, a tale in dialect, was included in the collection *In Ole Virginia* (1887); his first novel was *On Newfound River* (1891). Among Page's most popular works were *Red Rock* (1898), a fictional account of Reconstruction from the Southern point of view, and *John Marvel, Assistant* (1909), the action of which is set in Chicago. [H D]

The Novels, Stories, Sketches and Poems (18 vols., 1906–18).
Rosewell Page, *Thomas Nelson Page* (1923); Jay B. Hubbell, 'Thomas Nelson Page', in *The South in American Literature* (1954).

**Paine, Thomas** (1737–1809). Political philosopher, revolutionary. Born in Thetford, England, he had little schooling and worked at a number of jobs, including tax collector. ◊ Franklin persuaded him to emigrate to America, where on his recommendation, he edited the *Pennsylvania Magazine* in Philadelphia (1775). His essays on rights for women and Negroes, international arbitration and copyright, and humanitarianism were original and much needed in America. He won Washington's respect during the 1776 retreat in New Jersey, when he wrote the first of his *The American*

*Crisis* series of 13 pamphlets (1776–83), arousing new energy for the revolution. *Common Sense* (1776) had made him a major influence on the emerging republic, attacking monarchy and containing some famous words: 'Government, even in its best state, is but a necessary evil; in its worst state, an intolerable one'. In 1787 he returned to Europe, promoting his iron-bridge invention and entering French Revolution politics. His international revolutionary principles caused him to break with ◊ Jefferson's moderate reform. In England his books were burned by the public hangman. In reply to Burke's *Reflections on the French Revolution* (1790) he wrote *The Rights of Man* (1791–2) and dedicated it to Washington. Escaping to France, he took part in drafting a constitution but voted against the king's execution and supported the moderates. Robespierre's own death just prevented Paine's execution. Part of *The Age of Reason* (1794, 1796) he wrote in prison. In 1802 he returned to America and lived in New York State, poor, ill, attacked unfairly. Although he asked to be buried on his farm, William Cobbett took the coffin to England, and was not permitted to bury it. The remains are lost. In spite of being defended by Lincoln, Whitman and others, Paine remained largely hated and feared in America for his extremism and so-called atheism (he was in fact an ordinary deist), only rehabilitated a little after Moncure D. Conway's biography in (1892) and collection of his writings (1894–6). Today his New Rochelle cottage is a memorial. His pamphlets, poems and books are many, but his masterpieces are clear and outstanding. *The Rights of Man* affirms natural rights, the right to choose government, and the need to reject hereditary ruling classes. *The Age of Reason* is a popularization of 18th-century rationalist ideas on religion and philosophy – 'divine' revelations are myths, God's beneficence is manifest in his creation, every man has the right to follow the worship he prefers, Christianity like all traditional religions is a preposterous tool of enslavement against science and learning. The principles of this courageous and outspoken man were always directed towards humanitarian relationships in the world at large, not towards nation or class alone. His writings are clear, and he trusted that reason would bring about freedom and justice. His influence on American revolutionary thought was incalculably deep, ever since Washington said 'I find *Common Sense* working a powerful change in the minds of men'. [EM]

*Writings*, ed. P. Foner (2 vols., 1945).
W. E. Woodward, *Thomas Paine: America's Godfather* (1945).

**Parker, Dorothy** (1893–1967). Humorist, story writer, poet. Born at West End, New Jersey, she began her writing career with *Vogue* and reviewed for *Vanity Fair*, the *New Yorker* and *Esquire*. Famous for her spoken wit, she showed in reviews, poems and sketches the same note of trenchant commentary. Her cynicism and the concentration of her judgements were famous; and while she was not always a reliable critic or a wise judge of manners her contempt for the sentimental, the stupid and the provincial were always enlivening. Her poems, usually ironic commentaries on love and the relationship between the sexes, have been collected in the volume *Not So Deep as a Well* (1936). Her stories, many of them analogous to revue sketches, and often devastatingly pointed, are also collected, in *Here Lies* (1939). With Elmer ♦ Rice she wrote a play, *Close Harmony* (1924); and she was closely associated with the development of modern urbane humour. In 1944 the *Viking Portable Dorothy Parker* made available all her main work. [MB]

**Parkman, Francis** (1823–93). Historian. Son of a Boston 'Brahmin' minister, he became interested in Indians at Harvard and undertook an expedition to the frontier with his cousin Quincy Adams Shaw, recorded in his famous travel book, *The Oregon Trail* (1849), in which his 'tour of curiosity and amusement' turns into a taxing and dangerous journey. Its observations on the customs of behaviour of the Sioux and Pawnee Indians, its heroic conception of the journey, and its skill in catching the spirit of the rising West give it an almost Scott-like fictional intensity. Strained in health and going blind, Park-

man turned to horticulture, and became for a spell Professor in the subject at Harvard; but above all he went on to his main work as a historian, the magnificent history *France and England in North America* (9 vols., 1851–92). Conceived as an account of the French war in Canada, it extended to cover the whole conflict in America between France and Britain, and the struggle of both powers with the Indians. Of the eight separate works in the series, *Montcalm and Wolfe* (1884), about the climax of the imperial clash and the death of both leaders, won most contemporary acclaim and remains the classic account of the period; though all volumes have stood well and are still widely consulted.

Parkman saw history finally as the delayed triumph of progressive forces, but shared Scott's ambition to recapture the spirit of an era, and his favourite subject was (as for Scott and Cooper) the description of important battles amid magnificent natural scenes. 'I was haunted with wilderness images day and night,' he noted; but his complex story is a piece of superb construction, incorporating scenes and causes, particular facts and large historical movements, with the wilderness and the advent of civilization as his main theme. His epical dimensions sometimes lead him to be classed with literary historians, but he used carefully numerous manuscript sources in the U.S.A. and Europe, followed the paths of his heroes and armies and noted geographical features and oral traditions. Though there are clear prejudices on religious matters, notably about Catholicism, his sense of the interaction of individuals and groups, and his determinism mitigated by a sense of geographical, climatic and other factors also give his work historical strength. Parkman also wrote a novel, *Vassall Morton* (1856), and his *Journals* (ed. Mason Wade, 2 vols., 1947) are important memoirs. [MG/DKA]

*Works* (12 vols., 1922); *The Parkman Reader*, ed. S. E. Morison (1955).
Mason Wade, *Francis Parkman: Heroic Historian* (1942); Howard Doughty, *Francis Parkman* (1962); Otis A. Pease, *Francis Parkman's History: The Historian as Literary Artist* (1953).

**Parrington, Vernon L(ouis)** (1871–1929). Historian, critic. He is best known as the author of *Main Currents of American*

*Thought: An Interpretation of American Literature from the Beginnings to 1920*, first published in 3 volumes, two in 1927, the third posthumously and incomplete in 1930. Parrington, a Professor of English at the University of Washington, won a Pulitzer Prize and immediate renown with the book, the first attempt to write a large-scale intellectual history of colonial America and the United States round a general interpretative thesis. His introduction defines the aim as tracing in American letters the genesis of certain germinal ideas that are reckoned traditionally American, following 'the broad path of our political, economic, and social development, rather than the narrower belletristic'. The first volume discusses the rise of New England Puritanism and contrasts Jonathan Edwards and Roger Williams as representatives of authoritarianism and liberty, and then goes on to trace the emergence of agrarianism as a dominant national characteristic as settlement spread westwards. The second volume, covering 1800 to the Civil War, examines the impact of industrialization, seeing the 'coonskin Jacksonians' and the Southern 'Greek democracy' as attempts to prevent this change and maintain older agrarian values. The unfinished third volume relates literature to the post-Civil-War growth of reform movements that were trying to resist the development of a centralized capitalist state.

Brought up in Kansas, Parrington has a strong, confessedly liberal, Jeffersonian belief in an individualistic and agrarian free democracy. The book's weaknesses – such as its famous elevation of James Branch ◊ Cabell over Henry James, its stress on realism, etc. – are apparent; but its scholarly range and its exploitation of the cultural commitments of the period in which it was written make it both useful and a significant American monument. Though the patterns traced by Parrington no longer find general acceptance among historians, the approach did much to condition the outlook of the subsequent generation of scholars; it also influenced many literary critics towards an environmentalist, 'Taine-ian' approach. Lionel Trilling speaks of its deep impact on 'our conception of American culture', and points out some of the ways its influence has been harmful. [D K A/M B]

Lionel Trilling, 'Reality in America', *The Liberal*

*Imagination* (1950); Richard Hofstadter, *The Progressive Historians* (1968).

**Passos, John Dos.** ◊ Dos Passos, John.

**Patchen, Kenneth** (1911– ). Poet, novelist, painter. He was born in Ohio, and after one year at Alexander Meiklejohn's Experimental College, University of Wisconsin, he worked at 17 in a steel mill, as his father did. He has since held many jobs while maintaining himself as a poet. His poetic language was from the first contemporary and his material leftist in its social criticism. For the poems in *The Dark Kingdom* (1942) he painted water-colours and he has frequently designed his poems as visual pages of script and image. His early work also included *Before the Brave* (1936), *First Will and Testament* (1939), *The Teeth of the Lion* (1942) and *Cloth of the Tempest* (1943). His forms include short lyrics, odes, prose poems and ballads; his reputation was built largely on his love poetry (some of the finest of the century) and his scathing satire. In 1941 came his prose *The Journal of Albion Moonlight*, a brilliant allegorical journey to H Roivas, written in a surreal style of certain originality, with a hero who takes his place among the triumphs of existential literature. The novel *Memoirs of a Shy Pornographer* (1945) is nearly as good, written as a series of satirical episodes and dialogues. His other prose includes *Sleepers Awake* (1946) and *See You in the Morning* (1948), a novel, and the prose pieces in *They Keep Riding Down All the Time* (1946). The poetry continued in *An Astonished Eye Looks Out of the Air* (1945), *Pictures of Life and of Death* (1946), *Panels for the Walls of Heaven* (1947, prose poems), *Red Wine and Yellow Hair* (1949), one of his finest and most representative volumes, and *To Say If You Love Someone* (1950). *Selected Poems* appeared in 1946 and in an enlarged edition in 1957; further selections appeared as *Poems of Humour and Protest* (1956) and *The Love Poems of Kenneth Patchen* (1960), useful paperback editions.

After years of serious illness, he suffered a major spinal operation in 1951, but in spite of his painful incapacitation, Patchen continues to pour out his abundant gifts, against the worst odds. The poetry appears in *Orchards, Thrones and Caravans* (1952), *Fables and Other Little Tales* (1954), *The Famous Boating Party* (1954, prose poems), *When We Were Here Together* (1957,

includes *Orchards...*). *Doubleheader* (1966)
reprints *Hurrah for Anything* (1957, poems
and drawings), *Poemscapes* (1958, prose
poems), *A Letter to God* (1946; repr. from
the pamphlet by Henry Miller, *Patchen,
Man of Anger and Light*). *Because It Is*
(1960) is a remarkably free and exuberant
series of surreal poems and drawings; the
comparisons often made with Blake and
Edward Lear are not at all inept. *Hallelujah
Anyway* (1966) is a good collection of his
picture poems (see also *Tri-Quarterly*, Fall,
1964). The first major English edition of his
poems appeared in 1968 (*Selected Poems*,
ed. Nathaniel Tarn). *Love and War Poems*
(1967) is a first-rate selection which includes a useful collection of criticism of
Patchen. He is a typically American poet in
his native exuberance and freedom of form
and in his inheritance from European lyrical
and surrealist traditions. But finally he is
unique in his passion and intensely personal
character. [EM]

*Collected Poems* (1968).

**Patrick, John** (pseud. of John Patrick
Goggan) (1905–     ). Playwright. After
attending Harvard and Columbia and
writing two relatively unnoticed Broadway plays, he made his name with *The
Hasty Heart* (1945) which drew upon his
experiences as an ambulance driver in the
Second World War. *The Story of Mary
Surratt* (1947) and *The Curious Savage*
(1951) were among subsequent plays,
but another big success came with his
stage adaptation of Vern Schneider's novel
*The Teahouse of the August Moon* (1953).
This wartime comedy about American
soldiers building a teahouse on Okinawa
won various prizes, including the Pulitzer.
More recently most of his work has been
for the cinema, and his screenplays include
*Three Coins in the Fountain* and *Love Is a
Many-Splendored Thing*. [MB]

**Paul, Elliot** (1891–1958). Journalist, editor,
novelist. Born in Malden, Massachusetts.
He remained in Paris as a newspaperman
after the First World War, was associated
with several of the expatriate magazines,
and with Eugene Jolas he edited the last
and largest of them: *transition* (♢ Little
Magazines). Although Paul published
several novels in his early thirties, much of
his work may be described as an extended
autobiography, to which he himself gave the
title 'Items on the Grand Account'. This

sequence begins with what is probably his
best work, *The Life and Death of a Spanish
Town* (1937), an account of his life in a
village on Ibiza from 1931 to the irruption
of the Spanish Civil War. Other works in
this series which concern themselves with
his native land are *Linden on the Saugus
Branch* (1947), *Ghost Town on the Yellow-
stone* (1948), *My Old Kentucky Home* (1949)
and *Desperate Scenery* (1954). The success
of his parody *The Mysterious Mickey Finn*
(1939) led him to write crime novels, including *Hugger-Mugger in the Louvre* (1940)
and *The Black Gardenia* (1952).

Among Paul's most popular books are
his two tributes to his adopted city: *The
Last Time I Saw Paris* (1942; British title
*A Narrow Street*) and its sequel *Springtime
in Paris* (1950). These fictionalized accounts
of his experiences exhibit Paul's strengths
and weaknesses as a writer: a keen and
perceptive observer of life, he was not
entirely free from sentimentality when
recording it, with the consequence that he
will perhaps be remembered more for his
role in the literary history of the United
States than for any actual contribution
towards its literature. [HD]

**Paulding, James Kirke** (1778–1860). Satirist,
poet, playwright, essayist. He was born in
New York State, a contemporary and friend
of Washington ♢ Irving, with whom he
collaborated on *Salmagundi* (1807–8). The
second series of *Salmagundi* (1819–20),
sketches on New York written in character
in the manner of the 18th-century English
essayists, was entirely his. Unlike Irving,
Paulding stayed in the U.S.A., and his work
is strongly patriotic; *The Diverting History
of John Bull and Brother Jonathan* (1812) is a
satire on the settlement and revolution of
the United States. He parodied Scott in
*The Lay of the Scottish Fiddle* (1813) and
Anglo-American relations in *A Sketch of
Old England* (1822) and *John Bull in
America* (1825). He wrote plays (*The
Bucktails; or Americans in England*, 1847,
and *The Lion of the West*, 1831) and epic
verse (*The Backwoodsman*, 1818) but turned
more and more to tales and sketches,
drawing largely on American materials –
the New York Dutch, the woodsmen, the
pioneers. *The Dutchman's Fireside* (1831)
draws on the New York Dutch before the
Revolution, *Westward Ho!* (1832) is set in
Kentucky, and *The Old Continental* (1846)
is about the revolution in New York.

Paulding – who was late in life Secretary of the Navy – is a fascinating representative of the American literary mind at the time of Irving and Cooper, to both of whom he has close similarities, and by both of whom he has been overshadowed. [MB]

Amos L. Herold, *James Kirke Paulding: Versatile American* (1926).

**Payne, John Howard** (1791–1852). Dramatist. He grew up in Boston, and, in 1805, as a New York merchant's clerk, was already publishing his *Thespian Mirror*, 'to promote the interests of American drama'. At 15 his first play, *Julia, or, The Wanderer*, was performed. Sent to college by backers, he left through lack of funds and became a successful actor. In 1813 he began a 20-year period in London and Paris as playwright and adaptor; he courted Mary Shelley unsuccessfully, and returned to America in 1832, broke. Theatre benefit performances brought him $10,000, and he was given a consulship at Tunis. His most famous play was *Brutus, or, The Fall of Tarquin* (1818) but his fame rests with his words for Sir Henry Bishop's 'Home, Sweet Home', a song in his play *Clari, The Maid of Milan* (1823). His best play is *Charles II* (1924), a comedy (with Irving; see A. H. Quinn: *Representative American Plays*, 1917). The best biography is by Grace Overmyer (1957). [EM]

*America's Lost Plays*, ed. C. Hislop and W. R. Richardson (vols. 5 and 6, 1940).

**Peck, George Wilbur** (1840–1916). Newspaperman. Born in Huderson, N.Y. His newspaper, *Sun*, was so popular he was elected mayor of Milwaukee and governor of the state (1890–4); he remains moderately famous for his humorous tales *Peck's Bad Boy and His Pa* (1883), a series of which thousands of copies were sold. The last was *Peck's Bad Boy with the Cowboys* (1907). [EM]

**Peirce, Charles Sanders** (1839–1914). Logician, metaphysician. Born in Cambridge, Massachusetts, the son of Benjamin Peirce, Professor of Astronomy and Mathematics at Harvard, he attended Harvard and spent his working life in the U.S. Coast Survey until 1891, when he retired to write. He maintained his connexion with advanced thought in Cambridge, and though never widely known during his lifetime, made many original contributions to journals, on meta-physics, logic and other scientific matters. The bulk of Peirce's writing was not published until 1931–51, in *The Collected Papers of Charles Sanders Peirce*, ed. C. Hartshorne, P. Weiss and A. W. Burks. Peirce coined the term 'pragmatism' as a name for his philosophy. The approach was popularized by William ◊ James, with whom it is more commonly associated, but Peirce could not (with some justice) recognize his thought in James's formulation, and renamed his philosophy 'pragmaticism' by way of distinction. The standardization of philosophical language, so that philosophy might one day be put on a scientific basis, was always one of his *desiderata*: it shows, perhaps, both the stressed objectivity of his work and a certain naïveté in respect of philosophical idiosyncrasy. Peirce's logical analysis was not conducted in the symbolic language of post-Russell and Whitehead logicians, but in the discursive *exempla* of previous centuries. This non-mathematical prose of his essays makes them a considerable index of cultural opinion. It would not be too much to say that we have here the most keenly and solidly analytic mind in America in the 19th century operating, if only by the way, on the material of his civilization. Certain distinctions, fashioned to explain logical functions, tell us as much about the major socio-cultural dimensions of his time (see the distinction between acting, thinking and being). [AG]

Ed. Justus Buchler, *The Philosophy of Peirce* (1956); W. B. Gallie, *Peirce and Pragmatism* (1952).

**Penn, William** (1644–1718). Founder of Pennsylvania. Expelled from Oxford in 1662 for his beliefs, he travelled in France and Italy, tried the navy, the law, and managing his father's estates in Ireland, where he was imprisoned for the Quakerism he later expounded in *No Cross, No Crown* (1669). *The Great Case of Liberty of Conscience* (1670) was written during one of his many prison spells. In 1671 he founded a Quaker society in Holland, married, and in 1672 settled in Hertfordshire. Having become a proprietor of part of America, he went to the colony and drew up a constitution for what became a Quaker settlement in West Jersey. In 1677 he recruited more Quakers in Germany for Germantown, the early name of Philadelphia. In 1681 he asked for and received from Charles II a tract of land in America in payment of a debt to his father; it became the future Pennsylvania, designed by Penn as a Quaker state (*A Brief Account of the Province of Pennsylvania*, 1682, and *A Further Account . . .* , 1685). He made a famous pact with Indians whom in *Letter to the Committee of the Free Society of Trades* (1683), one of his many promotional tracts, he describes without sentimentality and conjectures their ancestors were the Lost Tribes of Israel. Absent on a final mission to Europe in 1686, he was removed from the governorship by the Council. In his retirement he wrote *Some Fruits of Solitude* (1693), a collection of maxims. Although his governorship was restored in 1694, he did not return until 1699, and made another Indian treaty, but was unable to abolish slavery. Again in 1701 he was forced out and he decided to give his colony back to England if the Quakers were protected, but a stroke spoiled his mind and he died with this scheme unfulfilled. In 1693–4 *The Present and Future Peace of Europe* appeared, a plan for a European parliament, one of the last schemes of a great and active humanitarian. [EM]

C. O. Peare, *William Penn: A Biography* (1957).

**Perelman, S(idney) J(oseph)** (1904–      ). Humorist. One of the funniest of modern American writers, he was born in New York and educated at Brown University, where he began writing for university and other humour magazines. His first book, *Dawn Ginsbergh's Revenge* (1929), was so successful he was taken up by Hollywood, where he became a script- and gag-writer, particularly for Marx Brothers films. From the 1930s onward, his work mainly took the form of books and essays, mostly for the *New Yorker*. He also wrote plays, and worked as a play-doctor; and he also posed as a farmer in agrarian Pennsylvania, a prey to the locals who lived off such cosmopolitan commuters; Perelman preyed back by making them the subject of humorous pieces. He now lives in London.

Perelman's manner is immediately identifiable. Its tone is vernacular; he exploits, to great comic effect, the wisecracking language of the New York Jew and of show business. He is an excellent parodist, mocking and celebrating the various manifestations of American mass-culture. Other pieces are autobiographical, and usually show the sophisticated Perelman wisecracking his way into defeat. His essays

often begin with some folly reported in the press, from which he builds up an absurd and extravagant playlet. As a social observer, Perelman is very sharp and also ambiguous; there is a kind of self-mocking foolishness about his denunciation – he ends up exposing all the potentially ridiculous features of himself. Yet all his works show an extreme literary sense, a quality that goes beyond simple craftsmanship; one can recognize the debt he has confessed to James Joyce. He is indeed an advanced absurdist, much admired by many serious writers. Among his numerous books are *Crazy Like a Fox* (1944), *Acres and Pains* (1947) and *Listen to the Mocking Bird* (1949). A useful approach to him is through *The Most of S. J. Perelman* (1958), a collection of his pieces across the years. [MB]

**Phillips, John** (1861–1949). Iowa publisher and editor. He co-founded (with Samuel S. McClure) *McClure's Magazine* (1886), which became the main organ of the 'muckraking' period of American journalism. His own book is *The Papers: Occasional Pieces* (1936). [EM]

**Pike, Zebulon Montgomery** (1779–1813). Travel writer. The son of a New Jersey army officer, he was commissioned in his father's company at 20, and in 1805 was directed by the governor of the Louisiana Territory to lead an exploration to the sources of the Mississippi. His second expedition (1806) reached into Kansas, Arkansas and Colorado, where he saw the peak which now bears his name. The Spaniards, intercepting him in New Mexico, forced him to abandon his journey. In the war of 1812 he was killed by an exploding powder magazine. His imagination and style in his account of his explorations (1810) are excellent – see Elliott Coues' edition of his *Account of an Expedition to the Sources of the Mississippi and through the Western Parts of Louisiana* (3 vols. with memoir and notes, 1895). [EM]

*The Journal of Zebulon Montgomery Pike*, ed. D. Jackson (2 vols., 1966).
W. E. Hollon, *The Lost Pathfinder: Zebulon Montgomery Pike* (1949).

**Plath, Sylvia** (1932–63). Poet. Born in Boston, Massachusetts, she was educated at Smith and (on a Fulbright award) Newnham, Cambridge. Here she met and married the English poet Ted Hughes and settled in England. Her early death cut short a growingly impressive poetic career; her two books, *The Colossus* (1960) and the posthumous *Ariel* (1965), show a remarkable development. The first is largely personal poetry, intense and delicately rendered, usually dealing with the relationship between the poet and a perceived object from which she seeks illumination, 'that rare, random descent'. It is controlled, serious verse, but her later work shows new strains and pressures at work in her, and becomes a poetry of anguished confession. Delicacy and control remain, but manage painful, suicidal materials. She is better known in England than in the U.S.A., but must surely be regarded as one of the most impressive of recent American poets. She also wrote a novel, *The Bell Jar* (1966). [MB]

Richard Howard, *Alone with America* (1969).

**Playwrights Company, The.** A group founded in 1938 by dramatists ◊ Anderson, ◊ Behrman, ◊ Howard, ◊ Rice and ◊ Sherwood to produce their plays in independence. [EM]

**Plutzik, Hyam** (1911–62). Poet. Brooklyn-born, he spent most of his early life in Connecticut, studying at Trinity College, Hartford, Connecticut and Yale. After the Second World War he taught at the University of Rochester. An intense, technically self-assured poet, he published *Death at the Purple Rim* (1941), *Aspects of Proteus* (1949), *Apples from Shinar* (1959) and a long narrative poem, *Horatio* (1961). Though his poems are usually short, they are ambitious in theme, dealing with the fact of suffering, the mystery of self, the meaning of nature, the effects of time and Plutzik's own Jewishness. [BP]

**Podhoretz, Norman** (1930–    ). Critic. He was born in New York and acquired three bachelor degrees before becoming editor of Looking Glass Library – and subsequently, in 1960, of *Commentary* magazine. His criticism, collected in *Doings and Undoings* (1964), can be characterized by its preferences: contemporaries to ancients and moderns, fiction to poetry and drama, and, frequently, non-fiction to fiction. *Making It* (1968) is an obsessive autobiography of success in the New York literary world. [BP]

**Poe, Edgar Allan** (1809–49). Poet, short-story writer, critic. Born in Boston. He began his literary career as a young man in Richmond, Virginia, writing verse modelled on that of Byron, Moore and other fashionable romantic poets. He published his first volume of poems in 1827, his second in 1829; by now he had spent one year at the University of Virginia, two in the U.S. Army, and was about to enter, and shortly afterwards to be dismissed from, the Military Academy at West Point. In 1831, he produced a volume of new and revised poems which showed him drawing more widely on the great romantic writers, yet finding a poetic voice of his own. Poems like the well-known 'To Helen', 'Israfel', and 'The City in the Sea' are clearly less self-engrossed and more formally controlled than 'Tamerlane' and 'Al Aaraaf', the most substantial poems of his earlier volumes. His poetic position was also more confident; the sophisticated critical introduction to this collection defends a poetry characterized by 'music' and 'indefiniteness'.

Meanwhile Poe was writing prose-tales and submitting them for money-prizes offered by newspapers, hoping for later book publication. Several are simply rather affected burlesques of the popular literature of the day, though there are signs he took them half-seriously. And 'Berenice' (1835), which he claimed to have written as a joke, was the first of those intense, melodramatic tales, culminating in 'Ligeia' (1838) and 'The Fall of the House of Usher' (1839), in which he states a prevailing theme, that of the neurotic intellectual hero confronted with 'the death of a beautiful woman' (Poe thought this 'the most poetical topic in the world'). 'William Wilson' (1839) definitively exploits the theme of the double. 'Hans Phaall' (1835), a cleverly fantastic piece of science fiction, also anticipates later stories – like 'The Balloon Hoax' (1844), 'Mesmeric Revelation' (1844) and 'Mellonta Tauta' (1849). The best of these early tales, 'MS. Found in a Bottle' (1833), also leads into later interests; it resembles his novel *The Narrative of Arthur Gordon Pym of Nantucket* (1838) in describing with considerable psychological depth a symbolic voyage of discovery.

By now well involved with the development of American literary journalism, Poe became in 1835 editor of the monthly

*Southern Literary Messenger*, an important focus for Southern writing published in Richmond, Virginia. He printed his own stories and poems, and in reviews showed himself capable of close critical analysis of prose style and original, if wild, theoretical criticism of poetry; his criticism, particularly his attacks on overrated popular novels, was found devastating. Now married to his 14-year-old cousin, Virginia, he moved to New York in 1837, Philadelphia in 1838, and back to New York in 1844, editing or contributing to various magazines, seeking a path for his serious interests in the prevailing pattern of American publishing. In 1840 and 1845 he published volumes of tales (*Tales of the Grotesque and Arabesque* and *Tales*), and in 1845 another volume of poems.

As he became more dependent on the mass-audience, he began to simplify the manner of his horror-stories, making their perverse protagonists less intellectual (see 'The Black Cat', 1843, 'The Cask of Amontillado', 1846, and 'Hop-Frog', 1849), though the detective stories, 'The Murders in the Rue Morgue' (1841), 'The Mystery of Marie Roget' (1842) and 'The Purloined Letter' (1844), contributed, through their hero Dupin, a quality of analytical seriousness, an intellectual and semi-scientific bent, to the genre. His speculations about the short story itself are of great importance; he provided the rationale for the formally economical modern tale in his review of Hawthorne's *Twice Told Tales* (1842), which is amongst his best criticism. His poetry was changing, too; some earlier work had been typical romantic obscurantism, but he now wrote several sonorous, clearly plotted pieces – 'The Raven' (1845), 'The Bells' (1849) and 'Annabel Lee' (1849). Though in his important 'The Philosophy of Composition' (1846) he said 'The Raven' had been deliberately constructed for popularity, he never lost his pretensions to learning. In the miscellaneous snippets of erudition he called 'Marginalia', in metaphysical dialogues like 'The Conversation of Eiros and Charmion' (1839), etc., he kept alive speculative ambitions which finally manifested themselves in *Eureka* (1848), his brilliantly egocentric attempt to explain the universe.

He was immensely versatile, a great assimilator and innovator, with many styles to suit various purposes. Yet the felicities of both verse and prose tend to emerge only momentarily from cadences or periods too mechanically contrived. His best short stories expose a disturbing strain of morbid feeling, but all his writing is permeated by a hint of theatrical vulgarity. He saw himself in numerous roles – as Byron, Coleridge, the quixotic yet violent Southern gentleman-scholar, as a great scientist, a superb journalistic manipulator of the American mass-audience, a promoter of a great American literary magazine – divisions which show clearly in his writings. In his work, conversation, and letters he liked to glamorize his past and his actions; he could express both the solipsistic intensity of extreme romanticism and pure opportunism, exploiting his romantic role for profit and prestige. Yet he could not catch the interest of the American public, except for occasional journalistic success. His literary executor, R. W. ◊ Griswold, won more permanent attention for him after his death by exaggerating his neurotic debility and inherited dipsomania to make him an almost Satanic figure. His subsequent reputation has been uncertain, yet generally high, especially since through the influence of his personality and writings on Baudelaire he contributed to the main stream of European symbolist literature. He has also been dominant in the development of American Southern literature. One cannot ignore the pretensions to greatness in his work; some, like Baudelaire, can accept these, but in others they provoke extreme hostility (see for instance Yvor Winters, *In Defense of Reason*, 1947). We should probably resist both tendencies, and place Poe somewhere beside Hawthorne, De Quincey and Wilkie Collins. [MA]

*The Complete Works*, ed. J. A. Harrison (17 vols., 1902); *Representative Selections*, ed. M. Alterton and H. Craig (1962); *The Centenary Poe*, ed. M. Slater (1949); *The Poems*, ed. F. Stovall (1965).

E. H. Davidson, *Poe: A Critical Study* (1957); A. H. Quinn, *Edgar Allan Poe: A Critical Biography* (1941); P. Quinn, *The French Face of Edgar Poe* (1957); Allen Tate, *The Forlorn Demon* (1953); ed. E. W. Carlson, *The Recognition of Edgar Allan Poe* (1967).

**Pohl, Frederik** (1919– ). Science-fiction writer. Editor of one of the leading magazines in his field, he has been called (by Kingsley Amis) 'the most consistently able writer science fiction, in the modern sense, has yet produced'. In collaboration with the late Cyril M. Kornbluth he wrote a series of novels of which the best is undoubtedly *The Space Merchants* (1953), a satiric account of a future society dominated by rival advertising agencies which is not without relevance to our own times. Others include *Search the Sky* (1954), *Gladiator-at-Law* (1955), *Presidential Year* (1956) and *Wolfbane* (1960). Pohl has also edited several anthologies, and his own works include *Alternating Currents* (1956), *Slave Ship* (1957) and *Drunkard's Walk* (1960). [HD]

Kingsley Amis, *New Maps of Hell* (1960).

**Porter, Gene Stratton** (1863–1924). Novelist. She was born in Wabash, Indiana, south of which is the Limberlost Swamp where she began her naturalist studies as a girl and which is the scene of *Laddie* (1913), a novel of her childhood of which a million and a half copies were sold in the following 30 odd years. *Freckles* (1904) rather duplicates this material, and so does *A Girl of the Limberlost* (1909), the tale of a girl hunting moths in the swamp to earn money for education. These and her other five books were bought in millions. The naturalist detail sometimes just compensates for the astonishing sentimentality. [EM]

**Porter, Katherine Anne** (1890– ). Storywriter, novelist. Born in Texas into a declining family proud of its descent from Daniel Boone, the 18th-century pioneering hero of Kentucky, she early rebelled against family and regional tradition and set out to find her own place; hence she had little formal education. She worked on a newspaper in Denver for three years, then lived as an expatriate in Mexico and Europe. Despite her rebellion, her best work is almost exclusively in those stories where she deals with a female protagonist of her own birth date and background, or where she uses the material of her Southern society, often that of her childhood. Thus she is unmistakeably a Southern writer, using the endlessly rich material of the defeated South with the social texture of a writer like Faulkner, yet with much more detachment than most of the Southern group of writers. The relationship of diminished present to glorious past allows her to achieve her finest effects – as in her excellent 'Miranda' stories. These interlinked tales, dealing with the human and social initiation of a girl who stands in close relation to the author, exploit a delicate symbolist method and show the past as a powerful inward force, its workings traced from story to story until in 'Flowering Judas' we find the emancipated Miranda bereft of the power to love.

Katherine Anne Porter's first volume was *Flowering Judas* (1930), containing, in addition to the complex title story, at least three other first-rate pieces: 'Maria Concepcion', about a Mexican Indian woman, one of the few cases where she successfully abandons her usual background; 'The Cracked Looking Glass', a similar but less extreme example, the story of an Irish farm woman; and 'The Jilting of Granny Wetherall', the death-bed reverie of a Southern matriarch. The most uniformly successful volume is *Pale Horse, Pale Rider* (1939), containing Miranda novellas. The title story of *The Leaning Tower* (1944) deals with Nazi Germany, and here there is dissipation of focus and a rather too detached attempt at social commentary. These weaknesses grow the more obvious in her novel *Ship of Fools* (1962), which was 20 years in the writing; it is a mechanical allegory about a shipload of travellers to Germany in the 1930s, dealing with human and social follies, seeking to encompass the character of Nazism. But her high reputation is based on her stories, at least half of which deserve the highest attention as explorations of the private consciousness. [DC/MB]

*Collected Essays and Occasional Writings* (1970). H. J. Mooney, Jr, *The Fiction and Criticism of Katherine Anne Porter* (1957); George Hendrick, *Katherine Anne Porter* (1965).

**Porter, William Sidney.** ♢ Henry, O(liver).

**Pound, Ezra** (1885– ). Poet. Although this seminal figure in 20th-century American poetry left Hailey, Idaho, soon after his birth and never afterwards lived in the West, he seems to have inherited from his frontier forebears his restless optimistic individualism. This background contrasts strangely, yet, in America, not untypically, with his career as a student of Romance languages at Hamilton College and the University of Pennsylvania. Here he became a friend of William Carlos ♢ Williams and Hilda ♢ Doolittle, took his B.A. and M.A. degrees and began to write verse translations in the tradition of Rossetti and Swinburne. As a budding romantic medievalist he was also drawn to Browning, whose combination of erudition and optimistic energy made him a peculiarly congenial model. From this period, too, dates his awareness of Whitman's central importance – at first as an antagonist, eventually as the most pervasive and enduring influence on his poetry.

In 1908, after a brief, abruptly terminated career as a college teacher, he left stuffy provincial America to seek his fortune in the Old World. After publishing his first book of poetry, *A lume spento*, in Venice (1908), he moved to London, where he soon found a sympathetic publisher in Elkin Mathews and an influential friend in Ford Madox Ford. Thereafter, his rise was meteoric. Together with Hulme, H. D., and Richard Aldington, he founded ◊ Imagism; became the European correspondent of *Poetry* (Chicago); and undertook his rewarding studies of Anglo-Saxon (*The Seafarer*) and Chinese (*Cathay*, 1915). His connexion with *Poetry* (◊ Little Magazines) enabled him to promote such major, but then unrecognized, talents as Robert Frost, T. S. Eliot and Marianne Moore. As a young but persuasive propagandist for the new anti-poetical poetry, he was able to help W. B. Yeats discover his mature style. By 1914 he had abandoned Imagism in favour of Vorticism, an ism which, by bringing the arts of poetry (Pound), painting (Wyndham Lewis), and sculpture (Gaudier-Brzeska) into relation, led Pound to think of large-scale poetic organization in terms of contrasting masses and planes. Whatever the intrinsic merits of Vorticist aesthetics, they left behind them, in the works of Gaudier-Brzeska and in *The Cantos* (1925, 1928, 1930, 1934, 1937, 1940), durable monuments.

*The Cantos* were begun shortly before his Vorticist phase and apparently were intended to be a Browningesque compendium of his cultural adventures, an essay in the Liberal Arts for philistine America. This plan, however, was abandoned as he became increasingly disturbed by the events of 1914–18: though he remained behind in London, the Great War put an end to his political innocence, greatly enlarged his human sympathies, and awakened typically American isolationist theories that social evils were caused chiefly by international (usually Zionist) conspiracies.

At first he resisted the pressures to abandon his somewhat narrowly literary preoccupations: *Homage to Sextus Propertius* (1917), his first major poem (in the form of a set of imitations from the Latin), explicitly repudiates the demand to write 'socially useful', 'engaged' poetry. But his next major poem, *Hugh Selwyn Mauberley* (1920), recognizes that the poet, if he is to survive as a poet, must abandon vulnerable 19th-century Aestheticist postures. By now he had moved to Paris, where he set about recasting *The Cantos*, composing operas and assisting the young American writers, notably Ernest Hemingway, who were congregating there (◊ Lost Generation). Too gregarious for his own good, in poor health, he virtually retired, in 1924, to Rapallo, Italy, where he was able to devote himself to research for, and the composition of, his major life-work, the epic *Cantos*. During the early thirties he grew convinced that Mussolini was the saviour of Italy, a constructive, inspiriting force that would sweep away poverty, disease and bloodshed. He held to this vision to the end, remaining in Italy after the American entry into the war, later to be captured and imprisoned by the U.S. military authorities in Pisa, where he wrote the first draft of his Bollingen Prize-winning *Pisan Cantos*. After being charged with treason for his Rome Radio broadcasts to American troops, he was declared insane and incarcerated in St Elizabeth's Hospital, Washington, D.C. There he completed the Pisan sequence (1948), the *Rock-Drill Cantos* (1955), and his greatest translation, *The Classic Anthology Defined by Confucius* (1954). In 1958, under pressure from a number of prominent public men, including the poet Robert Frost, the treason charges were withdrawn and he was allowed to return to Italy, where he now lives, still revising and adding to *The Cantos*.

After a half-century of labour, *The Cantos* is not far from a thousand pages in length: like *Leaves of Grass*, it is something more, and something less, than a poem, and of astonishingly uneven quality. The basis of the poem is a series of permutations of Greek, Chinese, early American, Renaissance and modern Italian, African and English legal materials. These are combined with autobiographical and lyrical sections to define a number of processes of political, economic and artistic values in action. Though notoriously difficult, many of the finest individual cantos (e.g. 1, 2, 13, 45, 47, 49) can be read without recourse to

John Edward's *Annotated Index to the Cantos* (1957). But the great Pisan sequence, to be understood adequately, requires patient investigation of secondary works and a good working knowledge of the previous cantos. *Drafts and Fragments of Cantos CX–CXVII* (1969) contains some of his most careful and serene poetry. Pound's earlier poetry, collected in *Personae* (1952), is more accessible, and it is here that his brilliant achievements as a prosodist can be most readily appreciated. His voluminous prose writings include *The Spirit of Romance* (1910; revised 1953), *Antheil and the Treatise on Harmony* (1924), *ABC of Reading* (1934), *Make It New* (1934), *Guide to Kulchur* (1938; revised 1951), *Patria Mia* (written 1913, publ. 1950) and *Impact: Essays on Ignorance and the Decline of American Civilization* (1960). A large selection of his prose is edited by T. S. Eliot in *The Literary Essays of Ezra Pound* (1954). His letters appear in *The Letters of Ezra Pound* (ed. D. D. Paige, 1950) and *Pound/Joyce: The Letters of Ezra Pound to James Joyce* (1968). Pound has done more than any other poet to advance the metrical revolution begun by Whitman. His cantos continue to appear in the little magazines and he continues to be a major influence on the development of American poetry. [GD]

Donald Gallup, *A Bibliography of Ezra Pound* (1963); Charles Norman, *Ezra Pound* (1960); Donald Davie, *Ezra Pound: Poet as Sculptor* (1964); G. S. Fraser, *Ezra Pound* (1961); Hugh Kenner, *The Poetry of Ezra Pound* (1951); ed. Lewis Leary, *Motive and Method in The Cantos of Ezra Pound* (1954); Julian Cornell, *The Trial of Ezra Pound* (1966).

**Powell, Dawn** (1897–1963). Novelist. She was born in Mount Gilead, Ohio, and the setting of her earlier novels is her native mid-West, but the main scene of her later and major fiction is ◊ Greenwich Village, New York, where she lived. She rejected her first novel in 1924 and considered *She Walks in Beauty* (1928) her first. Among her 14 novels are *The Bride's House* (1929), *Dance Night* (1931), *The Happy Island* (1938), *A Time to Be Born* (1942), *The Locusts Have No King* (1948), *The Wicked Pavilion* (1954) and *A Cage for Lovers* (1957). Her last novel, *The Golden Spur* (1962), a fine satire of city life focused on an old-fashioned bar-club and its clientele. As usual in her fiction, the characters are

indelibly accurate and the wit emerges from one of America's unique styles. Her target is the middle class; she never softened. Edmund Wilson believes her novels to be 'among the most amusing being written, and in this respect quite on a level with those of Anthony Powell, Evelyn Waugh and Muriel Spark'. Her short stories appear in *Sunday, Monday and Always* (1952), and of her plays, the ◊ Group Theatre produced *By Night* in 1933 and ◊ Theatre Guild *Jig Saw* in 1934. [EM]

Edmund Wilson, *The Bit Between My Teeth* (1965).

**Powers, J(ames) F(arl)** (1917–    ). Novelist, short-story writer. Born in Jacksonville, Illinois, he studied at Northwestern University and taught at Marquette University. He has written two volumes of short stories, *Prince of Darkness* (1947) and *The Presence of Grace* (1956), and a novel, *Morte D'Urban* (1962), all having predominantly Catholic themes and pursuing ironically the contrast between the mediocrity of ordinary day-to-day American living with the traditional ideals of the religious life. Several of the stories deal with the lives and problems of Catholic priests in provincial American rectories; they are witty and stylized. Others touch on lynchings, social cruelties, problems of immigrants. Powers's qualities come out most strongly of all in his novel, a superbly funny and devastating study of an entrepreneurish Catholic priest, Father Urban, who attempts to advance the fortunes of his order, the Clementines, by businesslike methods and alliances with the rich. It is a very well observed and ironic comedy of American life and the conditions under which the modern life of faith must be lived. [MB]

Alfred Kazin, 'Gravity and Grace: The Stories of J. F. Powers', in *Contemporaries* (1962); F. W. Dupee, 'In the Power County', *The King of the Cats* (1965).

**Prescott, W(illiam) H(ickling)** (1796–1859). Historian. Family fortune enabled Prescott to spend two years in Europe after an undistinguished undergraduate career at Harvard. He had literary and historical tastes and gradually focused his interests on Spain. In 1838 he published a 3-volume *History of the Reign of Ferdinand and Isabella*. This was followed by the works for which he is best known: a *History of the Conquest of Mexico* (3 vols., 1843; abridged and ed. C. H.

Gardiner, 1967) and a *History of the Conquest of Peru* (2 vols., 1847). He intended to complete his study with a *History of the Reign of Philip II*, but only the first 3 volumes had appeared at the time of his death. Prescott saw himself as a story-teller and history as a branch of literature. He had little concern for economic, social or even constitutional problems and was content to recount the heroic deeds of the past. Within this framework, however, his use of manuscript sources is impeccable. [D K A]

*The Literary Memoranda*, ed. C. H. Gardiner (2 vols., 1961).

**Price, Reynolds** (1933– ). Novelist, short-story writer. Born in Macon, North Carolina. A Rhodes Scholar at Oxford, he had previously graduated from Duke University, North Carolina, where he subsequently taught. His North Carolina childhood provides the major creative stimulus for his writing. Like many Southern writers he is constantly engaged in the discovery of the meaning of the present in the experience of the past, particularly the past of childhood. His best work brings together themes of family and the past, realized with a precision and delicacy never allowed to become indulgent or uncontrolled.

Set in the flat tobacco country of North Carolina, *A Long and Happy Life* – which won the 1962 William Faulkner Foundation award – is concerned with Rosacoke Mustian's gradual discovery of the responsibilities of love and is told with humour and humanity. The title story in *The Names and Faces of Heroes* (1963, short stories) is Price's most searching analysis of childhood family relationships; two other stories portray aged Negroes, and 'A Chain of Love' re-introduces Rosacoke Mustian. *A Generous Man* (1966) is a novel again concerning the Mustians but less restrained in symbolism and the mythic levels of what is really a simple tale. *Love and Work* (1968) overloads a novelist's efforts to justify his dead parents with nervous over-emphasis. [A H/E M]

**Prokosch, Frederic** (1908– ). Novelist, poet, translator. Born in Madison, Wisconsin. He has studied and taught in America and England, and travelled extensively in Europe and Asia; he now lives in Paris. All his work shows a cosmopolitan range of subject matter and influence, and he has been considerably affected by the work of many English writers, especially by Yeats and the whole movement of the 1930s. He is a writer with a political sense, who frequently reverts to themes of exile and loss, to the world of refugees and of men losing their selfhood. He has spoken of his attempt to write 'internationally', and this has given his books a strong travel and adventure dimension. His verse, lyrical yet with a contemporary awareness, has appeared in several volumes, including *The Assassins* (1936), *The Carnival* (1938), *Death at Sea* (1940) and in the selection *Chosen Poems* (1944). He has been a prolific writer of novels, some contemporary, some historical, all exploiting a wide range of settings – Asia (as in *The Asiatics*, 1935, centred on a young American traveller), Africa (*Storm and Echo*, 1948), Portugal (*The Conspirators*, 1943) and Europe generally (as in *The Skies of Europe*, 1941). His best-known books are probably the very successful *The Asiatics*, *The Seven Who Fled* (1937), about demoralized Russian exiles; and *Age of Thunder* (1945). *The Seven Sisters* (1962) concerns the death throes of an aristocratic American family, spread throughout the world, and *The Missolonghi Manuscript* (1968) takes the form of a private Byronic memoir rescued for posterity. His very wide range of subject and approach makes him a writer difficult to characterize, but his intelligence and cosmopolitan perspective make him always striking. Among his translations are renderings of Hölderlin. [M B]

James Radcliffe Squires, *Frederic Prokosch* (1964).

**Provincetown Players.** An important theatre group who produced between 1915 and 1929 nearly 100 plays by 50 playwrights, and thereby fostered the beginnings of serious American drama. George Cram Cook and his wife Susan Glaspell began the group in Provincetown, Massachusetts, at the Wharf Theatre (1916), where O'Neill's first play was performed. Their New York home was the Playwrights' Theatre at 139 MacDougall Street, and later in the Provincetown Playhouse. In 1929 they moved uptown to the Garrick Theatre, but unsuccessfully. Besides O'Neill, they produced ◊ Dreiser, ◊ Millay, ◊ Anderson, Paul ◊ Green, ◊ Cummings and Edna ◊ Ferber. [E M]

H. Deutsch and S. Hanan, *The Provincetown* (1931).

**Purdy, James** (1923– ). Novelist, story writer. Born in Ohio, he studied at Chicago and Madrid Universities. His first two books, *Colour of Darkness* (1957), short stories, including '63: Dream Palace' and *Malcolm* (1959), his first novel, brought him an immediate high reputation which has not declined. His theme is selfishness, lovelessness and alienation in small-town life; his mannered high-style supports a fantastic vision of character and time. *The Nephew* (1960), a novel, concerns the reconstruction of small-town life through an elderly spinster's writing a 'memorial' for her nephew killed in the Korean War. *Children Is All* (1962) contains 10 stories and 2 plays on accumulating themes of irrational fears and destructive eccentricities. His plays are more metaphysical than his fiction (Edward ◊ Albee adapted *Malcolm* for the stage in 1965). *Cabot Wright Begins* (1964) his third novel, is an ironic and fantastic story of the triumph of innocence in a man sentenced for 300 rapes. The satire on America, in the line of Nathanael ◊ West, explodes into sexual violence in *Eustace Chisholm and the Works* (1968), which concerns homosexuality in the Chicago of the thirties. Purdy connects the Depression with a wider collapse of personal life, and the controlled writing of the horror is strictly contemporary in both style and implication. *My Evening* (1968) contains a long story and 9 poems. [EM]

Jonathan Cott, in *On Contemporary Literature*, ed. R. Kostelanetz (1965).

**Putnam, Phelps** (1894–1948). Poet. Born in Boston, Massachusetts, he graduated from Yale, worked in an Arizona copper mine, served as associate editor on the *Atlantic Monthly*, and published two books of poetry, *Trinc* (1927) and *The Five Seasons* (1930). He left unfinished a long philosophical poem, 'The Earthly Comedy'. He has a distinctive personal voice in some of his lyrical and satirical poems. [EM]

**Pynchon, Thomas** (1937– ). Novelist. Born in Long Island, he served in the navy, graduated from Cornell University in 1958, and after a spell in ◊ Greenwich Village moved to Seattle and then to Mexico. *V.* (1963) is a huge brilliant novel with two heroes – Profane, hero of a plot incorporating his quest for identity and the similar exploits of a neurotic intellectual band called the Whole Sick Crew, and Stencil, hero of a plot in which his quest for the meaning of his father's memoirs involves the history of Malta, German colonialism in South-West Africa, and much more. The diverse materials are united through the struggle of the human against the inanimate. *The Crying of Lot 49* (1966) is a shorter novel, equally complex and erudite, concerning communications theory and the organization of energy. His short story 'Entropy' (1960, repr. *12 from the Sixties*, ed. R. Kostelanetz, 1967) is a brief dazzling elaboration of science into fiction. His other, uncollected, stories are 'Low-Lands' and 'Under the Rose'. Pynchon is one of the few important literary talents of the 1960s. [EM]

S. E. Hyman, in *On Contemporary Literature*, ed. R. Kostelanetz (1965).

# Q

**Queen, Ellery** (pseud. of Frederic Dannay) (1905–    ). Detective-story writer. With his cousin Manfred B. Lee (1905–    ) he has published approximately 100 books. Queen himself is the son of an inspector in the New York Police Department, and he and his father have appeared in a large number of stylistically unremarkable but usually well-constructed mysteries. Under the pseudonym Barnaby Ross, Dannay and Lee have also written novels which employ the detective Drury Lane, but many of these are now being issued under their more famous name. The highly successful *Ellery Queen's Mystery Magazine* began publication in 1941, and the University of Texas possesses the comprehensive Ellery Queen collection of detective fiction. [HD]

A. Boucher, *Ellery Queen: A Double Profile* (1951).

**Quinn, Arthur Hobson** (1875–1960). Critic. Born in Philadelphia, he spent most of his life as a distinguished teacher at the University of Pennsylvania. *Edgar Allan Poe* (1941) is an important critical exploration, but his major work is the immensely valuable *History of American Drama* (3 vols., 1923; revised 1943). [EM]

# R

**Rahv, Philip** (1908– ). Critic, editor. Born in Kupin, Russia, he teaches at Brandeis. He has written mainly on American and continental, particularly Russian, authors. In 1934 he was a founder of the *Partisan Review*, which he has co-edited for 30 years and helped to maintain as a journal of liberal-to-radical thought in both the literary and social spheres (◊ Little Magazines). In 1947 he edited *Discovery of Europe: The Story of American Experience in the Old World*. In a collection of his essays, *Image and Idea* (1949), he included 'Paleface and Redskin' and 'The Dark Lady of Salem', clever and incisive articles on the major dichotomies of the American literary imagination, torn between Eastern (and European) and Western (more specifically 'American') allegiances. *The Myth and the Powerhouse* (1965) is essays on European and American writers. He also edited two collections of essays from the *Partisan Review* and texts of various Russian writers. [AG]

*Literature and the Sixth Sense* (1969) (collected essays).

**Rand, Ayn** (1905– ). Philosopher, novelist. Born in Russia. She is important for the powerful influence her 'objectivist' philosophy has had in the America of the 1950s and 1960s, particularly though not only among college students. Her views, for which she has strongly proselytized, are a variant on the superman theory: she urges the rational recognition of self-interest, the limitation of emotional and altruistic judgements, and the uses of enlightened selfishness. Her position has strong conservative overtones. Her novels, which are polemical and usually show heroes in industry or town planning standing out against the common herd, include *The Fountainhead* (1943), *Atlas Shrugged* (1957) and *We the Living* (1959). [MB]

**Ransom, John Crowe** (1888– ). Critic and poet. Born in Tennessee and educated there at Vanderbilt University, where he taught for many years (1914–37). He subsequently went to Kenyon College, Ohio, founding there the *Kenyon Review*, one of the most important American academic critical and creative journals. He is associated with two major movements in American letters – the ◊ Fugitive group and the ◊ New Criticism. The latter took its name from the title of one of his books, and his critical position has been as influential as this suggests. As expressed in *God without Thunder* (1930), *The World's Body* (1938; revised 1969) and *The New Criticism* (1941), his approach, despite its practical-criticism emphasis, has large philosophical overtones and a considerable debt to Kant and probably to Bergson. He has a dominant concern with the 'ontological' discussion of a work; that is, with it as a thing in itself. This is in turn associated with an emphasis on concreteness, a distrust of abstraction, and a belief that art is essentially concerned with the act of perception as such, with showing that 'the object is perceptually or physically remarkable'. The position is in a sense an attempt to distinguish the language of literature from the language of science; its importance is that it has stressed the need for reading a text attentively and distinguishing its verbal procedures.

His poetry – contained in *Poems about God* (1919), *Chills and Fever* (1924), *Grace after Meat* (1924), *Two Gentlemen in Bonds* (1927), *Selected Poems* (1945), etc. – is, as his criticism might encourage us to suppose, metaphysically witty and presented with an enormous technical ability. What is surprising is its high style, its decorum; it is Southern, but Southern in its charm and aptness of language and form, rather than in its violence (cf. Robert Penn ◊ Warren). Many of the poems are elegies, a form in which Ransom is critically interested. Common themes are the contrast between the vigour of youth and the sad wisdom of age, the joy of summer and the reflective numbness of winter, themes that sometimes take a social dimension. Often opposites are held in a state of equilibrium in which we appreciate the intellectual and emotional complexity of a situation. Concepts of honour and tradition are presented with appreciative irony, so that we are conscious as much of detachment as of commitment; yet finally a human appreciation usually brings the poet into his poem. The high language, with its biblical overtones, creates a stylized and indeed melodramatic world. As a poet Ransom is idiosyncratic and enormously impressive; his influence on subsequent poets has been as strong as his influence on critics. [MB]

*Selected Poems* (revised edn 1970).
René Wellek, *Concepts of Criticism* (1963); George Watson, *The Literary Critics* (1962); Vivienne Koch, in *Modern American Poetry*, ed. B. Rajan (1952); 'Homage to John Crowe Ransom', *Sewanee Review*, LVI (1948); ed. T. D. Young, *John Crowe Ransom: Critical Essays and a Bibliography* (1968).

**Rawlings, Marjorie Kinnan** (1896–1953). Novelist. Born in Washington, D.C., she settled in Florida after working as a journalist, and began to write fiction about the region. In her autobiographical *Cross Creek* (1942) the significance and the security of the old Florida wilderness is central. A simple but delicate writer, steeped in local material and dialect, deeply concerned with the virtue of wilderness and pioneer life, she has taken as her main subject the semi-pioneer period of Florida's development in the late 19th century. Her works include *South Moon Under* (1933), *Golden Apples* (1935) and *When the Whippoorwill* (1940), a collection of Florida stories. Her best-known work is *The Yearling* (1938), a delicate, attractive novel set in the Florida of the 1870s, the story of a young boy with a tame fawn. Knowledgeably and carefully written, her books are good examples of American regional fiction. [MB]

**Realism (Veritism, Naturalism).** Though these terms, particularly the first and last, have been variously used by critics, their main significance in American literature is that they were employed by certain late-19th and early-20th-century writers to describe a self-conscious and developing literary tendency that was held to be particularly American and democratic. Though this movement, part of a general Western tendency in literature, derives largely from European models, it undoubtedly did strike particularly hard in the U.S.A., where one of its most clear-cut phases can be seen. The reason may be that these writers found themselves dealing with materials unworked by any earlier literary tradition (mid-Western city life, immigrant experience, etc.), that they were usually deeply affected by neo-Darwinian, neo-socialist or neo-Malthusian theories, taking a determinist approach to a society that seemed large, abstract and industrial and was run by others, and that they were conscious of the impersonal pressures of man upon man in a competitive environment. American realism, and the associated movements, can broadly be seen as a reaction against the eastern 'genteel tradition', and towards a more 'primitive' and scientistic literature, which was also a more modern literature. Certainly much modern American writing was ushered in by these movements.

REALISM: ⬦ Howells emerged as the chief American spokesman of this tendency, pioneered by Flaubert, Balzac and Tolstoy in Europe, and encouraged by Taine's critical theories. Demanding that attention be paid not to literary tradition but to things as they are, he best expressed his principles – a mixture of emphasis on verisimilitude and an ethical-aesthetic standpoint – in *Criticism and Fiction* (1891), arguing that we must first ask of a work of the imagination 'Is it true? – true to the motives, the impulses, the principles that shape the life of actual men and women? This truth, which necessarily includes the highest morality and the highest artistry – this truth given, the book cannot be wicked and cannot be weak. ...' Various local-colour writers are associated with this movement and principle; so was Henry James, though for some he represented an opposite principle, a totally aesthetic standpoint.

VERITISM: This term was used by Hamlin ⬦ Garland in his *Crumbling Idols* (1894) to assert a more scientific standpoint, in part a reaction against ⬦ Howells' moralism and his emphasis on the 'smiling' aspects of life (which to Howells were the 'typically American' aspects). Garland, drawing on Darwin and social determinism, stressed that literature was democratic when it was scientific and engaged with social problems; this meant that realism had no inherent optimism or ethics. This description came much closer to what writers like Stephen ⬦ Crane, Harold ⬦ Frederic and Henry Blake ⬦ Fuller were doing, though Garland was strongly opposed to the 'immoralism' of the Zola-esque tradition.

NATURALISM: Indebted to Zola, naturalism tended even further towards a determinist standpoint, drawing on economic and sociological analysis to show, normally, the effect of environment on the lower levels of society. Writers like ◊ Dreiser, ◊ London and ◊ Norris best exemplify this tendency, and it runs deep in 20th-century American fiction, particularly in proletarian writing. But in naturalism was also involved a franker and more psychologically determinist view of man's sexual and perhaps his violent impulses, and with what Dreiser called 'the clock of thought', the deeper-seated functions of will and desire.

Since it has long been characteristic for new movements in literature to assert the superior realism of their mode, and since 'reality' itself is a doubtful concept, these designations have only limited critical use; but in the specific usages of those who formulated them they show a steady realignment of aesthetic position. As used in the critical vocabulary of writers like ◊ Parrington (with his 'critical realists') and the neo-Marxists (with their 'social realists') this general area of terminology, though generally significant in modern aesthetics, is less enlightening than it is when used to denote the working principles of practising writers. [MB]

Alfred Kazin, *On Native Grounds* (1942, repr. 1956); Lars Åhnebrink, *The Beginnings of Naturalism in American Fiction* (1961); Charles C. Walcutt, *American Literary Naturalism: A Divided Stream* (1956).

Rechy, John (1934– ). He was born in El Paso, Texas, studied at Texas Western College, and served in the army in Germany. He established himself as an original writer with *The City of Night* (1963), a study, written in ambitiously elaborate styles, in the form of linked stories, of miscellaneous homosexuality and narcissism in American cities. *Numbers* (1968) again chronicles the limbo of male sexuality with first-hand detail. [EM]

Reed, John (1887–1920). Journalist. He attended Harvard and later worked for the *American Magazine* and *The Masses*. His reports from Mexico and Europe for the *Metropolitan* were published as *Insurgent Mexico* (1914) and *The War in Eastern* Europe (1916). His best-known work is *Ten Days That Shook the World* (1919), a product of his enthusiastic observation of events in Russia. On his return to America he was active in organizing the Communist Party there before being forced to leave for Russia, where he died of typhus in 1920. Reed, a flamboyant, romantic journalist, also published *Tamburlaine and Other Verses* (1917). Floyd ◊ Dell edited *Daughter of the Revolution and Other Stories* (1927), and John Stuart made a selection of his writings in *The Education of John Reed* (1955). [HD]

Granville Hicks, *John Reed: The Making of a Revolutionary* (1936); Richard O'Connor and Dale L. Walker, *The Last Revolutionary* (1965).

Reich, Wilhelm (1897–1957). Psychologist. He was born in Dobrzcynica, Galicia, into a German-speaking family which had largely relinquished its Jewish origins. His father, who was a prosperous farmer, and did not rear his children in the Jewish faith, died in 1914. Reich directed the farm and continued his schooling until the farm was destroyed in the war. In 1915, he joined the army of the declining Austro-Hungarian Empire. After the war, at the University of Vienna he first studied law and then changed to medicine, obtaining his M.D. in 1922 and taking graduate studies in neurology and psychiatry. He became First Clinical Assistant at Freud's Psychoanalytic Polyclinic in 1922 and its vice-director in 1928. In 1924 he joined the Austrian Socialist Party and began to consider the possibility of reconciling Freudian and Marxist ideas, convinced of the necessity of making psychoanalysis available to the working classes. In 1927 he published *The Function of the Orgasm*, in 1928 joined the Communist Party, and in 1929 opened the first sex hygiene clinics, for workers and employees, with his professional colleagues of the Socialist Society for Sex Consultation and Sexological Research. *The Mass Psychology of Fascism* (1933) explores political sociology and criticizes the party lines of both Communists and psychoanalysts. Reich's break with Freud was at least partly due to his double emphasis on socialism and the primary function of the orgasm in therapy. Between 1930 and 1937 he lectured in Berlin and then, to escape the Nazis, went to Denmark and Norway, until prejudice against his politics and his psychotherapy, together with his own recalcitrant personality, encouraged him to depart for America. He lectured as associate professor of Medical Psychology at the New School for Social Research in New York from 1939 to 1941, when his influence on American literature and sociology began. Reich's 'sex economy' and its sexual-political bases was bound to disturb the Establishment, since he worked *between* the dogmas and disciplines, stressed both the corruption of the Left and the puritanical cruelties of Western sexual repressions, and proclaimed a cosmic unity of all energy which appeared to be cranky. He had been expelled from the International Psychoanalytic Association in 1934, and the year before from the fascistic German Psychoanalytical Society. During this period and throughout the forties, he developed a highly original theory of the bioelectric nature of sexuality as the operative principle of the body, involving both the wide-ranging information of *Character Analysis* (1933) and the transformation of muscular energy by physical contact between patient and therapist which he termed 'vegetotherapy', a major development in psychosomatic medicine. His work in America was mainly forwarded through the Orgone Institute, founded in 1942, and established at Orgonon, Maine, in 1946, and the Wilhelm Reich Foundation, organized by students and friends in 1949. In 1940, Reich first used his orgone accumulator (a device for concentrating the universal energy element, the *bion*) on human beings, and it was this which caused the Federal Food and Drugs Administration to object to what they took to be a falsely offered cure and to bring an injunction against him. Reich was sentenced to two years' imprisonment and died in the Federal Penitentiary, Lewisburg, Pa. Since then his work has been developed considerably and his therapy become increasingly widespread. The effect of his writings, especially the model of the psychosomatic body and his terminology, have deeply influenced American writers since the forties, primarily Paul ◊ Goodman and certain writers of the Beat Generation (Allen ◊ Ginsberg and Jack ◊ Kerouac in particular), and William ◊ Burroughs. Besides works already mentioned, his books include *The Sexual Revolution* (1936), *Listen, Little Man!* (1948), *Ether, God and Devil* (1951), *Cosmic Superimposition* (1951), *The Murder of Christ* (1953), and *People in Trouble* (1953).

Documents of his relationship with Freud are contained in *Reich Speaks of Freud* (ed. M. Higgins and C. M. Raphael, 1967). [EM]

*Wilhelm Reich: Selected Writings* (1960).
Ilse Ollendorf Reich, *Wilhelm Reich: A Personal Biography* (1969); Michel Cattier, *La vie et l'œuvre du Docteur Wilhelm Reich* (1969); Philip Rieff, *The Triumph of the Therapeutic* (1966); Paul A. Robinson, *The Freudian Left* (1969).

**Reid, Mayne** (1818–83). Novelist. Born in Ireland, went to America about 1838, and served in the Mexican War. He was one of the most popular writers of romance on American frontier themes: *The Rifle Rangers* (1850), *The Castaways* (1870) and *Afloat in the Forest* (1866). He was a loyal friend of Poe's, and his *The Quadroon* (1856) was the basis of Dion ◊ Boucicault's popular play *The Octoroon* (1859). [EM]

**Rexroth, Kenneth** (1905–    ). Poet, critic, translator. Born in South Bend, Indiana, he spent his childhood and youth in the Middle West; orphaned at 13, he moved around the country working in a wide variety of casual labour, gradually picking up a personal knowledge of the arts and the world of radical politics. Apart from two years in school, his education began in the twenties, at the New School, the Arts Students League and the Chicago Art Institute. He moved to San Francisco in 1927 and has remained ever since. In the thirties he was active on the left and in the union movement. He has had several one-man shows of his paintings. His literary output is large, and as a teacher, translator, poet and critic his influence and encouragement has been radiating steadily since 1940. His early poems in *The Art of Worldly Wisdom* (1949) are surreal and experimental in the fashions of the twenties, but *The Phoenix and the Tortoise* (1944) has a maturity which shows the effect of his association with the Objectivists. There followed *The Signature of All Things* (1949), *Beyond the Mountains* (1951; 4 verse plays), and *The Dragon and the Unicorn* (1952), the verse journal of travel in Europe. *In Defence of the Earth* (1956) clearly shows the division in his work between the arguing and often irascible intellectual and the poet of quiet landscape and love. *Natural Numbers: New and Selected Poems* (1964) represents his poetry over 40 years, the newer poems having a personal, lyrical intensity. In 1957, the *Quarterly Review of Literature* issued his

'The Homestead Called Damascus' (in book form 1962), an autobiographical poem finished about 1926, one of his best works, and looking forward to *An Autobiographical Novel* (1966), an account of the first 21 years of his life, a small classic of anti-establishment experience. His other work includes *Original Sin*, a ballet performed in 1961, *The Minority of One* (1961), poems, *The Collected Shorter Poems* (1967) and *The Collected Longer Poems* (1968). His translations of classical, oriental and European poetry include the excellent *One Hundred Poems from the Chinese* (1956). His important critical essays are collected in *Bird in the Bush* (1959), which includes articles on ◊ Patchen, Henry ◊ Miller, and Martin Buber, and *Assays* (1962), with essays on contemporary poetry, Twain and William Carlos Williams. Rexroth fostered San Francisco literary life which blossomed between 1945 and the end of the fifties, and helped to pioneer the revival of jazz-and-poetry in the Bay Area and in New York. His life's work is a major contribution to American letters. [EM]

Lawrence Lipton, 'Notes towards an Understanding of Kenneth Rexroth . . .', *Quarterly Review of Literature*, IX, 2 (1957); Eric Mottram, *A Kenneth Rexroth Reader* (1970).

**Reznikoff, Charles** (1894– ). Poet. He graduated in law but, though called to the bar, did not practise. He is the author of a number of volumes of poetry, dating from 1927 onwards, and novels and a volume of verse plays. He was, along with George ◊ Oppen, etc., one of the Objectivist poets of the 1930s – that movement, which had a strong debt to ◊ Imagism, being strongly supported by Ezra Pound. At the same time there is a strong opposing vein of Jewish lyricism and Jewish learning in his work. He has been long a lonely and relatively unknown poet, but in recent years his reputation has come into ascendancy with *By the Waters of Manhattan* (1962), which is a selection from his verse, and *Testimony: The United States 1885–1890* (1965), the first volume of a long and documented poetic meditation on this period of American social economic and cultural history. *Family Chronicle* (1969) is a prose record of life in New York in the thirties. [EM/MB]

**Rice, Elmer** (1892–1967). Playwright, novelist. He was born in New York City, studied law at night school, but set out on a theatre

career, which began with *On Trial* (1914), a mystery play of victimization told through expressionist flashback. But his next success did not come until *The Adding Machine* (1923), where his typical concern for the social victim is embodied in the fate of Mr Zero, a 'waste product' of mechanized society. In *Street Scene* (1929) a slice of slum life moves towards murder and frustrated love without solution (Langston ◊ Hughes and Kurt Weill made it into a musical in 1947). *Left Bank* (1931) concerns feckless expatriates, and *Counsellor-at-Law* (1931) the legal profession. In 1933 Rice protested against Depression conditions in *We the People*, a Marxist play with democratic ideals, and *Judgment Day* (1934) is a warning against Nazism based on the Dimitroff trial. *Not for Children* (1935) attacks the theatre's divorce from reality, and *American Landscape* (1938) reasserts national traditions of 'freedom and the common rights of humanity', as against *Between Two Worlds* (1934), which had contrasted the Soviet system with the less humane American world. In 1951 he defended his leftist friends and colleagues at a time of national hysteria. His later plays have not been too good (*Dream Girl*, 1946, and *Cue for Passion*, 1959), but his autobiography, *Minority Report* (1963), is a significant document of the last three decades. The utopian satire *A Voyage to Purilia* (1930) is the best of his novels. [EM]

R. Hogan, *The Independence of Elmer Rice* (1965).

**Rich, Adrienne Cecile** (1929– ). Poet. Born in Baltimore, educated at Radcliffe, and now lives in Cambridge, Massachusetts. Her volumes include *A Change of World* (1951), *The Diamond Cutters* (1955) and *Snapshots of a Daughter-in-Law* (1963). She also published a pamphlet of poems in the English Fantasy Poets series during a year spent in England on a Guggenheim award. Her early verse is marked by a delicacy of insight, but her precocious talent has deepened and darkened in recent years. Her themes are those of personal and family relationships, and the nature of the subjective life. The poems in *Necessities of Life* (1966) have an extraordinary brevity and compassion of feeling (this volume includes translations from Dutch poetry). [BS/EM]

*Selected Poems* (1967); *Leaflets* (1969).
Richard Howard, *Alone with America* (1969).

**Richardson, Jack** (1935– ). Dramatist, fiction writer. He was born and works in

New York. *The Prodigal* (1960) showed the beginning of his highly intelligent wit in the theatre with its rehandling of the Agamemnon–Orestes story, and was followed by another play of conflicting idealism and opportunism, *Gallows Humor* (1961), a brilliant and funny satire on capital punishment. *Lorenzo* (1963) uses a Renaissance Italian touring actors' company to point the triumph of art-illusion over war-reality, but it is a less interestingly written play. His latest drama is *Christmas in Las Vegas* (1965). He has also written a novel, *The Prison Life of Harris Philmore* (1961). [EM]

**Richter, Conrad** (1890–1968). Novelist. Born in Pine Grove, Pennsylvania, he settled in the American South-west after a career in journalism, and began studying and writing about the past of the region. An interesting historical novelist, he is much concerned to convey the sensations and the texture of the imagined life of the past, and to show the growth of American attitudes and ambitions. His books include *The Sea of Grass* (1937), *Tacey Cromwell* (1942), *The Freeman* (1943), *Always Young and Fair* (1947) and the striking *The Water of Kronos* (1960). *The Awakening Land*, a pioneer trilogy, consists of *The Trees* (1940), *The Fields* (1946) and *The Town* (1950); the story of the Luckett family, who move into the Ohio wilderness, it follows the development of a new American liberal thought, and the movement from frontier to town culture. Richter comments interestingly on literary regionalism in *The Mountain on the Desert* (1955). In *The Grandfathers* (1964) a west Maryland mountain valley is the location of a 15-year-old girl's search for her father: a novel of unexpected humour and irony. [MB]

**Riding, Laura** (1901–　). Poet, novelist, critic. She was born in New York City and was one of the Southern ◊ Fugitive Group, but finally became an expatriate in Majorca, England and Switzerland. She established the Seizin Press in Deyá, Majorca, in 1927, and there edited the literary magazine *Epilogue* (1935–8) with Robert Graves. Her poetry is confessedly a private poetry, not only because it is modernist but also because it is very much the work of sensibility. Her volumes, published in various countries, some under the name Laura Riding Gottschalk, include *The Close Chaplet* (1926), *Poems: A Joking Word* (1930) and *Poet: A Lying Word* (1933). With Robert Graves she

wrote a novel, *No Decency Left* (1932), under the name Barbara Riche; but better known are her novels *A Trojan Ending* (1937), on the Trojan war, and *Lives of Wives* (1939). It was also with Graves that she wrote the famous and useful critical *Survey of Modernist Poetry* (1927), and she has produced other critical books and essays, including *Contemporaries and Snobs* (1928). [MB] *Collected Poems* (1938).

**Riesman, David** (1909–　). Sociologist. Born in Philadelphia, he attended a Quaker school, graduated from Harvard in 1931, practised law, and moved his interests towards the social sciences through Erich ◊ Fromm and readings in psychology. After working in this field at Chicago, his researches on American society produced (in collaboration) *The Lonely Crowd* (1950) and *Faces in the Crowd* (1952), a classic contribution whose terminology has contributed to the language. He became Professor of Social Science at Harvard in 1954. Before this wide recognition, he had written *Civil Liberties in a Period of Transition* (1942) and *Democracy and Defamation* (1942). His later work includes *Thorstein Veblen: A Critical Interpretation* (1953), *Constraint and Variety in American Education* (1956, 1958), two books of occasional pieces, *Individualism Reconsidered* (1954) and *Abundance for What?* (1964), and *Conversations in Japan* (1967, in collaboration with his wife). *The Academic Revolution* (1968, with Christopher Jencks) is a detailed survey of American higher education: the 'revolution' is the increasing professionalism of graduate schools. [EM]

**Riley, James Whitcomb** (1849–1916). The 'Hoosier poet'. Born in Indiana. His popular Indiana dialect poems won him enormous reputation at the height of the 'local-colour' movement. He began writing them, under the name 'Benj. F. Johnson, of Boone', while working as a journalist on the *Indianapolis Journal*. They were collected in *'The Old Swimmin'-Hole', and 'Leven More Poems* (1883). Then followed numerous other volumes, including *Home-Folks* (1900), *Riley Songs O' Cheer* (1905) and *A Hoosier Romance* (1910). The *Homestead Edition of The Poems and Prose Sketches of James Whitcomb Riley* (1897–1914) runs to 16 volumes. His *Letters* were collected (1930); there are numerous memoirs; he drew, and still draws State and national

pride. Riley wrote 'Little Orphant Annie'.
[MB]

Jeanette C. Nolan, *James Whitcomb Riley,
Hoosier Poet* (1941); Richard Crowder, *Those
Innocent Years: The Legacy and Inheritance of
a Hero of the Victorian Era, James Whitcomb
Riley* (1957).

**Rinehart, Mary Roberts** (1876–1958). Novelist, detective-story writer. Born in Pittsburg,
Pennsylvania, she began her long and prolific career in the then novel genre of literary
detection with *The Circular Staircase* (1908;
revised edn, 1935) and *The Man in Lower
Ten* (1909). Her sixty-first book, *The Swimming Pool* (1952), was also a mystery. She
was also the author of a popular series of
stories centred on an old maid and her two
friends, of which the first was *The Amazing
Adventures of Letitia Carberry* (1911) and
the last *The Best of Tish* (1955). A revised
version of her autobiography, *My Story*,
appeared in 1948. [HD]

**Ripley, George** (1802–80). Clergyman, editor, critic. From Greenfield, Massachusetts, and Harvard, he became a leading ◊
Transcendentalist Unitarian minister in
Boston (from 1826). He instigated and
organized the Brook Farm community experiment (1841–7), a utopian agrarian, self-
supporting community of intellectuals and
workers, in which ◊ Hawthorne, Theodore
Parker, Margaret ◊ Fuller, and William
Ellery ◊ Channing (I) among others, were
associated. Its aim was 'to prepare a society
of liberal, intelligent, and cultivated persons' who would resist 'the pressure of our
competitive institutions'. It was not finally
successful. Ripley also edited the *Harbinger*
(1845–9), a magazine of the Fourierist ideas
behind Brook Farm, and the Unitarian
weekly, *Christian Register*. His important
*Specimens of Foreign Standard Literature*
(1838–52) introduced European writers to
American readers. His *Discourses on the
Philosophy of Religion* (1836) was attacked
as heresy by Andrew Norton, and Ripley
replied in *Letters on the Latest Form of
Infidelity* (1840), a plea for religious tolerance. In 1841 he resigned his ministry,
feeling he had lost his sense of vocation,
became head of Brook Farm (see Hawthorne's novel which partly describes it, *The
Blithedale Romance*), and later edited the
*New American Cyclopaedia* (1858–63). He
is the very type of the earnest, experimenting,

soul-searching New England intelligence of
the mid 19th century. [EM/MG]

*Selected Writings of the American Transcendent-
alists*, ed. George Hochfield (1966).
O. B. Frothingham, *George Ripley* (1882);
Katherine Burton, *Paradise Planters: The Story
of Brook Farm* (1939).

**Roberts, Elizabeth Madox** (1886–1941).
Southern novelist. She was born in Kentucky, and most of her novels deal with her
home State, drawing on its history and
folklore. Her interest in folk-speech and
custom usually means that she is defined as
a regionalist, but it is possible to see her as an
interesting figure in that transitional phase
of Southern fiction between Ellen ◊ Glasgow and writers like Faulkner and Robert
Penn ◊ Warren. Her novels, sometimes set
in the pioneer period, deal with violence but
rather in the manner of the 'genteel tradition'. Among them are *The Time of Man*
(1926), *My Heart and My Flesh* (1927), *The
Great Meadow* (1930), and *Black Is My
Truelove's Hair* (1938). She also produced 3
volumes of poetry. [MB]

H. M. Campbell and R. E. Forster, *Elizabeth
Madox Roberts: American Novelist* (1956);
Robert Penn Warren, 'Life is from Within',
*Saturday Review*, 2 March 1963.

**Roberts, Kenneth** (1885–1957). Historical
novelist, journalist. Born in Kennebunk,
Maine. His novels have the reputation of
being extremely well researched (he has also
produced historical research and translations). Several of them deal with the historical development of Maine, his native
State, and Canada, over the period of the
Revolution. Among them are *Arundel*
(1930), about Benedict Arnold's expedition
against Quebec; *The Lively Lady* (1931);
*Rabble in Arms* (1933); *Northwest Passage*
(1937); and *Boon Island* (1956). His *I
Wanted to Write* (1949) is revealing about
his background and attitudes. [MB]

**Robinson, Edwin Arlington** (1869–1935).
Poet. The major poet of his generation, he
grew up in Gardiner, Maine, the 'Tilbury
Town' of his poems. A precocious, delicate
boy, he had to leave Harvard in 1893, after
two years, because his father's health failed
and the family's finances collapsed. His
mother died suddenly of black diphtheria,
and was buried hurriedly because the priest
and doctor feared the disease. His father
was a spiritualist who even experimented

with his beliefs on his deathbed. Robinson referred to these events as a 'living hell' which 'cut my universe clean in half'. His brother's disasters and loss of family money and the poet's own serious ear trouble and fear of brain damage resulted in his regarding himself as an exhausted misfit, 'a tragedy from the beginning'.

He printed his first poems, *The Torrent and the Night Before* (1896), at his own expense: it contained some of his finest works (revised edn 1897 as *The Children of Night*). Living in New York from 1898, his lonely retreat from company increased; he drank and was nearly destitute. Public recognition came with his verse novel, *Captain Craig* (1902). He made his first of many summer visits to the MacDowell Colony in New Hampshire, his refuge until his death. *The Man against the Sky* (1916) established him firmly with a readership, and his verse novel *Tristram* (1927) was a best-seller. He died of cancer in New York.

His intelligence and careful forms rejuvenated American *fin de siècle* poetry with works of austere honesty and precision. His melancholy is not tragic but ironic and dry; it resists romantic sentimentalities. 'Luke Havergal' and 'Children of the Night' are poems of failure balanced by briefly sustaining hope and oncoming life. His response to small-town suffering is beautifully articulated in poems like 'Miniver Cheevy', 'Flammande', 'Eros Turannos' and 'Mr Flood's Party'. He is a master of long narrative poems ('The Man against the Sky' and 'Tasker Norcross'), although the passive gloom of the Tilbury world can be monotonous and intellectually thin. His infatuation with medieval gothicry produced his narrative poems 'Merlin' (1917), 'Launcelot' (1927) and 'Tristam' (1927), visions of the decline of the West. His Jamesian verse novels are a unique and often interesting achievement – 'Roman Bartholow' (1923), 'Cavender's House' (1929), 'The Glory of Nightingales' (1930), 'King Jasper' (1935) - this last an allegory of capitalist and communist conflicts. *Tilbury Town: Selected Poems of E. A. Robinson* (ed. L. Thompson, 1953) is a useful introduction to his work.

For a shy and pessimistic man, his huge output and intense concern with human relationships and solitude are an achievement of extraordinary affirmation, most of it thoroughly readable. [EM]

C. P. Smith, *Where the Light Falls* (1965); H. C.

Franchere, *E. A. Robinson* (1968); Louis O. Coxe, *E. A. Robinson: The Life of Poetry* (1969); ed. E. Barnard, *E. A. Robinson: Centenary Essays* (1970).

**Roethke, Theodore** (1908–63). Poet. He was born and spent his childhood in Saginaw, Michigan; he taught in American universities; but his poetry is deeply associated with the landscape of the North-west. Poems appearing in *Open House* (1941), *The Lost Son and Other Poems* (1948), *Praise to the End!* (1951) and *The Waking* (1953) were selected for an excellently representative volume, *Words for the Wind* (1958). After the conventionalities of his first book, Roethke developed a unique poetry out of his sense of the links between the unconscious and nature – Richard Eberhart called it his 'worms period' – with Yeats as his formal model. His floppy whimsical poems, often in a sort of baby talk, were exceptional in a poetic career of almost desperate stabilities. His strength lay in creating an interior landscape out of a crowded greenhouse or a river estuary which locates, with lyrical precision and a degree of splendour, a sense of alienation, madness and reconciliation which he strives to unify. His last book, *The Far Field* (1964), contains some of his finest poems, with a new control of the long meditative line and a less obtrusive Freudian idea of men's lives. *On the Poet and His Craft* (ed. R. J. Mills, 1965) is a collection of his occasional prose. [EM]

*Collected Poems* (1968); *The Notebooks*, ed. D. Wagoner (1970).
Karl Malkoff, *Theodore Roethke: An Introduction to the Poetry* (1967); ed. Arnold Stein, *Theodore Roethke: Essays on the Poetry* (1966); Allan Seager, *The Glass House: The Life of Theodore Roethke* (1968).

**Rogers, Will(iam)** (1879–1935). Humorist. This modern American folk hero was born in Oklahoma of part Indian blood. He turned from a Wild West cowboy act into a comedian, with the Ziegfeld Follies, then in motion-pictures and a newspaper column. He continued the wisecracking folk-humour tradition of men like Artemus ◊ Ward and Petroleum ◊ Nasby, and his eye often turned to modern political affairs. He took the name of the 'Cowboy Philosopher' and wrote *The Cowboy Philosopher on Prohibition* (1919), *The Cowboy Philosopher on the Peace Conference* (1919), *Will Rogers' Political Follies* (1929), etc. Donald Day's

*The Autobiography of Will Rogers* (1949) selects from the writings of this great comic personality. [MB]

**Rølvaag, O(le) E(dvart)** (1876–1931). Novelist. Born in Norway of seafaring background, he became a sailor, then in 1896 came to the U.S.A. to farm in South Dakota. He eventually became Professor of Norwegian at St Olaf College in Minnesota. He began writing in Norwegian about Scandinavian immigrants in the States; *Giants in the Earth* (1927), and the two novels consecutive to it, *Peder Victorious* (1929) and *Their Father's God* (1931), written in Norwegian and translated, are the best known of his novels. Many still remain untranslated, but of those that are, *Pure Gold* (1930) and *The Boat of Longing* (1933), which celebrates his native Norway, are particularly notable. Rølvaag is usually identified as an American regional novelist, but he is also in the tradition of Scandinavian fiction, with its emphasis on the titanic struggle of individual men with both the forces within themselves and the environment in which they live. Thus the trilogy beginning with *Giants in the Earth* deals with the political, social and religious scene, but it is essentially pastoral – as the subtitle says, it is a 'Saga of the Prairie'. Rølvaag was in fact able to contribute to both traditions. [MB]

Theodore Jorgenson and Nora O. Solum, *Ole Edvart Rølvaag: A Biography* (1939).

**Roosevelt, Theodore** (1858–1919). Reformer, politician, historian. Born in New York. After Harvard he served briefly as a Republican member of the New York State legislature, but following the death of his first wife in 1884 bought a ranch in the Dakota territory where he stayed for several years. From childhood he had believed in the virtue of strenuous outdoor activity and had improved his naturally poor health by sport and physical exercises. He had also, while at Harvard, begun work on his first book, a naval history of the war of 1812. During his years in Dakota he indulged both interests, following an active career as a rancher and working in his spare time on a history, *The Winning of the West* (4 vols., 1889–96). In 1889 he was called back to the East by the offer of a post on the Civil Service Commission; other offices quickly followed. In 1898 he resigned his assistant secretaryship of the navy in order to take part in the Spanish–American War as

colonel of his own troop of volunteer cavalry, the Rough Riders. Fame in this campaign led to his election as governor of New York in 1898; in 1901 he became vice-president of the United States and succeeded to the presidency on the assassination of McKinley. He was re-elected in 1904, and in 1912 unsuccessfully stood as candidate for the Progressive Party.

In his public career a moderate reformer and a believer in manifest destiny, Anglo-Saxon superiority and social Darwinism, he expressed his philosophy in *The New Nationalism* (1910). The same qualities were displayed in his historical writing, as in *The Winning of the West*. He was a literary historian with a great admiration for Francis ◊ Parkman, and a staunch moralist who believed that the historian should take sides and should use his imagination in order to make his material dramatically alive. He emphasized the value of the individual and accepted the validity of applying evolutionary theories to national and international history. He believed implicitly that Anglo-Saxon America represented the highest point of human development. His values and judgements no longer find general acceptance, but his use of sources was excellent, and he had a gift for narrative that makes his work highly readable and historically valuable. [DKA]

*Autobiography*, ed. Wayne Andrews (1958).

**Rosenberg, Harold** (1906– ). Poet, critic, philosopher. He is a New Yorker, and in the thirties and forties began his reputation with work in *Poetry, Transition, The Symposium* and *View*. Later he wrote for *Partisan Review, Commentary*, the *Nation, Dissent* and *Les Temps Modernes*. He is a fine example of the art and literary critic completely dedicated to his profession of discrimination of contemporary culture. Merleau-Ponty asked him to write on Marx in *Les philosophes célèbres*, and his poetry has appeared in *Trance above the Streets* (1942) and in a number of little magazines. He has lectured at the New School for Social Research on literature and art. His major work consists of three highly important books of cultural analysis: *Arshile Gorky* (1962), the only significant study of the great Armenian-American painter; *The Tradition of the New* (1959), which demonstrates a tradition of art and poetry from Poe and Rimbaud through to American Action Painting (a term he himself coined),

Marxist judgements in the arts, Pop culture, etc.; and *The Anxious Object* (1964), a series of essays on art today and its audience, including pieces on De Kooning, Hofmann, Steinberg and Jasper Johns. *Art Works and Packages* (1969) continues his analysis of contemporary art. [EM]

**Ross, Barnaby.** ◊ Dannay, Frederic.

**Ross, Leonard Q.** ◊ Rosten, Leo Calvin.

**Ross, Lillian** (1898–      ). Reporter, novelist. Born in Syracuse. N.Y., she now lives in New York City and is on the staff of the *New Yorker*, where most of her work appears. Its main spirit is documentary, but her analytical talent also spreads towards fiction. *Picture* (1952) is a fictionalized true story and a classic study of Hollywood film-making. Her frank *Portrait of Hemingway* (1961) began as a *New Yorker* profile of the novelist. *The Player* (1962), written with Helen Ross, is a group portrait of 55 actors. Her first novel (best read as a series of short stories), *Vertical and Horizontal* (1963), is a marvellous detached analysis of contemporary New York, concentrating particularly on the world of medicine and psychoanalysis. *Talk Stories* (1966) is a collection of 60 interviews and descriptions (previously published in the *New Yorker* between 1958 and 1965) – the figures include Glenn Gould, Yehudi Menuhin, and Dag Hammerskjold – and *Reporting* (1966) reprints the account of John Huston in *Picture*, with six other pieces. [MB]

**Rosten, Leo Calvin** (1908–      ). Political scientist, sociologist, humorist. Born in Poland. Under this name he pursued his career as political scientist and sociologist, and published such books as his study of *Hollywood* (1941) and his *Guide to the Religions of America* (1955). But his sharp intellectual observation also shows in his writings as 'Leonard Q. Ross', author of *The Education of H\*y\*m\*a\*n K\*a\*p\*l\*a\*n* (1937) and *The Return of H\*y\*m\*a\*n K\*a\*p\*l\*a\*n* (1959). Kaplan is a somewhat dissident and confused student in the beginner's grade at the American Night Preparatory School for Adults, where immigrants encounter linguistic and social confusions of various kinds. 'Ross' is an enormously funny writer, and these stories, most of them from the *New Yorker*, are

sometimes too readily placed in the tradition of American-Jewish humour. His subject gives him an accurate measure for treating some of the follies of American life with strong satirical and sociological observation. *The Joys of Yiddish* (1968) is 'a lexicon for readers of English'. [MB]

**Roth, Henry** (1907–      ). Novelist. He left New York City in 1945 and lives in Augusta, Maine, teaching mathematics. His reputation lies solely with *Call It Sleep* (1934), one of the finest novels of the century and one of the few in the thirties to survive ideological fashion, the story of immigrants in New York seen through the eyes of a boy. After its publication, he worked at a new novel, and although Maxwell Perkins believed it was brilliant, Roth destroyed it (a section did appear in *Partisan Review*). It concerned a worker who had lost an arm and become a Communist Party organizer. The reprinting of *Call It Sleep* in England in 1963, with a preface by Walter Allen, revived an excellent reputation and its author's interest in writing. [EM]

A. S. Knowles, 'The Fiction of Henry Roth', *Modern Fiction Studies*, Winter, 1965–6; W. B. Rideout, *The Radical Novel in the United States 1900–1954* (1956).

**Roth, Philip** (1933–      ). Novelist, story writer. He was born in Newark, New Jersey, educated at Bucknell University and the University of Chicago, and has taught at the latter and the University of Iowa. He is one of the most highly reputed of post-war Jewish writers and a brilliant delineator of Jewish mores and psychology. *Goodbye, Columbus* (1959) contains a novella and 5 stories and won the National Book Award; the stories are wittily distilled vignettes of modern Jewish life, the novella an analysis in depth of wealthy life-styles and the American way of life seen through the glow of a romantic love affair. Roth's capacity to create a dense social texture, explore manners with a witty but saddened perception and probe deeply into psychological problems shows even more sharply in his long novel *Letting Go* (1962). In part an academic novel about depressed graduate students, it spreads into an elaborate complex of relationships in modern American life, without attempting slick moral solutions. *When She was Good* (1967), a further study in urban behaviour and values, is one of the few radical attacks on the American small town to achieve power without cheap sensationalism. *Portnoy's Complaint* (1969) *is* sensational and lacks Roth's previous precision and control, as if the contemporary situation has devastated his moral poise. But it is marvellously funny – an extended variant on classic jokes about the sterilizing Jewish mother, and her masturbatory consequences, turned this time into a less certain if obviously now more anguished and confused myth about the American dream. But it has been a great commercial success and has, paradoxically, enlarged critical interest in this important novelist. [MB]

**Rothenberg, Jerome** (1931–    ). Poet. He was born in New York City, studied at the City College and the University of Michigan, and after two years in the army has lived in his home city, teaching, writing, translating and founding the Hawk's Well Press and the important magazine *Poems from the Floating World*. In discussion with Robert ◊ Kelly, Armand Schwerner, Robert ◊ Bly and other poets, and through studies of Blake, Rimbaud, Neruda, Whitman, modern German poets (see his translations in *New Young German Poets*, 1959) and American Indian texts, he developed the 'deep image' concept of poetry (see 'An Exchange: Deep Images and Modes', with Robert Creeley, in *Kulchur*, 6, 1962, and 'Why Deep Image?', in *Trobar*, 3, 1961, reprinted *Eleventh Finger No. 1*, 1965). His intention was to re-establish forms of visionary poetry for the modern world. His poetry includes *White Sun Black Sun* (1960), *The Seven Hells of Jigoku Zoshi* (1962), *Sightings I IX* (1964), *The Gorky Poems* (1966), related to the works of the painter Arshile Gorky, *Ritual: A Book of Primitive Rites and Events* (1966), *Between: Poems 1960/63* (1967), *Further Sightings* (1967) and *The Flight of Quetzalcoatl* (1967). He also translated Rolf Hochhuth's *The Deputy* (1964) for the New York stage. Besides being an important poet in his own right, Rothenberg is part of a significant contemporary American effort to understand and incorporate world visionary literature. *Technicians of the Sacred* (1968) is a large and highly important collection of translations of ethnic poetry placed in the context of significant developments in 20th-century arts. [EM]

**Rourke, Constance** (1885–1941). Cultural historian. Born in Cleveland, Ohio, she taught English at Vassar, and after 1915 lived at Grand Rapids. She was a rare scholar of American literature, folklore and humour, and one of the first to write serious American cultural history with the bias away from formal literature (*The Roots of American Culture*, 1942). *American Humour: A Study of the National Character* (1931) is a standard work and concerns the relationships between Yankee, frontier and Negro humour, popular folklore and its figures, and writers like Henry James and Robert Frost. Her *Davy Crockett* (1934), *Audubon* (1936) and *Charles Sheeler* (1938) are permanent contributions to American studies. *Trumpets of Jubilee* (1927) consists of important pioneering studies of Lyman Beecher, Harriet Beecher ◊ Stowe, Horace Greeley and P. T. Barnum. [EM]

**Rowlandson, Mary** (*c.* 1635–*c.* 1678). Born in Lancaster, Massachusetts. Her fame rests entirely on being captured, with her daughter, by Indians in 1675, during King Philip's War, and writing her *Captivity and Restoration* (1682). America's first bestseller by a woman, it records this Massachusetts minister's wife's seven weeks and five days with the native Americans. Although she writes in the facile context of 'God's judgement', she carefully relates the ordeal of 20 'removes' with her captors, the sufferings both she and they underwent, and offers a certain amount of field anthropology. Her courage and endurance come clearly through her simple style and shrewd attitudes. [EM]

*Narratives of the Indian Wars, 1675–1699*, ed. C. H. Lincoln (1913); *The Oxford Anthology of American Literature*, ed. W. R. Benét and N. H. Pearson (2 vols., 1939).

**Rowson, Susanna** (1762–1824). Novelist, poet, dramatist. She was born in England and spent much of her varied life in America, where her father, a naval lieutenant, had been based, in Massachusetts. Her first novels – *Victoria* (1786), *The Inquisitor* (1788) and *Mary, or, The Test of Honour* (1789) – were not too successful, nor were her *Poems on Various Subjects* (1788) and *A Trip to Parnassus* (1788). But her fourth, and first American novel, *Charlotte, A Tale of Truth* (1791), made her name; it is a sentimental, didactic tale of a young lady seduced by an English officer and a French governess, told with some realism and much poetic justice, in the English romantic fiction manner. The Rowsons staged her plays in England and America (*Slaves of Algiers*,

1794, *The Female Patriot,* 1795, etc.). But she left the stage and opened a girls' school in Boston (1797), edited a magazine, and wrote three more novels, including the inevitable sequel, *Charlotte's Daughter* (known as *Lucy Temple*) (1828). [EM]

**Royce, Josiah** (1855–1916). Philosopher. Born in a frontier village of California and educated at the newly founded State university. With the support of interested businessmen, he went to Germany to study philosophy at Leipzig and Göttingen, returning to take a doctorate at Johns Hopkins University in 1878. After four years as instructor in English at California, he went to Harvard, where for the rest of his life he was a leading light in a department of philosophy that included William ◊ James and ◊ Santayana. He was the first American appointed to the Gifford lectureship in Scotland, and his lectures *The World and the Individual* (publ. 1900–1), given at Aberdeen in 1899, proved to be his masterpiece. His interests were manifold. He was a pioneer of mathematical logic; he gave the Lowell lectures in Boston and the Hibbert lectures in Oxford (*The Problem of Christianity,* 1913); his *Philosophy of Loyalty* (1908) sketches a system of ethics; he even wrote an outline of psychology, a novel and a history of California. As a metaphysician he was considered James's superior, but not his equal as a writer. His style is wordy, and the hortatory tone and the archaisms that he sometimes affected do not commend him to current taste.

He was the most eminent of American idealists. He did not begin, as did the British idealists, with sensation, but with an examination of the nature of ideas. He conceived an idea as a purpose, a striving to realize in our experience the character of an object. This he called the internal meaning of the idea. But there was also an external meaning, the reference to something that lay beyond our experience. The advance of knowledge is the gradual approximation of the first to the second. What would experience be like if the one overtook the other? The answer lies in three characteristics of his thought. First, as an idealist, he believed that no matter how far we went he should never find anything but experience; reality *is* experience. Secondly, the real order is an intelligible order, that is one in which everything is necessarily related to everything else in the experience of one all-

embracing mind. Thirdly, in this mind there is realized the complete fulfilment of man's strivings for goodness and beauty as well as truth. Finite mind is thus in its essence an attempt to realize an Absolute, which is the object at once of speculative search, of ethical striving and of religious worship. Such an idealism faces many problems, of which two proved particularly serious. Did not individuals lose their distinctness and simply disappear in this all-engulfing Absolute? And if the Absolute is perfect, does not this mean that the vast mass of suffering and injustice in the world must be accepted as part of the Divine goodness? Royce himself was troubled, since he took morality most seriously. As Santayana wrote of him: 'What calm could there be in the double assurance that it was really right that things should be wrong, but that it was really wrong not to strive to right them?' Royce's last days were unhappy, since in the First World War he felt compelled to turn bitterly against the Germany from whose teaching he had drawn his inspiration. [BB]

J. H. Muirhead, *The Platonic Tradition in Anglo-Saxon Philosophy* (1931); G. Santayana, *Character and Opinion in the United States* (1920) (essay on Royce).

**Rukeyser, Muriel** (1913–      ). Poet. Born and reared in New York City, a youth she writes about poignantly in *The Life of Poetry* (1949), an account of the wide social purposes for poetry and its connexions with science – a sense which permeates her poetry and prose. Her first poems, in *Theory of Flight* (1935), concern researches at the Roosevelt School of the Air, and *U.S.1.* (1938) projects her knowledge of working-class exploitation and her feeling for the thirties. As a young woman she had reported social conflict in America and in Spain; later in life, she developed her power to marshal a man's career through her own sensibility; the result is the magnificent *Willard Gibbs: American Genius* (1942) and the less detailed, more autobiographical *One Life* (1957), a study of Wendell Wilkie. *The Orgy* (1965) is an imaginative re-creation of experiences at the Kerry 'Puck Fair'. *Waterlily Fire: Poems 1935–1961* selects from her previous 8 books of poetry; the title poem is a brilliant reflection on the processes of humanly controlled change. She has also translated *Selected Poems of Octavio Paz* (1961) and his long poem 'Sun Stone' (1961). Her most recent poetry, collected in *The Speed of Darkness* (1968), includes 'The Outer Banks', a fine long poem, published separately in 1967. *The Traces of Thomas Hariot* (1970) is a pioneering study of the great Elizabethan. [EM]

**Rumaker, Michael** (1932– ). Story writer. He studied at ◊ Black Mountain College; his stories have appeared in *Black Mountain Review* and *Short Story 2*. His first book of fiction is *The Butterfly* (1962), and his *Gringos and Other Stories* (1967) includes the first-rate 'Exit 3', 'The Desert' and 'The Truck' (also in *Exit 3 and Other Stories*, 1966). [EM]

**Runyon, Damon** (1884–1946). Humorist, story writer. Born in Kansas, he grew up in Pueblo, Colorado, and had already been writing articles for local newspapers when he enlisted, at 14, for service in the Spanish-American war. He returned to work as a journalist on various Western newspapers, then became a sportswriter for the New York *American* in 1911. During the First World War he was a war correspondent for the Hearst newspapers, and after it was a regular Hearst columnist. His experiences in the world of New York sport fed into his best-known work – his many stories of Broadway characters, actors, petty crooks and athletes, first collected in *Guys and Dolls*, which did not appear until 1932. He had evolved a unique and bizarre style, a mixture of extravagant metaphor and racy slang, to describe intimately his particular world. A creator of types rather than stories, he belongs in the tradition of vernacular comedy exploited by many American writers. Other collections of his stories include *Blue Plate Special* (1934), *Take It Easy* (1938), and *Runyon on Broadway* (1950). Other selected collections are *The Best of Runyon* (1938), *Runyon à la Carte* (1944) and *Runyon First and Last* (1949). *Short Takes* (1946) is an entertaining selection of his newspaper columns. With Howard Linsay (1889– ), the Broadway director and actor, he wrote his only play, a farce called *A Slight Case of Murder* (1935).

His work is identified by its distinct social world and its superb exploitation of its vernacular; his striking literary use of this has been called 'Runyonese'. His range is not large, and his stories develop simply, but they have both authenticity and an entertaining and distinctive extravagance. [MG/MB]

Ed Weiner, *The Damon Runyon Story* (1948); Edwin P. Hoyt, *A Gentleman of Broadway* (1964); Jean Wagner, *Runyonese: The Mind and Craft of Damon Runyon* (1965).

# S

**Salinger, J(erome) D(avid)** (1919–    ).
Novelist, short-story writer. Born in New
York. After publishing 20 relatively undistinguished short stories, he 'found his
subject' with the short novel *The Catcher
in the Rye* (1951). In it, the teenage hero,
Holden Caulfield, leaves his 'prep school'
and spends a week-end in New York City.
Salinger's sympathies seem largely with
Holden, especially in the sardonic criticisms of the grown-up world of hypocrisy.
The book's main theme is Holden's resistance to growing up into the world of
'phoniness' and the betrayal by adults of
youthful integrity. The title implies Holden's
desire to protect other, younger children
from the blight of maturity. The book had
enormous popular success, particularly
among college students. It was followed by
a collection of short stories, *Nine Stories*
(1953; British title, *For Esmé, With Love
and Squalor*) which encapsulated many of
the themes later to be found in Salinger's
linked series of works. Some of the characters from the short stories reappear in the
longer stories of the fifties and sixties, all
concerned with the members of the Glass
family of New York, particularly the
children of Les and Bessie Glass, a Jewish-
Irish theatrical act. All are brilliant, former
radio 'stars' on a programme called 'It's
a Wise Child'. Seymour, the eldest, and *the*
genius, dies in his thirties, a suicide. The
problem that this act creates has become
increasingly the covert subject of the Glass
stories. It has fallen on the second son,
'Buddy' Glass, to explore the life of Seymour and his own relationship to his dead
brother. In *Franny and Zooey* (1961), the
youngest member of the family, Franny,
breaks down in a religious/nervous crisis,
and attempts to preserve herself by the
obsessive repetition of a 'Jesus prayer'
from the inanities of her college life. She is
rescued by her brother Zachary (Zooey),
who abases himself by citing the authority
of his older brothers, whom he holds responsible for his sister's condition, and so
ends her obsession. *Raise High the Roof-
beam, Carpenters and Seymour: An Introduction* (1963) contains two stories,

narrated by Buddy – the first an account of
his attempt to attend Seymour's wedding,
the second a general 'essay' on Seymour.
Most recently (June 1965), Salinger has
added to the canon a letter home from
summer camp by Seymour at the age of 7.
    In the Glass family, Salinger has created
an object of almost Janeite interest for
some, while others have found the increasingly elliptical and qualificatory manner of
writing and the air of total knowledge-
ability and of familial mutual appreciation
distasteful. There is some justice in thinking
that no real conflict or tension exist any
more in the saga, since all potential 'evils',
including Seymour's suicide, are now
entirely welcome as 'magnificent' by who-
ever narrates the stories. [A G]

Ed. Henry A. Grunwald, *Salinger: A Critical and
Personal Portrait* (1962); Frank Kermode, 'Fit
Audience', in *Puzzles and Epiphanies* (1962);
F. L. Gwynn and J. L. Blotner, *The Fiction of
J. D. Salinger* (1958); ed. M. Laser and N.
Freeman, *Studies in J. D. Salinger* (1963).

**Saltus, Edgar** (1855–1921). Novelist and
writer. Born in New York City, educated at
Columbia and in Germany, he set an influential, atheistic, hedonistic mood with
two fashionable studies, *The Philosophy of
Disenchantment* (1885) and *The Anatomy of
Negation* (1886). It persists through into his
novels. A number of these, like *Mr Incoul's
Misadventure* (1887), touch on diabolism
and sensationalism in exotic New York
society settings; he bore marked resem-
blances to Oscar Wilde, about whom he
wrote. Later novels turned to historical
settings with erotic undertones, notably
*Imperial Purple* (1892) and *The Imperial
Orgy* (1920). [M B]

**Sandburg, Carl** (1878–1967). Poet. The son
of Swedish immigrants in Illinois. Leaving
school at 13 he took a series of jobs, wandered West, and served in Puerto Rico during
the American War, returning to Lombard
College for four years. During his newspaper days in Chicago he was encouraged
by Harriet ◊ Monroe, through whose
*Poetry* magazine his poems first received

wide recognition in 1914. His first book
was a pamphlet of poems, *In Reckless
Ecstasy* (1904). In 1905 he married the
photographer Edward Steichen's daughter.
From 1910 to 1912 he was secretary to the
first socialist mayor of Milwaukee. He first
attracted attention with poems in *Poetry* in
1914. In 1916 *Chicago Poems* announced a
new voice in poetry of free-verse urban
speech rhythms harnessing the people and
the tempo of the 20th-century American
city. That popular line continued in *Corn-
huskers* (1918), *Smoke and Steel* (1920)
and, inspired by prairie rather than city,
*Slabs of the Sunburnt West* (1922). In *Good
Morning, America* (1928) his optimism is
darkened by American poverty and dis-
tress, but in *The People, Yes* (1936) a rich
variety of poetic forms sustains faith in an
ideal America, the folk-concept implicit in
*The American Songbag* (1927) and *The New
American Songbag* (1950), important collections of folk-ballads.

In 1932 he moved to the Michigan lake-
side and in 1946 from there to a farm in
North Carolina; in later years he paid a
visit to his forbears' relations in Sweden.
He was a major poet of the mid-West and
of urban Populist feelings. His earlier ▷
Imagism was augmented from popular
idioms and forms; his range from brief
images like 'Fog' to the rhetorical para-
graphs of *The People, Yes* is singular and
always socially conscious. Scorning the
genteel, he was a sentimental and un-
analytical socialist, confident in 'the
people', conscious of the ephemerality of
civilizations (his poems are full of images of
decay), and quietist in his melancholy.
He records rather than artistically shapes
and elaborates his materials; his rhetoric
is really a voice whose rhythms create a
basic recurrent form. Consequently his
verse has been most popular with a general
readership rather than the sophisticated
and academic. Besides his authoritative
imaginative biography of Abraham Lincoln (*The Prairie Years*, 1926, *The War
Years*, 1939), he wrote *Steichen the Photographer* (1929), four children's *Rootabaga
Stories* collections (1922–30), a novel,
*Remembrance Rock* (1948) and an account
of his youth, *Always the Young Strangers*
(1950). [EM/RWB]

*Complete Poems* (1950); *The Letters*, ed. H.
Mitgang (1968).
K. W. Detzer, *Carl Sandburg: A Study in Per-
sonality and Background* (1941); William Carlos

Williams, *Selected Essays* (1954); H. W. Wells,
*The American Way of Poetry* (1964).

**Sanders, Ed** (1939–    ). Poet. Born in
Kansas City, Missouri, he went East in
1957 after reading Ginsberg's *Howl* and
Pound's *Cantos*, and studied Greek at New
York University. His classical and Egypto-
logical interests are a main basis of his
poetic vision. He edits *Fuck You/A Magazine of the Arts*, an important journal of
poetry, and leads The Fugs, a counter-pop
group concerned with anti-war protest,
erotic freedom, and the musical setting of
lyrics by Blake and Swinburne. Sanders'
poetry moves with startling confidence in
an area which combines sexual verve and
mythological instances: *Poem from Jail*
(1963), *Peace Eye* (1965; revised edn 1969),
and *The Fugs Song Book* (1968), whose
lyrics are attributed to Sanders, Tuli
Kupferberg, Ken Weaver, William Blake
and God. [EM]

**Santayana, George** (1863–1952). Philosopher. Born in Spain of Spanish parents,
he came to the United States at the age of 8.
He studied philosophy at Harvard under
William ▷ James and ▷ Royce, and remained there as a teacher for some 25 years.
But he never felt at home in America; he
was repelled by its Puritanism and its
commercialism alike; and he returned to
Europe in 1912 to stay. He made his home
in Oxford, then in Paris and in Spain; from
1920 on, his time was chiefly spent in Rome,
where at the end he was cared for by the
sisters in a Catholic convent.

Santayana is the most polished writer
among American philosophers. His style
deliberately avoids technical terms and
prefers literary imprecision to pedantry.
He published 2 volumes of poetry, a verse
play, 5 commentaries on literature and
contemporary culture, a work of fiction,
*The Last Puritan* (1935), a 3-volume autobiography, and 18 substantial volumes of
philosophy. His most important works
are *The Life of Reason* (5 vols., 1905–6)
and *The Realms of Being* (4 vols., 1940).
*The Life of Reason* is a persuasive statement
of naturalism; Santayana described himself as 'a decided materialist – apparently
the only one living'. But he was not a
behaviorist; consciousness was not for
him a form of bodily behaviour, but a by-
product of changes in the brain, 'a lyric
cry in the midst of business'. His material-

ism lay in insisting that thought and emotion were produced by matter. Consciousness is the sole seat of value in the world, and the life of reason consists in such control of animal impulses as will lead to peace and satisfaction of mind. Brought up as a Catholic, he held that religious dogma was not fact but poetry, fabricated by the imagination and retained for its consoling power.

In *The Realms of Being*, the masterpiece of his old age, there is a notable shift of emphasis. Though our thoughts are controlled by our brains, their objects are not. And these objects are 'essences', a term that covers every quality and relation that we can be immediately aware of. Perception is the taking of some of these essences to exist in the object before us; if we are fortunate, our perceptions are 'true', although we can never be sure. Santayana is a sceptic who holds that all knowledge rests in the end on 'animal faith'.

In *Egotism in German Philosophy* (1916), he criticized idealism as contributing to German arrogance in the First World War. His main work on politics, *Dominations and Powers* (1950), hardly had a more promising theory to offer. Holding that there was no rational ground for preferring anything to anything else, nor therefore any rational way of settling international conflicts, he spoke scornfully of the United Nations. But his analyses of personal and national character were penetrating. In his *Character and Opinion in the United States* (1920), he etched vivid though rather acid portraits of James and Royce, and in his *Soliloquies in England* (1922), he pays a series of memorable tributes to the English temper. His studies in literature are often useful and perceptive: *Interpretations of Poetry and Religion* (1900) contains essays on Browning and Emerson; *Three Philosophical Poets* (1910) covers Lucretius, Dante and Goethe; and *Winds of Doctrine* (1913) includes pieces on Bertrand Russell and Shelley and 'The Genteel Tradition in American Philosophy'. [BB/EM]

*Persons and Places* (3 vols., 1944–53) (autobiography); *The Philosophy of Santayana*, ed. P. A. Schilpp (1940); *Selected Critical Writings*, ed. N. Henfrey (2 vols., 1969); *The Genteel Tradition*, ed. D. L. Wilson (1969); *The Birth of Reason and Other Essays*, ed. Daniel Cory (1969).
Ed. James Ballowe, *George Santayana's American: Essays on Literature and Culture* (1967);

Daniel Cory, *Santayana: The Later Years* (1963).

**Saroyan, William** (1908– ). Playwright, fiction writer. Born in California, he spent his early childhood in an orphanage. He left school at 12 to be a telegraph boy, and drifted from job to job until he became manager of a postal telegraph office in San Francisco. His first stories appeared in 1934, the year of his successful *The Daring Young Man on the Flying Trapeze*. He tells his life in *My Name is Aram* (1940), *Here Comes There Goes You Know Who* (1962), *After Thirty Years* (1962) and *One Day in the Afternoon of the World* (1964) with a boisterous self-assurance which is his main prose style. Novels and stories poured forth from California, his home since 1936. From 1939 to 1941 his main concern was drama; he refused a Pulitzer Prize (as bourgeois patronizing) for *The Time of Your Life* (1939). The Second World War seems to have tempered his exuberance a little in *The Human Comedy* (1942), a novel. His best work since 1945 is *The Assyrian and Other Stories* (1950), his autobiographies (including *Not Dying*, 1966, and *Don't Go But if You Must Say Hello to Everybody*, 1969), and *Boys and Girls Together* (1963), a novel exposing American married love with a surprising savagery. *The Daring Young Man* remains his typical best, stories reminiscent of Chaplin comedies or Joyce's *Dubliners*, with a range of poignant characters, creative sensitives caught in mass society. His stories are packed with America's racial and cultural outsiders, often treated sentimentally, but generally with sympathy and humanity. His plays demonstrate this faith in goodness over evil but without much moral reason, as he admits in the preface to *Don't Go Away Mad* (1949). In *The Time of Your Life* assorted types jostle for life in a San Francisco honkytonk, and *My Heart's in the Highlands* (1939) is a similar series of 'acts' which insist on slightly desperate vitality, dreams and frustrations. The motto of Saroyan is 'live – so that in that good time there shall be no ugliness or death for yourself or for any your life touches' – but his poverty-stricken Californians and outcasts generally hardly have the chance to find out how to. His bitter sentimentalities are not cynical or political in the twenties and thirties manner, but his derelicts and humble men and women struggle in the same Depression with a warmth which is heroic, on a small scale. He is a major writer of weakness and compensatory fantasy in a culture of success. [EM]

Howard R. Floan, *William Saroyan* (1966).

**Sarton, May** (1912– ). Novelist, poet. Born in Belgium, she went to the U.S.A. when her father, George Sarton, chemist and historian of science, joined the Harvard faculty. Her poems, generally personal or else highly abstract, include the volumes *Encounter in April* (1937), *The Lion and the Rose* (1948) and *Cloud, Stone, Sun, Vine* (1961). Her novels tend to see through the eyes of sensitive females and be fictions of sensibility. *The Single Hound* (1938) and *The Bridge of Years* (1946) both draw on Belgian experience; but most of her later fiction uses New England settings and relationships; notably her two college novels – *Faithful Are the Wounds* (1955), a striking study of the life and suicide of a politically radical Harvard professor; and *The Small Room* (1961), exploring the life of a woman's college near Cambridge, Massachusetts. *I Knew a Phoenix* (1959) is sketches for an autobiography. [MB]

**Schevill, James Erwin** (1920– ). Poet. Born in Berkeley, California, he graduated from Harvard and has worked in journalism and university teaching. An abstract and rhetorical poet who has often written of out-of-the-way subjects with learning and stylishness, he is also capable of very great intensity in dealing with the immediate world. He has spoken of his strong interest in bringing dramatic elements into lyric poetry, and his more recent verse has moved this way. Among his collections are *Tensions* (1947), *The American Fantasies* (1951), *The Right to Greet* (1955) and *Selected Poems, 1945–1959* (1960). He is most conveniently represented in the collection *Private Dooms and Public Destinations: Poems 1945–1962* (1962). The *Stalingrad Elegies* (1964), his best volume, is a sequence based on last letters from Stalingrad. He has also written plays and a biography of Sherwood ◊ Anderson (1951). [MB]

**Schjeldahl, Peter** (1942– ). Poet. He was born in North Dakota, educated in Minnesota and New York, and later worked as a newspaper reporter. In 1964 he co-founded *Mother*, a poetry magazine, and has worked as art critic for *Art News* and *Village Voice*. His poetry belongs with that of Ted Berrigan, Ron Padgett and other writers associated with '*C*' *Magazine* Press. But his first book, *White Country* (1968), shows individual talent. [EM]

**Schlesinger, Arthur Meier, Jr** (1917– ). Historian. He is both a professional historian and an active political figure within the Democratic Party and his published work has been mainly concerned with issues connected with his political leanings. In 1945 he received a Pulitzer Prize for a study of *The Age of Jackson*, in which he departed from the established interpretation relating the outburst of Jacksonian democracy to the expanding frontier, stressing instead the impact on national politics of the developing urban working class. He is at present engaged on a multi-volume series, *The Age of Roosevelt*, of which three volumes have so far appeared. *The Crisis of the Old Order* (1957) examines the Republican administrations of the 1920s, the onset of the Depression, and the election of Franklin D. Roosevelt in 1933. It is permeated by a faith in democracy; and by a rejection of *laisser-faire* individualism in favour of intervention by the state in the interests of the poorer sections of the community. Though supported by a formidable amount of research, the presentation is emotional and impressionistic: skilfully drawn pen portraits of individuals often take the place of analysis of issues. The early years of the Roosevelt administrations are described in *The Coming of the New Deal* (1959) and in *The Politics of Upheaval* (1960). These impressive volumes, more reserved in their technique, firmly establish Schlesinger as a major historian in the literary tradition. [EM]

**Schorer, Mark** (1908– ). Novelist, critic. He was born in Wisconsin, studied at the University of Wisconsin, taught literature at Harvard and is now at the University of California at Berkeley. He is an excellent theoretical critic of the novel – two essays of his, 'Technique as Discovery' and 'Fiction and the "Matrix of Analogy"', are critical classics – and a fine practitioner, in *A House Too Old* (1935), *The Hermit Place* (1941) and *The Wars of Love* (1954). He has also published an important study of Blake (*William Blake: The Politics of*

*Vision*, 1946) and the key biography of
Sinclair ◊ Lewis (*Sinclair Lewis: An
American Life*, 1961). [MB]

*The World We Imagine* (1968) (collected essays).

**Schulberg, Budd** (1914–    ). Novelist. He
was born in New York City but lived for
many years in Hollywood, where his
father was one of the first screenwriters and
later a producer. He himself has written
screenplays, including that of *On the
Waterfront* (1954), published as the novel
*Waterfront* (1955).

His principal works seem directly inspired by the American entertainment
industry, and he may be described as a
somewhat uneasy anatomist of the Hollywood dream of success. The title of his
first novel, *What Makes Sammy Run?*
(1941), has now become a conversational
cliché in American usage. This terrifying
portrait of the rise of Sammy Glick from a
New York slum to the unstable heights of
Hollywood remains his best work, despite
the attempt to universalize Sammy's
fortunately unique life into a 'blueprint of a
way of life that was paying dividends in
America in the first half of the twentieth
century'. Neither *The Harder They Fall*
(1947) nor *The Disenchanted* (1950)
possesses the concentrated force and
economy of this first novel. The former is an
exposure of the way in which 'the fight
game' may be manipulated for profit;
*The Disenchanted* offers a thinly veiled
portrait of an ageing Scott Fitzgerald,
with whom Schulberg once worked on an
abortive film script. In both, the ambivalent
nature of Schulberg's commitment is
reflected in an unsteady narrative focus
which tends to evoke an equally blurred
response. He has also published a collection of short stories, *Some Faces in the
Crowd* (1953). *Sanctuary V* (1970), his most
recent novel, describes the conflict between
a revolutionary president and a popular
hero. In 1965, following the riots in the
Watts area of Los Angeles, he set up the
Writer's Workshop in order to promote the
exploration of the social scene by local
talent. Plays, poetry and fiction emerged
to fulfil his vision. [HD]

C. E. Eisinger, *Fiction of the Forties* (1963).

**Schwartz, Delmore** (1913–66). Poet, short-
story writer, critic. Born in Brooklyn, N.Y.
An important figure in the group of Jewish

writers that emerged in American letters
around the Second World War. His first
volume of stories and poems, *In Dreams
Begin Responsibilities* (1938), shows some
characteristic features and themes; he
speaks of the difficulty of breaking through
from the essence of being into the outside
world, of the need for joy and celebration.
His next work was a translation of Rimbaud's *A Season in Hell* (1939); then
followed a verse-play, *Shenandoah* (1941),
and a collection of essays, *The Imitation of
Life* (1941). In 1943 came *Genesis Book I*, a
long poem about the growth of a Jewish
boy in New York City, and in 1948 his
excellent collection of short stories *The
World is a Wedding*, intelligent poetic
stories dealing often with the young Jew's
pursuit of wealth or intellectual prowess.
His later volumes include *Vaudeville for a
Princess* (1950) and *Summer Knowledge:
New and Selected Poems 1938–58* (1959),
poems which continued his free self-
revelation and lavish use of the European
writers he loved. His last work was *Successful Love and Other Stories* (1961). He
taught in a number of universities, lastly at
Syracuse. In criticism he is associated with
a reaction against 'academic' poetry.
[MB]

Marius Bewley, *The Complex Fate* (1952).

**Scott, Winfield Townley** (1910–    ). Poet.
Born in Haverhill, Massachusetts, educated at Brown University, he was for many
years literary editor of the *Providence*
(Rhode Island) *Journal* until in 1951 he
resigned to live in Sante Fé, New Mexico,
and write full-time. His poetry inherits the
stoic romanticism of poets like Frost and
Robinson, and many of its themes are of
New England derivation, often using local
vernacular. He frequently celebrates the
virtues of individualism and solitary
perception against the background of a
meticulously observed landscape. Though
his directness of statement sometimes comes
close to folksy wisdom, he can be a very
complex poet. Some of the poems (particularly the earlier ones) are comic episodes,
often character pieces directly recalling ◊
Robinson or ◊Sandburg. [MB]

*Collected Poems 1937–1962* (1962); *Biography for
Traman* (1937); *To Marry Strangers* (1945);
*Mr Whittier and Other Poems* (1948); *Change of
Weather* (1965); *Exiles and Fabrications* (1961)
(essays).

**Seidel, Frederick** (1936– ). Poet. Born in St Louis and educated at Harvard, he works and lives in New York. His first book, *Final Solutions* (1963), won him a reputation as a verse satirist. With ruthless calm, often employing dramatic monologue which leans on a kind of Jacobean ellipsis, he has attacked the largest social and political problems facing America in the sixties. [BP]

**Selby, Hubert** (1926– ). He was born in Brooklyn, went to sea after school, and worked at a number of jobs while writing. His work has appeared in *Black Mountain Review, New Directions, Kulchur,* etc. His *Last Exit to Brooklyn* (1964) is one of the most searing and carefully written moral exposures of urban violence and degeneracy in American literature. [EM]

**Seldes, Gilbert** (1893–1970). One of America's first systematic students of the popular arts. He was born in New Jersey and began his career as music critic, foreign correspondent and editor on *Collier's* magazine and the *Dial*. Later he became director of television for C.B.S. His best-known book is *The Seven Lively Arts* (1924, 1957), a study of comic strips, films, vaudeville and other pop entertainment. *The Movies and Talkies* (1929), *The Movies Come from America* (1937), *Your Money or Your Life* (1937) and *The Great Audience* (1937) take up the sociology and technique of films, and *The Future of Drinking* (1930) and *Against Revolution, The Years of the Locust* (1932) are studies of Prohibition and the Depression. *The Public Arts* (1956) is an invaluable work. He also wrote a novel, detective stories (as 'Foster Johns'), radio and TV scripts, and *Writing for Television* (1952). [EM]

**Seton, Anya** (1916– ). Popular novelist. Born in New York City, she is author of several historical novels, most with American settings, some best-sellers. They include *My Theodosia* (1941), about Aaron Burr's daughter; *Dragonwyck* (1944); *The Turquoise* (1946); *Foxfire* (1951); and *Katherine* (1954), which is about Chaucer's sister-in-law. [MB]

**Sewall, Samuel** (1652–1730). Born in England, he went to New England when he was 9, graduated from Harvard in divinity in 1671, and became a businessman and a judge. The richest man in Massachusetts, he became its chief justice in 1718. His *Diary* records his life (from 1674 to 1729) as a fairly humane secularist with considerable civic sense. As a private document its style is not literary but frank, with a detail which makes it a valuable record of an early American businessman who employed his worldly status, opposed witchcraft executions and slavery. *The Selling of Joseph* (1700) was the first anti-slavery tract printed in America. *Phaenomena quaedam Apocalyptica* (1697), 'a Description of the New Heaven', is an early celebration of American patriotism. [EM]

O. E. Winslow, *Samuel Sewall of Boston* (1964).

**Sexton, Anne** (1928– ). Poet. She was born in Newton, Massachusetts, and after a time in Baltimore and San Francisco has now returned to the Boston area. Her 3 volumes, *To Bedlam and Part Way Back* (1960), *All My Pretty Ones* (1962) and *Live or Die* (1967) have had considerable attention, in England as well as the U.S.A. A student of Robert ◊ Lowell, and indebted to him, she writes poetry of a strongly 'confessional' cast. The occasions are frequently familial and domestic; but out of them she manages to invest many of her poems with a kind of psychological mythology. Her second volume shows a mastery and a purposefulness less evident in the first; and though she is sometimes obvious she is an interesting poet in a rewarding American tradition. [MB]

**Shapiro, Karl** (1913– ). Poet, editor. Born in Baltimore, he made his first poetic reputation through his individual reactions to the crises of the 1940s, and to being a Jewish soldier in the American army (*V-Letter and Other Poems,* 1944). His review of American poetry and a theory of poetry appear in *Essay on Rime* (1945; in verse), *Beyond Criticism* (1953) and especially in the vigorously iconoclastic *In Defense of Ignorance* (1960), a challenge to academicism and 'criticism-poetry', augmented by *To Abolish Children*. He edited *Poetry* (1950–6) and taught at Johns Hopkins and Nebraska Universities. He edits *Prairie Schooner*. The poems in his first book, *Poems* (1935), are archaic in diction and form, but by *Person, Place and Thing* (1942) his style had clarified with his selection of social subjects. *Trial of a Poet*

(1947) defines his religious experience, and *Poems of a Jew* (1958) asserts a special identity; *White-Haired Love* (1968) is a set of erotic love poems. *The Bourgeois Poet* (1964) is a collection of freely associated sections of autobiography, polemics and illusions, designed to maintain relationships with the irrational and disjunctive. [E M]

*Poems 1940–1953* (1953); *Selected Poems* (1968).

**Shaw, Henry Wheeler.** ◊ Billings, Josh.

**Shaw, Irwin** (1913– ). Novelist, short-story writer, playwright. Born in Brooklyn, he took various jobs before graduating from Brooklyn College. Later he scripted radio serials and wrote screenplays in Hollywood. A one-act play, *Bury the Dead* (1936), was a macabre and surrealist plea for pacifism; a second, *The Gentle People: A Brooklyn Fable* (1939), a parable warning against the spread of fascist behaviour. Since *Retreat to Pleasure* (1940) and *Sons and Soldiers* (1944) he has turned from drama to fiction. *The Young Lions* (1948) is a long war novel, rather limitingly constructed around three characters – a bitter young Nazi, a New York stage manager, and a sympathetic liberal Jew – through whom Shaw condenses attitudes towards the Second World War. *The Troubled Air* (1951) is an interesting study of the American liberal and his dilemma at that time. He has continued to treat ambitious subjects with *Lucy Crown* (1956) and *Two Weeks in Another Town* (1960), a study of the film industry and its preoccupation with appearance and reality. He is a distinguished short-story writer, publishing *Sailor off the Bremen* (1939), *Act of Faith and Other Stories* (1946), *Mixed Company* (1950), *Tip on a Dead Jockey and Other Stories* (1957) and *Love on a Dark Street* (1965). [M G]

*Selected Short Stories* (1961).
C. E. Eisinger, *Fiction of the Forties* (1963).

**Sherman, Stuart.** ◊ New Humanism, The.

**Sherwood, Robert** (1896–1955). Playwright. Born in New Rochelle, N.Y. He began his career, after Harvard and war service on the Western Front, with an attack on militarism in *The Road to Rome* (1927). He had been drama critic (1919–20) and editor of *Life* (1920–8), and he continued to work in the theatre throughout a busy life elsewhere. During the thirties and forties

he was active in trying to convince Americans of the dangers of totalitarianism, and F. D. Roosevelt, many of whose speeches he wrote, made him director of overseas operations in the Office of War Information (see his *Roosevelt and Hopkins: An Intimate History*, 1948). His playwriting eased off during this period, and latterly he wrote mostly for films and television, his most famous scenario being for William Wyler's *The Best Years of Our Lives* (1946). *Acropolis* (1933) excoriated Hitler, and *Idiot's Delight* (1936) is a pacifist set of arguments about the coming war and the decline of the West. *The Petrified Forest* (1935) takes place in an Arizona desert filling-station: a New England writer sacrifices his life to let a girl escape her desert environment. A certain slickness and simplification of motivation haunt Sherwood's work and make it more superficial than his grand themes might suggest. [E M]

John Mason Brown, *The Worlds of Robert E. Sherwood: Mirror to His Times* (1965).

**Sigal, Clancy** (1926– ). Novelist, social commentator. Born in Chicago, he studied literature and film-making at the University of California. After army-service he worked as a reporter, then in film and television documentary in Hollywood. Recently he has lived in England and contributed articles on social and film matters to English and American periodicals. His first book, *Weekend in Dinlock* (1960), reportage about a Yorkshire mining village, was much praised for its sharp observations and its strong social sense. His novel *Going Away* (1962) is a detailed study of disillusion with the left and the Unions in America: one of the few major political novels since the Second World War. [M B/E M]

**Simms, William Gilmore** (1806–70). Novelist, poet, editor. Through his birth and youth in Charleston, South Carolina, he inherited an aristocratic tradition, although he was virtually an orphan and lacked the money to be a Southern gentleman. He resisted his 'discontented and ever-wandering' father's invitation to Mississippi and practised law at home, writing poetry, his early mistaken vocation. In 1832 he moved north to New England and New York and in 1833 published his first novel, *Martin Faber*, a crime story out of Godwin and Brockden ◊ Brown, followed by the first of his famous Southern romances,

*Guy Rivers: A Tale of Georgia* (1834). During the composition of over 80 books, mostly novels and intelligent without being outstanding, he became the foremost writer in the South. After his second marriage he became a planter, defended the slave-state, was ruined in the Civil War, and was neglected as a writer until the Southern Renaissance after the Second World War. He wrote many romances of the Revolution and the Indian wars, but his best and most celebrated novel is *The Yemassee* (1835), which dramatizes the encroachment of white settlements on the American Indians. Unlike Cooper, Simms shows in realistic detail the community life of the Indians, which he knew at first hand. The vanquishing of the Yemassees is an American tragedy paralleled by the confrontation of Puritan and Cavalier whites, the other major American theme. He produced a series of romance-novels about the Revolution, beginning with *The Partisan* (1835); a series of novels about colonial and 19th-century Southern life; some novels on Spanish history; and a body of short stories. He is deeply indebted to Scott and Cooper and helped to establish the relevance of these writers for Southern literature. He also wrote histories of South Carolina, a *Life of Captain John Smith* (1846), several other biographies, and 18 volumes of poetry. He edited the *Southern and Western Monthly Magazine and Review* and later the *Southern Quarterly Review*, and later still became involved with *Russell's Magazine* – all part of his task of promoting Southern literature. His literary criticism is in *Views and Reviews in American Literature, History and Fiction* (1845). Though much of his output is hack work, Simms is an important cultural figure, influentially active for Southern literature, a friend of Poe and other Southern writers, and helping to build a body of work which develops towards Ellen Glasgow and William Faulkner. [EM/MB]

J. V. Ridgely, *William Gilmore Simms* (1962); Jay B. Hubbell, *The South in American Literature 1607–1900* (1954); W. J. Cash, *The Mind of the South* (1941).

**Simpson, Louis** (1923– ). Poet. Born and educated in Jamaica, a background on which some of his work draws, he then went to Columbia University, New York, and now teaches at the University of California at Berkeley. He is an impressive, inventive and often very witty poet, making close use of personal experience but also exploiting literary allusion and literary elegance. His volumes include *The Arrivistes: Poems 1940–1948* (1949) and *A Dream of Governors* (1959). *At the End of the Open Road* (1963) contains poems which experiment with freer forms. [MB]

*Selected Poems* (1966).
Richard Howard, *Alone with America* (1969).

**Sinclair, Upton** (1878–1968). Novelist. Born in Baltimore. While still under 20 he wrote with incredible facility and under a series of pseudonyms more than two million words a year for juvenile pulp fiction. Converted to socialism, he used the profits from his successful protest novel *The Jungle* (1906) to establish Helicon Hall, an experiment in cooperative living which ended in a disastrous fire. In California he was an unsuccessful candidate for the Senate, but his most audacious venture occurred during the Depression when he ran for the governorship of California on the EPIC platform – End Poverty in California. Something of a prophet without honour in his own country, his books – which number over 100 – have sold by the million; over 1,000 translations in over 50 languages have been noted. He told the story of the first 35 years of his life in *American Outpost* (1932) and incorporated this volume in his *Autobiography* (1962).

It is extraordinarily difficult to fit him into any of the established categories. In nearly all his novels the polemicist dominates the artist; even *The Jungle*, a nightmarish account of conditions in Chicago's Packingtown and probably his best single work, is to some extent vitiated by Jurgis's conversion to socialism. This work had been preceded by several novels, of which the best is *Manassas* (1904; revised as *Theirs Be The Guilt*, 1959), the first volume of a projected but never completed trilogy on the Civil War; he followed it with a lengthy series of artistically crude assaults upon the institutions and abuses of a capitalist society, from the operation of Wall Street in *The Money-changers* (1908) to the automobile industry in *The Flivver King* (1937). *King Coal* (1917) exposed the treatment of the striking Colorado miners; *Oil!* (1927), one of the most readable of his novels, skilfully depicts the corruption of the Harding era; *Boston* (1928) is a somewhat ponderous account of the trial and execution of Sacco and Vanzetti. At times he is undoubtedly a brisk and attractive narrator; but persistent socialist bias rarely allows his novels to rise above the ideological treatise. A better medium for his combative talents and ideas on social reform was the vigorous series of polemics which he wrote between 1918 and 1927: *The Profits of Religion* (1918); *The Brass Check* (1919), on the press; *The Goose Step* (1923) and *The Goslings* (1924), on the American educational system; *Mammonart* (1925) and *Money Writes* (1927), on art and literature.

In 1940 he published the first of the 11 novels collectively known as *World's End*. Through his protagonist Lanny Budd, he offered a detailed investigation of the international scene from the beginning of the First World War. Stylistically undistinguished and, like most of his writings, wanting in the humorous and the sexual, frequently naïve and sometimes dull, this immense *roman fleuve* achieved great popularity which, it has been suggested, derived from the mass of information it purveyed in an age of tyrannical fact. At the age of 83, he published a romance, *Affectionately Eve* (1961), whose main interest is the behavioural pattern of small-town Georgia and big-city New York.

The Sinclair papers – over eight tons – now reside at the Lilly Library, Indiana University, and the commemorative catalogue (compiled by Ronald Gottesman) issued to accompany an exhibition in 1963 gives some indication of the range and variety of the extraordinary career of this extraordinary man. [HD]

*My Lifetime in Letters* (1960).
Floyd Dell, *Upton Sinclair: A Study in Social Protest* (1927); D. M. Chalmers, *The Social and Political Ideas of the Muckrakers* (1965).

**Singer, Isaac Bashevis** (1904– ). Story writer, novelist. Born in Radzymin, Poland, and raised in a poor section of Warsaw. His father and grandfather were rabbis, and he was educated at the Warsaw Rabbinical Seminary. Warsaw at this time was a major centre of religious and cultural Jewish life and had already produced many major Jewish writers when Singer turned to a writing career in preference to the rabbinical. In 1935, anticipating Hitler's invasion of Poland, he emigrated to the U.S.A., and since then has worked as a regular journalist and columnist for the New York Jewish daily paper, the *Forward,* where he has printed fiction over his own name and journalism under the pen-name Warshofsky. Apart from some early work published in Warsaw, nearly all his fiction has been

written in Yiddish for this journal, and usually produced under the strain of regular journalism. It is only recently that it has been translated on any scale and that his merit, and the endurance of his writing, has been recognized by a general audience. His reputation with non-Jewish audiences is now higher than that of any other Yiddish writer.

He writes chiefly about the Yiddish communities of his native Poland, exploring the folk-traditions and a deep-seated communal life of the past. His work is undoubtedly much indebted to his precursors in the Yiddish tradition, such as Aleichem and ◊ Asch, but is much more modern in approach and has undoubtedly been shaped by his experience in America. His themes of witchcraft, mystery and legend draw on traditional sources and traditional life, but they are established in a modern and ironic way. Worked with a deep and humane wisdom and insight, rich in the details of Jewish peasant and town life, they are also concerned with the bizarre and the grotesque, with irrationality and sexuality, and are often structurally convoluted and daring. His first major work, *Satan in Goray*, a short novel about the ferment in a Polish town in the 17th century when a messianic sect takes over, appeared in Yiddish in 1935 (in English, 1955). Among other books now translated are the novels *The Family Moskat* (in English, 1950), about a Warsaw family between 1914 and 1939, *The Magician of Lublin* (1960), *The Slave* (1960), *The Manor* (1967), the first part of a longer work concerning the exodus from their Polish ghetto of Jews after the insurrection of 1863, and *The Estate* (1969). His stories, which probably show him at his very best, are to be found in *Gimpel the Fool* (1957), *The Spinoza of Market Street* (1961), *Short Friday* (1964), and *The Seance and Other Stories* (1968). In 1966, Singer published *In My Father's Court,* a sensitive memoir of his youth in Warsaw. [MB]

Irving Howe 'I. B. Singer', *Encounter,* XXVI, 3 (March 1966); Dan Jacobson, 'The Problem of Isaac Bashevis Singer', *Commentary,* February 1965.

**Skinner, Cornelia Otis** (1901– ). Actress, humorist. She was born in Chicago, and wrote her first play, *Captain Fury,* in 1925. She became famous for her solo shows and her humorous books: *Tiny Garments* (1932), *Excuse It, Please* (1936), *The Ape in Me* (1959), etc. Her best-selling *Our Hearts*

*Were Young and Gay* (1942), with Emily Kimbrough, describes their European trip. She has also written a biography of Sarah Bernhardt. [EM]

**Slaughter, Frank** (1908– ). Novelist. Born in Washington, D.C. He has written non-fiction works on surgery and psychosomatic medicine, but it is his medical novels that have been best-sellers since *That None Should Die* (1941). They include *Air Surgeon* (1943), *A Touch of Glory* (1945), *The Healer* (1955), *Epidemic* (1961) and *Surgeon's Choice* (1969). [EM]

**Smith, Betty** (1904– ). Novelist. Born in Brooklyn, N.Y. After her early career as an actress she drew on her slum childhood for a best-selling novel, *A Tree Grows in Brooklyn* (1943). *Tomorrow Will Be Better* (1948) and *Maggie-Now* (1958) were only slightly less successful. [EM]

**Smith, Elihu Hubbard.** ◊ Connecticut Wits.

**Smith, (Captain) John** (1580?–1631). Soldier of fortune, explorer, chronicler. He was an Elizabethan adventurer before and after becoming governor of Virginia. He had travelled and lived in Poland, Russia, Transylvania and Turkey, returning to England in 1604 and, according to his own account, became one of the original promoters of the Virginia Company. He sailed with the first expedition to Virginia in 1605, helped to found the Jamestown settlement in the following spring, and was elected president of the colony. During important local explorations he established invaluable good relations with the Indians, securing food supplies which enabled the colonists to survive the first winter. His function was to consolidate the Virginia adventure on a business footing and substantiate semi-mythical geography. He was an enthusiast rather than a factual historian; his *A True Relation of . . . Virginia* (1608) is a business report raised by style to the level of literature, and it includes an account of the founding of Jamestown. He returned to England in 1609, revisiting America in 1614 to explore the coastline up to Maine and to trade for furs with the Indians. His series of maps and topographical accounts were to stimulate colonization, but his intelligent and explorative mind comes through clearly. *A Description of New England* (1616) is a valuable treatise urging the importance of

fish and furs as economic bases, arguing that to hunt for gold in the New World was futile. Codfish were unglamorous but a foundation for prosperity (see Charles Olson, *The Maximus Poems*, 1960). His *General History of Virginia, New England, and the Summer Isles* (1624) combines writings by himself and others. Smith helped to create American myths of heroism and endurance, and, through the Indian princess Pocahontas, the romance which tended to hide the exploitation of the Indians. But his stories tend to be more plausible than fictitious, and certainly evoke the spirit of early settlers who were not Puritans. [DKA/EM]

*Travels and Works*, ed. W. Arber, intr. A. G. Bradley (2 vols., Edinburgh, 1910); *Captain John Smith's America: Selections from His Writings*, ed. J. Lankford (1967).
Bradford Smith, *Captain John Smith* (1953); Philip Barbour, *The Three Worlds of Captain John Smith* (1964).

**Smith, Logan Pearsall** (1865–1946). Critic, scholar. Born at Millville, New Jersey, he came from a famous Philadelphia Quaker family, and was educated at Harvard and Oxford. Enabled by an annuity to become an expatriate, he settled in England. Like his brother-in-law Bernard ◊ Berenson, he wished to pursue a life of connoisseurship and aestheticism. His writings include a series of books of elegant, witty aphorisms and essays – *Trivia* (1902), *More Trivia* (1921), etc.; and a good deal of biographical, lexicographical and bibliographical work, including a biography of Sir Henry Wootton. He attacked the denigration of Milton by Pound and Eliot in *Milton and His Modern Critics* (1941). *Words and Idioms* (1925) is an excellent collection of articles on language. His autobiography, *Unforgotten Years* (1938), has some fascinating, Anglophile comments on American letters and on the habit of literary expatriation among American writers. [MB]

**Smith, William** (1727–1803). Scottish clergyman, historian. He went to Long Island as a tutor in 1751. His *A General Idea of the College of Mirania* (1753) impressed ◊ Franklin into helping him become provost of the College of Philadelphia. His pro-British views (*Sermon on the Present Situation of American Affairs*, 1775) and criticism of the Quakers made him suspect and vulnerable, and in 1779 the college's charter was withdrawn. He founded Washington

College, Maryland, but returned to his Philadelphian college and remained until it became the University of Pennsylvania in 1791. The best account of this eminent if irascible teacher is A. F. Gegenheimer's *William Smith: Educator and Churchman* (1943). [EM]

**Smith, William Gardner** (1926– ). Novelist. Born in Philadelphia and studied at Temple University. One of the most interesting Negro American writers. His novels include *Last of the Conquerors* (1948), *Anger at Innocence* (1950) and *The Stone Face* (1964). [EM]

**Smith, William Jay** (1918– ). Poet. Born in Louisiana, he studied at Washington University, Columbia, and as a Rhodes Scholar at Oxford, and has taught at Wesleyan, Columbia and Williams. A member of the Vermont legislature, he is married to the poet Barbara ◊ Howes. His books include *Poems* (1947), *Celebration at Dark* (1950), *Poems 1947–1957* (1957) and *The Tin Can and Other Poems* (1966). He has written children's books and published translations of Laforgue and Valéry Larbaud. His verse ranges between concise and precise lyrical poems and, more recently, long-line poems of a newly expansive and explorative kind. *The Spectre Hoax* (1961) and *Herrick: Selections* (1969) are books of criticism. [MB]

**Snodgrass, W(illiam) D(e Witt)** (1926– ). Poet. Born in Wilkinsburg, Pennsylvania, he won a high reputation on the strength of a single volume, *Heart's Needle*, published in America in 1959 and in England in 1960. It contains a number of poems written over the previous eight years, and the long title-sequence of poems to his daughter. The 'Heart's Needle' sequence shows his best qualities, particularly his power of using very indirectly connected images to link the central events of the poem – the birth of his child during the Korean War and his subsequent loss of contact with her after his divorce – with various social and political events and with the context of a bleak natural world. He studied at Geneva College and the State University of Iowa, and has taught at various American universities, including Cornell and Wayne State. The cosy domesticity and traditional cadences of the original poems in *After Experience:*

*Poems and Translations* (1968) are somewhat oppressive, but the translations from Rilke and others are excellent. [MB]

Paul Carroll, *The Poem in Its Skin* (1968).

**Snyder, Gary** (1930– ). Poet. He was born in San Francisco and grew up in the North-west. He studied Japanese and Chinese at Berkeley and in Japan, took his B.A. in anthropology, and has worked as logger, forester, carpenter and seaman. Since 1956 he has lived mostly in Japan. All these elements of his life are used in his poetry, which can be seen as a series of relationships between western and eastern cultures, machine technology and wild nature in America, the city and the soil, history and contemporary society. His images draw on this wide range of concerns and experience. His diction is economical and pure, his syntax flexible and terse, and his excellent craftsmanship has a freshness and respect for shapeliness rare in modern poetry. His poetry shows the open-air American fused with the scholar of *haiku* and Indian lore. His work is included in *Riprap* (1959; repr. with 'Cold Mountain Poems', 1958, in 1965), *Myths and Texts*, *Six Sections from Mountains and Rivers Without End* (1965), *A Range of Poems* (1966, which includes the earlier poems and two other sections, 'Miyazawa' and 'The Back Country') and *The Back Country* (1967). *Earth House Hold* (1969) is an important collection of essays and journals. [EM]

David Kherdian, *Gary Snyder: A Biographical Sketch and Descriptive Checklist* (1965).

**Sontag, Susan** (1933– ). Novelist, critic. Her first novel, *The Benefactor* (1963), is a semi-surrealistic analysis of inner consciousness. The title of *Death Kit* (1967), her second, refers to a death kit for the white race, which she described in an article as 'the cancer of human history'; the novel itself does not quite satisfy its experimental and symbolistic pretensions. Her influential essays on cultural matters have appeared in *Partisan Review, New York Review of Books,* etc., and show a sharp eye for cultural tendencies and great cleverness of manner; they are collected in *Against Interpretation* (1966). *Trip to Hanoi* (1969) is both reportage and an act of self-discovery. She has also published experimental short stories and *Styles of Radical Will* (1969). [MB]

**Sorrentino, Gilbert** (1929–    ). Poet. He was educated at Brooklyn College, founded the magazine *Neon*, and extends W. C. ◊ Williams' and ◊ Creeley's work in *The Darkness Surrounds Us* (1960) and *Black and White* (1964). *The Sky Changes* (1966) is a penetrating autobiographical novel. [EM]

**Southern, Terry** (1924–    ). Novelist, short-story writer. Born in Alvarado, Texas, he lives in New York City. His novel *Candy* written in collaboration with Mason Hoffenberg and published in Paris in 1955 under the pseudonym 'Maxwell Kenton', and in America in 1964, is a parody of *Candide* in which a naïve and innocent girl is subjected to an outrageous series of sexual advances in various contexts. The novel is also a parody of pornographic and salacious writing. Like *Candy*, Southern's *Flash and Filigree* (1958) contains parody of contemporary mores in its twin plots of persecuted medical specialist and college-level seduction. *The Magic Christian* (1959) is a short *conte* in which Guy Grand, a 'fabulous' billionaire, sets out to prove that everyone has his price and will perform any exploit, however scatological or malodorous, if you have the money to pay for it. Southern also collaborated on the film script of *Dr Strangelove: or, How I learned to Stop Worrying and Love the Bomb. Red Dirt Marijuana and Other Tastes* (1967) is a collection of short stories in excellent bad taste. [AG]

Arnold Goldman, 'What's New in American Fiction', *Views Quarterly* (Spring, 1965).

**Spencer, Elizabeth** (1921–    ). Novelist. Most of her fiction is set in Mississippi, where she was born. At Vanderbilt University, Nashville, she came under the influence of Donald Davidson, once a leading member of the ◊ Fugitive group, who helped her to publish her first novel, *Fire in the Morning* (1948). This and its successor, *This Crooked Way* (1952), show the influence of established Southern writers such as Eudora ◊ Welty and Carson ◊ McCullers. *The Voice at the Back Door* (1956) is an economically written novel about the problem of justice in the South. *The Light in the Piazza* (1960) is a short novel about an American woman and her mentally retarded daughter travelling in Italy. *Knights and Dragons* (1965) is an ambitious novel of blocked sensibilities, set in Rome. *No Place for an Angel* (1967) describes a pair of American marriages, and succumbs to self-conscious time-effects. *Ship Island* (1968) is a collection of neat stories. [AH/EM]

**Spicer, Jack** (1925–65). Poet. Born in California, where he lived and worked most of his life, his work as research linguist is strongly felt in his poetry, which is a highly complex but humane series of exploits with language. In *After Lorca* (1957) he says 'a poet is a time mechanic not an embalmer': the translations, poems and letters construct a witty commentary on the Spanish poet. *Billy the Kid* (1959) is a long poem on this Western myth; *The Head of the Town up to the Aether* (1962) is a set of poems and commentaries of considerable wit and formal experiment; *Language* (1965) and *Book of Magazine Verse* (1966) develop Spicer's complex sense of his particular society and extend his poetics. His other volumes include: *Lament for the Makers* (1962), *The Holy Grail* (1964), *Vancouver Lectures* 1966) and *A Book of Music* (1969). [EM]

**Spillane, Mickey** (Frank Morrison Spillane) (1918–    ). Detective-story writer. The exponent of a debased form of the 'hard-boiled' school of crime fiction and the creator of Mike Hammer, the private detective who appears in a series of novels which offer a best-selling mixture of sex and sadism. Hammer's relationship with his secretary Velda may be said to invoke the principle of procrastinated rape. Spillane's works include *I, The Jury* (1947), *Vengeance Is Mine* (1950), *The Long Wait* (1951), *Kiss Me, Deadly* (1952) and, more recently, *The Deep* (1961), *The Girl Hunters* (1962) and *The Snake* (1964). With *The Twisted Thing* (1966) it has become clear that Spillane's formula is an accurate myth of American violence. [IID]

**Stafford, Jean** (1915–    ). Novelist, story writer. Born in California, she studied at the University of Colorado and in Germany. She was married to Robert ◊ Lowell and later to A. J. Leibling, and has lived in various parts of the U.S.A. A delicate, highly accomplished writer, she has won high regard for her fiction – a fiction of sensibility and texture that frequently turns to the study of the growth of maturity and insight. Her novels include *Boston Adventure* (1944), dealing with a girl of cosmopolitan background who works as a private secretary to a woman in Boston; *The Mountain Lion* (1947), which treats the experience of two children living on a Colorado ranch; and *The Catherine Wheel* (1951). She is probably best known, however, as a short-story writer, for her two collections *Children Are Bored on Sunday* (1953) and *Bad Characters* (1964), both remarkable ventures in a form well suited to her talent and sensibility. Her non-fiction book on Lee Harvey Oswald's mother, *A Mother in History* (1966), captures a terrifying personality. [MB]

*Collected Stories* (1969).
C. E. Eisinger, *Fiction of the Forties* (1965).

**Stafford, William** (1914– ). Poet. A native of Kansas, educated at the Universities of Kansas, Wisconsin and Iowa. He now teaches at Lewis and Clark College in Oregon, and a good deal of his poetry – collected in *West of Your City* (1960), *Travelling through the Dark* (1962) and *The Rescued Year* (1966) – is set in the uncluttered Western and West Coast landscape. A lucid but not a simple poet, establishing his themes coolly and with detachment, he often draws for his subject matter on the contrast between modern mechanical civilization and more natural and primitive cultures, between the turns and ambiguities of our minds today and a more direct apprehension of things. [MB]

*Five American Poets*, ed. Thom Gunn and Ted Hughes (1963).

**Stallings, Laurence** (1894– ). Novelist, dramatist. Born in Georgia. His active early life is told in his novel *Plumes* (1924). His war experience went into his plays in collaboration with Maxwell ◊ Anderson, *What Price Glory?* (1924), *First Flight* (1925; on Andrew Jackson's youth), and *The Buccaneer* (1925; on Sir Henry Morgan). His photographic record *The First World War* (1933) was a best-seller, and he subsequently wrote many scenarios and librettos, none of them as popular as his early writings. His *Deep River* (1926) was one of the first works to use jazz in opera. His most famous film was *The Big Parade* (1925), and in 1963 he wrote *The Doughboys*, a first-rate account of the American Expeditionary Force, 1917–18. [EM]

**Starbuck, George** (1931– ). Poet. Born in Columbus, Ohio, and studied at the University of Chicago and at Harvard. His

stay in the Boston area produced some of his best poems, which form a part of his volume *Bone Thoughts* (1960). A poet of striking versatility and range of interests, he offers poems of a mordant whimsicality along with fables, odes, personal confessions, and celebrations and satires of places and their human populations. There is a macabre strain to his work; he presents with stylish vernacular effects the cruelty and violence he finds in the modern world. His most recent work is in *White Paper* (1966). [MB]

**Steffens, (Joseph) Lincoln** (1866–1936). Journalist. He was born in San Francisco and became an important newspaper man in New York, after a restless youth and studying abroad. He is associated with what President Theodore ◊ Roosevelt, in 1906, termed the 'muckraking' movement, journalists who were trying to expose the widespread corruption of American public life. He contributed a great deal to this cause through his editorship of *McClure's* magazine (1902–6) and associate editorship of the *American Magazine* (1906–11). His influence was the more considerable, coming at a time when the reformist progressive movement was increasing political strength. His *McClure's* articles analysing civic government in six major cities formed the basis of *The Shame of the Cities* (1904). There followed *The Struggle for Self-Government* (1906), *Upbuilders* (1909) and *Out of Muck* (1913). His rambling and readable *Autobiography* (1931) demonstrates his political radicalism as well as his interest in social reform. His articles were collected posthumously in *Lincoln Steffens Talking* (1936), and his *Letters* in 1938. [HD]

*The World of Lincoln Steffens*, ed. Ella Winter and Herbert Shapiro (1962).
Ella Winter, *And Not To Yield* (1963).

**Stegner, Wallace** (1909– ). Novelist, short-story writer, journalist. He was born in Iowa, and studied at Iowa and California Universities. He has been a university teacher, partly as a director of the creative writing centre at Stanford. His writing draws on wide first-hand and historical knowledge of the West. His distinguished novels of rural America include *Remembering Laughter* (1937), set on an Iowa farm, *On a Darkling Plain* (1940), about Saskatchewan during the 1918 influenza epidemic, *The Big Rock Candy Mountain* (1943), a family's search for opportunity through the Western frontierlands, *The Preacher and the Slave* (1950), about Joe Hill the labour leader, and *A Shooting Star* (1961), about wealthy Californians. His finest novel is *Wolf Willow* (1962), which besides being a classic of survival by adaptation is an analysis of the last frontier of the Great Plains and contains much autobiographical material. *All the Little Things* (1967) concerns the search for paradise gardens on the West Coast by a retired editor, a hippy and a university ethnologist. All his fiction is factually detailed, packed with characters and richly planned and written. His short stories are included in *Women on the Wall* (1950) and *City of the Living* (1956). Stegner is at least as famous for his non-fiction: *One Nation* (1945), a polemical survey of national and religious tension, *The Central Northwest* (1947), *The Gathering of Zion* (1964), a fascinating study of the Mormon treks, and *The Writer's Art* (1950). *Beyond the Hundredth Meridian* (1954) is a fine biography of John Wesley Powell, the explorer and nature conservationist, and an important study of the non-mythical west. Essays, letters and memoirs are collected in *The Sound of Mountain Water* (1969). [EM/MB]

**Stein, Gertrude** (1874–1946). Novelist, poet. Born in Allegheny, Pennsylvania, she was educated at Harvard's Radcliffe College (for women) and Johns Hopkins University in Baltimore. Psychology and medicine were then her primary interests, and at Harvard she had come under the influence of William ◊ James. In 1903 she moved abroad where, except for a short visit, she remained for the rest of her life, making Paris her 'home town'. She championed various young painters, most notably Picasso, Braque and Juan Gris, all then unknown, and her salon at 27 rue de Fleurus, where she hung her *inaccrochables*, became famous. Expatriate and visiting American writers like Sherwood Anderson and Scott Fitzgerald always sought her out (◊ Expatriates, Lost Generation). Her relationship with Ernest Hemingway, who helped type the vast manuscript of her novel *The Making of Americans* (1925, but written almost 20 years before), is legendary: she came to think his vaunted courage a sham; in his posthumously published *A Moveable Feast*, Gertrude Stein's relation with Alice B. Toklas, her female companion who died in

1967, is impugned. Nevertheless, her experiments in prose – originating perhaps in her Harvard project on automatic writing – particularly in the simplification of syntax, influenced Hemingway and others. These experiments may be seen in various stages of development in *Three Lives* (1909), *Tender Buttons* (1914) and *Geography and Plays* (1922). These books gave her a reputation for extreme unintelligibility, and she became in the eyes of many the leader of the *avant garde* in American writing. Her syntactical manipulations perhaps blinded her first readers to the homespun quality of her feelings about place and country – she was perhaps the only modernist who was always 'patriotic' – and for all her interest in subconscious processes her analysis of motive is hardly Freudian. The really radical departure in her stylistic experimentation was her attempt to develop a 'cubist' literature, a prose independent of meaningful associations, relying merely on sound-orchestration. Why she felt that 'meaning' had to be abandoned to create a multi-dimensional art remains something of a mystery, and there is no doubt that many who find pleasure in her work do so against her express intention, by enjoying the meaning they can piece out. *The Making of Americans* is her most assuming work; an attempt to write a *total* history of America by reporting in infinite detail and repetition the history of the Hersland family; the work runs to over 900 pages. In 1933 she wrote an autobiographical fragment of her Paris life, entitling it *The Autobiography of Alice B. Toklas*. While influenced by her other experiments, *The Autobiography* is not itself experimental and gained for her a wider readership. This book, combined with her lecture tour of America in 1934 – out of which came her *Lectures in America* (1935) (*Everybody's Autobiography*, 1938, deals with this period of her life) – and her 'mothering' of American G.I.s in the Second World War, brought her into public prominence. Her writing took a turn for the lucid, and her naïve posture – which many had thought drollery – combined with a new lucidity made her a lost leader in the eyes of many more determinedly aesthetic intellectuals. In this last period, she enjoyed herself as never before, and this is clear in *Paris France* (1940) and *Wars I Have Seen* (1945). Her lifelong appreciation of painting is demonstrated in many essays and particularly in *Picasso* (1939). The two best introductory collections of her writings are Carl

Van Vechten's *Selected Writings of Gertrude Stein* (1946; intr. F. W. Dupee 1962) and Patricia Meyerowitz's *Gertrude Stein: Writing and Lectures 1911–1945* (1967). [A G]

*The Yale Edition of the Unpublished Writings* (8 vols., 1951 ff.).
Donald Sutherland, *Gertrude Stein: A Biography of her Work* (1951); J. M. Brinnin, *The Third Rose: Gertrude Stein and Her World* (1959); Allegra Stewart, *Gertrude Stein and the Present* (1967); B. L. Reid, *Art by Subtraction: A Dissenting Opinion of Gertrude Stein* (1958); Alice B. Toklas, *What Is Remembered* (1963).

**Steinbeck, John** (1902–68). Novelist, short-story writer. Born in California, he attended Stanford University, studying marine biology without taking a degree. After a series of labouring jobs, he began writing. Most of his best work is related to the California either of his childhood or of the 1930s, when the social and economic conflicts inherent in the earlier period erupted. Born into a society in flux, he has turned usually to proletarian subjects and made a major theme of the search for values in the face of increasing dehumanization. The objectivity of this search has drawn attack from all sides; by dealing with the unfortunate, and showing how food was allowed to rot while men starved (*In Dubious Battle*, 1936, *The Grapes of Wrath*, 1939), he won the hostility of the haves, while his view that human happiness was not of necessity linked with the competitive life but could reside in idyllic poverty (*Tortilla Flat*, 1935) was attacked by the militant left. Though he wrote extensively about labour troubles, and even developed a theory of group man, both his life-long interest in biological observation and his deep romanticism make him at once too objective and too lyric for a simple political classification. Even *In Dubious Battle*, entirely devoted to the story of a strike of migratory fruit-pickers in California, is primarily concerned with creating actuality, and engages us with the strikers on humane, not doctrinaire, ground. Even more famous in this respect is *The Grapes of Wrath*, a landmark in American culture; the epic migration of the Joad family from Oklahoma to California, hunting work, is seen as a remarkable human endeavour, as meaningful and moving as any of the earlier westward migrations. He uses the same kind of language to re-create this crossing as he does in 'The Leader of the People' to describe a wagon-train crossing: 'Every man wanted some-

thing for himself, but the big beast that was all of them wanted only westering.' The book is simultaneously realistic and lyrical, gaining its scope by a technique of interposed chapters of commentary.

He is often a novelist of large ambitions; *Tortilla Flat*, about the happy lower depths of Monterey society, attempts a whimsically heroic dimension by bringing in Arthurian overtones. Fortunately, here as elsewhere, the book can be read without too much attention to its over-elaborate intellectual framework, and it is, with the two books already mentioned, among his best work. *Of Mice and Men* (1937), about a simpleton farmhand, has not stood up, but *The Pastures of Heaven* (1932) – best read not as a novel but as a collection of loosely related stories – and *The Long Valley* (1938) have. The latter work includes the four magnificent 'Red Pony' stories, and could serve as an admirable introduction to Steinbeck, showing his characteristic interests – the tensions of town and country, of past and present, of labour and ownership, as well as the objectivity of biological observation and a sort of Lawrencean mystic concept of personal power.

The later books are less impressive. *Cannery Row* (1945) returns to the mood and locale of *Tortilla Flat*, but the tone is less consistent, often more sentimental (though some scenes, notably the celebrated frog hunt, stand out). *The Wayward Bus* (1947), *The Pearl* (1947), *Sweet Thursday* (1954; a sequel to *Cannery Row*) and *The Short Reign of Pippin IV* (1957), a political satire, are all professional but minor works which do not recapture his earlier strength. The most ambitious post-war novel is *East of Eden* (1952), a parable of the fall of man, of Cain and Abel, and of human possibility, showing many of the virtues of his best books, but touched with sentimentality, melodrama and intrusive commentary. *The Winter of Our Discontent* (1961) partly renews his ability to write topical social fiction – the scene has shifted from California to Long Island. The best of his non-fiction works is *Sea of Cortez* (1941, with Edward F. Ricketts) and *The Log of the Sea of Cortez* (1951); and of his three books from the Second World War, *Once There Was a War* (1958) selects well from his war-correspondent articles. The play and film of his novel of the Nazis in Scandinavia, *The Moon is Down* (1942), were popularly successful, and recently his rediscovery of America, *Travels with Charley* (1962), was a best-seller. In 1966 he wrote the text for a book of photographs, *America and Americans*, a further stage in his idiosyncratic search for a usable native land. His mixed career won the Nobel Prize in 1962. [D C]

Warren French, *John Steinbeck* (1961); F. W. Watt, *Steinbeck* (1962); Peter Lisca, *The Wide World of John Steinbeck* (1958).

**Stern, Richard** (1928– ). Novelist, short-story writer. He was born in New York City, and studied at the Universities of North Carolina, Harvard and Iowa. He is Professor of English in the Department of General Studies in the Humanities at Chicago. *Golk* (1960), his first novel, is a satire on television through the career of a megalomaniac TV producer and his willingly duped assistants and audiences. *Europe or Up and Down with Baggish and Schreiber* (1961) describes the adventure of two Americans exploring Europe immediately after the last war. Then followed *In Any Case* (1963), a rather overwritten work, and *Teeth, Dying and Other Matters* (1964), which combined a collection of short stories, an essay on politics and a play, 'The Gamesman's Island'. *Stitch* (1965) concerns an advertising copy-writer who gives up his Chicago life and takes his family to Venice, unsuccessfully searching for answers to his perennial human problems. But the centre of the book is an American sculptor and his masterpiece, a stone garden, and Nina, a young poet, with Poundian ambitions. Stern has also edited an interesting anthology called *Honey and Wax: The Powers and Pleasures of Narrative* (1966). [E M]

**Stevens, Wallace** (1879–1955). Poet. Born in Reading, Pennsylvania. Now critically regarded as one of the greatest 20th-century American poets, he was an executive of a Hartford, Connecticut, insurance company, writing verse in his spare time. One of the experimental generation in modern poetry that appeared between 1910 and 1920, printing his verse in various little magazines, including *Poetry*, he published his first volume, *Harmonium*, in 1923. The volumes that followed – *Ideas of Order* (1935), *Owl's Clover* (1936), *The Man with the Blue Guitar* (1937), *Parts of a World* (1942), *Notes toward a Supreme Fiction* (1942), *Esthétique du Mal* (1945) and *The Auroras of Autumn* (1950) – show a continuous development in poetic thought and method. His chief concern as a poet – and as an aesthetician – has been with the central issue of post-romantic verse: the problem of how we perceive reality creatively in a universe in which God cannot be assumed to be pantheistically present. In a sense, he is the poet as philosopher, and his poems consistently deal with the way in which things outside the self resist meaningful definition, and how poetry and imagination, 'the supreme fiction', are primary and truthful instruments of comprehension – are, in fact, the highest way of knowing. Many of his poems deal, then, with the actual poetic act itself, and in this sense he is a modern romantic. Other poems demonstrate how the loss of Christian faith actually elevates poetry, affording the poet and indeed the ordinary man the clarity of the unencumbered imagination. Yet reality, particularly in a post-Christian universe, constantly changes; and it is the truthfulness and accuracy with which he pursues truthful accounting and truthful speculation – his basic themes throughout an extensive and continued body of work – that make him so major a poet.

His early reputation was as a dandy of poetry; much of his verse, particularly his early verse, was witty, balletic and comic in diction. He is well known for his use of recondite words; and his highly mannered style is the basis of the attraction he first exerts on his readers. But even the lightest and gayest and most colourful of his verse is consistent with his general line of speculation. To Coleridge, whom speculatively he resembles, such verse would show the operation of 'fancy', but, in a universe without basic revelatory symbols, fancy becomes important as a mode of creativity; the poet by loving the world enriches it. Stevens is concerned with the discovery of the universals operative in the world; but impressionism – and he *is* an impressionist – becomes very much more important to him than to the romantics. Yet reading through the body of his poetry, one finds a core of repeated, fundamental imagery – the imagery of the seasons, standing for different modes of imagining, different relations between perceiver and perceived; the imagery of colours; the images of harmony – central to the continued speculation. In his later poems, the ones usually preferred by his most dedicated followers, the gay enrichment of the world is less evident. These poems are much sparer than the early ones, and closer, in a sense, to the ideal relationship between the poet and his reality. But there are no conditions (and this point is essential to his aesthetics) in which the perfect relationship is fully attainable, because of the mutability of the world, and of the imagination. What he can propose is that there is an idea of order, a contained set of conditions (like the cycle of the seasons, which is a pattern of *predictable* change), within which the modern poet can work.

The problems of modern poetry make him a central figure of modern aesthetics. His essays, *The Necessary Angel* (1951), contain his prose speculations about the imagination, and make quite evident his relation to Coleridge and the romantics. His poetry is collected in two volumes, *Collected Poems* (1954) and *Opus Posthumous* (1957), which together with *The Necessary Angel* provide the body of his work. The *Letters of Wallace Stevens* (1967) is essential, but still leaves about 2,000 letters unpublished. [MB]

Frank Kermode, *Wallace Stevens* (1960); Robert Buttel, *Wallace Stevens: The Making of 'Harmonium'* (1967); John J. Enck, *Wallace Stevens: Images and Judgements* (1964); ed. R. H. Pearce and J. H. Miller, *The Act of Mind: Essays on the Poetry of Wallace Stevens* (1965).

**Stewart, Donald Ogden** (1894– ). Humorist, dramatist. He began his career as an actor and then in the 1920s won a reputation as a humorist with books like *A Parody Outline of History* (1921) and *Mr and Mrs Haddock Abroad* (1924). In the 1930s and early 1940s he was one of the many interesting figures in the Hollywood movie colony, where he wrote a number of film scripts. His plays for Broadway included *How I Wonder* (1947). He now lives in London. [MB]

**Stickney, Trumbull** (1874–1904). Poet. Brought from Switzerland to America when he was 5, he was educated by his father well enough to enter Harvard. After graduation in 1895 he returned to Europe and became one of the first Americans to receive the *doctorat de lettres* from the Sorbonne. He taught at Harvard until his early death from a brain tumour. As poet he is associated with the neo-classicism of William Vaughn ◊ Moody. His *Prometheus Pyphoros* (1900) presents the Greek hero as hero of scientific progress in dramatic scenes influenced by his friend Henry ◊ Adams. His collected poems (1905) was issued by his friends posthumously. [EM]

244

Ed. James Reeves and S. Haldane, *Homage to Trumbull Stickney* (1968).

**Stone, Irving** (1903– ). Novelist. Born in California, he studied at the University of California. Though he began his literary career by writing plays, he is best known as the author of a number of fictionalized biographies, the method of which is to present well-researched factual material while dramatizing – often very romantically – the thoughts and conversations of the characters. *Lust for Life* (1934) deals with Van Gogh; *The Agony and the Ecstasy* (1961) with Michelangelo. *Adversary in the House* (1947) takes as its subject Eugene V. Debs, the American labour leader, and *The Passionate Journey* (1949) John Noble, an American painter expatriate in Paris. *False Witness* (1940) explores the discord that breaks out in an idealistic California community in 1903. He has also written biographies of Jack London and Earl Warren. [MB]

**Stout, Rex** (1886– ). Detective-story writer. Born in Noblesville, Indiana. He published several 'straight' novels before turning at 48 to detective fiction. Since *Fer-de-Lance* (1934) his massive private investigator, Nero Wolfe, has dominated a large number of novels and stories. A verbally and gastronomically fastidious man who delights in growing orchids, Wolfe rarely ventures out of his New York house; the essential facts in his cases are gathered by his assistant Archie Goodwin. Stout's more recent publications include *Champagne for One* (1958), *Too Many Clients* (1960), *Gambit* (1962) and *A Right to Die* (1964). In *The Doorbell Rang* (1965), his twenty-second Nero Wolfe novel, the hero traps the F.B.I. to the point when J. Edgar Hoover himself comes to the rescue. A profile of Stout by Alva Johnston appeared in the *New Yorker*, 16 and 23 July 1949. [HD]

W. S. Baring-Gould, *Nero Wolfe of West Thirty-Fifth Street* (1969).

**Stowe, Harriet Beecher** (1811–96). Novelist. She was born in Litchfield, Connecticut, daughter of a famous orthodox Calvinist minister and sister of five brothers who became ministers. Although educated at private schools and her sister's female academy, where she taught later, she also read the *Arabian Nights*, Scott's novels and Lord Byron, as well as Cotton ◊ Mather.

In 1832 the family dutifully took religion and culture to the mid-Western frontier town of Cincinnati, where Harriet learned about slavery and the 'Underground Railway' at first hand. In 1836 she married a teacher at her father's theological seminary and in 1850 returned east with him to Maine (where he was professor at Bowdoin College) with her seventh child. Up to 1852 her writings were religious, didactic or textbookish, but these and her temperance tales were at least practice for her masterpiece, *Uncle Tom's Cabin*, immediately inspired by the Fugitive Slave Law of 1850 and by a vision of Uncle Tom's death during a communion service in 1851. With the steady income due to his wife's celebrity, Calvin Stowe left Bowdoin, and the family went to live at Hartford, Connecticut, near Mark Twain; Harriet bought a plantation in Florida. One of her sons drowned in 1857, another became an ex-army drunkard, her twin daughters were old maids and another daughter a morphine addict. But Mrs Stowe managed to find time, in 1869, to defend Lady Byron, whom she had met in England, by charging the poet with incest.

*Uncle Tom's Cabin* was serialized in the *National Era* (1851–2) and in book form (1852) 300,000 copies were sold in six months and it became an international best-seller. It is not the simple sentimental tract it is often held to be but a powerful analysis of every aspect of racialism, including a good understanding of the sexuality of slavery and a fair range of Yankee and Southern slaveholders. Mrs Stowe knew exactly how slavery degenerates, even if her death of Little Eva is sentimental and her integratable Negro rather crude. Her book undoubtedly contributed to national resistances to slavery which led to the Civil War, as Lincoln himself recognized. Translated into every European language, it caused Russian and Siamese masters to liberate their slaves and Scotland to raise a penny 'emancipation fund'. In *A Key to Uncle Tom's Cabin* (1853) Mrs Stowe documented her materials, and in 1856 she again tackled the problem in *Dred: A Tale of the Great Dismal Swamp*. Her later fiction concerns New England life, for example *The Minister's Wooing* (1859), *The Pearl of Orr's Island* (1862) and, the best, *Oldtown Folks* (1869). [EM]

Edmund Wilson, *Patriotic Gore* (1962); Constance Rourke, *Trumpets of Jubilee* (1927); E. Wagen-knecht, *Harriet Beecher Stowe: The Known and Unknown* (1965).

**Strachey, William** (fl.1609–18). Born in England, he was appointed secretary of the Jamestown colony (until 1611), but is otherwise known only through his writings. He wrote *History of Travel into Virginia Britannia* (printed 1849) and edited, and partly compiled, *For the Colony in Virginia: Laws Divine, Moral and Martial* (1612). *A True Repertory of the Wracks and Redemption of Sir Thomas Gates* tells of his experiences in *Sea Venture*, the flagship of a 1609 Virginia expedition wrecked in the Bermudas. After a pleasant nine months in the islands the 150 colonists sailed for Jamestown in two pinnaces built from the wreckage. Strachey's account is included in Samuel Purchas's *Hakluytus Posthumus, or, Purchas His Pilgrims* (1625). G. M. Gayley's *Shakespeare and the Founders of Liberty in America* (1917) discusses parallels with *The Tempest*. [EM]

C. R. Sanders, *The Strachey Family: Their Writings and Literary Associations* (1953).

**Stribling, T(homas) S(igismund)** (1881–    ). Novelist. From Tennessee. He has written a series of good tales of the South. *These Bars of Flesh* (1938), for example, attacks progressive education and New York trades unions, and *Teeftallow* (1926) was dramatized as *Rope* (1928). [EM]

**Sturgeon, Theodore** (Edward Hamilton Waldo) (1918–    ). Science-fiction writer. He began writing after a variety of occupations, including service as a merchant seaman. His works include *The Dreaming Jewels* (1950), *More Than Human* (1953), *E Pluribus Unicorn* (1953), *A Way Home* (a selection of stories edited by G. Conklin, 1955), *A Touch of Strange* (1958) and *Cosmic Rape* (1968). His best-known work is *More Than Human*, an account of the evolution of a group of disparate individuals into an entity which Sturgeon terms *Homo Gestalt*. [HD]

**Sturgis, Howard Overing** (1855–1920). Novelist. Born in London, he was the youngest son of an expatriate Boston banker, the half-brother of Julian Sturgis, a prolific Victorian novelist, and a cousin of George ◊ Santayana (whose Mario in *The Last Puritan* is said to have been based in part on Sturgis). Queen's Acre, the house near Windsor Great Park which

Sturgis occupied in 1889, for many years attracted a large number of British and American friends, among them Edith Wharton and Henry James, and was an important expatriate centre.

Sturgis never completely fulfilled the literary promise he was thought to possess. *Tim,* published anonymously in 1891, was aptly called by E. M. Forster 'an Etonian meditation'; *All That Was Possible* (1895) is a pallid account of a frustrated love affair. Both are concerned with the characteristically Jamesian theme of the conflict between the demands of the individual and those of society, a subject that achieves its best and fullest expression in *Belchamber* (1904). Though James dismissed the passive central figure as a 'poor rat', this novel remains a moving analysis of the plight of the suffering, sensitive individual in a corrupt and philistine society. *Belchamber* reveals a detailed knowledge of the habits and behaviour of the English upper classes; indeed, the degree of social criticism and sexual frankness alienated some friends and more readers. [HD]

Edith Wharton, *A Backward Glance* (1934); E. M. Forster, 'Howard Overing Sturgis', in *Abinger Harvest* (1936); Elmer Borklund, 'Howard Sturgis, Henry James, and *Belchamber*', *Modern Philology,* LVIII (May 1961).

**Styron, William** (1925– ). Novelist. Born in Newport News, Virginia, he graduated at Duke University, North Carolina after military service as a Marine lieutenant, and attended Hiram Haydn's writing class at the New School for Social Research, where he began *Lie Down in Darkness* (1951), a massive novel about the disintegration of a Southern family with conscious overtones of Greek tragedy. It begins with analysis of the chaotic lives of Milton and Helen Loftis, the suicide of whose daughter, Peyton, focuses the family's tragedy and is seen as a consequence of that same loss of traditional Southern values of family order and stability by which her parents' weakness is defined. Styron's prose is rich, often rhetorical, sometimes extravagantly so.

*The Long March* (1952) is, in contrast, short, economically written, restricted in scope, raising issues rather than exploring them. An exhausting Marines route march provides the occasion for a breakdown of liberal ideals when confronted with military

values. *Set This House on Fire* (1960) partly returns to the broad scope and abundant prose of his first novel. It is a story of American expatriates in Italy, taking the form of an exploration of past violence in the search for understanding and self-discovery. Mason Flagg, a convincing embodiment of the evil that is only a twist away from American innocence, is placed in conflict with the tortured struggles of an artist, Cass Kinsolving, for personal salvation. Peter Leverett, who largely embodies the author's point of view, has a Southern background, and once again it is in the Southern past that acceptable human values seem best defined.

In 1967, he returned to a subject he had contemplated earlier, *The Confessions of Nat Turner*, based on the 1831 rebellion in Southern Virginia led by the Negro Nat Turner, whose 'confessions' (1831) form the ground of the novel. Styron's structure and style are more involuted and artificial as he imagines the interpretation and motive of this example of the American dilemma. The novel was a highly acclaimed bestseller in America, although some – including Negro – critics objected to both its composition and its attitudes. [EM]

Maxwell Geismar, 'William Styron: The End of Innocence', in *American Moderns* (1958); Louise Y. Gossett, 'The Cost of Freedom: William Styron', in *Violence in Recent Southern Fiction* (1965); ed. John H. Clark, *William Styron's Nat Turner: Ten Black Writers Respond* (1968).

**Swados, Harvey** (1920– ). Novelist and story writer. Born in Buffalo, N.Y.; educated at the University of Michigan. Besides teaching at Sarah Lawrence, the University of Iowa and San Francisco State College, he has been active in journalism and in left-wing politics; a collection of polemical essays, *A Radical's America* (1962), explores his socialist position and his view of American society. His novels are *Out Went the Candle* (1955), an analysis of a scheming businessman in a struggling relationship with his children; *False Coin* (1959), a witty analysis of a Utopian writers' colony; and *The Will* (1963), another family novel, exploring the way an inheritance corrupts the lives of three brothers. An early collection of stories, *Nights in the Gardens of Brooklyn* (1951), has recently been reissued in England; *Out on the Line* (1957) contains stories interlinked by being about workers on a car-assembly line; and *A Story for*

*Teddy* (1965) brings together his recent short fiction. Though sometimes a ponderous writer, he has a strong social perception and a powerful capacity to render the complexities of modern experience. He has recently edited a first-rate collection of documents on the thirties, *The American Writer and the Great Depression* (1968). [MB]

Charles Shapiro, 'Harvey Swados: Private Stories and Public Fiction', in *Contemporary American Novelists*, ed. Harry T. Moore (1964).

**Sward, Robert** (1923– ). Poet. Born in Chicago, he was educated at the Universities of Illinois and Iowa, went to the University of Bristol on a Fulbright award and has taught at Cornell University. Volumes of verse include *Advertisements* (1958), *Uncle Dog* (1962), *Kissing the Dancer* (1964) and *Thousand-Year-Old Fiancée* (1966). He is a poet of varied styles and great verbal self-consciousness. [BP]

**Swenson, May** (1927– ). Poet. Born and educated in Utah. She now lives in New York, an editor for the publishing firm New Directions. Her collections include *Another Animal*, published in *Poets of Today, I* (1954); *A Cage of Spines* (1958); *To Mix with Time* (1963), which contains many new poems but also a substantial selection from the two earlier volumes; and *Half Sun Half Sleep* (1967). One block of her poems takes its occasions from European subjects; many others derive from rural and urban American subjects. Elaborate typography, grandiose metaphysics and high rhetorical intensity create many of her effects, and though the pitch is often shrill she certainly deals with problems of real importance for contemporary poetry. *Poems to Solve* (1966) consists of 35 poems in the form of riddles, allegories and extended metaphors, composed for children. [MB]

# T

**Tarkington, Booth** (1869–1946). Novelist. Born in Indianapolis, educated at Philips Exeter Academy, Purdue and Princeton Universities. His first successful novel, *The Gentleman from Indiana* (1899), was a cheerful, realistic story of a newspaper's crusade against political corruption and cynicism; *In the Arena* (1905) developed a similar theme. In 1902–3 he was a Republican member of the Indiana legislature. His reputation was made with *Monsieur Beaucaire* (1900), a period whimsy. In a style deriving partly from William Dean ◊ Howells and Mark Twain, there followed a series of mid-Western novels, of which two won Pulitzer Prizes, *The Magnificent Ambersons* (1918) and *Alice Adams* (1921). *Growth* (1927) is the overall title of a city trilogy which includes *The Turmoil* (1915), *The Magnificent Ambersons* (1918) and *The Midlander* (1923). New wealth and social mobility are his dominant concern. *The Magnificent Ambersons* charts the decline through three generations of a family fortune made by real estate in the Gilded Age, to be supplanted at last in wealth and status by the founder of the local automobile plant. *Alice Adams* is a sad morality tale of a drugstore assistant's attempt, with his own formula, to open a glue factory, and his daughter's attempt, with a web of fabrications, to win the love of a rich stranger and rise in society. The Horatio ◊ Alger sermon of 'Luck and Pluck' is squarely turned upside down. Further novels, *The Conquest of Canaan* (1905), *The Plutocrat* (1927), *The Heritage of Hatcher Ide* (1941), *Kate Fennigate* (1943) and *The Image of Josephine* (1945), carry the Indiana setting through the Depression and war years.

His series of novels, *Penrod* (1914), *Penrod and Sam* (1916), *Penrod Jashber* (1929), *Seventeen* (1916), *Gentle Julia* (1922) and *Little Orvie* (1934), had a wide readership: Penrod is the rowdy middle-class boy, with a mongrel dog and assorted intimates including the Negro brothers Herman and Verman (principal performers in a circus he organizes): he is the traditional American good 'bad' boy.

Tarkington dramatized several of his novels as well as writing 25 plays, some in collaboration, and an autobiography, *The World Does Move* (1928). He is the epitome of the middle-brow American novelist. [HB]

*Your Amiable Uncle: Letters to his Nephew* (1949). R. C. Holliday, *Booth Tarkington* (1918); James Woodress, *Booth Tarkington, Gentleman from Indiana* (1955).

**Tate, Allen** (1899– ). Poet, critic. He was born and educated in Kentucky, studied at Georgetown and Washington, and in 1922 graduated from Vanderbilt University, Tennessee, where with John Crowe Ransom, Robert Warren, Merrill Moore, Donald Davidson and Cleanth Brooks he was a member of the ◊ Fugitives group, dedicated to agrarianism, the ◊ New Criticism they were demonstrating, the South, and political conservativism (see *The Fugitive Magazine*, 1922–5, and the symposium, *I'll Take My Stand*, 1930). He lived in New York 1924–8, and in Paris, 1928–9, on a Guggenheim fellowship, taught in a number of American universities, edited *Hound and Horn* (1931–4), *Sewanee Review* (1944–6), with Herbert Agar, *Who Owns America?* (1936) and, with John Peale Bishop, *American Harvest* (1942). His important criticism, including essays on Hart Crane, Emily Dickinson, Poe and 'Tension in Poetry', appeared in *Reactionary Essays on Poetry and Ideas* (1936), *Reason in Madness* (1941) and *The Forlorn Demon* (1953). *Stonewall Jackson* (1928) documents aspects of the pre-Civil-War South and its myths, the subject also within his novel *The Fathers* (1938), in many ways his finest work. His poems, in *Mr Pope and Other Poems* (1928), *Poems 1928–1931* (1932) and *The Mediterranean and Other Poems* (1936), are tightly complex forms, embodying nostalgia for European culture, dedication to a vision of the viable South and a tradition of aristocratic experience. They need exegesis of their academic allusiveness and indirection, but the unravelling usually shows a distinguished intellect within its broadly religious moral orbit. [EM]

*Collected Essays* (1959); *Poems* (1960); *Essays of Four Decades* (1969).
J. C. Stewart, *The Burden of Time: The Fugitives and Agrarians* (1965).

**Taylor, Bayard** (1825–78). Novelist, travel-writer, poet, translator. Born in Pennsylvania, he was a member of the New York circle of the 1860s which included ◊ Aldrich, R. H. Stoddard and ◊ Howells. He worked on the *Saturday Evening Post* and the *Tribune*. He published his first volume of poems, *Ximena*, in 1844, and *Poems of the Orient* in 1854. His translation of Goethe's *Faust* (1870–1), for which he is perhaps best remembered, is in original metres, and serviceable. The first of his famous and popular travel books was *Views Afoot; or Europe Seen with Knapsack and Staff* (1846), a conventional touristic work. In 1849 he reported the Californian gold rush for the *Tribune*, and his experiences were recounted in *El Dorado; or Adventures in the Path of Empire* (1850), a useful record, frequently reprinted. He continued to travel and give popular lectures on his travels for audiences avid for news of the world. He worked for the diplomatic service in St Petersburg and in 1878 was appointed minister in Berlin. His poetry is the overripe obverse of his realistic journalism, but his novel *The Story of Kennett* (1866) treats country people with something of the detail of his travel works. [EM]

M. Hansen-Taylor and H. E. Scudder, *Life and Letters of Bayard Taylor* (2 vols., 1884); R. C. Beatty, *Bayard Taylor: Laureate of the Gilded Age* (1936); R. Cary, *The Genteel Circle: Bayard Taylor and His New York Friends* (1952).

**Taylor, Edward** (1645?–1729). Poet. He was born in Leicestershire and went to Boston, Massachusetts, in 1668. Samuel ◊ Sewall was his room-mate at Harvard, where he graduated in 1671, becoming a minister the same year. He ordered his poetry to be left unpublished. It was discovered in Yale library in 1937. The best colonial poetry of its kind, it is in fact characteristic English 17th-century devotional verse, with 'metaphysical' qualities and some significant New England linguistic usages. His ingenious metaphors and conceits dramatize abstract religious philosophy in original and attractive ways which partly redeem *God's Determinations Touching His Elect*, a series of poems on the New England covenant dogma. His 217 'Sacramental Meditations' are a lifetime's application of the Bible to daily life. [EM]

*The Poems*, ed. D. E. Stanford (1960).
N. S. Grabo, *Edward Taylor* (1962).

**Taylor, John** (1753–1824). He was born in Virginia, studied at William and Mary College, practised law, and made a career as a soldier and, after the Revolution, as a plantation owner. His ◊ Jeffersonian beliefs in the self-reliant agrarian property-owner are set out in *The Arator* (1813; agricultural essays), *Tyranny Unmasked* (1822; a pamphlet supporting protective tariffs), *New Views of the Constitution* (1823; on states rights governmental philosophy), and many more essays and pamphlets. His major work is *An Inquiry into the Principles and Policy of the Government in the United States* (1814), a thorough and plodding treatise on agrarian liberalism. [EM]

**Taylor, Peter** (1917– ). Novelist, short-story writer. Born in Nashville, Tennessee. His concern with the past, family and childhood gives a distinctively Southern quality to most of his fiction. Middle-class family life in the upper South provides his basic material, which is handled with subtlety and humour. His characteristic narrative method is one of careful reconsideration of event, distilled reminiscence rather than re-created dialogue and action. *A Long Fourth, and Other Stories* (1948), *The Widows of Thornton* (1954), *Happy Families are All Alike* (1960) and *Miss Leonora When Last Seen, and Fifteen Other Stories* (1963) are collections of stories. *A Woman of Means* (1950) is a short novel about the decay of a wealthy family in St Louis in the mid-twenties, told by an adult recollecting childhood experiences in the family. *The Death of a Kinsman* (1949) and *Tennessee Day in St Louis* (1957) are plays. [AH]

*Collected Stories* (1969).
*Sewanee Review*, LXX (Autumn, 1962) (three essays on his work).

**Theatre Guild.** Formed from among the Washington Square Players in 1918 'for drama, for beauty, for ideas' and the circumvention of commercialism in the theatre. Its first play was Jacinto Beneventi's *Bonds of Interest* (1919). The Guild Theatre itself opened in 1925 with Shaw's *Caesar and Cleopatra*. In 1931, many of the actors, playwrights and producers associated with Theatre Guild combined with others to produce plays of some social importance, the first important production of which was Paul ◊ Green's *The House of Connelly* (1931). [EM]

**Thomas, Norman** (1884–1969). Writer, politician. Born in Marion, Ohio, he graduated from Princeton in 1905 and was for some years a Presbyterian minister, until he resigned in order to devote himself to the causes of socialism and pacifism. Since the 1920s he unsuccessfully offered himself as a socialist candidate for most political offices, including that of the presidency. In 1918 he founded *World Tomorrow* and during 1921–2 was an editor of the *Nation*. His many publications include *The Challenge of War* (1925); *Socialism of Our Time* (1929); *The Choice before Us* (1934); *We Have a Future* (1941); *A Socialist's Faith* (1951); *Prerequisites for Peace* (1959); *The Great Dissenters* (1961); and *Socialism Re-Examined* (1964). [HD]

Harry Fleischman, *Norman Thomas: A Biography* (1964); M. B. Seidler, *Norman Thomas: Respectable Rebel* (1962).

**Thoreau, Henry David** (1817–62). As a child in Concord, Massachusetts, where he was born, he played the flute and shared his naturalist interests with his brother John. After Concord Academy, and Harvard (1833–7), he had a thorough training in mathematics, literature, classical languages, French and some Spanish and Italian. He also acquired some knowledge of Indian and Oriental literature. Through his friend Orestes Brownson, he came to ◊ Transcendentalism; Emerson encouraged him to keep the journals from which his books were made. In 1838, the Thoreau brothers opened a private school, together fell in love with Ellen Sewall, and made the trip which became the basis of Henry's first book, *A Week on the Concord and Merrimack Rivers* (1849). Ellen turned them both down, and Henry later wrote: 'It appears to be a law that you cannot have a deep sympathy with both man and nature.' After their school closed in 1841, he became Emerson's residential working companion. W. E. ◊ Channing (II) and Hawthorne became his friends. Needing to earn a self-reliant living he tried tutoring in Emerson's brother's New York family, and had introductions to Horace Greeley and Henry James, Sr. But he needed to return to his Concord woods. He improved his father's pencil business by developing a graphite process, contributed to the *Dial*, and made himself 'self-appointed inspector of snow-storms, and rain-storms', 'surveyor of forest-paths and all across-lot routes', and guardian of 'wild stock'. In 1845 he began a two-year experiment in simple economy and creative leisure in a self-made cabin on Emerson's land at Walden Pond, occasionally visiting friends, and interrupting his isolation with a gaol sentence for refusing to pay poll tax to a government waging war in Mexico. *Civil Disobedience* appeared in the Transcendentalist *Aesthetic Papers* in 1849. On their return from England he settled with the Emersons again and remained until his death. He turned professional surveyor, developed his botany skills with Louis ◊ Agassiz, the great American botanist and zoologist, and in 1853 went north to the Maine woods to experience a more primitive nature. After the Fugitive Slave Law of 1850 he assisted escapes via the 'Underground Railway', attacked slavery in 'Slavery in Massachusetts'. and supported John Brown's Harper's Ferry raid. He travelled to Niagara and Mississippi, but found no cure for his health and died upright, murmuring 'moose' and 'Indian', a memory of his horrified witness of a slaughtering at Chesuncook in 1853.

*Civil Disobedience* asserts 'that government is best which governs least', enables men to let one another alone instead of serving the state as 'machines', and urges passive resistance to tyranny. Its international influence extended at least as late as Gandhi. The journeys in *A Week on the Concord* are the frame for a programme of self-reliance, criticism, reading, poetry and the recording of American myth and history: it is the form itself of Thoreau's philosophy of free choice in a natural landscape known at first hand without the intervention of dogma or religion. The form of his masterpiece, *Walden* (1854), is again the organic articulation of personal experience, delineating what 'a necessary life' and a fundamental economy of work and leisure might be for 'freedom and a prospect of success'. Every closely observed natural and human event is to lead towards the recovery of a life of 'universal laws'. Thoreau's *Journals* contain the minute record of his daily life presented less formally, with some of the meditative metaphysical quality of his best poems. He is one of the masters of prose style, an exemplary individualist, and a living inspiration to resisters and dissenters everywhere, including, at one time, Gandhi, Tolstoy and the British Labour Party. His anarchist opposition to state coercion, and refusal to pay taxes which might contribute to national war or enforce the slavery-economy, have a direct bearing on American dissent in the 1960s. His final support of violence against slavery, in direct contrast to his earlier belief in passive resistance, is prophetic of the course many liberals were forced to take a hundred years later. [EM]

*Collected Poems*, ed. C. Bode (1964); *Selected Journals*, ed. C. Bode (1967); *The Correspondence*, ed. W. Harding and C. Bode (1957); *The Portable Thoreau*, ed. C. Bode (1947).
Walter Harding, *The Thoreau Handbook* (1959) and *The Days of Henry Thoreau* (1965).

**Thurber, James** (1894–1961). Humorist. He grew up in Columbus, Ohio, amid an eccentric family portrayed in some of his best essays. After working as a newspaperman in Columbus, Paris and New York, he met Harold Ross, editor of the *New Yorker*, and joined that paper, for which most of his essays, short stories and drawings were produced. His manner, interests and distinctive tone were inseparable from it and shaped it; the connexion is recorded in his memoir *The Years with Ross* (1959).

His very distinctive humour is a definable phase in the development of American literary tone. Like his *New Yorker* colleague and collaborator, E. B. ◊ White, he was elegant, genteel, devoted to 'good style'. His work appeals to a sense of gentleness, order and control, having a literary delicacy distinguished from most American writing; and it has a clear moral concern, a sense of the growth of anarchy, folly and absurdity which the slightly affected gentility can bring clearly out. Many of the essays and stories deal with the triumph of moral innocence in the world of mass-media, psychoanalysis and sexual revolution. Besides comic essays he wrote elegant fantasies where, again, the kind of moral innocence he valued shows plainly. His many drawings have the same sophisticated simplicity. A central theme is the

transition from the bourgeois and small-town America of the 1920s to the modern sophisticated society of the sex war, psychoanalysis and scientism. Though the approach has a vein of gentle mid-Western cracker-barrel philosophy, its great virtue is his capacity to place modernity and sophistication; as in his parody of pseudo-scientific sex articles, *Is Sex Necessary?* (1929, with E. B. White), and his spoof of psychoanalysis, *Let Your Mind Alone* (1937). A deft social commentator and inventor of superb comic locutions, he conveys strongly the atmosphere of America between the wars. The essays, short stories, cartoons and sequences of sketches are collected in *The Owl in the Attic and Other Perplexities* (1931), *The Seal in the Bedroom and Other Predicaments* (1932), *My Life and Hard Times* (1933), *Men, Women, and Dogs* (1943), *Alarms and Diversions* (1957), etc. With Elliot Nugent he wrote a stage comedy, *The Male Animal* (1940). *The Thurber Carnival* (1945) is a convenient English collection from his work over the years. [MB]

**Timrod, Henry** (1828–67). Poet. Born in Charleston, South Carolina, he lies in the chivalric, Keats-influenced tradition of Southern poetry deriving from Poe. One of the Russell's bookstore group, including William Gilmore ◊ Simms, Paul Hamilton ◊ Hayne and Basil Gildersleeve, who in 1867 founded in Charleston *Russell's Magazine* (an imitation of the English *Blackwood's*), he published poems and essays here and in other Southern journals. His earlier sentimental verse toughens as he encounters the experience of the Civil War, when he served in the Confederate Army and wrote loyal poetry, the two best-known poems being 'Ethnogenesis', which looks forward to the growth of a new stronger South, and his 'Ode Sung at the Occasion of Decorating the Graves of the Confederate Dead'. A Memorial edition of his poems, *Poems of Henry Timrod*, was issued in Boston in 1899; they can also be reached through the *American Writers Series, Southern Poets* (1936). [MB]

Jay B. Hubbell, *The South in American Literature 1607–1900* (1954).

**Tocqueville, Alexis, Comte de** (1805–59). French writer on America, politician. In 1831, a junior magistrate in Versailles, he was appointed to a commission of inquiry into American prisons and penitentiaries; and his work on *Du système pénitentiaire aux États-Unis et de son application en France* (1832) provided him with material for *De la démocratie en Amérique* (1835 and 1840), his lucid, concise and masterly analysis of American society and its institutions, in which he suggests that modern democracies will tend to sacrifice liberty to equality. Later a deputy and Minister for Foreign Affairs (June–October 1849), he was prevented by ill-health from completing his great *L'ancien régime et la révolution* (1856).

In Volume II, Book I, Chapters XI–XIX of *Democracy in America* (tr. H. Reeve, ed. P. Bradley, 2 vols., 1945), he analyses with penetrating cogency the present and future condition of American literature, developing a characteristic general thesis that 'the relations which exist between the social and political condition of a people and the genius of its authors are always numerous'. He claims American authors are 'English in substance and still more so in form', irrelevantly apeing the culture of a foreign aristocracy: in consequence 'the only authors whom I acknowledge as American are the journalists'. Two main factors are likely to vitiate the prospects of an American literature: the absence of a leisured intellectual class, and the inherent tendency of democracies to 'make the taste for the useful predominate over the love of the beautiful in the heart of man'. American authors (and their heterogeneous audience) will find themselves in an intellectual vacuum: prose style 'will frequently be fantastic, incorrect, overburdened and loose, almost always bold. . . . The object . . . will be to astonish rather than to please'. American poetry, turning from the past, will 'prefer the delineation of passion and ideas to that of persons and achievements'. 'Haunted by visions of what will be' it will 'range at last to purely imaginary regions'. Hence he probably suggests social reasons for American literature's symbolist preoccupation. [M G]

J. P. Mayer, *Tocqueville: Prophet of the Mass Age* (1940); Janes Bryce, *The Predictions of Hamilton and Tocqueville* (1887); G. W. Pierson, *Tocqueville and Beaumont in America* (1938).

**Tolson, M. B.** (1898–    ). Poet. Born in Moberly, Missouri, he was educated at Fisk, Lincoln and Columbia, with considerable distinctions and prizes. He has taught in a number of colleges and is well known for his drama clubs and public readings. He has served four terms as mayor of Langstone, Oklahoma, where he directs the Dust Bowl Theatre and teaches creative literature. His reputation as a leading Negro poet began with 'Dark Symphony', dramatizing the Negro condition (in *Rendezvous with America*, 1944). His long psychological poem *E. & O.E.* won him a *Poetry* award in 1952, and Allen ◊ Tate introduced his *Libretto for the Republic of Liberia* in 1953 (part of it was a commission he received as poet laureate of Liberia in 1947). *Harlem Gallery: Book 1, The Curator* (1965) is one of the most important events in Negro American literature and is itself a remarkably fine poem; the 24 sections, in an original literary idiom, dramatize ironically and passionately the relationships between African, Negro America and Western culture. (◊ Negro Literature.) [E M]

**Toomer, Jean.** ◊ Negro Literature.

**Totheroh, Dan** (1895–    ). The San Francisco dramatist whose fame rests with *Wild Birds* (1922), a mid-Western tale of an orphan girl, a reform school boy and psychology. There are also extant *Distant Drums* (1932 – a neurotic lady in a caravan *en route* for Oregon), *Moor Born* (1934 – the Brontës), and *Live Life Again* (1943 – Hamlet on a Nebraska farm). [E M]

**Tourgée, Albion W(inegar)** (1838–1905). Novelist. Born in Ohio, a lawyer and a judge, he moved in 1865 to North Carolina, where his experiences as a carpetbagger provided material for his most important works. He returned north to New York State in 1879, and in 1897 was appointed American consul in Bordeaux. His outstanding novel is *A Fool's Errand* (1879), a semi-autobiographical account of the Reconstruction, where exciting narration is interspersed with lucid socio-political analysis, managed from a northern point of view. Tourgée supplemented later editions with 'The Invisible Empire', a famous essay on the Ku Klux Klan. Related novels are *Toinette* (1874) – later revised as *A Royal Gentleman* – and *Bricks without Straw* (1880). Other novels deal with racial problems; and his 'The South as a Field for Fiction', in *Forum* (1888), is a seminal investigation. [D G]

Otto H. Olson, *Carpetbagger's Crusade: The Life of Albion Winegar Tourgée* (1965); Roy F. Dibble, *Albion W. Tourgee* (1921).

**Transcendentalists, The.** A group of writers who articulated the decline of 18th-century Calvinism in Massachusetts, the advent of Unitarianism and rationalism, and the effects of European romanticism. The leaders included Emerson, Thoreau, Alcott, W. E. ◊ Channing (I) and George ◊ Ripley; associated were Margaret ◊ Fuller, Orestes ◊ Brownson, Jones ◊ Very, Theodore Parker and others. Their ideas included the ideal nature of reality, the immanence of God in nature and man, the presence of Soul in all things, the unity of all things, the need to transcend what the physical senses and science can know through the truth of intuition. They borrowed freely from versions of Kant's concepts through Coleridge and Schelling to establish what Ripley called 'an order of truths which transcends the sphere of external sense' and 'the operations of understanding' (Brownson), and ascertain the 'facts' of 'certain great primal intuitions of human nature' (Parker). Alcott once 'saw the world as one great spinal column'. They rejected formal worship or any interceding between soul and God. The Christian gospels, with Shakespeare, Socrates and all great writing, were part of the totality of human and therefore divine work. They expressed their ideas not only in literature but in individual living, the founding of schools and Utopias, and the practice of dietary regimes. Emerson's *Nature* (1836) is the nearest to systematic formulation of a Transcendentalist philosophy and his essay *The Transcendentalist* (1842) suggests some of the attitudes of the group. The Transcendental Club was formed by Ripley in 1836 to exchange views. The quarterly *Dial* (1842–4) was their outlet, under the successive editing of Margaret Fuller and Emerson. Brook Farm was their joint stock company utopian experiment, organized at West Roxbury, Massachusetts, in 1841. [EM]

*The Transcendentalists: An Anthology*, ed. P. Miller (1950); *Selected Writings of the American Transcendentalists*, ed. George Hochfield (1966). *Transcendentalism and Its Legacy*, ed. M. Simon and T. Parsons (1967).

**Traven, Ben** (1890–1969). Novelist. A Chicago-born fiction writer who died in Mexico City. His guarded anonymity gave rise to wild speculations on his identity, especially since his fiction shows experience of extreme human situations and his style is not only vigorously contemporary, but has a certain clumsiness which is retained in the translations from the German. He gave his first press interview in 1966, still insisting on the privacy of his life. Traven's novels are exciting and vividly visualized narratives, strongly critical of capitalist motives: *The Death Ship* (1934), *The Treasure of the Sierra Madre* (1935), *The Carreta* (1935), *Government* (1935), *The Bridge in the Jungle* (1938), *The Rebellion of the Hanged* (1952). *The Night Visitor and Other Stories* appeared in 1966. Kenneth Rexroth calls Traven 'the greatest novelist of total disengagement' and adds that he was 'an elderly I.W.W. of German ancestry', a statement that probably needs corroboration from Judy Stone's 'The Mystery of B. Traven' (*Ramparts*, September 1967) and his American editor, Bernard Smith's article in the *New York Times*, 22 November 1970. [EM]

**Trilling, Lionel** (1905– ). Literary critic, novelist. He grew up in New York, and was educated there at Columbia University, where he is now Professor of English in the graduate school. He is one of the most influential of modern American critics. His critical writing, though founded on the ◊ New Criticism, has worked rather in the realm of advancing general ideas; it is notably informed by psychological, sociological and philosophical methods and insights. At its core is a deep concern with the totality of culture; he has urged the case for the liberal imagination of art as a primary social value. He is thus essentially a humanist and moralist, devoted to literature as an expression of the human mind in all its variousness and possibility, involved with the whole growth of human experience and judgement. Most of his criticism has been of romantic and post-romantic literature, and recently he has become concerned with the way this literature has, by adopting the pieties of alienation, tended to promote limited assumptions about our human nature.

He has written excellently on Arnold (*Matthew Arnold*, 1939) and Forster (*E. M. Forster*, 1943), in whose liberal humanist tradition he clearly lies. Essays on modern English and American fiction, romantic poetry and general socio-literary issues are collected in *The Liberal Imagination* (1950), *The Opposing Self* (1955), *A Gathering of Fugitives* (1956) and *Beyond Culture: Essays on Literature and Learning* (1965). He has also written a short study of Freud, *Freud and the Crisis of Our Culture* (1955). *The Experience of Literature* (1967) is an anthology from Sophocles to Ginsberg, with pedagogic commentary.

His one novel, *The Middle of the Journey* (1947), taking as its basic material the political development that the liberal mind in America went through in the 1930s and 1940s, puts political life to exacting moral examination. He has written two remarkable stories, widely reprinted but never collected together: 'Of this Time, of That Place', a classic story of the burden of responsibility a teacher bears for an eccentric student, and 'The Other Margaret', about a young girl initiated into consciousness of the moral and political inter-connectedness of people. [MB]

**Trumbull, John** (1750–1831). Poet. As a precocious Connecticut boy he passed the Yale entrance examinations at 7 and entered college at 13. With 'The Meddler' group of essayists he wrote *Spectator* imitations and stayed on as tutor, advocating a more liberal curriculum (e.g. introducing Augustan poetry) in *An Essay on the Uses and Advantages of the Fine Arts* (1770) and the long satirical poem *The Progress of Dulness* (1772–3). After 1773 he read law under John Adams, with whose Federalism he sympathized. Law and politics engrossed his later life and he died in Detroit having abandoned poetry and brief fame as a ◊ Connecticut Wit. *The Progress of Dulness* is a hudibrastic adventure of Tom Brainless, farmer's son, as he proceeds fecklessly through school, college, society and the ministry. Trumbull's better poem is the mock epic *M'Fingal* (1775–82), an extremely popular attack on the Loyalists, after Bulter and Macpherson. [EM]

A. Cowie, *John Trumbull, Connecticut Wit* (1936).

**Tuckerman, Frederick Goddard** (1821–73). Poet. Born in Boston, Massachusetts, he practised law in early life and then retired to Greenfield as a solitary observer of nature and a poet. His *Poems* (1860) is a collection of sonnets, highly regarded by poets and critics from Tennyson to Yvor ◊ Winters. Witter ◊ Bynner introduced his edition enthusiastically in 1931. Tuckerman's eccentric

phrasing and original imagery have a new following since N. Scott Momoday's *The Complete Poems* (1965). [EM]

S. A. Golden, *Frederick Goddard Tuckerman: An American Sonneteer* (1952).

**Turner, Frederick Jackson** (1861–1932). Historian. Born in Portage, Wisconsin, a frontier community, he was educated at Wisconsin University and Johns Hopkins University, where he was influenced by and reacted against Herbert Baxter Adams, a foremost exponent of the 'germ theory' of American development, which is primarily concerned with American institutions, tracing them back to primitive tribal Teutonic democracy at the time of the Roman empire. Turner maintained that exclusive concentration upon European origins distorted American experience. His own early experiences, Darwinian theory and the human geography of Friedrich Ratzel came together in his economic and social environmental theory of American history: the 'Turner thesis'. His 1893 paper, 'The Significance of the Frontier in American History', insisted that the characteristic of American history had been westward expansion and settlement into free land areas. Each settled locality evolved from primitive culture to more advanced and still individualized societies. Frontier conditions conditioned national legislation and distinctive values. These ideas were developed in *The Rise of the New West, 1819–29* (1906) into a theory of the sectional rather than state-political basis of national unity and common interests. *The United States 1830–50*, left unfinished at his death, was edited by Avery Craven, his former student, in 1935. In spite of his great influence, he wrote comparatively little, and his only other major books are two collections of essays, *The Frontier in American History* (1920) and *The Significance of Sections in American History* (1932). Since his death his theories have come under radical criticism (usefully summarized in *The Turner Thesis*, ed. G. R. Taylor, 1956). But he remains a monumental figure in American history and thought, although he is sometimes regarded as the founder of a myth rather than the discoverer of lasting historical facts. [DKA/EM]

**Twain, Mark (Samuel Langhorne Clemens)** (1835–1910). Novelist, humorist. He was the fifth of six children in a household with two slaves. His father was a Virginian lawyer working in Florida, Missouri, a frontier settlement on a tributary of the Mississippi. When Sam was 4 the family moved to Hannibal, on the great river itself (an idyllic boyhood told in the *Autobiography*, 1871). His father died when he was 12 and he was apprenticed to a printer, the beginning of his career of accurate reporting and entertaining sketches (written in the South-western humour tradition of ◊ Longstreet and George W. ◊ Harris). In 1857 he yielded to his boyhood ambition and trained with the great Horace Bixby as a river-boat pilot, a profession he loved 'better than any I have followed since' (*Life on the Mississippi*, 1883), a 'brief sharp schooling' during which he met 'all the different types of human nature that are to be found in fiction, biography or history'.

But the Civil War closed the river traffic and Twain's career terminated. His brief hilarious war experience is in 'The History of a Campaign That Failed'. He turned his hand to silver prospecting in Nevada, went back to journalism on the Virginia City *Enterprise*, and, in 1864, on the San Francisco *Morning Call* (*Roughing It*, 1872), and in 1865 published his first short story, 'The Celebrated Jumping Frog of Calaveras County'. After his 1865–6 voyage to Hawaii, he made the first of his hundreds of lecturing appearances. On his return from Europe and Palestine in 1867 (*Innocents Abroad*, 1869), he married and set up house in Hartford, Connecticut, his base until 1890. He began to play his Eastern, genteel present against his Western and wilder past, and thus became a major representative of post Civil War America entering the era of industrial expansion. His *The Gilded Age* (1873, with Charles D. Warner) is a novel exposing American business politics in the post Civil War era. He wrote a large number of short stories and essays, two travel books (*A Tramp Abroad*, 1880, and *Following the Equator*, 1897); he became a literary businessman, speculating in a publishing firm and over a hundred inventions, one of which, together with his extravagant living, bankrupted him. His daughter died tragically in 1896, and his writing reflects these disasters in its increasing irony and bitterness ('The Man That Corrupted Hadleyburg', 1900, 'What Is Man?', 1917 posth., and *The Mysterious Stranger*, 1916 posth.). His gusto as a public figure masked the private tensions which he wrote into pessimistic

works relegated to a locked desk drawer for posthumous exhumation.

Mark Twain's career was a central, representative one in American letters. He made the already well-developed role of humorist (◊ Billings; Nasby; Ward) into a central post of social observation. His worldwide reputation was based on a gift for mixing boyish rascality and innocence in a naïve, vernacular vision, one complicated, however, by his darkening, bitter view of man as hypocrite, victim and self-deceiver. The contradictions spread several ways: much of his work was about the Mississippi valley world of his childhood, but angled through the eyes of one deeply in the rapidly industrializing Gilded Age phase and its base in Eastern capital and Northern morality. Many of his books turn on complex ironies deriving from this: romance is questioned by realism, boyhood idyll by manhood despair, the agrarian past by the industrial present, the slaveholding South by the Northern progressivism of the post-bellum period. But the industrial and progressive present contains the highest irony of all: pretending to high morality, its real centre lies in money, machines and force. So, from the standpoint either of the wonderingly innocent childhood eye, or from that of an ironic disgust that holds that 'We have no *real* morals, but only artificial ones, morals created and preserved by the forced suppression of natural and healthy instincts,' Twain creates a world in which men are lost children or else bleak slaves to determinism.

The complexity and often inconsistency of the view; the fact that he often wrote carelessly or amateurishly; the instinct he felt to succeed at the most popular level of acclaim – all this meant his huge energies are not often raised to the level of major literature. He lacked the discipline of the persistent artist except in five great central works. Weakest are the historical novels: *The Prince and the Pauper* (1882) and *Personal Recollections of Joan of Arc* (1896). The Tom Sawyer books (1876; 1894; 1896), centred in his fascination with boyish play and imposture, are at times amusing, especially *The Adventures of Tom Sawyer* (1876), but thin stuff. His finest works are: *Life on the Mississippi* (1883), not a novel but a superbly evocative memoir, a brilliant account of pilotage and a criticism of the South; *A Connecticut Yankee in King Arthur's Court* (1889), which shifts Hank

Morgan, the machine-shop superintendent, into medieval England, which he promotes as an industrial American utopia and then destroys in a technological apocalypse; *The American Claimant* (1892), which resurrects Colonel Sellers, the confidence man of the earlier *Gilded Age; Pudd'nhead Wilson* (1894), a profoundly ironic work, drawing on Twain's recurring themes of exchanged identities and the paradox of slavery and freedom, that takes its story of the switched master and slave through to an ending of savage force; and the masterpiece *The Adventures of Huckleberry Finn* (1885), one of the world's great books. A deeply complex novel, it is at once the initiation of a 12-year-old boy into the hypocrisies of the Christian bourgeoisie, with its slavery, Southern feuds and money materialism, and a definition of morality learned empirically as the boy helps his Negro friend, Jim, down the Mississippi by raft. The multiple ironies, the vivid series of escape episodes, the variety of characters, and the brilliantly invented language of Huck's narrative make this an American classic and the triumph of Twain's special kind of humour. Twain's reputation is firmly based on these works. Year by year critical and biographical works about him pour from the universities, but he is worthy of such attention. [EM]

*Letters from the Earth*, ed. B. de Voto (1942); *The Autobiography*, ed. C. Neider (1961); *Mark Twain on the Damned Human Race*, ed. Janet Smith (1962).
H. N. Smith, *Mark Twain: The Development of a Writer* (1962); Walter Blair, *Mark Twain and Huck Finn* (1960); ed. Walter Blair, *Mark Twain: A Collection of Critical Essays* (1960); J. M. Cox, *Mark Twain: The Fate of Humour* (1967); J. Kaplan, *Mr Clemens and Mark Twain* (1967); S. J. Krause, *Mark Twain as Critic* (1968).

**Tyler, Moses Coit** (1835–1900). Literary historian. Born in Griswold, Connecticut. Important in the development of the syste-matic study of American literature, which took on impetus during the late 19th century, he helped – with John Seely Hart, Greenough White, E. P. ◊ Whipple, Brander ◊ Matthews and Albert Bigelow Paine – to establish the possibility of a serious study in the field. A sound and thorough scholar, his two great works on the Colonial and Revolutionary periods are still basic: *A History of American Literature, 1607–1765* (2 vols., 1878; abridged paperback edn, 1962) and *The Literary History of the American Revolution, 1763–1783* (2 vols., 1897). Tyler, who was Professor of English at the University of Michigan and then of American History at Cornell, also wrote *Three Men of Letters* (1895), on Joel ◊ Barlow, Timothy ◊ Dwight and Bishop Berkeley's three-year American visit. [MB]

Howard Mumford Jones. *The Life of Moses Coit Tyler* (1933).

**Tyler, Royall** (1757–1826). Playwright. He wrote one of the most famous early American plays, *The Contrast*, first performed in 1787 (published 1790). The first American comedy, written in the manner of Sheridan, it exploited American vernacular on the stage for comic purposes, and showed the triumph of the decent American characters over an English cad. One of the American characters, Jonathan, a New England rustic, is drawn from a basic type-figure of American humour; and the play asserts its Americanness from prologue onward. Tyler, who fought in the Revolutionary War and worked in the law office of John Adams, wrote other plays; a novel with a foreign setting, *The Algerine Captive* (1797); and a series of fictional letters, *The Yankey in London* (1809), joking about American customs. *The Contrast* appears in various collections of American plays, including Arthur H. Quinn's *Representative American Plays* (1938). It was revised successfully at the National Playwrights Conference at Waterford, Connecticut, in 1966. [MB]

# U

**Updike, John** (1932–    ). Novelist, short-story writer, poet. Born in Pennsylvania; educated at Harvard University and the Ruskin School of Drawing and Fine Art at Oxford. His poems and stories had appeared in the *New Yorker*, on which he worked, before his first book, *The Carpentered Hen and Other Tame Creatures* (1958), a collection of witty and satirical poems, was published. His prose and poetry have largely continued to reflect the polish and sophistication of the *New Yorker* at its best. *Hoping for a Hoopoe* (1959) and *Telephone Poles and Other Poems* (1963) are collections of poems; *The Same Door* (1959) is a collection of stories; and *The Poorhouse Fair* (1959) is a rather self-consciously bizarre novel about conflicts inside a poorhouse. *Assorted Prose* (1965) is a collection of parodies, autobiographical pieces and critical essays.

Updike's prose style is at all times precise and controlled. *Rabbit, Run* (1960) brilliantly evokes a world of total negation and moral confusion; the novel's protagonist is a man on the run from everything that might give him some kind of identity or definition as a human being. Some of the stories in *Pigeon Feathers and Other Stories* (1962), particularly those involving childhood recollections of Olinger, Pennsylvania, and expatriate days in England, have a greater sense of personal involvement than is common in his work. *The Centaur* (1963) is a more ambitious novel, linking the life of an Olinger teacher with the myth of Chiron, teacher of the Greek heroes. In 1964 appeared *Olinger Stories: A Selection*, and then came the books which have consolidated his career: *Of the Farm* (1965), a slow and over-written story of mother, son and son's wife during a farm weekend; *The Music School* (1966), short stories with bright surfaces; and *Couples* (1968), a novel on the topical matter of middle-class community sex. *Beck: A Book* (1970) dwells on writers' problems. His style still tends to replace character and clear motivation, but he is uncommonly readable. He has also written a children's book, *The Magic Flute* (1962). [A H/E M]

J. A. Ward, 'John Updike's Fiction', *Critique: Studies in Modern Fiction*, v (1962); D. D. Galloway, *The Absurd Hero in American Fiction* (1966).

# V

**'Van Dine, S. S.'** ◊ Wright, Willard Huntington.

**Van Doren, Mark** (1894– ). Poet, critic, novelist. Born in Hope, Illinois. He studied at the University of Illinois, then at Columbia University, New York, where he became Professor of Literature and a strong influence in the development of English studies. In the 1920s he was also literary editor of the important liberal weekly the *Nation*. A lucid, intelligent and very exact poet, his books of verse include *Spring Thunder* (1924), *Jonathan Gentry* (1931), a narrative poem, *The Last Look* (1937), *Seven Sleepers* (1944) and *The Country Year* (1946). In 1939 appeared *Collected Poems: 1922–1938*, which won the Pulitzer Prize. His novels include *The Transients* (1935), *Windless Cabins* (1940) and *Tilda* (1943); *Collected Stories* appeared in 1962. He has also written widely as scholar and critic, notably *Henry David Thoreau* (1916), *The Poetry of John Dryden* (1920; reissued 1946 as *John Dryden: A Study of His Poetry*), *Edwin Arlington Robinson* (1927), *Shakespeare* (1939) and *Nathaniel Hawthorne* (1949). *The Happy Critic* (1961) is a collection of essays, and he has edited several anthologies, including the *Oxford Book of American Prose*. [MB]

Collected and New Poems: 1924–1963 (1963); Selected Poems (1954); Autobiography (1958); The Narrative Poems (1965).

**Van Druten, John** (1901–57). English-born dramatist. His famous study of adolescence, *Young Woodley* (1925), was banned by the British censor, and Van Druten took it to New York and became American. His later plays are light work but good theatre and popular with actors: *Old Acquaintance* (1904), *The Voice of the Turtle* (1943), *I Remember Mama* (1944) and *Bell, Book and Candle* (1950). [EM]

**Van Vechten, Carl** (1880–1966). Novelist, critic. Born in Cedar Rapids, Iowa. Witty, elegant, under-rated, he wrote during the 1920s a number of delightful novels, in spirit a mixture of Firbank and Waugh.

Most deal with artistic New York in the jazz age, and are notable both for their sense of prevailing fashion and their excellent comedy; *Nigger Heaven* (1926), set in Harlem, is rather different and is part of a new wave of interest in Negro culture, while *Spider Boy* (1928) satirizes Hollywood, and *The Tattooed Countess* (1924) deals with Iowa, Van Vechten's home state. *Peter Whiffle* (1922), *The Blind Bow-Boy* (1923), *Firecrackers* (1925) and *Parties* (1930) are jazz-age novels. His several volumes of criticism derive chiefly from his activities as a music and drama critic; he wrote various memoirs (e.g. *Sacred and Profane Memoirs*, 1932), including some (e.g. his Introduction to the Modern Library edition of Gertrude Stein's *Three Lives*) about his friendship with Miss ◊ Stein, some of whose posthumous papers he edited. [MB]

Bruce Kellner, *Carl Van Vechten and the Irreverent Decades* (1969).

**Veblen, Thorstein** (1857–1929). Economist, social commentator. Born to Norwegian parents in Cato Township, Wisconsin. One of the most enduring of American social thinkers, he has had much impact on 20th-century intellectual and literary thought. Educated at Charleton College, Johns Hopkins and Yale, he joined the new University of Chicago in 1891 as an instructor in economics. In 1899 he published his best-known book, *The Theory of the Leisure Class*, an acute and witty analysis of the social values of America and its caste system based on pecuniary emulation. This was followed by *The Theory of Business Enterprise* (1904) and a series of socio-economic analyses, including *The Instinct of Workmanship* (1914). As a progressive social thinker, Veblen was influential for his literary manner as well as his analysis. The most incisive economist of his day in America, he wrote with a mordant irony that has preserved his writing. Steadfastly refusing to identify the American future with yet more capitalism, he projected not the usual agrarian alternative, but a third force of 'technocrats', scientifically trained workers who would take over control from the mere politicians. The question of 'who is to rule America?' is the invisible force behind his seemingly objective but ironical prose. Unpopular in many quarters in his day, he has been influential in most of the intellectual critiques of the 20th-century. H. L. ◊ Mencken challenged him; ◊ Dos Passos admired him; and he is extensively read today. [AG]

David Riesman, *Thorstein Veblen: A Critical Interpretation* (1953); J. Dorfman, *Thorstein Veblen and His America* (1934); Bernard Rosenberg, *The Values of Veblen* (1956); ed. Carlton C. Qualey, *Thorstein Veblen* (1968).

**Veil, Amanda** ◊ Miller, Warren.

**Veritism** ◊ Realism.

**Very, Jones** (1813–80). Poet, essayist. He was born in Salem, Massachusetts, and spent much of his childhood at sea with his father, a sea-captain. But on graduation from Harvard (1836) he became a tutor in Greek, entered the Divinity School and became isolated by the intensity of his religious vision. He moved from Unitarianism to a submissive mysticism. Forced to resign, and later released from a madhouse, he was befriended by the ◊ Transcendentalists Emerson and James Freeman Clarke, and began to write while he preached. His *Essays and Poems* (1839), prepared under Emerson's guidance, and the only volume to appear in his lifetime, are a surprisingly formal expression of his absolute faith in universal law and God's immanence in nature. His sonnets, with their celebrated extra-footed last line, have the power of complete integration of belief and feeling which can be called 'metaphysical'. In *Maule's Curse* (1938; repr. in *In Defense of Reason*, 1947), Yvor Winters printed a selection of Very's poems and praised them as being 'as convincing, and within their limits as excellent, as are the poems of Blake, or Traherne, or George Herbert'. This was an excessive judgement but helped to rehabilitate some of the poet's earlier reputation. [EM/MB]

*Poems and Essays*, ed. J. F. Clarke (1886); *Selected Poems*, ed. Nathan Lyons (1966).
W. I. Bartlett, *Jones Very: Emerson's 'Brave Saint'* (1942); Edwin Gittleman, *Jones Very: The Effective Years* (1967).

**Vidal, Gore** (1925– ). Novelist. Born in New York, he used his army service experience for the first of his 8 novels, *Williwaw* (1946). He has also written

mysteries as 'Edgar Box'. His stories are collected in *A Thirsty Evil and Other Stories* (1956). He ran for Congress as a democrat in 1960, gathering 25,000 votes more than J. F. Kennedy, an experience used in his neat play *The Best Man* (1960) and discussed in one of the excellent critical essays in *Rocking the Boat* (1962). *Reflections upon a Sinking Ship* (1969) is a second collection of essays. The title work of *Visit to a Small Planet and Other Television Plays* (1956) was rewritten as a Broadway success in 1957. Besides rewriting *Williwaw*, Vidal has rewritten or revised others of his novels: *The Judgement of Paris* (1952), *Messiah* (1954) and *The City and the Pillar* (1948), the first American novel to deal in detail with homosexuals and their world. *Julian* (1964) makes a novel out of the career of the apostate nephew of Constantine the Great: an erudite as well as an entertainingly physical book. In *Washington D.C.* (1967) the target is the corridor men of American power, the manipulations of a press lord and the game of the presidential elections. Behind the appalling picture of those who might control the world lies Vidal's disgust at the immoral procedures of government, and the same exacerbation propels *Myra Breckinridge* (1968), a novel of sexual interchange and doomed carnal America focused in the show-biz world. Vidal is today a leading satirist of pretentious, sophisticated America: in his latest play, *Weekend* (1968), he has a liberal senator insist that his son marry a black fiancée. *Two Sisters* (1970) is camp biography in the form of a novel. [EM]

**Viereck, Peter** (1916– ). Poet, critic. Born in New York City, he studied at Harvard and Oxford. After war service in Europe he taught English and German at Harvard, and later became Professor of History at Mount Holyoke. His poetry, which ranges from the comic and ironic to the extremely self-analytic, is collected in *Terror and Decorum* (1948), which in part reflects the violence of his war experience, and won the Pulitzer Prize, *Strike Through the Mask!* (1950), *The First Morning* (1952), *The Persimmon Tree* (1956) and *New and Selected Poems, 1932–1967* (1967). *The Tree Witch* (1961), in form between a poem and a play, concerns the conflict between the spirit of man's lost sense of the earth and the forces of conformity. Although he has spoken of his 'conservative' poetics, his work is capable of considerable savagery, a mixture of terror and decorum, power and control. Its themes are also reflected in his strong polemic against some of the tendencies of American liberalism, in works of social commentary which include *Metapolitics: From the Romantics to Hitler* (1941), *Conservatism Revisited: The Revolt against Revolt* (1949), *Dream and Responsibility* (1953) and *The Shame and Glory of the Intellectuals* (1953). These books have added a useful astringency to modern debate. *The Education of a Poet* (1951) is a critical work containing some useful analysis of ◊ New Criticism ploys. [MB/EM]

John Lawlor, 'Peter Viereck, Poet and Critic of Values', *Études Anglaises*, July 1954.

**Vonnegut, Kurt** (1922– ). Novelist. He was born in Indianapolis, was a prisoner of war in Germany, studied at Tennessee and Chicago Universities, and later began to write magazine short stories. His large reputation, established by *The Sirens of Titan* (1961) and *Cat's Cradle* (1963), was confirmed by *Slaughterhouse Five* (1969). Although he makes use of the apparatus of science fiction – *The Sirens of Titan*

contains a good deal of what has been called 'wide-screen baroque' – Vonnegut's novels reflect a highly individual talent which revels in irony. *Cat's Cradle*, for instance, is among other things a satire on both science and religion. Not least among his virtues is a sense – and use – of humour in a genre which notoriously suffers from the lack of it. His first novel, *Player Piano* (1960), is satirical science fiction on automation fantasies. *God Bless You, Mr Rosewater, or Pearls before Swine* (1965) is a brilliant example of black humour in the form of surrealist humour and short comic-strip-like sections: the theme is 'how to love people who have no use'. *Mother Night* was reissued in hardcover in 1966, a measure of Vonnegut's increasing reputation. The neat introduction comments on its Nazi and anti-semitic materials, used with familiar humour. *Welcome to the Monkey House*, a collection of short stories 'sold in order to finance the writing of the novels', appeared in 1968, and *Slaughterhouse Five* (1969) continues his phosphorescent analysis of twentieth-century addiction to warfare. [HD/EM]

Robert Scholes, *The Fabulators* (1967).

# W

**Wakoski, Diane** (1937– ). Poet. She was born and educated in California, and lives in New York. She has evolved into a major poet of what she terms 'the completely personal expression'; her powerful, sometimes surrealistically intense work is contained in: *Coins and Coffins* (1961), *Discrepancies and Apparitions* (1966), *George Washington Poems* (1967), *Greed* (1968–9) and *Inside the Blood Factory* (1968). She appears in *Four Young Lady Poets* (ed. LeRoi Jones, 1962). [EM]

**Waldo, Edward Hamilton.** ♦ Sturgeon, Theodore.

**Wallace, Lew** (1827–1905). Novelist. Born in Indiana, he practised law in Indianapolis, and served as general in the Civil War and on the court martial which tried those involved in Lincoln's assassination. He was governor in New Mexico and minister to Turkey, and is remembered for his *Ben Hur: A Tale of the Christ* (1880), a multiple bestseller. Among his other writings are 'The Wooing of Mulkatoon' (poem, 1898), and *The Prince of India, or, Why Constantinople Fell* (1893), a 300,000-word novel suggested by President Garfield. [EM]

**Wallant, Edward Lewis** (1926–1962). Novelist. Born in New Haven, Connecticut, he studied art and eventually became art director for a large New York advertising agency. When he died at 36, he had already made an important and substantial contribution to fiction, as one of the most interesting of post-war Jewish writers. His novels are *The Human Season* (1960); *The Pawnbroker* (1961), his best work; *The Tenants of Moonbloom* (1963); and *The Children at the Gate* (1964). All are dramas of religious conversion, in which the heroes, turned in upon themselves by suffering or timidity, are forced into contact with life through some redeeming act of love. Thus Joseph Berman, the hero of *The Human Season*, a Jewish plumber, struggles with despair on the death of his wife, finally achieving a redeeming sense of the power and energy alive in ordinary existence. He evokes memorably the archetypal Jewish experiences – particularly the horrors of the concentration camp and the degradation of the 'mercantile heritage'. [BW]

Jonathan Baumbach, *The Landscape of Nightmare: Studies in the Contemporary American Novel* (1965).

**Ward, Artemus** (Charles Farrar Browne) (1834–67). Humorist. Born in Maine, he became a printer as a young man, sent his earliest writings to the *Carpet Bag* (Boston) and began his reputation as a humorist on Ohio newspapers. 'Artemus Ward' first appeared, in a letter to the Cleveland *Plain Dealer* (of which he was city editor) in 1858, as a shrewd showman with a Yankee dialect and weird spelling. Ward began as a comic adventurer, but was soon commenting iconoclastically on political matters and the social developments of his time, from the Civil War to the Mormon Church. He became nationally famous; some of his best work appeared in *Vanity Fair*, including a mock interview with Lincoln. Like his fellow-humorists known as much by his appearances as his writing, Browne/Ward lectured across the country, knew 'Mark Twain' (whom he helped launch) in Virginia City, and in 1866 made a great success in England as lecturer and editor of *Punch*, but died there the following year. He is an outstanding example of American popular humour (e.g. 'the pretty girls in Utah mostly marry Young,' which he thought his best joke) and along with 'Petroleum V. ♦ Nasby' and 'Josh ♦ Billings' who took up the mode, he represents an important movement in American vernacular comedy. Only two books appeared in his lifetime, *Artemus Ward: His Book* (1862), and *Artemus Ward: His Travels* (1865), but more appeared posthumously, including *Artemus Ward in London* (1867). [MB]

*The Complete Works*, ed. T. W. Robertson and E. P. Hingston (1903); *Selected Works*, ed. Albert J. Nock (1912; 1924).
Don C. Seitz, *Artemus Ward* (*Charles Farrar Browne*): *A Biography and a Bibliography* (1919).

**Ward, Nathaniel** (1568–1652). Excommunicated by Laud he arrived in New England in 1634, became a minister in Ipswich, Massachusetts and returned when Cromwell came to power, in 1648. His significant book is *The Simple Cobbler of Aggawam in America* (1647), a discussion of Puritan doctrine and a defence of Congregationalism written in one of the finest idiosyncratic prose styles of the 17th century. His attack on tolerance includes a spicy satire on female costume and 'the nuduistertian fashion' of 'nugiperous gentledames'. [EM]

M. C. Tyler, *A History of American Literature 1607–1765* (2 vols., 1878; repr. 1949).

**Warner, Charles Dudley** (1829–1900). Novelist, essayist, biographer. Born in Plainfield, Massachusetts. Now usually recalled as a collaborator with Mark ◊ Twain on *The Gilded Age* (1873). He also wrote essays, reminiscent and literary (*My Summer in a Garden*, 1871, *Fashions in Literature*, 1902, etc.); a fictional trilogy (*A Little Journey in the World*, 1889, *The Golden House*, 1894, and *That Fortune*, 1899), on the misuse of a great fortune; and several good travel-books, including *Our Italy* (1891). Editor of the 'American Men of Letters' series, he contributed the biographies of John Smith and Washington Irving. [MB]

**Warren, Robert Penn** (1905–     ). Novelist, poet, critic. He was born in Kentucky, educated at Vanderbilt, California and Yale, and was a Rhodes scholar at Oxford in 1930. He has taught in a number of universities in America. His student contributions to the *Fugitive* (1922–5) already showed his affinities with the Southern Agrarians and *John Brown, the Making of a Martyr* (1929) and his essay in *I'll Take My Stand* (1930) confirmed them. He co-edited the *Southern Review* (1935–42) and, with Cleanth ◊ Brooks, compiled three highly influential ◊ New Criticism volumes, *Understanding Poetry* (1938), *Understanding Fiction* (1943) and *Fundamentals of Good Writing* (1950). His literary criticism in *Selected Essays* (1958) includes important essays on Conrad, Faulkner and 'The Rime of the Ancient Mariner'. Warren's handling of the long narrative poem and the short, metaphysically complex lyric distinguish a large poetic output in *Selected Poems 1923–1943* (1944), *Promises, Poems 1954–6* (1957), *Selected Poems; New and Old, 1923–1966*

(1966) and *Incarnations* (1968). His characteristic themes of personal and social guilt receive extended treatment in *Brother to Dragons* (1953), a book-length dramatic narrative in verse centred on the family history and ideas of ◊ Jefferson, and *Circus in the Attic* (1948, short stories). In *Audubon: A Vision* (1969), the great naturalist becomes the Adamic hero of a long poem on the American wilderness.

His eight novels explore obsessively the conflicts of the South as universal problems, but his moral point of view and style are uncomplex enough to make him a popular novelist. His materials are always vividly local: *Night Rider* (1939) concerns the Kentucky tobacco war of the 1900s, *At Heaven's Gate* (1943) contemporary Southern capitalism and pretensions to culture, *All the King's Men* (1946) the rise and fall of a Louisiana demagogue and his entourage, *World Enough and Time* (1950), his finest and most elaborate work, a famous Kentucky 19th-century murder case, *Band of Angels* (1955) the tragedy of miscegenation, *The Cave* (1959) the social effects of a cave accident, *Wilderness* (1961) a Bavarian Jew in the Civil War, and *Flood* (1964) a Tennessee town about to vanish under federal dam waters. These novels constitute a record of serious fiction-making on important themes, a lifetime's thinking which is clear, too, in his two important considerations of the Negro problems: *Segregation* (1956) and *Who Speaks for the Negro?* (1965). [EM]

L. Casper, *Robert Penn Warren: The Dark and Bloody Ground* (1960); ed. J. W. Longley, Jr, *Robert Penn Warren: A Collection of Critical Essays* (1967).

**Warshow, Robert** (1917–55). Critic, social commentator. An editor of the New York Jewish review *Commentary*, he wrote outstanding essays on films, comics, theatre and other aspects of popular culture, posthumously collected in *The Immediate Experience* (1962). [MB]

**Washington, Booker T(aliaferro)** (1856–1915). Negro leader. Was the son of a slave and a white man. He began work at an early age in salt furnaces and coal mines in West Virginia, and educated himself at night school and Hampton Normal Agricultural Institute (1872–5). After a period of teaching and a return to Hampton for experimental work for Indians, he created the Tuskegee

Institute (1881), which later became a large and important centre of Negro education (see his *Tuskegee and Its People*, 1905), and organized the National Negro Business League in Boston (1901). His books are the foundation of Negro American aspiration at the turning point in its history: *Sowing and Reaping* (1900), *Character Building* (1902) and *Working with the Hands* (1904). *Up from Slavery* (1901), an autobiography, is a major document in the history of America (see also *The Story of the Negro*, 1909, *My Larger Education*, 1911, and *The Man Farthest Down*, 1912). His biography of Frederick Douglass (1907) is a pioneering work in this field. Washington's philosophy of expediency, gradualism and submission, best in his famous 1895 speech at the Cotton State and International Exposition in Atlanta, was vitally challenged by W. E. B. ◊ DuBois in 1903, but he was the senior Negro leader for a quarter of a century. (◊ Negro Literature.) [EM]

S. R. Spencer, *Booker T. Washington and the Negro's Place in American Life* (1955).

**Webster, Daniel** (1782–1852). Lawyer, statesman, orator. Born in Salisbury, New Hampshire, he studied at Dartmouth College, practised law, entered politics in 1813, was Massachusetts senator from 1827 to 1841 and Secretary of State 1841–3 and 1850–2, but never gained the presidency he frequently sought. His willingness to compromise on any issue which might split the Union made him distrusted by both Northern Abolitionists and Southern planters. Whittier attacked him in 'Ichabod' but, after the Civil War, came to understand him ('The Lost Occasion', 1880), and Oliver Wendell ◊ Holmes wrote a similar pair of poems. Webster was New England capitalism's legal representative even while in public office. His special kind of eloquence and his dramatic appearance are celebrated in S. V. ◊ Benét's 'The Devil and Daniel Webster' (1937), in a sentence in Hawthorne's 'The Great Stone Face', and elsewhere, and some of his own words are legendary; 'Liberty *and* Union, now and forever, one and inseparable', and 'Liberty exists in proportion to wholesome restraint', etc. [EM]

*The Writings and Speeches*, ed. J. W. McIntyre (18 vols., 1903); S. H. Adams, *The Godlike Daniel* (1933); ed. W. Lewis, *Speak for Yourself, Daniel: A Life of Webster in His Own Words* (1969).

**Webster, Noah** (1758–1843). Lexicographer. Born in Connecticut, he served with his father in the army against General Burgoyne, studied at Yale (1778), and became a teacher and a lawyer. *Sketches of American Policy* (1785) is one of several pamphlets he wrote promoting strong central government, and between 1793 and 1798 he wrote in support of Washington's and Adams' policies and edited the *American Minerva*. But together with national government his deep concern was national language – 'our honour requires us to have a system of our own, in language as well as in government' – and literature. His *Grammatical Institute of the English Language, Comprising an Easy, Concise, and Systematic Method in Education, Designed for the Use of English Schools in America* (1783) is a patriot's compendium, a major aid to standardizing American spelling and pronunciation, and a best-seller as *The American Speller*. Webster's broad interests in science, literature, politics and local government and social life undoubtedly aided his monumental 20 years of preparation for his greatest work, *An American Dictionary of the English Language* (1828), which he completed in 1825 and revised in 1841. In 1843, G. and C. Merriam took over the right to the editions that have been appearing ever since. The 1962 *Third New International Dictionary* also defines English and Commonwealth words. Webster's original *Dictionary* was not only one of the first major works of American scholarship: it struck a blow for definition by usage rather than by linguistic purities. [EM]

*Noah Webster: On Being American. Selected Writings, 1783–1828*, ed. H. D. Babbage, Jr (1967).

**Weems, Mason Locke** (1759–1825). Clergyman, bookseller, biographer. Born in Arundel, Maryland. Ordained in 1784, Weems's rationalist views and his admiration for Thomas ◊ Paine alienated his fellow clergy and he left his parish to become an itinerant agent of the Philadelphia bookseller Mathew Carey. For 31 years he travelled throughout the sea-board states peddling 'improving' books. His fame lies in the moral tracts and biographies of revolutionary heroes which he himself wrote during this period. His famous life of George Washington (1800; ed. Marcus Cunliffe, 1962) embodied the virtues which he had consistently propagated. He portrayed

Washington as an almost impossibly moral, honest and wise leader, creating a folk myth which still lives. The work was continuously embroidered throughout successive editions, the famous story of the cherry tree and the hatchet appearing for the first time in the fifth edition of 1806. Parson Weems also wrote lives of Francis Marion (1809), Benjamin Franklin (1815) and William Penn (1822), but none achieved the great popular success of the earlier book. [EM]

**Weidman, Jerome** (1913–    ). Novelist, playwright. Born in New York, he studied there at City College and New York University. New York is a central part of his subject-matter. A witty observer of urban mores, particularly in the city's Jewish groups, he used his fiction to analyse ruthless business-men, ambitious writers, tough newspaper-men and go-getting poor boys. *I Can Get it for You Wholesale* (1937), and it's sequel, *What's In It for Me?* (1938), novels about Harry Bogen, an ambitious clerk in the New York garment trade, were found upsetting when they appeared. *I'll Never Go There Any More* (1941) shows an outsider confronted with Manhattan mores; *Too Early to Tell* (1946) mocks governmental agencies with its Bureau of Psychological Combat. Other novels include *Your Daughter Iris* (1955), which contrasts the Bronx and England, *The Sound of Bow Bells* (1962) and *Word of Mouth* (1964). Weidman's short stories have been collected in *The Horse That Could Whistle 'Dixie'* (1939), *The Death of Dickie Draper* (1965), etc. Latterly he has had Broadway successes with *Fiorello!* (1959), about La Guardia, Mayor of New York, and *Tenderloin* (1961). [MB]

**Weinberg, Bernard.** ◊ Chicago Aristotelians.

**Weiss, Theodore** (1916–    ). Poet. Pennsylvania-born, he was educated at Muhlenberg College and Columbia University. He taught at the University of North Carolina and Yale before joining the faculty of Bard College, where he edits the *Quarterly Review of Literature*. Five books of his verse have appeared – *The Catch* (1951), *Outlanders* (1960), *Gunsight* (1962), *The Medium* (1965) and *The Last Day and the First* (1968) – revealing his interest in the long poem, his inclination toward rhetoric and philosophy, and his debt to William Carlos ◊ Williams. [MB]

Richard Howard, *Alone with America* (1969).

**Welty, Eudora** (1909–    ). Story writer, novelist. Born in Jackson, Mississippi, of Northern parents, she is at once saturated in the familiar details of Southern life and history and removed from any deep commitment to the specifically Southern myths. Though she attended university at Wisconsin and Columbia, and worked briefly in advertising in New York, she has spent most of her life in Jackson as a part of that Mississippi delta community out of which her best writing grows. Works like *Delta Wedding* (1946) are sometimes said to present a nostalgic view of the remnants of a decadent aristocracy; in fact her interest is in the inward awareness of the individual, rather than in any social case. And though she is superb at creating an atmosphere and the texture of a community, her best stories explore the theme of what she calls in one of them ('The Still Moment') 'Separateness' and the potential reconciliation of love. She shows each individual as an endless mystery, and the necessity of love to include that mystery. Her works vary considerably, in part because she is technically accomplished and is constantly answering new creative problems. She can be quaint, as in some of her character-stories and in some of her use of legend (*The Robber Bridegroom*, 1942); she can also be superbly comic and effectively bizarre.

Her first book, *A Curtain of Green* (1941), is a collection of varied stories, many dealing with Southern grotesques. Then came a fairy-tale novel, *The Robber Bridegroom* (1942), set in Mississippi in 1798. *The Wide Net* (1943), stories, is a sure, impressive volume; so are the novels that followed, *Delta Wedding* (1946), a child's approach to the mysterious adult world of love and experience, and *The Golden Apples* (1949), interlinked short stories set in a single town and exploring elaborate narrative methods. The more recent books, the splendidly funny novel *The Ponder Heart* (1954) and the experimental collection of stories *The Bride of the Innisfallen* (1954), seem to be the work of an artist in complete command of impressive powers keeping her hand in while meditating some more important move. *Losing Battle* (1970) is a long novel celebrating the cohesion of a Mississippi family. [DC/MB]

A. Appel, Jr, *A Season of Dreams: The Fiction of Eudora Welty* (1966).

**Wescott, Glenway** (1901–    ). Novelist,

poet, story writer. He grew up in Wisconsin and studied at the University of Chicago, then became an expatriate, living in England, Germany and for eight years in the South of France, associated with but not closely allied to the ◊ 'Lost Generation'. He settled in New Jersey in 1934. He has published two volumes of poems, *The Bitterns* (1920) and *Natives of Rock* (1926), but is better known for his fiction. He is a delicate and lyrical writer who in his best work has made strong use of his native Wisconsin materials. His novels include *The Apple of the Eye* (1924), about a young boy's growth to maturity in a Wisconsin farm setting; *The Grandmothers* (1927), about a pioneer Wisconsin family; *The Pilgrim Hawk* (1940), set in Paris; and *Apartment in Athens* (1945), about the Greek underground resistance to the Nazis. A volume of stories, *Goodbye Wisconsin* (1928), exploits the contrast between Wisconsin and expatriate life; other volumes are *Like a Lover* (1926) and *Babe's Bed* (1930). *Images of Truth* (1962) is a collection of portraits of authors, including Katherine Anne Porter and Thomas Mann. [MB]

William H. Ruecket, *Glenway Wescott* (1965).

**West, Nathanael** (Nathan Wallenstein Weinstein) (1904–40). Novelist. Born in New York City. Increasingly recognized as a great precursor of the black comedy manner, West, who was killed in a car crash at 37, wrote four short novels which add up to one of the most telling indictments of the U.S.A. produced by an American. The American dream of a new world of liberty and the pursuit of happiness is envisaged as a grotesque nightmare; the land of opportunity turns comically into a land of failure, disillusionment, boredom, inhumanity and suffering

West's first novel *The Dream Life of Balso Snell* (1931) is untypical in being concerned with the disintegration of the isolated self, removed from any specific, social context; a surrealist dream story, it is a bitter, contemptuous exhibition of private despair. In his second, *Miss Lonelyhearts* (1933), the protagonist is the writer of a newspaper agony column gradually overcome by the weight of real suffering revealed by the halting letters he receives from his readers. His attempts both to evade and confront the immensities of pain in the world of which he is part end equally in failure. The story is told with economy

and the intellectual exhibitionism of *Balso Snell* has gone; the result is a modern fable of disturbing power. *A Cool Million* (1934) is a more overt denunciation of modern America in social and political terms. The form of the story is uninhibited parody of the Horatio Alger success myth. The innocent hero, having lost teeth, eyes, a leg and his scalp, in a *laissez-faire* world, and having become the witless tool of both Communist and Fascist organizations, ironically ends as a heroic martyr. The book makes its satirical points unerringly, and the wholly fabulous narrative mode is comically rich – but lacks that rooting in immediate human reality which makes *Miss Lonelyhearts* so compelling. West's last novel, *The Day of the Locust* (1939), is set in Hollywood, where he worked writing screenplays for the last five years of his life. The bizarre life of Hollywood and Southern California comes to focus the dangerous, explosive boredom and meaninglessness of modern life. Society's suppressed violence and hatred boil over in the last pages in an account of a mob riot at a film première. Character-types, action and setting are superbly chosen to define and articulate his vision of a modern world that is brutal, mindless and unredeemed. [AH]

*The Complete Works*, intr. Alan Ross (1957).
Randall Reid, *The Fiction of Nathanael West* (1968); J. F. Light, *Nathanael West: An Interpretative Study* (1961); Victor Comerchero, *Nathanael West: The Ironic Prophet* (1964).

**Wexley, John** (1907–   ). New York dramatist, celebrated for his plays on social themes, *The Last Mile* (1930), a plea for prison reform, and *They Shall Not Die* (1934), an impressive dramatization of the Scottsboro trial. [EM]

**Whalen, Philip** (1923–   ). Poet. He was born in Oregon, served in the air force 1943–6, studied at Reed College, and became associated with the San Francisco poetry revival of the 1940s and 1950s. Since 1966 he has been living in Japan. His published poetry begins with *Three Satires* (1951) and is established characteristically with *Self-Portrait from Another Direction* (1960), already notable for its invention of typographical and spatial layout forms to articulate the motion of thinking and feeling down the page. *Like I Say* (1960) and *Memoirs of an Interglacial Age* (1960) develop his poetic strengths: the direct graphical presentation of immediate experience, the abstract expressionist form of poetic diary, and the sense of the poem as an example of the poet's situation at a given moment, into which his current interests – Buddhism, jazz, sex, painting, anything he is taking part in – are projected and unified. There followed *Monday in the Evening* (1964), *Every Day* (1965), which includes calligraphically drawn works, a form which is most developed in *Highgrade* (1966) in order to obtain the sense of the poem being immediately made on the page. *On Bear's Head* (1969) is a collection of most of his twenty years' work. *You Didn't Even Try* (1966) is an interesting domestic novel, with little of the experiment of his poetry. [EM]

**Wharton, Edith** (1862–1937). Novelist. Born Edith Newbold Jones into a very well-to-do New York family, she was educated by governesses, her own extensive reading in the family library, and travel abroad. She came out into New York Society very young and married a member of her mother's circle, Edward Wharton, years older than herself, in 1885. Her first full-length novel, *The Valley of Decision* (1902), was a reconstruction of 18th-century Italy. Then followed subjects closer to home: as a wife and hostess Edith Wharton belonged to Society, but as a novelist she analysed its customs and attitudes with increasing penetration and devastating irony. The New York novels present a changing society, made significant morally; a strong sense of human dignity and integrity supplies the ultimate standard behind the social conventions and forms. She presents as the background to her stories a running conflict between two distinct upper middle classes, the old 'patrician' American families such as her own and the new rich for whom traditional ideals of culture, morals and manners, though they pay assiduous lip-service to them, are losing their sanctity.

The earlier work focuses attention on the relationship, usually hostile, between the individual and the community. The first great novel, *The House of Mirth* (1905), which shocked contemporary Society by its inwardness and realism, is an ironically tragic treatment of this theme in the disastrous social career of Lily Bart. *The Custom of the Country* (1913), the story of Undine Spragg's pyrrhic victory over family

and Society at home and abroad, is a satiric comedy. Between writing these, Edith Wharton produced her contribution to 'muck-raking', *The Fruit of the Tree* (1907), on the evils of industrialism; and also *Ethan Frome* (1911), which deals with the plight rather than the rebellion of the individual in Puritan, lower-middle-class New England. Its strong sense of tragedy and its highly dramatic development make it somewhat exceptional in her work (though it bears resemblance to *Summer*, 1917, also set in New England). All these novels possess a solidity and richness that makes them comparable with the great early novels of Henry James. Physical detail and the details of social gradation and custom are much more precisely and thoroughly presented than in his work; the 'visibility' of characters was always as strong an artistic principle with Edith Wharton as selection of 'crucial moments' and careful planning. Always elegant, she increasingly developed a clear, richly concrete and sharply ironic manner, which gives her books their distinctive moral acerbity.

After 1907 she spent much of her life in Paris and, after her husband's nervous collapse, followed by separation and divorce, she settled there, an important figure in the American expatriate community. She had known James from her youth; latterly he regarded her as an artist of equal standing. Other friends close to her interests were Bernard ◊ Berenson, Logan Pearsall ◊ Smith, Howard ◊ Sturgis, Geoffrey Scott, Walter Berry, and Percy Lubbock, who wrote the valuable *Portrait of Edith Wharton* (1947). After the First World War she bought a minor showplace, the Pavillon Colombe near Paris, where she entertained many younger writers. She had exhausted herself with large-scale welfare activities during the war; the 1920s at first bewildered her. Her brilliant *The Age of Innocence* (1920), once again dealing with New York society, has the faint air of an escape to the world of her childhood. But in *Twilight Sleep* (1927) and *The Children* (1928) she found a suitably rough satiric mode for portraying the disintegrating Society of America and Europe; her theme is now the helplessness of individuals amid social anarchy. The revival of her powers continues into her autobiography, *A Backward Glance* (1934), a record both of her social and literary life and an important document, and her unfinished novel *The Buccaneers* (1938), where the search for social order is brought into the English aristocracy.

She wrote altogether 46 books, many others worthy of attention. There are many good short stories, several admirable travel books, and the critical (and useful) *The Writing of Fiction* (1925). A recognized master of her art during her lifetime, she has been unduly neglected since her death; she needs to be seen not merely as Henry James's heiress but as a major novelist in her own right – the critic of a phase of civilization, an upholder of the idea of human civilization itself. [GW]

*Collected Short Stories* (2 vols., 1968).
Louis Auchincloss, *Edith Wharton* (1961); ed. Irving Howe, *Edith Wharton: A Collection of Critical Essays* (1962); Henry James, 'The New Novel', in *The Art of Fiction*, ed. Morris Roberts (1948); Blake Nevius, *Edith Wharton* (1953); Grace Kellogg, *The Two Lives of Edith Wharton* (1965); Geoffrey Walton, *Edith Wharton: A Critical Interpretation* (1970).

**Wheatley, Phyllis** (*c.* 1753–84). Poet. She was born in Africa, sold as a slave in Boston at the age of 8 to John Wheatley, a tailor, who educated her in his family, and became a precocious student of English, Latin and Greek. Her poems were admired for their freakishness – Negro and juvenile as well as pietistic. But her small achievement is genuine and saddening. She came to London when she was 18, much admired in society, and returned to America, marrying unhappily with a free Negro, John Peters, and died of her struggle against poverty in Boston. *Memoir and Poems of Phyllis Wheatley* appeared in 1834 and her letters in 1864. Voltaire mentioned her once as 'une Négresse qui a fait de très bons vers anglais'. (◊ Negro Literature.) [EM]

M. Bacon, *Puritan Promenade* (1964).

**Wheelwright, John** (1897–1940). Poet. Born in a wealthy Boston suburb, he graduated from Harvard College and studied architecture at M.I.T. Until it was cut short by a drunken driver, his life was given half to poetry and architecture and half to Trotskyism: he was Boston's most elegant and legendary leftist. Except for the posthumous *Selected Poems* (1941), all of his poetry was privately published, and won him a reputation only among critics and

other poets. It is important minor poetry: often in the form of parable, metrically difficult, and displaying a relish for the particular and for the epigrammatic. [BP]

**Whipple, Edwin Percy** (1819–86), Critic. Born in Gloucester, Massachusetts. Like Moses Coit ◊ Tyler and Brander ◊ Matthews, he was important for his part in establishing American literature as a field of study. In his day he was regarded as an authoritative American critic and lecturer; a typical work is his *Lectures on Subjects Connected with Literature and Life* (1850). Though he gave most of his attention to European literature, his late *American Literature and Other Papers* (1887) represents his interests in native authors, particularly in Emerson. In 1963, Mark Schorer introduced a useful collection of his essays on American writers entitled *Spokesmen*. [MB]

**White, E(lwyn) B(rooks)** (1899–    ). Humorist, critic. Important in a sometimes neglected tradition in modern American letters, the tradition of elegance, urbanity and formal concern, he exploited the traditional periodical essay-form and helped make it relevant for modern literary journalism. Associated from the 1920s with the *New Yorker*, he resembles ◊ Thurber – with whom he collaborated on *Is Sex Necessary?* (1929) – in exactness of style, satirical sharpness and response to the anti-humane tendency of much modern life. But if less euphoric than Thurber, he is more openly intelligent. His humorous commentary is to be found in such collections as *Alice through the Cellophane* (1933), *Quo Vadimus? or the Case for the Bicycle* (1939) and in the satirical stories of *The Second Tree from the Corner* (1954). Editorial commentaries from the *New Yorker*, etc., are collected in *The Wild Flag* (1946) and his essays in *The Points of My Compass* (1962). In addition to writing humour, he wrote a scholarly work on the popular religious literature of the 16th century; revised William Strunk Jr's classic little *The Elements of Style* (1959); published children's books and a volume of poems, *The Fox of Peapack* (1938); and compiled with his wife *A Sub-Treasury of American Humor* (1941). [MB]

**Whitman, Walt** (1819–92). Poet. The great poet's father was a Long Island carpenter, builder and radical who read ◊ Paine and Owen and admired the Quaker, Hicks, imparting to his son his own respect for democracy and the interior life of the soul. After a childhood period in the (then) country town of Brooklyn, apprenticed to a printer, he returned to 'fish-shaped Paumanok' and taught in schools from 1836 to 1841, at intervals working as printer and journalist and on his own paper, the *Long Islander*. His poetry showed little originality and his prose, including a temperance novel (1842), is slight and topical. At 23 he edited the Democratic *Aurora* in New York but was sacked after a few months, as he was from the Brooklyn *Eagle*, apparently for his independent, radical opinions. In 1848 he travelled to New Orleans to work on the *Crescent*, a trip which opened his provinciality to the Mississippi heartlands. His New York journalism ended. He had been prolific, conventional and rhetorical; his personal manner was dandified; he moved in the company of painters, opera buffs and Bohemians; he was excited by the international art and industry of the World's Fair; he had supported his family as a shrewd real estate man. Then at the age of 31 his image changed, as his notebooks show, towards his new prophetic, bardic role as poet of an ideal America. He grew a beard and became Walt, the poet of *Leaves of Grass* (1855), his name appearing only in small print in the copyright, the frontispiece portraying the new bard as 'an American, one of the roughs, a kosmos, disorderly fleshy and sensual . . . eating and drinking and breeding' (*Song of Myself*). This was not the language of genteel letters, and his poems were attacked for their free structure and physicality, although he was backed by Emerson and Thoreau. By 35, he embodied the mythical national poet he wanted to be. For the rest of his life he augmented the book of his personality until he received the ninth and final edition on his deathbed. The 1860 version contained 124 new poems and many revisions; the fifth edition (1872) includes the Civil War poems, *Drum Taps* and its sequel.

Whitman's workman's costume became less emblematic when the Depression left him poor in 1853. From 1857 to 1859 he edited the Brooklyn *Times*, his last journalistic job. The 1860 portrait for *Leaves* shows him more Byronic than rough. In the Civil War he demonstrated the comradely tenderness and love of his poems by tending the wounded in camp hospitals, offering his friendship to men suffering from war and primitive medicine (*Hospital Visits*, 'The Wound Dresser'). His poetry was enriched but his health was impaired: Matthew Brady's 1863 photograph shows him a white-haired old man at 44. Little critical attention was paid to *Drum Taps*; a shocked Secretary of the Interior sacked him from his Washington clerkship; and he resigned from the series of minor posts from ill-health in 1873. During this period he produced 'When Lilacs Last in the Dooryard Bloom'd', an elegy for Lincoln and a celebration of regenerative powers, *Democratic Vistas* (1871), a pamphlet on the nature of democracy, and 'Passage to India' (1868), representative of his later manner. By 1866 he had sufficient allegiance in America and England but recognized his descent from 'the high plateau of my life and capacity', a decline speeded by a paralysing stroke in 1873. He lived in Camden, New Jersey, wrote a few more poems, and *Specimen Days* (1882–3), and during a brief recovery of energy travelled to St Louis and the Rocky Mountains (1879). In 1884 he bought a little house in Camden where he lived well looked after until his death.

*Leaves of Grass* is a continuous performance maintaining the stance of the new American poet, inheritor of Emerson's self-reliance and ◊ Transcendental universalism: 'who touches this touches a man'. 'Out of the Cradle Endlessly Rocking' displays the poet's origins in the boy's intimations of loss of love and life, countered by the active sense of being part of universal processes of rejuvenation, that ebb and flow of oceanic energies which is Whitman's central philosophical image. His 'evangel-poems of comrades and love' are designed to reveal an ecstatic vision of diversified life exemplified by the Manifest Destiny of the United States, the opportunity for recovering Adam's innocence and 'a world primal again'. The fine erotic 'Calamus' poems are a central personal demonstration whose wider circle is an ideal Brotherhood of 'America' round the globe: 'One's self I sing, a single separate person, Yet utter the word Democratic, the word En-Masse'. 'Song of Myself' is a magnificent series of examples of exact individual, social and natural life unified through an organic linear form which itself is the shape of exuberant energy, that 'procreant urge of the world' the poem's philosophy contains. Whitman's greatness springs from his need to make a 'song of Sex and Amativeness, and even Animality' which is the song, too, of the 'libidinous' power of nature. His poetic forms appear to be loose, even rhetorically diffuse, but at their best their rhythms firmly articulate his naturally spreading genius. [EM]

Complete Poetry and Selected Prose, ed. E. Holloway (1938); Leaves of Grass: Readers' Edition, ed. H. Blodgett and S. Bradley (1964). G. W. Allen, The Solitary Singer: A Critical Biography (1955); R. Chase, Walt Whitman Reconsidered (1955); ed. M. Hindus, Leaves of Grass One Hundred Years After (1955); ed. R. H. Pearce, Whitman: A Collection of Critical Essays (1962).

**Whittemore, Reed** (1919– ). Poet. Born in New Haven, Connecticut, he attended Yale University. He served in Europe in the Second World War and now teaches English at Carleton College in Minnesota, where he edited two leading literary reviews, *Furioso* and its successor the *Carleton Miscellany*. In 1964–5 he was Poetry Consultant to the Library of Congress. A witty and critical commentator both in prose and verse, his criticism has stressed the need for poetry to emphasize its rational elements, and his own work, varied as it is in theme, is concerned with quality and accuracy of mind. His books of poems are *Heroes and Heroines* (1946), *An American Takes a Walk and Other Poems* (1956), and *The Self-Made Man and Other Poems* (1959). *The Boy from Iowa* (1962) contains essays as well as poems, and *The Fascination of the Abomination* (1963) brings together poems, essays and short stories. [MB]

**Whittier, John Greenleaf** (1807–92). Poet, journalist. Raised on his Quaker father's farm at East Haverhill, Massachusetts, he early became familiar with the poetry of Burns. In 1831, while he was working as an editor, he published *Legends of New-England*, early verse. From 1833 until the Emancipation of the slaves in 1865, his main concerns were political, and he was an extremely influential spokesman in the anti-slavery cause. His anti-slavery poems, collected in *Voices of Freedom* (1846), were declamatory 'trumpet calls', and he tended to justify himself as a poet on the grounds of his devotion to freedom and brother-

hood, his decent if homespun Quaker concern. In his later work his concern with his region turned him towards historical and legendary narratives and to what he called 'Yankee pastoral'. As a nature poet, despite his strong religious vein, he is by no means as convincing as his many 19th-century admirers thought, and his reputation has not really survived. Even so there is much of interest. The personal quality of *Snow-Bound* (1866), written after the death of his beloved sister Elizabeth and recalling his childhood, makes it an interesting and significant poem; it brought him poetic success. Some of his best work, including *Home Ballads* (1860), *In War Time* (1864; containing 'Barbara Frietchie'), *The Tent on the Beach* (1867) and *Among the Hills* (1869), appeared during and just after the Civil War, which he both criticized and celebrated in verse. The radical changes which the war brought in American society made his recollective nature-poetry, about the pastoral land-owning life of the Jeffersonian dream, seem nostalgic and therefore the more popular. Though conventional in its metrics, evidently excessive in its 'poetic diction', his verse remains worthy of interest. Widely circulated in England during the last century, it is to be found in numerous old editions. [MB]

Writings, ed. H. E. Scudder (7 vols., 1888–9); The Poetical Works, ed. W. G. Horder (1919). Samuel T. Pickard, Life and Letters of John Greenleaf Whittier (1894); Edward Wagenknecht, John Greenleaf Whittier (1967).

**Wieners, John** (1934– ). Poet. He was born in Boston, graduated from Boston College, studied at ◊ Black Mountain College, founded *Measure* magazine in 1961 with Robin Blaser and Stephen Jonas, and has recently been living and working in Buffalo. His plays, including *Anklesox* and *Jive Shoelaces* (1968), a lyrical work on drug addiction, have been produced by New York poets' theatres. His reputation was established immediately with *The Hotel Wentley Poems* (1958; 2nd edn, original versions, 1965), a series recording days and nights (dated) of experience. *Ace of Pentacles* (1964) develops his range of material rather than his technical ability. The poems in *Pressed Wafer* (1967), written in 1965, show a further extension of his delicate, edgy style. *Unlived* is a set of three variations. [EM]

**Wigglesworth, Michael** (1631–1705). Poet. He went from England to Connecticut when he was 7, graduated from Harvard in 1651 and became minister at Malden, Massachusetts, in 1656. Typically, he used his bad health to write his poem 'Meat Out of the Eater' (1669), on the uses of sickness. Fame arrived with two long poetic warnings of great popularity. *The Day of Doom* (1662) is the first American religiose bestseller, repeatedly reprinted, 224 stanzas of doggerel which allowed the faithful to enjoy the tortures of the non-elect in hell, their own smug depravity or self-irghteousness, and the torment of damned children. *God's Controversy with New England* (1662, publ. 1871) laments the advent of secularism and celebrates a new love for New England as New Eden betrayed by carnality. A Harvard dormitory bears his name. His *Diary 1653–1657* (ed. E. S. Morgan, 1965) is a classic of Puritan introspection and criticism. [E M]

R. Crowder, *No Featherbed to Heaven: Wiggles-worth, 1631–1705* (1962).

**Wilbur, Richard** (1921–    ). Poet, translator, critic. One of the best and most highly regarded of post-war American poets. He was born in New York and served in the army in Italy. He has studied and taught at Harvard and now teaches writing at Wesleyan College. His volumes include *The Beautiful Changes, and Other Poems* (1947), *Ceremony and Other Poems* (1950), *Advice to a Prophet* (1961), a collected volume, *The Poems of Richard Wilbur* (1963) and *Walking to Sleep* (1969). His elegance, fineness of manner and formality are the distinguishing features of his work, and have made him the target of those who speak for a rawer sort of poetry and who identify him as a leading figure among the 'academic' poets. He projects a sensibility in which the claims of aesthetic beauty are pitted against the difficulties of living authentically in an age of confused values. His way of universalizing particular experience is not that of Robert ◊ Lowell, the other major figure of the period; his is rather the attempt to create out of some impulse towards emotion a revelation of something 'lofty or long-standing', displaying the essential nature of experience. He has also written a number of light, extremely witty poems (e.g. the songs he wrote for the musical *Candide*). He has done some distinguished translations, particularly of Moliére, and some striking criticism, particularly of Poe. [M B]

*The Moment of Poetry*, ed. Don Cameron Allen (1962).

**Wilcox, Ella Wheeler** (1850–1919). Poet. Born in Wisconsin. 'Laugh and the world laughs with you, Weep and you weep alone.' With this sort of verse she became one of the most influential and best-selling poets of the late 19th century in America and elsewhere. Now regarded as of the poker-work school, she was thought an erotic poet in her time, and readers throbbed to her verses. Her *Drops of Water* volume (1872), her first, had a temperance emphasis; but with the daring *Poems of Passion* (1883) she disturbed America. Spiritualism and oriental metaphysics of vaguely erotic cast informed her more than 40 volumes, which included fiction and short stories. *The Worlds and I* (1918) is autobiographical. [M B]

**Wilder, Thornton** (1897–    ). Novelist, playwright. He was born in Wisconsin and grew up in China, graduated from Yale in 1920, studied archaeology at Rome, and took an M.A. in French at Princeton. Briefly a teacher, he began making a living from writing in 1928, but taught at Chicago University (1930–6). A best-selling novelist and Pulitzer Prize dramatist, he is one of the most successful professionals in the business, writing what he pleases out of a wide culture and yet captivating a popular audience. His first novel, *The Cabala* (1926), is an elaborate multilevelled analysis of a great European past. The manner of James and Proust is again apparent in *The Bridge of San Luis Rey* (1927), a philosophic novel of fate and chance. *The Woman of Andros* (1930) again concerns decadence before a new coming, in pre-Christian Greece in this case, and *Heaven's My Destination* (1934) deals satirically with the clash of salesmanship and evangelism in America. *The Ides of March* (1948) is an elaborate epistolary novel about Julius Caesar. *The Eighth Day* (1967), his first novel for nearly 20 years, is a large-scale structure built round a murder case in Southern Illinois. It is ambitious, inflated and impregnated with a facile optimism curiously remote from the American sixties. Wilder's first play was *The Trumpet Shall Sound* (1926) and collections of one-act plays appeared in 1928 and 1931. His most famous plays are *Our Town* (1938), an American pastoral without scenery, influenced by Gertrude Stein's ideas, and *The Skin of Our Teeth* (1942), a satirical morality on man's escapades with wife and mistress. Recently Jose Quintero produced three short plays as *Plays for Bleecker Street.*

Wilder's themes are philosophically weighty, but nothing disturbs very deeply and his forms are imitative, as he himself will admit; but he is a skilful entertainer, a tolerant philosopher without anguish, and totally undidactic. Life is cyclic, he says, man will prevail, there is no need to worry. This is the source of his comedy. [EM]

M. G. Goldstein, *The Art of Thornton Wilder* (1965).

**Williams, Jonathan** (1929– ). Poet. He was born in Asheville, North Carolina, educated at Princeton, Chicago Institute of Design and ♦ Black Mountain College. His Jargon Press, founded in 1951, is one of the most important publishers of poetry and *avant garde* writing in America, making available for the first time a considerable number of now established American writers. His publications also set a particularly high standard of design and illustration. He has served as poet in residence at Aspen Institute for Humanistic Studies. His own poetry is some of the wittiest, most formally accomplished and original in America, with subjects ranging from baseball to the English Lake District, from American ecology to social injustice in the South. His early work appeared in *Red/Gray* (1951) and *Four Stoppages* (1953); his stature is clear in *The Empire Finals at Verona* (1959), a particularly fine volume with brilliant drawings and photocollages by Fielding Dawson. There followed *Amen/Huzza/Selah* (1961), *Elegies and Celebrations* (1962), with characteristic references to ♦ Olson, Sherwood ♦ Anderson, Thoreau, the painter Franz Kline, Whitman, Messiaen, the composers Charles Ives and Carl Ruggles – a Williams pantheon. *In England's Green* & (1962) partly shows his interest in curious flora and fauna; *Lullabies Twisters Gibbers Drags* (1963) contains satires worthy of ♦ Patchen and ♦ Cummings; *Lines about Hills above Lakes* (1964, intro John Wain) is an October postcard series, mainly in prose, sent in critical love from Cumberland and Westmorland. He has recently produced poems on *Mahler* (1965) with illustrations

from R. B. Kitaj, and *The Lucidities* (1968), the latest in his books of epigrams on art and eccentricities. [EM]

*An Ear in Bartram's Tree: Selected Poems 1957–1967* (1969).

**Williams, John A.** ♦ Negro Literature.

**Williams, Roger** (1603–83). Puritan dissenter. A London tradesman's son, he graduated at Cambridge and went to Boston, Massachusetts, in 1630, preaching in Plymouth and Salem as unordained minister because of his unorthodox theology. Banished in 1635, he founded Providence Plantation in 1636 on Narragansett Indian land – but he was the first New Englander to meet the indigenous Americans with understanding rather than exploitation and conversion: *A Key into the Language of America* (1643) mainly concerns Indian words and opinions. Williams is one of the greatest early dissenters, a man of educated intelligence who believed in the rights of Indians to their lands, in the spiritual freedom of the individual, and in a church freely joined by those truly converted. Cromwell granted him a charter for Rhode Island in 1643. He was the first to welcome Jews to a New World colony. *The Bloudy Tenent of Persecution, for Cause of Conscience* (1644) is a dialogue between Peace and Truth concerning freedom of conscience and authority: to John ♦ Cotton's famous reply, Williams himself replied with *The Bloudy Tenent Yet More Bloudy* (1652). *George Fox Digg'd out of His Burrowes* (1676) attacks Quakers for their self-righteous reliance upon 'inner light' infallibility. [EM]

*The Puritans: A Sourcebook of Their Writings*, ed. P. Miller and T. H. Johnson (1938, revised bibliography, 1963).
P. Miller, *Roger Williams: His Contribution to American Tradition* (1953).

**Williams, Tennessee** (1914– ). Playwright. His grandfather was an episcopalian minister, his father a travelling salesman and his mother a Quaker. He was born in Columbus, Mississippi, but the family moved to St Louis when he was 12. During the Depression he worked in a shoe factory while writing short stories which did not sell, and eventually he reached Iowa University, graduated in 1940, and received a Rockefeller grant (1940) to work on a play, *Battle of Angels*. After its disastrous opening in Boston, his first success came with *The Glass Menagerie* (1945) in New York, and since then his reputation has become international. His novels and stories include *The Roman Spring of Mrs Stone* (1950), *Hard Candy* (1954), and *Three Players of a Summer Game* (1960), and his poems appeared in *In the Winter of Cities* (1956). *The Knightly Quest* (1967) is a novella and four short stories.

Central in his drama is the lonely vulnerable woman whose present hell of insecurity is sustained by a dream of the past or the future. Illusion is confronted by reality to bring about a violent climax associated with the young male intruder. These are the materials of *The Glass Menagerie, A Streetcar Named Desire* (1947), *Summer and Smoke* (1948) and *The Rose Tattoo* (1951), a tender and boisterous play about a Sicilian widow's remarriage. In *Camino Real* (1953), Williams experimented with expressionist methods to explore his own attitudes towards the artist's activity. His finest plays so far appeared between 1955 and 1959, the superb dramatic analysis of American conflicts in *Cat on a Hot Tin Roof, Orpheus Descending* (a reworking of *Battle of Angels*), *The Garden District*, and *Sweet Bird of Youth*, all plays set in the South and dealing with the attempts of sensitive trapped women to escape isolation. *Period of Adjustment* (1960) is a full-length domestic comedy, *Night of the Iguana* (1961) and *The Milk Train Doesn't Stop Here Any More* (1962) tend to repeat earlier formulas, and the latest are *Slapstick Tragedy* (1965) (2 plays, *The Mutilated* and *The Gnadiges Fräulein*), and *The Two Character Play* (1967), about two actors trying frantically to keep their life theatre going. *Kingdom of Earth* (1968) is the complete version of the play whose Broadway version was entitled *The Seven Descents of Myrtle*. *In the Bar of a Tokyo Hotel* (1969) is a lacerating study of a painter's life.

Although Williams is often attacked for violence, sexual neurosis and personal shock tactics, his plays are no more sensational than Jacobean tragedies of blood. The language of his best plays is consistently brilliant and careful, a clear and sometimes poetic vehicle for his vision of primitive violence which cuts through superficial civilization in the American South as elsewhere. His symbolic dramas are universally recognized as necessary allegories of rough conditions and as such have their beauty,

not always revealed in hysterical film and stage performances. [EM]

N. Tischler, *Tennessee Williams, Rebellious Puritan* (1961).

**Williams, William Carlos** (1883–1963). Poet, fiction writer. Began his long creative life as doctor and writer in Rutherford, New Jersey, where he was born. His father was English; his mother's family came from various Caribbean islands and contained French, Spanish and Jewish elements. After Swiss, Parisian and New York schools, he studied medicine at Pennsylvania University (where he met Pound and H.D.), taking his internship at hospitals in New York (where he met Wallace Stevens), and a year in pediatrics in Leipzig, before becoming a G.P. in Rutherford in 1909, the year of his first book, *Poems*, printed privately. In London, he had met Yeats, and throughout his busy life he never ceased to keep in touch with writers and painters among his friends and correspondents. The first book to show his poetic character, at least in embryo, was *The Tempers* (1913), and in *Spring and All* (1923) revealed a major poet, combining what he needed from Cubism (recorded in *A Novelette and Other Prose*, 1921–31), the surreal methods of his prose poems in *Kora in Hell* (1920), ◊ Imagism and Pound, and, finally, his own direct apprehension of common life in America. His elucidatory detail from everyday life and speech deliberately avoided the mandarin expatriate manners of Eliot and Pound and allied him with a group of thirties poets – including ◊ Reznikoff and ◊ Oppen – whose aims were stated in the 'Objectivist' number of *Poetry* (21 March 1931) and Louis ◊ Zukofsky's *Five Statements for Poetry*. Williams extended these principles in his prose and poetry through his own poetically guiding concept: 'No ideas but in things', the root of the four books of *Paterson* (1946–58) as well as his critical essays.

In 1926 he won the *Dial* award, in 1950 the National Book Award, and with ◊ MacLeish the Bollingen Prize in 1952, the year he was appointed consultant in poetry at the Library of Congress but prevented from serving because of alleged leftism. *A Voyage to Pagany* (1928) and the *Autobiography* (1951) provide some account of his personal life and opinions; *Selected Essays* (1954) and *Selected Letters* (1957) contain his criticism and a running commentary on his creative life in the context of contemporary literature. His fiction includes short stories (collected in *The Farmer's Daughters*, 1961) and documentaries (*The Knife of the Times*, 1932, and *Life along the Passaic River*, 1938), and the novel trilogy, *White Mule, In the Money* and *The Build-Up* (1937–52). His plays, some of them radically experimental, and a considerable influence on recent American drama, are collected in *Many Loves and Other Plays* (1961), and the poems in *Collected Earlier Poems* (1951), *Collected Later Poems* (1950) and *Pictures from Breughel* (1962), which includes *The Desert Music* (1954) and *Journey to Love* (1955).

In the American Grain (1925) is a prose account of the Americanness of America told through the works and lives of explorers and writers, an essential and beautifully written part of Williams' lifelong concern for the definition of a man and his cultural and topographical environment and heritage, and for the nature of being an American and a writer. The 4 books (a fifth in notes) of *Paterson* epically explore the life of a man in a city, experiencing the historical and contemporary in order to design his life productively but without religious or philosophical dogma. The variety of characterization, poetic skills and humane but discriminating sympathies make this poem a masterpiece. Throughout his life, Williams came near to despair only over the betrayal and waste of human natural resources in America. His superb ear and explorative linear controls articulate his essential unsentimental serenity. His work has been an endless source of formal inspiration to American poetry since 1950. [EM]

M. L. Rosenthal, *A William Carlos Williams Reader* (1966).
Alan Ostrom, *The Poetic World of William Carlos Williams* (1966); L. W. Wagner, *The Poems of William Carlos Williams* (1964); T. R. Whitaker, *William Carlos Williams* (1968); J. Guimond, *The Art of William Carlos Williams* (1969).

**Wilson, Edmund** (1895–   ). Critic, playwright, poet, novelist, short-story writer. He was born in Red Bank, New Jersey, studied at Princeton, where he edited the *Nassau Literary Magazine* and collaborated in *The Undertaker's Garland* (1922), a dull collection of dirges and epitaphs, reported for the New York *Sun*, and during the First World War worked in a French hospital and

for U.S. Intelligence. Returning to New York, he edited *Vanity Fair*, reviewed for the *New Republic* and the *New Yorker*, and became Edmund Wilson, the formidably erudite pundit. He has written a novel, *I Thought of Daisy* (1929), short stories of the New York suburban and educated, *Memoirs of Hecate County* (1946; slightly revised 1960), *Five Plays* (1954; his plays include *Discordant Encounters*, 1926, *This Room and This Gin and These Sandwiches*, 1937, *The Blue Light*, 1950, his best, and *The Duke of Palermo and Other Plays*, 1969) and neat collections of private prose and verse, *Note-Books of Night* (1942) and *Night Thoughts* (1961). He collected his friend Scott Fitzgerald's posthumous writings (*The Crack-Up*, 1945) and his own verse (*Poets, Farewell*, 1929). His travel reflections, sociological studies and autobiographical essays appeared as *The American Jitters: A Year of the Slump* (1932), *Travels in Two Democracies* (1936), about Russia and America, *Europe without Baedeker* (1947), 'sketches among the ruins of Italy, Greece and England' (reissued in 1967 with 'Notes from a Diary of 1963–64: Paris, Rome, Budapest'), *Apologies to the Iroquois* (1960) (with a study of 'The Mohawks in High Steel' by Joseph Mitchell), a personal ethnological exercise of considerable significance, and *The Cold War and the Income Tax* (1963), an attack on America's military expenditure. *Red Black Blond and Olive* (1956) is an important book of comparative cultural studies based on experiences among the Zuñi Indians in New Mexico, in Haiti, in Russia and in Israel, between 1935 and 1954. *The Scrolls from the Dead Sea* (1955) and *O Canada!* (1965) again testify to the extraordinary range of interest and application of intelligent research Wilson consistently shows as he penetrates other people's cultures. The training for this began with *To the Finland Station* (1940), a magnificent study of history in the making, through considerations of Michelet, Taine, Marx, Bakunin, Trotsky, Lenin and others. Of his literary criticism, *Axel's Castle* (1931) is a standard work on symbolist literature, *The Triple Thinkers* (1938; enlarged 1948) combines essays on American and European writers, and *The Wound and the Bow* (1941) is a study of the relationship between neurosis and literary imagination.

His analytical commentary and criticism of American and European literature, arts and politics appears as the superb and enlightening series *The Shock of Recognition* (1943), an annotated anthology of works concerning the recognition of an explicitly American literature, *Classics and Commercials* (1950), reviews of literature in the forties, *The Shores of Light* (1952), on the cultured life of the twenties and thirties, *The American Earthquake* (1958), *Patriotic Gore* (1962), prefaced by an attack on American militarism and concerned with Civil War literature, and *The Bit between My Teeth* (1965), covering 1950 to 1965. These works constitute a huge chronicle of responsive reading in literature written between the early 19th century and the 1960s, an intellectual biography of a scholar and critic of wide tastes, uncommon linguistic abilities and a few notoriously querky neglects, especially in 20th-century literature. The autobiographical materials in *A Piece of My Mind* (1956) and *A Prelude* (1967) offer circumspect and selective details about private life. Productive in so many fields of writing, Wilson is distinguished for his commitment, his exemplary absence of academic objectivity, and his ability to remain detached from political and psychological schools in a period beset by dogmatic theory and absurd abnegation before leaders. He is deeply American in his active sense of a free culture based on the continuous life of knowledge and research uninhibited by precedent. [E M]

Sherman Paul, *Edmund Wilson: A Study in Literary Vocation in Our Time* (1965).

**Wilson, Sloan** (1920–    ). Novelist. Born in Norwalk, Connecticut, he graduated from Harvard in 1942 and became a reporter on the *Providence Journal* (1946–7). Later he was an Assistant Director of the National Citizens Commission for Public Schools (1947–52), and Assistant Professor of English at the University of Buffalo (1952–5). Wilson achieved an early success with *The Man in the Gray Flannel Suit* (1944), a study of a business executive, and after *Voyage to Somewhere* (1946) produced four more best-selling novels about contemporary American manners: *A Summer Place* (1958), *A Sense of Values* (1961), *Georgie Winthrop* (1962) and *Janus Island* (1967). [M G]

**Wimsatt, W(illiam) K(urty)** (1907–    ). Critic, scholar. Educated at Georgetown University, Washington, and then at Yale, where in 1939 he received his Ph.D. and became an instructor; in 1955 he was appointed Professor. His first book, *The Prose Style of Samuel Johnson* (1941), analyses the qualities of a good prose style – a subject almost ignored in modern criticism. A reviewer's criticism prompted him to rethink and develop one chapter as *Philosophic Words* (1948). Other work on the English 18th century includes his editions of *Alexander Pope, Selected Poetry and Prose* (1951), *Boswell for the Defence* (with F. A. Pottle, 1959) and *Samuel Johnson on Shakespeare* (1960).

His major work has been in theoretical literary criticism, where his rigorously philosophical approach has been coupled with a strong 'structuralist' theory stressing the distinctively metaphorical character of literary language. Though this has differentiated him from ◊ New Criticism, his stress on the need for criticism to be ' the general anatomy of verbal powers' links him in some respects. With Cleanth ◊ Brooks he wrote *Literary Criticism: A Short History* (1957) which again combines great learning with original insight. He is best known for his collection of articles *The Verbal Icon* (1954) which dismisses two 'fallacious' approaches to literature – the 'Intentional Fallacy' of judging not an author's achievement but his hopes, and the 'Affective Fallacy' of describing not ' the verbal object' but individual and collective reactions to it – and also examines the relation of poetry to morals, and to ' universal' rather than 'local' truth; and various problems of style. He develops his themes and approach further in *Hateful Contraries* (1965), more essays on criticism. No other book – save possibly Northrop ◊ Frye's *Anatomy of Criticism* – has defined so well the formidable problems facing the serious critic. [M G/M B]

**Wingfield, Edward-Maria** (*c.*1560–*c.*1620?). First governor of Jamestown. Elected president of the Council of Virginia on arrival, he was deposed later by the Virginia company councillors. Besides *A Map of Virginia . . .* (1612), he wrote *The Generall Historie of Virginia, New-England, and the Summer Isles* (1624), which includes work by other voyagers to America and elaborated Captain John ◊ Smith's version of the early days of the community, and *The True Travels, Adventures, and Observations of Captaine John Smith* (1630). [E M]

**Winters, Yvor** (1900–68). Poet, critic. Chicago-born and educated at the Universities of Chicago, Colorado and Stanford, he is one of the first notable poets of distinctively Western, particularly Californian, landscape and history, in verse which is severely restrained and patterned. A second major subject area of his poetry derives from his experience as a scholar and teacher at Stanford since 1927: 'The young are quick of speech./Grown middle-aged, I teach/Corrosion and distrust.' His critical work is best read as the effort of a poet to understand and thus free himself from past (romantic) and contemporary ('modernistic') ideas and techniques which interfered with his own poetic development. He is married to the American novelist Janet Lewis.

Winters' best critical work is as a metrical analyst and pioneer interpreter of American literary history. His defence of conventional metres, his essays on Poe, Cooper and Dickinson have classic status, heavily indebted in theory to Arnold and ◊ Babbitt. *In Defense of Reason* (1947) collects important essays on 19th- and 20th-century American writers, from Cooper to Hart Crane. *The Function of Criticism* (1957) includes major studies of Hopkins and Frost. *Forms of Discovery* (1967) is a set of essays on the short poem in English. *Yvor Winters on Modern Poets* (1959) is a useful paperback collecting six critical essays, prefaced by a short introduction by Keith McKean. [GD/EM]

*Collected Poems* (1963).
Alan Stephens, 'The Collected Poems of Yvor Winters', *Twentieth Century Literature*, October 1963; Denis Donoghue, 'The Black Ox', *New York Review of Books*, 29 February 1968.

**Winthrop, John** (1588–1649). Lawyer, colonial administrator, chronicler. A group of leading English Puritans obtained from Charles I in 1629 a charter for a colonizing venture called the Massachusetts Bay Company. Winthrop was elected their governor, and in 1630 the entire company transferred itself to America, founding Boston and a number of other settlements nearby. Winthrop became the first governor of the Massachusetts Bay Colony and continued in this office, or as deputy governor, for most of the time until his death in 1649. Under his guidance a theocratic commonwealth developed in which, despite restriction of the franchise to church members,

a system of representative institutions enabled the creation of a fairly democratic society. In addition to a number of religious works, Winthrop wrote a famous journal which recounted the migration from England and the story of his private and public life in the colony down to the year of his death. While less elegantly composed than William ◊ Bradford's history of Plymouth, it is a highly readable and historically valuable account of the early development of one of the most important of the New England colonies. [EM]

*Winthrop's Journal: 'History of New England 1630–1649'*, ed. J. K. Hosmer (2 vols., 1908); ed. P. Miller and T. H. Johnson, *The Puritans: A Sourcebook of Their Writings* (1938; revised bibliography 1963).
Samuel Eliot Morison, *Builders of the Bay Colony* (1930).

**Wise, John** (1652–1725). Theologian. Born in Roxbury, Massachusetts, and Harvard-educated, he was one of the most courageous and witty ministers of his time. His base was Ipswich, Massachusetts, but he went as chaplain on two military expeditions. His leading protests against arbitrary colonial taxation, which brought him imprisonment, and his petition on behalf of the victims of the Salem Witch trials, are typical of his life. *The Churches Quarrel Espoused* (1710), a plea for independent churches against the ◊ Mathers' central organization proposals, was held in high regard by the pre-revolutionary patriots; it was reprinted in 1772. So was *A Vindication of the Government of New England Churches* (1717), proposing to replace Calvinist doctrines of election with ideas of equality; it influenced the writers of the Declaration of Independence. He also wrote *A Word of Comfort to a Melancholy Country* (1721). Wise's merits as a writer of prose are urged by Moses Coit ◊ Tyler in *A History of American Literature: 1607–1765* (1878, 1962), and his style of controversy is as humorous as it is humane. [MB/EM]

George Allan Cook, *John Wise: Early American Democrat* (1952).

**Wister, Owen** (1860–1938). Novelist. Born in Pennsylvania, he graduated from Harvard. Several trips to Wyoming provided material for *Lin McLean* (1898), a series of related stories of the Western cattle country; *The Jimmy-john Boss* (1900), short stories; and, easily his most popular work, *The Virginian* (1902), a classic Western novel, featuring a prototype Western hero, ideally brave, handsome, honourable and chivalrous. *Lady Baltimore* (1906) is a romantic novel of life in Charleston, and *Philosophy 4* (1903) is a story with a Harvard background. [A H]

*Writings* (11 vols., 1928).
Larzer Ziff, *The American 1890s* (1967).

**Wolfe, Thomas** (1900–38). Novelist. His father was a stone-cutter in Asheville, North Carolina, and his mother, from the hill country around, ran a boarding-house. At 15 he went to North Carolina University where he developed his inclination to write plays, further mistakenly fostered in G. P. ◊ Baker's '47 Workshop' at Harvard (1922). He played the lead there in his own *The Return of Buck Gavin* (1924) and *Welcome to Our City* (1923), the city being the native 'Altamont' of his first novel, *Look Homeward, Angel* (1929). From 1924 to 1930 he taught English at New York University, wrote his play *Mannerhouse*, travelled in Europe, began writing his first novel in England (published by Maxwell Perkins at Scribner's), married Aline Bernstein, and commenced *Of Time and the River* (1935). He worked with Perkins on this latter novel until it was published and in that year settled in New York, famous and successful. In 1935–6 he travelled to the West Coast, the South, and to Germany, and in 1937 paid his first visit to Asheville since his first novel appeared. He had two operations for a brain infection after pneumonia in 1938. His last two novels and a second volume of short stories were edited after his death by Edward C. Aswell.

His four novels, and parts of the stories in *From Death to Morning* (1935) and *The Hills Beyond* (1941), are a continuous autobiographical fiction on a huge scale, the anguish of whose composition is partly told in 'The Story of a Novel' (1936). In *Look Homeward, Angel*, the hero is Eugene Gant, immersed in the tumultuous pressures of his exuberant family from which he escapes into literature and college. It is a great overflowing work with superb characterizations of Gant's parents, his sister Helen, and his brother Ben. *Of Time and the River* moves Gant to university, Europe and New York, and in *The Web and the Rock* (1939) he has become George Webber, experiencing his first love affair in New York (the first half parallels the first novel), and in *You Can't Go Home Again* (1940) he is a published

novelist, lonely in the city and nostalgic for North Carolina. Wolfe's large scheme has the scope, massive detail and sense of space and time of an epic structure, but also the redundancy of its cyclic conception. The interest lies with the accurate dialogues, realistic descriptions and passages of poetic rhetoric sometimes of considerable power. Wolfe is neither a Southern writer nor a ◊ 'Lost Generation' expatriate: he reaches for a dimension beyond America and the contemporary 'wilderness of ugliness and provincialism', a degree of romantic ambition towards completely unified experience. [E M]

*Letters*, ed. E. Nowell (1956); *The Enigma of Thomas Wolfe: Biographical and Critical Selections*, ed. R. Walser (1953); *The Notebooks*, ed. R. S. Kennedy and P. Reeves (1970). Andrew Turnbull, *Thomas Wolfe* (1968); R. S. Kennedy, *The Window of Being: The Literary Career of Thomas Wolfe* (1952); *Modern Fiction Studies*, Autumn, 1965 (Thomas Wolfe issue).

**Wolfe, Tom** (1931–    ). Critic. Born in Virginia, he took his doctorate in American studies at Yale, became a newspaper reporter, and after an award-winning report from Cuba, moved to the *New York Herald-Tribune*. The first piece in his celebrated pop style was for *Esquire* in 1963. Subsequent pieces built into *The Kandy-Kolored Tangerine-Flake Streamline Baby* (1965), a classic of American studies. In *The Electric Kool-Aid Acid Test* (1968) his baroque style of disc-jockey harangue plus acute observation of salient detail is used to present Ken Kesey and his Merry Pranksters, the world of psychedelia. *The Mid-Atlantic Man* (1969) explores the cults of the faddists on both sides of the ocean. [E M]

**Woods, John** (1926–    ). Poet. Born in Martinsville, Indiana, educated at the University of Indiana. During the years he has taught at Western Michigan University, at Kalamazoo, he has published *The Deaths at Paragon* (1955), *On the Morning of Color* (1961), *Cutting Edge* (1966) and *Keeping Out of Trouble* (1968). His best and most characteristic poems are terse, ironic, wittily cryptic statements of social concerns. [B P]

**Woodworth, Samuel** (1784–1842). Born in Massachusetts, he edited a children's magazine, *The Fly*, wrote plays and poems in New York, and became a successful editor and publisher. He is remembered for two popular poems, 'The Old Oaken Bucket' (1818) and 'The Hunters of Kentucky' (1821). [E M]

**Woolcott, Alexander** (1887–1943). Journalist, critic, story writer. He was born in the Utopia of the North American Phalanx in an 85-room building. He became a bank clerk, and a drama reporter on the New York *Times*. After the First World War, his fame exploded as a journalist, raconteur and make-or-break critic. His cruelty was sometimes witty and is accurately displayed in Kaufman and ◊ Hart's revenge, *The Man Who Came to Dinner* (1939), whose title role he absorbed by playing it himself. His journalism and tales are collected in 10 volumes. The glint shines somewhat in *The Portable Woolcott* (ed. J. Hennessy, 1946). [EM]

**Woolman, John** (1720–72). Preacher, mystic. He was born in New Jersey into a devout Quaker farming family, and became a tailor, shop assistant and preacher, teaching social reform, tolerance and anarchistic pacifism. He died in England, at York, of smallpox. His *Essay on Some Considerations on the Keeping of Negroes* (1754; second part, 1762) was an important early anti-slavery document and contributed towards the abandonment of this practice by the Quakers. His *Journal* (1774) is an important record of the spirit of American Quakerism and a classic of Quaker intimacy with God and insistent truth-telling. The account of his spiritual and mystical experiences have a simple lucidity, and yet there is also a concrete respect for work and a realistic confrontation which resembles the 19th-century ◊ Transcendentalists. The *Journal* was widely read in the 19th century; the Everyman edition appeared in 1910 and it is edited, with other works on social and religious matters, by A. M. Gummere in *The Journals and Essays of John Woolman* (1922), with a biographical introduction and bibliography. [MB/EM]

Janet Whitney, *John Woolman: American Quaker* (1942); Edwin Cady, *John Woolman* (1965); G. M. Trevelyan, 'John Woolman, the Quaker', in *Clio, a Muse and Other Essays* (1913).

**Woolson, Constance Fenimore** (1840–94). Novelist, story writer. Born in Claremont, New Hampshire, the grandniece of James Fenimore ◊ Cooper, she is usually associated by critics with the local colorist movement which flourished, notably among female writers, in the late-19th-century America. Her earlier novels, some historical, some

contemporary, deal with various parts of the States. The sketches in *Castle Nowhere: Lake-Country Sketches* (1875) treat the French inhabitants of the Great Lakes region of the U.S.A. Those in *Rodman the Keeper: Southern Sketches* (1880) deal with Florida, also the setting of her novel *East Angels* (1886). *For the Major* (1883) has a North Carolina background. After 1879 she was attracted to Europe by 'that old-world feeling' and lived in Oxford, Florence and Venice. Her *Dorothy and Other Italian Stories* (1896) deals interestingly with Americans in Italy. She became a friend of Henry James, whom she idolized, and he represented her in 'The Aspern Papers'. [MB]

John D. Kern, *Constance Fenimore Woolson: Literary Pioneer* (1934).

**Wouk, Herman** (1915– ). Novelist, playwright. Born in New York. Before the war a professional radio scriptwriter, he served in the navy in the Pacific and began writing fiction. His first two novels are comic – *Aurora Dawn* (1947) satirizes the world of radio and advertising with a stylish, 18th-century comic-novel approach; *The City Boy* (1948) treats the humour of a Bronx boyhood. Then came *The Caine Mutiny* (1951), a concentrated, tough, and well-managed treatment of a mutiny aboard a Second World War minesweeper. Wouk made from it a Broadway play, *The Caine Mutiny Court Martial*, which became a successful film. He has never quite regained this form. *Marjorie Morningstar* (1955) follows a Jewish girl through an elaborate love-life and show business ambitions to a final resting place in suburban security. *Slattery's Hurricane* (1956) reworks an earlier film-script. *Youngblood Hawke* (1962) shows a Thomas ◊ Wolfe-like Southern novelist destroyed by success and the big city. *Don't Stop the Carnival* (1965) has surface attractions in its Carribbean setting; for the rest it is matter for compulsive readers. [MB]

**Wright, James** (1927– ). Poet. He studied at Kenyon College, in his native state Ohio, and at the University of Washington, and now teaches at the University of Minnesota. His elegant and excellently controlled poetry, with its strong moral concern, has won high reputation. It is collected in *The Green Wall* (1957), *Saint Judas* (1959) and *Shall We Gather at the River* (1968). [MB]

Paul Carroll, *The Poem in Its Skin* (1968).

**Wright, Richard** (1908–60). Novelist, story writer, social critic, commentator. Nearly all his work is concerned with the role of the Negro in a white-dominated world. Born near Natchez, Mississippi, he began to write soon after moving to Chicago in 1934. In the early 1940s he lived mainly in Mexico; in 1946 he moved to Paris where he remained until his death. He joined the Communist Party in the early thirties, and remained a member until 1944.

The ironically titled *Uncle Tom's Children* (1938; enlarged, 1940) is a collection of stories all portraying Southern racial prejudice and brutality in harshly naturalistic style. *Native Son* (1940) describes the career of Bigger Thomas, a Negro boy raised in the Chicago slums. This powerful novel is written in the mode of social determinism; in his violence and cruelty Bigger Thomas is the inhuman product of an inhuman world. More interesting is the sense in which he emerges as an early existential hero; the way of violence becomes for him the only way towards self-consciousness and claiming his human rights. *The Outsider* (1953) is about an intellectual Negro's much more self-conscious search for identity and meaning in life; but the language in which the action, and the socio-political problems involved, is handled is shrill and over-pitched for the whole to be convincing. In *The Long Dream* (1958) Wright returns to the special problem of being a Negro in America. *Land Today*, written before *Native Son*, but published only in 1963, is a powerful documentary novel of Chicago's South Side during the Depression: its hero, Jake Jackson, is a classic of the insulted and injured black American.

Wright's other work includes *Black Boy* (1945), an autobiography; *12 Million Black Voices* (1941), a short text and picture folk-history of the American Negro; *Black Power* (1954), a rather unsympathetic account of Ghana; *The Color Curtain* (1956), a report on the Bandung Conference in Indonesia; *Pagan Spain* (1957), a severely critical account of Franco's Spain; *White Man, Listen!* (1957), a lecture on racial injustices; and *Eight Men* (1961), a fine collection of stories. (◊ Negro Literature.) [A H]

Robert A. Bone, *The Negro Novel in America* (1958), and *Richard Wright* (U. of Minnesota Pamphlet, 1969); Constance Webb, *Richard Wright: A Biography* (1968); James Baldwin, *Notes of a Native Son* (1955); Dan McCall, *The Example of Richard Wright* (1969).

**Wright, Willard Huntington** ('S.S. Van Dine') (1888–1939). Critic, detective-story writer. Born in Virginia, Wright became an influential critical journalist writing on art and drama. With H. L. ◊ Mencken and George Jean ◊ Nathan he edited the important periodical *The Smart Set* (1912–14), with them wrote *What Nietzsche Taught* (1914), and also published collections of critical essays and a novel, *The Man of Promise* (1916). An illness in 1923 started him writing detective stories, his detective being the learned dilettante Philo Vance. In 1926 appeared *The 'Benson' Murder Case*, a year later came *The 'Canary' Murder Case*, and thereafter came many more Philo Vance novels, all reaching a wide and varied public. [M B]

**Wylie, Elinor** (1885–1928). Poet, novelist. Born in New Jersey and educated in Philadelphia, Elinor Hoyt was married three times, secondly to Horace Wylie. Her literary career was short, but within one decade, the 1920s, she established a reputation equally as poet and novelist. After the early and anonymous *Incidental Numbers* (1912) she published *Nets to Catch the Wind* (1921), a collection of delicate, elegant poems about birds and animals. Similar work appeared in *Black Armour* (1923) and *Trivial Breath* (1928), and there were new elements of fantasy and mysticism in her *Angels and Earthly Creatures* (1928), which contained the interesting sonnet sequence, *One Person*. Her *Last Poems* appeared in 1943.

She wrote four historical novels; each could be described by the subtitle, 'A Sedate Extravaganza' of her first, *Jennifer Lorn* (1923), which concerned English aristocrats in India during the 18th century and was highly praised by Sinclair Lewis. *The Venetian Glass Nephew* (1925) was a fantastic parable. *The Orphan Angel* (1926; British title *Mortal Image*, 1927) imagined Shelley's escape from drowning and an enthusiastic visit to America; its successor *Mr Hodge and Mr Hazard* (1928) described England in the sober decade following the deaths of Byron and Shelley.

Her last husband, the poet William Rose ◊ Benét, edited her *Collected Poems* (1932) and *Collected Prose* (1933), and wrote a brief critical study, *The Poetry and Prose of Elinor Wylie* (1934). [M G]

Nancy Hoyt, *Elinor Wylie: The Portrait of an Unknown Lady* (1935).

# Y

**Yerby, Frank** (1916– ). Novelist, short-story writer. Born in Georgia. Educated at Paine College and at the Universities of Fisk and Chicago. After teaching in Southern argicultural colleges (1939–41) he worked in industry, and has since been a full-time writer, living in France and Spain. Yerby won national attention and the O. Henry Memorial Award with his first short story, 'Health Card' (1944), describing the brutal humiliation of a Negro couple by military policemen; but his first novel, *The Foxes of Harrow* (1946), was a romance about the South before the Civil War, and despite criticism from other Negro writers he has produced a long and immensely popular series of such works, including *The Golden Hawk* (1948), *The Saracen Blade* ( 1952), *Gillian* (1960), *The Old Gods Laugh* (1964) and *Judas, My Brother* (1968). *Speak Now* ( 1969) uses the black jazz life but the setting is romantic Paris. [MG]

**Young, Stark** (1881– ). Critic. He was educated at the University of Mississippi and Columbia; he taught English at a number of universities, published poems, a verse drama, and a number of plays (after 1919) while he was drama editor of *The New Republic*. His serious essays on theatre appeared in *The Flower of Drama* (1923). In *I'll Take My Stand* (1930), he criticized the South's 'mad self-respect and honour complex' as well as its victimization by Washington government. His best work is the theatre criticism in *Immortal Shadows* (1948) and his translations of Chekhov. [EM]

# Z

**Zaturenska, Marya** (1902– ). Poet. Born in Russia, she came to the U.S.A. in 1909. She is married to Horace ◊ Gregory, with whom she wrote the important *History of American Poetry: 1900–1940* (1946). Her poems have been published regularly since 1924 and her latest book is *Terraces of Light* (1960). [EM]

**Zukofsky, Louis** (1904– ). Poet. He was born on the lower East Side of Manhattan and has lived in New York City most of his life, for over 30 years in Brooklyn. He has taught at the University of Wisconsin, San Francisco State College and Brooklyn Polytechnic Institute. His poetry, one of the most magnificent bodies of work in American literature, is a long and persistent search for and achievement of accuracy and refinement of language and a continuous lyrical expression of faith in men and women. It appeared firstly in *An 'Objectivist's Anthology* (a *To* publication, 1932), in such little magazines as *Origin, Poetry, Black Mountain Review, Dial, Transition* and *Trobar*, and *First Half of 'A' – 9* (1934). After *55 Poems* (1941) there appeared a number of volumes, still published largely through the support of small publishers of poetry, who included Jonathan ◊ Williams, Cid Corman and Iain Hamilton Finlay: *Anew* (1946), *Some Time* (1956), *Barely and Widely* (1958), *'A' 1–12* (1959), *16 once published* (1962), *I's (pronounced eyes)* (1963), *After I's* (1964) and *Found Objects 1962–1926* (1964). *All: The Collected Short Poems 1923–1958* (1965) and *All: The Collected Short Poems 1956–64* (1967) are, as Zukofsky says, 'an autobiography: the words are my life', and an expression of 'the desirability of making order out of history as it is felt and conceived'. These aims are achieved through poems built mainly from short cadences of unique precision and frugality which control warmth of feeling in a delightfully spare objectivity. *'A' 1–12* (1959) and *'A' 13–21* (1969) are the first sections of the only long poem to compare with the *Cantos* of Pound and *Paterson* of Williams for intellectual scope, lyrical intensity, formal invention and poetic intelligence. *All* and *'A'* constitute a great onward-going major poetry constructed from 'historical and contemporary particulars', a 'process of active literary omission', a rejection of crude metaphor and symbolism, and a use of the poetic line and typography to demonstrate 'how the voice should sound' (see *Five Statements for Poetry*, 1958; original publication 1951 and repr. *Kulchur* 7, 8 and 10, 1962). His quietly incisive poetry is the form of a lifetime's regard for definition. *Catullus* (with Celia Zukofsky, 1969) is a large collection of translations. His criticism is in *Le Style Apollinaire* (1934), *A Test for Poetry* (1948), a book of documentation for his theory of poetry and good writing in general, and *Prepositions* (1967), a collection of critical essays. *It was* (1961) is fiction, issued complete as *Ferdinand* (1968). His finest prose work is *Bottom: On Shakespeare* (1963), volume 1 of which is a brilliant reading of Shakespeare out of a lifetime of study and research; volume 2 is a musical setting of *Pericles* by the poet's wife, Celia Zukofsky. *The Gas Age* (1969) transcribes some observations on poetry made at a reading, and *Autobiography* (1970) interposes brief personal prose statements between musical settings of his lyrics by Celia Zukofsky. [EM]

Ezra Pound, *Polite Essays* (1937); Robert Creeley, 'A Note on Louis Zukofsky', *Kulchur* 14 (1964); Cid Corman, *At: Bottom* (1966); ed. Charles Tomlinson, *Agenda*, III, 6 (1964) (Zukofsky issue).

# RECOMMENDED READING

## ANTHOLOGIES AND COLLECTIONS

Oscar Cargill, ed. *American Literature: A Period Anthology* (4 vols., revised edn, 1949).

Geoffrey Moore, ed., *American Literature* (1964).

A. H. Quinn, ed., *Representative American Plays from 1767 to the Present Day* (7th edn, 1953).

G. W. Allen, W. B. Rideout and J. K. Robinson, ed., *American Poetry* (1965).

Donald M. Allen, ed., *The New American Poetry: 1946–1960* (1960).

Hennig Cohen, ed., *The American Experience* (1968) and *The American Culture* (1968).


## HISTORICAL AND CRITICAL WORKS

Alexis de Tocqueville, *Democracy in America* (1835; 1840; various modern edns).

Oscar Handlin, *The American People* (1963).

John Blum et al., *The National Experience* (1968).

David M. Potter, *People of Plenty* (1954).

H. B. Parkes, *The American Experience* (1955).

Marcus Cunliffe, *The Literature of the United States* (revised edn, 1970).

R. S. Spiller, W. Thorp, T. H. Johnson and H. S. Canby, ed., *Literary History of the United States* (2 vols., revised edn, 1964).

Philip Rahv, ed., *Literature in America* (1957).

Oliver W. Larkin, *Art and Life in America* (revised edn, 1960).

Bernard Rosenberg and David M. White, ed., *Mass Culture: The Popular Arts in America* (1957).

Wilfrid Mellers, *Music in a New Found Land* (1964).

Henry Nash Smith, *Virgin Land: The American West as Symbol and Myth* (1950).

Leo Marx, *The Machine in the Garden: Technology and the Pastoral Ideal in America* (1964).

Howard Mumford Jones, *The Theory of American Literature* (1948).

Leon Howard, *Literature and the American Tradition* (1960).

R. W. B. Lewis, *The American Adam: Innocence, Tragedy, and Tradition in the Nineteenth Century* (1955).

F. O. Matthiessen, *American Renaissance: Art and Expression in the Age of Emerson and Whitman* (1941).

Charles Feidelson, Jr, *Symbolism and American Literature* (1953).

Richard Chase, *The American Novel and its Tradition* (1957).

Marius Bewley, *The Complex Fate: Hawthorne, Henry James and Some Other American Writers* (1952).

Alfred Kazin, *On Native Grounds: An Interpretation of Modern American Prose Literature* (revised edn, 1956).

Leslie Fiedler, *Love and Death in the American Novel* (revised edn, 1966).

Nelson Manfred Blake, *Novelists' America: Fiction as History, 1910–1940* (1969).

W. B. Rideout, *The Radical Novel in the United States, 1900–1954* (1956).

Roy Harvey Pearce, *The Continuity of American Poetry* (1961).

C. Feidelson and P. Brodtkorb, ed., *Interpretations of American Literature* (1959).

Robert M. Williams, *American Society: A Sociological Interpretation* (1951).

Max Lerner, *America as a Civilization* (1957).

*Latin America*

# EDITORIAL FOREWORD

The Latin American section of the Penguin Companion is intended for the general reader who may have little or no previous knowledge of the continent. Although there has been a body of literature since before the conquest, the section concentrates on writers of the nineteenth and twentieth centuries. There are short entries which refer to indigenous literatures in Maya, Náhuatl and Quechua and there are also biographical entries which cover representative writers of the colonial period. But Latin American literature as such begins with Independence and has grown in excellence with time. The increasing number of translations which are now appearing in English are nearly all of contemporary writers and it was felt proper that the most substantial entries should be devoted to these rather than to the obscurer writers of the past whom the English-speaking reader may never come across. The difficulty has been to know which of the many contemporary writers are to be included. In general the line has been drawn to exclude those born after 1930 except where their work has appeared in translation or has earned international recognition. It is hard to guess the future importance of young writers and no doubt some deserving names have been omitted.

The interpretation of literature in this section is a broad one for it would have been foolish to have omitted names such as Bernal Díaz del Castillo or Bartolomé de las Casas on the grounds that they had not written a novel or a play. Cultural historians such as Ricardo Rojas and Ezequiel Martínez Estrada have been included when their work has had special influence.

Each entry aims to give the relevant facts of the author's life and provide a concise guide to the outstanding works. There is generally a short bibliography which gives prominence to work included in anthologies and to critical works, especially those which are readily available and are in English. There is also a short reading list for those who wish to carry their inquiries further.

Finally a brief word about the alphabetical order of the entries. In Spanish American names the father's family name usually precedes that of the mother. The entries are therefore placed under the father's name, e.g. Gabriel García Márquez under G. In the case of Brazilian names, where the father's name is generally the last name, entries are under the last name, e.g. Ribeiro Couto under C.

I should like to thank all my collaborators, especially J. M. Cohen, who originally planned the section. I also owe a debt of gratitude to Dr Luis Rebelo for unstinting help with the Brazilian section.

JEAN FRANCO

# ABBREVIATIONS

Alegría, *BHNH.* Fernando Alegría, *Breve historia de la novela hispano-americana* (Mexico, 1959; 2nd edn, 1965).

Alone, *HPLC.* 'Alone' (Hernán Díaz Arrieta), *Historia personal de la literatura chilena* (Santiago, 1954).

Bandeira, *APBP.* Manuel Bandeira, *Antologia dos Poetas Brasileiros da Fase Parnasiana* (Rio de Janeiro, 1951).

Bandeira, *APBR.* Manuel Bandeira, *Antologia dos Poetas Brasileiros da Fase Romântica* (Rio de Janeiro, 1949).

BAE. Biblioteca de Autores Españoles (Madrid).

Borges and Casares, *PG. Poesía gauchesca,* ed. Jorge Luis Borges and Adolfo Bioy Casares (2 vols., Mexico, Buenos Aires, 1955).

Brotherston, *SAMP.* G. Brotherston, *Spanish American Modernista Poets* (1958).

Brushwood, *MN.* John S. Brushwood, *Mexico in Its Novel* (University of Texas P., 1966).

CA. Colección Austral (Madrid/Buenos Aires).

Cândido, *PLB. Presença da Literatura Brasileira,* ed. Antônio Cândido and José Aderaldo Castello (São Paulo, 1964; 2nd edn, 1966).

Castro, *PLC.* Raúl Silva Castro, *Panorama literario de Chile* (Santiago, 1961).

Castro, *PNC.* Raúl Silva Castro, *Panorama de la novela chilena, 1843–1953* (Mexico, Buenos Aires, 1955).

Cohen, *LAWT. Latin American Writing Today,* ed. J. M. Cohen (Penguin Books, 1967).

Cohen, *PBSV. The Penguin Book of Spanish Verse,* ed. J. M. Cohen (Penguin Books, 1960).

Cohen, *WNC. Writers in the New Cuba,* ed. J. M. Cohen (Penguin Books, 1967).

DLL. *Diccionario de la literatura latinoamericana* (Washington, D.C., 1958 ff.) (Chile, Bolivia, Colombia, Ecuador, Central America only).

Driver, *IBL.* David M. Driver, *The Indians in Brazilian Literature* (New York, 1942).

Ellison, *BNN.* Fred Ellison, *Brazil's New Novel: Four Northeastern Masters: José Lins do Rego, Jorge Amado, Graciliano Ramos, Rachel Queiroz* (Berkeley, Los Angeles, 1954).

Fitts, *APAC. Antología de la poesía americana contemporánea,* ed. Dudley Fitts (New York, 1942, London, 1947).

Franco, *MCLA.* Jean Franco, *The Modern Culture of Latin America* (1967).

*GPRB. Grandes Poetas Românticos do Brasil,* ed. Antônio Soares-Amora (São Paulo, 1949).

Harss, *LN.* Luis Harss, *Los Nuestros* (Buenos Aires, 1966; tr. author, *Into the Mainstream,* New York, 1967).

Manzoni, *INA.* Manzoni, *El indio en la novela de América* (Buenos Aires, 1960).

Menton, *HCNG.* Seymour Menton, *Historia crítica de la novela guatemalteca* (Guatemala, 1960).

Moreno, *RP*. C. Fernández Moreno, *La realidad y los papeles* (Madrid, 1967).

Nist, *MBP*. *Modern Brazilian Poetry*, tr. and ed. John Nist, with Yolanda Leite (Bloomington, Indiana, 1962).

Nist, *MMB*. John Nist, *The Modernist Movement in Brazil* (Austin, Texas, and London, 1967).

Paz and Beckett, *AMP*. *Anthology of Mexican Poetry*, ed. O. Paz and S. Beckett (Bloomington, Indiana, 1959).

*PM*. *Poesia en movimiento. Mexico 1915–66*, ed. O. Paz, Ali Chumacero, José Emilio Pacheco, and Homero Aridjis (Mexico, 1966).

*PV*. *Antología de la poesía viva latinoamericana*, ed. Aldo Pellegrini (Barcelona, 1966).

Rojas, *NE*. Ángel F. Rojas, *La novela ecuatoriana* (Mexico, Buenos Aires, 1948).

Sánchez, *LP*. Luis Alberto Sánchez, *La literatura peruana* (6 vols., Buenos Aires, 1929).

Suárez-Miraval, *LP*. Manuel Suárez-Miraval, 'Las letras peruanas en el siglo xx', in *Panorama das literaturas das Américas* (Angola, 1963).

Suárez-Murias, *NRH*. Marguerite C. Suárez-Murias, *La novela romántica en Hispanoamérica* (New York, 1963).

Trend, *OBSV*. *The Oxford Book of Spanish Verse*, ed. J. B. Trend (1940).

Ureña, *BHM*. Max Henríquez Ureña, *Breve historia del modernismo* (Mexico, Buenos Aires, 1962).

# A

**Abreu, Casimiro José Marques de** (1839–60). Brazilian romantic poet. Born in the state of Rio de Janeiro, in 1853 he was sent to Lisbon to study commerce and there wrote many of his poems. In 1857, he returned to Brazil and died of tuberculosis at 22. His small output consists of a short dramatic piece, *Camões e o Jau* (1854), a collection of poems, *As Primaveras* (1859), and a number of posthumous poems. ◊ Bandeira calls him 'the most ingenuous of our poets'; he is chiefly remembered for his charming nostalgic verses idealizing childhood. These include the well-known anthology piece 'Meus oito anos' ('When I was eight'). [JF]

Bandeira, *APBR*; Cândido, *PLB*, ii.

**Acevedo Díaz, Eduardo** (1851–1921). Uruguayan novelist. He was active in politics and fought on the revolutionary side during civil wars. He was twice exiled, and after 1903 never returned. Much of his literary work was written abroad. Three novels, *Ismael* (1888; repr. 1953), *Nativa* (1890; repr. 2 vols., 1931), *El grito de gloria* (1893; repr. Buenos Aires, 1954), deal with different periods in Uruguay's struggle for independence. *Ismael* is about the liberation of Uruguay from the Spaniards. *Nativa* takes place in 1824 during the Brazilian occupation of Uruguay. *El grito de gloria* deals with the achievement of complete independence. A final novel, *Soledad* (1894; repr. 1954), is an example of the *mester de gaucheria* (the *gauchouque* genre), its hero being an outlaw gaucho minstrel who falls in love with a girl of the *estancia*. [JF]

Alberto Zum Felde, *Proceso intelectual del Uruguay*, i (revised edn, Montevideo, 1944); Emir Rodríguez Monegal, prefaces to the Montevideo editions of his work; Emir Rodríguez Monegal, *Eduardo Acevedo Díaz* (Montevideo, 1963).

**Acosta, José de** (1539–1600). Jesuit author of a *Historia natural y moral de las Indias* (1590; repr. Mexico, Buenos Aires, 1940), an encyclopedic account of the history, geography, politics, religion and the flora and fauna of Latin America. Acosta's work is remarkable for its insistence on factual material and on observation, although it was written at a time when writers tended to rely heavily on the authority of the ancients. [JF]

*Obras* ed. P. F. Francisco Mateos (BAE, Madrid, 1954).

Mariano Picón Salas, *A Cultural History of Spanish America* (Berkeley and Los Angeles, 1962).

**Acuña, Manuel** (1849–73). Mexican poet. His single volume of poems, in the Spanish romantic tradition, includes 'Nocturno', a love-poem written on the eve of suicide, and 'Ante un cadáver', a meditation upon a corpse which concludes with the materialistic reflection that matter, at least, is immortal. He wrote one play, *El pasado*. [JMC]

*Obras* (1965).

José Luis Martínez, 'Vida y obra de Manuel Acuña', in *La expresión nacional* (Mexico, 1955).

**Adonias Filho** (Adonias Aguiar) (1915– ). Brazilian novelist. Born on his father's farm near Bahia, he went to the primary school at Ilheus but was unhappy there; he then attended the College Ipiranga in Salvador (at the same time as Jorge ◊ Amado), frequently interrupting his studies with long stays on the farm, during which he read many French, Russian and English novels and observed the life of the rural population. Both experiences were important for his novels. He contributed to journals and was interested in the theatre. He directed the publishing firm A Noite and the Instituto Nacional do Livro. He is now the director of the National Library and the Agência Nacional. He was recently elected to the Brazilian Academy. On the publication of his last novel (*O Forte*, 1965) Octavio de Faria wrote a survey of Adonias Filho's three earlier works, which constitute a trilogy, and traced a progression from the youthful exuberance of the first work to the perfect balance between content and expression in the last. All his novels deal with life in the cocoa-producing region of the North-east, which he depicts with a harsh, direct and uncompromisingly amoral power of style, and in which the lawlessness, brutality and vengeance of the backlands' people are common themes. His style tends towards the creation of a new Brazilian literary language; and though it differs from that of ◊ Guimarães Rosa, it is from this point of view of equal importance. [AA]

Novels: *Memórias de Lázaro* (1946); *Corpo Vivo* (1952); *Os Servos da Morte* (1946); *O Forte* (1965). Essays: *Itinerário Lírico de Tasso da Silveira* (1958); *O Bloqueio Cultural*; *Modernos Ficcionistas Brasileiros* (1958).

**Afro-Cubanism.** A movement which owed its origin to the European cult of the primitive but which developed into an important revaluation of Negro culture. Many of the poets of Afro-Cubanism were white men who nevertheless believed that an original Cuban culture must include Negro elements. Afro-Cubanism incorporated African words and rhythms and a naïve sensuality into poetry, but it also stimulated a deeper interest in Negro folk tradition and art which had already been explored by Fernando Ortiz in his studies, *Los negros brujos* (1906) and *Los negros esclavos* (1916). Afro-Cuban poets included Ramón Guirao (1908–49), José Z. Tallet (1893–　　), Alejo ◊ Carpentier, Emilio Ballagas (1908–54), who compiled an important anthology of *negrista* poetry, and Nicolás ◊ Guillén. There were similar movements in other parts of Spanish America, notably Puerto Rico (◊ Palés Matos), and parallel movements in both painting and music. [JF]

José Antonio Portuondo, *Bosquejo histórico de las letras cubanas* (Havana, 1960); G. R. Coulthard, *Race and Colour in Caribbean Literature* (London, 1962).
*Mapa de la poesía negra*, ed. E. Ballagas (Buenos Aires, 1946); Franco, *MCLA*.

**Aguiar Filho, Adonias.** ◊ Adonias Filho.

**Aguilera Malta, Demetrio** (1909–　　). Ecuadorian writer, journalist and film director. Born in Guayaquil. In 1930, with several other Guayaquil writers, he published a number of stories in *Los que se van: cuentos del cholo y del montuvio*. This book heralded a new and flourishing period in the history of the Ecuadorian novel and short story, a period dominated by realistic writers from Guayaquil. Some of Aguilera Malta's major works consisted of straight reporting; these included *¡Madrid!* (1937), a report on the Spanish Civil War, and

*Canal Zone* (1935), on Panama. His major novels are *Don Goyo* (1933) and *La isla virgen* (1942). The first centres on a vigorous old man who incarnates the tough, earthy qualities of the *mestizos* (part white, part Indian inhabitants) of the coastal jungle regions. The second is the story of the defeat of the 'civilizers' by the powerful jungle. [JF]

Rojas, *NE*; *DLL*.

**Aguirre, Nataniel** (1843–88). Bolivian novelist. Author of *Juan de la Rosa*, the best Bolivian novel of the 19th century. It first appeared anonymously in the *El Heraldo* of Cochabamba in 1885. This first-person narrative, sub-titled *Memorias del último soldado de la independencia*, links the story of the orphan boy of the title with the struggle for independence. [JF]

Porfirio Díaz Machicao, *Nataniel Aguirre* (Buenos Aires, 1945); E. Viscarra, intr. to *Juan de la Rosa* (Cochabamba, 1943).

**Agustini, Delmira** (1886–1914). Uruguayan poetess. Her tragic life and early death exemplified her isolation from society. Of conventional family background and education, her passionate temperament contributed to the breakdown of her marriage. The husband, from whom she separated, killed her and then himself. No poet of the ◊ Modernism period, not even ◊ Darío, expressed so frankly the delights and torments of sexual experience. In *Los cálices vacíos* (1913), her finest collection of poems, the themes of physical love and death are interwoven. [JF]

*Poesías completas*, intr. A. Zum Felde (2nd edn, 1955).

**Alcântara Machado, Antônio Castilho de** (1901–35). Brazilian short-story writer. His *Brás, Bexiga e Barra-Funda* (1927), whose title is the names of three poor districts of São Paulo, is a collection of chronicles of daily life, particularly among the Italian immigrant population. The author claimed no high-flown literary intentions: 'It is a journal. Nothing more. . . . It reflects no political viewpoint or ideology. It does not comment or argue. Nor does it go deeply into anything.' The stories build up a composite picture through small incidents, snatches of conversation and apparently insignificant details, in documentary-film manner. *Laranja da China* (1928) was a collection of stories each built around a

Brazilian character whose high-sounding nickname – 'O Revoltado Robespierre' (the Revolutionary Robespierre), 'O Filósofo Platão' (Plato the Philosopher) – is used to give comic point to the anecdote. The style of the stories is dry, clear and humorous. Alcântara Machado also wrote a travel book, *Pathé Baby* (1926), and his newspaper articles and chronicles were published as *Cavaquinho e Saxofone* in 1940. Some stories and an unfinished novel were also published posthumously as *Mana Maria* in 1936. [JF]

*Brás, Bexiga e Barra-Funda e Laranja da China,* intr. S. Milliet (1944).

**Alceu Amoroso Lima** (1893–    ). Brazilian essayist. Until 1945 he wrote under the pseudonym Tristão de Athayde. He showed an early interest in his native Brazilian literature and after graduating in law in 1913 he turned to criticism and to the encouragement of modern movements in Brazilian literature. He became a Catholic in 1928 and has held the chair of Brazilian literature at both the National and Catholic Universities of Rio. Head of the publishing firm Agir, which he founded in 1944, he has contributed substantially to Brazilian literary criticism and has published essays on history, education, religion and politics. His approach is idealistic and like ◊ Rodó he has stressed the cultural links that bind the nations of the Latin-American continent. The main body of his criticism is included in *Estudos* (5 series, 1927–35). [ΛΛ]

**Alegría, Ciro** (1909–67). Peruvian novelist and politician. Most of his work dealt with the lives of the Indians. Son of a small landowner of Northern Peru, he also lived for a time on the edge of the jungle with his grandfather. His first novel, *La serpiente de oro* (1935; tr. H. de Onís, *The Golden Serpent*, New York, 1963), was the story of a village and its inhabitants who sailed rafts down the river Marañón. Soon after finishing his education, Alegría joined the A.P.R.A. (Alianza Popular Revolucionaria Americana) party led by Raúl Haya de la Torre and was imprisoned in 1931 for his political views. In 1934, he went into exile to Chile and remained permanently abroad for many years thereafter. In 1939, he published *Los perros hambrientos*, which dealt with the sufferings of the Andean Indians when their crops fail. His finest novel, *El mundo es ancho y ajeno* (1941; tr. H. de

Onís, *Broad and Alien is the World,* New York, 1941, London, 1942), won an international prize offered by a North American publishing house. It deals with the attempt to expel an Indian community from the lands they had traditionally held in common. The author shows a sympathetic appreciation of the good qualities of Indian communal living and shows how this could become the basis of a modern socialist community if the Indians could manage to add to their traditional lore some knowledge of modern techniques and if they could dispense with harmful superstitions. However, the novel ends in tragedy with the defeat of the Indian resistance. [JF]

*Novelas completas* (2nd edn, Madrid, 1964). Alegría, *BHNH*.

**Alencar, José Martiniano de** (1829–77). Brazilian novelist and politician. He was born in Ceará of a distinguished family and graduated from São Paulo University, after which he began writing for magazines and newspapers. His 2 series of *Cartas a Erasmo* (1865, 1867) analyse the Brazilian political situation. From 1868 to 1870, he served as Minister of Justice but retired from political life to devote himself to literature. In 1856, he published *Cartas sobre a Confederação dos Tamoios* under the pseudonym 'Ig' and in these attacked Gonçalves de ◊ Magalhães's Indianist epic, and revealed his desire for an original Brazilian literature and literary language. Under the influence of the French romantics (especially Chateaubriand), and of Scott and Fenimore Cooper, he became interested in the Indian, seeing in him the origins of the Brazilian nation, and the incarnation of freedom. His first publication in this genre was the poetic novel *O Guarani* (1857), the story of a noble Indian chief and his love for Cecilia, daughter of a Portuguese nobleman. The story is set in the 16th century and the Indian's consistently noble behaviour is in vivid contrast to that of the villain of the story, a false Italian priest. The chief virtue of the novel is probably the poetic description of Brazilian scenery. *Iracema* (1865; tr. 1. Burton, *Iracema, the Honey-Lips, a Legend of Brazil,* London, 1886) concerns the love between an Indian princess and a Portuguese officer who abandons Brazil after her death only to be drawn back to this newly adopted homeland by her memory. Alencar also wrote one purely Indian novel, *Ubirajara* (1874), and completed 3 cantos of an Indian epic, *Os Filhos de Tupan* (1863). He also wrote novels on historical and regionalist themes, notably *A Guerra dos Mascates* (1871–3), *O Tronco do Ipé* (1871), *Gaúcho* (1870) and *O Sertanejo* (1875). *As Minas da Prata* (1866) was a novel inspired by the myth of buried treasure and the journeys of the *bandeirantes* (pioneers). He was also a dramatist and his works include a version of the *Dame aux Camélias* theme, *As Asas de um Anjo* (1860), a drama of the Negro, *Mãe* (1862), and a historical drama, *O Jesuíta* (1875; tr. E. R. de Britto, *The Jesuit*, no date). [J F]

*Obra completa* (3 vols., 1958–9).
Prefaces to *Obras de José de Alencar* (1929); Driver, *IBL*.

**Almafuerte** (pseud. of Pedro Bonifacio Palacios) (1854–1917). Argentinian poet. Of deliberate and original bad taste, he expresses his grim humour, misanthropy and contempt for religion in a continuous hyperbole. He was a self-educated man who believed strongly in the virtues of education; hoping to help wipe out illiteracy, he became a country schoolmaster. He defended the poor and the oppressed but was also an aggressive individualist who sometimes struck Messianic attitudes. He gained considerable popularity and is still admired by some Argentinian writers who value his experiments in colloquialism and his metrical innovations. Though well-read, he posed as semi-literate in order to annoy the 'decadents' from whom he claimed to have rescued American literature. His *Lamentaciones* (1906) reveal the influence of Lamartine. [J M C]

*Obras completas*, ed. A. J. Torcelli (1928); *Obras de Almafuerte*, ed. R. Brughetti (1954); *La hora trágica* (1906) (autobiography).
*DLL*.

**Almeida, Guilherme de** (1890–      ). Brazilian poet. Born in the State of São Paulo. His early collections were romantic and sentimental. These included *Nós* (1917), *A Dança das Horas* (1919), *Messidor* (1919), *Livro das Horas de Soror Dolorosa* (1920) and *Era uma Vez* (1922). From 1921, he became an active promoter of *avant garde* poetry. He was one of the first to praise the work of Manuel ◊ Bandeira and he took part in the Modern Art Week of 1922 (◊ Modernism in Brazil). His later collections, *A Flauta que eu Perdi* (1924), *Meu* (1925) and *Raça* (1925), show a mastery of

technique. He compromised between regular and free versification, but the influence of the Modernist movement is seen in the introduction of nativist and national themes. He was elected to the Brazilian Academy of Letters. [J F]

Cândido, *PLB*, iii; Nist, *MMB*.

**Almeida, José Américo de** (1887–      ). Brazilian novelist. He was born in Areia, Paraiba, and had a distinguished public career as a leader in the liberal revolution of 1930, a cabinet member under Vargas, presidential candidate for the Liberal Party in 1936, and an official in the Ministry of Public Works and Transportation when Vargas was re-elected in the 1950s.

His first literary endeavour was *A Parahyba e Seus Problemas*, a sociological presentation of his message of reform. The main ideas – those of the neglect of the interior and of the contrast between life in the *sertão* (the backlands) and the littoral – are also found in later works. His first and best novel, *A Bagaceira* (1928; Lisbon, 1963), is more concerned with the moral and economic decay of the sugar-cane plantations. He attributes both to the periodic droughts and the ravages of the climate. Another theme is the contrast between the old, paternal, aristocratic plantation society and the new, mechanized, impersonal business operation that it has become. He also laments the new workers' organizations, feeling that the workers' days of happiness and security are ended forever with their new power. Almeida exaggerates this aspect of plantation life; for the worker in 1915 was little different socially or economically from the former slave. Underlying the social themes of the novel is an ill-fated love affair between the plantation owner's son, Lúcio, and the *retirante*, or drought refugee, Soledade; their affair is ended abruptly when Lúcio's father takes Soledade for his mistress. Interesting up to this point, the story becomes melodramatic when Lúcio and Soledade meet again years later. The reformer's message loses its immediacy because the book covers such a protracted period of time. Stylistically, the work is weak, and the author is neither original nor succinct in his descriptions. The importance of *A Bagaceira* is that it was one of the first novels to attract national attention to the problems of the North-east, and that it has inspired many authors to write of the people and life of the *sertão*. Américo de Almeida's other works include *O Boqueirão* (1935) and *Coiterios* (1935). [DH]

H. de Campos, *Obras* xxi (São Paulo, 1962); Ellison, *BNN*.

**Almeida, Manuel Antônio de** (1831–61). Brazilian novelist and journalist. Son of a Portuguese army lieutenant, he graduated as a doctor but left the medical profession to become a journalist. He became manager of the national printing press and was thus able to help the young Machado de ◊ Assis, whose talent he was one of the first to recognize. Almeida's outstanding work is the novel *Memórias de um Sargento de Milícias* (intr. M. de Andrade, 1941; tr. L. J. Barrett, *Memoirs of a Militia Sargeant*, Washington, D.C., 1959), which began to appear as a serial in 1852 in the *Correio Mercantil*. The *Memórias* were set in Rio de Janeiro during the period 1808–20 and admirably recapture the spirit and language of these years. The book takes the form of a picaresque narrative centring on the childhood, adolescence and early manhood of Leonardo, an illegitimate boy protected by a series of women. The *Memórias* broke decisively with romantic plot conventions and presented realistic characters in a precise, unadorned prose. Apart from the artistic merit of the work, the novel represents a rich documentary source for the period. [JF]

M. de Andrade, *Aspectos da Literatura Brasileira* (São Paulo, c. 1959); Marques Rebêlo: *Vida e Obra de Manuel Antônio de Almeida* (Rio de Janeiro, 1943).

**Alone.** ◊ Diaz Arrieta, Hernán.

**Altamirano, Ignacio Manuel** (1834–93). Mexican novelist. Of pure Indian blood, he was brought up in a small Indian village. His precocity brought him to the notice of the authorities, who helped him to complete his education. During the 'Wars of Reform', he fought on the side of Juárez and afterwards became a teacher and writer. His main interest was the improvement of educational standards and the formation of a national consciousness through literature. He believed that people's standards of culture could be raised through the novel. He edited the periodicals *El Correo de México* (1867) and *El Renacimiento* (1869), and he was an active participant at the literary discussions held in the Liceo Hidalgo. *Clemencia* (1869) is set during the period of the War of French Intervention and has a plot rather similar to

that of Dickens' *A Tale of Two Cities*. *La navidad en las montañas* (1870) is the story of Christmas in a small village and the author also included criticism of the hypocrisy of the clergy, the education system and army recruitment. *El Zarco* (tr. Mary Allt, *El Zarco, the Bandit*, London, 1957), published posthumously in 1901, was completed in 1888 (and parts of it had been read at a meeting of the Liceo Hidalgo). It was based on the adventures of the '*plateados*' ('silvery ones'), some famous bandits of the time, and concerns a conflict between an evil blue-eyed bandit and a good steady dark-skinned villager who were rivals for the love of a girl. It possesses historical rather than literary interest in that it attempts to vindicate the dark-skinned members of the Mexican nation against the prejudices of a period which assumed the superiority of the Anglo-Saxon type. [JF]

*Obras literarias completas* (1959).

M. Azuela, 'Cien años de novela mexicana', in *Obras completas*, iii (Mexico, 1960); Brushwood, *MN*.

**Alvarenga, Manuel Inâcio da Silva** (1749–1814). Brazilian poet. From Minas Gerais, he studied at Coimbra, where he took a degree in law and where he also published a poem, *O Desertor das Letras* (1774), a humorous criticism of the educational system, which also supported Enlightenment ideas of reform. He returned to Brazil, where he taught rhetoric and poetics and where he helped to found an Academy of Sciences, later reorganized under the name of Sociedade Literária. A man of progressive ideas, a supporter of the French Enlightenment and later of the Revolution, he came under suspicion and was imprisoned between 1784 and 1797, in which year he received a royal pardon. He collaborated in *O Patriota* (1812–13), the most important of the early Brazilian literary magazines. Much of his work is didactic, but he also published *Glaura* (1799; ed. A. A. de Melo Franco, 1944), a collection of rondos and madrigals, the rondos being his own original adaptation from an Italian form. Many of his verses are in the pastoral convention and have elegance and musicality. [AA]

*Obras Poéticas*, ed. and intr. Joaquim Norberto (2 vols., 1864).

**Alvarenga Peixoto, Inácio José de** (1744–93). Brazilian poet. Educated in Coimbra, he became judge in São João del-Rei (Minas Gerais) and later dedicated himself to looking after his farms and mining interests. He was involved in the famous conspiracy, the 'Inconfidência Mineira' (the Mineira Betrayal), was imprisoned in 1789 and was exiled in 1792 to Angola, where he died. He is a typical example of the Enlightenment poet and in some of his poems he reflects the desire for peace, order and agricultural prosperity. [JF]

Cândido, *P L B*.
M. Rodrigues Lapa, *Vida e Obra de Alvarenga Peixoto* (1960).

**Álvares de Azevedo, Manuel Antônio** (1831–52). Brazilian romantic poet. He died when still a student. His best poems, *Lira dos Vinte Anos*, brought him posthumous fame when published in 1853. His complete works were not published until 1862 and this edition did not include the unfinished narrative poem in Byronic style *O Conde Lopo*, which appeared in 1886. Álvares de Azevedo also wrote a play, *Macário,* and a collection of stories, *A Noite na Taverna* (both 1855). He represents a lachrymose romanticism which frequently descends into sheer sentimentality; at his best, as in the first part of *Lira dos Vinte Anos*, he writes of haunting dreams and visions ('Sonhando'), of death and love ('Saudades'), or his feeling of communion with nature ('Crepúsculo nas Montanhas'). [JF]

Cândido, *P L B*, ii; *G P R B*.

**Álvarez, José Sixto** (1858–1903). Argentinian writer. He depicted national and regional types and scenes. He is best known by his pseudonym, Fray Mocho. Brought up on a farm he became a journalist and writer. His stories appeared weekly in the magazine *Caras y Caretas*. His best-known works are *Un viaje al país de los matreros* (1897), about a community of gaucho river-dwellers, *En el mar austral* (1898), about the *Tierra del Fuego*; and the weekly magazine stories on which his reputation is based. [JF]

*Obras completas,* intr. F. J. Solero (1954).

**Amado, Jorge** (1912–     ). Brazilian novelist. Born in Bahia, he has set most of his novels in this region. He is a prolific writer and began his first novel, *Pais do Carnaval* (1932), at 18. It is interesting as a study of a Brazilian youth's search for ideals in politically turbulent times. The novels *Cacau* (1933), the story of the life of the

workers on the cocoa estates south of Bahia, and *Suor* (1934) initiate the politically committed novel in Brazil, which attempted to show the workers' sufferings in the light of the class struggle. Most of the novels he wrote during the thirties are of this type. They include *Jubiabá* (1935), which dealt with the problem of the Bahian Negro, *Capitães de Areia* (1937) and *Mar Morto* (1936), which dealt with the lives of the fisherfolk of North-eastern Brazil. Amado's concept of class struggle leads him to categorize his characters as either good or bad, the former including the poor, the downtrodden and the Bahian Negroes, the latter including all representatives of power and authority. An increasing concern with style and technique marks his mature novel, notably *Terras do Sem Fim* (1942; tr. *The Violent Land*, New York, 1945), written during a period of exile in Uruguay. The novel, with its sequel *São Jorge dos Ilhéus* (1944), has a broad historical background and deals with the rise, the apogee and the ruin of the cocoa estates. Unlike some of the previous novels, this one depicts complex, believable protagonists who compel the reader's interest in a story of conflict between two families fighting for control of a valuable tract of plantation. The absence of earlier political themes is notable in Amado's latest works, *Gabriela, Cravo e Canela* (1958; tr. W. L. Grossman, *Gabriela, Clove and Cinnamon*, New York, 1962); *Os Velhos Marinheiros* (1961; tr. H. de Onís, *Home is the Sailor*, New York, London, 1964); *A Morte e a Morte de Quincas Berro Dagua* (1965); *Os Pastores da Noite* (1966; tr. H. de Onís, *Shepherds of the Night*, New York, 1966); and *Donna Flor e seus Dois Maridos* (1966). These works are similar in their loose episodic framework, witty amusing characters and larger-than-life characterization reminiscent of folk-tale. They base their humour on human foibles, passions and ambitions and give the impression that the fantasy world is superior to the real one. [D H]

*Jorge Amado. Trinta Anos de Literatura* (São Paulo, 1961); Ellison, *B N N*.

**Amorim, Enrique** (1900–60). Uruguayan novelist. His major novels are concerned with rural life, although he is by no means simply a regional novelist. He has considerable powers of observation and insight, though on the surface his novels often appear formless. His major novels are *El* *paisano Aguilar* (1934), which deals with the return to his estate of a landowner who has been educated in the city and the difficulties he encounters; *El caballo y su sombra* (1941), which sheds new light on the conflict between the immigrant and the native creole landowners (the landowner of the story, proud possessor of a stallion, causes the death of an Italian immigrant child and is in turn killed by the child's father); and *La desembocadura* (1958), a haunting story evoking the days of the pioneers and the inevitable though regretted transformation of their life with the coming of industry and better communications. Amorim has also tried his hand at many different types of novel, including a story of juvenile delinquency, *Corral abierto* (1956), and *Los montaraces* (1957), set among foresters. [JF]

Alicia Ortiz, *Las novelas de Enrique Amorim* (1949); Mario Benedetti, *Literatura Uruguaya, siglo X X* (Montevideo, Buenos Aires, 1963).

**Anchieta, Padre José de** (1534–97). Jesuit poet, historian, humanist and philologist. He was born in Tenerife in the Canary Islands and educated in Coimbra. In 1551, he entered the Jesuit order and went to Brazil in 1553 in the company of the Governor-General, Duarte da Costa. He played a prominent part in the founding of the cities of São Paulo (1554) and Rio de Janeiro (1565). His *Fragmentos Históricos* (1584–6) are of great importance. He was also the author of a grammar of the Tupi language – the language used by the Brazilian Indians (*Arte de Gramática da Lingua mais Usada na Costa do Brasil*, 1559). He wrote poems in Tupi, Spanish, Portuguese and Latin, all on religious themes. Many of the poems are songs in praise of the Eucharist or of the Virgin. [A A]

*Cantos*, intr. A. Peixoto (Rio de Janeiro, Academia Brasileira de Letras, n.d.); *Poesias*, ed. M. Lourdes de Paula Martins (Comissão do I V Centenário da Cidade de São Paulo, 1954); Cândido, *P L B*, i.
D. L. Hamilton, *A Vida e as Obras de José de Anchieta* (Washington, D.C., 1942).

**Andrade, Mário de** (1893–1945). Brazilian poet and novelist. One of the leading figures of the Brazilian Modernist movement (◊ Modernism in Brazil). He studied music, but after the publication of the poems *Há uma Gôta de Sangue em Cada Poema* (1917) he dedicated himself to the creation of a truly Brazilian literature. In 1922, he took an active part in the Modern Art Week in São Paulo, which launched the Modernist movement, and in the same year he published a collection of poems on São Paulo themes (*Paulicéia Desvairada*; tr. Jack E. Tomlins, *Hallucinated City*, Vanderbilt U.P., 1968), influenced by Verhaeren's *Villes tentaculaires*. Its novelty lay not only in the themes but in the *avant garde* language and forms of the poems. His next collection, *Losango Cáqui* (1926), comprised the lyrical recollections of a soldier. In 1927, he published *Clã do Jaboti* and in 1930 *Remate de Males*. As a poet, Mário de Andrade was, with Oswald de ◊ Andrade, one of the pioneers of the Brazilian *avant garde* movement of the twenties and is perhaps more important for this than for the quality of his verse. Though often playful and humorous his poetry by no means ignores social themes. His most challenging and controversial contribution is, however, the novel *Mucanaíma* (1928; repr. 1957), which he subtitled 'heroi sem nenhum caráter' ('hero without a character'). It coincided with a spate of cultural nationalism in Brazil which had arisen out of the Modernist movement and which crystallized around a number of magazines, notably the *Revista de Antropofagia*, which advocated a return to indigenous roots. *Mucanaíma* is a poetic myth about an Amazonian Emperor whose fantastic adventures form the theme of the novel and include a visit to the ultra-modern São Paulo. The novel thus represents an attempt to write the myth of modern Brazil, and its language aims at a 'composite Brazilian tongue'. The novel has somewhat baffled critics down to the present and there is as yet no good study of it. [JF]

*Obras Completes*, ed. Mário de Andrade (1966); *Poesias Completas* (1955) (almost complete); *Poesia*, intr. D. Motta (1961).

**Andrade, Olegario Victor** (1841 ?7). Popular patriotic poet of Argentina. He lived as a humble government employee and provincial journalist before he became famous on publication of his poem 'El nido de cóndores'. His main poems, 'Prometeo' (1877), 'San Martín' (1878), 'Victor Hugo' (1881) and 'Atlántida' (1881) owe much to Hugo's influence. 'Prometeo', for instance, is a hymn to human progress. In his 'Atlántida' he anticipated ◊ Rodó and ◊ Darío in his exaltation of the Latin races. [JF]

*Obras poéticas* (1943).

**Andrade, Oswald de** (1890–1954). Brazilian poet and novelist. With Mário de ◊ Andrade one of the initiators of Brazilian Modernismo (◊ Modernism in Brazil). As a young man, he had visited Europe, where he came into contact with the *avant garde* and especially with the Futurist movement. He returned to Brazil in 1912 and almost immediately began writing and working for an artistic and literary movement which would correspond to the modern spirit shown by the expanding city of São Paulo. He encouraged young Brazilian painters and helped to organize the Modern Art Week of São Paulo in 1922. In 1924 he issued his own manifesto, *Pau Brasil*, intended not only as a programme for a new Brazilian poetry but also as an *avant garde* poetry which would influence Europe in the way that Europe had hitherto influenced Brazilian literature. His poems were short, often ironic evocations of such subjects as landscapes, streets, a tram car, the Berlitz school or burlesque incidents from Brazilian history. Sometimes he parodied, as for instance in his 'Meus oito anos', a comic rewriting of Casimiro ◊ Abreu's anthology piece. The virtue of his poetry is the economy with which he suggests the complexity of Brazil. He also wrote novels, beginning with *Os Condenados* (1922) and *Memórias Sentimentais de João Miramar* (1924; repr. 1964), a comic novel which satirizes Brazilian society and uses parody of pompous Brazilian language to great effect. Other novels include *Serafim Ponte Grande* (1933) and *Marco Zero*, a trilogy in which he tried to write a novel of Brazilian society from 1930 onwards. He called it a 'mural novel' and began writing the first volume, *A Revolução Melancolica*, in 1933 although he published it only in 1943. Somewhat overshadowed by other writers, Oswald de Andrade's prose and poetry had undergone a revaluation in recent years by Augusto and Haroldo de Campos, who have recognized his talent and originality and have begun to republish his work. [JF]

*Poesias Reunidas*, intr. H. de Campos (1966); *Un Homem sem Profissão. Memórias e Confissões, 1890–1919* (1954).
Mário da Silva Brito, *História do Modernismo Brasileiro* (São Paulo, 1958); Nist, *MMB*.

**Anjos, Augusto dos** (1884–1914). Brazilian poet. Author of a single volume of poems, *Eu* (1912; ed. F. de Assis Barbosa, 1963; Cândido, *PLB*, ii). In his writing, he aimed at precision of language. Many of his poems reflect a spiritual crisis: 'My deepest anguish is without a name . . . ' he wrote in one of them. He questioned contemporary values and was particularly disturbed by contemporary materialist philosophies which seemed to detract from the significance and stature of human life. [JF]

**Aranha, José Pereira da Graça** (1868–1931). Brazilian writer. Born in Maranhão in North-eastern Brazil of a well-to-do family. He was a man of broad culture who spent many years abroad as a diplomat. Like others of his generation, he was an ardent supporter of Republicanism and Abolitionism in Brazil and was also deeply concerned with Brazil's comparative backwardness. He believed that the mixture of races contributed to this, and that, by changing Brazil's ethnic composition, immigration from Europe might be the first step on the road to national progress.

His best-known work is the novel *Chanaan* (1902; tr. M. J. Lorente, *Canaan*, Boston, 1920, London, 1921), a vehicle for his views on immigration, told through the adventures of two German immigrants, Lentz and Milkau, who arrive to pioneer on the land. Milkau hopes to find a free and moral society where the violence and degeneration of Europe can be forgotten. Lentz is imperialistic and power-seeking and sees America as an area ripe for domination. Both are disillusioned, for both native Brazilians and their fellow-immigrants are far from being ideal people; hope, if any, must lie in the distant future. The plot of *Chanaan* is thin, the dialogue wooden and the language over-elaborate, but the novel retains its interest as a document of the epoch. A subsequent work, *Malazarte* (1911), was an allegorical drama which combined Brazilian folklore figures with real characters, and expresses belief in a nebulous, universal, cosmic harmony as the solution to man's problems. *A Estética da Vida* (1920) studies the origins and development of Brazilian national character. With the inauguration of Modernismo (◊ Modernism in Brazil) in 1922, Graça Aranha identified himself with the *avant garde* and in 1924 resigned from the Academy in protest against its policy. In 1925, he published his *O Espírito Moderno*, and his final novel, *A Viagem Maravilhosa*, appeared in 1931. His sympathy towards the Modernist movement in Brazil did not extend to the nativism and primitivism which characterized certain phases of the movement. Profoundly Europeanized in outlook, he wished to raise the cultural level of his country but without destroying national originality and creativity. [D H]

*Obras Completas* (8 vols., 1939–41).
M. de Lourdes Teixeira, *Graça Aranha* (8th edn, São Paulo, 1952).

**Arciniegas, Germán** (1900–    ). Colombian essayist, journalist and literary critic. At one time Colombian Minister of Education, he also served for several years as editor-in-chief of the *Revista de América* (1944–8) in Bogotá. He has acted as an interpreter of Latin-American history and culture, and his valuable anthology *The Green Continent* (New York, London, 1944), published in English, provided a good introduction to the literature, history and geography of the sub-continent. He has published many works on the *conquistadores*, including *Don Pedro de Valdivia, conquistador de Chile* (1943), *Francisco Pizarro* (1941), *El Caballero de El Dorado, vida del conquistador Jiménez de Quesada* (Buenos Aires, 1942). His *Biografía del Caribe* (Buenos Aires, 1945) was translated by Harriet de Onís as *Caribbean, Sea of the New World* (New York, 1946). A panoramic survey of Latin America, *El continente de siete colores* (1965), has been translated as *Latin America; A Cultural History* (New York, 1966). [J F]

**Arévalo Martínez, Rafael** (1884–    ). Guatemalan poet, short-story writer and novelist. For nearly 40 years he was head of Guatemala's National Library. His literary apprenticeship occurred at the height of the ◊ Modernism period. Nevertheless his work always had a distinctly personal (not to say eccentric) touch. His best-known work is a collection of stories, *El hombre que parecía un caballo*, the title story of which is a caricature of the Colombian poet, Porfirio ◊ Barba Jacob. The story consists of a word portrait of a man who both physically and temperamentally resembles a horse. In the same collection of stories is 'Un Guatemalteco en Alaska', a strange account of a group of Central Americans who work in the salmon fisheries and canneries. This originality marks most of Arévalo Martínez's subsequent work,

which includes, *El señor Monitot* (1922), *La oficina de paz de Orolandia* (1925), *Las noches en el palacio de la nunciatura* (1927), *La signatura de la esfinge* (1933) and *El mundo de los maharachías* (1938). [J F]

*Obras escogidas, prosa y poesía: 50 años de vida literaria* (1959); *Cuentos y poesías*, intr. C. G. Prada (Madrid, 1961).
Menton, *H C N G*.

**Arguedas, Alcides** (1879–1946). Bolivian journalist, historian and novelist. His *Pueblo enfermo* (1909) was a pioneer social study of Bolivia which paid particular attention to racial questions and to the influence of the environment on the character of the inhabitants. An early novel on an Indian theme, *Wata-Wara* (1904), was completely rewritten and published in 1919 as *Raza de bronce*. A pioneer novel of protest on behalf of the Bolivian Indians, it deals with a community living on the shore of Lake Titicaca and their oppression at the hands of the landowner, who not only exploits them economically but does not regard them as human beings. In this novel, Arguedas showed a knowledge of Indian language and customs. Although he does not probe very deeply into their minds, he undoubtedly helped to draw attention to the plight of the Indians. His two other novels are *Pisagua* (1903) and *Vida criolla* (1912). He has also written a standard history of Bolivia (1920). [J F]

*Obras completas*, intr. L. A. Sánchez (2 vols., Mexico, 1959–60).
Manzoni, *I N A*.

**Arguedas, José María** (1911–69). Peruvian scholar and novelist. He spent much of his childhood among Indians in mountain towns and villages. Though not an Indian, he spoke Quechua before he spoke Spanish. He later studied in Lima, especially social anthropology and folklore, and became Professor of Quechua and Anthropology at San Marcos University, Lima. He has a deep conviction that the music, song and dance of the Peruvian Indians is the authentic culture of Peru. Much of his writing is concerned with the vindication of Indian culture, and with the tragic gulf between the Indian and the non-Indian. From his very first story, *Agua* (1935), he tried to write a Castillian which would capture the flavour of Quechua and thus serve as a more authentic medium for presenting the

Indian mind than Castillian Spanish. In this and subsequent novels, he used Quechua words and expressions, especially when recording conversations. His next novel, *Yawar Fiesta* (1941), was the story of a community of Indians who were expelled from lands they had held for generations. There followed *Diamantes y Pedernales* (1954) and his major novel, *Los ríos profundos* (1958; intr. M. Vargas Llosa, 1967). This is based on Arguedas's own life and deals with the conflict in the mind of an adolescent between his natural sympathy for the Indians among whom he has been brought up and the Catholic boarding-school education which aimed at severing his Indian roots. In 1961 came *El Sexto*, which was also based on an autobiographical experience – this time an imprisonment for political reasons. His novel *Todas las sangres* (1964) returns to the theme of the alienation of the white landowning élite and the oppression of the Indians who, nevertheless, retain their dignity and identity. Dr Arguedas has also published *Canto Kechwa* (1938), a volume of translations from Quechua, and a collection of short stories, *Amor mundo* (Montevideo, 1967). [JF]

**Arinos, Affonso** (1868–1916). Brazilian writer. Born in the Minas Gerais region. His novels *Os Jagunços* and *Pelo Sertão* (1898) were first published as newspaper serials under the pseudonym Olivio de Barros. The characters are idealized versions of the *sertanejo* or inhabitant of the backlands of North-eastern Brazil. His other novels include *Joaquín Mironga* which deals with the slaves, and *Pedro Barqueiro*. His short stories were published in a posthumous collection, *Histórias e Paisagens* (1921). Also published posthumously were *O Mestre de Campo* (1918) and *O Contratador de Diamantes* (1917). [JF]

**Arlt, Roberto** (1900–42). Argentinian novelist and dramatist. He was the son of German immigrants and his stormy life provided the basis for his novels, the first of which, *El juguete rabioso* (1926), was based on the experiences of his youth and adolescence. His most ambitious novel, in 2 parts, *Los siete locos* (1929) and *Los lanzallamas* (1931), tells the story of a visionary, Erdosain, and a group of madmen who plot to destroy Buenos Aires. It is a vision of a nightmarish Buenos Aires

full of fantastic people; yet perhaps because of the imaginative technique it presents a far more authentic picture of that immigrant melting-pot than most of the realistic novels of the period. The linguistic jokes and parodies anticipate the experiments of ◊ Cortázar, although there is a greater savagery and destructiveness in Arlt, who re-creates a city that is utterly corrupt and a world that is hurtling towards cataclysm. His statement that 'los seres humanos son monstruos chapoteando en las tinieblas' ('human beings are monsters splashing about in the dark') applies not only to his novels but also to the plays. The first, *Prueba de amor*, appeared in the early thirties. Among his other publications are *El amor brujo* (1932), *El jorobadito* (1933) and *La fiesta de hierro* (1940). There is a good edition of his novels and stories (*Novelas completas y cuentos*, 3 vols., 1963), with an introduction by his daughter, Mirta Arlt, who has also edited his plays (*Teatro completo*, 1968). [JF]

N. Etchenique, *Roberto Arlt* (Buenos Aires, 1962); R. H. Castagnino, *El teatro de Roberto Arlt* (La Plata, 1964); A. Núñez, *La obra narrativa de Roberto Arlt* (Buenos Aires, 1968).

**Arreola, Juan José** (1918– ). Mexican short-story writer and dramatist. His best pieces are witty imaginative prose poems which show verbal inventiveness. These include his 'Bestiario' and 'Confabulario', both of which are included in the volume *Confabulario total* (*1941–61*). He has also published *La feria* (1963). [JF]

*P M.*

**Ascasubi, Hilario** (pseud. Paulino Lucero, Aniceto el Gallo) (1807–75). Argentinian ◊ gauchesque poet, soldier and politician. He fought on the unitarian side against the Federalists, was captured by the Federalists but escaped and went into exile in Montevideo and helped to defend that city during a nine-year siege by the armies of the Federalist Rosas. Under the pseudonym Paulino Lucero, he wrote a number of poems and verse dialogues in which gauchos voiced their hatred of Rosas and commented on incidents in the fight against the tyrant. A second series of gauchesque poems and prose pieces written in the 1850s under the pseudonym Aniceto el Gallo are mainly satirical comments on contemporary affairs. Ascasubi's most ambitious work is a narrative poem, *Santos Vega*, mainly written in *décimas* (10-line verses) in which the legendary gaucho minstrel, Santos Vega, tells the story of twin brothers, one good and one evil; set in the colonial era, the adventures of the brothers enable the poet to re-create the world of the gaucho, the pampa, the cattle-herding and branding, the Indian raids. The poem is often rambling and flat, yet it has its highlights, in particular a vivid description of an Indian raid. [JF]

Borges and Casares, *P G.*

**Assis, Joaquim Maria Machado de** (1839–1908). Brazilian novelist. He became his country's leading literary figure despite his very humble birth, and the fact that he was a mulatto and an epileptic. Orphaned early in childhood, he was brought up by a mulatto stepmother and worked as a printer, where his talents attracted attention. He went into journalism, published his first short stories and novels and, after winning recognition, secured a good post in the Civil Service. He became first President of Brazil's Academy of Letters. His enormous output included 9 novels and more than 200 short stories. Between his first poem, published at 15, and his first important novel, *Memórias Póstumas de Brás Cubas* (tr. *Epitaph for a Small Winner*, New York, 1952), which appeared in serial form in 1880, there was a long apprenticeship in which his genius was somewhat hampered by romantic convention. However, even in the early romantic novels, there is psychological verisimilitude. *Helena* (1876) reflected a tragedy of the author's own life, for the heroine, in order to be accepted into wealthy society, pretends to be the illegitimate daughter of a rich man, concealing the fact that her real father is alive and living in poverty. Social success is achieved at the cost of a real human relationship which has to be stifled, just as Machado de Assis himself had to forget his humble relations when he moved into more respectable circles. Another novel of this period, *Iaiá Garcia* (1878), attempts to break away from the romantic happy ending by showing some of the 'prose' of married life. It was however after 1880, under the influence of Sterne, Xavier de Maistre and Stendhal, that he began to adopt a freer form more suitable to his discursive and detached approach. From 1880 onwards, he produced masterpiece after masterpiece, including *Memórias Póstumas de Brás Cubas, Quincas*

*Borba* (1891; tr. *The Heritage of Quincas Borba,*London, 1954),*Dom Casmurro* (1899; tr. *Dom Casmurro*, New York, 1953), *Esaú e Jacó* (1904; tr. H. Caldwell, *Esau and Jacob*, London, 1966), *Memorial de Aires* (1908). These later novels reflect his philosophy, which, on his own confession, was 'harsh and bitter'. Like Schopenhauer, he believed that men were irrational creatures, actuated by will, and that individual existence had no transcendental design. Like Schopenhauer he saw self-denying love and art as the two methods by which the individuation principle could be transcended. Each of the later novels describes a circle of defeat and despair. Brás Cubas spends his youth and energies in a long adulterous affair with the wife of a friend, a woman he could have married in the first place had he set his mind to it. His life slips by in plots, intrigues and secret meetings until he suddenly realizes that he is an old man. In *Quincas Borba*, the protagonist, Rubião, inherits a fortune at the outset of the novel and wastes this and the rest of his life pursuing the chimera of a married woman who cynically fleeces and then deserts him. In *Dom Casmurro*, Bento schemes for years to escape from the seminary to marry his childhood sweetheart, Capitú – only to live a married life as a tortured Othello. *Esaú e Jacó*, a political allegory, is also despairing. The protagonists are twin brothers who squabble and fight through the momentous moments of Brazilian history and who symbolize the warring elements in Brazilian life. In many of these later novels and some of the short stories, Machado de Assis suggests that there is a sharp difference between a man's social image and his self and that this split is the inevitable consequence of living in society. In the short story 'O Espelho' (in *Papéis Avulsos*, 1882; tr. W. L. Grossman and H. Cauldwell in *The Psychiatrist and Other Stories*, London, 1963), for instance, the reflected image of the narrator is dim until he puts on his lieutenant's dress uniform and then the outlines of his reflection become sharp and clear. Machado de Assis was nevertheless no cynic. He simply refused to accept a sentimental and self-deceiving view of himself and others, and resembled his own character, Aires – ironic, detached, observant. [JF]

*Obras completas* (1952); *Obras completas* (Aguilar, 1959).

J. Galante de Sousa, *Bibliografía de Machado de Assis* (Rio de Janeiro, 1955); Wilton Cardoso,

*Tempo e Memória em Machado de Assis* (Belo Horizonte, 1958).

**Asturias, Miguel Ángel** (1899– ). Guatemalan poet and novelist. Graduating in law, he went to the Sorbonne, where he studied under the distinguished Maya scholar Georges Raynaud, who had translated the Maya 'Bible', the *Popul Vuh*, from Quiché to French. In 1937, Asturias published a translation of the *Popul Vuh* into Spanish, based on Raynaud. Maya studies undoubtedly helped to stimulate his first creative writing, *Leyendas de Guatemala* (1930), poetic retellings of Guatemalan legends of both Indian and Spanish origin. His most important work is the novel *El Señor Presidente* (tr. F. Partridge, *The President*, London, 1963), published in 1946, which was written many years earlier but could not be published during the dictatorship of Ubico. The character of the 'President' was based on the dictator, Estrada Cabrera, under whose regime Asturias had grown up, but the novel is far more than the denunciation of a particular regime. By the use of an imaginative language and technique, Asturias conveys a nightmare world of fear in which all the inhabitants of a city from Minister to beggar are enmeshed. Christian and humane values are debased. The President, the incarnation of evil, is God; and those who rebel against him are sinners who must be punished. In 1949, Asturias published *Hombres de maíz*, a novel which described the transformation of Indian life on contact with commercialized mestizo and white civilization. The novel attempted to show this process not through a Europeanized consciousness but in terms of myth, as the Indian mind would conceive it. His later work includes a trilogy of novels on the foreign control of the banana plantations. *Viento fuerte* (1950), the first novel of the trilogy to appear, is the only one to have been translated into English (tr. D. Flakoll and C. Alegría, *The Cyclone*, 1967). This was followed by *El Papa verde* (1954) and *Los ojos de los enterrados* (1955). More recently there has appeared a novel which carries his technique of 'magical realism' to even greater extremes. This is *Mulata de tal* (1960; tr. G. Rabassa, *The Mulatta and Mr Fly*, London, 1967). He has also recently published a *nouvelle, El Alhajadito*. His poems were published in the collection *Sien de alondra* (1949). A novel published

in 1957, *Week-end in Guatemala,* dealt with the overthrow of the Arbenz government in 1954. In 1967, he was awarded the Nobel Prize for literature. [JF]

*Obras escogidas* (3 vols., Madrid, 1955–66).
Atilio Jorge Castelpoggi, *Miguel Ángel Asturias* (Buenos Aires, 1961); Menton, *HCNG*; Harss, *LN*.

**Athayde, Tristão de.** ◊ Alceu Amoroso Lima.

**Azevedo, Aluísio de** (1857–1913). Brazilian writer, journalist and diplomatist. The first of his 11 novels, *Uma Lágrima de Mulher,* was published in 1880, and in the following year he published *O Mulato,* a melodramatic story set in São Luis de Maranhão of the illegitimate son of a white man and a Negress whose love for his cousin and his career end tragically after the discovery of the secret of his birth. There followed an undistinguished group of novels, *O Mistério da Tijuca* (1882), *Memórias de um Condenado* (1882) (the title of which he later changed to *A Condessa Vésper*), *Filomena Borges* (1884) and *A Mortalha de Alzira* (1894). Under the influence of naturalism, he wrote *O Homen* (1887), a novel which analysed a case of sexual frustration. This was followed by *O Coruja* (1890) and *O Cortiço* (1890; tr. H. W. Brown, *A Brazilian Tenement,* London, 1928). The latter described the rise of a slum landlord who began by living off the money of his Negro mistress and finally became wealthy from rents from cheap property. It presented a realistic picture of the lives of the Rio de Janeiro poor. His last novel, published in 1895, was *Livro de uma Sagra.* The complete works were published in São Paulo in the 1950s, each novel being published separately, and with an introduction. [JF]

*Obras Completas,* ed. M. Nogueira da Silva (14 vols., 1939–41).
Eugenio Gomes, *Aspectos do Romance Brasileiro* (Bahia, 1958).

**Azuela, Mariano** (1873–1952). Mexican novelist. He started his career as a doctor, and began writing while still a medical student in Guadalajara. He had published several novels before joining one of Villa's bands as an army doctor during the Revolution. This experience forms the basis for the outstanding novel of the Mexican Revolution, *Los de abajo,* which first appeared in 1915 as a serial in an El Paso,

Texas, newspaper and was published in book form in 1916 (tr. E. Munguía, *The Underdogs*, 1929, New York, 1963). The novel successfully conveyed the attitudes of the peasants and barbaric side of the Revolution. It was one of the first Latin-American novels successfully to use a mass protagonist. In a subsequent novel, *Los caciques* (1917), he depicted the economic oppressors of pre-Revolutionary Mexico and in *Las moscas* (1918) he described the flight by train of a group of opportunists and members of the old order as revolutionary forces enter Mexico City. Azuela's great talent as a novelist lies in his ability to show the life of the mass. In the twenties, he turned to experiment, notably *La malhora* (1923) and *La luciérnaga* (1932). *Las tribulaciones de una familia decente* (1938) dealt with the chaos and conflicting values of the post-Revolutionary years and his two final novels, *La maldición* and *Esa sangre*, published posthumously, were increasingly bitter on the evils that still existed in Mexico despite the Revolution. [JF]

*Obras completas* (3 vols., 1958–60); *Two Novels of Mexico: Las moscas. Los caciques*, tr. L. B. Simpson (Berkeley and Los Angeles, 1964) (*The Flies* and *The Bosses*).
A. Magaña-Esquivel, *La novela de la Revolución*, i (Mexico, 1964); Brushwood, *MN*.

# B

**Balbuena, Bernardo de** (1562–1627). Mexican poet. He was born in Spain but arrived in Mexico as a child. He was trained for the Church and became Bishop of Puerto Rico, where he died. His main works are *Grandeza mexicana* (1604), a description in tercets of Mexico City; and *Siglo de oro en las selvas de Erífile* (1608), which is in the pastoral convention and consists of a series of eclogues, mainly descriptive in character. *El Bernardo, o victoria de Roncesvalles* (1624) is a long epic on the legend of Bernardo del Carpio, imitative of Ariosto. [JF]

*Grandeza mexicana y fragmentos del Siglo de Oro y El Bernardo*, ed. F. Monterde (2nd edn, 1954).
José Rojas Garcidueñas, *Bernardo de Balbuena: la vida y la obra* (Mexico, 1958).

**Ballagas, Emilio.** ◊ Afro-Cubanism.

**Banchs, Enrique** (1888–1968). Argentinian poet. His first collection, *Las barcas*, appeared in 1907. This was followed by *El libro de los elogios* (1908), *El cascabel del halcón* (1909) and *La urna* (1911), after which he did not publish another collection, although some poems and stories appeared in reviews, sometimes unsigned. Profoundly influenced by European and especially French poetry, he cultivated pure poetry and wrote studies on Valéry, Claudel and Rilke among others. Without great literary influence on younger Argentine poets, he nevertheless won their respect by his wholehearted dedication to poetry. [JMC]

Nicolás Cócaro, 'Enrique Banchs: Verso y prosa', *Revista Oeste*, 11 (Buenos Aires, 1950); Moreno, *RP*.

**Bandeira, Manuel** (1885–1968). Brazilian poet. Son of an engineer, he spent much of his childhood in Recife before going to São Paulo to study architecture. He was unable to complete his studies, since he was found to be tubercular, and for many years he was an invalid. Between 1913 and 1914, he lived in a Swiss sanatorium, where he met Paul Éluard. In 1917, he published a collection of poems, *A Cinza das Horas*, which, though showing no great originality of form, represented a refreshing break from the Parnassianism and Symbolism which still held the literary field. Many poems of the collection express 'desencanto' ('disenchantment'), melancholy and nostalgia for 'os dias de minha infancia' ('the days of my childhood'). Nursery rhyme and children's stories, always a source of inspiration to him, already appear in some of the poems, e.g. 'João Felpudo. Viajem a roda do mundo/Numa casquinha de noz'. Bandeira himself described his next collection, *Carnaval* (1919), as 'um livro sem unidade' ('a book with no unity'). But the ironic and irreverent carnival poems, the comic parody of Parnassian poets in 'Os Sapos', already heralded the iconoclastic mood of the 1922 Modern Art Week (◊ Modernism in Brazil), although Bandeira did not as yet consider that he had found his style. In 1924, he published *O Ritmo Dissoluto*, a group of poems which he added to his other collections in an edition of his complete works, *Poesias*. Though this was a transition work he was to regard one of the poems in it, 'Noite Morta', as one of his best pieces. However, it was in *Libertinagem* (1930) that he fully mastered a free poetic technique and modern idiom. The volume began with an onslaught on traditional poetry in 'Poética', in which he declared 'Estou farto do lirismo comedido – Do lirismo bem comportado' ('I am tired of measured lyricism, of well-behaved lyricism'). In the best-known poem of the collection, 'Vou-me embora pra Pasárgada', the poet evokes a childhood fantasy world in which everything is possible. *Estrêla da Manhã* (1936), his last important volume, was distinguished by its emphasis on death and religious faith, a faith occasionally glimpsed rather than consistently experienced. Bandeira is also the distinguished translator of much modern poetry, and has written Portuguese versions of Shakespeare's *Macbeth* and Schiller's *Maria Stuart*. He is also an important literary critic, responsible for major editions and anthologies of Brazilian poetry of the past. [JF]

*Poesia e Prosa*, intr. S. B. de Holanda and F. de Assis Barbosa (1958); Cândido, *P L B*, iii.

**Barba Jacob, Porfirio** (pseud. of Miguel Angel Osorio Benítez; also known as Maín Ximénez or Ricardo Arenales) (1883–1942). Colombian poet. He modelled his life on the French *poètes maudits*, often causing scandal by his riotous behaviour. He founded newspapers and literary reviews in Colombia and Mexico, made a fortune in the Mexican Revolution and later lost it; he lived in many Latin-American countries including Guatemala (◊ Arévalo Martínez). 'En nada creo, en nada' ('I believe in nothing. Nothing'), he wrote, but the rebellion, doubt and isolation so evident in his life are not often successfully carried into his poetry. He never succeeded in freeing himself from the influence of ◊ Darío and was almost the last of the Modernists. No edition of his poems was ever supervised by the poet and existing editions contain errors. [JMC]

*Canciones y Elegías* (1932); *Rosas negras* (1933); *Poemas intemporales* (Mexico, 1944).
Javier Arango Ferrer, *Panorama das literaturas das Américas*, i.

**Barbosa de Oliveira, Antônio Rui** (1849–1923). Brazilian lawyer and politician. He had an indirect influence on literature. He became President of the Republic and was noted for his oratory. He cultivated fine language and careful use of words and was regarded as a purist. [AA]

*Obras Completas*, ed. A. J. Lacoinbe (36 vols., 1943–     ).
Charles William Turner, *Rui Barbosa, Brazilian Crusader for the Essential Freedoms* (New York, 1945).

**Barreto, Affonso Henriques de Lima** (1881–1922). Brazilian novelist. He entered the Civil Service as a young man, having had to abandon his studies to earn his living. His novels reflect the bitterness of a life spent in obscurity. Because of poverty, he had difficulty in publishing them. It was obvious that Lima Barreto, a mulatto, felt himself an outsider, and his best novels show his rebellion against the *status quo*. All his work is set in Rio de Janeiro and the majority is openly critical of the injustices, the rigidity and the hypocritical attitudes of Rio society. His most interesting novel is undoubtedly *Triste Fim de Policarpo Quaresma* (published in book form in 1915). The hero is an army officer genuinely concerned about the future of his country. But his life is a series of setbacks. Whether attempting to exploit the land or to join an armed rebellion against the government, he is doomed to failure. At the end of the book he is imprisoned as a traitor by the man he had supported. The adventures of the hero are an expression of the author's feeling of impotence in a society which denied him any outlet. His other novels include *Recordações do Escrivão Isaías Caminha* (1909), *Numa e a Ninfa* (1915), *Vida e Morte de M. J. Gonzaga de Sá* (1919), *Histórias e Sonhos* (1920), *Bagatelas* (1922) and the posthumously published *Clara dos Anjos* (1948). [AA]

*Obras Completas*, ed. and intr. F. de Assis Barbosa (1956).
Francisco de Assis Barbosa, *Vida de Lima Barreto* (2nd edn, Rio de Janeiro, 1959).

**Barreto de Meneses, Tobias** (1839–89). Brazilian thinker. He became Professor of Law at the University of Recife in 1881 and was influential for his introduction of various European philosophies into Brazil. He first followed the eclectic spiritualism of Cousin, then became a positivist, and finally turned to Haeckel's monism and the works of Eduard von Hartmann. His main works are *Ensaios e Estudos de Filosofia e Crítica* (1875), *Questões Vigentes* (1888), *Estudos Alemães* (1883), *Vários Escritos* (1900) and *Polêmicas* (1901). [JF]

*Obras Completas* (1926)
J. Cruz Costa, *Panorama of the History of Philosophy in Brazil* (tr. Fred G. Sturm, Washington, D.C., 1962).

**Barrios, Eduardo** (1884–1963). Chilean novelist and dramatist. His widowed Peruvian mother had him educated in Lima. He was destined for the army like his father, but broke with his family and wandered about from job to job as trader, bookkeeper in the nitrate fields of northern Chile, and salesman. Some of these experiences are reflected in his novel *Un perdido* (1917). His reputation as a novelist is based on his skill at psychological studies of strange cases. The first of these was *El niño que enloqueció de amor* (1915), the story of a boy who goes out of his mind because of his obsession for an older girl. *El hermano asno* (1922) takes place in a Franciscan monastery and concerns the relationship between two friars and the love one of them experiences for a girl outside. His major novel, *Gran señor y rajadiablos* (1948), re-creates the paternalistic world of 19th-century Chile and the boisterous life of a country landowner. In *Los hombres del hombre* (1950) he splits a man's personality into a number of 'characters' each of which assumes a separate identity. [JF]

*Obras completas* (2 vols., 1962).
Castro, *PNC*; Alegría, *BHNH*.

**Belli, Carlos Germán** (1927–    ). Peruvian poet. His work shows a thoroughly modern consciousness. He first attracted attention with *O hada cibernetica* (1962). His poems often dramatize man's helplessness in modern society. His complete poetry to date was published in Montevideo in 1967 under the title *El pie sobre el cuello*. [JF]

*PV*; twenty poems tr. Clayton Eshleman, *Tri-quarterly*, Winter/Fall, 1968/9.

**Bello, Andrés** (1781–1865). Venezuelan scholar and neo-classical poet. He was one of the leading intellectuals of the inde-pendence movement and because of the breadth of his vision can truly be con-sidered a figure of Continental signific-ance. Politically he was no revolutionary but favoured an enlightened monarchy. His early poetry was patriotic, but not bellicose. In 1810 he left for exile in London, where he stayed for nearly 20 years, taking part in politics as an agent of the revolutionary governments and spending much of his time in study. In 1826, he founded *El Repertorio Americano* (1826–8), in which he published one of his best-known poems, 'Silva a la agricultura de la zona tórrida' (1826), which evokes the beauties of the American landscape. During this London period he also wrote 'Carta escrita desde Londres a Paris por un americano a otro', a lament for his exile and for the failure of the independence movement to bring about peace and virtue. Although he was in Europe at the height of the romantic movement, he was not basically in sympathy with the movement, although he was closer to English romanticism than to the French. In 1829, Bello returned to America at the invitation of the Chilean government, and in Chile he taught, wrote books on law philosophy and published his famous *Gramática de la lengua castellana* (1847). This, together with the notes added to it

by the Colombian Rufino José Cuervo (1844–1911), is still considered one of the standard treatises on the language. As a defender of classicism and humanism, he came into conflict with ◊ Sarmiento and other Argentine exiles in Chile and there resulted an outstanding polemic, one of the first and most fundamental literary disputes in the new republics. As an imagi-native writer, Bello left little of great merit, but he is important as an outstanding early post-independence thinker, and inter-national lawyer and grammarian. [JF]

*Obras completas*, i, *Poesías*, intr. F. P. Castillo (1952).
Pedro Grases, *Doce estudios sobre Andrés Bello* (Buenos Aires, 1950); E. Rodríguez Monegal, *Este otso Andrés Bello* (Caracas, 1969).

**Benavente, Fray Toribio de** ('Motilinía') (?–1565). Spanish-born Franciscan. He became one of the most influential mis-sionaries in the New World. He gave him-self the nickname Motolinía ('poor') because this was the first Indian word he learnt. Like ◊ Las Casas he was sympathetic to the Indians, though he differed from the Dominican father on the question of speedy baptism. Motilinía believed in converting the Indians and baptizing them as quickly as possible. He denounced the cruelty of the Spaniards towards the Indians but in more measured terms than Las Casas. His most important work is the *Historia de los indios de la Nueva España*, written about the middle of the 16th century but first published in 1848 by Lord Kingsborough in his *Mexican Antiquities*. Ten years later the work was included in the first volume of Joaquín García Icazbalceta's *Colección de documentos para la historia de México* (1858). A scholarly biobibliographical study which argues convincingly that Motilinía died in 1565 (and not in 1569, the date usually given) is to be found in Francis Borgia Steck's introduction to his own translation of the *Historia*, published as Motilinía's *History of the Indians of New Spain* (Washington, D.C., 1951). [JF]

**Benedetti, Mario** (1920–    ). Uruguayan novelist, critic and short-story writer. A member of a generation which realized that Uruguayans could no longer be identified with the country-dwellers and gauchos and that the majority of them were urbanites and civil servants. His best-known work is a collection of short stories, *Montevideanos*

(1959), which successfully convey the quiet desperation of Montevideo office workers, servants and football players. They also show accurate observation and an acute ear for colloquialisms. His other works include several novels: *Quién de nosotros* (1953), *La tregua* (1960) and *Gracias por el fuego* (1965), which is about the relationship between a father and son. The father is a political and business tycoon, the son a man of liberal conscience who struggles in vain against his father's influence. Mario Benedetti has also published much excellent criticism, including *Literatura uruguaya, siglo xx* (1963) and *Letras del continente mestizo* (1968). [JF]

Cohen, *L A W T*.

**Bento, Texeira** (c. 1556–1600). Poet. Little is known of his life. He was probably born in Oporto (Portugal) but left for Brazil at an early age. Here he worked as a teacher in Pernambuco, but having killed his wife he was sentenced to 20 years' imprisonment. It is not known whether or not he served the whole of his sentence. In 1594, he appeared before the Inquisition as a new Christian and was sent for trial to Lisbon. In 1599, he underwent an auto-da-fé and he died in the following year just before the publication of his only work, *Prosopéia* (1601), a minor epic of 94 verses, written in praise of Jorge de Albuquerque Coelho, governor of Pernambuco. The poem is an early example of nativism. [JF]

Cândido, *P L B*, i.

**Bernárdez, Francisco Luis** (1900–    ). Argentinian poet. After a brief period in the *avant garde* Ultraist movement and a period of residence in Spain, he began to write on Catholic themes in an unadorned classical style. His long religious poem, *El buque* (1935), describes the coming of grace to the human soul and echoes the rhythms of St John of the Cross. In later poems he adopted a long cadenced line that rises and falls like a prayer. Sometimes he is dry and formal; sometimes he deliberately echoes the religious poetry of 16th-century Spain. In his best work, *Poemas elementales* (1942), however, his religious inspiration seems to run underground, nourishing without intruding. Here his long line is well sustained and his voices rises psalmodically to the grandeur of the theme. [JMC]

*Poemas nacionales* (1950); *Los mejores versos* (1952).

**Bilac, Olavo Brás Martins dos Guimarães** (1865–1918). Brazilian poet. A leading exponent of the Parnassian school. Born in Rio de Janeiro, he abandoned his medical studies to go into journalism, teaching and politics. The first poem of his collection *Poesias* (1888) was entitled 'Profissão de Fe', in which he declared, 'When I write, I envy the goldsmith'. In 1902, he published 'O Caçador de Esmeraldas', a patriotic poem, in a new edition of the *Poesias*. It describes the life of a *bandeirante* (pioneer) who penetrated the interior of Brazil in search of emeralds and silver. *Tarde* (1919) contains poems on the themes of death and the significance of existence. [JF]

*Poesias* (27th edn, 1961); Bandeira, *A P B P*; Cândido, *P L B*, ii.

**Bioy Casares, Adolfo** (1914–    ). Argentine novelist, dramatist and short-story writer. A member of the editorial committee of the magazine *Sur*. A friend of ◊ Borges, with whom he has collaborated under the joint pseudonym of 'Honorio Bustos Domecq', he too uses the novel to probe intellectual problems, and uses the form of the mystery or the detective novel as a framework for this. His two major novels are *La invención de Morel* (1940) and *El sueño de los héroes* (1954). *El diario de la guerra del cerdo* (1969) contains stories. [JF]

**Blanco Fombona, Rufino** (1874–1944). Venezuelan politician, diplomat and writer. His stormy early career has been recorded in his autobiography, *Camino de imperfección: diario de mi vida* (1906–13). A member of the Arielist generation (◊ Rodó), he fiercely attacked the North Americans and upheld the cultural unity of Latin America. He wrote a history of Venezuela and was instrumental in founding the *América* publishing house in Madrid, which published Latin-American literary classics. His own novels, *El hombre de hierro* (1907) and *El hombre de oro* (1916), deal with the defects of the Venezuelan ruling élite. He is also typical of his generation in turning from cosmopolitan and 'eternal' themes to the American scene. His *Cuentos americanos* (1904) are evidence of this trend. He also edited the letters of Bolívar (1922). [JF]

*Obras selectas*, ed. G. Márquez (Madrid, 1958). Ureña, *B H M*.

**Blest Gana, Alberto** (1830–1920). Chilean novelist. He graduated as an engineer from a French Military Academy and returned briefly to Chile, where he first taught mathematics at a military school and then published his first novels, intended as the Chilean *Comédie Humaine*. He wrote 10 novels during this period, of which the best are *Martín Rivas* (1862; tr. Mrs Charles Whitman, *Martín Rivas*, New York, 1918), which depicts the rise of a country boy in the society of Santiago, and *El ideal de un calavera* (1863). In 1866 he was appointed commercial attaché to the Chilean Embassy in Washington and thereafter was to remain abroad, serving for many years as Chilean Ambassador to France and to England. A second period of literary production began with *Durante la Reconquista* (1897), a historical novel followed by *Los transplantados* (1904), which dealt with rich émigrés, and *El loco estero* (1909), in which he evoked the Santiago he had known as a very young boy. His novels are of historical interest but are quite without the imagination and insight of Balzac, whom he admired. [JF]

'Alone', *Don Alberto Blest Gana* (Santiago, 1940); Raúl Silva Castro, *Alberto Blest Gana* (2nd edn, Santiago, 1955).

**Bolívar, Simón** (1783–1830). One of the leading fighters in the American independence movement and usually known as 'The Liberator'. He led the armies which liberated Venezuela, Colombia and Ecuador from Spanish rule and by the victory of Ayacucho ensured the freedom of Peru and dealt the final blow against the Spanish armies in the New World. Although destined for a life of action, Bolívar, who came from a wealthy creole family of Venezuela, had received an excellent education. His tutors were Andrés ◊ Bello and Simón Rodríguez, a Latin American disciple of Rousseau. His extensive correspondence reveals a complex personality and sheds invaluable light on the course of the independence movement. His best-known letter is probably the 'Carta de Jamaica' (1814), in which he made remarkably accurate prognostications on the future of the Spanish-American countries after Independence. [JF]

*Cartas del Libertador* (12 vols., Caracas, 1929–59); *Selected Writings*, compiled Vicente Lecuna, ed. H. A. Bierck, Jr, tr. L. Bertrand (New York, 1951); W. S. Robertson, *The Rise of the Spanish American Republics as Told in the Lives of Their Liberators* (London, 1918).

**Bombal, María Luisa** (1910–    ). Chilean novelist. Educated at the Sorbonne, she returned to Chile at a time when Criollism was still the reigning literary school. Her first collection of stories, *La última niebla* (1935), written in poetic and sensitive style, was utterly opposed to the often brutal realism of the criollist writers. Her other works include *La amortajada* (1938; tr. *The Shrouded Woman*, New York, 1948), the imagined memories of a woman who has just died, and a final novel, *The House of Mist* (1947), written in collaboration with her husband after she had been living in New York for several years. [JF]

**Bonifácio de Andrada e Silva, José** (1765–1838). Brazilian statesman and poet. He was born in Santos in the state of São Paulo and died in Niterói. He was educated at Coimbra where he studied civil law and natural philosophy. He later became Professor of Mineralogy there and was also elected to the Portuguese Academy of Sciences. He was widely known as a scientist, but he gained greater fame for his indispensable role in Brazilian independence; many historians consider him the father of independence. He was the most influential political advisor to Dom Pedro I, and he was instrumental in effecting Pedro's declaration of independence in 1822. Bonifácio and his brothers later broke with Pedro I over his increasingly autocratic ways. His incessant criticism of Pedro made many enemies for him, and he spent several bitter years in exile in France. He was an old man when he returned to Brazil after the abdication of Pedro I in 1831, and he spent his remaining days as a tutor to the royal family of Dom Pedro II.

José Bonifácio is most famous as a statesman and scholar. But he is also the author of poems written during his exile in France. He uses the pen name Américo Elisio and writes bitterly of his native land. The style is neo-classic, with careful attention to form, and with many allusions to exotic Greek places, authors and mythology. He invokes the muses to preside over his creations and one of his odes eulogizes Virtue, which he feels is lacking in his homeland. In an ode to friendship, 'A Amizade', the poet uses many classical descriptions and lists such divergent figures as Descartes, Virgil and Pope as belonging to the exclusive fraternity of reason. This poem is much less bitter and much more formal in style than is Bonifácio's ode to the Bahians, 'Aos Bahianos'. He viciously criticizes his compatriots for lacking virtue, and says that his only crime was to stand for liberty and justice. He believes he will never again see Brazil: he expresses his love for the land with emotional descriptions of its mountains, rivers and flowers that intimate a nascent romanticism. He closes the poem with the fervent desire that Brazil will learn to base its young empire on liberty, justice and independence – and also on gratitude to those who helped create it. [D H]

*Poesias*, ed. S. Buarque de Holanda (1946).
Octávio Tarquino de Sousa, *História dos Fundadores do Império do Brasil*, i (1957).

**Bopp, Raul** (1898– ). Brazilian poet. His best-known work is *Cobra Norato* (1931), a poem published at the height of the 'Antropofagia' ('Cannibalist') Movement. Bopp and his associates held a 'back-to-the-roots' view of Brazilian literature, believing that they must call the attention of the reading public to a 'different Brazil'. *Cobra Norato* represented an attempt to write an epic of Brazilian nature, using as a framework an Indian myth. *Avant garde* in technique, it evoked the vastness and lush fertility of Bopp's native country. [JF]

*Cobra Norato e Outros Poemas* (6th edn, 1956). Nist, *MMB*.

**Borges, Jorge Luis** (1899– ). Argentinian poet, writer and critic. He was educated in Europe and there came into contact with the *avant garde* writers and in particular with the Ultraist movement in Spain, a movement interested in the invention of startling new metaphors. Borges' first poems were published in Spain and he returned to Buenos Aires in 1921 to introduce Ultraism to the younger generation there. He helped to found and collaborated in a number of periodicals such as *Prisma* (1921–2), *Proa* (1922–3) and *Martín Fierro*. At this time he was mainly publishing poetry about Buenos Aires. It was only gradually that he evolved as a story writer, his first collection of stories being *Historia universal de la infamia* (1935). This was followed by *Ficciones* (tr. A. Kerrigan, *Ficciones*, London, 1962), written between 1935 and 1944 and published as a collection in 1944, and *El Aleph* (1949). It is the stories of these latter two collections which are his principal claim to fame. In them he has developed a truly original form, the 'fiction' in which, in the guise of an essay, a detective story, a piece of literary criticism or biography he plays his 'games with infinity'. Though fundamentally nihilistic, Borges finds endless fascination in man's ingenuity in devising philosophic systems, though he confesses to being most interested in the aesthetic possibilities of these. Borges' most recent work, *El hacedor* (1960; tr. M. Boyer and H. Morland, *Dreamtigers*, Austin, 1964), was a collection of poems and short parables, the title piece being an account of Homer's blindness, a subject to which Borges' own increasing blindness has undoubtedly drawn him. Borges is also a distinguished Anglo-Saxon scholar and has lectured on Anglo-Saxon literature at Buenos Aires University. He has also written a number of highly personal essays on English, Argentinian and other literatures, and on the Spanish language in Argentina. For many years, he worked as a librarian. The Perón regime, however, undertook a persecution of intellectuals and he was made chicken inspector in 1946 – a deliberate insult. After the fall of Perón, in 1955, he became director of the National Library. International recognition has come recently, especially after 1961, when he was awarded the Formentor Prize. His latest work is *Informe sobre Brodie* (1970), a collection of stories. [JF]

*Obras completas* (1954–60) (*Historia de la eternidad, Poemas, Historia universal de la infamia, Evaristo Carriego, Ficciones, Discusión, El Aleph, Otras inquisiciones, El hacedor*); *Labyrinths*, ed. D. A. Yates and J. E. Irby (Norfolk, Conn., 1962) (translated selections); *Labyrinths: Selected Stories and Other Writings* (New York, 1962); *A Personal Anthology*, tr. A. Kerrigan (London, 1968); *The Book of Imaginary Beings*, tr. N. T. di Giovanni and the author (New York, 1969).
Ana María Barrenechea, *Borges, the Labyrinth-Maker* (New York, 1965); R. Burgin, *Conversations with Jorge Luis Borges* (New York, 1969).

**Botelho de Oliveira, Manuel** (1636–1711). Brazilian poet from Bahia. His *Música do Parnaso* (1705; ed. A. Nascentes, 2 vols., 1953) was the first book published in Brazil by a Brazilian-born author. The collection included poems in Portuguese, Spanish, Italian and Latin. The author's style is typical of the baroque period in Iberian literature, being both *conceptista* and *culterano*. [JF]

Cândido, *PLB*, i.

**Botelho Gosálvez, Raúl** (1917– ). Bolivian novelist and essayist. He has also worked as a journalist and served in many diplomatic posts. His novels are predominantly social and deal with a variety of Bolivian regions and problems. They include *Borrachera verde* (Santiago, 1938), *Coca* (Santiago, 1941), an Indianist novel, *Altiplano* (Buenos Aires, 1945) and *Tierra chúcara* (Santiago, 1957). [JF]

Augusto Guzmán, *La novela en Bolivia, proceso 1847–1954* (La Paz, 1955).

**Braga, Rubem** (1913– ). Brazilian writer. He has had a varied career as author, publisher, translator and columnist. Unlike many of his contemporaries, he does not concern himself with the problems of society or with individual psychological studies, claiming that he is one of the few remaining superficial writers and that he wants to preserve this heritage. A *crônista* (chronicler), he writes short pieces in the nature of vignettes which offer a satirical picture of human frailty. He satirizes particularly the middle-class population of Rio de Janeiro, always with humour and often through the medium of fantasy. In *O Homem Rouco* (1949), Braga contemplates modern man's psychological complexes and the profession of psychiatry, wryly questioning the value of the latter. In one *crônica*, 'O Temperamento do Canário', he concludes that the personal life of the canary is disappointingly similar to that of man. In another – 'Da Vulgaridade das Mulheres' – he satirizes the fashion industry and women who blindly follow its dictates. But though critical of the manners of his fellow-countrymen, Braga can also speak with tenderness and affection of Rio, as in 'O Homem na Cidade', in which he describes the sights, sounds and sensations of a day in the city. [DH]

*50 Crônicas Escolhidas* (1951); *Aí de ti, Copacabana* (2nd edn, 1962); Cândido, *PLB*, iii.

**Brunet, Marta** (1901–66). Chilean novelist and short-story writer. She grew up in the provinces. Her first published work, *Montaña adentro* (1923), a novel of peasant life, appeared with the help and encouragement of the literary critic Díaz Arrieta. There followed *Bestia dañina* (1920), *Bienvenido* (1929), *Humo hacia el sur* (1946) and *María Nadie* (1957). Marta Brunet's claim to distinction is in her depiction of ordinary peasant women and in her descriptions of nature. [JF]

*Obras completas* (1966).
Raúl Silva Castro, *Panorama literario de Chile* (Santiago, 1951).

**Buarque de Holanda, Sérgio** (1902– ). Brazilian writer. After graduating in law, he became a historian and essayist, and since 1948 has held professorships at the University of São Paulo. His most famous work, *Raizes do Brasil* (1936), was a historical exploration of the origins of Brazilian society and national character. He has also written a *História do Brasil* (1944) in collaboration with Tarquinio de Sousa. [AA]

# C

**Caballero Calderón, Eduardo** (1910–    ). Colombian novelist, diplomatist and journalist. He has served his country in diplomatic posts in South America and Spain, has spent some years as Buenos Aires and Rio correspondent for *El Tiempo* of Bogotá, and has also lived in Madrid, where he founded the Guadarrama publishing house. He has published many essays on the nature of Latin America and on the relationship between Latin America and Europe and North America, of which the best known are *Suramérica, tierra del hombre* (1942) and *Latinoamérica, un mundo por hacer, Americanos y Europeos* (1957). It is, however, as a novelist that Caballero Calderón excels. His *Siervo sin tierra* (1954) is a graphic account of the life of a landless peasant whose sole ambition is to own a plot of land. A previous novel, *El Cristo de espaldas* (1953), became a Latin-American best-seller. The novel deals with the tragic civil strife which broke out in Colombia in 1947 and the efforts of a priest to practise the mercy his religion represented. His finest novel to date is *Manuel Pacho* (1964), a myth-like story of a wild and primitive boy who carries the body of his dead grandfather to the nearest town in order to claim his inheritance. A recent novel, *El buen salvaje* (1966), won the Spanish Nadal Prize. [JF]

*Obras* (2 vols., 1963).
*D L L.*

**Cabral de Melo Neto, João** (1920–    ). Brazilian poet. The most brilliant poet of the generation of 1945. Although he has absorbed the influence of French poets, particularly Valéry and Ponge, and also that of Spanish folk poetry, he has developed along original lines. Using deceptively simple, stark vocabulary, he builds the poem on permutations of words, creating effects of irony. In all his poetry, conceptual creativity is central. He has published *Pedra do Sono* (1942), *O Engenheiro* (1945), *Fábula de Anfion e Antiode* (1947), *Psicologia da Composição* (1947), *O Cão sem Plumas, O Rio* (1954). All but the last of these were included with the dialogue *Os Três*

*Mal-Amados* in *Poemas Reunidos* (1954); a second collection entitled *Duas Águas* (1956) added *O Rio*, the unpublished *Paisagens com Figuras* and *Uma Faca só Lâmina*, as well as the verse play *Morte e Vida Severina*. The theme of the play is the death of a refugee from the drought-afflicted Northeast. It was performed with great success by the University of São Paulo Dramatic Society at the International Student Drama Festival held in Paris in 1961 (part tr. E. Bishop, *Encounter*, September 1965). Other collections of his poetry include *Quaderna* (1960) and *Dois Parlamentos* (1961), subsequently incorporated with the unpublished *Serial* in *Terceira Feira* (1961). His latest volume, carrying further the techniques introduced in 1961, is *Educação pela Pedra* (1966). His personal anthology was published in Rio as *Antologia Poetica* (1965). [JF]

*Poesias Completas* (1968); *Encounter,* September 1965; Cohen, *L A W T.*
Alexandre Pinheiro Torres, 'A Poesia de João Cabral de Melo Neto', in *Poesia: Programa para o Concreto* (Lisbon, 1966).

**Cabrera Infante, Guillermo** (1929–    ). Cuban novelist and short-story writer. His main works are the short-story collection *Así en la paz como en la guerra* (1960) and the novel *Tres tristes tigres* (Barcelona, 1967), a panoramic and ironic view of Cuban society on the eve of the Castro Revolution chiefly remarkable for a virtuoso use of pastiche and parody and for the author's manipulation of language. [JF]

Cohen, *W N C.*
Luis Gregorich, '"Tres tristes tigres", obra abierta', in *Nueva novela latino americana,* ed. Jorge Lafforgue (1969).

**Cambaceres, Eugenio de** (1843–88). Argentinian novelist. He first wrote for the magazine *Sud América* under the pseudonym Lorenzo Díaz. Besides journalism and writing, he also took an active part in politics and was elected deputy to one of the provincial legislatures. His first novel, *Pot pourri, Silbidos de un vago* (Paris, 1881), was followed by *Música sentimental* (1884) and

*Sin rumbo* (1885), which critics regard as the first true interpretation of ordinary life in the countryside around Buenos Aires. The novel tells the story of an estate owner and the girl he seduces. In 1887, Cambaceres published *En la sangre*, a novel which pursued the favourite naturalist theme of the man whose ruin is brought about by his 'bad blood'. [JF]

*Obras completas* (1956).
Guillermo Ara, *La novela naturalista hispano-americana* (Buenos Aires, 1965).

**Campo, Estanislao del** (1834–80). Argentinian ◊ gauchesque poet. A supporter of Mitre, he fought for the states of Buenos Aires at the battles of Cepeda (1859) and Pavón (1861). In 1867, he became deputy for Buenos Aires province. His admiration for Hilario ◊ Ascasubi made him decide to adopt the gauchesque style, and his first poems, signed 'Anastasio el Pollo'(Ascasubi signed himself 'Aniceto el Gallo'), appeared in *Los Debates* of Buenos Aires in 1857. His most popular poem was *Fausto: impresiones del gaucho Anastasio el Pollo en la representación de esta ópera* (1866). A comic account of an ignorant countryman's reaction to the opera *Faust*, it went into 136 editions before 1910. However, the poem earned the disapproval of José ◊ Hernández, author of *Martín Fierro*, who believed that it made the gaucho into a caricature figure. [JF]

Borges and Casares, *P G*, ii.
*DLL*.

**Cândido, Antônio** (1918–    ). Brazilian critic. Professor of Comparative Literature at the University of São Paulo. A graduate in sociology as well as literature, his criticisms combine literary insight with a knowledge of the social background. Often challenging and controversial, his *Formação da Literatura Brasileira* (2 vols., 1959) is not concerned with colonial literature, which he does not believe is truly Brazilian. Other important works include an anthology (compiled in collaboration with José Aderaldo Castello), *Presença da Literatura Brasileira* (1964; 2nd edn, 1966), and a theoretical work *Literatura e Sociedade* (1965). He is also the author of a number of sociological studies. [AA]

**Cardenal, Ernesto** (1925–    ). Nicaraguan poet. After a period as a political militant, he became a Trappist and is now head of a contemplative group which lives on an island off the Nicaraguan coast. He has published *La ciudad deshabitada* (1946), *Proclama del conquistador* (1947), *Hora O*, *Epigramas* (1961), *Oración por Marilyn Monroe y otros poemas* (1965). His poetry has a strong social element and is very much concerned with the semi-colonial position of Nicaragua, but it is by no means confined to simple social protest. His social conscience is backed by strong religious convictions and a literal interpretation of Christ's teaching. [JF]

*El estrecho dudoso* (1967).
*Poemas* (Havana, 1967); *PV*; 'Drake in the Southern Sea', tr. Thomas Merton, *New Directions*, 17 (1961).

**Cardoza y Aragón, Luis** (1904–    ). Guatemalan poet, essayist and art critic. He was active in the *avant garde* movements of the twenties and thirties and was particularly influenced by surrealism. His best-known work is a sensitive and poetic study of the Guatemalan character and environment, *Guatemala, las líneas de su mano* (1955), and a study of Mexican painting, *La nube y el reloj* (Mexico, 1940). He has also published some poetic prose reminiscences, *Dibujos de ciego* (Mexico, 1969). [JF]

*DLL*.

**Caro, José Eusebio** (1817–53). Colombian poet. A passionate individualist, Caro was first influenced by the English utilitarians, by the French encyclopedists and, in his poetry, by Byron, but later became a fervent Christian. He was a journalist who founded a literary periodical, *La Estrella Nacional*, in 1836 and became editor of a political paper, *El Granadino*. On the election of José Hilario López in 1849, he went into exile in the United States and died of yellow fever when returning to his own country four years later. Like many 19th-century poets, Caro could not devote much time to writing, being caught up in political activities. His constant theme is freedom and his model was the European romantics. [JMC]

*Antología; verso y prosa* (1951).
*DLL*.

**Carpentier, Alejo** (1904–    ). Cuban musicologist and novelist. His mother was Russian and his father French. He first studied architecture, but later turned to music and anthropology and became the first to write a history of Cuban music. In the twenties, he became interested in Negro music and wrote *La passion noire,* an oratorio which was first performed in Paris. At this point Carpentier turned to literature and was active in the Afro-Cuban literary movement (◊ Afro-Cubanism), at its height during the late twenties and early thirties. He wrote poems in the Afro-Cuban manner and in 1933 published a novel, *Ecué-Yamba-O,* which dealt with the adventures of a Negro plantation boy who runs away to the city where he becomes involved in the gang life and the *santería* (the Cuban equivalent of voodoo) cults. There followed many years of silence, during which Carpentier lived and worked in France, the United States, Venezuela and many other countries. In 1949, he published a historical novel, *El reino de este mundo* (tr. H. de Onís, *The Kingdom of this World,* New York, 1957), which dealt with the 18th-century uprisings of slaves in Haiti. *Los pasos perdidos* (1953; tr. H. de Onís, *The Lost Steps,* New York, London, 1956) was set in Venezuela and dealt with the adventures of a musicologist who is searching the upper reaches of the Orinoco for primitive musical instruments. His journey takes him to the most primitive tribes and he finally reaches a remote region in which a group of modern adventurers are trying to found a Utopia far from the modern world. The musician, though tempted to settle among them, finds that as an artist he cannot go backwards in time but must return to civilization to carry on 'Adam's task of naming things'. The novel is important in that it is in the nature of an allegory of the Latin-American artist's conflict between roots and modernity. In 1956, Carpentier published a political novel, *El acoso* (tr. H. de Onís, *Manhunt, Noon III,* April 1959), dealing with the flight of an informer from the vengeance of those he had betrayed. *Guerra del tiempo* (1958) consisted of a collection of experimental short stories. *El siglo de las luces* (tr. H. de Onís, *Explosion in a Cathedral,* New York, 1963) appeared in 1962. Set in the period of the French Revolution, the novel is an ambitious attempt to see the Caribbean area as a whole. The action moves from Cuba to Jamaica and Guadalupe and to the Guiana mainland, and shows how the revolutionary ideals which inspired the independence movements degenerated into autocratic dictatorships. [J F]

Cohen, *L A W T.*
Alegría, *B H N H*; Harss, *L N.*

**Carrasquilla, Tomás** (1858–1940). Colombian novelist. He set out to copy nature and 'present man in his setting'. The setting that he chose was the province of Antioquia, of which he drew the types and customs and speech. His first novel, *Frutos de mi tierra* (1896), was written without thought of a public, almost as an experiment. His characters, who are numerous and drawn from every walk of life, reveal themselves in racy conversation, anecdote and jest. The author himself stands apart, and, while preaching no moral, views them with a humorously philosophical detachment. Though he creates some subtle characters, chiefly women and children, he sees humanity as like the animals, a viewpoint which he develops in some grotesque and ridiculous scenes reminiscent of Valle-Inclán.

Carrasquilla's best novels were, in his own opinion, *Salve, Regina* (1903) and *La marquesa de Yolombó* (1926), the action of which takes place in the 18th century. The latter, though most ambitious, is digressive, didactic and anachronistic. Nevertheless, it contains some of his best scenes. The folktales in the volume *En la diestra de Dios Padre* (1897) are witty and ironical, and give a delightful picture of the customs of his province. During a period of blindness, he dictated a 3-volume novel, *Hace tiempos* (1935–6), which some regard as his most important work. [J M C]

*Obras completas* (2 vols., 1958).
Kurt L. Levy, *Vida y obras de Tomás Carrasquilla* (Medellín, 1958).

**Carrera Andrade, Jorge** (1902– ). Ecuadorian poet. As a student, he took part in student politics and helped to found the Ecuadorian Socialist Party. He lived abroad in Germany, France and Spain and was secretary for a time to Gabriela ◊ Mistral. On returning to Ecuador, he again took part in politics but then embarked on a diplomatic career and again spent many years outside the country. He also edited the Spanish edition of the *UNESCO Courier* for some time. A talented poet, in his first work he celebrated the wonders of ordinary life in brilliant and original language and imagery. He adapted the Japanese hai-kai into Spanish. The titles of many of the volumes of his poetry reflect his experiences as a traveller, but these travels are used to illuminate his own inner experience and his sense of the transitoriness of things. His collections include *Estanque inefable* (1922),

*Boletines de mar y tierra* (1930), *Registro del mundo* (1940), *Latitudes* (1940) (essays), *Rostros y climas* (1948) (essays) and *Viajes por paises y libros* (1962). *Lugar de origen* includes all his poetry since 1940. Numerous translations have appeared in *Poetry, Adam* and *International Review*. [JF]

*Edades poéticas (1922–1956)* (1958); *Poesías escogidas*, intr. P. Salinas and J. Carrera Andrade (1945) (anthology); *Visitor of Mist*, tr. G. R. Coulthard and K. Nott (London, 1950); *Secret Country* (*País secreto*), tr. M. Lee (New York, 1946); *To the Bay Bridge* (*Canto al Puente de Oakland*), tr. E. L. Turnbull (Stanford, Cal., 1941). *D LL.*

**Carrió de la Vandera** ('Concolorcorvo') (*c.*1715–after 1778). Spanish-born official of the Spanish crown who served in Mexico and was a *corregidor* in Peru. In 1771 he was given the position of inspector of posts and the book for which he is famous, *El lazarillo de ciegos caminantes* (Buenos Aires, 1946; tr. W. C. Kline, *El Lazarillo: A Guide for Inexperienced Travelers between Buenos Aires and Lima*, Bloomington, Ind., 1966), is in part a report of the posts on the roads between Buenos Aires and Lima. *El Lazarillo* was first published in Lima in 1776 with a false place (Gijón) and false date (1773) of publication. It was not reprinted until 1908 in Buenos Aires and until recently it was accepted as being the work of Carrió de la Vandera's friend and travelling companion, Don Calixto Bustamante, an Indian, to whose pen the original was attributed. It is not clear why Carrió de la Vandera should have made such a mystery out of the authorship except that the work is critical of certain aspects of life in the region. It is of particular interest for its use of American expressions, its description of the inhabitants of the pampa and its discussion on the Spaniards' treatment of the Indians. It is also what it sets out to be – a comprehensive and witty guide book. [JF]

José J. Real Díaz, 'Don Alonso Carrió de la Vandera, autor del Lazarillo de ciegos caminantes' (BAE, 122).

**Carvalho, Ronald de** (1893–1935). Brazilian poet and critic. His works include *Poemas e Sonetos* (1919), *Epigramas Irónicos e Sentimentais* (1922), *Jogos Pueris* (1926), *Toda a América* (1926). Early on in his career, Carvalho had associated himself with both Futurism and Brazilian Modernism (◊ Modernism in Brazil) but his later poetry is

Whitmanesque. He is also the author of a good introduction to Brazilian literature, *A Pequena História da Literatura Brasileira* (1919). [JF]

**Carvalho, Vicente** (1866–1924). Brazilian poet. Born in the state of São Paulo. His collection *Poemas e Canções* (1908; 15th edn, 1946) was a success. Influenced by Parnassianism, this collection as well as two previous collections, *Relicário* (1888) and *Rosa, Rosa de Amor* (1902), also included elements of romanticism. Somewhat apart from the mainstream of Parnassianism in Brazil (represented by Olavo ◊ Bilac), Carvalho was known as the 'São Paulo Parnassian' or the 'poet of the sea'. Other collections include *Versos de Mocidade* (1909) and prose pieces included in *Paginas Sôltas* (1911). [AA]

Hermes Vieira, *Vicente de Carvalho, o Sabiá da Ilha do Sol; Biocritica* (2nd edn, São Paulo, 1943); Bandeira, *A P B.*

**Casal, Julián del** (1863–93). Cuban poet. One of the early Modernists. His life was dogged by illness and misfortune. His mother died and his family lost their small sugar estate when he was young. He himself had tuberculosis and was to die of this at 30. Although he admired French literature and the Paris of the decadents, on his only visit to Europe (1888–9) he refused to visit Paris for fear of shattering his illusions. Like Baudelaire, whom he admired, he tried to explore new areas of sensual experience, was an admirer of Chinese and Japanese art and loved the exotic. Some of his poems were inspired by the paintings of Gustave Moreau, a then fashionable decadent painter. In many of his poems he aspired to a marmoreal perfection. In some he used a startling and violent imagery. Though he knew ◊ Darío, his own output was too small and his life too short for him to have wielded much of an influence on Modernism. He published two volumes of poetry, *Hojas al viento* (1890) and *Bustos y rimas* (1893). [JF]

*Poesías* (1963).

J. M. M. Sans, *Julián del Casal y el modernismo hispanoamericano* (Mexico, 1952) (includes selection of poems); Ureña, *BHM*; Brotherston, *SAMP.*

**Castellanos, Juan de** (1522–1607). Poet. One of the best of colonial poets, he was born in Spain and died in Colombia. He went to America as a young man and after a roving life in the Caribbean took holy orders and settled in Tunja, where he lived for 40 years among the Chibcha Indians. He composed his *Elegías de Varones Illustres de Indias* between 1570 and 1590. This is a verse epic recounting the story of the Spanish expansion in the New World and the exploits of the *conquistadores*. The poem is an imitation of the Spanish poet Alonso de Ercilla's *La Araucana* but is of some historical interest. [JM]

*Obras*, intr. M. A. Caro (Bogotá. 4 vols., 1955).

G. Restrepo, *Historia de la literatura colombiana*, i (2nd edn, Bogotá, 1945).

**Castellanos, Rosario** (1925–    ). Mexican poetess and novelist. Her work was at first insubstantial and feminine but gathered weight and opacity in *Poemas, 1953–55* (1957), in which she turned to objective themes. Deeply concerned for the Indians of her native province of Chiapas, for whose education she had worked, she saw in them both a conquered people and a reservoir of ultimate hope. From poetry of love and loss and friendship, she turned in *Testimonios* to an impersonal simplicity and commitment. In *Lívida luz* (1960) she returned to more personal themes. Rosario Castellanos has also published two collections of stories, *Ciudad Real* (1960) and *Los convidados de agosto* (1964), and two novels, *Balún Canán* (tr. I. Nicholson, *The Nine Guardians*, London, New York, 1959) and *Oficio de tinieblas* (1962). A third, *Rito de iniciación*, is due to appear. *Balún Canán* and *Oficio de tinieblas* are both set in Chiapas. The first is partly autobiographical and relates the break-up of the old feudal life under the impact of the land reforms introduced during the government of Lázaro Cárdenas. *Oficio de tinieblas* described the growth and suppression of an Indian religious cult and the reactions of white and mestizo to this. [JMC]

**Castillo Andraca y Tamayo, Francisco del** (1716–70). Peruvian satirical poet and friar. He was blind from infancy but his skill as an improviser was justly renowned. He wrote ballads on people and customs which he mildly satirized and is of interest for his pictures of 18th-century Lima manners. He also wrote plays, some in imitation of French neo-classicists, but also some *sainetes*, or short farcical scenes. [JF]

*Obras*, ed. R. V. Ugarte (1948).

**Castro, Francisco de** (late 17th century). Mexican Jesuit. Author of *La octava maravilla*, a poem in 5 cantos in honour of the Virgin of Guadalupe (written before 1675, publ. 1729). Gongorist in its Latinisms and erudition, the poem contains splendid passages, e.g. that in praise of the maguey, the plant from which comes a liquor – pulque – 'sweeter than the honey of Hybla'. [JMC]

*Antología de la poesía hispanoamericana*, i, ed. G. de Albareda and F. Garfias (Madrid, 1957) (extracts).

**Castro Alves, Antônio de** (1847–71). Brazilian poet. He was born in the province of Bahia, studied law in Salvador and Recife and there carried on a famous polemic on poetry with Tobias ◊ Barreto. He fell in love with the actress Eugenia Câmara, for whom he wrote his one play, *Gonzago ou a Revolução de Minas* (1867). He published only one collection of poetry in his lifetime, *Espumas Flutuantes* (1870). Posthumous publications included *Os Escravos* and *Hinos do Equador*, which were first included in their entirety in Afranio Peixoto's edition of his *Obras completas* (1921), although some had previously been published separately. A collection of poems with the title *A Cachoeira de Paulo Afonso* was published in 1876. *Espumas Flutuantes* included poems on typically romantic themes such as 'Mocidade e Morte' and others such as 'Coup d'Etrier' in which he sings of the 'floresta americana'. In *Os Escravos* were included many poems such as 'Tragedia no Lar' in which Castro Alves painted in pathetic colours the sufferings of the slaves and the ruthless breaking-up of families by the traders. His best-known poem of protest against the slave-trade is 'O Navio Negreiro' with its dramatic picture of the 'sonho dantesco' (Dantesque nightmare). In 'A Cruz da Estrada' he describes the lonely, neglected grave of one of the slaves. Castro Alves's poetry is not without literary merit, especially when he draws near to the simplicity and spontaneity of folk poetry, as in his 'Canção do Violeiro'. [JF]

*G P R B* (includes complete poems).

Federico Pessoa de Barros, *Poesia e Vida de Castro Alves* (São Paulo, 1962).

**Céspedes, Augusto** (1904–    ). Bolivian journalist, novelist and politician. His *Sangre de mestizos*, a collection of stories about the Chaco war against Paraguay, appeared in 1936. These are excellent realistic

313

accounts of the soldiers' fight not only against the Paraguayan enemy but against an overwhelmingly hostile environment. His novel *Metal del diablo* (1946) is based on the life of the tin millionaire, Patiño, and covers a period from the end of the 19th century to the 1940s. [JF]

Augusto Guzmán, *La novela en Bolivia, proceso 1847–1954* (La Paz, 1955).

**Chocano, José Santos** (1875–1934). Peruvian Modernist poet. The childhood of his adventurous life was unhappy, for it was spent during the period of the Peruvian–Chilean war and its aftermath. As a young man he was threatened with execution for political activities and his *Iras santas* (1895) were written in prison. He supported both Pancho Villa and the Guatemalan dictator Estrada Cabrera, whose friend and adviser he became and on whose downfall he was sentenced to execution. He was saved when eminent people in Europe and America petitioned on his behalf. The most notorious incident in his career was his shooting of a young Peruvian critic and writer in 1925, for which he was first held in a military hospital; later, on his release, he left for Chile (1927). There he was assassinated on a tram by a man who believed himself to have been cheated in a business deal. Most of Chocano's poetry is of a piece with his life, rhetorical and grandiloquent, yet it is by no means worthless. He considered himself the 'poet of America' and wrote primarily on American themes, thus leading the way in abandoning the cosmopolitan themes of poets like ◊ Darío. He was one of the first Spanish-American poets to speak with pride of his mixed blood and to exalt the Peru of the Incas. Though he confessed to being more drawn to the Peru of the past than contemporary Peru, he showed intuitive sympathy for present-day Indians in such famous poems as 'Así será', 'Quién sabe!' and 'Ahí no más'. His most important collections are *Alma América* (1906), *Fiat Lux* (1908) and the posthumously published *Oro de Indias*. [JF]

*Obras completas*, intr. L. A. Sánchez (Madrid, 1954).

**Chumacero, Alí** (1918–     ). Mexican poet. His output was small but remarkably concentrated and disciplined. Deriving from the introspective manner of ◊ Villaurrutia and taking some influence from the surrealism of ◊ Paz, he has submitted his inspiration to a close intellectual discipline. Reflecting on themes of isolation and loneliness, he transcends the personal, and suggests in the manner of a less discursive Perse the legendary qualities by which a man's life can be seen as a moment in the long migratory history of tribes and peoples. 'El viaje de la tribu' is in this respect an outstanding poem. [JMC]

*Palabras en reposo* (1956); Cohen, *P B S V*; Cohen, *L A W T*.

Ramón Xirau, 'La poesía de Alí Chumacero', in *Poetas de México y España* (Madrid, 1962).

**Coelho Neto, Henrique Maximiano** (1864–1934). Brazilian short-story writer. He described life in the backlands in an elaborate style. Some of his stories also dealt with city life. As a writer, he was eclipsed by the Modernist movement (◊ Modernism in Brazil) and became one of its chief opponents, with the result that he has virtually been ignored by modern critics. His main collections of stories were *A Capital Federal* (1893), *Miragem* (1895), *Sertão* (1896), *Inverno em Flor* (1897), *O Morto* (1898), *A Conquista* (1899), *A Tormenta* (1901) and *A Esfinge* (1908). Details of his many other collections can be found in Paulo Coelho Neto, *Coelho Neto* (Rio de Janeiro, 1952). [AA]

Isaac Goldberg, *Brazilian Literature* (New York, 1922; Brito Broca, 'Coelho Neto, Romancista', in *O Romance Brasileiro*, in collaboration with Aurelio Buarque de Holanda (Rio de Janeiro, 1952).

**Colón, Cristóbal** (1451–1506). Italian-born discoverer of the West Indies. His log book referring to his first voyage is the first description of the American landscape and peoples. As many commentators have shown, these descriptions reflect the influence of the literature of the period and do not penetrate this new reality with any depth. Colón tended to see what was similar to Europe, rather than the differences. Hence Colón's Indies are like European gardens and are inhabited by nightingales. Nevertheless there can be few more dramatic historical documents. [JF]

*Primer viaje de Cristóbal Colón, según su diario de a bordo*, intr. G. Marañón (Barcelona, 1944); *The Log of Christopher Columbus' First Voyage to America as Copied out by Bartholomew Las Casas* (London, 1944).

**Concrete Poetry.** Brazilian Concretism began in 1952 with the foundation of the

*Noigandres* review by Augusto and Haroldo de Campos and Décio Pignatari. They claimed Mallarmé, Pound and Apollinaire as their masters, and their poetry also owes something to the Chinese ideogram and gestalt theory. They claim that the poem is not to be read as a succession of ideas but to be perceived as a whole, thus 'communicating time and space simultaneously'. The poem is not an intentional vehicle of meaning but rather a visual experience, the creation of an object. [JF]

*Concrete Poetry*, ed. S. Bann (London, 1968); Augusto de Campos, Haroldo de Campos, Décio Pignatari. *Teoria da Poesia Concreta: Textos Críticos e Manifestos 1950–60* (São Paulo, 1965).

**Congrains Martín, Enrique** (1932– ). Peruvian author. He deals particularly with problems of urban life. He has published *Lima hora cero* (1954) and *Kikuyo* (1955), both collections of short stories. [JF]

**Contreras, Francisco** (1877–1933). Chilean writer and critic. Most of his adult life after 1905 was spent in Paris, where he became a member of the editorial staff of the *Mercure de France*. His first works were *Esmaltines* (1897), a collection of sonnets and poems in the style of Banville and Gautier, and *Raúl* (1902), a narrative poem. Contreras's chief claim to attention is as a publicist who did much to make Europeans aware of Latin-American literature by publishing articles on the subject in French. He published *Les écrivains contemporains de l'Amérique espagnole* (1920). He was also responsible for coining the word *mundonovismo* to describe the change that took place in Latin-American literature just after 1900 and the increased interest in New World themes. [JF]

John M. Fein, *Modernismo in Chilean Literature. The Second Period* (Durham, N.C., 1965).

**Correia, Raimundo** (1860–1911). Brazilian poet. Born on a boat close to the Maranhão coast. He graduated in law and worked as a civil servant, lawyer and later as a teacher. He died in France. Correia's first collection of poems, *Primeiros Sonhos* (1879), was romantic, but he later turned to Parnassianism in his *Sinfonias* (1883), which had a preface by Machado de ◊ Assis. In 1891, he published *Versos e Versões*, which included not only original verse but translations from Hugo, Gautier, Leconte de Lisle and Heine.

In 1891, he published *Aleluias*, after which his output declined. Unlike contemporary poets who adopted the Parnassian style, he attempted to go beyond a mere preoccupation with form and rhythm and his best verses are those in which he expressed a Leopardi-like anguish. One of his most effective poems of this type is 'Plenilúnio' (in Cândido, *PLB*). He was also skilled as a descriptive poet. [AA]

*Poesia Completa e Prosa*, ed. W. Ribeiro do Val (1961); Cândido, *P L B*, ii.
Waldir Ribeiro do Val, *Vida e Obra de Raimundo Correia* (Rio de Janeiro, 1960).

**Cortázar, Julio** (1914– ). Argentinian novelist, and short-story writer. This brilliant and original writer now lives and writes in Europe. His first work was published under the pseudonym of Julio Denis and for many years his work consisted mainly of critical essays. In 1951 he published a volume of short stories, *Bestiario*, in which there were fantastic and grotesque elements. This was followed by *Final del juego* (1964) and *Las armas secretas* (1964), both collections of short stories. Cortázar's first novel, *Los premios* (tr. E. Kerrigan, *The Winners*, London, 1965), appeared in 1960 and was his first attempt at an 'open' work. It is the story of a sea cruise won as a lottery prize by certain inhabitants of the Buenos Aires region. They are not told of their destination and the passengers quickly divide into two groups – those who obey the rules of the ship and those who try to break them. In a collection of allegorical stories, *Historia de cronopios y famas* (1962), Cortázar made a similar distinction between 'warm and disorderly cronopios' and the routine-loving 'famas'. His major work to date is the novel *Rayuela* (tr. G. Rabassa, *Hopscotch*, New York, 1966, London, 1967), which is a completely open novel. The reader may take the chapters in chronological order or follow the order the novelist suggests – in which case he has two completely different experiences. The novel represents the inner search of Horacio Oliveira and his attempt to enter into relationships. Though the novel takes place partly in Paris, partly in Buenos Aires, neither the place nor the order in which the events take place have any importance. Oliveira is already on the outside of any social order. The girl he sometimes loves, Maga, represents an end, a goal, but it is a goal that is always elusive, never realized.

315

The novel sheds a significantly new light on modern consciousness. Cortázar has also recently produced a collection of short stories, *Todos los fuegos el fuego* (1966). [JF]
*End of the Game*, tr. P. Blackburn (London, 1967) (selected short stories).
Harss, *L N*.

**Cortés, Hernán** (1485-1547). Conqueror of Mexico. Between 1519 and 1526, while on the Mexican campaign, he wrote six long letters describing the country he found, its inhabitants and the course of his campaign. Two of these letters have been lost but the first is often replaced in modern editions by an account sent to Charles V by the town of Vera Cruz. These letters relate the marvels of New Spain in plain soldierly language and Cortés confessed the poverty of language to express the strange new reality of Mexico: 'por no saber poner los nombres, no las expreso' ('because I do not know the names of things, I do not express them') he said of the things he saw. The *Cartas* show some sympathy for and appreciation of Indian civilization but they are naturally self-justificatory. Hence their main interest today is for the insight they give into the mind and attitudes of the conqueror. [JF]
*Cartas de relación de la conquista de México* (C A, Buenos Aires, 1945); *Five Letters*, tr. J. Bayard Morris (London, 1928).

**Costa, Cláudio Manuel da** (1729-89). Brazilian poet. Born in Minas Gerais, he studied in Coimbra, where he graduated in law, and on his return to Brazil served in the administration and legislature. Accused of taking part in an anti-Portuguese conspiracy known as the 'Inconfidência Mineira', he was imprisoned. The shock of this led to him implicating other conspirators and he then committed suicide. Costa belonged to the 'Arcadia' group of poets, a movement initiated by Tomás Antônio ◊ Gonzaga and da Silva Alvarenga. He took the name Glauceste Satúrnio, as a pseudonym, for his pastoral poetry. Costa was a poet formed in a predominantly European tradition but one who felt the need to break with the culterano style of the past. He achieved an elegant style in which, on the basis of classical models, he was able to express human conflicts. Of historical importance is his epic poem, 'Vila Rica', which was influenced by the 'Uruguay' of Basílio da ◊ Gama. [AA]
*Obras Poéticas*, ed. J. Ribeiro (2 vols., 1902); Cândido, *P L B*, i.

Alberto Lamego, *A Academia Brasílica dos Renascidos* (Paris, Brussels, 1903).

**Couto, Rui Ribeiro** (1898-1963). Brazilian novelist and poet. His first poems are symbolist, although he became a leading member of the Modernist movement. His collections of poems include *O Jardim das Confidências* (1921), *Poemetos de Ternura e de Melancolia* (1924), *Um Homem na Multidão* (1926), *Canções de Amor* (1928), *Nordeste e Outros Poemas do Brasil* (1933), *Poesia* (1934), *Cancioneiro de Dom Afonso* (1939), *Cancioneiro do Ausente* (1943), *Dia Longo* (1944), *Arc-en-ciel* (1949), *Mal du pays* (1949), *Rive étrangère* (1953), *Entre Mar e Rio* (1952). His poem *Dia Longo* won the International Poetry Prize in Paris in 1948. He has also written novels and proseworks, including *O Crime do Estudante Batista* (1922), *Baianinha e Outras Mulheres* (1927), *Cabocla*(1931), *Prima Belinha*(1940) and *Provincia* (1933). [AA]

**Cruz, Sor Juana Inés de la** (Juana Inés de Asbaje y Ramírez de Santillana) (1648-95). Mexican poetess. After gracing the viceregal court she took the veil and pursued both poetry and learning from the cloister. In her *Respuesta a Sor Filotea de la Cruz* (1691) she defended herself against the attacks of an obscurantist bishop by an eloquent and rational plea for intellectual freedom and the rights of women to education. Though orthodox in belief, she took a side-blow at the Inquisition by remarking that if she wrote verses and plays it was partly out of an incapacity for sacred subjects, but also because artistic heresy, unlike doctrinal, was not punishable by the Holy Office.

Sor Juana's 'Primer sueño', a metaphysical poem in the style of Góngora's 'Soledades', describes the soaring of her soul towards knowledge. Like the *Respuesta* it defends the private viewpoint. The poem has a metaphysical fervour that is quite individual, and that looks forward to the intellectual nihilism of a modern Mexican poet, José ◊ Gorostiza. Much of her poetry was occasional. A number of sonnets, however, the *redondillas* against male stupidity, 'Hombres necios', and a few *romances* and *villancicos* give her high rank in the school of Góngora. As a dramatist, she follows Calderón, but in the best of her *autos*, *El divino Narciso*, she daringly introduces the Aztec rite of eating the Corn-god as a parody invented by the devil to ridicule the Communion. Sor Juana was the last considerable poet of the Spanish Golden Age, and the first of Mexico. [JMC]

*Obras completas* (1951–7); Cohen, *P B S V*; Trend, *O B S V*; *Encounter*, I, 3.

Ludwig Pfandl, *Sor Juana Inés de la Cruz. La décima musa de México* (Mexico, 1963); Alfonso Reyes, 'The Tenth Muse of America', in *The Position of America* (New York, 1950).

**Cruz e Sousa, João da** (1861–98). Brazilian poet. The son of Negro slaves, he was educated and sent to school with the help of the former slave owner. His intellectual qualities brought him to the notice of the sociologist Dr Da Gama Rosa, who tried to help him enter the legal profession. In 1885, he published *Tropos e Fantasias* and in 1890 left his native state of Santa Catarina for Rio de Janeiro, where he lived in very modest circumstances. Although a Naturalist in his early years, at 30, influenced by his reading of Baudelaire, he turned to Symbolism. He was also influenced by the Portuguese poet Antero de Quental. In 1893, this new phase in his creative activity was marked by the publication of *Missal* (prose poems) and *Broqueis*.

His personal life was unhappy. His wife, a Negress, went mad and two of his children died in childhood. And despite his talent and originality as a poet, he was recognized only by a small and devoted group of admirers, notably Nestor Vítor. Posthumous publications include *Evocações* (prose poems, 1898), *Faróis* (1900) and *Ultimos Sonetos* (1905). Musicality, powerful and beautiful imagery mark his poetry. His symbolism has been seen by some critics to correspond to the need to transcend his origins. Thus Roger Bastide in *Quatro Estudos sobre Cruz e Sousa* shows the poet's obsession with the word 'white', which the poet refers to obliquely or directly in images of the moon, snow, cloud, ivory, foam, pearl etc. For Bastide, Cruz e Sousa ranks with Mallarmé and Stefan George as one of the masters of Symbolism. [AA]

*Obra completa*, ed. A. Muricy (1961); Cândido *PLB*, ii.

Nestor Vítor, *Cruz e Sousa* (Rio de Janeiro, 1899); Roger Bastide, 'Quatro Estudos sobre Cruz e Sousa', in *Poesia Afro-Brasileira* (São Paulo, 1943).

**Cuadra, José de la** (1903–41). Ecuadorian novelist. Born in Guayaquil, after graduating from law school he became a university teacher and held important official posts. With Joaquín Gallegos Lara, Enrique ◊ Gil Gilbert, and Demetrio ◊ Aguilera Malta and Alfredo ◊ Pareja Diezcanseco, he formed part of the *grupo de Guayaquil* which made such an important contribution to the Ecuadorian novel. The motto of the group was ' Reality and nothing more than reality' and much of their work centred round the lives of the *montuvios* or mestizo inhabitants of the coastal area around Guayaquil. De la Cuadra wrote some excellent short stories, but his major work is a novel, *Los Sangurimas* (1934), a story of violence. It tells of a family descended from a foreign father and a Sangurima (Indian) mother. The mother's family kill the foreigner soon after the birth of a son, Nicasio, and the mother in turn kills one of her own family. From now on there is a feud between different branches of the family, a feud which ends in bloodshed and tragedy. José de la Cuadra also wrote an essay on the *montuvio* with the title *El montuvio ecuatoriano* (1937). [JF]

*Obras completas*, intr. A. Pareja Diezcanseco (1958).

**Cuadra, Pablo Antonio** (1912–     ). Nicaraguan poet and dramatist. He has also written many essays, collected in *Hacia la cruz del sur* (Madrid, 1936), *Promisión de Mexico* (1945) and *Entre la cruz y la espada* (Madrid, 1946). His most important collections of poetry are *Poemas nicaragüenses* (Santiago de Chile, 1933) and *Canto de temporal* (1933). An anthology of his poetry with the title *Corona de jilgueros*, which covered the poetry written between 1929 and 1949, appeared in Madrid in 1949. [JF]

*New Directions*, 17 (1961) (translations).

**Cunha, Euclydes da** (1866–1909). Brazilian writer. He was born in the province of Rio de Janeiro. After attending Polytechnic School, he entered military school in 1886, but left before completing his course and went to São Paulo to become a journalist. Having re-entered and again left the army, da Cunha was working as a civil engineer when the Canudos rebellion occurred in 1896. He was sent as a reporter by a São Paulo newspaper to cover the military campaign, and the result of his reporting is a national epic.

*Os Sertões* (1902; 26th edn, 1963; tr. S. Putnam, *Rebellion in the Backlands*,

Chicago, 1957) is more than mere reportage which attracts ephemeral notice. It is an immense treatise on the history, sociology, geology and geography of the Brazilian *sertão*, or backlands. A small band of *sertanejos*, led by the religious fanatic Antônio the Counsellor, defied federal troops at Canudos for almost a year. The courage and tenacity of these backwoodsmen inspired da Cunha to write sympathetically of their customs, superstitions, ceremonies and celebrations. His description of their way of life in itself is sufficient reason for the success of his book. But it also contains valuable information for military studies, with its descriptions of guerrilla warfare, skirmishes and ambushes. Da Cunha's scientific background also enabled him to describe the geography and geology of this region, and to make such original contributions that even today his work is considered essential reading for students of these sciences.

But perhaps the most outstanding feature of *Os Sertões* is the portrayal of the violent contrast between civilization and barbarism. More than an apology for the *sertanejo*, da Cunha's work is a protest against the civilized littoral and its new republican government which had ignored the interior. It is true that his Spencerian positivistic background and the prevailing pseudo-scientific laws of heredity caused him to be pessimistic about the possibilities of the mixed, or inferior races. But he was also a humanitarian who realized the backlander

should be helped. More important, he discovered that the mestizo is the backbone and the basis of Brazilian nationality. The fact that the *sertanejo* is Brazilian too, perhaps more Brazilian than the European-oriented littoral, caused him to plead for integration and education of the backlander as a means of achieving national unity.

The impact of *Os Sertões* on Brazil has been profound. It was an immediate success and has been (excepting perhaps Gilberto ◊ Freyre's *Casa Grande e Senzala*) the most influential work in 20th-century Brazilian letters. It has encouraged Brazilians to look inward, to discover the possibilities of their own country and to create a Brazilian literature. Da Cunha's epic awakened a spirit of national discovery and self- criticism which later found expression in Brazil's modernist and regionalist movements.

He spent his remaining years as a sanitary engineer, a surveyor and a professor of logic. He also wrote *Peru versus Bolivia* (1907; repr. 1959), concerning a boundary dispute between the two countries, and *Contrastes e Confrontos* (1907; repr. 1923), a collection of South American studies. He was murdered in 1909 before completing his *Paraíso Perdido*, which, again, was to deal with the backlands. [DH]

Ellison, *B N N*; S. Putnam, intr. to translation of *Os Sertões* (*Revolt in the Backlands*, Chicago, 1957); S. Putnam, *Marvelous Journey* (New York, 1948); O. de Souza Andrade, *História e Interpretação de 'Os Sertões'* (São Paulo, 1960).

# D

**Darío, Rubén** (Félix Rubén García Sarmiento) (1867–1916). Nicaraguan poet. A key figure of the Modernist movement (◊ Modernism). Born in the small town of San Pedro de Metapa, his parents separated when he was a child and he went to live with an aunt in León. He quickly revealed himself as an infant prodigy, publishing his first poems anonymously at 13. He attracted wide attention in León with his early poems and so was taken to the Nicaraguan capital, Managua, and given a job in the National Library, where he read the Spanish classics. He left for Chile in 1886, encouraged by a friend, and here he was soon established as a journalist and writer. In 1887, he published *Rimas y Abrojos*. His previous poems had combined romantic elements with a naïve political and religious idealism. He had translated some of Victor Hugo's poems and Hugo was to remain an influence, but *Rimas y Abrojos* also showed Spanish influences and there were echoes of Bécquer as well as of Campoamor. However, Darío was increasingly interested in contemporary French poets and in the adaptation of French styles into Spanish poetry. *Azul* (1888), a collection of poems and stories, represented a decisive break with Spanish literary tradition. The poems evoked an ideal world of guiltless erotic love and many of them radically transformed traditional metres or introduced new lengths of line. The stories, in a poetic and sensual prose quite new to Spanish, often dealt with the artist's opposition to bourgeois society and its values. Soon afterwards he coined the word 'Modernism', which came to mean the exaltation of art and aesthetic values and the striving for musicality and technical perfection in verse. After *Azul*, he spent some years in Central America and in Buenos Aires, where he was at the centre of an active literary circle. Here he published a collection of essays on contemporary European poets and writers, *Los raros* (1896), and *Prosas Profanas* (1896), a collection of poems which marks one of the heights of Modernism. In 1892 he was sent to Spain by the Argentine paper *La Nación* and he returned there as *La Nación* correspondent in 1898. Much of the rest of his life was spent in Europe, where his health was undermined by dipsomania and where he underwent increasing disillusionment. He seems to have attained some spiritual peace in Mallorca, where he settled in 1913, but he was already ill and he died after a long, painful return journey to Nicaragua.

*Prosas profanas* had been a virtuoso performance and had included a wide range of poetic metres, rhymes and a great extension of the poetic language. The influence of the French Parnassians was marked but Darío's use of the mythological figures of the classical world was no mere imitation of Parnassianism. He uses the centaur and the swan, for instance, as complex objective symbols, for they united animal and divine attributes which he felt warring within himself. In *Cantos de vida y esperanza* (1905), the guiltless and unified world of his previous collections is torn with anguish and many of the poems express torment at the prospect of death. Others reflect the political preoccupations of the Arielist generation (◊ Rodó). *El canto errante* (1907) showed much less inventive genius and included poems previously written but not collected. Finally came *Canto a Argentina* (1914), a sonorous tribute to a country which had been one of his chief patrons. Few of his poems give pleasure today, but his influence as an innovator in prose and poetry was immense. [JF]

*Obras completas* (5 vols., Madrid, 1950–55); *Obras poéticas completas* (Madrid, 10th edn, corrected and enlarged, 1967).
Pedro Salinas, *La poesía de Rubén Darío* (2nd edn, Buenos Aires, 1958); Arturo Torres-Ríoseco, *Vida y poesía de Rubén Darío* (Buenos Aires, 1944); R. Ledesma, *Genio y figura de Rubén Darío* (Buenos Aires, 1964); Ureña, *BHM*.

**Denevi, Marco** (1922– ). Argentine novelist. He first gained recognition with *Rosaura a las diez* (1955). In 1960, he won the *Life* magazine prize with *Ceremonia secreta* (New York, 1960). He has written several plays, including *Los expedientes* (1957), *El emperador de la China* (1959) and *El cuarto de la noche* (1962). [JF]

**Desnoes, Edmundo** (1930– ). Cuban novelist and short-story writer. Author of *Todo está en el fuego* (1952), which included poems and stories; and the novels *No hay problema* (1964), *El cataclismo* (1965) and *Memorias del subdesarrollo* (1967; tr. the author, *Inconsolable Memories*). [JF]

**D'Halmar, Augusto** (1880–1950). Chilean journalist and novelist. His *Juana Lucero* (1902) dwelt on a popular theme of the time, the life of a prostitute. D'Halmar was greatly influenced by Tolstoy, and with his friend Santiván started a Tolstoyan colony. In 1917, he published a novel on an Indianist theme, *Gatita*. Of his other works, many of which were published abroad where he served in the consular service, the most noteworthy is *Pasión y muerte del cura Deusto* (1924). [JF]

Alone, *H P L C,* and *Los cuatro grandes de la literatura chilena* (Santiago, 1962) (selections). Castro, *P L C.*

**Díaz Arrieta, Hernán** ('Alone') (1891– ). Chilean critic. He has encouraged many new writers and has written regularly for *La Nación* and *El Mercurio.* His most important works are his *Panorama de la literatura chilena durante el siglo XX* (1931) and *Historia personal de la literatura chilena* (1954). [JF]

**Díaz del Castillo, Bernal** (1492?–1584). Chronicler of the conquest of Mexico. He reached the New World in 1514 with Pedro Arias Dávila, governor of Darien, but soon left for Cuba, where he took part in Grijalva's expedition to Yucatán in 1518. He joined Cortés and was present during the whole of the conquest of Mexico. Awarded an *encomienda* or allotment of Indians in Guatemala, he lived there for the rest of his life and wrote his *Verdadera historia de la conquista de la Nueva España* (ed. J. R. Cabañas, 2 vols., Mexico, 1955; tr. J. M. Cohen, *The Conquest of New Spain,* Penguin Classics, 1963), stating in a preliminary note that he was then 84. He set out to write a true eyewitness account 'muy llanamente, sin torcer a una parte ni a otra' ('plainly, without distortion'), as against the official account of López de Gómara. The result is a vigorous, colloquial work which brings the main actors of the Conquest alive and has the excitement of direct reporting. Díaz del Castillo was a common man of his time, not given to speculating on

events, but this adds to the immediacy of the narrative. The *Verdadera historia* was not published until 1632. [JMC]

**Díaz Mirón, Salvador** (1853–1928). Mexican poet. His early work was greatly influenced by Victor Hugo. Like Hugo, he dealt with the themes of the poor and oppressed ('Los parías') and with the role of the poet as seer ('A Victor Hugo' and 'A Gloria'). Díaz Mirón's first poems appeared between 1876 and 1886 and were to influence ◊ Darío and Santos ◊ Chocano. At this period Díaz Mirón's ambitions seem to have been partly political (deputy 1884–5), but his political career ended in 1892 when in an electoral campaign he killed an opponent in self-defence. His subsequent imprisonment transformed his life and his poetry. He became increasingly isolated and his poetry more introspective. *Lascas* (1901), his principal collection, contains poems which are more intense and original than anything he had written before, from the grotesque and realistic descriptions of corpses in 'El muerto' and 'Ejemplo' to the tortured sensuality of 'Vigilia y sueño'. After the publication of *Lascas,* his output was scarce. [JF]

*Poesías completas,* intr. A. Castro Leal (Mexico, 1952).
Ureña, *B H M.*

**Díaz Rodríguez, Manuel** (1868–1927). Venezuelan novelist and short-story writer. Of a wealthy family, he graduated in medicine but did not practise. His culture was cosmopolitan and he travelled widely in Europe. In 1898, his first stories, *Cuentos de color,* began to appear in *El cojo ilustrado,* which had begun as a trade periodical and which became an important platform for young Venezuelan writers. Many of these stories dealt with a characteristic Modernist theme – the conflict between ideals and the arid environment. This was also the major theme of his novels and especially of *Ídolos rotos* (1901) and *Sangre patricia* (1902). In common with many Modernists, Díaz Rodríguez abandoned cosmopolitanism and turned to his native countryside. *Peregrina o el pozo encantado, novela de rústicos del valle de Caracas* (1922), his best novel, was the fruit of this later period. [JF]

Alegría, *B H N H;* Lowell Dunham, *Manuel Díaz Rodríguez, vida y obra* (1942; 2nd edn, Mexico, 1959).

**Dickmann, Max** (1902–    ). Argentine journalist and novelist. He collaborated in the literary review *Nosotros* and made Spanish translations of many North American writers (Dos Passos, Faulkner, etc.). He preferred novels in which the characters were 'sencilla y fuerte' ('simple and strong'). His episodic *Madre América* (1930) centred on life in the Paraná delta and the town of Itatí. *Gente* (1936) dealt with a whole spectrum of human types from aristocrat to vagabond and *Los frutos amargos* (1941) with the problem of the immigrant. *Esta generación perdida* (1945) presented a conflict of generations between the disappearing values of the old and the failure of the new generation. [JF]

*DLL.*

**Domínguez de Camargo, Hernando** (?– 1657). Colombian Jesuit poet. His *Poema heroico de San Ignacio de Loyola* (1666; intr. F. Arbeláez, Bogotá, 1956) describes the life of the founder of the Jesuits in a richly Gongorist style. Domínguez took his story from a chronicle. What he added were the embellishments – banquets, hunting scenes, descriptions of wealth and apparel. Loyola's asceticism was ignored. Domínguez frequently refers with appreciation to the American scene, the subject of several of his lyrics, the best known of which is a description of a waterfall: 'A un salto por donde se despeña el arroyo de Chillo ' ('To a waterfall over which crashes down the river Chillo '). [JMC]

**Donoso, José** (1924–    ). Chilean novelist and short-story writer. His first stories were written in English. In 1955, he published his first collection, *Veraneo*, and in 1957 his first novel, *Coronación* (tr. J. Goodwin, *Coronation*, New York, London, 1965). In 1960 there appeared *El Charleston* (short stories) and an anthology of previously published short stories, followed in 1966 by *Los mejores cuentos de José Donoso*. His most recent publications have been *El domingo* (tr. *This Sunday*, New York, London, 1968). He is at present working on the novel *El obsceno pájaro de la noche* an extract of which appeared in *Mundo Nuevo* 13 (July 1967). [JF]

**Drummond de Andrade, Carlos** (1902–    ). Brazilian poet. Born in Itabira (Minas Gerais) of a family long-established in this region, he became a journalist and civil servant and one of the great innovators in Brazilian poetry. His first collection, *Alguma Poesia* (1930), appeared after the initial phase of Modernism (◊ Modernism in Brazil). In it, he had already absorbed and transcended the *avant garde* experimentalism of the Brazilian Modernist movement. With elements drawn from everyday experience, the poet explored themes of human isolation and communication. All his poetry is imbued with irony and humour, a humour that often depends on anti-climax. Indeed one of his chief contributions even in his first published volume was to break with the rhetoric of literary tradition and thus to question certain basic assumptions about experience. This rebellion against tradition, playful in his first poems, deepened with subsequent collections, which included: *Brejo das Almas* (1934), *Sentimento do Mundo* (1940), *Poesias* (1942), *A Rosa do Povo* (1945), *Poesia até Agora* (1948), *A Mesa* (1951), *Claro Enigma* (1951), *Fazendeiro do Ar* (1955), *Ciclo* (1957), *Poemas* (1959), *Lição de Coisas* (1962). The invention and irony which characterize his poetry are also present in his prose works – essays and short stories. His main concern is the fragmentation of human experience, the impossibility of fulfilment or of understanding fully even the most ordinary elements of experience. Thus in 'Confidência do Itabirano', the poet meditates, 'I lived for some years in Itabira. A hove all, I was born in Itabira' to conclude, 'Once I had móney, I had cattle and farms / Now I am a civil servant / And Itabira is only a photograph on the wall / And how it hurts,' He has recently published *José e Outros* (1967). [JF]

*Poemas* (1959); *Contos de Aprendiz* (3rd edn, 1963); Cândido, *P L B*, iii.
Mário de Andrade, *Aspectos da Literatura Brasileira* (São Paulo, c. 1959); Othon Moacyr Garcia, *Esfinge Clara* (Rio de Janeiro, 1955).

# E

**Echeverría, Esteban** (1805–51). Argentinian poet and thinker. He lived in France in 1826–30 and there became enthusiastic for the European romantics, especially Schiller, Byron and Scott. Romanticism was to imbue his political and social thought as well as his literary output. He believed that a country must develop its own national genius and that Argentina's first task was to cultivate an original literature and thought and so liberate herself intellectually as well as politically from Spain. He thus helped to found the Asociación de Mayo, a society of young Argentinians opposed to the strongman rule of the Federalist, General Rosas. He set out his political and cultural ideals in a pamphlet, *Dogma socialista de la Asociación de Mayo* (1837–46), which advocates Christian socialism, honour and sacrifice as motivating forces in society and democracy as a political system. In 1840, the Rosas persecution forced him to flee to Uruguay and he died there before the fall of Rosas. His literary reputation was based on his poetry. In 1832, shortly after returning to Argentina, he had published *Elvira o la novia del Plata*, followed by *Los consuelos* (1834). These are more remarkable for being the first poetry of newly independent Argentina than for literary merit. *Rimas* (1837) included his best-known poem, 'La cautiva', a verse narrative of the escape of a creole woman and her lover from an Indian encampment where they had been held in captivity, their flight and final death in the pampa. Though Echeverría is best known as a poet and a thinker, his finest work is a short story, *El matadero* (probably written c. 1840 but published posthumously; ed. and tr. A. Flores, *The Slaughter House*, New York, 1959), an intense allegory about Argentina under Rosas which takes place in a slaughter house. The pursuit of an escaped bull excites the butchers, who recapture it and make a ritual killing. Aroused by the sight of blood, they turn on a young man who happens to be passing and who bears no outward sign of support for Rosas and is therefore assumed to be an enemy. They torture him, cause him to have a haemorrhage and leave him for dead. The story is a powerful indictment of the barbarism and lack of respect for civilized values which marked the Rosas era. [JF]

Obras completas (*1870–74*), ed. J. M. Gutiérrez (5 vols., 1951); '*El matador*' et '*La cautiva*', with 3 essays by Noé Jitrik (Besançon 1969).

**Edwards Bello, Joaquín** (1887–    ). Chilean novelist. Although a member of a distinguished and wealthy family, Edwards Bello preferred to deal with the lower depths of Chilean society. He was a prolific journalist, a rebel and a novelist in the documentary manner. His main works are *Criollos en Paris* (1933), *Un Chileno en Madrid* (1928) and *Valparaiso, la ciudad del viento* (1943), but his best-known work is *El roto* (1920), in which he introduced statistics and documentary evidence in order to paint a devastating picture of the Chilean *lumpenproletariat*. [JF]

Alone, *HPLC*.

**Eguren, José María** (1882–1942). Peruvian poet. His first collection, *Simbólicas* (1911), revealed an imagination far removed from reality. In their evocative powers, his words fulfilled a function akin to that of musical notes and were deprived of connotative significance, e.g. 'Los sueños rubios de aroma / despierta blandamente / su sardana en las hojas' ('Blond dreams of perfume softly awaken their dance in the leaves'). A second collection, *La canción de las figuras*, appeared in 1916. The eminent politician and critic, José Carlos Mariátegui, gave the most exact appreciation of Eguren's poetry when he declared that 'por las rutas de lo maravilloso, por los caminos del sueño, toca el misterio. Mas Eguren interpreta el misterio con la inocencia de un niño alucinado y vidente' ('through the marvellous and through dream, he touches mystery. But Eguren interprets mystery with the innocence of a hallucinated and prophetic child'), and indeed there is the freshness of a child's vision in many of his poems. A collection of poems, *Poesía*, appeared in

1929, containing his first two collections and some new poems, *Sombra y Rondinelas*, which include some of the most extraordinarily powerful poetry published in Latin America. 'La ronda de espadas' for instance expresses a nocturnal sense of mystery and fear. [J F]

*Poesías completas*, intr. E. Núñez (1951).

# F

**Fagundes Varela, Luis Nicolau** (1841–75). Brazilian romantic poet. He enrolled as a student in Recife and then in São Paulo, but abandoned his studies because of inner conflicts. He spent the rest of his life in Bohemian wanderings, dedicating himself primarily to poetry. His many collections include *Noturnas* (1851), *O Estandarte Auriverde* (1853), *Vozes da America* (1854), *Cantos e Fantasias* (1855), *Cantos Meridionais* (1859), *Cantos do Êrmo e da Cidade* (1859), *Anchieta ou o Evangelho das Selvas* (1875), *Cantos Religiosos* (1878), *Diário de Lázaro* (1880). Of these the *Cantos e Fantasias* includes a series of moving elegies on the death of his wife and son, particularly the 'Cântico do Calvario' in memory of the latter (one of his best poems). *Cantos do Êrmo e da Cidade* are poems on the theme of solitude. Many of his other collections are of poems on patriotic themes. His *Anchieta ou o Evangelho das Selvas* was written in collaboration with his sister and is a poem of 10 cantos which centres on the religious aspects of this theme. [JF]

*Poesias Completas*, ed. F. J. da Silva Ramos (1955); *Poesias Completas*, ed. M. Tati and E. C. Guerra (3 vols., 1957); *G P R B*; Cândido, *P L B*, ii.

**Faria, Otavio de** (1908–   ). Brazilian novelist. He early began to collaborate in literary review and made several journeys to Europe. His first works were *Machiavel e o Brasil* (1931) and *Destino do Socialismo* (1933). Even as a youth he had in mind the creation of a cycle of novels which would relate the 'Tragedia Burguesa' ('Bourgeois Tragedy'). This vast project, only partially completed to date, was intended to convey a total picture of the Brazilian middle class seen not so much through class conflict as in a moral context. Volumes published include: *Mundos Mortos* (1937), *Caminhos da Vida* (1939), *O Lôdo das Ruas* (1942), *O Anjo de Pedra* (1944), *Os Renegados* (1947), *Os Loucos* (1952), *O Senhor e o Mundo* (1958). [JF]

Olivio Montenegro, *O Romance Brasileiro* (2nd edn, Rio de Janeiro, 1953).

**Fernández, Macedonio** (1874–1952). Argentinian novelist and poet. A member of the Argentine *avant garde* during the twenties, he wrote an *avant garde* novel, *No todo es vigilia la de los ojos abiertos* ('It is not always wakefulness to have the eyes open', 1928). In 1941, he published *Una novela que comienza* and his autobiographical *Papeles de recienvenido* appeared in 1929. Among his collections of poetry are *Destino de llorarte* (1941) and *Passacaglia* (1955). [JF]

*Museo de la novela de la Eterna* (1967). Moreno, *R P*; J. L. Borges, *Macedonio Fernández* (Buenos Aires, 1961).

**Fernández, Pablo Armando** (1930–   ). Cuban poet. One of the most talented of her post-revolutionary poets, he served for a time as Cuban cultural attaché in London. His best-known collection to date is the *Libro de los héroes* (1963), a series of poetic meditations on the heroes of the Cuban revolution. He has recently won the Casa de las Américas prize with a novel, *Los niños se despiden* (Havana, 1968). [JF]

*P V*.

**Fernández de Lizardi, José Joaquín** (El Pensador Mexicano) (1776–1827). Mexican novelist and political journalist. Generally regarded as the first Latin-American novelist, he was largely self-taught and was particularly interested in the Enlightenment thinkers of France and Spain. A supporter of Hidalgo's premature independence uprising in 1810, he later (1812) founded a journal devoted to the revolutionary cause, *El Pensador Mexicano* (1812–14). He was imprisoned several times for his political views and largely because of censorship difficulties he turned to the novel to express his ideas on reform. *El Periquillo Sarniento*, the first Latin-American novel, thus came to be written in 1816 (ed. J. R. Spell, 1959). There followed *Noches tristes* (1818), *La Quijotita y su prima* (1819) and *Don Catrín de la Fachenda*, written about 1820 but published posthumously. During the second stage of the struggle for Mexican independence, Lizardi sided with Iturbide, with whom he later became disillusioned.

Thus when Iturbide had himself crowned Emperor of post-Independence Mexico, Lizardi was again in opposition; an anticlerical pamphlet of this period, the *Defensa de los Francmasones* (1822), earned him excommunication. Nevertheless, in reward for his services in the War of Independence, he was appointed editor of the government paper, *La Gaceta del Gobierno*, and in 1826 founded his own organ, *Correo Semanario*. All Lizardi's novels are didactic criticisms of morals and manners. His outstanding work is *El Periquillo Sarniento*, a complete and vivid picture of middle-class Mexican life at the end of the colonial period. His main targets of attack were the old-fashioned and often absurd education system, the survival of scholasticism, ignorance of scientific methods, poor professional training of doctors and surgeons, disdain for agricultural toil and Mexico's economic dependence on the mining industry. He also attacked the clergy and the monastic orders but showed enlightened attitudes to the Indian and the Negro. *El Periquillo Sarniento* is a picaresque novel. Each stage of the main character's career serves to throw into relief one abuse or another. [JF]

*Obras I: Poesías y fábulas*, ed. J. Chencinsky and L. M. Schneider (1963).
J. R. Spell, *The Life and Works of José Fernández de Lizardi* (Philadelphia, 1931).

**Fernández Moreno, Baldomero** (1885–1950). Argentinian poet. Of Spanish descent, he lived in Spain in 1892–9. He studied medicine and practised as a doctor until 1924, then became a teacher. The rest of his life was spent in teaching and writing. His first collection of poems, *Las iniciales del misal*, appeared in 1915 and there followed *Aldea española* (1925), *Poesía* (1928), *Décimas* (1928), *Dos poemas* (1935), *Seguidillas* (1935), *Romances* (1936). The titles of some of these collections ('Décimas', 'Seguidillas' and 'Romances' are all Spanish verse forms) show the strong Spanish influence on his poetry. Indeed he is one of the modern Latin-American poets who is closest to Peninsular tradition. His poetry gives the effect of simplicity and spontaneity and deals with the ordinary places and the day-to-day incidents of living. [JF]

*Antología* (1915–50) (5th edn, 1954).
Moreno, *R P*.

**Fernández Retamar, Roberto** (1930– ).

Cuban poet. He is now editor of the *Casa de las Américas* magazine. A selection from all his poetry was included in his own anthology, *Con las mismas manos* (1962), since when he has published *Aquellas poesías y Si a la Revolución*, *Historia antigua* and *Buena suerte viviendo* (1967). He has also published a study of Cuban poetry, *La poesía contemporánea en Cuba, 1927–1953* (1954). [JMC]

*P V*.

**Florit, Eugenio** (1903– ). Cuban poet. He applied a refined Gongorism to description of the landscapes and waters of his native country in his first collection, *Trópico* (1930). Among the religious poems in his *Doble acente* (1937), 'Martirio de San Sebastián' stands out for the balanced use of 17th- and 20th-century techniques. Florit's later poetry is simpler and more meditative, relying for inspiration on childhood memories and the contemplation, of the sea. *Asonante final y otros poemas* (1956) contains as its title piece a delicate self-portrait of the poet at work. [JMC]

*Antología poética 1930–1955* (1956).

**Fray Mocho.** ◊ Álvarez, José Sixto.

**Freyre, Gilberto de Mello** (1900– ). Brazilian sociologist and essayist. Born in Recife, the capital of the North-eastern state of Pernambuco. He received his early education in Brazil but graduated from Baylor University, Texas. He then studied under Professor Franz Boas of Columbia, returned to Brazil in 1923 and in 1926 helped to organize an important regionalist conference which issued a regionalist manifesto. This manifesto stated the urgency of preserving regional values and traditions, of studying regional cultures, which were the real roots of Brazilian nationalism. The Regionalist movement gave an impetus to North-eastern culture and both ◊ Almeida and ◊ Lins do Rego were influenced by Freyre.

Freyre is principally known, however, for his sociological works, especially the monumental *Casa Grande e Senzala* (1933; tr. S. Putnam, *The Masters and the Slaves*, 1945). Probably no other book has had a greater effect on recent Brazilian attitudes and literary production. In this sociological and historical treatment of Brazilian society, he concentrates on the strands of race and cultures which met in the sugar plantations of the North-east. He shows the effects of miscegenation of the African, Indian and Portuguese-Caucasian races upon the culture of the North-east and relates this to the structure of the plantation 'big house' with its surrounding slave quarters. He places particular emphasis on sexual relations within the sugar-planting society. In analysing the daily activities of the plantations, the development and organization of society in the North-east and the uniqueness of the racial mixtures, Freyre contributed to dispelling the national inferiority complex (particularly strong in the preceding generations) regarding race. His work has taught Brazilians much about themselves, their national characteristics and social history, and has given a powerful impetus to regional literature and sociological studies. Though *Casa Grande e Senzala* is primarily a sociological study, its easy, and often poetic, style makes it read like a novel. One of its principal themes – that describing the slave-holding system as benign, especially in comparison with other slave-holding societies – has lately been much criticized in light of recent historical research and evidence.

Of Freyre's other works, two are available in English. *Brazil: An Interpretation* (1945) was written directly in English, while *Sobrados e Mucambos* (1936; repr. 1961) was translated in 1963 as *The Mansions and the Shanties*. The former deals with Freyre's attempt to define and describe his society, while the latter tells of the rise of the mulatto in Brazilian society. [DH]

Ellison, *BNN*; S. Putnam, *Marvelous Journey* (New York, 1948).

**Frías, Heriberto** (1870–1928). Mexican novelist. As a lieutenant in the Mexican army, he was sent on an expedition to northern Mexico to help put down a rebellion among the Yaqui Indians. His account of this brought him into conflict with the authorities and formed the basis for his first novel, *Tomóchic*. In 1893, he left the army and started a career in journalism and in 1899 published *Tomóchic: Episodios de la campaña de Chihuaha*, in Texas. The novel is weak and crudely written but presents a striking picture of poverty and religious fanaticism in northern Mexico. It is also of interest because it shows the awakening of social conscience in the young protagonist who, like Frías himself, came to sympathize with the Indians he had fought against.

Frías then worked for many years as a journalist; on the outbreak of the revolution, he became a supporter of Madero. He wrote several other novels, mainly interesting as social documents. The most noteworthy is *¿Aguila o sol?* (1923), an account of miseries of village life during the regime of Porfirio Díaz. [JF]

Antonio Magaña Esquivel, *La novela de la Revolución*, i (Mexico 1964).

**Fuentes, Carlos** (1929– ). Mexican novelist. His collection of short stories, *Los días enmascarados* (1954), includes a good horror tale, 'Chac Mool'. His first novel, *La región más transparente* (1958; tr. *Where the Air is Clear*, New York, 1960), a panorama of all classes in Mexico City, uses techniques derived from Dos Passos, Joyce and others. It concentrates on the fate of the pre-Revolutionary land-owning class and the 'new men' who had emerged after the Revolution. *Las buenas conciencias* (1959) deals with the adolescence of a young provincial in rebellion from his bourgeois family but unable to sympathize wholly with those of lower social classes. At the end of the novel, he in his turn is about to be absorbed into the middle-class élite. *La muerte de Artemio Cruz* (1962; tr. S. Hileman, New York, London, 1964) fulfils the promise of Fuentes's earlier work. It is the story of a political boss, beginning on his death bed and by a series of flash-backs recalling his past life. The personality of Artemio Cruz is divided into an 'I' and a 'You' to represent the conflicts within his mind. The novel is both a social novel and a study of character. The short story *Aura* (1962) exploits a somewhat decadent fantasy. Fuentes's recent work includes the short-story collection, *Cantar de ciegos* (1964), and a novel, *Zona sagrada* (1967), which deals with the lonely obsession of a young man, haunted by the image of his film-star mother. He has also recently published *Cambio de piel* (1967; tr. S. Hileman, *Change of Skin*, New York, 1968), his most ambitious work to date. This is an attempt at an 'open novel' which shows a constantly changing permutation of relationships between four people on a trip to Cholula. A brilliant essayist and critic, Fuentes has also published *La nueva novela hispanoamericana* (1969) and *Casa con dos puertas* (1970). His most recent novel is *Cumpleános* (1970), and he has also begun to write for the theatre. [JF/JMC]

# G

**Gallegos, Rómulo** (1884–1968). Venezuelan novelist and politician. From his student days, Gallegos worked for the advancement of his country. He helped to found a review, *La Alborada*, in 1909 and many of his early essays show his faith in education as a weapon for the transformation of Venezuela. He was a teacher for several years and did not publish his first novel, *El último Solar*, later called *Reinaldo Solar*, until 1920. This concerned the hero's attempt to transform the country and make his mark on society, but unlike similar attempts in later novels this one ended in disillusionment. *La trepadora* (1925) was more optimistic and was concerned the fusion of the different races into a new Venezuelan type. But it was with *Doña Bárbara* (1929) that Gallegos achieved fame. The novel was conceived during a stay in Europe but written after Gallegos had returned to Venezuela and learned at first hand about life on the cattle ranches in which it is set. The characters are partly symbolic, Bárbara standing for the forces of disorder and barbarism. She is a ruthless cattle rancher who has encroached on the lands of her neighbour, the city-educated Santos Luzardo. The struggle between them parallels the struggle between the two elements of lawlessness and civilization in Venezuelan life. A sub-theme is Santos Luzardo's taming and eventual marriage with Doña Bárbara's daughter, who has grown up as a child of nature. The final triumph of civilization did not accord with the actual situation of the country, at that period suffering under the Gómez dictatorship, and soon after publication of the novel Gallegos went into voluntary exile (1931–5) in order to escape the attentions of the dictator. *Cantaclaro* (1931) – another novel of the plains and the cattle estates – and *Canaima* (1935) were both written in exile. The latter was set in the Guiana region and the hero, Marcos Vargas, experiences adventures typical of life in the area – he kills a powerful rival, searches for gold, becomes foreman of a rubber plantation. But towards the end he goes to live among the Indians in a search for self-knowledge. His half-caste son, who

returns to civilization to be educated, symbolizes a new Venezuela that combines the ancient indigenous wisdom with modern education. Gallegos has also written a novel set among the coastal Negroes (*Pobre negro*, 1937) and many short stories. In 1947, he became President of Venezuela at the head of the Acción Democrática party but a military coup soon sent him into exile, where he remained until 1958. [JF]

*Obras completas* (2 vols., 2nd edn, Madrid, 1959).
Lowell Dunham, *Rómulo Gallegos, vida y obra* (Mexico, 1957).

**Galván, Manuel de Jesus** (1834–1910). Dominican novelist. His *Enriquillo, leyenda histórica dominicana (1503–1533)* (1882; tr. Robert Graves, *The Cross and the Sword*, London, 1956) is a romantic novel of the early days of the Spanish colonization of the island. Written in good Spanish prose, it is based on various chronicles and histories of the Conquest period and has an authentic atmosphere. It concerns the rebellion of an Indian chief, Enriquillo, against the injustices and cruelty of the Spaniards, and historical personages such as Bartolomé de las Casas and Juan de Grijalva appear. The historical realism of the background makes the novel stand out from the sentimental exaltations of the noble savage current in the 19th-century literature of Latin America. [JF]

Suárez-Murias, *NRH.*

**Gálvez, Manuel** (1882-1962). Argentine writer. He graduated as a lawyer after writing a thesis on the white slave traffic. From the first, he was interested in social problems. He helped to found the periodical *Ideas* and became supervisor of secondary education in Argentina. In 1917, he founded a publishing house and he also found time to travel extensively abroad. His first popular success was *La maestra normal* (1914), a realistic novel of a country schoolmistress and her conflict with the environment. This was followed by *El mal metafísico* (1917), again relating a clash between the hero, this time a writer, and the arid cultural climate of Buenos Aires. There followed *La sombra* *del convento* (1917) and *Nacha Regules* (1919), a novel of prostitution. Amongst his many other works, there is an interesting historical reconstruction of the war between Paraguay and the triple alliance of Argentina, Brazil and Uruguay which took place in the 19th-century. Gálvez wrote a trilogy on this theme called *Escenas de la Guerra del Paraguay* (1928–9). Many of Gálvez's later novels are Catholic in theme, notably his *Miércoles santo* (1930; tr. W. B. Wells, *Holy Wednesday*, London, 1934), which tells of the daily life of a simple parish priest. [JF]

*Obras escogidas* (Madrid, 1949).
Alegría, *B H N H*.

**Gama, José Basílio da** (1740–95). Brazilian poet. He was still a novice in a Jesuit school when the Jesuits were expelled from Portugal. Thereafter, he spent many years abroad in Italy and Portugal, where he was accused of Jesuitism and condemned to exile in Angola. A poem on the marriage of the Marquês de Pombal's daughter saved him from going into exile, and in the same year (1769) he wrote a Brazilian epic, *O Uraguai* (repr. 1941), which included many attacks on the Jesuits. He was thereafter protected by Pombal. He died in Lisbon. His most important work is *O Uraguai*, the blank verse epic which dealt with a war waged by the Portuguese and the Spaniards against the Indians of the Seven Missions along the Uruguay river. There are 5 cantos, of which the first deals with preparations in the Spanish and Portuguese camps; the second with the advice of the Portuguese general, Gomes Freire de Andrade, and his attempts to parley with the enemy. In the third canto, the Indian, Cocambo, fires the prairie in order to destroy the enemy camp and then flees to the Jesuit mission where his promised bride, Lindoya, awaits him. The Jesuits murder Cocambo, and Lindoya then has a vision of the Lisbon earthquake and the expulsion of the Jesuits. The last two cantos deal with the death of Lindoya and the victory of the Portuguese. The two major themes of the poem – the attack on the Jesuits and the tragedy of the Indian – reflect the conflict in da Gama's mind between his European culture and his American upbringing. The extent of his sympathies for the Indian is the subject of some controversy among critics. They are, however, agreed on his importance as a poet who introduced the theme of the Indian into

Brazilian poetry. In this epic, praise of the noble savage is more than mere imitation of European fashion; and in one of his sonnets, he wrote of the revolt of the Indian Tupac Amaru against the Spaniards and exalted the American hero over the European oppressor. [JF]

*Obras Poéticas*, intr. J. V. de Malto (1920).
Manoel de Souza Pinto, *O Indianismo na Poesia Brasileira* (Coimbra, 1928); Driver, *I B L*.

**Gamboa, Federico** (1864–1939). Mexican novelist. He was greatly influenced by Zola and attained great popularity, particularly with his life of a prostitute, *Santa* (1903). Many of his novels, for instance *Suprema ley* (1896) and *La llaga* (1910), are concerned with the moral dilemmas of the middle classes. He was also a dramatist, his most notable play being *La venganza de la gleba* (1907). [JF]

*Obras completas*, intr. F. Monterde (1965).

**García Calderón, Francisco** (1883–1953). Son of a former President of Peru, he lived mostly in France, where he was in the diplomatic service and acted as an important propagandist for Latin America in Europe. He was a disciple of ◊ Rodó and identified himself with the attitudes of the Latin races. His *Les Démocraties latines de l'Amérique* (1912) was one of the first surveys of Latin America specifically written for people abroad. [JF]

**García Calderón, Ventura** (1886–1959). Peruvian short-story writer. Brother of the above. His most famous collection, *La venganza del cóndor* (1924), was a series of tales of rural Peru. The title story dealt with an Andean Indian's vengeance against an oppressive white man. Despite the fact that the author sees the Indian from the outside, the story does represent a stage in the awakening of Peruvian social consciousness to the plight of the Indian. [JF]

Suárez-Miravel, *L P*.

**García Márquez, Gabriel** (1928–    ). Colombian novelist and short-story writer. He was brought up in a small declining town in a tropical Atlantic region of Colombia, a town that was almost cut off from the rest of the world. The childhood impressions of heat and isolation and their effect on human personality formed the basis of much of his later writing. After studying in Bogotá, he became a journalist. Since 1955, he has lived abroad in Venezuela, Paris, Mexico and Spain. His first novel, *La hojarasca* (1955), told of the death of a doctor in Macondo (where other novels are set). Because of earlier scandals, the priest refuses to allow the doctor to be buried in holy ground. In the conflict that follows, the past history of the town over two decades is evoked. García Márquez next published a brief novel, *El coronel no tiene quien le escriba* (1961), in which he recounts the lonely agony of a retired colonel waiting for a pension which never comes in a small remote town full of hatred and intrigue. He has also published a collection of short stories, *Los funerales de la Mamá Grande* (1962), and *La mala hora* (1962). His work has reached its finest expression in *Cien años de soledad* (1967), a novel in which he relates, with humour and irony, the rise and fall of the town of Macondo and the family of Buendía. Though Macondo is clearly a microcosmic reflection of Colombia and of the whole of Latin America, García Márquez never allows allegory or symbolism to intrude too obviously. *Cien años de soledad* (tr. G. Rabassa, *A Hundred Years of Solitude*, 1970) is one of the best Latin-American novels; it conveys a perpetual sense of wonder at the strangeness of this Continent. [JF]

Cohen, *LA WT*.
Harss, *LN*.

**García Terrés, Jaime** (1924–      ). Mexican poet and critic. His two volumes of poetry, *Las provincias del aire* (1956) and *Los reinos combatientes* (1961), are tightly and sometimes hermetically concentrated. His strength lies in his economy and restraint, and in his powers of generalization, as in the poem 'Este era un rey', from his own experience towards a general statement. Some of his best pieces are developed from travel-notes, taken on Pulteney Bridge at Bath, in Greece or in the Parc Montsouris. He is the most European of contemporary Mexican poets. His prose collection, *La feria de los días*, contains literary and political essays, the latter left-wing in character. [JMC]

*PM*.
Ramón Xirau 'Nuevos poetas de México', in *Poetas de México y España* (Madrid, 1962).

**Garcilaso de la Vega, El Inca** (pseud. of Gómez Suárez de Figueroa) (1539–1616). Peruvian historian. Born in Cuzco, the illegitimate son of an Indian woman and a Spanish captain, Garcilaso de la Vega. In 1560 he went to Spain, where he spent the rest of his life befriended and assisted by relations on his father's side. His last 20 years were spent in Córdoba. His first published work, a translation of the famous *Dialoghi d'amore* by the neo-Platonist León Hebreo, appeared in 1590. In 1605, he published *La Florida del Inca*, an account of the adventures of Hernando de Soto, the discoverer of Florida, which some have seen as one of the first imaginative works to be published from the New World. His *Comentarios reales que tratan del origen de los Incas* appeared in 1609 and a second part with the title *Historia general del Perú* (1617) was published posthumously in 1617. The *Comentarios reales* include valuable accounts of the history, beliefs, customs, laws, astrology, music and medicine of the Incas and of their system of government. The information had been absorbed by the Inca Garcilaso as a child and a young man from his mother and her people. The intention of the work was to show the parallels between Inca civilization and religion and that of Western Christendom. [JF]

*El Inca Garcilaso en sus 'Comentarios', Antología vivida*, intr. J. B. Avalle-Arce (Madrid, 1964); *First Part of the Royal Commentaries of the Yncas*, ed. and tr. C. R. Markham (Hakluyt Society, 2 vols., London, 1869–71); *The Florida of the Inca*, ed. and tr. J. G. and J. J. Varner (Austin, Texas, 1951); *Royal Commentaries of the Inca and General History of Peru*, tr. H. Livermore, intr. A. J. Toynbee (Texas, 1966). J. Fitzmaurice-Kelly, *El Inca Garcilaso de la Vega* (London, 1921); Luis A. Arocena, *El Inca Garcilaso y el humanismo renacentista* (Buenos Aires, 1949).

**Gauchesque.** Poetic style common in 19th-century Argentina and Uruguay. The poets were not gauchos (nomadic cowboys) but city men who were familiar with gaucho dialect through contact with these in war or on ranches. The style was originated by the Uruguayan Bartolomé ◊ Hidalgo (1788–1822), who wrote a number of dialogues in octosyllabic verse in which gauchos commented on contemporary and political and social events. The style was used for political polemic and satire by Hilario ◊ Ascasubi (1807–75) and Estanislao del ◊ Campo (1834–80). In these three poets, there is a mock *naïveté* under cover of which they satirize politics and manners. The genre was transformed by two writers, the Uruguayan Antonio Lussich (1848–1928), whose *Los tres gauchos orientales* portrayed a more authentic and heroic type of gaucho, and José ◊ Hernández (1834–86), author of the masterpiece *Martín Fierro*. It was the publication of *Los tres gauchos orientales* in 1872 which directly stimulated José Hernández to write his poem which raised the gaucho from a mere mouthpiece to a legendary hero figure. [JF]

Poesía gauchesca, intr. J. L. Borges and A. B. Casares (2 vols., Mexico, 1955).

Ricardo Rojas, *La literatura argentina*, i: *Los gauchescos* (2nd edn, Buenos Aires, 1924).

**Gerchunoff, Alberto** (1883–1950). Argentine journalist and novelist. He was born in Russia of Jewish parents. The family emigrated to Argentina in order to escape the pogroms and there settled in a Jewish farming colony in which Gerchunoff grew up. He later left for Buenos Aires, where he educated himself and worked in a variety of occupations before entering journalism. With the help of Roberto ◊ Payró, he joined the staff of *La Nación*, on which he worked for 50 years until his death. His most original work is a novel, or a series of sketches, based on his life in the Jewish colony and called *Los gauchos judíos* (tr. P. de Pereda, *The Jewish Gauchos of the Pampa*, New York, 1955, London, 1959), which appeared in 1910 on the occasion of the centenary of Argentinian independence from Spain. The novel is something of an idyll of rural life and describes the Jews returning to the life of the land from which they had been separated for centuries and their assimilation into the Argentinian nation. [JF]

*DLL.*

**Gil Gilbert, Enrique** (1919–    ). Ecuadorian novelist and short-story writer. One of the Guayaquil group who collaborated on *Los que se van* (1930) (◊ Aguilera Malta). A member of the Communist Party, his work generally has a social message. In the thirties he published two volumes of short stories, *Yunga* (1933) and *Relatos de Emanuel* (1939). In 1940, he received second prize in a North American novel contest for *Nuestro pan* (1942; tr. D. Poore, *Our Daily Bread*, New York, Toronto, 1943), a novel about the workers in the rice fields of the coastal plain. [JF]

Rojas, *NE.*

**Girri, Alberto** (1919–    ). Argentinian poet. The close economy of his form contrasts strikingly with the repressed violence of his content. He presents an inner disorder, fear, and anguish in lines of great compression. *Línea de la vida* (1955) gives a selection from five small books published between 1946 and 1952, in which the poet's style develops away from rhetoric and dream-imagery towards a poetry of essences. Several pieces in its more assured successor, *Examen de nuestra causa* (1956), while still extremely subjective, at the same time reflect the outer world more clearly. 'Epístola a Hieronymus Bosch' is a subtle piece of interpretation, and 'En el puente' states most directly Girri's characteristically agonized awareness of impermanence. Other collections of his poetry include *De playa sola* (1946), *Coronación de la espera* (1947), *Trece poemas* (1949), *El tiempo que destruye* (1950), *Escándalo y soledades* (1952), *La penitencia y el mérito* (1957), *Propiedades de la Magia* (1959), *Elegías italianas* (1962), *El ojo* (1964). A selection of poems from all these was included in his *Poemas elegidos* (1965). Poems not included in this selection are to be found in *La condición necesaria* (1960). [JMC]

**Gonçalves Dias, António** (1823–64). Brazilian romantic poet. Born in Maranhão, he went to Coimbra to study law and there began to write poetry. His *Primeiros Cantos* (1847) were published soon after his return to Brazil and his *Sextilhas de Frei Antão* and his *Segundos Cantos* appeared a year later. He became a teacher in the Colégio de Pedro II and was later sent to the northern provinces of Brazil to report on primary and secondary education there. Between 1854 and 1858, he was in Europe studying educational methods, and it was here in 1857 that he published his *Cantos* and part of his narrative poem, *Os Tambiras*, as well as his *Dicionário de Língua Tupí*, a dictionary of one of the Brazilian Indian languages. Between 1859 and 1861 he took part in an exploratory expedition to the Amazon region but soon after fell ill and went to Europe for treatment. He was drowned on his return in the shipwreck of the *Ville de Boulogne* – a disaster which occurred within sight of Maranhão. Gonçalves Dias is the Brazilian romantic poet *par excellence* and his 'Canção do Exílio' which begins 'Minha terra tem palmeiras / Onde canta o Sabiá' ('My fatherland has palm trees in which the *sabiá* sings') is known to every schoolboy. Many of his best poems are on the pathetic theme of the Indian defeat at the hands of the Portuguese. 'O Canto do Piaga', 'O Canto do Indio', 'Tabira', 'I-Juca-Pirama' all deal with the courage of the Indians and the tragedy of their defeat. This too is the theme of the ambitious narrative poem 'Os Tambiras', of which he published only 4 cantos. It is thought that another 12 cantos may have been lost in the wreck of the *Ville de Boulogne*. The extant portion of the poem relates the struggle between the Timbiras, led by Itajuba, and the Gamellas and includes many passages describing the idyllic life and environment of the Indians. Indian life is compared favourably with that of Europe and the poet laments the evils brought by the white man. The poem is the best of the romantic epics on an Indian theme. In 'A Escrava', Gonçalves Dias also dealt sympathetically with the Negro slave and her longing for the 'doce pais do Congo' (sweet land of the Congo). Apart from these poems, he also wrote on the subject of nature, on the usual romantic themes, and in his 'Sextilhas de Frei Antão' he wrote in old Portuguese. As a young man, he wrote many historical plays (*Boabdil, Patkull, Beatriz Cenci, Leonora de Mendoça, A Noiva de Messina*) and he also translated contemporary European poets, particularly Heine, into Portuguese. [JF]

*Poesia Completa e Prosa Escolhida*, intr. M. Bandeira (1959); *GPRB* (complete poems); Cândido, *PLB*, i.
Driver, *IBL*.

Gonzaga, Tomás Antônio (1744–1810), Brazilian poet. Born in Portugal of Brazilian parents, he lived in Brazil as a child and then took a law degree in Coimbra. When he returned to Brazil, he was sent to Minas Gerais in an official position and here became involved in local society and helped to initiate the 'Arcadia' movement along with Claudio Manuel da ◊ Costa and M. I. da Silva ◊ Alvarenga. Like these two poets, he was involved in the conspiracy against the Portuguese known as the 'Inconfidência Mineira' and as a result, in 1792, he was sent into exile to Mozambique, where he died. His 'Arcadian' pseudonym was Dirceu and his finest poems, *Marília de Dirceu* (3 pts, 1792, 1799, 1812), are written in the pastoral vein and addressed to an ideal beloved, affirming his ideal of a peaceful, uncomplicated life, devoid of anguish and sin. Gonzaga has also been identified as the author of the anonymous *Cartas Chilenas*, poetic satires of Portuguese administration in Minas Gerais. [AA]

*Obras Completas*, ed. Rodrigues Lapa (2 vols., 1957); Cândido, *PLB*, i.

González, Joaquín V. (1863–1923). Argentinian writer. He graduated in law and wrote many legal treatises. His main contribution to literature is *Mis montañas* (1893, intr. G. Ara, 1953), a poetic description of the scenery, life and customs of the mountain region of La Rioja where he was born. [JF]

*Obras completas* (25 vols., 1935–7).

González de Eslava, Fernán (1534?–1601?). Playwright. He was born in Spain but came to Mexico about 1559. He was the author of 16 allegorical plays (*coloquios*), commissioned mostly by the ecclesiastical authorities to celebrate secular and religious events. Despite the allegorical nature of these works, there are realistic characters and scenes and colloquial dialogue. Only a few of his comic, secular plays (*entremeses*) have survived. [JF]

*Coloquios espirituales y sacramentales*, ed. J. R. Garciadueñas (2 vols., 1958).
J. J. Arrom, *El teatro de Hispanoamérica en la época colonial* (Havana, 1956).

González Martínez, Enrique (1871–1952). Mexican poet. He first studied and practised medicine in the Mexican provinces. In 1911 he went to Mexico, where he joined the group of young intellectuals who had founded the Ateneo de la Juventud, where lectures and discussions were held. From then onwards, González Martínez held official posts and worked as a teacher. He also served as Mexican Minister to Argentina and Spain. The title of his first collection, *Silénter* (1909), is indicative of the inner and philosophical nature of his preoccupations. *Los senderos ocultos* (1911) revealed him as a reflective poet of inner contemplation. The collection included the famous 'Tuércele el cuello al cisne' which was regarded as an attack on Modernists (◊ Modernism) and in particular on the less skilful imitators of ◊ Darío. The poet here urges his fellow poets to abandon the search for purely formal perfection in order to concentrate on the deep rhythms of life and on the pursuit of wisdom. His poetry underwent no appreciable change of style up to his last book, *El nuevo narciso* (1952). From 1920 onwards his reputation and influence grew among Mexican poets. Many of his poems, among them 'Hortus conclusus',

'Parábola del huesped sin nombre', 'Un fantasma' etc. are anthology pieces. [JMC]

*Poesía* (3 vols., 1939–40); *Antología* (Buenos Aires, 1943); *La obra*, intr. A. Castro Leal (1951).

**González Prada, Manuel** (1848–1918). Peruvian poet and political thinker. Although a member of the aristocracy and one-time seminary student, González Prada became a vigorous anti-clerical polemicist and defender of the Indians and the poor. A decisive event in his life was the war against Chile, the War of the Pacific (1879–83), during which the Chilean army occupied Lima. As a protest, he locked himself in his house and refused to appear in public. At the end of the war, he led a movement which worked for national regeneration. In the political and social field he fought for the integration of the Indian into national life, the suppression of the power of the clergy and educational reform. In this field he exercised great influence over the founders of the A.P.R.A. party and on Mariátegui, founder of the Peruvian socialist party. He also believed that an authentic Peruvian culture must have its roots in popular culture, the writer should use a natural language and one suited to the time he was living in. A literary circle founded by him as an instrument of national regeneration developed in 1888 into the National Union Party, which, however, disbanded during his long sojourn in Europe. On his return he became head of the National Library, succeeding Ricardo ◊ Palma. It is somewhat of a paradox that his poetry, except for *Baladas*, should reflect so little of his social and political thinking. It is true that he published *Presbiterianas*, a collection of anti-clerical verse, in 1909, but his *Minúsculas* (1901) and *Exóticas* (1911) are both akin to contemporary Modernist poetry in their themes, style and metric innovations. The latter collection betrays a preoccupation with perfection of form and a refined paganism reminiscent of some of Darío's poems. Much of his poetry was published posthumously. *Baladas* (1935) drew its inspiration from European folk poetry, and *Grafitos* (1937) included the lines 'Única moral del Arte: / la perfección de la forma' ('Art's only moral: / formal perfection'). [JF]

Robert G. Mead, *González Prada: el pensador y el prosista* (New York, 1955); Jorge Mañach, Federico de Onís, Arturo Torres-Ríoseco, et al., *Manuel González Prada, Vida y obra bibliografía, antología* (New York, 1938); Suárez-Miravel, *LP*; Sánchez, *LP*, vi.

**González Vera, José Santos** (1897–1970). Chilean writer. He came into prominence in the twenties with *Vidas mínimas* (1923; 3rd edn, 1950) and *Alhué* (1928; 4th edn, 1951), collections of sketches of ordinary people in villages and towns. However, there is nothing of the regionalist writer in González Vera, who is more interested in psychological touches and small telling details. He writes with irony and economy and tends to reduce rather than expand subsequent editions of his work in an attempt to achieve the utmost conciseness. His outstanding work is the autobiographical *Cuando era muchacho* (1951), which presents a fascinating sidelight on Chile and Chileans and is also remarkable for its quiet and disconcerting humour. [JF]

E. Ljungstedt, *Un prosista chileno: José Santos González Vera* (Madrid, 1965); Alegría, *BHNH*.

**Gorostiza, José** (1901–    ). Mexican diplomat and civil servant. He published a book of delicately traditional lyrics, *Canciones para cantar en las barcas* (1925), and one longer poem of remarkable purity, *Muerte sin fin* (1939), which is comparable to the best of Valéry or Jorge Guillén. *Muerte sin fin* is the ultimate expression of nihilism which even denies the possibilities of poetic creation or communication. Man in his solitude sees his own reflection in the water, which is the reflection of 'death without end'. If once men were the reflections of God, now they reflect only a dead deity. Gorostiza searches for possibilities of ecstasy and finds only the fulfilment of a return into nothingness. His sober, almost imageless verse contains great transparency and beauty of modulation. [JMC]

*Poesía* (1964); *PM*.
Ramón Xiran, *Tres poetas de la soledad* (Mexico, 1955).

**Groussac, Paul** (1848–1929). Argentine critic and man of letters. He was born in France and arrived in the Argentine in 1866. He became Professor of Mathematics in the Colegio Nacional and collaborated in the *Revista Argentina*. In 1884, he became editor of *Sud América*. His novel, *Fruto vedado* (1884), was based on his experiences in the Argentine provinces. However, Groussac's most important contribution was less in the field of the novel than in stimulation of Argentine cultural activities in general. He was head of the Biblioteca Nacional, a pioneer historian and became one of the leading figures in Argentine culture. [JF]

*DLL.*

**Guevara, Miguel de** (1585?–1646?). Mexican poet. He was almost certainly the author of the sonnet 'A Cristo crucificado' – 'No me mueve, mi Dios, para quererte' ('Do not move me my God to love thee'), which has been attributed to many, including Loyola. A number of other sonnets by this friar, preserved in manuscript, are hardly inferior and tend to confirm his claim. [JMC]

*Poetas novohispanos, primer siglo,* ed. A. Méndez Plancarte (Mexico, 1942); Cohen, *PBSV*; Trend, *OBSV*.

**Guillén, Nicolás** (1902–    ). Cuban mulatto poet. Born in Camaguey, he studied law in Havana. Here he came into contact with ◊ Afro-Cubanism and his first published volume, *Motivos de son* (1930), was in the Afro-Cuban manner. But unlike other adherents to this movement, Guillén had Negro blood and so penetrated beneath the superficial exploitation of African words and rhythms to give a psychological insight into Negroes and mulattos. Many of these early poems capture in a charming and lyrical manner popular attitudes and speech. *Sóngoro Cosongo* (1931) shows traces of the influence of the Spanish poet Federico García Lorca, who spent a short time in Havana after leaving New York in 1930. The poems of this collection still have predominantly Negro themes, but there is also a strong feeling of sympathy for the poor and humble and a vision of social revolution in the poem 'Llegada'. In the poems of *West Indies Ltd* (1934) there appear the themes of slavery and of colonial exploitation. In 1937 Guillén, who was increasingly left-wing in his sympathies and who was to become a member of the Communist Party, published *España*, a series of poems on the war and on the hope that Communism offered for the future. In *Cantos para soldados y sones para turistas* (1937) and *El son entero* published in 1947 (which included previously unpublished poems) the social themes predominate. Since 1948, when he published *La paloma de vuelo popular: Elegías*, his output has been meagre. His most recent collection is *Tengo* (1964).

Guillén, one of the most successful of Latin-American social poets, has created a genuinely popular poetic flavour. [JF]

Cohen, *PBSV*; *Cuba libre*, ed. Langston Hughes and B. F. Caruthers (Los Angeles, 1948) (translation).
Angel Augier, *Nicolás Guillén* (2nd revised edn, 2 vols., Havana, 1965).

**Guimarães, Afonso Henriquez da Costa** (Alphonsus de Guimaraens) (1870–1921). Brazilian Symbolist poet. He greatly admired the poetry of ◊ Cruz e Sousa, but his own poetry is intensely religious, even mystic in tone. His collections include *Setenário das Dores de Nossa Senhora e Câmara Ardente* (1899), *Dona Mística* (1899), *Kiriale* (1902), *Pauvre Lyre* (1921) and the posthumously published *Pastoral aos Crentes do Amor e da Morte* (1923). [JF]

*Obra completa,* ed. A. de Guimarães Filho (1960); Cândido, *PLB*, ii.

**Guimarães, Bernardo** (1825–84). Brazilian novelist. Author of regionalist novels and of historical and anti-slave novels. His works include *O Ermitão do Muquém* (1869), *Lendas e Romances* (1871), *O Garimpeiro* (1872), *Lendas e Tradições da Província de Minas Gerais*, *O Seminarista* (1872), *O Índio Afonso* (1873), *A Escrava Isaura* (1875), *Maurício ou Os Paulistas em São João d'El Rei* (1877), *A Ilha Maldita* (1879), *O Pão de Ouro* (1979), *Rosaura, a Enjeitada* (1883) and *O Bandido do Rio das Mortes* (1904). He also published poetry and wrote one play, *A Voz do Pajé*, which he published in 1914. [JF]

Basílio de Magalhaes, *Bernardo Guimarães* (Rio de Janeiro, 1926).

**Guimarães Rosa, João** (1908–1967). Brazilian novelist. He was born in Cordisburgo, Minas Gerais, studied medicine and served as a career diplomat, but his deepest involvement was in literature. Though he wrote of his native Minas Gerais and its inhabitants, he cannot be classified solely as a regionalist. His subjects and descriptions are Brazilian, but his works have a more universal application than do those of other North-eastern writers. He does not discuss his topic in purely social terms, but concentrates more on the mythology of the *sertanejo* (inhabitant of the backlands). Guimarães Rosa mastered the mentality of the backlander and his intimate relationship with the land; and in doing so he posed conflicts and situations common to all men. One of his best-known works is *Sagarana* (repr. 1961). It is a collection of short stories dealing with the people, climate, customs and natural environment of the interior. More than other Brazilian writers, Guimarães Rosa utilizes the land not only as a background, but also as a character and a moving force in his stories. The life of the *sertanejo* is so inextricably bound up in and determined by the environment that it is *the* all-pervasive element in backland society. The natural calamities of the *sertão* shape the mentality of its inhabitants and order their mode of existence. He has captured this drama through the psychological emphasis of his stories, through exacting attention to detail and dialogue, and through creation of the authentic language of the interior. The combination of Portuguese and Indian words, the distortion of pure Portuguese and the use of completely new words to define things native to the *sertão* are all part of the *sertanejo*'s language. Even the title of the book expresses the author's linguistic creativity, with its Germanic 'saga' and Tupi ending 'rana'. Some critics feel his language is so difficult as to obscure the actual story, and its complexity poses problems even to Brazilian readers.

Guimarães Rosa does not focus only on natural catastrophes; he feels that there is tragedy, emotion and human interest even in the smallest occurrences. It is in this attitude that the universal qualities of the work transcend the regional. These characteristics are also present in his most ambitious work, the novel *Grande Sertão: Veredas* (1956; tr. J. L. Taylor and H. de Onís, *The Devil to Pay in the Backlands,* New York, 1963). This work takes the form of an uninterrupted monologue of the bandit Riobaldo. As leader of a group of bandits, Riobaldo has been haunted by the need to avenge the death of Joca Ramiro, and to do this he makes a pact with the devil. The bandit is also haunted by his overwhelming affection for Diadorim, a member of the band who dies and is revealed to be a woman, the daughter of Joca Ramiro. The author creates an original literary language, invents words and draws on dialect in order to create a vision of the North-east not in the realist terms of previous writers but in terms of an epic struggle between the forces of good and of evil. In the same year as the publication of *Grande Sertão*, Guimarães Rosa also published *Corpo de Baile,* a 2-volume collection

of stories, which also fuse the regional and the universal. He later published *Primeiras Estórias* (1962; tr. *The Other Side of the River,* London, 1969). [DH]

**Güiraldes, Ricardo** (1886–1927). Argentine novelist and poet. Son of a landowner, he spent his first years in France and the rest of his childhood on a family estate. Later he went to Buenos Aires and from 1910 shared much of his time between the Argentine capital and Paris. He published a volume of poems, *El cencerro de cristal,* in 1915 and a collection of short stories, *Cuentos de muerte y de sangre,* in the same year. He collaborated in many of the *avant garde* journals of the twenties, such as *Proa* and *Martín Fierro.* After *Raucho* (1917), which was partly autobiographical, Güiraldes emerged as a stylist in *Rosaura* (1917), a short novel, and in *Xaimaca* (1923), a novel which centres on a sea journey. His outstanding work is *Don Segundo Sombra* (1926; tr. H. de Onís, New York, 1935, London, 1948), in which he drew on his knowledge of life on the cattle ranches of his country. The novel is much more than a story of gaucho life, for it concerns a boy's growth to maturity through the tutelage of a wise cowhand, Don Segundo Sombra, who is also the incarnation of the pampa and whose wisdom has been culled from the land and from nature. [JF]

*Obras completas* (1962).
Giovanni Previtali, *Ricardo Güiraldes and Don Segundo Sombra* (New York, 1963); G. Ara, *Ricardo Güiraldes* (Buenos Aires, 1961); Alegría, *BHNH.*

**Guirao, Ramón.** ◊ Afro-Cubanism.

**Gutiérrez, Juan María** (1809–78). Argentinian poet, writer and critic. His *Poesías* (1869) were without originality and his best work is a short novel, *El capitán de patricios,* written in 1843 but not published until 1874, telling the idealized love story of an independence patriot. Gutiérrez is also of interest as one of the first critics and historians of Spanish-American literature. [JF]

*Poesías,* intr. R. A. Arrieta (Biblioteca de Clásicos Argentinos, 1945).

**Gutiérrez González, Gregorio** (1826–72). Colombian poet. His early work was in a sober romantic style imitated from Espronceda and Zorilla, but sometimes more intimate in the manner that Bécquer was to develop later. His masterpiece, however, is a 'Georgic', realistic in detail and rich in dialect and Indian words: 'Memoria sobre el cultivo del maíz en Antioquia' (1866; annotated edn ed. R. Jaramillo, 1950). On the humorous pretext that he is preparing an account for a learned body, he describes the cultivation of maize from the first clearing of a plot in the forest to the final cooking of the grain. The poem 'Memoria' idealizes country life though without poetic distortion. More than a curiosity, it is one of the best narrative poems in Spanish-American literature. [JMC]

*DLL.*

**Gutiérrez Nájera, Manuel** (1859–95). Mexican poet and short-story writer. His education in a French school in Mexico helped to inculcate an admiration for French writing, though he never visited France. In 1883 he published *Cuentos frágiles*, which, with ◊ Darío's *Azul*, helped to transform Spanish prose style by introducing a more sensuous vocabulary and more colour. Gutiérrez Nájera was obliged to spend most of his working life as a hack journalist. Nevertheless he was also responsible for founding Mexico's first Modernist literary journal, the *Revista Azul*, in 1894. He wrote many of his pieces and Modernist stories under the pseudonym 'El Duque Job', thus indicating both the aristocracy of the artistic profession and the fact that he was doomed to suffer. His poetry is chiefly remarkable for the use he makes of colour, as in 'De blanco' and for his use of Gallicisms, which, help to convey a light and charming sensuality, as in 'La corregidora'. However he had a more serious side, for he was tormented by his ugly appearance, drank heavily and was beset by religious doubts and a desire for faith. Though not a poet of the first rank, he undoubtedly made a distinc-

tive contribution to the Modernist revolution. (◊ Modernism.) [JF]

*Poesías completas*, intr. F. González Guerrero (2 vols., 1953); *Cuentos completos y otras narraciones*, intr. E. K. Mapes (1958).
Ureña, *BHM*; Boyd G. Carpenter and Joan L. Carpenter, *Manuel Gutiérrez Nájera* (Mexico, 1966); Carlos Gómez del Prado, *Manuel Gutiérrez Nájera. Vida y obra* (Mexico, 1964).

**Guzmán, Martín Luis** (1887–    ). Mexican writer. He studied law and at the outbreak of the Mexican Revolution became a journalist with the forces of the Revolution in the north. He spent many years as an exile after 1914, for as a supporter of Madero he disapproved of many of the Revolutionary leaders. Up to 1934, indeed, he spent many years in New York and Madrid. He was author of one of the early eyewitness accounts of the Revolution, *El águila y la serpiente* (1928; tr. H. de Onis, *The Eagle and the Serpent*, New York, 1930). A semi-fictionalized account of his experiences, it relates his visits to various Revolutionary leaders, including Carranza and Pancho Villa, and his final break with Villa. It is a remarkably vivid account of the character of the leaders and of some of the incidents in the fighting by a man who, though in sympathy with change, could not approve of the barbarism he saw around him. In *La sombra del caudillo* (1929), he turned to the post-Revolutionary society, in which the generals of the Revolutionary period were now struggling for political supremacy. His 4-volume fictionalized chronicle, *Memorias de Pancho Villa* (1938–40), is put into the mouth of the General himself. [JF]

*La novela de la Revolución Mexicana*, ed. A. Castro Leal (1958–60) (includes *El águila y la serpiente* and *La sombra del caudillo*).
J. L. Martínez, *Literatura mexicana siglo xx*, i (Mexico, 1949); A. Magaña Esquivel, *La novela de la revolución* (Mexico, 1964); Brushwood, *MN*.

# H

Henríquez Ureña, Pedro (1884–1946). Dominican writer. With his brother Max (1885–    ), he became an outstanding Hispanic critic and man of letters. He left his native country in 1905 to go to Cuba and thence to Mexico, where he was associated with a group of intellectuals who founded the Ateneo de la Juventud. He studied in Madrid in 1917–20 and after the ending of the Mexican Revolution warmly supported the new cultural and social era which he believed it heralded. In 1924, he went to Buenos Aires, where he remained until he died as a leading member of the Instituto de Filología of the University of Buenos Aires. His lectures on Latin-American culture at Harvard were published in English as *Literary Currents in Hispanic America* (Cambridge, Mass., 1945) and his *Historia de la cultura en la América hispánica* appeared after his death, in 1947. [JF]

*Obra crítica*, intr. J. L. Borges (Mexico, 1960); *Pedro Henríquez Ureña*, intr. E. Sábato, notes by C. and L. A. de Castellanos (Buenos Aires, 1967) (selections).

Heredia, José María (1803–39). Cuban poet. He was permanently exiled from his country in 1823 for having taken part in a revolutionary movement, and lived in the United States for three years and thereafter in Mexico, where he died. Heredia had been educated by his father in classical authors but his poems are romantic and melancholy in spirit. His best-known poems are 'Niágara' and 'En el Teocalli de Cholula', a meditation on a ruined pyramid of the Aztecs in which the poet reflects on the lost glories and on the futility of human pride. [JF]

*Poesías completas* (2 vols., 1940–41); *Antología de la poesía cubana*, ed. J. Lezama Lima, ii. Manuel Pedro González, *José María Heredia, primogénito del romanticismo hispano* (Mexico, 1955).

Hernández, José (1834–86). Argentinian poet. Author of *Martín Fierro*. He was brought up on an estate in the province of Buenos Aires, his early life troubled by the political upheavals of the period. During the civil disturbances that followed the fall of Rosas, he fought on the side of the provinces against the domination of Buenos Aires. He worked as secretary, journalist and government official and in 1869 founded a newspaper, the *Río de la Plata*, in which he campaigned on behalf of the gauchos and in particular against their conscription for service against the Indians. His poem, *Martín Fierro* (repr. 1953), was conceived in Montevideo after reading *Los tres gauchos orientales* by Antonio Lussich. Hernández first thought of writing a protest poem in ◊ gauchesque style, but the poem very quickly outstripped this original idea. The first part (1872) expressed the spirit and way of life of the gaucho. Martín Fierro, a *payador* (gaucho minstrel), sings of his own sufferings first as a conscript and later as an outlaw, and of the lonely life of the boundless pampa. At the end, he falls into a police ambush but successfully defeats his enemies, thanks to the defection to his side of one of the policemen, Cruz, whose sad life has been similar to his own. The two men decide that they cannot live amongst their own people any longer, Martín Fierro ritually breaks his guitar and they go to join the Indians in the desert. The first part of the poem was a huge success among ordinary people, who paid to hear it recited and who learnt it by heart. A second part, *La vuelta de Martín Fierro*, appeared in 1879 and related the death of Cruz, the return of Martín Fierro from captivity among the Indians, and his meeting with his sons, who in turn relate their sad adventures. By 1879, when the second part was published, the nomadic gaucho had already begun to disappear. The pampa was in the process of being divided up into estates. The building of railways drew towns and villages closer together and made life there somewhat less isolated. Thus *Martín Fierro* was in a sense a myth of the past, but as such it has continued to hold the imagination of Argentinians, for the poet conveyed the starkness and desolation of the pampa as well as his nostalgia for a disappearing way of life. [JF]

Borges and Casares, *PG*.
Ezequiel Martínez Estrada, *Muerte y trans-*

*figuración de Martín Fierro* (1948; 2nd edn, 2 vols., Mexico, 1958); J. L. Borges, *El Gaucho Martín Fierro* (London, 1964).

**Hernández Catá, Alfonso** (1885–1940). Short-story writer. Of Spanish father and Cuban mother, he was brought up in Cuba and Spain and became a journalist in Madrid. The first steps in his literary career were guided by the Spanish novelist Benito Pérez Galdós. Though Hernández Catá spent many years in Spain, he never became a Spanish citizen. He served for some time in the Cuban diplomatic corps and was outspoken in attacking the Machado dictatorship. He became a skilful short-story writer, influenced in his first collection, *Cuentos pasionales* (1907), by Maupassant. He was particularly interested in unusual psychological cases, as is revealed by the stories of his best collections, *Los siete pecados* and *Piedras preciosas* (1927). He was killed in an aeroplane accident in Rio de Janeiro bay. [JF]

*Sus mejores cuentos*, intr. E. Barrios (Santiago, Nascimento, 1936).

**Herrera y Reissig, Julio** (1875–1910). Uruguayan poet. Son of a distinguished family which fell into political disgrace, he dedicated himself to literature and carried to an extreme the Modernist belief that art was for a select minority and the artist was a man apart from the masses. He founded the journal *La Revista* in 1899 and organized a literary group, Torre de los Panoramas, so called because they met in the attic of his home. Herrera y Reissig's most characteristic collections, *Los éxtasis de la montaña* (1904–7) and *Los sonetos vascos* (1906), create a pastoral world inspired in the patriarchal communities of the Basque countryside which the poet had never visited. His imagined country is one of great rural simplicity, of villages where time has stood still and peasants carry out their immemorial tasks. Undoubtedly in many respects, this poetry represents an escape from the confusion and uncertainties of modern life, but it is successful as a poetic vision of peace and ordered calm. [JF]

*Poesías completas*, intr. G. de Torre (2nd edn, Buenos Aires, 1945).
Ureña, *BHM*; Brotherston, *SAMP*.

**Hidalgo, Bartolomé** (1788–1822). Poet. The first man to write ◊ gauchesque poetry. He was born of humble parents in Montevideo

and participated in the independence movement. He sold his poetic compositions on the streets of Buenos Aires. His *Diálogos* (1822) are on patriotic themes and are put into the mouths of simple gauchos. He became a Minister, and a Director of the Coliseo theatre, and represented the Uruguayan government in Buenos Aires. [JF]

Borges and Casares, *PG*, i.

**Hojeda, Diego de** (1571?–1615). Peruvian poet. He was born in Spain but went to Peru as a young man. After entering the Dominican order, he rose to become prior of convents in Cuzco and in Huánuco de los Caballeros. He wrote a sacred epic, *La cristiada* (1611; ed. P.T.C.M., 2 vols., 1947), which consists of 12 books relating the life and passion of Jesus Christ. [JMC]

**Hostos, Bonilla Eugenio María de** (1839–1903). Puerto Rican writer and thinker. Although Puerto Rican, he had family ties with Santo Domingo and with Cuba and in fact fought all his life for the unity of the Spanish-speaking Caribbean islands and their independence from Spain. As a young man, he went to Spain to study law and there wrote for newspapers and completed his one novel, *La peregrinación de Bayoán* (1864), a curious work which aptly reflects his own inner struggles. The novel is the story of the hero's restless travels, his love for a Cuban girl and the conflict within himself between his love and the conviction that his country's freedom must be his first goal. When his fiancée dies, he feels intense guilt and yet realizes that he would have been incapable of devoting himself wholeheartedly to her. Hostos was to write no more novels, and in the prologue to a second edition he stated that the pursuit of literature was for the idle and for those who had completed their life's work. Hostos remained in Madrid, where he took part in Republican politics in the period just before the fall of Isabel. He appears as a character in a novel by Galdós, *Prim* – one of the *Episodios nacionales* – but was disillusioned when the Republic did nothing for Cuba and Puerto Rico. He spent much of the rest of his life in New York and travelling in South America. [JF]

*Obras completas* (20 vols., Havana, 1939).
J. Bosch, *Hostos el sembrador* (Havana, 1939); *Eugenio María Hostos: Vida y obra. Bibliografía. Antología* (Hispanic Institute, New York, 1940).

*Huidobro*

**Huidobro, Vicente** (1893–1948). Chilean poet. His first work appeared when he was only 18. In 1913 he founded a review, *Azul*, dedicated to the cause of literary revolution. He was already working towards a poetic theory which he was later to call *creacionismo*, a theory which regarded art not as an imitation of naturally created phenomena but as the creation of new phenomena which the artist thus added to nature. His first declaration of his artistic aims was made in Buenos Aires at a lecture in the Ateneo Hispano, after which he went to Paris and joined the literary groups around the magazines *Sic* and *Nord Sud*, whose editor was Pierre Reverdy and whose master was Guillaume Apollinaire. In 1918 and 1921 Huidobro was in Madrid, where he lectured on *creacionismo*. The exact degree of influence that Huidobro had on the Hispanic *avant garde* is difficult to assess, particularly since most writing on the subject is over-charged with emotion; but he is clearly of importance as a man who put into words the broad aims of the *avant garde* of the twenties (*Manifestes*, Paris, 1925). He was less successful at putting the theory into practice. A volume of *creacionista* poetry, *El espejo de agua*, appeared in 1916, after which he published both in French and in Spanish. These poems are built up in a series of startling metaphors. Following the Futurists, the poet introduces into his poems objects from modern life, such as the aeroplane or the Eiffel Tower. In some he uses typographical devices, thus anticipating Concretism (but probably he derived this from Apollinaire). Besides *Ecuatorial* (1918), *Automne régulier* (1918–22 – in French) and *Tout à coup* (1922–8 – in French), he published an ambitious poem in 7 cantos called *Altazor o el viaje en paracaídas* (1919), which anticipates ◊ Neruda's *Residencia en la tierra* in its imagery of flux and death. He also wrote a number of experimental novels and plays. [JF]

*Poesía y prosa*, intr. A. de Undurraga (Madrid, 1957); *Obras completas* (2 vols., 1964).
H. A. Holmes, *Vicente Huidobro and Creationism* (New York, 1933).

# I

**Ibarbourou, Juana de** (1895– ). Argentinian poetess. Born in the Argentine provincial city of Melo, she moved to Montevideo on her marriage at 18. She has led a contented life as wife, mother and poet, and was named 'Juana de América' in 1929. Her first collection of poems, *Las lenguas de diamante*, was published in 1919, and she has since published continuously up to 1956, when *Oro y tormenta* appeared. She is first and foremost a poet of nature and is completely subjective in her approach. She has also written poems and stories for children. [J F]

*Obras completas*, intr. V. G. Calderón (Madrid, 1953).

**Icaza, Jorge** (1906– ). Ecuadorian novelist. Born in Quito, he worked as a humble civil servant and at the same time acted with the National Theatre. He began writing drama but soon published a collection of stories, *Barro de la sierra* (1933). He had difficulty in publishing his first novel, *Huasipungo* (1934; tr. M. Savill, *Huasipungo*, London, 1962), which has won international renown as one of the most brutally frank accounts of the exploitation and ill-treatment of the Andean Indians. The theme of the story is the expulsion of the Indians from their lands (*huasipungos*), their forcible employment as labourers on the road and the terrible starvation they suffer when they are unable to harvest their own crops. Their revolt against the ill-treatment is ruthlessly suppressed. Though the novel has been translated into many languages and widely acclaimed, its crude realism tends to alienate the reader from the people who should arouse his sympathies. Subsequently Icaza published *Cholos* (1938), a novel about the *mestizo* or half-caste, *Media vida deslumbrados* (1942), *Huairapamushcas* (1948) and *El chulla Romero y Flores* (1958). His *En las calles* published in 1935 was a satirical novel of political life in the city. [J F]

*Obras escogidas*, intr. F. F. Alborz (Mexico, 1961). Rojas, *NE*.

**Inglês de Sousa, Herculano Marcos** (1853–1918). Brazilian novelist. He graduated as a lawyer and later worked as a journalist and university teacher. Influenced by Eça de Queirós and less directly by Émile Zola, he planned a series of novels about the men and the landscape of the Amazon region. His novels fail because they are demonstrations of naturalist theories rather than creative works. Only *O Missionário* (1891; 3rd edn, intr. A. Buarque de Holanda, 1946), which centres on the story of a small town and the surrounding region in the state of Pará, is worthy of serious consideration. His other novels include *O Cacaulista* (1876), *História de um Pescador* (1876), *O Coronel Sangrado* (1877) and *Contos Amazônicos*. [A A]

**Isaacs, Jorge** (1837–95). Colombian poet and novelist. He was of English Jewish origin and his father, after emigrating to Jamaica, later settled in Colombia, where he bought an estate, El Paraíso. His medical studies in Bogotá and London were unfinished because the family lost their money in a civil war. On his return to Colombia, he became a works inspector on a road from Cali to the sea and there wrote most of his literary work. In 1864, he joined a literary circle in Bogotá, El Mosaico, which helped him to publish his poems and later the novel, *María*, on which his fame as a writer rests. He became editor of a moderate conservative paper, *La República*, in 1867, served as Colombian consul in Chile and took part in a civil war in 1876 on the Liberal side. During later life, he explored the Colombian hinterland and studied the Indian tribes. *María* (1867), the best romantic novel of Latin America, is set in the countryside of his childhood. The heroine is an orphan who is given a home by relatives. The son of the house falls in love with her but is made to go abroad to study. In his absence, María, who has been suffering from a fatal illness all along, dies. The attraction of the novel is in its descriptions of nature and the Colombian countryside. [J F]

Mario Carvajal, *Vida y pasión de Jorge Isaacs* (Santiago Ercilla, 1937); Suárez-Murias, *NRH*.

**Itaparica, Frei Manuel de Santa Maria** (1704– after 1768). Poet. Born in Bahia, he became a Franciscan. In 1769, he published in Lisbon a book entitled *Eustáquidos* which included the poem of this title and a shorter poem, 'Descrição da Ilha de Itaparica'. 'Eustáquidos' relates the life of Saint Eustaquio while the 'Descrição' (Cândido, *P L B*, i) attempts to capture the beauty of the Brazilian landscape in language which imitates the dignity and sonority of the classics. [JF]

# J

**Jaimes Freyre, Ricardo** (1868–1933). Bolivian Modernist poet, historian and diplomatist. He spent much of his life abroad, especially in Argentina. In 1894, he helped to found the *Revista de América* with Rubén ♭ Darío. In his best-known collection of poems, *Castalia bárbara* (1899), the poet used Nordic mythology with great effect in order to convey man's sense of loss and alienation. Although critics accuse him of borrowing his Nordic mythology from Wagner and Leconte de Lisle, the imitation is not slavish. The coldness and barrenness of his imagined landscapes are objective correlatives for the states of mind he wishes to evoke. Jaimes Freyre lived in the Argentine town of Tucumán, where he was Professor of Literature, for 20 years. He became an Argentine citizen in 1916, which did not prevent him from joining the Bolivian Republican Party in 1920. In 1921, he became Minister of Education in the Bolivian Government and later served as this country's delegate to the League of Nations and thereafter as Foreign Minister. In 1927, he broke with President Siles of Bolivia and returned to Buenos Aires, where he spent the rest of his life. Despite his social eminence, he was a life-long socialist. Besides being a poet, he was author of a number of works on Tucumán and wrote a treatise on poetic techniques, *Leyes de la versificación castellana.* [JF]

*Poesías completas*, ed. E. J. Colombres (Buenos Aires, 1944) (with biographical study).
E. Carilla, *Ricardo Jaimes Freyre* (Buenos Aires, 1962); Ureña, *BHM*.

**Junqueira Freire, Luis José** (1832–55). Brazilian romantic poet. His poems reflect a tormented and confused spirit. His first publication, *Inspirações do Claustro* (1855), was written after a period in the Benedictine order, which he left without taking final vows. The themes are predominantly religious, although in some of the poems he reveals torment and doubt. His posthumously published *Obras Poéticas* (1867) included a collection aptly named *Contradicções Poéticas* ('Poetical Contradictions'), in which many of the poems are expressive of extreme despair and a longing for death or even madness ('Louca'). He also wrote some poems on national and social themes. [JF]

*Obras*, ed. R. A. Correia (3 vols., 1944); *GPRB*.
H. Pires, *Junqueira Freire, sua vida, sua época, sua obra* (Rio de Janeiro, 1929).

# L

**Landívar, Rafael** (1731–93). Guatemalan poet. A Jesuit who was educated in Mexico. After the expulsion of the Jesuits from the domains of the Spanish crown, Landívar went to Italy where he lived in penury, and wrote in Latin a description of Mexican life, *Rusticatio Mexicana* (1781; intr. O. Valdés, Mexico, 1965), the finest Latin poem written in the New World. Bull-fights, cock-fights, the cultivation of sugar and indigo, gold and silver-mining, and all the birds and beasts of Mexico came under his interested gaze. His poem is not an academic exercise but a living achievement. A verse translation into Spanish was made by the neo-classic poet F. Escobedo (1874–?), a canon of Puebla cathedral. [JMC]

**Larreta, Enrique** (1875–1961). Argentinian novelist. A wealthy man who served as minister plenipotentiary to France in 1910–11 and who often lived abroad. An admirer of Spain and Hispanic culture, he wrote an excellent historical novel, *La gloria de don Ramiro* (1908; tr. *The Glory of Don Ramiro*, New York, 1924). The novel centred on the Moorish communities which survived in Spain during the reign of Philip II and was based on historical research. Its prose style has been greatly admired and reflects the concern for fine writing characteristic of the Modernist period. Larreta was not a prolific writer although he did write several other novels, the most important of which was *Zogoibi* (1926), a love tragedy set among wealthy ranch-owners in Argentina. [JF]

*Obras completas* (2 vols., 1959).
Amado Alonso, *El modernismo en La gloria de don Ramiro* (Buenos Aires, 1942).

**Las Casas, Bartolomé de** (1474–1566). Dominican friar and defender of the Indians. He first went to Santo Domingo and Cuba as a layman. After joining the Dominican order, he was moved by the sufferings of the Indians. His *Brevísima relación de la destrucción de las Indias* (1552; tr. J. Phillips, *The Tears of the Indians*, Stanford, Calif.) was a

moving account of the treatment of the indigenous inhabitants of the New World by the colonizers and was influential in initiating the 'Black Legend' of Spanish colonization. He wrote a *Historia de las Indias* (intr. Lewis Hanke, 3 vols., Mexico), which he began in 1527 and continued almost to the time of his death. Bartolomé de las Casas championed the Indian cause at the celebrated debate in Valladolid (1550–1), when he maintained successfully that the Indians were rational creatures and not natural slaves and should therefore be converted by peaceful means and not bought and sold. It has been pointed out by Las Casas' critics that the decision may have had little practical effect on the treatment of the Indians and actually encouraged the importation of African slaves as substitutes. [JF]

Lewis Hanke, *Bartolomé de las Casas, an Interpretation of his Life and Writings* (The Hague, 1951).

**Latorre, Mariano** (1886–1955). Chilean short-story writer. Of French ancestry, he was born in the south of Chile and early discovered that his European-type education had little to do with the land and the people around him. He observed scenery and types which had never been reflected in literature. After completing his education in Valparaíso and Santiago he worked as a librarian and later became a teacher. His first book of short stories, *Cuentos de Maule* (1912), portrayed fishermen. His *Cuna de cóndores* (1918) was a series of stories with an Andean setting. In other collections, he described other rural types, especially from the south. He was one of the first Chilean short-story writers to be interested in describing the natural landscape. [JF]

*Sus mejores cuentos* (1925; 3rd edn, 1962); *Autobiografía de una vocación* (1956).

**Lêdo Ivo** (1924–    ). Brazilian poet. A member of the generation of 1945 who had his roots in the surrealist movement. His first collection was *As Imaginações* (1944), followed by *Ode e Elegia* (1945), *Ode ao Crepúsculo e Acontecimento do Soneto*

(1948) and *Cântico* (1949). His search for new forms of expression culminates in the appropriately named *Linguagem* ('Language', 1951). This was followed in 1955 by *Um Brasileiro em Paris ou O Rei da Europa*. [AA]

**Leguizamón, Martiniano** (1858–1935). Argentinian novelist and historian. Author of a historical novel, *Montaraz* (1900), of the gaucho warriors who defended Entrerrios against Artigas. He also wrote plays, in one of which, *Calandria* (1896), the hero was a gaucho outlaw. The play is of historical importance, since it marks the beginning of a series of native plays in Argentina. His *Recuerdos de la tierra* (1896) are historical sketches which were important in giving Argentinians a sense of their national past. [JF]

José Torre Revello, *Martiniano Leguizamón, el hombre y su obra* (Paraná, 1939).

**Lezama Lima, José** (1912– ). Cuban poet. He helped to found a number of *avant garde* reviews, notably *Verbum* (1937), *Nadie parecía* (1943) and, most important, *Orígenes* (1944), which helped to revitalize Cuban poetry. Much of his recent poetry draws on the technique of surrealism. In his essays, he has put forward the view that the poet's task is the exploration of the unknown. His major work is the novel *Paradiso* (1966), on which he worked for many years. Written in a highly imaginative poetic prose, it explores the formation of a poet's vision, the significant experiences of his life, his sexual initiations and the exploration of the world of the senses which are later to contribute to his poetic work. The novel is undoubtedly one of the remarkable works of contemporary Spanish-American fiction. [JF]

*Tratados en La Habana* (Santiago de Chile, 1970). Fitts, *APAC*; *PV*.

**Lihn, Enrique** (1929– ). Chilean poet. His third collection, *La pieza oscura* (1963), which included poems written between 1955 and 1962, was a new departure in Spanish-American poetry. Lihn succeeded in presenting states of consciousness in which events of daily life, memories and reflections on the past were part of a dialectic that led to new states of consciousness. He has since published a collection of short stories, *Agua de arroz* (1964), and a collection of

poems, *Poesía de paso, la derrota y otros poemas*, which won the Casa de las Américas poetry prize in Havana in 1966. [JF]

Cohen, *LAWT*; *PV*.

**Lillo, Baldomero** (1867–1923). Chilean short-story writer. Of middle-class family, as an employee of a Chilean mining company he gained first-hand knowledge of the miners and workers who were to figure in most of his short stories. He was influenced by French and Russian realists and particularly by Zola. In 1898, he went to Santiago, took part in working-class movements and worked in the publications department of the University. He published two collections of short stories, *Sub terra* (1904) and *Sub sole* (1907), both predominantly about mines and miners. Lillo has a quality rare among Latin-American writers of the period, for his stories show men doing manual labour, and inhuman conditions are exposed without sentimentality. In the best of the stories (e.g. 'La compuerta numero 12'), the alienation of man in industrial society is powerfully conveyed. [JF]

*Antología*, ed. N. Guzmán (1955).
Fernando Alegría, *Las fronteras del realismo: Literatura chilena del siglo xx* (Santiago, 1962).

**Lima, Alceu Amoroso.** ◊ Alceu Amoroso Lima.

**Lima, Jorge de** (1893–1953). Brazilian poet. Born in the North-eastern state of Alagoas. He attended medical school, first in Bahia and then in Rio de Janeiro, where he published his first volume of poetry, *XIV Alexandrinos* (1914). He continued to practise medicine, first in his native state and then in Rio and even after his appointment to a chair of Brazilian Literature in 1937. In 1935, he became a Catholic, an event marked by the publication of *Tempo e Eternidade* in collaboration with Murilo ◊ Mendes. Although both a painter and a novelist, his reputation rests upon his poetry. His early work still showed the influence of Parnassianism but after the Modern Art Week (1922) he became associated with the Modernist movement (◊ Modernism in Brazil), although, possibly because he had roots in the Northeast, his Modernism had regional characteristics. From this period comes his Afro-Brazilian poetry, of which the best known was *Essa Negra Fuló* (1928), the title poem of which captured the language and rhythm of Negro life. Some poems of this period express protest at the oppression of the Negro. Following his conversion, much of his poetry was written around religious themes, although in *Poemas Negros* (1947) he returned to the themes of his earlier work. His last work, *Invenção de Orfeu* (1952), is believed by some critics to represent the height of his poetic achievement. Through the symbol of Orpheus descending into the underworld, he describes the stages of his own poetic development in relation to the European and American cultures in which he had been formed. Jorge de Lima is also a distinguished translator of works by Bernanos, Claudel and of works in English and German and has written a novel, *Calurga* (2nd edn, 1943). [AA]

*Obra Completa*, i, *Poesias e Ensaios*, ed. A. Coutinho (1958).

**Lins do Rego, José** (1901–57). Brazilian novelist. Born in Parahyba, the son of an aristocratic planter family, he was steeped in the patriarchal atmosphere of the plantation 'big house'. He also experienced an intimate contact between the white plantation owner and the former slaves. His first three works, *Menino do Engenho* (1932), *Doidinho* (1933), *Banguê* (1934), the first novels of a 'Sugar Cane Cycle', trace the heyday and decline of plantation life, and were closely associated in spirit with the Regionalist movement initiated by Gilberto ◊ Freyre. These early novels are dominated by the figure of the head of the family, José Paulino, a powerful estate-owner of the old school, although most of the action is seen through the eyes of his grandson Carlos, who first roves freely over the plantation and among the children of the black labourers and is later sent to school in the city. Two later novels in the cycle, *O Moleque Ricardo* (1934) and *Usina* (1936), centre around the adventures of one of Carlos's boyhood companions, the black boy Ricardo, who goes to seek his fortune in the city, is involved in a strike and is sent to a prison colony. It is he who witnesses the transformation of the old paternalistic system by industrialization and the increased poverty of the former plantation hands that results. In *Pedra Bonita* (1938), the novelist turns to the fanaticism of the inhabitants of the *sertão* (the backlands) and tells a tale reminiscent of Euclydes da ◊ Cunha's *Os Sertões*. Other novels of this period include *Pureza* (1937), *Riacho Doce* (1939) and *Agua-Mãe* (1941). Lins do Rego's masterpiece was *Fogo Morto* (1943; tr. 1944). In it, he returned to his study of plantation life and portrays the decay and disappearance of the old plantation aristocracy. The principal character is a Don Quixote type who combines both the author's respect for the old nobility and his compassion for the poor. *Eurídice* (1947) is a psychological study of a sex-murderer who tries to understand his own problem. *Cangaceiros* (1953) returned to a typical North-eastern theme – that of the bandit. Lins do Rego's first three novels have been translated into English and are published in one volume as *Plantation Boy*. [DH]

*Romances Reunidos e Ilustrados* (1960–61); *Meus Verdes Anos* (1956) (autobiography).
José Aderaldo Castello, *José Lins do Rego: Modernismo e Regionalismo* (São Paulo, 1961); Ellison, *BNN*.

**Lispector, Clarice** (1925–    ). Brazilian novelist. In 1943, she obtained a success with *Perto do Coração Selvagem* (1944). This was followed by *O Lustre* (1946), *A Cidade Sitiada* (1949), *Alguns Contos* (1962), *A Maçã no Escuro* (1961), *A Paixão Segundo G.H.* (1964), *A Legião Estrangeira* (1964) and *Laços de família* (1960). [JF]

**López, Luis Carlos** ('El tuerto López') (1883–1950). Colombian writer. Born in Cartagena. His poems and poetic sketches of provincial life reveal a fine irony. He published *De mi villorio* (1908), *Posturas difíciles* (1909) and *Por el atajo* (1920). The simplicity of his poems and the provincial themes is in sharp contrast to Modernism which was at its height when he began to write. [JF]

*42 Poemas*, intr. C. García-Prada (Mexico, 1943).

**López, Vicente Fidel** (1815–1903). Argentinian historical novelist. As one of the young post-Independence intellectuals he had been forced to go into exile during the Rosas regime. He went to Chile, where he formed part of the group which included ◊ Sarmiento, Alberdi and ◊ Mitre. Here he conceived the idea of the historical novel as a way of guiding future policies through an understanding of the past. He wrote a novel *La novia del hereje o La Inquisición de Lima*, which appeared as a serial in a Chilean newspaper and was published as a book in

Montevideo in 1954 with a long prologue on the historical novel, which he saw as a combination of historical fact which cannot be tampered with and the details of day-to-day life in which the author can use his imagination. *La novia del hereje*, set in Lima, dealt with the struggle between the Inquisition, the State, the Church and the family of a young heroine, María, who had fallen in love with one of Drake's officers. The novel ends happily when María is saved by her lover during the earthquake of 1579. Although he wrote other novels, Vicente López became more important as a historian and educator. [JF]

Suárez-Murias, *NRH*.

**López Albújar, Enrique** (1872–1965). Peruvian mulatto writer and history teacher. He lived in the town of Piura, where he also edited a newspaper and served as a judge. His experiences as a judge formed the basis for his *Cuentos andinos* (1920) and *Nuevos cuentos andinos* (1927), many of which deal with Indians and the injustices committed against them. His novel *Matalaché* (1925) dealt with the daring theme of a love affair between a white woman and a Negro. He also wrote an autobiographical work, *De mi casona* (1924). [JF]

Suárez-Miravel, *LP*.

**López Portillo y Rojas, José** (1850–1923). Mexican writer. He studied law and became a professor of law. He travelled widely in Europe and the East and became governor of Jalisco. Although he wrote in all literary genres and published travel sketches, history and criticism his most important work is the novel *La parcela* (1898), which portrayed rural life in the 19th century. Like many other novels written before the 1920s, the emphasis was on the disorder that resulted from the moral failings of the landowning class. Hence the theme concerns the clash of a good landowner and a bad landowner over a piece of land ('*la parcela*') and the eventual triumph of good over evil. He also wrote *Nieves* (1897) and *Los precursores* (1909). [JF]

*Cuentos completos*, intr. E. Carballo (2 vols., 1952); *Obras* (4 vols., 1898–1909); *La vida al través de la muerte*, intr. L. M. Spell (Mexico, 1964) (with select bibliography).
M. Azuela, 'Cien años de novela mexicana', in *Obras completas*, iii (Mexico, 1960); Brushwood, *MN*.

**López Velarde, Ramón** (1888–1921). Mexican poet. His language was based on colloquial rhythms, and his sentimental irony, though deriving from Laforgue by way of Leopoldo ◊ Lugones, is natural and personal. In his most popular 'Suave patria', a poem addressed to his country, he speaks of himself as singing 'in the style of a tenor who imitates the throaty modulations of the bass'. It is the most realistic and charming of patriotic odes, a series of pictures of Mexico in its daily life and traditional dress.

López Velarde's earliest poetry employs modernistic tricks, which he never entirely abandoned. His off-beat Latinisms and unexpectedly abrupt rhymes are a permanent feature of his style. The poems of his first published book, *La sangre devota* (1916), are provincial and autobiographical. The theme of love is treated with tender sensuality and psychological exactitude. The poet reveals himself as a man divided between the sordid and the unattainable ideal. His sense of sin derives from an uncomplicated and direct faith. In his next book, *Zozobra* (1919), he reaches a higher level. His sensuality is expressed with greater subtlety, and the provinces are now seen in retrospect from the streets of the capital, nostalgically in 'El minuto cobarde' and half-menacingly though still as a lost paradise in 'El retorno maléfico'. His final, uncollected poems, which include 'Suave patria', are in the same tone. A collection of prose-poems and sketches, *El minutero*, which was published posthumously in 1923, contains some pieces that are on the level of his best poetry. [JMC]

*Poesías completas y El minutero* (2nd revised edn, 1957); Cohen, *PBSV*; Paz and Beckett, *AMP*; *PM*.
Elena Molina Ortega, *Ramón López Velarde, estudio biográfico* (Mexico, 1952); Octavio Paz, 'El lenguaje de Ramón López Velarde', in *Las peras del olmo* (Mexico, 1957); Allen W. Phillips, *Ramón López Velarde, el poeta y el prosista* (Mexico, 1962).

**López y Fuentes, Gregorio** (1897–      ). Mexican novelist. Born in Veracruz state. His first important publication was the novel *Campamento* (1931), which described the reactions and conversations of a group of Revolutionary soldiers waiting to go into action. It makes effective use of a mass protagonist. *Tierra* (1933) dealt with the followers of Zapata and the fight for distribution of the land among the peasants. *El* *indio* (1935; tr. A. Brenner, *They That Reap*, London, 1937) won a national prize although it was critical of the fact that life in remote Indian villages had not radically changed after the Revolution. Another novel, *Mi general* (1934), centred on the problem of the military generals who interfered in peace-time politics. *Entresuelo* (1948) was one of the few of his novels to be set in a city, although it again dealt with the humbler classes and with the drift of the peasants from the land. López y Fuentes belongs to a generation of Mexican writers who, while identifying themselves with the aims of the Revolution, have remained critical about the way these aims have been carried out. He also belongs to a generation which made a determined and often successful attempt to penetrate into the psychology of humble people. [JF]

*La novela de la Revolución Mexicana*, ed. M. Esquivel (1964) (includes *Campamento, Tierra, Mi general*). Brushwood, *MN*.

**Loveira, Carlos** (1882–1928). Cuban labour organizer and novelist. Loveira fought in the Cuban liberation expedition in 1898 and afterwards had a variety of jobs, including shop-worker, labourer and interpreter with the U.S. occupation forces. He also worked on the railways and became a labour organizer and founder in 1908 of the Liga Cubana de Empleados de Ferrocarriles (Railway Workers' Union). His first writing was for labour journals. In 1913, because of his labour activities, he left Cuba and lived in Yucatán. In 1916, he toured South America on behalf of the Federación Panamericana de Trabajadores. His first book (1917) was about his experiences as a labour organizer: this was *De los 26 a los 35 lecciones de la experiencia en la lucha obrera*. ('Of the 26 to 35 lessons of experience in the working-class struggle'). On his return to Cuba, he served in the Labour Department of the Ministry of Agriculture. His first novel, *Los inmorales* (1919), was a plea for the introduction of divorce into Cuba. This was followed by *Generales y doctores* (1920; ed. and intr. S. M. Bryant and J. R. Owre, New York, 1965), *Los ciegos* (1922), *La última lección* (1924) and *Juan Criollo* (1927). His two best novels, *Generales y doctores* and *Juan Criollo*, are largely autobiographical. The first goes back to the days before Independence and evokes the Cuba in which he grew up. *Juan Criollo* is a vigor-

ous attack on the corrupt society of post-independence Cuba. [JF]

**Lugones, Leopoldo** (1874–1938). Argentinian poet. A poet of great force and output whose influence on Spanish American poetry was equal to that of Rubén ◊ Darío. In the 1890s, he arrived in Buenos Aires from Córdoba, where he had spent his early years and there formed part of a Modernist circle, became a friend of Rubén Darío and also became well known as a socialist militant. His first work, *Las montañas del oro* (1897), is a grandiose work influenced by Hugo and Whitman. In 1905, there followed an altogether different work, *Los crepúsculos del jardín*, a collection of poems of unequal merit mostly evocative of Samain. *Lunario sentimental* (1909) again bears traces of French influence – this time of Laforgue – but contains some of Lugones' best poetry and was admired by the *avant garde* poets of the twenties. In 1910, there is a marked change with the *Odas seculares*, published to coincide with the centenary of Argentinian Independence. The poems celebrate the 'cattle and the corn', the age-old rustic tasks, in a tone which indicates Lugones' growing sense of nationalism, and his identification of the national with the rural and the traditional which was to turn him from the socialist camp into that of the right wing. Several prose works written at this period are also indicative of this growing nationalism, notably his historical novel *La guerra gaucha* (1905), and his study of the gaucho troubadours, *El payador* (1916), both of which glorify the gaucho in whom Lugones finds incarnated the spirit of the pampa. There followed *El libro fiel* (1912), *El libro de los paisajes* (1917) and *Las horas doradas* (1922) three volumes of poems which reflect the poet's inner life. In common with other poets of this period, Lugones was attracted to the ballad form and wrote a *Romancero* (1924) and *Romances del Río Seco* (1938), published after his death. *Poemas solariegos* (1927) represented a nostalgic return to the scenes of his childhood. There is an elegiac mood about the collection. Lugones also wrote some strange tales (almost science fiction) collected in *Las fuerzas extrañas* (1906) and *Cuentos fatales* (1924). Always a turbulent personality, he was involved in many controversies. In the twenties the younger generation turned against him and when he committed suicide at 63 he was a very bitter man. After his death, however, his genius has increasingly been acknow-ledged and one of the best tributes to him has been paid by Jorge Luis Borges, one of his former critics. [J F]

*Obras poéticas completas* (Madrid, 1952).

Jorge Luis Borges, *Leopoldo Lugones* (Buenos Aires, 2nd edn, 1965) (with bibliography); Carlos Horacio Magis, *La poesía de Leopoldo Lugones* (Mexico, 1960).

**Lynch, Benito** (1885–1951). Argentinian novelist. Member of a well-to-do land-owning family who spent some of his early years on an estate. Of Irish, French and Spanish ancestry, he identified himself in his novels with the creole. His début was made in journalism and his first novel, *Los caranchos de la Florida*, did not appear until 1916. His best novel, *El inglés de los güesos*, deals with the love of a simple country girl with an English anthropologist. As always in Lynch's novels, the civilized European brings conflict and unhappiness into the otherwise simple rustic world. *El romance de un gaucho* (1933) was again the story of a tragic love between a countryman and a sophisticated woman. The best feature of Lynch's work is his skill in portraying country people and in recording their lan-guage. [J F]

Alegría, *BHNH*.

# M

**Magalhães, Domingos José Gonçalves de**
(1811–82). Brazilian romantic poet. He
graduated as a doctor in Rio de Janeiro in
1832 and in the same year published his *Poesias*. He went to Europe (1833–6) and came
into contact with the romantic movement.
His second collection of poetry, *Suspiros
Poéticos e Saudades*, influenced by romanticism, was published in Paris in 1836. On his
return to Brazil, he founded *Niterói – Revista
Brasiliense*, which introduced romanticism
to Brazil and he also helped to initiate a
school of Brazilian drama. He wrote two
tragedies, *Antônio José ou o Poeta e a Inqui-
sição* (1838) and *Oligato* (1839). In addition
t o his literary activities, he took part in politics and became a deputy in 1846. After
teaching at the Colégio de Pedro II, he entered the diplomatic service and served in
various diplomatic posts from 1850 until the
end of his life. He died in Rome. Much of his
work was written while living abroad as a
diplomatist; and to this later period belongs
*A Confederação dos Tamoios* (1856), *Urânia*
(1862), *Cânticos Fúnebres* (1864), *Opúsculos
Históricos e Literários* (1865). He also published books on philosophy and psychology.
Much of his lyric poetry, especially that of
the *Suspiros*, deals with the theme of the
poet's '*saudades*' (nostalgias) for his distant
homeland: 'O terra do Brasil, terra querida'
('O land of Brazil, dear land'). His most
ambitious poem, *A Confederação dos
Tamoios*, is an epic describing the early
struggles between the Tamoios and the
Portuguese, the conversion of the Tamoios
by Padre ◊ Anchieta, and their ultimate
defeat, which was followed by the founding
of Rio de Janeiro. The poem includes all the
major themes of Brazilian romanticism;
nevertheless it was bitterly criticized by
some contemporaries, among them José de
◊ Alencar, as being old-fashioned in its
expression. [JF]

*Obras* (9 vols., 1864–76); Cândido, *PLB*, i;
*GPRB*.
José Aderaldo Castello, *Gonçalves de Magalhães*
(São Paulo, 1946); Driver, *IBL*.

**Mallea, Eduardo** (1903–     ). Argentinian
novelist and essayist. Born in Bahía Blanca,

where his father was a doctor, he studied in
Buenos Aires and began, but did not finish,
legal studies there. After visits to Europe he
became in 1931 editor of the Sunday supplement of the famous Buenos Aires paper *La
Nación* and thereafter devoted his life to
writing. Mallea's first published work was a
collection of stories, *Cuentos para una
inglesa desesperada* (1925), followed by a
10-year silence. In 1936, he published a series
of stories, *La ciudad junto al río inmóvil*,
which centred on the anguish and sense of
isolation of a number of Buenos Aires inhabitants. In these stories, it was clear that
Mallea's main interest was an ethnological
one; subsequent novels and essays were to
explore the essence of Argentina. His essays
include *Conocimiento y expresión de la
Argentina* (1935), *Meditación en la costa*
(1937), *El sayal y la púrpura* (1941) and an
autobiographical essay, *Historia de una
pasión argentina* (1937), which relates his
quest for his own and his country's essence.
*Fiesta en noviembre* (1938) and *La bahia del
silencio* (1930; tr. E. Grummon, *The Bay of
Silence*, New York, 1944), carried his quest
into the novel, the protagonists of which are
transmutations of Mallea. With *Todo verdor
perecerá* (1941; tr. J. Hughes, *All Green
Shall Perish*, London, 1967) and *Las
Aguilas* (1943) the themes were no longer so
closely related to personal experience,
although they still centred on Argentina.
*La Aguilas*, for instance, traced the decline
of a wealthy landowning family. Another
group of novels centres on the nature of
being; these include *El alejamiento* (1945),
*El retorno* (1945), *Los enemigos del alma*
(1950), *Chaves* (1953), *Simbad* (1957) and
*La barca de hiel* (1967). [JF]

*Obras completas*, intr. M. Picón-Salas (2 vols.,
1951).
J. H. Richard, *The Writings of Edward Mallea*
(Berkeley, Cal., 1959); *DLL*.

**Mansilla, Lucio Victorio** (1831–1913).
Argentinian soldier and writer. His father
had belonged to the circle around the dictator Rosas (1830–52), and the family
suffered on the fall of the tyrant. As a young
man, Lucio was exiled from Buenos Aires

as a result of an incident with the poet José ◊ Mármol. He later became a journalist and on his return to Buenos Aires took an active part in politics in support of Adolfo Alsina and served in the war against Paraguay (1855–8). He was made commander on the frontier of the country occupied by the *ranqueles*, a tribe of Indians, and served here in 1858–70. His negotiations with the Indians form the subject of his best-known work, *Una excursión a los indios ranqueles* (1870). This account, which has been compared to Francis Parkman's *Oregon Trail*, is both a precise description of unknown lands and a protest against the treatment of the Indians. Mansilla also wrote *Retratos y recuerdos* (1957–9), an autobiography. [JF]

Enrique Popolizio, *Vida de Lucio V. Mansilla* (Buenos Aires, 1954).

**Marechal, Leopoldo** (1900–1970). Argentinian poet, novelist, essayist and dramatist. Member of the group which contributed to the *avant garde* periodicals of the twenties, *Proa* and *Martín Fierro*. For many years he was a schoolteacher but he held important official positions when the Perón government came into power, being one of a minority of intellectuals who cooperated with Perón. In his youth he was a socialist, but later became a fervent nationalist and Catholic.

*Días como flechas* (1925), his most important early collection of poems, reflects the Ultraist preoccupation for the startling metaphor and a frank enjoyment of the sensual pleasures of existence. Other collections of this period are *Odas para el hombre y la mujer* (1929) and *Cinco poemas australes* (1937). His second period begins with *Laberinto de amor* (1935), poems centring around the poet's inner quest for the eternal. There followed *El Centauro* (1940), *Sonetos a Sophia* (1940), and *Viaje de la primavera* (1945). Critics are now increasingly recognizing the importance of Marechal's novel *Adán Buenosayres* (1948), an ambitious Joycian attempt to write a novel on different planes and at once the story of Buenos Aires and a spiritual quest. He later published *Heptameron* (1966), *El banquete de Severo Arcangelo* (1965) and *Megafon o la guerra* (1970). [JF]

Juan Pinto, *Breviario de literatura argentina contemporánea* (Buenos Aires, 1958).

**Mariátegui, José Carlos** (1895–1930). Peruvian politician and critic. A disciple of ◊ González Prada, he was largely self-educated, but his intellectual and political interests drew him towards a group of young writers and poets, and in 1918 he was awarded a scholarship to Europe by the Leguía government, which hoped to woo him away from his left-wing opinions. In Europe, he came into contact with Marxism, and in 1923 returned to Peru where he became one of the leaders of the left-wing nationalist A.P.R.A. party (Alianza Popular Revolucionaria Americana). He later broke with A.P.R.A. to found the Peruvian Socialist party (a member of the Comintern). In 1926, he founded *Amauta*, one of the most interesting of Peruvian literary magazines. Mariátegui's essay 'El proceso de la literatura' included in his *Siete ensayos de interpretación de la realidad peruana* (1928; 9th edn, 1964) is one of the first attempts at a sociological interpretation of Peruvian literature and is still of value. [JF]

Eugenio Chang Rodríguez, *La literatura política de González Prada, Mariátegui, y Haya de la Torre* (Mexico, 1957).

**Marín, Juan** (1900–63). Chilean novelist and doctor. The most famous of his many novels, *Paralelo 53 Sur*, was begun when he was a ship's doctor with the Chilean navy. In this capacity, he visited the little-known southerly region of Chile, the Magellan Straits, where his novel was to be set. The novel is a history of violence and exploitation amongst the lawless communities of this region whose isolation made it difficult to establish the rule of law. Juan Marín then served in the diplomatic corps and travelled widely. He published *Un avión volaba* (1935), *Naufragio* (short stories, 1939) and *Viento negro* (1944). This last novel was a story of labour unrest and violence among the coalminers and seamen. [JF]

José A. Balseiro, 'Dos novelas chilenas', in *Expresión de Hispanoamérica* (San Juan de Puerto Rico, 1963).

**Mármol, José** (1818–71). Argentinian poet. He wrote his first verses on the walls of the prison in which Rosas had confined him. A romantic in the Spanish manner, he owed something to Byron and a great deal to Byron. His *Cantos del peregrino* (1846), which tell of a sea-voyage along the coasts of South America, are in the manner of *Childe Harold*, though completely undramatic. The poet describes the tropical coasts, speculates on the future of America and the decadence of Europe and rages against the tyrant, Rosas. The poem is like a travel diary, though it includes lyrical outbursts of the imaginary 'pilgrim', Carlos. The mood alternates between the gay and the elegiac. Mármol's *Armonías* (1851–4) contains much scornful invective against Rosas, but also some romantic lyrics. His novel *Amalia*, which he began to publish in Montevideo in 1844 (a second edition with a preface by the author appeared in 1851), was also an attack on the Rosas regime and was set in the 'black year' of 1840, when oppression was at its worst. The story relates a tragic love affair between a young man in hiding from Rosas and the beautiful Amalia. But into the love story there is woven autobiographical material and historical characters and events. There is in fact a certain incongruity between the conventional love tragedy and the horror of dictatorship and secret police which the novel powerfully conveys. [J M C]

Suárez-Murias, *NRH*.

**Marqués, René** (1919–    ). Puerto Rican writer. He has published two important collections of short stories, *Otro día nuestro* (1955) and *En una ciudad llamada San Juan* (1960). The title story of this latter collection is a bitter allegory of Puerto Rican life and concerns a man who murders his wife and then castrates himself. Marqués is probably better known as a dramatist who has helped to vitalize Puerto Rican theatre. Nearly all his plays are indeed related to the Puerto Rican situation. In technique, he is indebted to contemporary North American drama, the influence of O'Neill being apparent in *El sol y los MacDonald* (1957). His best-known play is probably *La carreta* (1953) which is the drama of the Puerto Rican peasant who emigrates to the United States. *La muerte no entrará en palacio* (1957; in *El teatro hispanoamericano contemporáneo,* Mexico) concerns the betrayal of revolutionary ideals and the political theme also dominates *Un niño azul para esa sombra* (1958), the drama of a political rebel. Among his other plays of note is *Los soles truncos* (1958). [J F]

Carlos Solórzano, *Teatro latinoamericano del siglo xx* (Buenos Aires, 1961); Francisco Manrique Cabrera, *Historia de la literatura puertorriqueña* (Río Piedras, 1956).

**Martí, José** (1853–95). Cuban poet, patriot and rebel. Son of a humble Spanish settler in Cuba, he was fortunate in receiving an education at a free school started by an educator, Mendive, who also helped him to go to a secondary school. In 1868, Martí was arrested in an uprising in Cuba and sentenced, at 16, to six years' forced labour after a compromising letter of his had been found. His one year as a convict inspired his lifelong fight for independence. On release, he was sent into exile to Spain, which permitted him to continue his studies. His adult life was devoted to journalistic activity and work on behalf of Cuban independence, first in Mexico, and later in New York and Venezuela. In 1878, an amnesty permitted him to return briefly to Cuba but he was again deported to Spain. In Venezuela, where he lived for a short time (1877–80), he founded the *Revista Venezolana*. From 1881 to 1895 he was in New York, which he left to take part in a military expedition to Cuba in which he was killed. Martí's poetry, like his political beliefs, stemmed from faith in the ordinary man. His theory of poetry was similar to that of Wordsworth and he was also influenced by the ideas of Emerson. His first collection was *Ismaelillo* (1882), a series of charming poems addressed to his son. *Versos libres*, written shortly afterwards, was published after his death. *Versos sencillos* appeared in 1891. Although often regarded as a precursor of Modernism, Martí's vigorous and direct verse had no contemporary imitators. His poetic innovations were, nevertheless, far-reaching. A good example is his 'Sueño con claustros de mármol' (in *Versos sencillos*) in which the free verse and abrupt caesura convey the effect of agitation and nightmare. His articles and letters are as interesting as his poetry. Indeed some critics believe that he was an even greater innovator in prose-writing than in poetry. Stylistically his prose is fresh, free from cliché. Perhaps more remarkable than the style, they reveal a man who stood head and shoulders above most of his contemporaries. His articles on American identity, on its literature and race problems looked far to the future and are often remarkably prophetic. [J F]

*Obras completas* (27 vols., 1954).

J. Marinello, *José Martí, escritor americano: Martí y el modernismo* (Mexico, 1958); Ivan A. Schulman, *Símbolo y color en la obra de José Martí* (Madrid, 1960).

**Martínez, Luis** (1869–1909). Ecuadorian writer. He was active in politics as a Liberal and became Minister of Education. Earlier he had spent some years farming in the coastal region of Ecuador, where he wrote on agriculture and tried to put new ideas into practice. He believed that his countrymen should turn their attention to practical matters, a conviction which is reflected in his one novel, *A la costa* (1904; 2nd edn, intr. M. J. Calle, 1906). This polemical novel is something of a pioneer work in Ecuadorian literature, since it contrasts the parasitic society of Quito with the more productive and satisfying life of the farmers. It also attacks the clergy, a favourite target in the years following the domination of the fanatically religious dictator García Moreno. Through the person of the hero, a disappointed law student who is never able to complete his studies, Martínez shows the weaknesses of a society in which neither education nor social attitudes fit the reality of life in the hostile Ecuadorian environment. Only by changing education and attitudes, Martínez suggests, will Ecuador progress. [JF]

**Martínez Estrada, Ezequiel** (1895–1964). Argentinian poet and essayist. His very civilized and allusive poetry is ironic, at times humorous, and generally detached. It marked a reaction from the fervid violence and popularism of ◊ Lugones, but lacks feeling and is undistinguishedly conventional in form. His pessimistic study of the condition of his country, *Radiografía de la Pampa* (1933), has, by contrast, a baroque magnificence of language and a morbidly prophetic justice in its even-handed condemnation of the ruling oligarchs and the restlessly protesting masses. It is one of the great achievements of Spanish American prose, comparable in importance to ◊ Sarmiento's presentation of the Argentinian myth in *Facundo*. The rapidity of his survey and his gift for phrase and metaphor make the book more poetic than his poetry. Though pitiless and at times subjective in its pessimism, it was not only just in its analyses but accurately prophetic of the Perón era and the epoch of popular irresponsibility that has followed. Martínez Estrada wrote both plays and novels, which are marred by his subjective preoccupations with disaster. His literary criticism, on the other hand, with its wide political extension, has an individual quality, in particular *Muerte y transfiguración de Martín Fierro* (1948). [JMC]

**Matos Guerra, Gregório de** (1633–96). Brazilian poet. Born in Bahia, he studied law in Coimbra and lived in Lisbon before leaving for Brazil. In Bahia, he lived a disorderly life and though he became Treasurer of the Cathedral his satirical tongue soon lost him the post. Known to his contemporaries as the Boca do Inferno (Mouth of Hell), he was a pitiless critic of society, his targets being corruption and injustice. For a time he was exiled to Angola, but he returned to Brazil in 1695 and died in Recife in the following year. Apart from satirical verse, he wrote lyric poetry in praise of sensual love, and in some poems idealized woman. Towards the end of his life, he was increasingly aware of the contrast between the pleasure of the senses and divine love. Study of Gregório de Matos's poetry has been difficult because his work circulated in manuscript. No copy in his own hand has been discovered and attribution of poems presents difficulty. They were little known until some of his verses appeared in an anthology compiled by Januário da Cunha Barbosa in 1829. His satirical poems were published in 1881 and the rest of his poetry in 1923 and 1933 in uncritical editions. His complete works have recently been published. [JF]

*Obras*, ed. A. Peixoto (5 vols., 1923–33); Cândido, *PLB*, i.
S. Spina, *Gregório de Matos* (São Paulo, 1945).

**Matto de Turner, Clorinda** (1854–1909). Peruvian novelist. She was the author of one of the first novels to deal sympathetically with the plight of the modern Indian. Influenced by the teaching of Manuel ◊ González Prada, to whom it was dedicated, *Aves sin nido* (1889; tr. C. J. Thynne, *Birds without a Nest: A Story of Indian Life and Priestly Oppression in Peru*, London, 1904) is the story of a remote village in which the Indians are exploited by the triumvirate of church, judge and landowner. A white couple from Lima attempt to befriend the orphans of a murdered Indian couple and bring up the daughter Margarita to be an educated young lady. She falls in love with the governor's son only to learn at the end of the novel that he is her half-brother, both of them being the offspring of a lascivious priest. The anti-clerical bias of the novel is characteristic of the liberal writers of this period. Despite the melodramatic plot, the novel is of interest as a picture of life in the remoter villages of Peru and as a reflection of early humanitarian attitudes. [JF]

Manzoni, *INA*.

**Maya, Rafael** (1897–    ). Colombian poet and teacher. He has written for many Colombian periodicals. Much of his early poetry is written in a Whitman-like *vers libre*, yet without violences of language. Though sensitive to the predominant French influences, and distinguished by a classical and hellenistic style, he has read and appreciated the great Spanish poets. His collections include *La vida en la sombra* (1925), *Coros de mediodía* (1928) and *Después del silencio* (1938), but his finest work is *Navegación nocturna* (1959), a self-analysis in which he faces the solitude of man but rejoices in the contemplation of the world which he re-creates from his memories. He detects the presence of God in the order of the Universe and calls up an outward vision to counterbalance inward desolation. [JMC]

*DLL.*

**Maya Literature.** The surviving Maya texts were written down after the Conquest in the native languages but in Latin script. In Yucatán, several chronicles were preserved, some books on Indian medicine and a series of texts known under the general title of the Books of Chilam Balam (ed. A. M. Bolio, Mexico, 1941; tr. R. L. Roys, Washington, 1933); 18 such books survive, and only 4 have been studied and translated, the best-known being *El libro de Chilam Balam de Chumayel*. In Guatemala, several texts in the Quiché and Cakchiquel languages have survived; but the most notable Guatemalan Maya text, the *Popul Vuh* (ed. A. Recinos, Mexico, 2nd edn, 1953; tr. D. Goetz and S. G. Morley, London, 1951), survives only in the transcription and Spanish translation made by Padre Ximénez in the 18th century, the Quiché manuscript compiled some time after the Conquest from which Ximénez copied his document having now disappeared. The same fate attended the original Quiché text of the *Título de los señores de Totonicapán*, for which only a Spanish translation of *c.*1835 by a priest remains. A Maya drama, *Rabinal Achí* (ed. F.Monterde, Mexico, 1955), has also been written down, thanks to the efforts of the abbot Brasseur de Bourbourg. Like the surviving literature in ◊ Náhuatl, Maya literature, consisting of creation myths, legends, histories and hymns, is religious in character. [JF]

Miguel León-Portilla, *Las literaturas precolumbinas de México* (Mexico, 1964).

**Meireles, Cecília** (1901–64). Brazilian poet. She was an orphan and unhappily married, which perhaps helps to account for the sense of isolation repeatedly expressed in her poetry. Apart from writing poetry, she was a university teacher and took an active interest in Brazilian folklore. Her first book of poetry, *Espectros*, was published in 1919 when she was 18. This was followed by *Nunca mais e Poemas dos Poemas* (1923) and *Baladas para El Rei* (1925). She later rejected this early work and did not include it in her collected editions, believing that her poetry really began with *Viagem* (1939), a collection in which space, solitude and the sea are the main elements. But behind these elements is the poet's search for an elusive identity expressed in a fluid verse form. The poet Amadeu Amaral declared of *Nunca mais e Poemas dos Poemas* that the apparent simplicity concealed a deep, elemental emotion and her later poetry has confirmed the opinion of critics who see her as one of the great poets of modern Brazil. Her more recent collections include *Vaga Música* (1942); *Mar Absoluto* (1945); *Retrato Natural* (1949); *Amor em Leonoreta* and *Doze Noturnos na Holanda* (1952); *Romanceiro da Inconfidência* (1953); *Poemas Escritos na India* (1953); *Pequeno Oratório de Santa Clara* (1955); *Pistóia, Cemitério Militar Brasileiro* (1955); *Canções* (1956); *Giroflê* (1956); and *Romance de Santa Cecília* (1957). She also wrote many essays and works of criticism, among them *Metal Rosicler* (1960) and *Escolha o seu sonho* (1964), a series of reflections on contemporary life. She has also written plays, of which the most important is *O menino atrasado, auto de Natal* which influenced the *Vida e Morte Severina* of João ◊ Cabral de Melo Neto. [AA]

*Obra Poética* (1958); *Antologia Poética* (1963); Nist, *MBP*.

**Melgar, Mariano** (1791–1815). Peruvian poet. Of mixed blood, he abandoned the seminary after training for the priesthood to take part in the struggles which led to the independence of Peru. He did not live to see independence, for he was caught after a defeated insurrection in 1814 and executed on the battlefield at Umachiri. Despite his early death and his classical training (he translated Ovid and Virgil), Melgar was an initiator who introduced into Peruvian poetry several new styles and themes. He was the first Peruvian poet to write with great frankness on amatory themes. He introduced the fable into Peruvian poetry as a way of criticizing society and its abuses, e.g. 'El cantero y el asno', in which the poor ass which is starved and beaten is the spokesman for the Indian. He was also the first to adapt the *yaraví*, a Quechua verse form, to Spanish poetry. Though his adaptations are not good, he set a precedent which was not really pursued until more recent times. [JF]

Sánchez, *LP*, v.

**Mendes, Murilo** (1902– ). Brazilian poet. Born in the province of Minas. From 1920, he worked in a variety of jobs in Rio. From 1953, he has lived abroad as a teacher of Brazilian literature. The death of his friend, the artist Ismael Nery, in 1934 helped to bring about his conversion to Catholicism and in 1935 he published *Tempo e Eternidade* in collaboration with Jorge de Lima. He became famous with his first collection, *Poemas* (1930); subsequent collections included *A Poesia em Pânico* (1938), *O Visionário* (1941), *As Metamorfoses* (1944), *Mundo Enigma* (1945), *Poesia Liberdade* (1947) and *Contemplação de Ouro Prêto* (1954). Though his early work was experimental and humorous in the manner of the *avant garde*, the influence of surrealism was also apparent. After his conversion to Catholicism, religious preoccupations were expressed through surrealistic techniques. [AA]

*Poesias* (1959); Cândido, *PLB*, iii.

**Mera, Juan León** (1832–94). Ecuadorian writer. He was born and died in Ambato, came from a poor family, was self-educated and at first earned his living as a painter. He later became a political journalist, folklorist and editor of an official newspaper. He rose to become Governor of a province, Deputy, President of the Senate and a Minister. He was one of the first historians of Ecuadorian literature and the first Ecuadorian to use indigenous themes in poetry and the novel. His work includes a collection of legends, *Mazorra* (1875), a legend in verse, *La virgen del sol* (1861), and his most important work, *Cumandú o Un drama entre salvajes* (1879). This novel is an interesting example of the 'noble savage' theme transposed to an American setting. It deals with the story of an elder of an Indian tribe married to a young girl who is doomed to be buried with

him on his death. Instead she runs away to a Christian settlement, where she is baptized and adopted. The novel also represents a pioneer attempt to describe the jungle. [JF]

Concha Meléndez, *La novela indianista en Hispanoamérica* (*1832–1889*) (Madrid, 1934); Rojas, *NE*.

**Miró, Ricardo** (1883–1940). The Panamanian national poet. He was born at a period when Panama was still under Colombian rule and he worked for its independence. In 1903, Panama was declared an independent republic and from then on Miró dedicated himself to journalism and literature. In 1904, he founded the newspaper *El Heraldo del Istmo* and published his first poem in it. In 1908, he published a collection of poems, *Preludios*, followed in 1916 by *Los segundos preludios* and in 1929 by *Caminos silenciosos*. Through his poetry he can be said to have contributed to forming a sense of Panamanian nationality. [JF]

Rodrigo Miró, 'La literatura panameña de la república', in *Panorama das Literaturas das Américas*, iii.

**Mistral, Gabriela** (Lucila Godoy Alacayaga) (1889–1957). Chilean poet. Nobel Prize winner for 1945. She was the daughter of a schoolmaster and herself taught for many years in rural and secondary schools. She became headmistress of an important Santiago school. The suicide of her fiancé for personal reasons which had nothing to do with Gabriela had a profound effect and inspired her early poetry. In 1914, she received first prize in the Juegos Florales in Santiago for her 'Sonetos de la muerte'. The collection *Desolación* (1922) centred on the themes of suffering, frustrated motherhood, on nature and on religious experience. *Ternura* (1924) continues the line of *Desolación*, but in its later editions contains some charming songs for children. *Tala* (1938) has religious overtones. A final collection, *Lagar*, appeared in 1954. She travelled widely, and at one point filled a post with the League of Nations. She was made an honorary consul by the Chilean government with power to open a consulate wherever she might settle. She spent many of her later years in Italy and France. Much of her prose-writing remains unpublished. [JMC]

*Poesías completas* (Madrid, 1958); Fitts, *APAC*; *Some Spanish-American Poets*, tr. A. S. Blackwell (New York, London, 1929; 2nd edn, Philadelphia, London, 1937).

Fernando Alegría, *Genio y figura de Gabriela Mistral* (Buenos Aires, 1966) (with anthology and short bibliography); Margot Arce de Vázquez, *Gabriela Mistral: The Poet and Her Work* (New York, 1964).

**Mitre, Bartolomé** (1821–1906). Argentinian soldier, politician and writer. His youthful *Rimas*, on native themes, were published in 1854. Like many of his generation, he believed that the novel could help nationalism by presenting in an exciting form the major events of the country's history. He set out his ideas on the historical novel in the preface to *Soledad* (1847), which told the story of the wars of independence by interweaving historical events with a love story. Mitre played an active part in the political events of his country and served as President of the Republic. [JF]

*DLL.*

**Modernism.** A term first applied to Hispanic literature by the poet Rubén ◊ Darío and adopted to describe a movement of innovations in prose and poetry which originated in Spanish America and spread to Spain. The innovations were partly stylistic in that greater flexibility was introduced into poetry with the use of new metres, rhythms and line lengths and the poetic vocabulary was widened, especially through the influence of French poetry. At a deeper level, Modernism represented a radical departure from existing attitudes to poetry in Spain and Spanish America. The poem came to be regarded as an artefact and the experience of poetry akin to religious experience. Most Modernist poets regarded themselves as standing apart from society, which belonged to the world of flux, in contradistinction to true values which they felt to be eternal. Hence the attempt of many Modernist poets, e.g. Julián del ◊ Casal, Darío, ◊ Jaimes Freyre, to use symbols and vocabulary divorced from local and temporal associations. Some critics, notably Juan Ramón Jiménez and Federico de Onís, have claimed that Modernism represents a basic shift in sensibility comparable to that of Romanticism in Modern Europe. [JF]

*Antología de la poesía española e hispanoamericana (1882–1932)*, ed. Federico de Onís (Madrid, (1934); Brotherston, *SAMP*.
Ricardo Gullón, *Direcciones del modernismo* (Madrid 1963); Ureña, *BHM*; I. A. Schulman and Manuel Pedro González, *Martí, Darío y el modernismo* (Madrid, 1969); Franco, *MCLA*.

**Modernism in Brazil.** This movement has no connexion with Hispanic Modernism, although it also represents a movement of regeneration in the arts. It was initiated largely by the activities of a group of young writers and painters, notably the critic and poet Oswald de ◊ Andrade and the painter Anita Malfatti. The former called for a modern art which would match the modern city of São Paulo and deplored the identification of the writer with the backward country-dwellers. The main foreign influence on the movement was Futurism. In 1922, Modernism became widely known through the organization of a Modern Art Week in São Paulo, in which the works of revolutionary young painters and sculptors were exhibited. These showed two of the characteristic streams of Modernism – its identification with the European *avant garde* and at the same time a back-to-the-roots primitivism. There was also the conscious feeling that São Paulo, an ultra-modern city, ought to outstrip Europe not only in its architecture and way of life but also in its literature and painting. Many of the first literary productions were iconoclastic, the most revolutionary writers of the early twenties being Mário de ◊ Andrade and Oswald de ◊ Andrade. Modernism was never a school, but the Modern Art Week was the starting point for a period of intense literary and artistic activity in Brazil during which many little magazines, e.g. *Pau Brasil, Verde-Amarêlo* and *Festa*, were founded, and led ultimately to the absorption of new techniques and the rise of a generation of poets of genuine talent and originality such as Manuel ◊ Bandeira, Carlos ◊ Drummond de Andrade and Cecília ◊ Meireles. [JF]

Mário da Silva Brito, *História do Modernismo Brasileiro* (São Paulo, 1958); John Nist, *The Modernist Movement in Brasil* (Austin, Texas London, 1967); Franco, *MCLA*.

**Montalvo, Juan** (1833–89). Ecuadorian polemicist. His youth was spent as a diplomatist in Paris. On his return to Ecuador at 27 he became the dictator García Moreno's bitter opponent and spokesman for the liberal cause. In 1855, he founded *El Cosmopolita*, a political and literary journal of short duration but very influential. He was forced to leave the country, but even after the tyrant's death in 1875 he was still in opposition to the authorities and was condemned to permanent exile. His

*Catilinarias* (polemical essays) were published in Panama in 1880, but his last years were spent in Paris, where he founded the paper *El Espectador* (1886–8). His *Siete tratados* (written *c*. 1873, published in France, 1882), his main work, is a series of moral essays in which readings from his favourite authors are applied to political situations. Their aim was to provide humanist moral standards and ideals for Spanish Americans. *Capitulos que se le olvidaron a Cervantes* (1895), though apparently an imitation of Cervantes, also included characteristic disquisitions in which his old enemies, the tyrant García Moreno and the dictator Veintemilla, are attacked. [J F]

*Juan Montalvo*, ed. and intr. Gonzalo Zaldumbide (Mexico, 1959) (anthology).
Enrique Anderson Imbert, *El arte de la prosa en Juan Montalvo* (Mexico, 1948).

**Monteforte Toledo, Mario** (1911–   ). Guatemalan novelist and scholar. He studied at the Sorbonne and later graduated as a lawyer. He has also done research work in sociology and written a study of Guatemala, *Guatemala, Monografía sociológica* (1959). Many of his novels are concerned with Indian life in Guatemala. *Anaité* (1948) was set in the Petén, in the northern jungle region of Guatemala, and was about man's struggle with nature. *Entre la piedra y la cruz* (1948) concerns an educated Indian's conflict between two cultures. There followed another novel of Indian life, *Donde acaban los caminos* (1953), and a political novel, *Una manera de morir* (1957). [J F]

Menton, *HCNG*.

**Monteiro Lobato, José Bento** (1882–1948). Brazilian writer. He was reared in the coffee-growing atmosphere of his native São Paulo. He was a plantation owner himself for a while, and often during his career as publisher, author, translator, business entrepreneur and conscientious critic of Brazilian politics and society he longed to return to rural life. He was an admirer of new ideas and of such differing figures as the Fords, the Rockefellers and Brazil's social reformer Luís Carlos Prestes. He was gaoled and exiled for his outspoken criticism of political dictatorship and corruption. Intolerant of social injustice as well, he was one of the first to recognize that the core of Brazilian nationality lay in the scorned *caboclo*, or hillbilly. He realized that the backlander's characteristic lethargy and ignorance were due more to lack of health and educational facilities than to qualities inherent in the lower classes.

In *Urupês* (1918), a collection of brief sketches on the prototype *caboclo* Jeca Tatú, the author anticipates and influences later Brazilian themes. His approach is new because it is sympathetic to Jeca, his attitudes and customs, but it also deals with his faults and does not idealize him. The author considers the existence of the rural poor to be Brazil's national sin. He feels that society has abdicated its responsibility toward the *sertanejo* (inhabitant of the North-eastern *sertão*) and says that the upper classes in their superficial way of life carry Jeca's physical illnesses in their souls. In focusing national attention on the forgotten mestizo of the interior, the author awoke a storm of controversy and has inspired much regionalist literature.

Monteiro Lobato is also known for his delightful children's stories, which comprise 17 volumes. Of his essays, one of the best known is *Ideias de Jeca Tatú* (1919), which expresses alarm over and disgust at foreign literary influence in Brazil. Though the author also reacts strongly against artificial language, he uses elaborate phrases where the rude hillbilly would have spoken more simply. After *Urupês*, his other collections include *Cidades Mortas* (1919), *Negrinha* (1920), *A Onda Verde* (1921). [D H]

*Obras Completas* (2 vols., 1946).
Edgard Cavalheiro, *Monteiro Lobato, Vida e Obra* (2 vols., São Paulo, 1955).

**Montes de Oca, Marco Antonio** (1932–   ). Mexican poet. Of considerable vigour and violence of imagery, he has not yet developed an adequate sense of form. Under the influence of Octavio ◊ Paz, he submitted himself to the licences of surrealism. The abundance and harshness of the Mexican landscape provides a variety of pictures far richer than those of the Paris school, and the poet's growing preoccupation with Mexican themes offers him a possible way out of the surrealist impasse. [J M C]

*Delante de la luz cantan los pájaros* (1959); *Cantos al sol que no se alcanza* (1961); *Fundación del entusiasmo* (1963); *La parcela en el Edén* (1964); *Vendimia del juglar* (1965); *Pedir el fuego* (1969); Cohen, *LAWT*; *PM*; *Triquarterly*, Fall/Winter, 1968/9 (translations).

**Moock, Armando** (1894–1942). Chilean playwright. His first play, *Crisis económica* (1914), aroused little interest, but he was to become very popular both in his own country and in Buenos Aires, in which city many of his plays were to be produced, notably *La serpiente* (1920). He was a prolific writer of light comedies with wholesome endings. [JF]

*DLL.*

**Moraes, Vinícius de** (1913–    ). Brazilian poet. He showed an early interest in the cinema and worked for a time as a film critic before entering the diplomatic corps. His play *Orfeu da Conceição* (1956) was adapted for the cinema as *Black Orpheus*. His early collections, *O Caminho para a Distância* (1933), *Forma e Exegese* (1935), *Ariana, a Mulher* (1936) and *Novos Poemas* (1938), seem to have been influenced by French Catholic poets. But from *Cinco Elegias* (1943, but written in 1938), his verse showed an increased intensity and a widening of the field of interest. *Poemas, Sonetos e Baladas* (1946) is one of his best collections. He later achieved great popular fame with his lyrics for the 'bossa nova'. The third edition of his *Antologia Poética* (1963) included poems from *Livro de Sonetos* (1957) and *Novos Poemas II* (1959). [AA]

Cândido, *PLB*, iii; Cohen, *LAWT*; Nist, *MBP*.

Octavio de Faria, *Dois Poetas – Augusto Frederico Schmidt e Vinícius de Moraes* (Rio de Janeiro, 1935).

**Moro, César** (pseud. of César Quispes Asiú) (1903–56). Peruvian surrealist poet. He lived and worked for much of his life in Paris and wrote a great deal of poetry in French. In Spanish, he published *La tortuga ecuestre*. [JF]

*Prosas reunidas*, ed. André Coyné (1958); *PV*.

**Motilinía.** ◊ Benavente, Fray Toribio de.

**Murena, H. A.** (pseud. of Hector Alberto Álvarez) (1923–    ). Argentinian novelist and essayist. He continues the pessimistic tradition of ◊ Mallea and ◊ Martínez Estrada. His trilogy, *Historia de un día* (1955–    ), and his book of short stories, *El centro del infierno* (1956), carry realism to the verge of horrified fantasy. Accepted as a spokesman for his generation, in 1954 he published a book of essays on the theme of his continent, *El pecado original de América*. In his own words it is 'a kind of mental autobiography'. A self-educated man, disgusted with his uncultured surroundings, he cries for 'the entry of America into the world of humanity'. [JMC]

# N

**Náhuatl Literature.** Creation myths, religious poems, hymns and dramatic songs in the language spoken by the Aztecs and other peoples of central Mexico. Little is known of the origin of Nahua culture but it has been shown that it goes back to the time before the Aztec empire. The extant literature mostly comes from documents written down after the Conquest, the most important of such compilations being that made by the Franciscan Fray Bernardino de ◊ Sahagún. He used a team of assistants to collect and record in the Náhuatl language traditions, proverbs, hymns and all aspects of Aztec religious belief. The original compilation occupied 12 volumes and formed the basis for Sahagún's *Historia general de las cosas de la Nueva España*, a summary and a commentary on this Náhuatl material. The immense compilation in the Indian language has not yet been completely translated and it has proved already a mine of information for students of pre-Columbian culture. Sahagún's work was continued by several of his pupils who transcribed the *Colección de cantares mexicanos* and the *Manuscrito de los romances de la Nueva España*. Another friar, Andrés de Olmos, also collected ceremonial speeches in Náhuatl. From these varied sources, it has been possible to study something of the remarkable pre-Columbian literary tradition both in poetry and in prose. Náhuatl poetry can be divided into a number of categories – creation myths, sacred hymns addressed to the Gods, war songs, lyric poems on the subject of friendship, death and the ephemeral nature of life. The writing of poetry had an important place in pre-Columbian society and its technique and symbolism are highly developed. Pioneer work on this subject and Spanish translations of poems have been made by the Mexican scholar Angel M. Garibay, and some of the poems have been translated by Irene Nicholson in her study *Firefly in the Night* (London, 1959). [JF]

Angel M. Garibay, *Historia de la literatura náhuatl* (Mexico, 1953–4); Miguel León-Portilla, *Las literaturas precolumbinas de México* (Mexico, 1964).

**Nalé Roxlo, Conrado** (1898–    ). Argentinian poet and dramatist. The best of his poetry is tenderly ironic in the manner of Heine. His first published volume, *El grillo* (1923), had a prologue by ◊ Lugones. Later he fell a light-hearted victim to surrealism. But more interesting are his plays, particularly three poetic dramas: *La cola de la sirena* (1941), the story of a man who fell in love with a mermaid and gave her up when she had her tail cut off and was turned into a woman; *El pacto de Cristina* (1945), a fancy-dress drama of Crusading times in which the devil refuses the soul of a young woman in love because it is too pure but takes option on that of her unborn child, whereupon she commits suicide; and *Judith y las rosas* (1956). Nalé Roxlo has also written short stories, notably *Las puertas del Purgatorio* (1956). [JMC]

*Teatro* (1957); *Cuentos y poesías de Conrado Nalé Roxlo*, ed. R. C. Gillespie (New York, 1954); Fitts, *APAC*.

**Navarrete, Fray Manuel de** (1768–1809). Mexican poet. His earlier work was in the pastoral tradition and his later, written after the War of Independence, more elegiac. Among his best poems, 'Noche triste' and the group of 'Ratos tristes' show the influence of Young's *Night Thoughts*. Navarrete, who had been interested in drawing as a young man, had a feeling for landscape. He was a Franciscan and taught Latin, pursuing the writing of poetry without the knowledge of his superiors. He wrote love poems and nature poems with a Rousseauesque joy in the contact of man with nature. Yet the poems also have a religious stamp, for he sees nature as a hymn to the divine Maker, and his praise of the simple life is within the Spanish tradition of 'alabanza de aldea y menosprecio de corte' ('praise of village and contempt of the Court'). [JMC]

*Poesías profanas*, ed. and intr. F. Monterde (1939).

**Neruda, Pablo** (pseud. of Neftalí Ricardo Reyes) (1904–    ). Chilean poet. Born in the provincial town of Parral. His father

357

worked on the railways and while Neruda was still very young he was sent to Temuco in the far south, which was still virtually pioneer territory. Here, in the atmosphere of the frontier (which was to leave its traces on his poetry), Neruda grew up, and here also he came into brief contact with Gabriela ◊ Mistral, who taught for a time in Temuco. Neruda was a precocious child who became literary editor of the Temuco daily *La Mañana* at 14. In 1920, he went to Santiago to study and there published his first book of poems, *La canción de la fiesta*, in 1921; a second collection, *Crepusculario* (1923), brought him immediate recognition. In 1924, he published the enormously popular *Veinte poemas de amor y una canción desesperada*. These poems used an intensely subjective imagery derived from the poet's own personal associations. From 1927 until 1945, he lived abroad and served as Chilean consul first in Rangoon and Java; in 1933 he was sent to Barcelona. This is the period of the first two volumes of *Residencia en la tierra* (1925–31; tr. A. Flores, *Residence on Earth and Other Poems*, Norfolk, Conn., 1946), first published as a collection in 1933. These poems are the outcome of a period of spiritual nihilism; the poet sees human experience as an absurdity because man exists in time and is subject to decay. The poems attempt to communicate the senseless chaos which Neruda sees as the only 'unity'. However, even at the depths of despair, the poet finds a certain reassurance in the humble vegetable world. The great change in Neruda's poetry occurred just after the Spanish Civil War. He had been in Spain during the war and in 1939 he was in Paris working on behalf of the Spanish Republican refugees. After the war, he joined the Communist Party and announced a change in his poetry, a change which was already evident in the poems of the third *Residencia en la tierra*, finally published as *Tercera Residencia* (1947). From now on, he regarded poetry not as an élite pursuit but as a statement of human solidarity addressed to 'simple people'. One of the first fruits of the change was his *Canto General* (1950), a poem of epic dimensions parts of which he had begun to publish in 1947. It was conceived as a song of Chile but developed into an ambitious hymn to virgin America, to its flora and fauna, to the conquerors and to its peoples. It traces the history of Latin America, the class struggles and even brings

in world politics, Russia and America. The finest parts of the poem are those which evoke the landscape of America and meditate on the grandeurs and the fall of the pre-Columban civilization, *Alturas de Macchu Picchu* (tr. N. Tarn, *The Heights of Macchu Picchu*, London, 1966), but there are also long passages of now-outdated political polemic which weaken the work. In the fifties he published his *Odas elementales* (2 vols., 1954; tr. C. Lozano, *The Elementary Odes*, selection, New York, 1961) and *Tercer libro de las Odas* (1959). The odes represent a serious attempt to write an 'elemental' poetry which could communicate to ordinary people. Always a prolific poet, Neruda has since published *Cantos ceremoniales* (1961), *Cien sonetos de amor* (1959), *Memorial de Isla Negra* (5 vols., 1964), *Plenos poderes* (1962), *Estravagatio* (1958) and *Canción de gesta* (1960). Though poetry has always been Neruda's principal activity, he was elected Communist senator in 1945 and was forced to flee Chile when he quarrelled with González Videla in 1946. He has read his work to workers' meetings in many parts of the world and his poetry is better known internationally than that of any other Latin-American poet. The most complete edition of his work is the *Obras completas* (Losada, Buenos Aires, 1957; new edn, 2 vols., 1968). He has recently completed his first play, *Fulgor y muerte de Joaquín Murieta* (Santiago, 1967). He has also recently published two collections of poetry, *Fin de mundo* (Buenos Aires, 1969) and *La espada encendida* (Buenos Aires, 1970). [JF]

*Selected Poems*, tr. B. Belitt, intr. L. Monguió (New York, 1961); *We Are Many*, selections tr. Alastair Reid (London, 1967); *Twenty Love Poems and a Song of Despair*, tr. W. S. Merwin (London, 1969); *Selected Poems*, ed. N. Tarn, various translators (London, 1970); Cohen, *LAWT*; *Adam*, April, 1943; *Encounter*, September 1965).

Amado Alonso, *Poesía y estilo de Pablo Neruda* (Buenos Aires, 1940); Margarita Aguirre, *Genio y figura de Pablo Neruda* (Buenos Aires, 1946); Emir Rodríguez Monegal, *El viajero inmóvil* (Buenos Aires, 1957).

**Nervo, Amado** (1870–1919). Mexican poet. Beginning as a follower of ◊ Darío, he diluted his talent, though intending to purify it. His moral, amorous and vaguely religious poetry has enjoyed great popularity, but today hardly a handful of his poems are readable. 'The delicate mystery', which Darío believed they communicated, has evaporated. His stories combine theosophy with a scientific interest which recalls that of H. G. Wells. They are best when most direct. As a writer of decorative prose, Nervo was unsuccessful. His work on the whole lacks form. [JMC]

Obras completas (2nd edn, Madrid, 1962); *Los cien mejores poemas de Amado Nervo*, intr. E. González Martínez (1919); *Fuegos fatuos y pimientos dulces* (1955); Trend, *OBSV*; Paz and Beckett, *AMP*.
Bernardo Ortiz de Montellano, *Figura, amor y muerte de Amado Nervo* (Mexico, 1943); Ester Turner Wellman, *Amado Nervo, Mexico's Religious Poet* (New York, 1936); M. Durán, *Genio y figura de Amado Nervo* (Buenos Aires, 1968).

**Novo, Salvador** (1904–    ). Mexican poet. He was associated with the post-Revolutionary poetry movements along with ◊ Torres Bodet, ◊ Villaurrutia and ◊ Gorostiza. He wrote for the magazines *La Falange* (1922–3), *Ulises* (1927–8) and *Contemporáneos* (1928–31). His first important collection, *XX poemas* (1925) comprised descriptions of the country or the city written in a humorous *avant garde* idiom. *Espejo* (1933) included many poems on autobiographical themes treated with humour and irony. However, Novo's poetry also has serious overtones and many express a sense of post-Revolutionary disillusion. In *Poemas proletarios* (1934) he expresses concern over the fact that his contemporaries preferred slogans to reality. He is also important as a critic and has been instrumental in acquainting Mexicans with the best European and North American writing. In recent years, his major work has been in the theatrer [JF]

*Poesía* (1961); Fitts, *APAC*; *PM*.

Merlin H. Foster, *Los Contemporáneos (1920–32)* (Colección Studium, 45, Mexico, 1954); F. Dauster, *Ensayos sobre poesía mexicana* (Colección Studium, 41, Mexico, 1963).

**Núñez Cabeza de Vaca, Alvar** (1490?– 1559). Author of one of the strangest shipwreck stories. He was a member of Pánfilo de Narváez's expedition to Florida, was shipwrecked and captured by Indians, with whom he lived, becoming so integrated into their way of life that he almost went unrecognized by a Spanish expedition in 1536. His first-person account of his wanderings is one of the most vivid of the 16th-century chronicles. [JF]

*Naufragios y comentarios, con dos cartas* (CA, 1942; tr. C. Covey, *Adventures in the Unknown Interior of America*, New York, 1962).

**Núñez de Pineda y Bascuñán, Francisco** (1607–82). Author of an account of life among the Chilean Indians, based on his own account of his captivity. Son of one of the conquerors of Chile, he took part in skirmishes against the Araucanian Indians, who resisted the Spaniards fiercely. He was taken prisoner on an expedition and lived for some time with different Indian chiefs. His *Cautiverio feliz y razón de las guerras dilatadas de Chile* was written after his release (*c.* 1650) and is remarkable for the sympathy shown towards the Indians. Núñez de Pineda reveals himself as a man of stoical dignity who tried to persuade his captors of the truth of Christianity by example and he shows great indignation at examples of cruelty and unscrupulousness on the part of the Spaniards. [JF]

*Cautiverio feliz etc.*, intr. D. Barros Araña (Colección de Historiadores de Chile, III, Santiago, 1863).

# O

**Obligado, Rafael** (1851–1920). Argentinian romantic poet. He came of a wealthy family and held a literary salon in his own home. His one volume of poems, *Poesías*, was first published in Paris in 1885, and included 'Los horneros', 'El camalote' and 'El seibo', which were poems on his native countryside. He wrote heroic poetry and the ambitious 'Santos Vega', a poem in several cantos which described the pampa scenery, the gauchos and their fiestas. Santos Vega, the hero, was a traditional Argentinian folk hero whose legendary song contest with the devil in the guise of Juan sin Ropa ('Naked Johnny') is the theme of the final canto. But the 'devil' of Obligado's poem is symbolic of the progress which was destroying the old gaucho life. [JF]

*Poesías escogidas*, ed. F. E. Gutiérrez (1953).

**Oliveira, Antônio Mariano de** (known as Alberto de Oliveira) (1857–1937). Brazilian poet of the Parnassian school. The publication of his *Sonetos e Poemas* (1885) marked the beginnings of a reaction against romanticism in Brazil. He had previously published *Canções Românticas* (1878) and *Meridionais* (1884). His *Sonetos e Poemas* show a preoccupation with objectivity and form which runs through all his subsequent poetry. In 1900, he published his *Poesias Completas* and this was followed by three volumes of *Poesias* (1911, 1913, 1922). These later poems, though formally extremely polished and technically perfect, are not always as objective as his previous work. His 'Alma em Flor', for instance, is a poetic cycle set in the Brazilian countryside which relates an ideal love story against a setting of an old plantation. [AA]

Bandeira, *A P B P*; Cândido, *P L B*, ii.

**Olmedo, José Joaquín de** (1780–1847). Ecuadorian poet. He played an important part in the activities which led to Peruvian and Ecuadorian independence. He participated in the Spanish Cortes of Cadiz held in 1811, and in 1823 he acted as an envoy to Bolívar to persuade him to help Peru against the Spaniards. Bolívar's victories at Junín and Ayacucho in 1824 were the last big battles in the Spanish-American independence movement and they form the subject of one of his two well-known odes, *La victoria de Junín: Canto a Bolívar* (1825), which celebrates the rebel's victory over the Spaniards and prophesies, in lines given to the ghost of the last Inca, Bolívar's complete triumph in a future battle – already in the past when the poem was written. Olmedo's second important ode, *Al general Flores, vencidor en Miñarica* (1835), deplores the fratricidal anarchy which was already breaking out among the former colonists. Olmedo's style is neoclassical; and even his grandiloquent excesses are cold and studied. He wrote little else that is read today. He translated parts of Pope's *Essay on Man*. [JMC]

*Poesías completas* (Mexico, 1947).
Darío Guevara, *Olmedo* (Quito, 1958).

**Onetti, Juan Carlos** (1909–    ). Uruguayan writer. He moved to Buenos Aires as a young man, where he worked at odd jobs before becoming a journalist. His first novel, *El pozo* (1939), has a lonely 'outsider' hero, Eladio, the prototype of many characters in subsequent novels who cannot communicate or enter into satisfactory relationships. Onetti first attracted attention with *Tierra de nadie* (1941), which he said was concerned with a generation of Argentinians living in 1940 and in particular with a type of 'morally indifferent individual who has lost faith and all interest in his own fate'. This was followed by *La vida breve* (1950), in which he created the fictional world of the port of Santa María and a character, Bransen, who is a tragic Walter Mitty. There followed *Los adioses* (1954), *Una tumba sin nombre* (1959), *La cara de la desgracia* (1960) and what is probably his finest novel, *El astillero* (1961; tr. *The Shipyard*, New York, 1968). *Juntacadáveres* (1965) dealt with many of the characters who appeared in *El astillero*. This latter novel centres on Larsen, who becomes manager of a ghost shipyard and it is set in a kind of limbo between reality and illusion. All Onetti's novels are concerned with disillusionment and with the inevitable corruption that goes with advancing years or experience. He has two excellent volumes of short stories, *Un sueño realizado y otros cuentos* (1951) and *Un infierno tan temido* (1962; title story tr. in Cohen, *LAWT*). [J F]

M. Benedetti, 'Juan Carlos Onetti y la aventura del hombre', in *Literatura uruguaya siglo xx* (Montevideo, Buenos Aires, 1963); A. Rama, essay on Onetti in 1965 Montevideo edition of *El pozo*; Harss, *LN*.

**Ortiz, Adalberto** (1914–    ). Ecuadorian poet and novelist. Born in Esmeraldas. After graduating as a teacher, he began to write poetry on Negro themes, inspired by the example of the poets he had read in Emilio Ballagas's anthology of Negro poetry (◊ Afro-Cubanism). Many of these poems were later published in the collection *El animal herido* (1959). Ortiz has also written a novel, *Juyungo* (1943), with a Negro hero whose picaresque adventures in the tropical regions of Ecuador finally lead to his death at the hands of Peruvian soldiers. [J F]

*DLL.*

**Othón, Manuel José** (1858–1906). Mexican poet. He expressed a romantic self-identification with his native countryside in classical forms. His *Himno de los bosques* (1891), a self-consciously anti-modernistic celebration of the Mexican landscape, is authentic despite its echoes of the Spanish 16th century. His eye, ear and feelings are alert. *Poemas rústicos* (1902) is his outstanding collection, in which he prefers to present the country without man. In *Idilio salvaje* (1905) his poetry rises to higher levels under the impact of human feeling: the love of the ageing and conventional poet for a young woman. Here the bare mountains of northern Mexico fittingly symbolize the self-accusing desolation that afflicts him. This group of seven sonnets assures him immortality. [J M C]

*Poesías y cuentos*, ed. Antonio Castro Leal (1963); *Paisaje*, ed. and intr. Manuel Calvillo (1944); Cohen, *P B S V*; Paz and Beckett, *A M P*.
Alfonso Reyes, 'Los *poemas rústicos* de Manuel José Othón', in *Obras completas*, i (Mexico, 1955).

# P

**Pacheco, José Emilio** (1939–      ). Mexican poet. Author of *La sangre de Medusa* (1958), *El viento distante, Los elementos de la noche* (1963), *El reposo del fuego* (1966). He has recently completed the novel *Morirás lejos* (1967) and a collection of poetry, *Para matar el tiempo* (1969). [JF]

*P M; Tree Between Two Walls*, tr. G. Brotherston and E. Dorn (Santa Barbara, 1969).

**Pagaza, Joaquín Arcadio** (1839–1918). Mexican poet and priest. He set out to describe his country's scenery in the manner of Virgil and Horace, both of whom he translated. His best poems are his sonnets on sites in the Valle de Bravo and the state of Vera Cruz, e.g. 'El Papaloapan'. Here he contrives idyllic miniatures, even though the rivers and volcanoes have Aztec names and the fruits are not those of the Mediterranean. His most ambitious poem, *María*, fails because it cannot convey the majestic beauty of the 'tierra caliente' but only its squalors and discomforts. Pagaza is the best 19th-century Mexican poet prior to ◊ Gutiérrez Nájera and ◊ Othón, the latter of whom he influenced. [JMC]

*Selva y mármoles, antología* (1940); Paz and Beckett, *A M P.*

**Palés Matos, Luis** (1898–1959). Puerto Rican poet. His poetry was undistinguished until, in the twenties, he began to write an Afro-Spanish poetry using African words or African-sounding words of his own invention interwoven with Spanish to give the effect of Negro rhythms of song, chant and dances. Like many of the Afro-Cuban poets (◊ Afro-Cubanism), Palés Matós was not himself a Negro and many of his poems are no more than picturesque attempts to re-create a world of magic and rite which was remote from European culture. In common with many European intellectuals of the time, he turned to the Negro in reaction against the 'over-cerebralization' of white civilization. Although it was often said that his poems were devoid of any social comment many of them do attempt to convey the effect of the clash of cultures in the West Indies or, as in 'Elegía del Duque de la Mermelada', the sadness of the civilized Negro separated from his primitive origins. His best collection of Afro-Spanish poems was *Tuntún de pasa y grifería* (1937). [JF]

*Poesía, 1915–56*, intr. F. de Onís (1964); Fitts, *A P A C.*

**Palma, Ricardo** (1833–1919). Peruvian writer. He invented a new genre, the *tradición*, a free treatment of some incident drawn from history or legend. In his youth, he took part in politics and fought in civil wars. He reached the high point of his political career between 1868 and 1872 when he was a senator. In 1872, he published his first series of *tradiciones*, although many of these had already appeared previously in magazines. By 1876, he had attained a continental reputation and was in correspondence with prominent men in both Europe and America. During the war between Peru and Chile, he suffered the loss of books and manuscripts, but after the war was put in charge of the National Library, which he built up and reorganized. Further series of *tradiciones* appeared in 1872, 1874, 1875, 1877, 1883 and 1885 and again in 1906 and 1910. He also re-edited works of colonial literature and wrote critical studies. His later life was overshadowed when he was made to retire from directorship of the National Library. The *tradiciones* form a witty and often light-hearted series of anecdotes based on Peruvian history and historical figures from pre-Conquest times to the middle of the 19th century. Palma is not concerned with the big moments of history but with human behaviour; his attitude even to hallowed figures is, according to Luis Alberto Sánchez, 'escéptica, heterodoxa y socarrona' ('sceptical, heterodox and sly'). His preference was for anecdotes set in Lima in Viceregal times. He liked the setting, too, of convent intrigue. He was extremely interested in language and wrote with great art and skill. [JF]

*Tradiciones peruanas completas* (1957); Sánchez, *L P; The Knights of the Cape*, tr. H. de Onís (New York, 1945).

José Miguel Oviedo, *Genio y figura de Ricardo Palma* (Buenos Aires, 1965) and *Ricardo Palma* (Buenos Aires, 1968).

**Pardo y Aliaga, Felipe** (1806–68). Peruvian poet and playwright. Son of a Spanish Royal Official who had left Peru after the Declaration of Independence, Pardo began writing poetry in Spain but returned to Peru in 1827. He took part in politics, served as a diplomat and retained a critical attitude towards the backwardness of the creole. His pamphlet *El espejo de mi tierra* (1840) was a bitter attack on the immaturity of the new Republic and many of his poems also take up this theme, the farcical transplantation of European institutions to Peru. He also attacked the 'creolist' school of writing led by ◊ Segura. His satire in both prose and verse is biting and lively; he castigates the laziness of Peruvians, the frivolity of the upper classes and the ignorance of the masses. He also wrote plays, notably *Frutos de la educación* (1829). [JF]

*Poesías y escritos en prosa* (1869).
Sánchez, *L P*, v.

**Pareja Diezcanseco, Alfredo** (1908–    ). Ecuadorian novelist, journalist and historian. Born in Guayaquil, he was obliged to earn his living at a variety of occupations, including that of cabin-boy on a merchant ship. His first important novel was *El muelle* (1933), a story of the Guayaquil dock-workers. Since then he has published many novels, of which the outstanding are *La Beldaca* (1935), the story of a coastal river-boat; *Hombres sin tiempo* (1941), a novel based on the author's experience as a political prisoner, and *Las tres ratas* (1944), set in the slums of Guayaquil. Pareja Diezcanseco's most ambitious work is *Los nueve años*, volumes of which appeared in 1956 and 1959; this is a novel which covers a vast segment of Ecuadorian life during the 1920s and 1930s and which attempts to present the interplay of social forces. Pareja Diezcanseco is an admirer of Thomas Mann and has written a book on him. [JF]

Rojas, *NE*.

**Parra, Nicanor** (1914–    ). Chilean poet. He created the anti-poem, which he describes as 'nothing more than a traditional poem enriched by surrealist sap'. At first he composed poetry which, reacting against

the 'creacionismo' of Vicente ◊ Huidobro and ◊ Neruda, was intended as accompaniment to singing and dancing. This poetry is boisterous, cynical and picturesque, echoing the style of popular ballads. His later anti-poems are more brutal. He takes narrative themes and turns them upside down. 'Life has no meaning', the prosaic conclusion of his 'Soliloquio del individuo', appears to be his motto, and those pieces which despairingly face up to this belief are probably his best. Many others are nostalgic and surrealistically whimsical. *Cancionero sin nombre* (1937), *Poemas y antipoemas* (1954; 2nd edn, 1956), *La cueca larga* (1958), *Canciones Rusas* (1967) and *Versos de salón* (1962). [JMC]

Cohen, *LAWT*; *Encounter*, September 1965; *Poems and Antipoems*, tr. F. Alegría (New York, 1967, tr. various translators, London, 1968); *PV*; *Obra gruesa* (1969).

**Parra, Teresa de la** (1895–1936). Venezuelan novelist. Of wealthy family background, she was born on an estate near Caracas and educated in Paris. Her childhood memories of the idyllic life of the 'big house' formed the basis for her charming *Las memorias de Mamá Blanca* (1929; tr. H. de Onís, *Mama Blancá's Souvenirs*, Washington, D.C., 1959). An earlier novel, *Ifigenia* (1924), was also based on personal experience, being the story of an intelligent Paris-educated young lady who returns to a life of boredom in the backward society of Caracas, with its rigid etiquette and provincial staidness. [JF]

**Payno y Flores, Manuel** (1810–94). Mexican novelist. Famous for his adventure stories first published in serial form. *El fistol del diablo* appeared in 1845–6 and *Los bandidos del Río Frío* in 1889–91 (2nd edn, intr. A. C. Leal, 1964). The latter, despite a sensational and complex plot, gives an extraordinarily vivid picture of Mexican society in the early 19th century. [JF]

Brushwood, *MN*.

**Payró, Roberto J.** (1867–1928). Argentinian journalist and novelist. He became the secretary of the first Centre of Socialist Studies in Argentina. Caught in Belgium during the First World War, he was imprisoned as an enemy spy because of his criticism of German militarism. His best works are a series of novels which humour-ously set up for criticism aspects of Argen-tinian provincial life: *Pago Chico* (1908), the *Divertidas aventuras del nieto de Juan Moreira* and the picaresque short novel *El casamiento de Laucha* (1906). Payró also wrote many plays on national themes, of which the best are *Sobre las ruinas* (1904) and *Vivir quiero conmigo* (1923). [JF]

*Tales from the Argentine*, ed. W. Frank (New York, 1930) (includes *El casamiento de Laucha*, tr. A. Brenner, and *Pago Chico*, part tr. A. Brenner, etc.).

Raúl, Larra, *Payró: El novelista de la democracia* (3rd edn, Buenos Aires, 1966); Germán García, Roberto Payró. *Testimonio de una vida y realidad de una literatura* (Buenos Aires, 1961).

**Paz, Octavio** (1914– ). Mexican poet. His work came to an early maturity under the impact of the Spanish Civil War, which he witnessed in Madrid. A series of diplo-matic posts has kept him abroad for many years and subjected him to the prevalent European influences, in particular to surrealism. Paz's surrealism however differs from that of his master André Breton in that he was never fascinated by dream-imagery for its own sake. For like Carlos ◊ Pellicer, he carried the sun of his native country with him. Everything that his hands touch flies. The world is full of birds – 'Todo lo que mis manos tocan, vuela Está lleno de pájaros el mundo'.

The central problem of Paz's later and more mature work is that of solitude, which is for him not an obsession, but a point of departure. Man alone is a divided being, who can only become whole by way of the poetic image, of sexual love or of divine participation. In the poem 'Himno entre ruinas' of 1949, the first of the book *La estación violenta* (1958), he contrasts pictures of a ruined Europe and a still barbarous Mexico, of discursive thought and the midday heat in which all thought ceases 'like rivers that do not flow into the sea' ('ríos que no desembocan') and draws the contraries together under the sign of man, 'a tree of images, words that are flowers, that are fruit, that are actions' ('Hombre, árbol de imágenes, palabras que son flores que son frutos que son actos'). In 'El cántaro roto' day and night are resolved, and the toad-god, the only survivor of men's deities, exorcised by the poetic image which springs from the poet's side like the wheat of the resurrection and

takes him 'beyond beginning and end' ('más allá de fin y comienzo'). The book cul-minates in Paz's greatest and most ambitious poem, 'Piedra de sol' (tr. and intr. M. Rukeyser, *Sun-Stone*, New York, 1963), in which he reconciles the opposites of social and hermetic preoccupations, of the mo-ment and the aeon, of sexual love and isola-tion, of history and eternity under the sign of the 'sun-stone', the engraved stone calendar of the Aztecs. The method of this poem owes something to the musical con-struction of Eliot's *Four Quartets*. Paz varies and contrasts his pictures and in-cidents in Eliot's manner, but the resem-blance goes no further.

Paz's concern for Mexico and her dual cultural heritage is expressed in his essay on the destiny of his country, *El laberinto de la soledad* (1950; revised edn, 1959). He has collected his short essays on literary and artistic themes in *Las peras del olmo* (1957), *El arco y la lira* (1956), *Cuadrivio* (1965), *Los signos en rotación* (1965) and *Puertas al campo* (1966). His most recent poetry is included in *Libertad bajo palabra: obra poetica, 1935–58* (1960), *Salamandra* (1962), *Viento entero* (New Delhi, 1966) and *Ladera este* (1969). And he has recently experi-mented with 'Discos Visuales'. [JMC]

Cohen, *PBSV*; *The Labyrinth of Solitude*, tr. L. Kemp (New York, 1962, London, 1967); *Selected Poems*, tr. M. Rukeyser (Bloomington, Ind., 1963); Cohen, *LAWT*; *Triquarterly*, Winter/Spring, 1968/9.

R. Xirau, *Tres poetas de la soledad* (Mexico, 1955).

**Pellicer, Carlos** (1899– ). Mexican poet. Possessing a keen and ironic painter's eye and a great joy in nature, he has continu-ously striven to achieve order, sobriety and mental discipline. His poetry descends in a purely Mexican tradition from that of ◊ Othón and ◊ López Velarde. The early *Colores en el mar* (1921) finds colour and joy even in the port of Buenos Aires. But Pellicer's happiest evocations are of his native Tabasco, of the 'green flash of par-rots' in the forest. He uses a free verse rich in assonances, word-play and echoes, in-terrupted by colloquial asides. His more mature work begins after a return from long travels, which are recorded in poems that are sometimes little more than travel notes. *Hora de junio* (1937) contains one of his finest poems, 'Esquemas para una oda tropical', in which he sets out 'in one clear shout' ('un solo grito claro') to speak for 'the palm and the antelope, the silk-cotton tree and the alligator, the fern and the lyre-bird, the tarantula and the orchid, the zenzontle and the boa-constrictor'. In the same book appear his first sonnets, which do not attain the distinction of his more public utterance in *vers libre*. The later religious sonnets of *Práctica de vuelo* (1956), however, combine a joy in God with a completely unmystical joy in tropical nature. Those addressed to the archangels are pure Mexican baroque, shimmering with imagery of light and darkness; others glow with alternate emotions of hope and fear, with the flashing dance of matter and spirit. 'Every poet brings something new to poetry,' wrote Octavio Paz. 'One of the great gifts that Pellicer has brought us is the sun.'

Carlos Pellicer is custodian of a museum which he himself founded in his native town of Villahermosa, and which contains pre-Columbian antiquities from the civilizations of the Tabasco province. [JMC]

*Material poético 1918–1961* (1962); Trend, *OBSV*; *PM*; Fitts, *APAC*.
Octavio Paz, 'La poesía de Carlos Pellicer', in *Las peras del olmo* (Mexico, 1957).

**Pena, Luis Carlos Martins** (1815–48). Brazilian playwright. He wrote comedies of manners on the subject of everyday life. He is significant chiefly for historical reasons as a pioneer of Brazilian theatre. His works include: *O Juiz de Paz a Roça* (1838), *O Judas em Sábado de Aleluia* (1844), *Os Irmãos das Almas* (1844), *Os Dois ou o Inglês Maquinista* (1845), *O Noviço* (1845), *Quem Casa Quer Casa* (1845), *Os Três Médicos* (1845), *O Namorado* (1845), *A Barriga do meu Tio* (1846). He also wrote some serious plays (in *Teatro*, ed. Melo Morais Filho and Silvio Romero, 1898). [AA]

*Teatro cómico* (1943); *O Juiz de Paz da Roça* and *O Judas em Sábado de Aleluia*, ed. A. Costa (1951); *Teatro*, ed. Darcy Damasceno (2 vols. 1956).
Silvio Romero, *Vida e obra de Martins Pena* (Porto. 1901).

**Peralta de Barnuevo, Pedro** (1663–1743). Peruvian scholar. He was well known as an astronomer, mathematician, engineer and historian besides being one of the finest poets of the colonial period in Spanish America. His most famous poetic works are his *Lima fundada* (1732), an epic of Pizarro's conquest of Peru which has Gongoristic touches, and his *Pasión y triunfo de Cristo* (1738). Despite the fact that this work

showed the limitations of scientific investigations, it brought him into conflict with the Inquisition. At the trial, which dragged on until 1740, he was accused of endangering the dignity of the faith. He was then 77 and a sick man; yet in the midst of his troubles he published his *Lima inexpugnable* (1740). He also wrote several plays and some *entremeses* and *bailes*. [JF]

*Obras dramáticas*, ed. I. A. Leonard (1937); F. García Calderón, *Biblioteca*, VII.
Sánchez, *LP*, iii.

**Pesado, José Joaquín** (1801–61). Mexican poet. Reflective and classical in style, he wrote, in addition to love poems and devotional pieces, a series of sonnets on the Mexican landscape, *Sitios y escenas de Orizaba y Córdoba*, and a collection entitled *Los aztecas* in which he tried to revive something of the tradition of pre-Colombian poetry in ◊ Náhuatl. The outstanding poem of this type, 'Vanidad de la gloria humana, Canto de Netzahualcóyotl', treats the old theme of 'Ubi sunt' in a traditional manner. It marks, however, the first of many attempts to incorporate the Mexican past into Spanish tradition. [JMC]

*Poesías originales y traducidas* (Mexico, 1886).

**Pezoa Véliz, Carlos** (1879–1908). Chilean poet. Of humble family background, he worked as a modest civil servant until he was badly wounded in an earthquake. His only collection of poetry was published posthumously. His best poems are evocations of Chilean rural scenes and characters from humble life. The language is simple, unpretentious and yet effective and his work is increasingly appreciated by modern writers. [DJ]

*Alma Chilena* (1911); *Antología* (*poesía y prosa*), intr. N. Guzmán (1957).

**Picchia, Paulo Menotti del** (1892–    ). Brazilian poet and novelist. He graduated in law in 1913 and for some years owned and worked on newspapers. He became well known in 1917 with the *Juca Mulato* poems, which expressed a new mood of cultural nationalism and anticipated the nationalist substratum of the Modernist movement. In 1922, he became associated with Modernism. In 1925, he published *Chuva de pedras*. (◊ Modernism in Brazil.) [AA]

*Poemas* (15th edn, 1935); Fitts, *APAC*; 3 poems tr. A. R. Lopes and W. D. Jacobs, *Books Abroad*, XXVI, 3 (Summer, 1952).

Pericles Eugenio da Silva Ramos, 'O Modernismo na Poesia', in *A Literatura no Brasil*, ii, ed. A. Coutinho (Rio de Janeiro, 1959).

**Plácido.** ◊ Valdés, Gabriel de la Concepción.

**Pompéia, Raul D'Avila** (1863–95). Brazilian novelist and poet. He also worked as a journalist and wrote on behalf of the emancipation of the slaves and in support of the Republic. He is best known as author of a masterly novel of school life, *O Ateneu* (intr. Mário de Andrade, Lisbon, n.d.), first published in 1888 in the *Gazeta das Notícias*. It is a brilliant, sometimes ironic and bitter account of life in O Ateneu, a boarding school run by a megalomaniac headmaster and owner of the school, Dr Aristarco Argolo de Ramos, a man who uses his position and the school for personal ends. It is not conceived as social protest but as a penetrating and sensitive study of the sexual and intellectual awakening of the boy protagonist, the narrator. The school system is merely the framework within which the relations between the boys and between boys and masters are worked out. The style is remarkable for its lucidity and economy, while the theme undoubtedly helped to inspire at least one similar novel – *Doidinho* by ◊ Lins do Rego. Pompéia's other works include *Uma Tragédia no Amazonas* (1880), *Microscópicos* (stories) and the prose poem *Canções sem Metro*, published posthumously in 1900 (see Bandeira, *APB*). [JF]

**Pôrto Alegre, Manuel José de Araújo** (1806–79). Brazilian poet. He took an active part in Brazilian romanticism and collaborated with Gonçalves de ◊ Magalhães, in the magazine *Niterói–Revista Brasiliense* published in Paris in 1836. However, he is considered by critics to be more of a neoclassicist than a romantic, and his *Colombo* has been called the last classical work. Other collections include *O Caçador* (1843), *O Voador* (1844), *A Destruição das Florestas* (1845). Except for *Colombo* (1855), he

collected his poems in a single volume (*Brasilianas*, 1863). [AA]

Manuel Bandeira, *Apresentação da Poesia Brasileira* (Rio de Janeiro, 1946).

**Prado, Pedro** (1886–1952). Chilean poet and novelist. He was trained as an architect, and as a young man he collaborated on many little magazines. He was a member of the important literary group Los Diez, founded in 1916, and he anticipated some *avant garde* experiments in his *Flores de cardo* (1908). He began writing novels in 1914 with *La reina de Rapa-Nui*, an exotic fantasy. It was followed by *Alsino* (1920), which concerns a boy who grows wings and learns to fly, and is heavily symbolic of the conflict between man's spiritual aspirations which allow him to soar and his earthbound nature. In 1924, there appeared his *Un juez rural* (tr. L. B. Simpson, intr. A. Torres-Ríoseco, Berkeley, Cal., 1968), the story of a provincial judge who becomes disillusioned with himself and questions the right of one human being to judge another. [JF]

Raúl Silva Castro, *Pedro Prado (1886–1952)* (New York, 1959).

**Prieto, Jenaro** (1889–1946). Chilean novelist. Trained as a lawyer, he wrote two good novels, *Un muerto de mal criterio* (1927) and *El socio* (1929; tr. B. de Roig and G. Dowler, *The Partner*, London, 1931). The first is the story of a judge who finds himself administering justice in Heaven. It makes the point that human beings can only understand and pardon and cannot judge. The second is the story of a man who invents a partner, 'El socio', who can be used as a scapegoat for his faults and to excuse and explain anything he wants hidden from his family. The invented 'socio' soon takes on a life of his own, however. Jenaro Prieto's novels make their moral points in a witty and amusing manner. [JF]

Castro, *PLC*.

# Q

**Quechua Literature.** Survivals of the literature of the Inca civilization and of post-
Conquest writing in Quechua (the modern
name given to Runa-Simi, the language
spoken in the Inca empire). The survivals of
pre-Conquest poetry are rare because the
Incas had no system of writing, but several
examples are to be found in the works of the
Inca ◊ Garcilaso and in the *Nueva Coronica
y Buen Gobierno* of Huamán Poma de Ayala
(?1526–1614), an Indian whose work contrasted the glories of Inca civilization with
the post-Conquest situation. The survivals
of Quechua poetry of Inca times include
some fine love lyrics as well as hymns and
religious poetry. Poems continued to be
written in Quechua even after the Conquest
and there was a well-known mestizo poet,
Juan Wallparanichi Potosí (1793–1814),
who composed in this tongue. Post-
Conquest dramas in Quechua have also
survived, the best known being *Ollantay*,
composed in the form in which it has survived probably in the 18th century, although
it obviously has sources both in Spanish
dramatic tradition and in pre-Conquest Inca
legend and drama. [JF]

J. M. B. Farfán, *Colleción de textos quechuas del
Peru* (Lima, 1952).

**Queiros, Raquel de** (1910– ). Brazilian
novelist. Born in the North-eastern city of
Fortaleza in 1910, but spent much of her
childhood inland on her father's plantation.
Here, the ancient, patriarchal social system
made a great impression on her, especially
the aspect requiring women to play a submissive, defined role, Raquel de Queiros's
four novels are preoccupied with defying
the tradition of woman's inequality, as she
achieves her aim through artistic and compassionate characterization of her heroines.
The principal theme in most of her works is
love – sexual love, maternal love and love
of mankind – and she considers it to be the
basic need of all women. Usually, it is a disappointed love, in which the heroine must
make some noble sacrifice for having challenged the traditional norms of social
behaviour. But the author is not melodramatic or maudlin; for she has perfect

control over her characterizations, choice of
words and emotions. This maturity of expression is remarkable for one who wrote
all her novels between the ages of 19 and 28.

In her first work, *O Quinze* (1930), the
theme of love is expressed through the ill-
fated affair of Vicente and Conceição. But
this novel, unlike the later ones, is mainly
social; it is concerned with the drought of
1915 and its consequences, a vivid childhood memory for the author, and she paints
a harsh picture of the suffering it caused. In
combining the social theme and the romance
she alleviates the stark description of the
*sêca*. Her second novel, *João Miguel* (1932),
also has a social theme – that of injustice –
but it is skilfully kept subordinate to the
character study of Santa and John Michael.
More than in *O Quinze*, the novelist is interested in portraying the social plight of the
woman. In this case it is Santa, a prostitute,
who is revealed through the comments of
other characters. They resent her air of
superiority and feel she should accept her
lowly position in society. Raquel de Queiros
is concerned with the vast disparity between
the rich and the poor, and with the social
system that perpetuates it. In this novel the
author, without sentimentality, gives the
reader an insight into the attitudes and plight
of the North-eastern poor. *Caminho de
Pedras* (1937), written during a period of
government censorship, is much less social
and more psychological than the novelist's
first two works. Though the main characters
are labour organizers, their activities only
provide the backdrop for the theme of
womanly love expressed through Noemi.
She is torn between the love she has found
with Roberto and her responsibilities to
her husband and son. Noemi chooses to
follow her emotions and goes to live with
Roberto, incurring social censure, while
society's double standard virtually ignores
Roberto's role in the affair. To the author,
Noemi's action in rejecting the hypocrisy of
an unhappy marriage is brave; for, in so
doing, she sacrificed her respectability. In *As
Três Marias* (1937; tr. F. P. Ellison, *The
Three Marias*, New York, 1963), the novelist
again deals with womanly love which re-

quires defiance of social norms. The main character, Maria Guta, is more fully presented than is Noemi in *Caminho de Pedras*. In this psychological study of Maria Guta, the reader follows her from childhood to womanhood, and thus understands her motives for finally challenging society. Though the story involves the lives of three Marias during and after their days in a convent school, it is mainly concerned with Guta's search for love; she finds love with Isaac, a Jewish refugee who faces deportation. Rather than bear their unborn child, Guta destroys it in what the author considers a woman's supreme sacrifice. Though disturbed by her own childlessness, Raquel de Queiros feels that it would be a greater crime to bring an illegitimate child into a hostile world. The drama of Maria Guta and the emotions of love and despair are skilfully presented. Since her last novel, the author has worked mainly as a translator and a literary critic. [D H]

*Quatro Romances* (1960) (*O Quinze, João Miguel, Caminho de Pedras, As Três Marias*).
Ellison, *BNN*.

**Quiroga, Horacio** (1878–1937). Uruguayan short-story writer. His life was dogged by personal tragedy, beginning with his father's early death as a result of a shooting accident. Quiroga grew up at the height of ◊ Modernism and his first published work, *Los arrecifes de coral* (1901), shows Modernist influence. He was an admirer of Poe and ◊ Lugones and became interested in madness and in abnormal psychology. In 1903, another tragic accident – this time he himself accidentally shot a friend – obliged him to go to Buenos Aires and soon afterwards he was appointed to a commission which was studying the ancient Jesuit ruins in the tropical region of Misiones, an appoint-

ment which decisively changed the course of his life. He was so fascinated by the pioneer life of the wilderness that he returned to the tropics, first as a cotton planter in the Chaco region, and later to Misiones, where he built his own bungalow in the wilderness. Tragedy was still to mark his life. His first wife committed suicide and he himself was to commit suicide when he discovered in a Buenos Aires clinic that he was suffering from cancer. Before *Cuentos de amor, de locura y de muerte* (1917) many of his stories show the direct influence of Poe, but in this collection, while still interested in the evocation of horror, he shows tragedy and death as arising out of the natural circumstances of the characters' lives or the environment. There followed *Cuentos de la selva* (1918; tr. A. Livingstone, *Stories of the Jungle*, New York, 1922, 1940, London, 1923 ; also in *Tales from the Argentine,* ed. W. Frank, New York, 1930), *El salvaje* (1920), *Anaconda* (1921), *El desierto* (1924) and *Los desterrados* (1926), which include his most characteristic stories, most of which were based directly on his own experiences in the Chaco and in Misiones. Nearly all the stories concern man's reactions in the face of extreme conditions and the struggle with the natural environment. In some of the stories the protagonists are animals and there is a contrast drawn between the animals' adaptation to nature and man's wilful attempt to alter nature. His finest stories (e.g. 'El hombre muerto') attain a high degree of objectivity. [J F]

*Cuentos escogidos*, intr. G. de Torre (2nd edn, Madrid, 1958).
José Enrique Etchevery, *Horacio Quiroga y la creación artística* (Montevideo, 1957); Emir Rodríguez Monegal, *Genio y figura de Horacio Quiroga* (Buenos Aires, 1967); N. Jitrik, *Horacio Quiroga* (Buenos Aires, 1967).

# R

**Rabelo, José da Silva Laurindo** (1826–64). Brazilian poet of mixed blood. He wrote bitter satirical poetry. *Trovas* (1853) was published in his lifetime. Much of his other work, including *Alberto* (a poem), a novel, *O Coveiro*, and some plays, were lost. [AA]

*Obras,* ed. and intr. O. M. Braga (1946).

**Ramos, Graciliano** (1892–1953). Brazilian writer. He spent much of his life in the North-eastern state of Alagoas. His early life had a strong influence upon his later literary career. From his corrupt father, a one-time municipal judge, and from his ill-tempered mother, Ramos acquired his suspicion of authority and his critical view of human nature. From the harsh physical realities of the *sertão*, or backlands, he learned the pessimism of man's struggle for existence. His formal education was slight; but he read voraciously, especially the works of Dostoevsky, Balzac and Eça de Queiroz, which influenced his writings. Ramos is considered by many to be Brazil's best novelist since Machado de ◊ Assis. The two artists share many of the same traits: irony, pessimism, introspection, emphasis on characterization and subordination of the plot to psychological study. But Ramos is different from Machado de Assis in the sociological orientation of his novels. Ramos is concerned with man's struggle against his hostile environment, and he expresses this concern through psychological observation of the effect of North-eastern life on the *sertanejo*. A second theme is that of the contrast between the *sertão* and the civilization represented by the littoral, which he views as superficial and poisonous to the purity of the uncivilized *sertanejo*. The central point of both his major themes is revolutionary: the basis of injustice, poverty and illiteracy in the North-east must be eradicated before the inhabitants can live as human beings rather than animals. Ramos is a skilful artist; he subordinates his social themes to the study of character, human conflicts and emotions, and he creates a profound effect on the reader.

His first novel, *Caetés* (1933), is atypical because it is the least psychological and there is not a constant sociological undercurrent. It is typical, however, in its bleak outlook and its description of the stifling atmosphere of small North-eastern towns. Through the main character, João Valério, Ramos communicates his central idea: that human morals and standards are determined only by self-interest. Ramos's second novel, *São Bernardo* (1934; tr. *Saint Bernard*, is considered a masterpiece of Brazilian literature. It is stylistically more sophisticated than *Caetés* in its first-person approach and psychological probings. Ramos presents the internal conflicts of Paulo Honório, the protagonist, a landowner whose psychology and relations with his wife are affected by his class position. His idealistic wife, Magdalena, finally commits suicide. In the novelist's third work, *Angústia* (1936; tr. L. C. Kaplan, *Anguish*, 1946), he uses the stream of consciousness technique to portray the mental devastation of the protagonist, a man who is from the backlands but who now lives in the city and becomes obsessed by the tantalizing glimpses of a girl next door whom he finally kills. The novel is thus on the theme of alienation and city man. Ramos's last novel, *Vidas Sêcas* (1938; tr. R. E. Dimmick, *Barren Lives,* Austin, Texas, 1965), was written in the third person with little dialogue. The protagonist Fabiano scrapes a living as a cattleman in the drought-afflicted North-east and periodically during the great droughts has to emigrate. The story is a skilful study of the growing feeling of rebellion in an illiterate and his final migration with his family to the city. After *Vidas Sêcas*, all Ramos's writings are in short-story form, except for his outstanding *Memórias do Cárcere* (1953), which relate his experiences in a concentration camp during the Getúlio Vargas regime. [JF]

*Complete Works* (São Paulo, 1961–2).
Rolando Morel Pinto, *Graciliano Ramos – Autore e Ator* (São Paulo, 1962); Ellison, *BNN.*

**Reyes, Alfonso** (1889–1959). Mexican poet, literary critic and scholar. The son of one of Porfirio Díaz's generals, he rebelled against the stuffy intellectual atmosphere of the regime and with other young intellectuals formed the famous Ateneo de la Juventud in 1910. Here lectures and discussions were held in the newest trends in philosophy. During and after the Mexican Revolution, Reyes spent many years in Spain, where he studied with the famous scholar Menéndez Pidal and became an authority on the Golden Age. On his return, he became a respected teacher, encouraging the new generations of post-Revolutionary Mexico to develop a culture of universal scope. He himself contributed important studies on Latin-American culture. He stressed not only the importance of the intellectual in national life but also the responsibility of the man of culture. His essays cover an enormous variety of subjects from classical studies to contemporary works. At the end of his life, Reyes became director of the Colegio de Mexico which carried on important research and publishing projects. Reyes was a poet whose poetry is often stimulated by persons and places; he also wrote drama. [JF]

*Obra poética* (1952); *Obras completas* (15 vols., 1955–63); *Selected Essays*, tr. C. Ramsdell (Berkeley, Los Angeles, 1964); *The Green Continent*, ed. G. Arciniegas (New York, London, 1944) (translations).

**Reyles, Carlos** (1868–1938). Uruguayan novelist. He was heir to a fortune which he inherited in 1886 after which he lived for some time in Spain. He was greatly influenced by naturalism, and his first works, *Por la vida* (1888) and *Beba* (1894), were attempts to apply Zola's theories. *Beba* draws a parallel between the hero's experiments with the breeding of horses and his own union with his niece Beba, both of which are doomed to failure. *La raza de Caín* (1900) is a psychological study of an envious man who fails to rise above the circumstances of his birth and environment. *El terruño* (1916) is a study in contrasts between the urban intellectual Tocles and his mother-in-law, Mamagela, who runs an estate in the country. The intellectual is a failure; his ideas are of no practical use, whereas Mamagela's practical wisdom not only enables her to live happily in her environment but also benefits the country as a whole. Reyles' best-known novel, *El embrujo de Sevilla* (1922; tr. J. LeClercq, *Castanets*, New York, 1929), represents a break with his naturalistic works; in it, he evokes the spirit of Andalucía and especially of Seville. Reyles' final novel, written after he had lost his fortune, *El gaucho Florido* (1932), is an excellent account of the life of a gaucho. [JF]

Guillermo Ara, *La novela naturalista hispano-americana* (Buenos Aires, 1965); Luis Alberto Menagra, *Carlos Reyles* (Montevideo, 1957).

**Ricardo Cassiano** (1895–    ). Brazilian poet. His first poems, *Dentro da Noite* (1915), and *A Frauta de Pa* (1917), were Parnassian. With *Vamos Caçar Papagaios* (1926), he became a Modernist and was to be associated with the Verde-Amarêlo group led by Plínio ♢ Salgado. During this period he was concerned primarily with the expression of Brazilian themes and the celebration of Brazilian life and nature. In later collections, such as *Um Dia Depois do Outro* (1947) and *A Face Perdida* (1950), he expresses the perplexities of modern life and man's search for a sense of identity. His *Poesias Completas* were published in Rio de Janeiro in 1957. He has also written several volumes of essays. [JF]

Cândido, *PLB*, iii; *Meu Caminho até Ontem* (1955) (selected poems).

**Riva Palacio, Vicente** (1832–96). Mexican novelist and historian. He was also a lawyer and politician and took part in the wars against Maximilian. He is chiefly interesting for two historical novels which attack the Spanish colonial regime, *Monja y casada, virgen y mártir* (1868) and *Martín Garatuza, Memorias de la Inquisición* (1868), and for his *Cuentos del General* (Madrid, 1896). [JF]

*La novela del México Colonial*, ii, intr. A. Castro Leal (Madrid, 1964).

**Rivera, José Eustasio** (1889–1928). Colombian poet and novelist. He was born in the provincial town of Neiva but completed his studies as a teacher and later as a lawyer in Bogotá. He then served on a government commission sent to trace the boundaries between Venezuela and Colombia. This took him into the Amazon basin where he learnt of the exploitation of the rubber workers, and he returned to Bogotá to campaign on their behalf. Rivera had published a collection of sonnets, *Tierra de promisión*, in 1921, very reminiscent of the sonnets of ♢ Herrera y Reissig except that the setting was Colombia. After a period in the cattle country, where he had gone to settle a legal dispute, Rivera began the work for which he is famous, the novel *La vorá-*

*gine.* This was completed after his expedition to the jungle and was published in 1924 (tr. E. K. James, *The Vortex*, New York, 1935). The protagonist of this novel, Arturo Cova, is a poet and incarnates Rivera's own horrified reactions to the barbarism and the violent natural environment of his native land. It tells the story of Cova's flight from Bogotá with Alicia, their sojourn among the violent inhabitants of the cattle country. Alicia leaves Cova to follow the rubber workers into the Amazon basin and the novel becomes an account of Cova's despairing search in the hostile jungle which finally swallows both Alicia and himself. [JF]

Eduardo Neale-Silva, *Horizonte humano: Vida de José Eustasio Rivera* (Wisconsin, 1960), and *Estudios sobre José Eustasio Rivera: I, El arte poético* (New York, 1951).

**Roa Bastos, Augusto** (1917–    ). Paraguayan writer. He came from a humble background, his father being a worker on a sugar plantation. He went barefoot until he was 8 and attended only a primary school. At 17, he joined the army, fought in the Chaco war against Bolivia and later became a journalist and radio commentator. He was awarded a British Council scholarship and spent some time in Britain but he did not begin to write seriously until exiled in Buenos Aires. Here, he published a volume of short stories, *El trueno entre las hojas* (1953), and a novel, *Hijo de hombre* (1959; tr. R. Caffyn, *Son of Man*, London, 1965). The novel is a lyrical re-creation of Paraguay over the last hundred years. The novelist breaks away from the conventions of realism and social protest and gives a lyrical interpretation of Paraguayan consciousness. In a series of interwoven episodes and legends the author presents a wide spectrum from the 19th-century struggles of the Paraguayan people to the Chaco war. The unity of the novel is the country itself, a Paraguay seen not through the eyes of an intellectual but through the struggles of peasants, soldiers, lepers, villagers and children. He has since published selections of short stories, *Madera quemada* (Santiago, 1967) and *Los pies sobre el agua* (Buenos Aires, 1967). [JF]

Alegría, *BHNH.*

**Rodó, José Enrique** (1872–1917). Uruguayan thinker. His influence extended to several generations of Latin Americans. He was educated in Montevideo but owing to the death of his father did not go to university. Despite this he became one of Uruguay's leading men of letters at a very early age. In 1895, he helped to found *La revista nacional de literatura y ciencias sociales*, in 1898 became Professor of Literature at the National University and in 1900 was director of the National Library. He twice served as a Deputy. He died in Europe when on a visit to which he had looked forward all his life. Rodó was one of the first to understand and appreciate ◊ Darío's *Prosas profanas*; he wrote a preface for the second edition stating that despite his skill Darío was not 'the poet of America'. In 1900, he published his most famous work, the essay *Ariel* (ed. and intr. G. Brotherston, Cambridge, 1967; tr. F. J. Stimson, Boston, New York, 1922), in which he elaborated his ideas on the basis of the symbolism of Shakespeare's *Tempest*, with Ariel representing the spirit and Caliban utilitarian materialism. The essay was directly inspired by the events of 1898, in which Spain lost the last of her colonies and a new power appeared in the Caribbean – the United States. The essay is a meditation on what makes a civilization great. For Rodó, it is the extent to which a civilization pursues a disinterested ideal as Greek civilization did. A civilization which, like the United States, pursues materialistic ends will produce no lasting work. Rodó believed that in a democratic community, education could be an instrument for selecting an élite who would pursue the disinterested ideal and he urges the youth of Latin America to pursue this goal. *Ariel* was immediately popular all over Latin America, influencing many outstanding men of letters, and also helped to propagate two widely held assumptions – that intellectuals can change society through the power of ideas and that Latin America was a unity which transcended the separate nations and their cultures. Rodó also wrote an ambitious treatise, *Los motivos de Proteo* (1909; tr. A. Flores, *The Motives of Proteus*, London, 1928), in which he examined the nature of individual vocation and motivation, and *El mirador de Próspero* (1914), a series of essays on outstanding men and particularly on the great Latin-American men of letters. [JF]

*Obras completas*, ed. and intr. E. R. Monegal (Madrid, 1956).

**Rodríguez Freile, Juan** (1566–1640?). Colombian writer. Author of the *Conquista y* *descubrimiento del Nuevo Reino de Granada* (tr. W. C. Atkinson, *The Conquest of New Granada*, London, 1961), a chronicle which goes up to 1636, when he finished writing it. It has become known as 'El Carnero'. Of little historical value, it reveals to us the presence in colonial Spanish America of a frustrated Boccaccio. The narrative is full of spicy anecdotes, tales of murders and adulteries, legends and gossip. Like the Arcipreste de Hita Rodríguez Freile liked to link his most scandalous stories to a moral, usually a condemnation of the wiles of women. [JMC]

**Rodríguez Galván, Ignacio** (1816–42). Mexican romantic poet and dramatist. An extreme rebel, he was one of the outstanding figures of the Reforma era. His denial of God, the Spanish tradition and the political regime earned him a fame which survives only in his 'Profecía de Guatimoc'. Here in the name of the last Aztec emperor he defies the powers of Europe and the United States, and with biblical plangency identifies his own fate with that of his country. The 'Profecía' is the finest poem of the Mexican Romantics. His plays were on colonial themes and include *Muñoz, visitador de México* (1838) and *El privado del virrey* (1842). [JMC]

**Rojas, Manuel** (1896–    ). Chilean novelist. His father died before he was 5, and at 16 he was working as a labourer. He crossed to Chile, where he subsequently worked as bargeman, night-watchman, sailor, actor, house-painter, typographer and journalist. He became director of the University of Chile press. His first publication was *Hombres del sur* (1926) and there followed *Lanchas en la bahía* which, like many of his works, was based on his own experiences. His finest novel is *Hijo de ladrón* (1951; tr. Frank Gaynor, *Born Guilty*, London, 1955). The novel tells of a boy's early life, his father's arrest and imprisonment for burglary and the boy's lone journey to Chile. Here he is caught up by accident in a street riot (the description of which is exceedingly skilful) and is again imprisoned. On his release he is taken in by beachcombers. The novel is not only an excellent account of the lower depths of Chilean and Argentinian society but also a penetrating examination of crowd and working-class psychology. [JF]

*Obras completas* (1961).
Alegría, *Las fronteras del realismo* (Santiago, 1962).

**Romero, José Rubén** (1890–1952). Mexican novelist. Born in Michoacán, where his father was a merchant. He was a supporter of Madero when the Mexican Revolution broke out and after the Revolution he served as Ambassador in Brazil and Cuba. Romero became the interpreter and chronicler of life in Mexico's sleepy, provincial towns. His semi-autobiographical *Desbandada* (1934) and *Apuntes de un lugareño* (1932) show the peaceful life and the characters of the Mexican provincial town into which the Revolution erupts with unexpected brutality. His most famous novel is *La vida inútil de Pito Pérez* (1938; tr. J. Coyne, *The Futile Life of Pito Pérez*, New York, 1966), the life of a Mexican small-town drunkard, told in the picaresque tradition. *Rosenda* (1946) is the story of a girl who falls in love and gives herself ungrudgingly to a man who finally leaves her. [JF]

*Obras completas*, ed. A. Castro Leal (1957); *Cuentos y poesías ineditos*, ed. W. O. Cord (1964) (with bibliography); *La novela de la Revolución Mexicana*, ii (1964) (includes *Apuntes de un lugareño* and *Desbandada*).
*José Rubén Romero, vida y obra, bibliografía, antología* (New York, 1946).

**Romero, Silvio** (1851–1914). Brazilian literary critic. He wrote the pioneer *História da Literatura Brasileira* (1888), a 2-volume study which stressed sociological factors. He had been a disciple of Tobias Barreto, worked as a teacher of philosophy in the Colégio Pedro II and later taught philosophy of law in Rio de Janeiro. He took part in politics as well as in many polemics. He is mainly remembered for his history of literature but his other works include *Estudos de Literatura Contemporâneu* (1885), *Outros Estudos de Literatura Contemporânea* (1905) and *Ensaios de Sociologia e Literatura* (1901). [AA]

**Ruiz de Alarcón, Juan** (1551?–1639). Mexican-born dramatist. He wrote his plays in Spain between 1615 and 1625, while working in the Council for the Indies. A quiet man and a hunchback, he was much lampooned for his deformity but did not often strike back. He worked carefully, leaving a mere 24 plays, where Lope, who had some influence over him, wrote hundreds. His verse is not spectacular, but his construction and his psychology are the best of his age. He is in some respects an 18th-century dramatist writing in the 17th. His best plays are comedies of Madrid life, and their subject is often a defect – not of body but of character. *La verdad sospechosa*, which is the source of Corneille's *Le menteur*, is about an inveterate liar; and *Las paredes oyen* is concerned with slander. *Los pechos privilegiados*, a rather slow-moving historical piece, contains the figure of the model court-favourite, and *El tejedor de Segovia*, a romantic historical play, has a rebel as hero. Ruiz de Alarcón wrote only one religious play. The sobriety of his style and the realism of his treatment is sometimes attributed to his Mexican upbringing. His psychological subtlety, however, is entirely his own. [JMC]

*Obras completas*, ed. A. Millares Carlo (2 vols., 1957–9); Cohen, *PBSV*.

**Rulfo, Juan** (1918–    ). Mexican novelist. He first published a collection of short stories of life in his native province of Jalisco, *El llano en llamas* (1952; tr. G. de Schade, *The Burning Plain*, Austin, London, 1968). Violent and colloquial, they express the callous despair of the poor with great objectivity and economy of language. The title story is a particularly impressive account of a group of peasants caught in the Revolution and emerging, bewildered, into post-Revolutionary Mexico. *Pedro Páramo* (1955; tr. L. Kemp, New York, 1959) is one of the best contemporary Latin-American novels. Here the time sequence is entirely fluid; the principal character in search of his father – the Pedro Páramo of the title – sees and hears scenes from the past and captures the conversations of the ghost inhabitants of a deserted village. In this way, the author evokes in a manner that is at once poetic and realistic, the now vanished world of the pre-Revolutionary landowner of the title whose exploits he can thus show without bitterness or hatred. [JMC/JF]

Cohen, *LAWT*.
Alegria, *BHNH*; Harss, *LN*.

# S

Sábato, Ernesto (1911– ). Argentinian writer. His novel, *El túnel* (1948; tr. H. de Onís, *The Outsider,* New York, 1950), describes the stages in the growing madness of an artist who has murdered his mistress. *Sobre héroes y tumbas* (1961; 3rd edn, 1964) is an ambitious work which probes the greatness and decline of a whole sector of Argentinian society through the love of a young man for Alejandra, a beautiful but unbalanced epileptic descendant of a noble creole family, the 'heroes' of 19th-century Argentina. Alejandra's father has the vision and the courage of the heroes but in modern Argentina, these qualities degenerate. Her father becomes a criminal lunatic whom she kills before committing suicide at the end of the novel. The novel represents an attempt to see a whole period of Argentinian history and an élite (the creole aristocracy) as a whole. Despite its strangeness – and at times incomprehensibility – the novel is an extremely powerful and compelling work. Sábato has expressed his own views on the novel in *El escritor y sus fantasmas* (2nd edn, 1964). [JF]

Alegría, *BHNH*.

Sabines, Jaime (1925– ). Mexican poet. His sober irony derives from that of ◊ López Velarde. He contrasts the goodness and simplicity of life in the provinces – he comes from Chiapas – with the ugly urban existence of the capital. Against poverty, disease and the brooding certainty of death, he sets the positive values of physical love and comradeship. His sequence *Tarumba,* addressed to his unborn son, is an unmetaphysical portrait of the poet as noble savage. Later poems are more social and less personal. His attitudes are tentative in everything except his belief that 'reality is superior to dreams'. [JMC]

*Recuento de poemas* (1962); *Doña Luz* (1969); Cohen, *LAWT; PM*.
Ramón Xirau, 'Nuevos poetas de México', in *Poetas de México y España* (Madrid, 1962).

Sahagún, Fray Bernardino de (1499–1590). Spanish-born Franciscan scholar. He left for the New World in 1529 at a time when the newly triumphant conquerors were destroying the remains of Aztec civilization. Sahagún believed that the best way of converting the Indians was through their language and an understanding of their religious beliefs. To further this aim, he set about collecting Indian traditions in the native language, Náhuatl. To do this, he used a team of native scribes who set the traditions down in the original language. The vast work took many years but constituted an invaluable record which remained unpublished for 200 years and which even now has not been fully studied. It is very largely from this record that modern Mexican scholars have gained their knowledge of Aztec religious beliefs and it is also a valuable source of ◊ Náhuatl literature. His monumental *Historia general de las cosas de la Nueva España*, compiled between 1570 and 1582 (ed. A. M. Garibay, 4 vols., Mexico, 1956) was a summary and commentary of the material he had collected and was intended for the Consejo de las Indias. [JF]

Salgado, Plínio (1901– ). Brazilian writer. He helped to found the Verde-Amarêlo movement, named after the colours of the Brazilian flag and dedicated to a nationalist cultural programme. He later became involved in the right-wing integralist movement, and his novels *O Estrangeiro* (1926), *O Esperado* (1931), *O Cavalheiro de Itararé* (1932) and *A Voz do Oeste* (1933) were all written to illustrate his political ideas. [JF]

Sánchez, Florencio (1875–1910). Uruguayan dramatist. He made his reputation in the Argentinian theatre. He worked as a journalist in Montevideo; as a member of the *blanco* party he fought in the civil war of 1896–7, an experience that disillusioned him with party politics. After the war, he joined an anarchist group, the Centro Internacional de Estudios Sociales, but soon afterwards left Uruguay for Argentina, where he worked on several newspapers. His first play, a *sainete*, was written about 1902 when he was living in Rosario, but his first real success was *M'hijo el dotor*, written to make money for his marriage. It was first performed on 13 August 1903 and had an immediate success. The play was on the theme of the conflict of generations between the conservative ideas of an old gaucho father and the modern ideas – and morals – of his city- and university-educated son. In 1904, there appeared *La gringa*, possibly Sánchez's best-known work. This play dealt with the conflict between the slip-shod, easy-going gaucho, Don Cantalicio, and the hard-working Italian immigrants (or *gringos*) to whom he loses his farm. The play ends with the reconciliation of the two opposing forces through the marriage of 'la gringa' to Don Cantalicio's son. Another important play of Sánchez was *Barranca abajo* (1905), which was more sombre than his other plays, although like them it dealt with the decline of the old gaucho. Don Zoilo, the protagonist, is a tragic figure who loses his estate and sees his family turn against him. He commits suicide when he finally realizes that he has no place in modern society. Sánchez wrote other plays, mostly dealing with the moral and social problems of middle-class life. [JF]

*Teatro completo*, intr. V. Martínez Cuitiño (Buenos Aires, 1951); *Representative Plays*, tr. W. K. Jones (Washington, D.C., 1961).

Ruth Richardson, *Florencio Sánchez and the Argentine Theatre* (New York, 1933); Karl E. Shedd, 'Thirty Years of Criticism of the Works of Florencio Sánchez', *Kentucky Foreign Language Quarterly*, III (January–March, 1956); Jorge Cruz, *Genio y figura de Florencio Sánchez* (Buenos Aires, 1966).

**Sandoval y Zapata, Luis de** (fl. 1650–60). Mexican poet. Author of a group of sonnets in the Gongorist manner, the most original of which is addressed 'A la materia prima' ('to prime matter'), and of a 'Relación fúnebre', on the beheading of the two brothers Ávila in the Plaza Mayor of Mexico. His conceits have a characteristically metaphysical touch. He left few poems, some of which still lie unpublished in the National Library of Mexico. [JMC]

*Poetas novohispanos*, II, i, ed. A. Méndez Plancarte (1944).

**Santa Cruz y Espejo, Francisco Javier Eugenio** (1747–95). Ecuadorian journalist and writer. His father was Indian and his mother mestizo. His father worked as an assistant in a hospital and Santa Cruz y Espejo gained the title of doctor of medicine and also studied theology and law. One of the most erudite men of his day, he was a severe critic of the Spaniards, and hence incurred the displeasure of the authorities. He founded a journal, *Primicias de la Cultura en Quito*, and also became head of the public library. In 1795 he was imprisoned and then transferred to a hospital, where he died. Much of Espejo's work remains unpublished, but his most interesting work, *El nuevo Luciano*, appeared in 1797. It is a critique of the Jesuit system of education. [JF]

*Escritos del doctor Francisco Javier Eugenio Santa Cruz y Espejo* (3 vols., 1912–13). *DLL.*

**Sarmiento, Domingo Faustino** (1811–88). Argentine politician, polemicist and thinker. His collected works fill 52 volumes. Sarmiento came from a poor family of the town of San Juan and was largely self-educated. Very early he became convinced of the importance of education for the future of his country and at 15 was teaching in a country school. A firm believer in progress, he soon came up against the dictator Rosas, who, for Sarmiento, was symbolic of backwardness and ignorance. Forced to go into exile in Chile, he remained abroad almost continuously until the fall of Rosas in 1852, working in a variety of occupations – as schoolteacher, clerk and miner. He travelled to the United States and Europe, where he studied educational ideas, and, on the fall of Rosas, became Argentinian Ambassador to the United States. In 1868, he became President of Argentina and at the end of his presidency continued to work in the field of educational reform. His outstanding piece of writing, *Facundo* (1845; 4th edn, 1958; tr. Mrs Horace Mann, *Life in the Argentine Republic in the Days of the Tyrants*, New York, 1868), is a biography of the gaucho leader Juan Facundo Quiroga, who was one of Rosas's allies but was later assassinated at Rosas's orders. *Facundo* is of more than passing historical interest for, in describing the career of the gaucho leader, Sarmiento also makes a poetic and penetrating study of the pampa and of the way of life of its inhabitants. The description of Facundo's last ride to the ambush in which he met his death reaches dramatic intensity. However, Sarmiento's political and social thinking now seem over-simplified. He equated

375

civilization with urban living, with 19th-century commercial and industrial progress and with European or North American ways of life. Barbarism, on the other hand, was a product of isolated rural ways of life. Among his other writings is *Viajes por Europa, Africa y América* (1849–51), which offers observations on his travels; his *Recuerdos de provincia* (1850) give an interesting account of his childhood and early manhood. [JF]

*Obras* (52 vols., Santiago, 1885–1914); *A Sarmiento Anthology*, tr. S. E. Grummon, ed. and intr. A. W. Bunkley (Princeton, 1948).

A. W. Bunkley, *The Life of Sarmiento* (Princeton, 1952); Ricardo Rojas, *El profeta de la pampa; vida de Sarmiento* (5th edn, Buenos Aires, 1951).

**Schmidt, Augusto Frederico** (1906–65). Brazilian poet, businessman and diplomat who became associated with the Modernist movement (◊ Modernism in Brazil). He began to write poetry and founded a publishing firm which published novels by Raquel de ◊ Queiros, Jorge ◊ Amado and Graciliano ◊ Ramos. He turned away from the verbal dexterity and humour of early Modernism and developed a direct poetry which showed his spiritual preoccupations. His collections include *Canto do Brasileiro* (1928), *Cantos do Liberto* (1928), *Navio Perdido* (1929), *Pássaro Cego* (1930), *Desaparição da Amada* (1931), *Canto da Noite* (1934), *Estrêla Solitária* (1940), *Mar Desconhecido* (1942), *Poesias Escolhidas* (1946) and *Fonte Invisível* (1949). After the publication of his complete works in 1956, he wrote *Aurora Lívida* (1958) and *Babilônia* (1959). He also published prose works and criticism. [AA]

*Poesías Completas* (1956); Cândido, *PLB*, iii; Nist, *MBP*.

**Segura y Cordero, Manuel Ascensio** (1805–71). Peruvian playwright of Spanish descent. He fought alongside his father and against the Independence armies but later supported the nationalist leader, Felipe Santiago Salverry. His first serious play was *El sargento Canuto*, which attacked militarism with great success. In *La saya y el manto* (1841) he attacked those who secured political advance through feminine intrigue. His *Ña Catita* (1845) was a creole Celestina. Segura championed the cause of creolist writing against the attacks of ◊ Pardo and others. [JF]

Sánchez, *LP*, v.

**Sigüenza y Góngora, Carlos de** (1645–1700). Mexican-born poet and scholar. Of Spanish and Creole parentage, he was educated as a Jesuit but left the Order and became Professor of Mathematics in the University of Mexico. He was renowned for his learning, was appointed Royal Cosmographer and was, it is reported, invited to France by Louis XIV. He was in correspondence with the leading intellectuals of his day and even took part in expeditions of exploration. He was a friend of Sor Juana Inés de la ◊ Cruz, but his own poetry was a poorer imitation of the Spanish Góngora. He was a historian and a chronicler of contemporary events and wrote the interesting *Infortunios de Alonso Ramírez* (1690; in *La novela del México Colonial*, i, 1964; tr. E. H. Pleasants, *The Misfortunes of Alonso Ramírez*, Mexico, 1962), a transcription of the adventures recounted to him by a Puerto Rican captured by English pirates in the East who accompanied them to the coast of Brazil where they put him on a boat with some companions and left him to find his own way to shore. The work is sometimes considered a novel, but its interest is primarily in the light it sheds on the sea conflicts between England and Spain in the 17th century. Also of interest is his *Primavera india* (1662), which describes the vision of Our Lady of Guadalupe which led to the foundation of the pilgrimage church of that name. [JF]

*Obras con una biografía*, ed. I. A. Leonard (1928).

Irving A. Leonard, *Don Carlos de Sigüenza y Góngora, a Mexican Savant of the Seventeenth Century* (Berkeley, Cal., 1929).

**Silva, José Asunción** (1865–96). Colombian poet. He was the son of a wealthy merchant, Ricardo Silva, who had himself been a member of the El Mosaico literary circle which did much to stimulate Colombian writing. He visited France in 1886, where he came into contact with contemporary trends in poetry and was particularly influenced by the decadents in England and France and by Poe. His return to Bogotá was unhappy. He found himself unable to fit into the narrow, provincial environment and when the family fortunes were lost he had to spend many years in business activities which he hated. The death of a sister increased his despair. Furthermore he lost many of his manuscripts, including poems and short stories, when a ship on which he was returning to Colombia was wrecked. In 1896, he shot himself. Silva was a contemporary of the Modernists but stands apart from them. Much of his poetry is on conventional romantic themes and especially on love and death. His poems include *Día de difuntos*, which in some respects recalls Poe's 'The Bells'; Silva's poem however builds up a musical contrast between the world of the living and the world of the dead. It is in fact this twilight region where death and life meet that his best poem, 'Nocturno III', evokes. Here the versification and rhythms achieve a high degree of suppleness and musicality, breaking away from all conventional forms. The lines lengthen with the shadows which accompany Silva on his lonely twilight walk on which he was reunited in spirit with his dead sister. Silva wrote several prose pieces which shed an interesting light on his distaste for his own period and society and he also wrote an autobiographical novel, *De sobremesa* (1887–96). [JF]

*Poesías completas: seguidas de prosas completas* (Madrid, 1952).
Ureña, *BHM*.

**Sousa, Antônio Gonçalves Teixera e** (1812–61). Brazilian novelist. He rose from modest origins and was obliged to work at many occupations including carpenter, writer, teacher and journalist. *O Filho do Pescador* (1843), the first Brazilian novel, is however a romantic sentimental novel of little interest today. He also wrote *A Providência* and *As Fatalidades de Dois Jovens* (1856). He wrote two plays and published several volumes of poetry. [AA]

**Sousândrade** (Joaquim de Sousa Andrade) (1833–1902). Brazilian poet. His work was largely forgotten until its rediscovery by Augusto and Haroldo de Campos. His *Harpas Selvagens* was conventionally romantic in theme but showed an unusual and vivid command of language and descriptive poetry. He came from the remote frontier region of Maranhão and journeyed along the Amazon in 1853. He spent some years in Europe and, after briefly returning to Brazil, settled in the United States in 1870. He later returned to Brazil and worked on a remarkable poem, *O Guesa Errante* – Guesa being an Indian poet who according to the religion of certain Colombian Indians must wander over the world before returning to be

sacrificed. There are 13 cantos of this poem extant, some of them incomplete, its main theme being the contrast between the unspoiled world of nature with which Indian civilizations are identified and the corruption of the city. The latter theme was given remarkable expression in the canto 'O Inferno de Wall Street', a kind of *Walpurgisnacht* of capitalism, written in an odd mixture of Portuguese and English. Certainly the poem is a literary oddity and deserved republication. The first four cantos appeared in a New York edition of *Obras Poeticas* published in 1874 under the name J. de Souza Andrade. There are two undated New York editions containing further cantos and a London edition which is the most complete but is also undated. [JF]

A. and H. de Campos, *Revisão de Sousândrade* (São Paulo, 1964) (with bibliography).

**Storni, Alfonsina** (1892–1938). Argentinian poet. She had an adventurous early life as a member of a theatrical troupe, then as a schoolteacher in the provinces. She was also a journalist and was actively interested in a young people's theatre movement. Her first book of poetry, *La inquietud del rosal*, appeared in 1916. Of her subsequent collections, *Ocre* (1925) is the most outstanding. Her poetry is chiefly remarkable for the frankness with which she states her erotic problem – desire for a lover and humiliation at her imagined feminine inferiority. Her later poetry is more intellectual. She committed suicide by drowning after learning that she had cancer. [JMC]

*Obra poética* (1952).
*DLL*.

**Subercaseaux, Benjamín** (1902–    ). Chilean novelist. He has written a remarkably interesting essay on Chile, *Chile o una loca geografía* (1940). His best novel, *Jemmy Button* (1950; tr. M. and F. del Villar, New York, 1954, London, 1955), is a penetrating study of the relationship between primitive and civilized man. Set in Victorian times, it tells the story of a British exploration vessel which takes on board some Indians from Tierra del Fuego and carries them back to London to be converted and civilized. They are later returned to their native land where they quickly return to their primitive ways. [JF]

Alone, *HPLC*.

# T

**Tallet, José Z.** ▷ Afro-Cubanism.

**Taunay, Alfredo D'Escragnolle** (Visconde de Taunay) (1843–99). Brazilian novelist of French descent. He took part in the war against Paraguay after attending a military academy. He fought in the Mato Grosso expedition and took part in a retreat about which he wrote in *La Retraite de Laguna* (1871), first published in French. A previous book, *Cenas de Viagem* (1868), also dealt with his army experiences and showed great precision of style. His major work is the novel *Inocência* (1872; tr. H. Chamberlain, *Innocence*, New York, 1945), a romantic regionalist novel translated into many languages which included some of the first accurate descriptions of life and customs in the interior of Brazil. His dialogues are spontaneous and realistic and there are fine descriptions of nature. The book is based on his own experiences in the little-known areas of Brazil and among Indians, for whom he had a remarkable sympathy and understanding. Other novels include *Lágrimas do Coração* (1873), the title of which was later changed to *Manuscrito de uma Mulher*, and *O Encilhamento* (1894). He wrote plays, but apart from his novels his outstanding work is his posthumously published *Memórias* (1948). [AA]

**Távora, João Franklin da Silveira** (1843–88). Brazilian novelist. He wrote realistically of the North-east. His novels include *Os Índios de Jaguaribe* (1862), *A Casa da Dalha* (1866), *Um Casamento no Arrabalde* (1869), *O Cabaleiro* (1876), *O Matuto* (1878) and *Lourenço* (1881). [JF]

**Terrazas, Francisco de** (1525?–1600?). Mexican poet. Author of some fragments of an epic on the New World and the Conquest of Mexico. Terrazas is at his best in the idyllic scenes between the lovers Quetzal and Huitzel, and at his dullest when following the events of history. His father had fought with Cortés, but he was pacific in his outlook, a Petrarchist whom Cervantes considered 'the Apollo of New Spain'. [JMC]

*Poesías*, ed. Castro Leal (1941).
García Icazbalceta, *Francisco de Terrazas y otros poetas del siglo XVI* (Madrid, 1962).

**Torres Bodet, Jaime** (1902– ). Mexican poet. One of the most prolific poets to emerge in the years following the Mexican Revolution. He had published nine books by the age of 24. Much of his early poetry is of poor quality and some critics consider his best work to have been published in the collection *Cripta* (1937) which came out after a period of seven years' silence. It is a poetry of solitude and separation. In 1949, there appeared *Sonetos*, followed by *Fronteras* (1954) and *Tregua* (1957). Torres Bodet has also written stories and essays, has been active in Unesco and has served as Minister of Education. [JF]

*PM.*
Frank Dauster, *Ensayos sobre poesía mexicana* (Colección Studium, 41, Mexico, 1963); Merlin H. Foster, *Los contemporáneos* (Colección Studium, 46, Mexico).

**Triana, José** (1931– ). Cuban dramatist. His early drama was influenced by contemporary European theatre. He has published three important plays, *Medea en el espejo*, *La muerte del Ñeque* and *Noche de los asesinos*, which won the Casa de las Américas Prize in 1945 and was produced in London by the Royal Shakespeare Company in 1967. [JF]

# U

**Usigli, Rodolfo** (1905–    ). Mexican dramatist. He is a pioneer of the modern Mexican theatre. Besides writing plays, he has also been a director, critic and actor. His views on the theatre were influenced by those of Shaw and he believed that a healthy society gave rise to drama which had a direct social role. Many of his plays have either remained unperformed or have been performed many years after they were written. Usigli's first plays date from 1930, but it was not until 1936 that his comedy *Estado de secreto* was performed. He wrote a series of plays, *Tres comedias impolíticas*, which criticized the Mexican political situation in the early thirties, and a serious drama, *El gesticulador* (1937), to which he later added an essay by way of epilogue. *El gesticulador* satirized the Mexican's love of myths and lies through the central character, a retired professor who wins fame and posthumous glory by posing as a revolutionary general. Usigli wrote many plays on contemporary Mexican society and its problems, one of the most successful of which, *Jano es una muchacha* (1952), dealt with the problem of sexual licence. He also wrote two weighty historical dramas, *Corona de sombra* (1943; tr. W. F. Stirling, *Crown of Shadows*, London, 1946) on Maximilian and Carlota and *Corona de luz* (1965) on Bartolomé de ◊ las Casas. Usigli has also written books on the theatre, notably *México en el teatro* (1932) and *Itinerario del autor dramático* (1940). [JF]

*Teatro completo* (1963).

**Uslar Pietri, Arturo** (1905–    ). Venezuelan novelist. Author of two important historical novels, *Las lanzas coloradas* (1931; tr. H. de Onís, *The Red Lances,* New York, 1963) and *El camino de El Dorado* (1947). The former concerns the wars of independence and represents a break with the conventional didactic historical novels which were usual in Latin America. *Las lanzas coloradas* has no overt message but merely shows the conflicting groups and masses, notably the creole landowner who supports Bolívar and the semibarbarous estate foreman who fights for the Spaniards. The novelist thus shows implicitly that the conflict between civilization and barbarism was already a reality. He has also published several collections of stories, notably *Treinta hombres y sus sombras* (1949), and a novel of contemporary Venezuela, *Un retrato en la geografía* (1962), which relates the story of a political prisoner of the Gómez regime who, on his release, is precipitated into the confused world of contemporary Venezuela. Political issues are debated; the novel becomes the study of a country, of Venezuela, of its oil, its peasants and its newly rich townsfolk who despise their native land. The best passages, however, are those that deal with such events as the general strike in Caracas and the storming of the University rather than those dealing with ideas and geography. [JMC/JF]

Alegría, *BHNH.*

# V

**Valdelomar, Abraham** (1888–1919). Peruvian poet and story writer. He worked as a civil servant and edited an official newspaper, *El Peruano*. He was a man of varied interests who wrote a work on the bullfighter Belmonte, a life of Doña Francisca de Gamarra, *La Mariscala*, and two unsuccessful novels. His fame rests on two collections of stories, *El Caballero Carmelo* (1918) and the posthumously published *Los hijos del sol*, and the poems first published in the anthology *Las voces múltiples* (1916). He was also editor of an important literary review, *Colónida*, which appeared in 1916, attacked established reputations and included translations of many foreign writers, including Mallarmé. *Los hijos del sol* evoked the Inca past of Peru in a poetic prose. [JF]

Suárez-Miravel, *LP*; Manzoni, *INA*.
César Angeles Caballero, *Vida y obra* (Peru, 1964).

**Valdés, Gabriel de la Concepción** (1809–44). Cuban poet. The illegitimate son of a mulatto barber and a Spanish dancer, he took the name Plácido as a tribute to the apothecary who befriended him. He lived a humble life, earning his living by odd jobs, and began to write verses after coming across the poetry of the Spanish poet, Francisco Martínez de la Rosa. His poems are chiefly remarkable for their moving protests against injustice. He was executed in 1844 after being tried for his complicity in a plot to bring about Negro domination in Cuba. [JF]

*Poesías selectas de Plácido* (1930).
Frederick S. Stimson, *Cuba's Romantic Poet, the Story of Plácido* (Chapel Hill, North Carolina, 1964).

**Valencia, Guillermo** (1873–1943). Colombian poet. One of the first generation of ◊ Modernists. He was of a wealthy family and spent some time in Paris, where he came under the influence of Mallarmé and Oscar Wilde, whose *Ballad of Reading Gaol* he translated. He published *Ritos*, his one book of original poems, in 1898. A stylistic perfectionist, he was a Parnassian

by sympathy, though his intellectual power and his social conscience prevented him from being a pure aesthete. Fully mature in his *Ritos*, he produced only translations afterwards. His *Catay* (1929) were versions of Chinese poems translated by way of French. In 1914, he reprinted *Ritos* with a few additions. His work appears coldly chiselled judged by modern standards. He shows none of the passion and none of the vulgarity of his great contemporary ◊ Darío. [JMC]

*Obras poéticas completas* (1948; 3rd edn, Madrid, 1955); Trend, *OBSV*.

**Valle y Caviedes, Juan del** (1652?–97?). Peruvian satirical poet born in Spain. Very little of his biography is known. He was evidently taken to Peru early in his lifetime, but it is not known how he lived there. Few of his poems were published in his lifetime, probably because they were too acrimonious and, in some cases, lewd. The first publication of many of his poems had to wait until 1873 when they appeared in volume 5 of *Documentos literarios del Perú*, edited by Manuel de Odriozola and Ricardo Palma. The most complete edition of Caviedes' poetry to date is that of Fr Rubén Vargas Ugarte, which appeared in 1947. Much of Caviedes' satirical poetry is *conceptista* in nature and the weight of his satire was directed against doctors. Caviedes also wrote religious poetry and is author of a 'Carta' to Sor Juana Inés de la ◊ Cruz. He also wrote some short dramatic pieces. Undoubtedly his wit and verbal skill put him among the best of Latin-American poets of the colonial era. [JF]

*Obras*, ed. R. V. Ugarte (1947).
Daniel R. Reedy, *The Poetic Art of Juan del Valle Caviedes* (U. of North Carolina P., 1964).

**Vallejo, César** (1892–1938). Peruvian poet. He was born in the small town of Santiago de Chuco in northern Peru. According to the poet both his parents were the children of the union of a priest and an Indian woman. Despite the fact that the family were not comfortably off, Vallejo was able to attend Trujillo University and he also attended the University of San Marcos in Lima for a short time. His first collection, *Los heraldos negros*, appeared in 1918 and showed the varied influences of ◊ Darío and ◊ Herrera y Reissig but also included one or two moving poems on his family which anticipate much of his later poetry. In 1920 Vallejo was arrested while in his home town and accused of being implicated in some political disturbances. Although apparently innocent, he was imprisoned for several months and many of the poems of his second collection, *Trilce* (1922), refer to this event, which had important repercussions in his life and on his poetry. *Trilce* is an uneven collection in which the poet experimented in many *avant garde* techniques, employing typographical effects, and inventing new vocabulary. The best poems, 'Las personas mayores', 'Oh las cuatro paredes de la celda', 'He almorzado solo ahora', 'Madre, me voy mañana a Santiago', are amongst the finest poems in the Spanish language. The often tortured imagery, the broken syntax, reveal the anguish of Vallejo's sense of separation from others. A forlorn desire for brotherly love and a sense of futility and absurdity informs nearly all his poems and is expressed in an entirely new and revolutionary way, in what constitutes an attack on conventional Spanish language and speech forms. In 1923, Vallejo went to Paris where, except for short periods spent in Spain, he was to remain for the rest of his life. He lived in Paris in great penury and seems to have earned his money mainly by writing for the press. For many years he wrote little poetry, but as his sympathies became increasingly left-wing he turned to other forms of literature. Two short trips to Russia in 1928 and 1929 had a decisive effect on the course of his development and henceforth he was to spend much of his life in militant political activity. In 1930, he was expelled from France for his activities and lived for a short time in Madrid, where he published a novel of social protest set in Peru, *El tungsteno*, and wrote a number of left-wing plays. In 1933 he was back in Paris but again left for Spain at the beginning of the Civil War, first to visit Republican territory and later to attend the International Writers' Congress. It was during this period of his life that he again began to write poetry intensively, but his remaining poetry was published only after his death, when his poems on Spain appeared in a special number of the review *Nuestra España* (1938). Under the title *España, aparta de mi este cáliz*, they were published in Mexico in 1940. His other poetry, collected under the title *Poemas humanos*, was published in Paris in 1939. This posthumous collection contains some of his most impressive poetry; here the absurdity of man's posturing in the face of death and the irrationality of life in society are magnificently expressed. 'Los nueve monstruos' and 'La rueda del hambriento' evoke the grim depression-haunted days of the thirties and express the poet's impotence in the face of universal disorder. [JF]

*Poesías completas*, intr. F. Retamar (Cuba, 1965); *Obra poética completa*, ed. F. Moncloa (1968); *12 Spanish American Poets*, tr. H. R. Hays (New Haven, London, 1963); Fitts, *APAC*; *Encounter*, 1965; C. Eshleman, *Human Poems* (London, 1969).
Luis Monguió, *César Vallejo, vida y obra, bibliografía, antología* (New York, 1952).

**Vargas Llosa, Mario** (1936–    ). Peruvian novelist. He spent his early years in Bolivia. He was educated in Bolivia, Piura and Lima, and then in Madrid. He has also spent some time in Paris. His collection of short stories, *Los jefes*, was published in Barcelona in 1958 but he first became known with his novel *La ciudad y los perros* (tr. *The Time of the Heroes*, 1967), which won a Spanish literary prize in 1962. The story is set in a military academy in Lima of which the author had personal experience. The *perros* (dogs) of the title are the military cadets whose life in the college is one of external discipline which hides the inner uncertainties and perversion of their lives. The pattern of bullying, of oppressor and victim, of personal codes of honour is both contrasted and compared to the free life of the city outside the gates of the school. The similarity with Musil's *Törless* comes to mind but the novel is by no means an imitation of this, being directly relevant to the tensions within Peruvian society. Vargas Llosa has since published *La casa verde* (1966; tr. Gregory Rabassa, *The Green House*, 1969), which again contrasts two communities – in this case the remote jungle region of the upper Marañón and the city of Piura. The different time strata of the jungle world and the city, the symbiotic relationship between the innocent savage and city corruption, make this one of the most ambitious Peruvian novels, probably the first to try and encompass the conflicts of the nation as a whole. *Los cachorros,* a short novel, was published in Barcelona, 1967. Vargas Llosa has just completed a new novel, *Conversación en la Catedral.* [JF]

Harss, *LN.*

**Vasconcelos, José** (1882–1959). Mexican thinker and politician. Along with Alfonso ◊ Reyes, he was one of the members of the Ateneo de la Juventud which did so much to stimulate intellectual life in pre-Revolutionary Mexico. During the Revolution, he supported Madero and briefly became Minister of Education in one of the Revolutionary governments. He met all the Revolutionary leaders and has left one of the most interesting accounts of the Revolutionary years in his autobiography, *Ulises Criollo* (1935). He was appointed Minister of Education in the post-Revolutionary government of Obregón and was to have a decisive influence on cultural life. It was he who first commissioned murals for public buildings, thus directly stimulating Mexico's muralist movement; he opened many schools, particularly in rural areas, and encouraged orchestras and musicians. He also invited other Latin-American intellectuals and writers to Mexico and Gabriela ◊ Mistral spent some time there. Vasconcelos resigned from the government in the face of the growing influence of Plutarcho Calles, against whose nominee he fought an unsuccessful election campaign in 1929, after which he went abroad. He was a prolific essayist who wrote many theoretical works, notably *La raza cósmica* (1925), in which he forecast that Mexico and Latin America, with its fusion of races, were destined to be the leaders of the highest stage of human development. [JF]

*Obras completas* (4 vols., 1957–61).

**Vega, Ventura de la** (1807–65). Argentinian dramatist. He became director of the national theatre in Madrid. He wrote rhetorical and classical tragedies, attempted the romantic, and scored his one success with *El hombre de mundo* (1845), a light comedy of middle-class life in sparkling verse. This was the ancestor of all Spanish drawing-room comedy down to the time of Benavente and his school. [JMC]

**Veríssimo, Erico** (1905–    ). Brazilian novelist. He was born in Pôrto Alegre,

which provides the background for most of his novels. He had been greatly influenced by authors such as Ernest Hemingway, John dos Passos and Aldous Huxley, and has translated Huxley's *Point Counter Point* into Portuguese. Widely read and well travelled, he has also been a guest lecturer at many foreign universities. Besides his novels, he is the author of *Gato Prêto em Campo de Neve* (1941), a series of impressions received during his travels in the United States, which is used as a textbook in many Portuguese language classes. *Mexico* (tr. Lomas Barrett, 1960) is also a collection of observations containing sketches of the Mexican character, Mexican history and customs.

Veríssimo is best known for his novels, the most important one being *Caminhos Cruzados* (tr. L. C. Kaplan, *Crossroads,* London, 1956). As in most of his works, the author is here concerned with man's destiny – his ability to discover his identity and assert his will in a complex, changing urban society. This concern is expressed through various characters whose lives in a five-day period are briefly intertwined and then separated, usually by some misfortune. This idea of temporarily crossed pathways is well suited to his writings of city life, where rapid change makes human relations tenuous and ephemeral. Most of Veríssimo's characters react against their disorientation either by fighting their condition and asserting their individuality, or by succumbing to their fate and melting into the anonymous urban mass. Some characters react by blotting out the real world and living in one of fantasy, where beauty and kindness still exist. Veríssimo is skilful in his study of urban types, in weaving the lives of his characters, and in balancing his work with amusing personalities and situations. *Olhai os Lírios do Campo* (1938; tr. J. N. Karnoff, *Consider the Lilies of the Field,* 1947) is also concerned with lives that are drawn together in everyday occurrences as well as personal tragedies; Veríssimo portrays his characters' defiance or submission to their plight with keen insight. *Noite* (1940; tr. L. L. Barrett, *Night,* London, 1956) is more pessimistic in tone than Veríssimo's other works, and the element of humour found in *Crossroads* is totally lacking in *Noite,* in which the protagonist is an anonymous stranger. Veríssimo's most ambitious work is *O Tempo e o Vento,* a trilogy of novels that includes *O Continente* (1949), *O Retrato* and *O Arquipélago* (1962). The trilogy traces 200 years in the history of a family of southern Brazil. *O Resto é Silencio* (tr. L. C. Kaplan, *The Rest is Silence*, London, 1956) is Veríssimo's other novel, published in 1943. [DH]

**Veríssimo Dias de Matos, José** (1857–1916). Brazilian literary critic. He opposed the Scientism of Tobias ◊ Barreto, setting up spiritual as opposed to material values. His *História da Literatura Brasileira* was published in 1916 (3rd edn, 1954). He also published a 2-volume *Estudos Brasileiros* (1889, 1894) and a further collection of *Estudos de Literatura Brasileira* (1901–7). [AA]

**Viana, Javier de** (1871–1925). Uruguayan short-story writer. He was the son of a landowning family who began to write under the influence of naturalism. His creative works can be divided into two periods: those written before 1905, including the best of his stories, and those written after this date, when his work suffered because he was writing under economic pressure. In 1904 he lost his money and from this point onwards he was forced to write in order to live. The 15 publications after this date included the collections *Macachines* (1910), *Leña seca* (1911), *Yuyos* (1912) and *Abrojos* (1919), and show a gradual decline in the author's creative powers. Viana's best stories, therefore, are to be found in *Campo* (1896) and *Gurí* (1901); from this period there also date a novel, *Gaucha* (1899), and two volumes in which the author relates his experiences in the uprisings of 1886 and 1904, *Crónicas de la revolución del Quebracho* and *Con divisa blanca* (the first had appeared as a serial in 1891 and the second was published in 1904). Viana's stories deal with life in the countryside and on the cattle ranches of Uruguay; he is no sentimentalist and his stories frequently dwell on the brutal and repugnant aspects. He shows the native country-dwellers as lazy, negligent and brutal, dominated by the *caudillos*. The stories are often weak as regards psychological penetration but the best of them have a sombre power. [JF]

*Selección de cuentos*, intr. A. S. Visca (2 vols., 1965).

**Villaurrutia, Xavier** (1903–50). Mexican poet and dramatist. In reaction against the provincialism of ◊ López Velarde, he introduced themes and manners that derived from Supervielle and from such American poets as Archibald MacLeish. He founded the magazine *Ulises* (1927), in collaboration with Salvador Novo, and in this were published translations from many contemporary European writers including Joyce, Gide and Giraudoux. He was associated with the *Contemporáneos* group of poets who published in the Mexican review of that name and who worked in isolation from the social preoccupation of post-revolutionary Mexico. *Nostalgia de la muerte* (1938), his best-known collection of poems, contains two groups of *nocturnos*, fluent and delicately pessimistic of which all the merits lie on the surface. Villaurrutia was in love with death and ended his life by suicide. His subjects are hopeless love, insomnia, and the sense of loss experienced in foreign cities. One poem alone, 'Décima muerte', rises above the level of minor poetry. Written in a form very close to that of the traditional *décima*, it recalls without pastiche the Spanish poetry of the 17th century. His later poetry is simpler but less distinguished. In 1936, Villaurrutia went to study drama in the United States and he has written many plays. His theatre, like his poetry, was founded on a preoccupation with precise language. He is noted for his skilful dialogues. Amongst his many plays, the most outstanding are *El ausente* (1937), *La hiedra* (1941), *El yerro candente* (1944) and *Invitación a la muerte* (1940). [JMC]

*Poesía y teatro completos* (1953); Cohen, *PBSV*; *PM*.
Ramón Xirau, *Tres poetas de la soledad* (Mexico, 1955).

**Villaverde, Cirilo** (1812–94). Cuban novelist and patriot. A member of a literary circle which met at the home of Domingo Delmonte, he also identified himself with the cause of Cuban independence. He was imprisoned in 1848 but managed to escape to the United States, where he spent nine years. After a brief return to Cuba, he again went to live abroad, and his most famous novel, *Cecilia Valdés*, was published in New York in 1882 (tr. S. G. Gest, New York, 1962). This novel is outstanding as one of the first to deal with the problem of race in Cuba. Although begun as early as 1839, Villaverde was not able to continue work on it until 1879. It tells the story of a mulatto woman, Cecilia, a woman of out-standing beauty, and her love affair with a young man of a wealthy landowning and merchant family who unknown to her and to him is the son of the same father. Despite the somewhat melodramatic and sensational nature of the plot, the novel is one of the best 19th-century Spanish-American novels and abounds in accurate, lively and realistic descriptions of the life of all classes of Cuban society in the early years of the 19th century. The descriptions of university lecture halls, slave quarters, dance salons, executions of criminals and sugar plantations indeed make it a valuable social document quite apart from their artistic value. [J F]

G. Coulthard, *Race and Colour in Caribbean Literature* (London, 1962); Suárez-Murias, *N R H.*

# Z

**Zorrilla de San Martín, Juan** (1855–1931).
Uruguayan poet. He wrote and revised his
poem *Tabaré* from 1879, the date of its first
publication, to 1923, the year of its last
corrected edition. It tells the story of the
love of a *mestizo* for the daughter of a
Spaniard at the time of the Conquest. But
the story is less important than the symbolism, which is complicated and theological.
Zorrilla was a romantic, a disciple of
Bécquer, who came to symbolism in his own
way, independently of French examples.
From Bécquer he learnt the art of musical
construction and the use of the leitmotiv.
For he was primarily a lyrical poet with a
strong pictorial sense, and narrative served
him only as a pretext. Zorrilla's essays and
books of travel are of less interest than this
very individual poem. [JMC]

R. Ibañez, *La leyenda patria y su contorno
histórico* (Montevideo, 1959).

# RECOMMENDED READING

The main anthologies are included in the list of abbreviations, but mention should also be made of a substantial 5-volume anthology edited by A. Flores, now in course of publication (New York, 1969 ff.).

## LITERATURE AND THE HISTORY OF IDEAS

Anderson Imbert, Enrique, *Spanish American Literature: A History* (Detroit, 1963).
Arciniegas, Germán, *Latin America. A Cultural History* (New York, 1966; London, 1969).
Clissold, *Latin America. A Cultural Outline* (London, 1965).
Cruz Costa, João, *A History of Ideas in Brazil* (Berkeley and Los Angeles, 1964).
Ellison, Fred P., *Brazil's New Novel* (Berkeley and Los Angeles, 1959).
Franco, Jean, *An Introduction to Spanish American Literature* (London, 1969).
Franco, Jean, *The Modern Culture of Latin America* (London, New York, 1967).
Henríquez Ureña, Pedro, *A Concise History of Latin American Culture* (New York, London, 1967).
Leonard, Irving A., *Baroque Times in Old Mexico* (Ann Arbor, 1959).
Nicholson, Irene, *Firefly in the Night. A Study of Ancient Mexican Poetry and Symbolism* (London, 1959).
Picón Salas, Mariano, *A Cultural History of Spanish America from Conquest to Independence* (Berkeley and Los Angeles, 1962).
Putnam, Samuel, *Marvelous Journey, A Survey of Four Centuries of Brazilian Writing* (New York, 1948).
Torres-Rioseco, Arturo, *The Epic of Latin American Literature* (Berkeley and Los Angeles, 1959).
Zea, Leopoldo, *The Latin American Mind* (Oklahoma, 1963).

## HISTORY

Blakemore, Harold, *Latin America* (London, 1966).
Boxer, C. R., *The Portuguese Seaborne Empire* (London, 1969).
Herring, Hubert, *A History of Latin America from the Beginnings to the Present* (2nd edn, New York, 1963).
Humphreys, R. A., and Lynch J., *The Origins of the Latin American Revolutions 1808–1826* (New York, 1966).
León-Portilla, Miguel, *The Broken Spears. The Aztec Account of the Conquest of Mexico* (London, 1962).
Parry, J. H., *The Spanish Seaborne Empire* (London, 1966).
Pendle, George, *A History of Latin America* (Penguin Books, 1963).
Robertson, William Spence, *Rise of the Spanish-American Republics* (London, 1961).